Y0-BVN-882

Parliament
of the
Commonwealth
of Australia

BICENTENARY PUBLICATIONS PROJECT

ACTS
OF PARLIAMENT

A narrative history of the
Senate and House of Representatives
Commonwealth of Australia

Gavin Souter

MELBOURNE UNIVERSITY PRESS 1988

First published 1988
Reprinted August 1988
Printed in Australia by
Brown Prior Anderson Pty Ltd, Burwood, 3125, for
Melbourne University Press, Carlton, Victoria 3053
U.S.A. and Canada: International Specialized Book Services, Inc.,
5602 N.E. Hassalo Street, Portland, Oregon 97213-3640
United Kingdom, Europe, Middle East, Africa:
HB Sales
Littleton House, Littleton Road, Ashford, Middlesex,
England TW151UQ

© Commonwealth of Australia 1988

National Library of Australia Cataloguing-in-Publication entry

Souter, Gavin, 1929–
    Acts of Parliament: a narrative history of the Senate and
    House of Representatives.
    Bibliography.
    Includes index.
    ISBN 0 522 84367 0

    1. Australia. Parliament — History. 2. Legislative bodies —
    Australia — History. I. Title.
328.94'09

Contents

Illustrations

Abbreviations used in acknowledgements for the reproduction of illustrations are as follows:

AA	Australian Archives	PA	Promotion Australia
AIS	Australian Information Service	PHCA	Parliament House Construction Authority
ANIB	Australian News and Information Service	REBT	Royal Exhibition Building Trust
HMC	Historic Memorials Committee	SMH	Sydney Morning Herald
NLA	National Library of Australia	VPL	Victorian Parliamentary Library

Plates

Text illustrations

Conversions

1d (penny)	0.83 cent
1s (shilling)	10 cents
£1 (pound)	$2
1 inch	2.54 centimetres
1 foot	0.30 metre
1 yard	0.91 metre
1 mile	1.60 kilometres
1 lb (pound)	0.45 kilogram
1 stone	6.35 kilograms

Preamble

There are many acts of parliament, and in a sense this book is one of them. It is not a legislative measure, of course, but an act of parliament in the wider sense of action or deed, forming part of Parliament's Bicentenary Publications Project for the 200th anniversary of European settlement in Australia. The Project was initiated in 1981 by the Speaker of the House of Representatives, the Right Honourable Sir Billy Snedden, and the President of the Senate, the Honourable Sir Harold Young, in accordance with recommendations made by the Library Committee of Parliament. An Advisory Board was appointed to assist the Presiding Officers, and among various works which it decided to sponsor was 'a narrative history of events and people connected with the Australian parliament'.

Such a narrative presents obvious problems of superabundance. How, for example, does the narrator deal with a cast of characters which alters at least every three years, and often more frequently? Since its inauguration in 1901, the Parliament of the Commonwealth of Australia has been electorally reincarnated thirty-four times—from the first Parliament, meeting in Melbourne, to the thirty-fifth Parliament, now sitting in the provisional Parliament House at Canberra which is soon to be replaced by a permanent building on the nearby site of Capital Hill. During that time the Australian Parliament has seated more than 1200 members and passed about 7000 acts. The record of its debates, augmented regularly like the script of a never-

ending play, consists so far of 460 bound volumes containing at least 400
million words.

Somewhere in the perpetual cycle of election, legislation and dissolution
there is a narrative. Its threads of events, people and issues may be inter-
twined with much that is expendable, but they can be drawn out, as all narra-
tives are, by judicious selection and omission. In attempting this, I have had
to remember that my proper subject is Parliament, not government, and certainly not the whole body politic. Yet Parliament has close connections with
the government of the day, with political parties, the electorate, the High
Court and the Governor-General. To the extent that these affect or are affected by Parliament, they also form part of the subject.

The tale is full of sound and fury, tragedy and comedy, high hope and low
cunning—all the elements of that ordinary life for which Parliament serves
as an extraordinary arena and stage. The cast is well endowed with jesters,
conjurors, gladiators, a number of stars and one or two Titans. I trust that this
selective version of their play, unlike Macbeth's desolate vision of life, will
signify something. Members of parliament are ourselves writ large, and (in
theory, at any rate) it is by our leave that they strut and fret their hour upon
the stage. This being the case, we should be able to learn from their performance how well or otherwise Parliament has served its masters, and also to
learn something about the masters themselves, which is to say ourselves as a
people.

Acknowledgement of the assistance which I have received from many
sources must begin with the Advisory Board which selected me for this
undertaking in 1983, and for the next four years allowed me complete inde-
pendence as author. I thank its members, past and present: Mr Manfred
Cross, M.P. (Chairman), the Honourable Dr N. Blewett, M.P., the Honourable Mr Gordon Bryant, Mr H. G. P. Chapman, Mr B. J. Conquest, M.P., Mr
Allan Fleming, Dr Geoffrey Hawker, Dr Colin Hughes, the Honourable
Barry Jones, M.P., Mr W. Smith, M.P., Senators Shirley Walters (formerly
Chairman), J. A. Mulvihill, G. R. Maguire and B. C. Teague, Professor Patrick
Weller, Mrs Katherine West, and Mr Hillas de S. C. MacLean. Mr MacLean
was a constant source of help in his capacity as Parliamentary Librarian, as
also were other members of the Library staff, notably John Brudenall, Brenda
McAvoy (manager of Parliament's Bicentenary Publications Project), Jan
MacDonald, Reina Hill, Martin Lumb and Chris Field.

I also thank John Fairfax & Sons Ltd for having allowed me leave of
absence to write this book.

My closest colleagues in the project, to all of whom I am especially
indebted, were four consecutive research assistants: Dr Sally Kennedy,
Gillian Higginson, Stephen Holt and Ann Millar. I am also grateful to the
colleagues who converted my manuscript into floppy disks, Jennifer Tyrrell
and Margaret Fifita.

Anyone reasonably familiar with the subject of this book will appreciate
the extent of my recourse to the following: Professor Geoffrey Sawer's *Australian Federal Politics and Law*, Volumes One (1901–1929) and Two (1929–
1949); the 'Political Review' appearing regularly in *The Australian Quarterly*
since 1954, and the 'Australian Political Chronicle' appearing in *The Aus-*

tralian *Journal of Politics and History* since 1956; *House of Representatives Practice*, edited by J. A. Pettifer; *Australian Senate Practice*, by J. R. Odgers; *Commonwealth Parliamentary Debates, Votes and Proceedings of the House of Representatives*, and *Journals of the Senate*.

I am particularly grateful to Professor Sawer himself for reading and commenting on the manuscript, and for similar assistance from Mark McRae and John Porter, officers of the House of Representatives, and from the Clerk of the Senate, Alan Cumming Thom.

For help in the course of research, I have many grateful acknowledgements to make: Professors K. S. Inglis and D. A. Aitkin, for extending the privilege of visiting fellowships in the Departments of History and Political Science at the Research School of Social Sciences, Australian National University; Catherine Santamaria, Pam Reay, Bill Tully and Mark Cranfield at the National Library of Australia; Anne Lynch and Harry Evans in the Department of the Senate; Kate McLoughlin at the National Film and Sound Archive; Josephine McGovern and Bruce Davidson at the Library of the Victorian Parliament; Kate Owen in the *Sydney Morning Herald* Library; Richard Thorp and Leslie McKay at Mitchell, Giurgola and Thorp; Norman Barwick at the Parliament House Construction Authority; Don Piper, Secretary of the Joint Standing Committee on the New Parliament House and Director of the New Parliament House Secretariat; Pamela Morris-Kennedy, Mt Stromlo Observatory; Peter Bowers, Mike and Kate Steketee, Alan Reid, Ian Fitchett, Russell Schneider and Barry Cassidy; and staff at the Australian Archives, the Australian Electoral Commission, the Australian War Memorial, La Trobe Library, Oxley Library, R. G. Menzies Library, Government House at Yarralumla, and Promotion Australia.

I am grateful for having had the advantage of speaking with the Prime Minister, the Honourable Mr R. J. L. Hawke, the Right Honourable Mr Malcolm Fraser, the Honourable Mr Andrew Peacock, M.P., the Honourable Mr Ian Sinclair, M.P., the Honourable Mr James McClelland, and the Honourable Mr Fred Daly; Senators the Honourable John Button, the Right Honourable R. G. Withers, the Honourable F. M. Chaney, the Honourable Michael Tate, Graham Richardson, and D. J. Hamer. My thanks for various forms of assistance also go to the following: the late Professor L. F. Crisp, Professor Russel Ward; Messrs M. V. Suich, H. J. Gibbney, L. F. Fitzhardinge, the late J. R. Odgers, Norman Parkes, David Burke, D. W. N. Robinson, C. W. Allen, Max Thompson, Ronald McKie, Sir Harold White, Dr Allan Martin, Dr Peter Edwards, Dr Clem Lloyd and Dr Philip Ayres; Mrs V. Ulm, Mrs Heather Henderson, and Mrs D. Fortescue; for help in Tasmania, Geoffrey and Gretel Blackburn; and for timely, invaluable help, Dr G. C. Hipwell of Sydney and Dr T Middlemiss and Dr J. Wong See of Canberra. Finally, my thanks as ever to Ngaire and Anne Souter.

Gavin Souter

Part One

Melbourne 1901–1927

1

Moloch

Forecast

Between the inauguration of the Commonwealth of Australia in Sydney on 1 January 1901 and the opening of federal parliament in Melbourne four months later, omens of the future seemed to abound. A new century began, and an old Queen died; the worst Australian drought on record scorched into its seventh year, and two apocalyptic horsemen, war and plague, could be seen on the horizon; a steamship named the *Federal* foundered off the coast of Victoria, and—as if that was not enough—a great three-tailed comet appeared in the heavens. The Great Southern Comet, as it became known, was one of the most brilliant ever seen from Australia. In pre-scientific days, said the Melbourne *Argus*, such an apparition would surely have been followed hot-foot by news that all the statues were sweating blood. Yet this was the twentieth century, a sceptical age already acquainted with electric light, telegraphy, telephones and even a few motor cars. People were merely interested in omens, not awed by them.

The Melbourne *Age* regretted that it could not connect the brilliant astral visitor 'with the coming to Australia of the Heir to the Throne or with the opening of the Commonwealth Parliament, as our remote ancestors would have done . . .'. The Great Southern Comet would indeed have made a good harbinger for His Royal Highness the Duke of Cornwall and York, grandson of the late Queen Victoria, who was then on his way to open parliament. Its appearance coincided in time with the voyage of the royal yacht—a refurbished P. & O. liner, the *Ophir*—from Singapore around Cape Leeuwin, on the south-western edge of the Australian continent, and across the Great Australian Bight. Even the *Bulletin*, which could take Dukes or leave them, remarked upon this coincidence:

Oh, have you seen the comet with three fiery streamers from it?
'Tis a portent in the heavens that cannot be mistook!
'Twould have been a mighty omen had the period been Roman,
Had his highness been a Caesar instead of just a Jook.

Australia first heard about the comet from the lighthouse keeper at Cape
Leeuwin, who saw it early on Wednesday morning, 24 April, the *Ophir's* second day out from Singapore. Thereafter, whenever skies were clear, the
comet's morning and evening appearances were observed by government
astronomers or meteorologists (usually one and the same person) in the six
former colonies which had federated to form the Commonwealth—in order
of their comet-sighting, Western Australia, South Australia, New South
Wales, Victoria, Queensland and Tasmania.

The Western Australian astronomer, W. E. Cooke, happened to be visiting
his opposite number in South Australia, Sir Charles Todd, and together they
located the comet within hours of receiving news of it from Perth by overland telegraph. It was brighter than Sirius. On Friday morning, as the *Ophir*
cleared Sunda Strait for the Indian Ocean, the Victorian astronomer, Pietro
Baracchi, caught a glimpse of it near Mercury in the constellation of Pisces,
its triple tail extending over several degrees. The New South Wales astronomer and meteorologist, H. C. Russell, was beaten by two amateurs who saw
part of the comet's tail before he did, in a gap between Sydney's eastern horizon and overlying cloud. Queensland and Tasmania did not have government astronomers, but on 5 May, the day the *Ophir* dropped anchor at
Melbourne, a good telescopic sighting was obtained in Brisbane by the
Queensland meteorologist, Clement L. Wragge.

'Inclement' Wragge, as some called this self-styled 'Boss Weather Prophet
for Australia', had more than a passing interest in the Duke's arrival and the
ceremonies over which His Highness was to preside that week. For the last
few days Wragge had been issuing special *Ophir* bulletins. The forecast was
far from clement, and for reasons to be explained later it must be suspected
that on this occasion the prophet was even more anxious than usual to be
proved right. Let the new parliament be opened under a grey sky, Wragge
seemed to be saying: he had welcomed the coming of federation, but already
it had disappointed him.

Meteorology was one of many activities conducted independently by the
Australian States, and now scheduled for eventual coalescence under the
Commonwealth. Of the six government meteorologists, Wragge had the
widest range of reporting stations and the largest public following. An Australian meteorology conference in 1888 resolved that each observatory
should confine itself to providing forecasts for its own colony. Men like Todd
and Baracchi kept within their own borders, preferring astronomy to meteorology, issuing tersely statistical weather bulletins, and seldom taking the risk
of prediction. Wragge, on the other hand, ignored the 1888 resolution: he
addressed himself in the most personal way to a public avid for his
continent-wide news and clairvoyance. He specialised in low-pressure systems travelling from the Antarctic towards Australia, and often announced
their approach while they were still thousands of miles away.

Each day his observatory at Wickham Terrace in central Brisbane received weather reports by telegraph and cable from points as far afield as Cape Leeuwin, Streaky Bay and Cape Borda in South Australia, New Zealand, New Caledonia and the Malay Archipelago. It was a bad week that did not throw up at least one new antarctic depression or tropical cyclone, and Wragge may well have been the first meteorologist in the world to identify such disturbances by name. From the mid-1890s he worked his way through Greek and Roman mythology, historical and biblical allusion, Polynesian words, the Ethiopian and Hebrew alphabets, and even certain Australian politicians. Xerxes, Hannibal, Ozias, Barton and Deakin all made their appearance in 'Mr. Wragge's General Remarks', like so many players with their exits and their entrances.

A New South Wales politician, A. H. Conroy, once denounced Wragge as 'a sort of Hottentot rain-god' who 'locates many storms away in the Antarctic Ocean where there are no meteorological stations, so that his predictions cannot be checked'. In return, Wragge named a cyclone after him: 'Conroy, black and treacherous, is likely to cross the Southern District'.

Some of his claims certainly were long shots (he once announced an approaching Antarctic depression while it was still near Tristan da Cunha in the south Atlantic); furthermore he was mildly eccentric in appearance and manner, a tall, rather gawky red-haired and bearded Englishman who liked wearing old clothes and blucher boots. Yet he was also a scientist of no mean achievement. He had been the first meteorologist in Australia to issue isobaric maps, and had established the Torrens Observatory near Adelaide and the Mt Wellington Observatory at Hobart. His 'General Remarks' may have been discursive and whimsical, but they were reprinted all over the country and in this time of drought they were widely read. After Conroy's harsh words, the canny Victorian politician, Simon Fraser, spoke up for the Rain-God: 'Pastoralists in the Gulf country, in Central Queensland, in Southern Queensland, New South Wales, Victoria, Tasmania and even New Zealand look to Mr Wragge's forecasts, and generally find them reliable'.

Wragge had national aspirations, and made no secret of it. To the annoyance of his counterparts in other colonies he subscribed his weather maps 'Meteorology of Australasia, Chief Weather Bureau, Brisbane'. On his return to Brisbane from an international meteorological conference in 1897, he offered to relieve all the colonial astronomers of their meteorological duties. 'We are in a position in Brisbane', he wrote in a letter published by the *Age*, 'to issue forecasts for all the colonies more accurately by far than can be done locally'. Although Victoria's astronomer-cum-meteorologist rebuked Wragge for bad manners, the *Age* seemed to find some merit in his proposal. 'As all the scientific world knows', it wrote,

Mr Baracchi is a distinguished mathematician and astronomer, and his very competence in these exact sciences makes him both unfit and disinclined to study the problems of meteorology, which cannot as yet be reckoned an exact science, although it is making rapid strides towards that end. Mr Wragge is, on the contrary, fitted to grapple with the nascent science which, being still in the empirical stage, requires the enthusiasm and divine afflatus of the seer.

Yet Wragge's ambition came to nothing. Not only was his proposal ignored, but federation, upon which he had largely pinned his hopes, left him worse off than before. On 1 March 1901 he returned to the observatory from holidays. 'Well', said his first bulletin of the month,

> today we resume duty at the Chief Weather Bureau under a new regime, since the Post and Telegraph Department of Queensland has been transferred to the Federal Government. It is always pleasant to resume interesting public work after a well-earned respite, and we do so with every confidence, and with firm determination to serve the Australasian people to the best of our power so long as we remain connected with the Chief Weather Bureau.
>
> Now, before saying a word anent the distribution of pressure at present covering this new-born nation the time is clearly opportune for an expression of public thanks to all those officers of the Queensland Post and Telegraph Department and their confreres in the sister States who have for many years past worked so harmoniously with this office by the accurate transmission of the multitudinous meteorological data from all parts of the continent, and we do thank them most cordially—most truly—feeling that the future will be productive of mutual benefit in the momentous interests of the great Commonwealth.

But that was not to be. What Wragge had apparently failed to realise, and what the *Brisbane Courier* made clear two days later, was that although constitutionally a State department dealing with posts, telegraphs and telephones could be transferred quickly to the Commonwealth by proclamation, any meteorological appendage of such a department could be transferred only by the slower process of an act of the federal parliament. This left the Chief Weather Bureau, as the *Courier* put it, 'hung like Mahomet's coffin between heaven and earth', still part of the Queensland bureaucracy, but with no ministerial head. There was speculation that Wragge might resign, and in New South Wales the *Sydney Mail* wondered how in that event Australia could manage without him. 'To dispense with him', it said, 'would be merely to invite the idle winds to blow a hole in the Commonwealth'.

Wragge stayed in his post for the time being, but thenceforth any close reader of his 'General Remarks' would have noticed a deepening mood of inclemency. This was partly because the antarctic depressions were on their seasonal move again, bringing havoc from west to east across southern Australia, but also because of the names which Wragge applied to them. Day after day the Southern Ocean was swept by gales, real and merely predicted.

On 21 March the S.S. *Federal*, a collier bound from Port Kembla in New South Wales to Albany in Western Australia, passed the lighthouse on Gabo Island, heading west into a gale which Wragge had named Zamoth. Five days later the lighthouse keeper found a drowned seaman and a splintered piece of wood bearing the pencil-written message—'SS Federal Melbourne'. Five more bodies were found on the wild coastline of Croajingolong County, east Gippsland, some of them torn to pieces by wild dogs. The *Federal* had carried a crew of twenty-eight, and there were no survivors.

After Zamoth came Amok, a monsoonal depression over the Northern Territory of South Australia; Necodan, an antarctic disturbance 'running the easting down near the forty-eighth parallel south from the Great Bight'; and, on 29 April—moving towards the easterly route of the royal yacht, which was then within a day's steaming of Albany—another antarctic system, which Wragge claimed to have detected several days earlier off the Crozet Archipelego, south of Madagascar. This one he called Moloch.

The *Ophir* may have put Wragge into an Old Testament mood, for Zamoth, Necodan and Moloch all came from that source. But was it too fanciful to suggest a more subtle reason for his choice of the latter name for a low-pressure system that might well determine the sort of weather in which federal parliament would be opened? Moloch was a Canaanite idol to which children were sacrificed as burnt offerings, and one ground for scepticism about federation had always been the fear that uniting colonies might have to make inordinate sacrifices in the dread name of Commonwealth.

The arch-anti-federalist of New South Wales, J. H. Want, spoke about 'this hydra-headed monster called federation basking in its constitutional beastliness', and even such a federalist as South Australia's Josiah Symon was wary of the sacrifices which might be exacted from his own colony by its larger partners. At a federal convention in 1897 Symon referred in one of his speeches to the American humorist Artemus Ward, who once declared that 'he was perfectly ready on the altar of patriotism to sacrifice all his relations, beginning with his mother-in-law'.

'All his wife's relations', corrected a Victorian delegate, Isaac Isaacs.

'Then that makes it much stronger. Some members of the other colonies, I say, seem to emulate Artemus Ward, and are prepared to sacrifice the smaller colonies on their own little altar of federation.'

Wragge, suspended as he was between heaven and earth, perhaps felt he was being prepared for just such an altar. Be that as it may, he now proceeded with gloomy relish to herald the eastward advance of Moloch. 'So the noble *Ophir* has reached Albany!' he wrote on 1 May.

> We are by no means pessimists; we never believe in taking the minor or negative side of life, but at the same time it must be admitted, in view of Moloch, now looking so ugly and threatening over the lower forties south from the Leeuwin, that matters do not appear very promising for the Melbourne celebration.

The South Australian and Victorian astronomers were more hopeful, both predicting on Saturday 4 May that a high pressure area over central and southern Australia would keep the weather fine for the *Ophir*'s arrival and a procession through Melbourne on Monday. The royal yacht reached Melbourne one day early, and was escorted to anchorage by the flagship of the Australian Squadron, H.M.S. *Royal Arthur*, and other naval vessels including a South Australian gunboat, H.M.C.S. *Protector*, lately returned from the Boxer Rebellion in China. A quarantine officer came on board to look cursorily for any signs of the pandemic bubonic plague which only two days earlier had claimed its third Australian victim of the year (a jockey in Perth), thus bringing to more than one hundred the number of Australia's plague deaths during the last eighteen months. Later the new Governor-General of Australia, Lord Hopetoun, visited the Duke and Duchess of York to discuss the coming week's events, and next afternoon, in fine weather, the royal couple and their retinue drove along St Kilda Road to Government House, cheered every inch of the way.

The news from Wragge was still bad. 'Numerous epithets have been applied to us with reference to the forecasts and the historical proceedings at Melbourne', he wrote on Wednesday 8 May, the day before parliament was to be opened.

> But work must be done, truth must be told, however unpleasant, and shirk it we shall never. Therefore we say that unless some law comes into play different to those with which we have had to deal, the northern side of Moloch will surely cause wet and nasty weather at Melbourne on the occasion of the opening of the Federal Parliament.

The Victorian Astronomer, Baracchi, now conceded the possibility of early showers, but promised fairly pleasant weather for the climactic ceremony which was to start in Melbourne's Exhibition Building at noon. But Wragge did not waver. 'Moloch', he wrote on Wednesday evening, 'is now, unfortunately for Marvellous Melbourne, in full swing over Victoria. Fierce westerly squalls, with driving rain, are tearing through the channel between Cape Otway and Flinders Island, and the Federal Parliament will be opened amid the blustering grandeur of a blow from Antarctica'.

'Marvellous Melbourne'—or 'Marvellous Smelbourne', as some in Sydney jeered—had come by this sobriquet during the economic boom when the huge Italian renaissance Exhibition Building opened its doors for the International Exhibition of 1880; when banks and bubble companies lined Collins Street, the 'Golden Street', from one end to the other; and terrace housing spread beside the new factories of Richmond and Fitzroy. For the time being Melbourne was Australia's most populous city. Sydney was rapidly regaining its former ascendancy, but the census of March 1901 had shown Melbourne to be still eight thousand ahead, with a population of almost half a million. One recent visitor, the American author, Nat Gould, remarked on the city's wide, even streets, but found it to be suffering from 'the Chinese curse and also from larrikinism'. 'Collingwood roughs are about the worst specimens of human brutes on earth', he wrote. 'Off Bourke Street there are many notorious Chinese dens, and some of the private bars in the lower-class hotels are hotbeds of vice.'

Melbourne also had temperance hotels, spacious parks, and a quiet, efficient system of public transport by means of cable tram. Through narrow tunnels between the rails ran an endless steel cable on to which the tram's grip fastened for its ride along busy streets. Motor cars were still a rarity, and the main cause of road accidents was horse-bolting. A good bolt down Bourke Street was worth several column-inches in the city's two morning newspapers, the liberal *Age* and the conservative *Argus*.

Although Melbourne had been deeply scarred by the depression of the 1890s, it and other Australian cities were now on their way to economic recovery, thanks largely to a mining revival. Drought continued to starve the pastoral industry, however, and poverty was still easy to find in country and town alike. During the Duke's visit the radical journal *Tocsin* insisted that flags and banners were 'only the tawdry finery of the courtesan and prostitute, whose painted face and gaudy attire hide the blackened soul and diseased body. Behind and beneath all the glare and the glitter stands the gaunt phantom of hunger, and the cry of the unemployed'. This was an extreme view, and one that was hard to reconcile with Melbourne's wild enthusiasm for its royal visitors.

At 11 o'clock on Thursday morning, Lord and Lady Hopetoun left Melbourne's three-storeyed Government House in their viceregal carriage to be driven through crowded streets to the Exhibition Building in Carlton Gardens, on the eastern heights of the city. Ten minutes later, to the roar of a cannonade, Their Royal Highnesses joined the procession in a semi-state landau attended by scarlet-coated outriders and an escort of mounted Australian troops. The carriage was drawn by four bay horses from the Governor-General's stables—by name Captain Cook, Macquarie, Argonaut and Waldersee—and in the rumble stood two liveried and bewigged footmen. The Duke, later to become King George V, wore the gold-trimmed uniform of a rear-admiral. His Duchess, Princess Victoria May of Teck, popularly known as Princess May, was still in mourning for Queen Victoria. She wore a gown of black brocaded gauze, diamond chains and a small black toque.

The escort was led by Colonel J. C. Hoad, assistant Adjutant-General of Victoria's armed forces, wearing on his tunic one of the medals presented by His Royal Highness earlier that week to veterans of the South African war in which Australian troops were still fighting. It bore the likenesses of Queen Victoria and Britannia, and had an orange ribbon with narrow stripes of scarlet and blue. Behind the colonel came a detachment of 116 men, including the brass band of the New South Wales Lancers and soldiers from every other State as well. All the States maintained their own little armies, which in colonial times the first great federalist, Sir Henry Parkes, had belittled as 'painted soldiers'. Directly behind Colonel Hoad were troopers of the Victorian Mounted Rifles, in brown tunics, maroon facings and soft felt hats turned up on the right; Queensland Mounted Rifles, wearing felt hats with grey emu feathers; Tasmanian Mounted Rifles, in grey tunics with red facings and felt hats with black cock tail feathers; South Australian Mounted Rifles, with two lines of red braid on their riding pants, and red puggarees on their hats; New South Wales Lancers, fawn tunics with red piping, black cock feathers and lances with pennons; and the West Australian Mounted Rifles, khaki and unadorned.

The *Argus* thought this cavalcade 'passing through our dun-coloured democratic city' looked like 'the South Head light on a murky sea', and indeed the morning was as murky as Inclement Wragge could have wished. Moloch had arrived, bringing the first of several showers that were to fall during the day. A great bluish-grey cloud hung over Government House, and as the procession reached St Kilda Road a violent gust of wind blew poplar leaves from the wet road into the royal carriage. Many in the crowd wore ulsters or carried umbrellas. 'The cold and searching wind from the Antarctic daunted them not', said the *Age*. 'It might blow cold as its own huddled icebergs, tossing far south that morning in the deep, purple sea, but while there was not continuous rain the people cared nothing for mere showers.'

Opposite the Town Hall in Swanston Street another strong gust of wind caught up with the procession. The crowd had just begun to cheer the Governor-General, who earlier in life had been a popular Governor of Victoria, and a number of hats were being waved in the air. Several of these were blown on to the road, and one was trampled by His Excellency's horses. 'It's not every man', its owner was reported as saying, 'who has had his hat trodden on by Lord Hopetoun's horse when His Lordship was on his way to the opening of the first Australian Federal Parliament'. Another who stood out in this mainly well-dressed and good-natured crowd was a withered little man with tobacco-stained lips and a stubbly chin. 'On his back he carried a red blanket rolled in a piece of hessian', said the *Argus*. 'In one hand he held a black lidless billy-can, from the handle of which were slung two dirty tucker bags. The man was a typical sundowner . . . and so he saw what he declared he had tramped 500 miles to see.'

The largest crowds were in Spring Street, where the procession passed the Treasury buildings, a statue of General Gordon ('somewhere dead, far in the waste Soudan', but here gazing pensively out to Port Phillip Bay, his riding crop under one arm), and the Parliament House which Victoria's Legislative Council and Legislative Assembly had recently vacated to provide a temporary home for federal parliament. But only the main hall of the Exhibition Building—500 feet long, and 200 feet high from floor to roof of dome—had been deemed large enough for the ceremonial opening. At 12 o'clock the royal landau drew up outside the south doors, where the Duke and Duchess were received by the Governor-General. Photographers and at least one cinematographer recorded the arrival, eight trumpeters sounded a fanfare, and the royal party walked through a crimson-carpeted vestibule to join the greatest concourse of people Australia had ever mustered in one building.

A Bill for an Act

On the eve of this gathering one of its most distinguished participants, Alfred Deakin, composed a despatch to the London *Morning Post*, for which he had recently become an anonymous, indeed clandestine, 'special correspondent'. Deakin—a veteran of Victorian ministries in spite of his relative youthfulness, and foremost among the federalists of that colony—was now Attorney-General of the Commonwealth. The mood in which he addressed readers of the *Morning Post* was one of 'personal exultation at the achievement of Federation' and 'joy at the final abandonment of internecine conflicts'. 'The self-government granted to the Colonies individually by the Mother Country was so unfettered', he wrote, 'that they were able to treat each other as foreign nations, and did so, conducting their communications by means of diplomatic correspondence, visits and conferences, and maintaining at their own free will fiscal wars against each other'. At the turn of the century their combined population of 3 783 000 was uniformly British, apart from the one major exception of 21 000 surviving Aborigines. Within that general sameness, however, there was considerable variation and rivalry.

'Australia' was merely a geographical expression, like 'Europe', with little or no political meaning. The self-governing colonies dealt directly with London; they maintained their own artillery, cavalry and gunboats; ran their own rail systems (by 1901 Adelaide was connected to Brisbane by three different rail gauges, but not to Perth); paid their way with notes issued by a variety of private banks in all States except Queensland (which issued its own Treasury notes) and with coins minted at Sydney, Melbourne and Perth, inscribed 'Australia' but otherwise identical with British sovereigns, shillings and pennies; flew their own flags alongside the ubiquitous Union Jack, and issued their own postage stamps. Most colonial stamps showed one version or another of Queen Victoria, but Western Australia preferred black swans and Tasmania's scenic stamps were among the first of their kind in the world.

The differences that affected people most closely were the fiscal ones referred to by Deakin. Customs and excise duties were imposed for protection as well as for revenue, but not to the same extent by all colonies. Victoria was the most restrictive, protecting its manufacturers with a tariff that averaged 30 per cent on nearly a thousand articles of commerce, from acetic acid to zinc sheet. New South Wales, whose larger pastoral community had no wish to pay more for imported manufactures, pursued a policy of free trade. South Australia and Tasmania, although sharing the senior colony's preference, found that they needed to protect themselves against Victorian exports by raising duties beyond the levels required for revenue alone. In the *Australian Handbook* for 1901 the list of customs duties for Victoria filled fifteen pages; New South Wales only half a page; South Australia, Tasmania and Queensland three pages each; and Western Australia two pages.

There were customs offices at Corowa, Echuca and Mildura on the River Murray, at Albury and Wodonga on the Melbourne–Sydney railway line, at Wallangarra on the Queensland border, and Serviceton in South Australia: 'no visitor can pass from Sydney to Melbourne', wrote a Sydney apologist for freedom of trade, B. R. Wise,

> —although these cities are as closely related by ties of business and friendship as Liverpool is to Manchester, or Boston to New York— without being subjected to a tiresome delay of thirty minutes while his person is inspected by detectives and his luggage searched as if he were a suspected thief.

One advantage of the fiscal issue was that, at a time of factional politics, when amorphous groupings were not easily defined, it was a sort of litmus paper that turned pink for Protection and blue for Free Trade. The fiscal issue produced a readily recognisable division on a single important national issue. Regional identity of economic interest gave the division some coherence, but these were exceptions to the rule. Broadly, the strongest advocates of Free Trade were the established merchant and agricultural interests in New South Wales, whose politics were generally conservative. The main challenge to them came from Victorian manufacturers who argued that Protection was necessary to foster secondary industries and extend employment. These were arguments which appealed to influential people (often of a liberal and even radical cast of mind) not only in Victoria but in the less developed economies of Tasmania and South Australia, and to a lesser extent in parts of Queensland. Western Australia, which was only just beginning to enjoy the fruits of its gold boom and of the expansion of agriculture and industry which accompanied the sudden rise in population there, tended to regard Protectionism as just another opportunity for the eastern colonies to profiteer at the expense of consumers on the far side of the continent. Other groups such as the embryonic labour movement were found in both fiscal camps according to regional interests. W. M. Hughes, for example—secretary of the Sydney Wharf Labourers' Union and a Labor member of the New South Wales Legislative Assembly—advocated free trade because it was 'the natural order of things'.

Fiscal war between the colonies, and a common interest by those colonies in military security, each gave impetus to the federal movement which hitherto had produced only rhetoric. In the early 1880s rumours of intended annexations in the Pacific by France and Germany led to a form of association between some of the colonies, but this was so loose as to be barely perceptible. Then, in the following decade, a great Depression argued very persuasively the folly of pursuing several different tariff policies, and conversely the need for closer federal union with better co-ordination of the continent's economy.

Federal systems of government had usually commended themselves to states whose people desired union but not unity, and without doubt this feeling prevailed in the Australian colonies. Those who thought about the matter realised that there were two kinds of federal system: the weaker confederation, in which a central government dealt only with governments of the component States, not with individual citizens; and the stronger federation which, although giving the central government considerable power over citizens, attempted to reconcile that national power with the maintenance of State rights.

Confederate systems adopted in the past by Switzerland, Germany and the thirteen American States linked by a Continental Congress had all proved unsuccessful; and so it was, too, with the even flimsier Federal Council of Australasia. This Council—first advocated by Sir Henry Parkes in 1881, and agreed upon in principle two years later by governments of the Australian colonies, New Zealand and Fiji—was a small representative body with power to legislate on some matters that were beyond the competence of individual colonies, and on certain other matters, such as regional defence, which could be referred to it by member governments. It did not meet for the first time until 1886 and, although surviving until 1901, it possessed neither executive powers nor revenue. New South Wales, whose premier, Parkes, now argued that such a 'ricketty body' would merely 'impede the way for a sure and solid federation', declined to join. So also, for other reasons, did New Zealand; and South Australia withdrew after belonging for only three years.

In June 1889 Sir Henry Parkes, a robust seventy-five years of age and Premier for the fifth time, was talking in his office to the Governor of New South Wales, Lord Carrington. They were discussing Canada's position *vis-à-vis* the imperial government, which was stronger than that of the Australian colonies because of the Canadian provinces' federal status. 'I could confederate these colonies in twelve months', said the old man.

'Then why don't you do it?' replied His Excellency. 'It would be a glorious finish to your life.' Parkes smiled and said: 'There are some difficulties'.

What Parkes had in mind was clearly not a confederation, but a federation comparable in solidity to those of the United States of America since 1787 and Canada since 1867. In the determined campaign for federation upon which he then embarked, Parkes found ready ammunition in a report on Australia's defences by a British military officer, Major-General Bevan Edwards. Indeed it was not inconceivable that Parkes himself had helped to inspire Edwards's recommendation for 'federation' of the colonial forces under one command. The Edwards Report, completed in October 1889, also recommended the establishment of a federal military college and standardisation of the colonies' rail gauges.

During that month Parkes visited Brisbane to speed the federal message, and on his way home he delivered an oration that caught the attention of people all over Australia. At the School of Arts in Tenterfield, amid the granite hills of New England, he told his listeners on 24 October that

> the great question which they had to consider was, whether the time had not now come for the creation on this Australian continent of an Australian Government, as distinct from the local governments now in existence.(Applause.) In other words, to make himself as plain as possible, Australia had now a population of three and a half millions, and the American people numbered only between three and four millions when they formed the great commonwealth of the United States. The numbers were about the same, and surely what the Americans had done by war, the Australians could bring about in peace without breaking the ties that held them to the mother country.(Cheers.) As to the steps which should be taken to bring this about, a conference of the Governments had been pointed to [during his discussions in Brisbane], but they must take broader views in the initiation of the movement than had been taken hitherto; they must appoint a convention of leading men from all the colonies, delegates appointed by the authority of Parliament, who would fully represent the opinion of the different Parliaments of the colonies. This convention would have to devise the constitution which would be necessary for bringing into existence a federal government with a Federal Parliament for the conduct of national business. (Applause.)

There is no need to trace every step that led eventually to the drafting of a constitution bill, its approval by a majority of votes in all Australian colonies, and its enactment in 1900. Our main interest here is in the kind of parliament prescribed by the Commonwealth of Australia Constitution Act, and why such a kind was preferred to any other by the majority opinion that emerged from the constitutional conventions of 1891, at Sydney, and 1897–98, in sessions at Adelaide, Sydney and Melbourne. Certain things were taken for granted from the start. As Parkes had said at Tenterfield, the colonies did not want to break their ties with the mother country. This meant they would federate under the Crown. Their Constitution, like Canada's, would be passed into law by the British parliament, and some parliamentary elements of that 'great governmental machine', as one delegate to the Sydney convention described the coming constitution, would undoubtedly resemble those of London, Ottawa and the existing six colonial parliaments in Australia. There would be a Governor-General, representing the Queen and the British Government, and there would be two houses of parliament. An Australian Constitution might also embody the British concept of responsible government, whereby a Governor-General would choose as his advisers certain members of the parliamentary party or coalition with a majority in the lower or popularly elected house (these members formed a governing ministry or cabinet, and dealt with His Excellency as a privy council or executive council) and would accept their advice only so long as they continued to enjoy the confidence of that house. Thus under the doctrine of responsibility a ministry was accountable for its actions to the popular house (in London and Ottawa, the House of Commons), and would lose office if signally defeated in a vote there.

But there was no certainty that the drafters of an Australian Constitution would avail themselves of responsible government. It did have the recommendations of being both British and familiar; yet the United States seemed happy enough without it. The American Constitution had in fact done all it could to separate the executive from the legislature. The President was not chosen by Congress, and he was not responsible to it; neither he nor the members of his cabinet could sit in either the House of Representatives or the Senate. America had built a workable federal machine, which was more than a centralised state like the United Kingdom had ever needed to do, and some of those attending the 1891 convention were familiar with its technicalities. Deakin, Victoria's 34-year-old Attorney-General, commended to his fellow delegates a work he had just finished reading—*The American Commonwealth*, by the British M.P. and Oxford Professor of Civil Law, James Bryce—and throughout the 1897–98 convention Bryce's three volumes were always on the table.

American and other federal models provided a variety of solutions to some of the Australian problems for which Westminster precedents were not relevant. The British parliament—consisting of sovereign, House of Lords and House of Commons—had supreme and unlimited power throughout the Empire. It passed what laws it pleased, and no court could rule them unconstitutional. The British Constitution was a collection of statutes, customs and conventions, and parliament could repeal or modify any part of these at any time. For that reason it was said to be a flexible constitution, as distinct from the more or less rigid constitutions of other nations, particularly federations.

The word 'federation' derives from the Latin *foedus*, meaning a league, treaty or compact, and a federal constitution may be thought of as a treaty between high contracting parties—the States and the nation. If the federation is to survive, such a treaty must reassure its signatories at two levels: it must somehow reconcile national power with States' rights, and also reconcile the larger states' expectations of predominance, on the one hand, with the claims of smaller states to equality, on the other. This the federal 'treaty' seeks to do by defining the kind of laws a national parliament may properly make, by providing a federal judiciary to see that parliament does not exceed its powers, and by ensuring that the Constitution itself can be amended only with some degree of difficulty. America's Constitution further assuaged the States' fears of Moloch by adapting the bicameral system to their need for reassurance. One chamber represented the nation, its members popularly elected from individual districts; the other represented the States, an equal number of senators for each State being at first chosen by the respective State legislatures. Canada followed this example to some extent, though its Senate did not represent all provinces equally and was not so close in legislative power to the lower house as was its counterpart in Washington.

As a means of reassuring suspicious States, a States' house might seem only as good as its ability to amend legislation, particularly financial legislation. Canada and the United States had both followed the British system under which revenue and money bills were initiated only in the lower house. But whereas by convention the Canadian Senate did not amend such bills, the United States Senate had constitutional power to do so. America had the stronger federal spirit. Canada's provincial legislatures exercised only those powers expressly given to them by the federal Constitution; all other powers belonged to the national parliament. The United States Constitution bestowed specific powers on the centre, and what was left belonged to the State legislatures. With *The American Commonwealth* displayed so prominently before them, and given their own provincial apprehensions, it seemed more than likely that the delegates gathered at Sydney's Parliament House would prefer America's centrifugal way of sharing legislative power.

Other sources of inspiration available at this convention were the latest edition of A. V. Dicey's *Introduction to the Study of the Law of the Constitution*; a draft constitution bill prepared on his own initiative by the Tasmanian Attorney-General, Andrew Inglis Clark, who was an admirer of most things American; another draft by the Premier of South Australia, Charles Cameron Kingston, drawn like Clark's mainly from the Constitutions of the United States, Canada and the Australian colonies; and *Manual of Reference*, a useful compendium of federal systems by Richard Chaffey Baker. Nowhere did the federal flame burn more brightly than in this former Attorney-General of South Australia. Baker wanted a States' House co-ordinate with the popular house not only in power to amend, but also in power to bring about changes of government. His ideal was the Swiss form of executive, with an equal number of ministers elected by, and responsible to, both houses of parliament.

The choice of Sydney as a meeting place for the National Australasian Convention was clinched by Sir Henry Parkes's continuing lameness from a serious carriage accident. He could not have gone anywhere else, and the convention would have been sadly incomplete without the man who, as early as 1867, had spoken of 'a new constellation of six stars in the heavens, and the footprints of six young giants in the morning dew'. As Premier of the host colony Sir Henry was president of the convention, but after his opening address he spoke infrequently and had little influence on the proceedings. The real leader was the Premier of Queensland, Sir Samuel Griffith. This 'lean, ascetic, cold, clear' lawyer, as Deakin described him, was elected chairman of the committee on constitutional powers and functions. He did more than anyone else to shape the draft Constitution of 1891.

On the first sitting day, 4 March, Parkes proposed several resolutions expressing the sense of an informal discussion held in his office with most of the premiers, and others, including Clark and Kingston. One of these resolutions called for the establishment of a parliament consisting of a Senate and House of Representatives, the former to have an equal number of members from each province, regardless of population, and the latter elected by districts formed on a population basis and possessing the sole power of originating and amending all bills appropriating revenue or imposing taxation; a federal supreme court, which would be a final court of appeal for Australia; and an executive, consisting of a governor-general and such members of parliament as might from time to time be appointed to advise him, their term of office depending upon possession of majority support in the House of Representatives.

This was certainly a start, but it begged some very difficult questions. The next speaker, Sir Samuel Griffith, came straight to what was probably the hardest question of all: the role of the Senate. As an earnest federalist, Griffith believed that the States' House should have full power to amend. Such nearly co-ordinate power worked satisfactorily in the American system of separate executive and legislature. But how could it do so without risk of deadlock, he asked, in the traditional system of responsible government which was preferred by at least half the delegates, including himself?

> We propose, as I understand it, assuming that the house representing the states is to have the authority which I think it must and ought to have, to associate with it a system which has never in the history of the world been tried in conjunction with it. We propose to have an executive government having possibly, seats in Parliament. How shall we guarantee that the machine will work if we insist that these ministers will hold their offices, in form as well as in reality, by the will of one house only? Does not the possibility of a very serious deadlock occur here to every honourable gentleman at once? The majority of one house of the legislature will certainly be made up of the representatives of the larger colonies. Probably two colonies in that house [New South Wales and Victoria] will be able to overshadow all the rest.
> Mr PLAYFORD: Possibly one!
> Sir SAMUEL GRIFFITH: Possibly one some day; but almost certainly two at no distant date. Now, that majority representing the people of these two states in that house would have the making and unmaking of governments. On the other hand there would be an independent body in the constitution representing the states. Suppose that independent body . . . differed from the house of representatives representing two states, there would be certainly a deadlock at once . . . I point out that the experiment we propose to try has never yet been tried. We must take into consideration the existence of those two forces possibly hostile, even probably hostile, before, say fifty or a hundred years are over, and we must frame our constitution in such a way that it will work if that friction does arise.

One of the shrewdest politicians listening to this speech—another

Queenslander, the frail J. M. Macrossan, who was to die during the convention—thought correctly that he detected a flaw in Griffith's argument. 'The influence of party will remain much the same as it is now', he said, 'and instead of members of the senate voting, as has been suggested, as states, they will vote as members of parties to which they belong. I think, therefore, that the idea of the larger states being overpowered by the voting of the smaller states might very well be abandoned'. Macrossan's observation was all the more astute for having been made so early in the evolution of Australian party politics, yet undeniably Griffith had touched on something crucial. The sensitivity of the four less populous States—in descending order, Queensland, South Australia, Tasmania and Western Australia—ensured that the Senate's power, no matter which way it might come to be exercised, remained a central issue.

New South Wales and Victoria were not prepared to let the upper house, which in their view could be dominated by members representing little more than a quarter of the national population and elected by State legislatures, thwart the democratically elected lower house. Western Australia, to take the most extreme case, had a population of only 49 800 (although before the end of the decade its population, increased by immigration from eastern Australia to the goldfields of Kalgoorlie and Coolgardie, would have relegated Tasmania's to last place); yet this vast, thinly peopled State was to have the same number of senators as New South Wales or Victoria, whose populations were each well over a million.

This quandary was resolved by what became known as the compromise of 1891, taken directly from the South Australian parliament. The Senate's power to amend would match that of the House of Representatives for all proposed laws except those imposing taxation and appropriating revenue or money for the ordinary annual services of government, which the Senate could affirm or reject, but not amend. However—and here was the compromise—although the Senate could not amend such 'money bills', it could at any stage return them to the House of Representatives with a message *requesting* the omission or amendment of any items or provisions. And the House of Representatives might, if it saw fit, comply with that request. With this compromise approved by 22 votes to 16, the prospect of deadlock between the houses receded, and the final draft Constitution contained no procedure for dealing with such an eventuality.

The final draft was composed during Easter on board the Queensland Government steamer *Lucinda* as it cruised the waters of the Hawkesbury estuary, Pittwater and Sydney's Middle Harbour. Those on board included Griffith, Kingston, another South Australian, Sir John Downer, and Edmund Barton, a Sydney barrister, former New South Wales Attorney-General and Speaker in the Legislative Assembly of that State. Inglis Clarke was ill with influenza and Griffith, who did most of the final shaping, came down with the same complaint before the cruise was over.

Nothing of importance in the draft Bill was changed by debate. The Bill provided that members of the executive council (that name was preferred to the British and Canadian 'privy council') '*may* sit in parliament', and by that means the choice between responsible government and a separate executive was left open. Similarly the establishment of a Supreme Court of Australia was made possible rather than mandatory. The federal partners were to be called 'States' rather than 'Provinces', and the federation was to be known as 'the Commonwealth of Australia'. The name 'Commonwealth' had been first suggested by Parkes, and it was strongly supported by Griffith and Deakin against the misgivings of some to whom its Cromwellian overtones seemed vaguely revolutionary. After much argument in the judiciary committee it was narrowly adopted in time for Griffith to use it in the draft instead of such proposed alternatives as 'Federal Dominion', 'Federated States' and 'United Australia'. 'It is no doubt new to some honourable members', said Griffith in debate, 'but I think they will find, as I myself found, that, after being accustomed to it for two or three days, it will come to be regarded as the most natural and proper name'.

There was, of course, nothing binding about the draft Bill. The 1891 delegates had been appointed by colonial parliaments, and those parliaments were free to amend the draft or even to ignore it. New South Wales did not take the lead for which other colonies were waiting. An election soon after the convention left Parkes dependent for survival on a completely new parliamentary group, the Labor Party, which made its debut in that colony with no fewer than thirty-five seats. Parkes resigned in October and was succeeded by an anti-federalist and Protectionist, G. R. Dibbs. The new leader of the Free Trade Opposition, George Houston Reid, admitted the advantages of federation but was wary of its possible effect on New South Wales tariff policy. With the customary sharp wit that so belied his appearance of obese somnolence, Reid said that for New South Wales to join the other more or less Protectionist colonies would be like 'a teetotaller setting up house with five drunkards'.

As Attorney-General in the new Protectionist ministry, Barton managed to bring about some debate on the draft Bill, but received no support from Labor members. Some of these newcomers, finding the Bill too rigid for socialist hopes, and suspicious of the power it conferred on the governor-general, were actively opposed to the kind of federation contemplated at the convention. 'I believe in home rule', said Arthur Rae, the Labor Member for Murrumbidgee.

> I believe, too, that if federation comes about on any such lines as those laid down by the convention, before this generation has passed away we shall see one of the most terrible struggles that has ever convulsed any nation on the earth, in order to obtain the rights which men are asked voluntarily to resign.

Four colonial parliaments debated some aspects of the draft. Queensland took no action at all, and neither did Western Australia.

With the interdependence of colonial economies being demonstrated so palpably by the 1890s Depression, the federal movement soon revived. Federal leagues appeared, and in 1893 a conference was held at the border town of Corowa, whose citizens were greatly incommoded by the presence of customs houses on the River Murray. There a Victorian lawyer, Dr John Quick, outlined a series of steps which could lead consecutively to federation.

George Reid—by then Premier of New South Wales, and allowing enthusiasm to overcome his caution—called a conference of premiers at Hobart in January 1895. The Premiers agreed to try to secure the passage of enabling acts by their parliaments, embodying the kind of steps which Dr Quick had proposed: election by popular vote of ten representatives from each colony, who would attend another convention to frame another draft constitution; adjournment of the convention to let parliaments consider the draft; reassembly of the convention to consider all suggested amendments; and finally, submitting the revised draft to all colonial electors at referendum.

By the time the first session of the Australasian Federal Convention began at Parliament House, Adelaide, in March 1897, Sir Henry Parkes had died and Sir Samuel Griffith had left politics to become Chief Justice of his colony. In any case Queensland, because irreconcilable differences between its two parliamentary chambers had prevented the passing of an enabling act, sent no delegates to the convention. Neither did New Zealand, which had been represented in 1891 but thereafter showed little interest in uniting with its neighbours across the Tasman Sea. Western Australia decided to attend only at the last minute.

Presiding over the convention were the men who had been Griffith's two main adjutants at Sydney, Kingston and Barton. Kingston was an idealistic and autocratic radical, once described by the Colonial Office as 'perhaps the most quarrelsome man alive'. It did not follow from the fact that he was Premier that he would also be the convention president, for that position was now elective rather than ex officio, and Kingston had made some powerful enemies in his own colony. On one occasion he had been arrested with a loaded duelling pistol in his pocket while on his way to an intended rendezvous, of his own making, with Richard Baker. He had also quarrelled bitterly with another conservative South Australian parliamentarian—the barrister Josiah Symon, who suspected that the coming Commonwealth might be willing to sacrifice all its relations on the altar of federation— describing him in a letter to the *South Australian Register* as 'a gruesome ghoul' and 'a forensic compound of squid and skunk'.

Nevertheless, Kingston was elected president. Barton was termed leader, and that was precisely the role he was now generally acknowledged to have assumed in the federal movement thoughout Australia. 'Australia's noblest son', the Sydney *Daily Telegraph* called him, not without malice. 'To hell with this noblest son business', Barton replied; and yet to many the phrase did not seem inapt.

Like Kingston he was a big man, not as tall but perhaps heavier than the South Australian, for he weighed 17 stone. His mane of iron-grey hair rose from a wide brow which Deakin described as Apollo-like, his black eyes glowed 'like jewels in the ardour of his inspiration', but to Deakin's sharp eye the lower part of Barton's face fell below this high standard. The mouth was 'fish-like, though its pout often had a pretty effect; the jowl was large, pointing not only to strength of will but to love of ease and indulgence'. He was dignified and courteous, a good constitutional lawyer, and an easy conversationalist who enjoyed social life. Strangers sometimes hailed him in the street as 'Toby', a childhood nickname that had stuck, and behind his back some even used the name 'Toby Tosspot', in exaggerated allusion to his liking for good food and wine. Barton was the second youngest of eleven children, born of English stock in the middle-class suburb of Glebe and educated at Sydney Grammar School and Sydney University. His father had been a moderately successful stockbroker. Noblest or not, Toby Barton was certainly one of Australia's most favoured sons.

At the popular election of convention delegates, Barton received the largest majority of any candidate in any colony. Among his colleagues from New South Wales were Richard O'Connor, a close friend since school days, and one of only three Roman Catholics to be elected (the others were the South Australian Patrick McMahon Glynn and the Tasmanian Matthew Clarke); George Reid, who was still Premier; William Lyne, the Protectionist Leader of the Opposition, a truculent backblocks politician whose instincts were parochial rather than federal; and Bernhard Wise, a former double-first and blue from Oxford, the quality of whose metal never matched the promise of its lustre. Another New South Welshman, 30-year-old Robert Garran, achieved prominence at the convention although he was only Reid's secretary. His recently published book on federalism, *The Coming Commonwealth*, was so well received by delegates that he 'felt rather like Lord Byron when he woke one morning and found himself famous'.

Victoria's delegation included its liberal Premier and Treasurer, Sir George Turner; Deakin, a liberal backbencher in the Legislative Assembly who was Barton's counterpart and federal lieutenant in Victoria; two radical lawyers, Isaac Isaacs and Henry Bournes Higgins; and William Trenwith, M.L.A., union secretary and a former bootmaker, who was the only official Labor man at the convention. Other prominent delegates were the Premier of Tasmania, a former soldier in the British Raj, Sir Edward Braddon (Tasmania's best known federalist, Inglis Clark, was absent on a voyage to America); Sir John Forrest, the amiable but rough Premier of Western Australia; and a very strong South Australian delegation. In addition to Kingston and Glynn, the latter included Sir Richard Baker, who served as chairman of committees; Sir John Downer; Josiah Symon; and the Colonial Treasurer, Frederick Holder. Another South Australian, E. G. Blackmore, was clerk of the convention. The latter, Clerk of the Legislative Council and Clerk of the Parliament at Adelaide, was reputed to have the most sonorous voice in official Australia.

The convention took as its starting point not the 1891 draft Bill but several resolutions moved by Barton, the first of which proposed as a prerequisite of federation that 'the powers, privileges, and territories of the several existing colonies shall remain intact, except in respect of such surrenders as may be agreed upon to secure uniformity of law and administration in matters of common concern'. Yet the earlier draft had exerted too great an influence on public opinion not to affect the proceedings at Adelaide. The Adelaide Bill might differ in many respects from that which had been completed on board the *Lucinda*, but it would still owe more to Sir Samuel Griffith than to anyone else.

The Adelaide session came down on the side of responsible government by deciding that no minister of state should hold office in the executive council for longer than three months 'unless he shall be or become a member of one of the Houses of Parliament'. It also made sure (rather than optional) that the Commonwealth's judicial power would be vested in a High Court of Australia, and would extend to all matters arising under the Constitution or under laws made by the parliament. The upper house was first called 'States Assembly', then changed to 'Senate', though George Reid thought that name too 'frenchified'. For the lower house, Higgins favoured 'National Assembly', and Symon 'House of Commons'; but once again the majority preferred America's 'House of Representatives'.

As in 1891 the most crucial debate concerned the composition and powers of the Senate *vis-à-vis* those of the lower house. This question in fact occupied more than one-third of the 7053 pages of the federation convention debates in the 1890s. There was a fundamental difference between the supposed interests of large and small States. If the Senate was to have co-ordinate power, argued Isaacs, it should not also have equal representation for all States:

> I believed, and within certain limitations I believe it still, that equal representation is right to protect the smaller States from fears which are groundless, but . . . are not unreasonable in certain minds. But I am not willing that that equal representation shall be coupled with co-ordinate powers. If you have co-ordinate powers, or what are tantamount to co-ordinate powers, you have no need for equal representation . . . To say that three-fifths of the Senate representing one-fifth of the population of Australia and representing one-fourth of the federal revenue should be able to dominate the remaining four-fifths of the population and the remaining three-fourths of the revenue, is equally absurd, and therefore when I am asked, as we are all asked, to supply the reason in logic and in justice for not making this concession, I think when these facts are stated, the reason, the logic and the justice are self-evident.

The concession to which Isaacs referred had been proposed in the constitutional committee, and was now under debate. It meant a narrowing of the exceptions made earlier to the Senate's power of amendment. The draft Bill of 1891 had excepted 'laws imposing taxation and laws appropriating the necessary supplies', and now the constitutional committee had suggested omitting the words 'laws imposing taxation and'. This would enlarge the scope for the kind of financial amendment which a delegate like Symon of South Australia regarded as essential:

> I agree with Mr Holder that there is a fear existing in the minds of many in this country that we are going to be harnessed to the car of the larger colonies, that that time may be long in arriving when we shall be equal in population, and when we shall be able to meet them on an equal footing in the House of Representatives. At present we are not. We would love to meet you with seventeen members to forty-nine. I am willing to meet you in that way. I believe in your fairness and judgement, but at the same time I agree with the framers of the American Constitution as to original sin. We do not ask under colour of a favour what we think we should have as a right . . . We have been told during the debate that this is the time for plain language, and I say that we should have a powerful Senate possessed of a

will and having the means to exercise and enforce it, sitting as one of the most invulnerable parts of the State in relation to money.

On 13 April, the first day the draft Bill came before the convention sitting as a committee of the whole, Reid moved an amendment to restore the words 'laws imposing taxation and'. If this were passed it would revive the compromise of 1891, under which the Senate would be prevented from amending taxation as well as appropriation and supply bills, but in addition to the simple alternatives of passing or rejecting such bills would also be able to request their amendment by the lower house. On those four words depended nothing less than the fate of federation. 'If the other colonies are not prepared to accept what has been fairly regarded as the 1891 compromise', said Sir George Turner, speaking as much for New South Wales as for Victoria, 'then we are placed in such a position that we have no hesitation in saying that Federation will be impossible'.

At 9.30 p.m.—with a vote looming, and seemingly certain to go against Reid's amendment—Barton deferred his closing speech because of a bronchial cold. This 'providential catarrh', as Robert Garran later described it, had the effect of delaying the vote until next day. After some late lobbying in the delegates' hotels, two South Australians, three Tasmanians and one New South Welshman changed their minds, and the amendment scraped through by 25 votes to 23.

From Adelaide the draft Bill went to the parliaments of all participating colonies. Of the amendments suggested by them, twenty-one were accepted during later sessions of the convention, thirty-six were lost after exhaustive debate, and seventy were lost with little or no debate. During the Sydney session Higgins tried unsuccessfully to replace the Senate's equality of representation with population-based representation; Forrest took up the lost cause of widening the Senate's amending power, and was heard to mutter 'Rats!' from time to time while supporters of the majority were speaking; and Paddy Glynn, an Adelaide lawyer with a barely comprehensible Irish brogue, wrote an important letter beginning, 'Dear Miss Dynon'.

'On Tuesday, during the sitting', explained Glynn in another letter, to his mother,

> I wrote a proposal of marriage to a girl whom I had only spoken to once; had a telegram accepting on Wednesday; made what the audience considered a great speech on Thursday at 5.30 p.m.; took the 7.15 p.m. express to Melbourne same night, got married on Saturday and returned same day, arriving here on Sunday. You will think I am mad . . . She is at all events what will please you: a Catholic, a good one, with enough religion for the two of us.

In January 1898, half way through one of the most ferocious Victorian summers on record, the convention reassembled in the Legislative Assembly chamber at Melbourne. For seven days in a row the temperature was well over 100 degrees Fahrenheit. Birds and animals died of heat exhaustion, and the searing north-west wind blew a pungent odour of bushfire smoke into the Legislative Assembly. Clement Wragge ushered in two welcome Antarctic changes, by name Zayan and Niphrata, but on each occasion the wind soon swung back to the north.

This last session of the convention extended the list of subjects on which federal parliament could make laws to include 'invalid and old-age pensions' and 'conciliation and arbitration for the prevention and settlement of industrial disputes extending beyond the limits of any one State'; agreed that differences between the two houses should be settled by a three-fifths majority vote at a joint sitting of the houses; laid down procedure for altering the Constitution by referendum after a proposed amendment had been passed by absolute majorities of both houses of parliament; declared not only that the seat of government should be determined by parliament, as the Adelaide draft had stated, but that it should also be within territory vested in the Commonwealth; and reassured the colonies that they would continue to receive an adequate share of customs revenue after federation. Tariff was the colonies' main source of income. Now it had been decided that customs duties on intercolonial trade would end when federation began, and that the right to levy duties on imports from overseas would pass to the Commonwealth. What guarantee was there that the federal government would pass on enough of that revenue to the States? The answer came in a clause moved by the Tasmanian Premier, Braddon: the Commonwealth would retain not more than one-quarter of customs and excise revenue for its own purposes, and distribute the balance to State governments for use as they might decide. The young and distant colony of Western Australia, because of its relatively greater reliance on imports, was acknowledged to be a special case. It was therefore agreed, on a motion by Deakin, that for five years after the introduction of a uniform tariff Western Australia would be allowed to impose customs duty on goods from other States at a rate which would diminish by one-fifth each year.

As the next step to federation, the Melbourne draft Bill was submitted by referendum to the voters of New South Wales, Victoria, Tasmania and South Australia in June 1898. The Western Australian parliament, still worried about loss of revenue in spite of the Braddon and Deakin clauses, wanted to discuss the Bill; and Queensland was still keeping its own counsel. The Bill received a majority in four colonies, but in New South Wales the Yes vote was less than a statutory minimum of 80 000 which parliament had prescribed as necessary. Although Reid claimed, with some justice, to have 'lifted federation out of the gutter' by arranging the Premiers' meeting of 1895, some federalists blamed him for the fixing of a minimum vote, and for not evincing sufficient pro-Bill enthusiasm during the campaign. In his opening speech, which earned him the nickname of 'Yes-No' Reid, he pointed out every part of the Bill likely to have an adverse effect on New South Wales, and then said that nonetheless he personally would vote 'Yes'. It is only fair to say that Reid felt a responsibility to his colony, and that the negative aspects of his speech were quite consistent with views he had previously expressed at the convention. But this did not stop some federalists, particularly Deakin, from bringing in the unwarranted verdict of treachery.

In an editorial which he wrote for the *Age*, Deakin said:

Having declared his adhesion to the Commonwealth Bill under the evident assurance that the conditions which he had imposed must block its acceptance, so soon as its success began to be secured by the labors of others, [Reid] hastened to take the platform as its hostile critic. His antagonism to it grew in exact proportion as its prospects improved, until at last, acting from the highest motives, he contrived to bring about the failure of a movement which he claimed to have inaugurated by defeating a Bill he had pledged himself to support.

That withering tone remained characteristic of Deakin's attitude towards the man who was later to become his chief federal opponent.

In January 1899 a conference of the six colonial Premiers in Melbourne tinkered with the draft Bill to enhance its prospects in New South Wales and Queensland at another referendum. There were four main amendments. In a joint sitting of the two houses to resolve disagreement, the decision of an absolute majority (instead of three-fifths, as previously agreed) would be final. Neither house alone should have power to prevent a proposed constitutional amendment being referred to the people: a proposed amendment, if passed twice by one house and rejected or obstructed by the other, could be submitted to referendum by the Governor-General. The Braddon clause would operate not perpetually, but for ten years. And finally, the seat of government would be within New South Wales, and not less than 100 square miles in area. Out of respect for Victorian feelings, the site would be not less than 100 miles from Sydney, and until the Commonwealth parliament was able to meet there it would sit in Melbourne.

Between June and September 1899 the amended Bill was approved by New South Wales and all other colonies except Western Australia. To those who had such a timetable in mind, it now seemed far more likely that a Commonwealth of Australia—even if it had to be a constellation of only five stars—would keep its appointment with the twentieth century. By October all colonies except Western Australia had adopted addresses to the Queen praying for the imperial parliament's enactment of the Constitution Bill. Five months later a delegation consisting of Barton, Deakin, Kingston and a former Tasmanian Premier, Sir Philip Fysh, began discussions in London with the Colonial Office. The Australians pressed for passage of the Bill without amendment, and except for certain technical adjustments and a compromise about appeals from the High Court to Britain's Privy Council, they succeeded. The Bill had a quick passage through both houses of parliament, and the resulting 'Act to Constitute the Commonwealth of Australia' received royal assent on 9 July 1900.

Provision was made in the Act for Western Australia to join the other colonies if the Queen was satisfied that its people had agreed to do so. They did agree later that month, casting what turned out to be (mainly because of the urban vote in Perth and the 'T'othersiders' on the goldfields) proportionately the most affirmative vote from any of the colonies. On 17 September Queen Victoria proclaimed that 'on and after the first day of January one thousand nine hundred and one' the people of all six colonies would be united in a Federal Commonwealth under the name of the Commonwealth of Australia.

The Constitution was a conservative document that would be described several decades later as only 'minimally appropriate' even in 1901, 'carrying . . . so heavy and restricting a burden of nineteenth century Colonial thinking and parochial compromise'. Nevertheless, or perhaps partly for that very reason, it received a measure of praise from James Bryce, whose book, *The American Commonwealth*, had been a basic reference at both federal conventions. In Bryce's estimation, the new Constitution stood federally somewhere between those of the United States and Canada. 'In the United States', he wrote,

> the Federal Government has less power as against the States than in Australia. In Canada the Federal Government has more power, or at least a wider range of action. In other words, the Australian system approaches nearer, in point of form, to a Unitary Government than does the United States, but not so near as does Canada . . .
>
> Technically regarded, the Constitution is an excellent piece of work. Its arrangement is logical. Its language is for the most part clear and precise . . . Although it is much longer, as well as less terse, than the Constitution of the United States, going into fuller detail, and with more of the flavour of an English statute about it, it nevertheless, like that Constitution, leaves much to be subsequently filled up by the action of the legislature. A very large field of legislation remains common to the States and the Commonwealth Parliament; and though statutes passed by the latter will of course override or supersede those which may have been passed by the former, it may be many years before the higher Parliament finds leisure to cultivate all the ground which lies open before it.

A High Court, intended by the Constitution to have jurisdiction in such matters as the constitutional validity of Commonwealth laws, would be established in due course by parliament. Until then, any matters arising under laws of the Commonwealth parliament would have to be dealt with by State courts.

Parliament itself would consist of the Queen (which, for practical purposes, was to say the governor-general); the Senate, composed of six members from each State, elected for a term of six years by the people of each State voting as one electorate; and the House of Representatives, composed of members elected for three years, the number chosen for each State being in proportion to State populations, and the total number being as nearly as practicable twice the number of senators. The seventy-two seats in the lower house would become vacant simultaneously; but the upper house was to enjoy greater continuity because the thirty-six senators would vacate their seats by rotation, half every three years.

The powers, privileges and immunities of the two houses would be such as might be declared by parliament, and until so declared would be those of the House of Commons of the United Kingdom. Section 51 of the Constitution enumerated thirty-nine subjects on which parliament would have power to make laws 'for the peace, order and good government of the

Commonwealth'. The list started with interstate and foreign trade and commerce, and taxation, and proceeded through such other powers as naval and military defence, banking other than state banking, postal and telegraphic services, immigration and emigration, currency and coinage, and astronomical and meteorological observations.

In these areas the Senate would have equal legislative power with the House of Representatives, except as provided in Section 53. That section prevented the Senate from originating 'laws appropriating revenue or moneys, or imposing taxation', amending 'proposed laws imposing taxation, or proposed laws appropriating revenue or moneys for the ordinary annual services of the Government', and amending any proposed law 'so as to increase any proposed charge or burden on the people'. At any stage, however, the Senate could 'return to the House of Representatives any proposed law which the Senate may not amend, requesting, by message, the omission or amendment of any items or provisions therein'.

Section 57 provided the machinery to settle disagreement between the houses. If the Senate rejected or failed to pass, or passed with amendments that were unacceptable to the House of Representatives, any proposed law submitted to it by the lower house, and if it did this again when the same bill was returned to it by that House after an interval of three months, the governor-general had power to dissolve both houses simultaneously. And if after an election the result was still deadlock, the governor-general could convene a joint sitting of the members of both houses at which an absolute majority of all members would be taken to have enacted the bill.

The governor-general would possess much greater powers than the prime minister, who as a matter of fact was not even mentioned in the Constitution. Whether His Excellency chose to exercise those powers would, of course, be another matter; but under the Constitution he could prorogue (discontinue without dissolution) the parliament; he could dissolve the House of Representatives short of its full term, either by itself or (in the case of deadlocks) with the Senate; and, 'according to his discretion, but subject to the constitution', he could assent in the Queen's name to any law passed by the parliament, withhold that royal assent (without which no law would have force), or reserve the law 'for the Queen's pleasure'—which meant that Her Majesty's imperial advisers would decide whether it was to have force or not.

More important, and likely to be of greater practical significance, members of the Federal Executive Council would hold office during the governor-general's pleasure. Executive councillors would be members of parliament summoned by the governor-general to advise him in that capacity, and in practice they would also form the ministry—but only for so long as His Excellency pleased. As the Constitution said nothing about the kind of circumstances which might determine pleasure or displeasure at Government House, it was reasonable to assume that on occasion there would be need for viceregal discretion.

According to British practice the concept of responsible government, which the Commonwealth of Australia had embraced by making its ministers of state sit in parliament, required governments to possess the confidence (that is, support by a majority of members) of the lower house. If they lost that, they lost the governor-general's pleasure and lost office. That was how it worked in the British and colonial parliaments, but they were not federal parliaments. To some eminent Australian federalists it seemed that the house representing the States should also have a say in the fate of governments.

The views of such men as Sir Samuel Griffith, Inglis Clark and Sir Richard Baker on this matter were summed up by Dr John Quick and Robert Garran in their *Annotated Constitution of the Australian Commonwealth*, a work of 1008 pages published in 1901. It was argued, they wrote,

> that the same principle of State approval as well as popular approval should apply to Executive action as well as to legislative action; that the State should not be forced to support Executive policy and Executive acts merely because ministers enjoyed the confidence of the popular Chamber; that the State House would be justified in withdrawing its support from a ministry of whose policy and executive acts it disapproved; that the State House could, as effectually as the primary Chamber, enforce its want of confidence by refusing to provide the necessary supplies . . .
> On these grounds it is contended that the introduction of the Cabinet system of Responsible Government into a Federation, in which the relations of two branches of the legislature, having equal and co-ordinate authority, are quite different from those existing in a single autonomous State, is repugnant to the spirit and intention of a scheme of Federal Government. In the end it is predicted that either Responsible Government will kill the Federation and change it into a unified State, or the Federation will kill Responsible Government and substitute a new form of Executive more compatible with the Federal theory . . .
> It is not our province to comment on the opinions and contentions of these eminent federalists. Their views have not been accepted; and, for better or for worse, the system of Responsible Government as known to the British Constitution has been practically embedded in the Federal Constitution, in such a manner that it cannot be disturbed without an amendment of the instrument. There can be no doubt that it will tend in the direction of the nationalisation of the people of the Commonwealth, and promote the concentration of executive control in the House of Representatives. At the same time it ought not to impair the equal and co-ordinate authority of the Senate in all matters of legislation, except the origination and amendment of Bills imposing taxation and Bills appropriating revenue or money for the ordinary annual services of the Government.

Birth and Cradle

On 15 December Australia's first Governor-General—John Adrian Louis Hope, Earl of Hopetoun, a man of elegance, fragile health and less than perfect political judgement—arrived in Sydney, where the Commonwealth was to be inaugurated in two weeks' time. His most pressing duty was to choose the first prime minister. In this important task he had a free hand, and, despite the advantage of having had some previous experience of Australian politics as Governor of Victoria, he made a botch of it—the so-called

'Hopetoun Blunder'. In spite of Barton's undoubted personal standing, by which His Excellency seemed to be swayed at first, some argued that the honour should go ex officio to the premier of the senior colony. Lord Hopetoun was converted to the latter view (probably by George Reid and the acting Governor, Sir Frederick Darley) and on 19 December he commissioned William Lyne, the Premier of New South Wales, to form a ministry.

'Big Bill' Lyne would have seemed more at ease in moleskins and bowyangs than the dark suit and waistcoat of a colonial politician. Born in Tasmania, he had become a pioneer settler in the Gulf country of northern Queensland, and later a pastoralist in the New South Wales riverina. To a cultivated Melburnian like Deakin he seemed 'crude, sleek, suspicious, blundering'; but others recognised beneath Lyne's clumsy and often inarticulate manner a native shrewdness and strength of purpose. His old political rival Reid called him a rogue elephant. 'He is on the rack when on his feet', said Melbourne *Punch*, 'and you can feel each twist of the crank in his earnest effort to find language for his thoughts'. On one occasion he praised another member for his 'admirably trite speech'.

At least Lyne was a Protectionist, and that might help him outside New South Wales; but he was not personally well known in the other colonies, and had not been a prominent federalist. Imagine, then, the feelings of Deakin, who on 19 December had already sent his luggage to the railway station and was waiting for one telegraphed word, 'Imperative', which would be Barton's signal to join him, and his ministry, in Sydney. Instead the telegram said: 'It is Lyne. I have declined to join him'.

Some of Deakin's Victorian allies, including the influential proprietor of the *Age*, David Syme, felt that he should support Lyne in order to keep out the even less preferable George Reid with his pernicious free trade—and it could have come to that. On 21 December Deakin wrote to Barton: 'I have braced Turner up and will try Holder in an hour or two to secure you the leadership, but failing that in my judgment it is your duty to join Lyne. Your own judgment and conscience must decide. Australia will suffer if you refuse to crucify yourself'.

Deakin and Sir George Turner, the Victorian Premier, met Holder, the Premier of South Australia, on the express from Adelaide when it stopped briefly at North Melbourne to let ticket collectors on board for the few remaining minutes to Spencer Street station. Perhaps they were heading off any supporters of the Lyne faction who might have been waiting at Spencer Street. At any rate, they made common cause with Holder. He and Turner took the evening train to Sydney, where they told Lyne they would not serve under him. Turner would not accept unless Deakin did; Deakin refused, and also persuaded the *Age* to change its tack. Without Victorians, Lyne could not hope to muster a sufficiently representative ministry. On Christmas Eve he returned his commission, and the Governor-General sent for Barton.

The 'Cabinet of Kings' which Barton enlisted with ease, and also some ruthlessness, consisted of four Premiers (Lyne, Turner, Forrest, and Neil Lewis of Tasmania), two former Premiers (Kingston, and Sir James Dickson of Queensland), Barton himself, his close friend and colleague Richard O'Connor, and of course Deakin. That made nine, and the Constitution provided for no more than seven ministers of state, whose combined salaries should not exceed £12 000. O'Connor and Lewis would therefore be ministers without portfolio and without salary, though they would receive (as also would their salaried colleagues) the annual parliamentary allowance prescribed in the Constitution.

This allowance of £400 was £100 more than parliamentarians received in New South Wales, Victoria, Queensland and New Zealand; £200 more than in Western Australia and South Australia; and £300 more than in Tasmania. At that time American congressmen received the equivalent of £1000, and British parliamentarians were unpaid. The federal allowance seemed ample enough by comparison with the average annual income of, say, a carpenter, saddler or blacksmith (£150); combined with ministerial salary, it seemed positively princely. The Prime Minister could expect to receive £2500 in all, and the other ministers of state £2050.

Although the future of this cabinet would not be certain until parliament was elected, the only changes in its composition were in fact to take place before the election. Dickson died, and was replaced by another Queenslander, J. G. Drake. Lewis had never had any intention of entering federal parliament, and after only three months without portfolio he was replaced by another Tasmanian and former Premier, Sir Philip Fysh.

One 'king' conspicuously missing from this cabinet was Frederick Holder, the South Australian Premier whose long rail journey to Sydney had helped rectify the Hopetoun Blunder. Before returning to Adelaide, Holder was assured by O'Connor that he would not be overlooked in the event of Barton being asked to form a ministry. When that event did occur Holder was summoned back to Sydney, and then ignored. 'He was not approached or in any way consulted', wrote his fellow South Australian, Glynn, 'and heard nothing of the completion of the Ministry until it was announced in the papers of Monday, 31 December 1900. He was simply sold, and is in consequence, as far as his somewhat neutral nature is capable of strong feeling, furious and disappointed'. Lyne's acceptance of a portfolio, combined with O'Connor's closeness to Barton, meant that New South Wales would have three ministers. Victoria had only two, so how could the other colonies have more than one each? In the choice that had to be made between Holder and Kingston, Kingston's claim was the stronger.

The Governor-General and his nine executive councillors were sworn into office as the climax to a grand inaugural ceremony in Sydney on New Year's Day, 1901. A five-mile-long procession made its way out through sweltering midsummer heat to Centennial Park, and there in a white wedding-cake pavilion, surrounded by a multitude under straw hats and parasols, Clerk Blackmore read the Queen's proclamation of the Commonwealth. Lord Hopetoun and his advisers took their oaths of office, the band played 'God Save the Queen', and a choir of ten thousand sang 'Federated Australia'.

Later that afternoon the Executive Council held its first meeting in a room provided by the New South Wales Government. Most of those present were physically imposing men—particularly the heavyweights Forrest, Lyne, Kingston and O'Connor, all of whom were bearded, as also were Deakin and Dickson. All except Dickson had been born in Australia, but the two pending replacements, Drake and Fysh, were English-born. Deakin was the youngest

An invitation to the Federation celebrations, Melbourne, 1901

(forty-four); Fysh, when he joined them, would be the oldest (sixty-five); Barton was fifty-one. Barton had been sworn as Minister of State for External Affairs and Deakin, second in cabinet rank, was Attorney-General. Each had very competent departmental secretaries—in the case of External Affairs, Atlee Hunt, and for the Attorney-General, the young Robert Garran.

It was Garran's responsibility that day to compose in longhand and take to the New South Wales Government Printer the first issue of the *Common-wealth Gazette*, containing among other announcements a list of the new federal departments and their ministers. The departments of customs and excise in each State had been transferred automatically to the Commonwealth, as provided by the Constitution to ensure an immediate source of income, and the new federal Minister of Customs, with a ready-made staff around the continent, was Kingston. The Constitution also provided for the transfer of certain other services from the States by proclamation of the Governor-General. Two transfers of this kind were to be made on 1 March—posts, tele-graphs and telephones, coming under the Postmaster-General, Drake; and naval and military defence, under Forrest. Turner was the Treasurer; and Lyne, although he remained Premier of New South Wales until March, was also simultaneously federal Minister for Home Affairs from the start.

Cabinet met in Sydney until April. Barton conducted most of his business on a partially enclosed veranda in New South Wales premises, and most of the embryonic government's administrative work was performed by Hunt, Garran and the very few departmental officers at their disposal. Garran, a tall stork-like young man of great perspicacity and vigour, saw to the drafting of certain bills which would be required no matter what kind of parliament might be elected. 'We took the existing models for such Bills', he wrote, 'and cut them to the bare bone and made them like a drawing by Phil May, with every superfluous line rubbed out'.

Garran and Hunt found government offices in Melbourne, planned the Duke of York's programme, and made arrangements for a general election. Under the Constitution, parliament was required to meet in Melbourne not later than six months after the establishment of the Commonwealth. The election was conducted according to electoral laws applying to the various State lower houses, and because of certain requirements by some of those laws the earliest it could be held was at the end of March. All States had the secret ballot, but in other electoral characteristics they differed widely. Only in South Australia and Western Australia were women entitled to vote. New South Wales, Victoria and Queensland had manhood suffrage, but in Tasmania that right was qualified by a small property requirement. Some States allowed plural voting by property owners, but the Constitution precluded this at federal elections. Aborigines, except those in the Northern Territory of South Australia, had the right to register for the vote, but in four States that was subject to qualification. Only South Australia and Tasmania allowed their Aborigines to vote on the same basis as other citizens. In South Australia few of them were believed to exercise that right, and in Tasmania, for numerical reasons, this was of little more than academic interest.

The Constitution allowed States to determine their own electorates for the House of Representatives. Based upon an estimate of population made in 1900 by statisticians from all colonies, but with the proviso that no State should have fewer than five seats, the electorates were distributed as follows: New South Wales, twenty-six; Victoria, twenty-three; Queensland, nine; South Australia, seven; Western Australia, five; Tasmania, five. The lists of electorates and polling places published in early issues of the *Commonwealth Gazette* read indeed like a gazetteer of the new Commonwealth: Gwydir (Wee Waa, Moree, Walgett, Pilliga), Eden-Monaro (Queanbeyan, Urayarra, Brindabella, Molonglo), Maranoa (Longreach, Apple Tree Creek, Musket Flat, Boulia), Capricornia (Rockhampton, Bogantungan, Crocodile, Meteor Downs), Indi (Chiltern, Yackandandah, Wodonga), Swan (Katanning Court House, Fortescue telegraph station, Monyonooka school house) . . . South Australia and Tasmania, choosing not to determine electoral boundaries, would each vote as one electorate, the same way all States were to vote for the Senate.

There were 127 candidates for the 36 Senate seats and 181 for the 75 seats in the lower house, and all were men. They were required by the Constitution to be at least twenty-one years old, residents of the Commonwealth for at least three years, British-born or naturalised subjects of the Queen, and electors entitled to vote at an election for the House of Representatives. South Australian and Western Australian women, having been enfranchised since 1894 and 1899 respectively, were thus entitled to nominate; but none did. The quality of candidates in general was not easy to assess. The *Sydney Mail*, while conceding the excellence of some, thought that the average quality was 'decidely lower than any well-wisher of the Commonwealth would like to see'. There were complaints about 'a profusion of little men', but on the other hand the *Sydney Morning Herald* expressed concern that State parliaments would lose their best men to 'the superior attractions of the two Federal Houses'. Most of the leading convention delegates stood for seats in the parliament which they had helped bring into being.

Most candidates were identified with one or other of three embryonic parties: the Protectionists or Ministerialists, led by Barton and enjoying a head start thanks to the proceedings at Centennial Park; the Free Traders, under the *de facto* leadership of George Reid; and a smaller group of Labor candidates, numbering twenty-seven for the lower house and fourteen for the Senate. All three groups held policy conferences early in 1900, but the resulting platforms contained little to excite or inform the electorates.

The Protectionists had no federal name (in Victoria they were called the National Liberal Organisation, in New South Wales the Australian Liberal Association), and like the other parties they had no federal council. Both the Protectionists and Free Traders laid claim to the popular designation 'liberal', but 'conservative' would have been closer to the truth.

Barton delivered his Protectionist policy speech on 17 January at Maitland—in the New South Wales electorate of Hunter, where he was unopposed—with Deakin and Kingston on the platform beside him. Never before in history, Barton reminded his listeners, had it been allowed to one body of men to govern a whole continent. His Government would do nothing to harm the States. Unless under the stress of some great emergency, it would not exercise the power of direct taxation, for that would be to invade a province of taxation (income tax) wherein alone the States would still be able to augment their incomes after losing the right to levy customs and excise duties. Estimates of the Commonwealth Government's initial running cost ranged from £300 000 to £750 000. The uniform tariff would bring in sufficient revenue, and would not discourage industries. It would be 'a tariff calculated to maintain employment, in other words a business tariff'.

Barton spoke of legislation being prepared by Kingston to provide conciliation and arbitration beyond the limits of any one State in the event of a national industrial crisis; the completion of a transcontinental railway system by linking Kalgoorlie to Port Augusta, though not until the federal Government was convinced that the gain from it would outweigh expenditure; his personal belief that women should be entitled to vote at federal elections, though not to sit in parliament; and finally (to loud and continued applause) the subject of white Australia. There would be legislation against any influx of Asiatic labour. The Government would have equally strong objection to Polynesian or Kanaka labour on the canefields of North Queensland. It would not be guilty of any oppression of those Pacific Islanders already in Australia (or, by implication, of reducing the profits of the sugar industry dependent on their labour), but would take steps to prevent the importation of any more islanders.

George Reid, who was opposed by three candidates in East Sydney, made no formal policy speech for the Free Traders, who called themselves the Australian Free Trade and Liberal Association. In the course of wide campaigning he admitted the need for some revenue duties, but argued that local industries should be encouraged by bounties, not a protective tariff. He also spurned the federal power to legislate for old-age pensions because pensions would have to be financed out of heavy customs duty or direct federal taxes.

Labor candidates had no official leader, or even an unofficial one like Reid, and the Commonwealth parliamentary platform adopted by an interstate labour conference carefully skirted controversy. Australia's first labour platform of any kind—that of the Australian Labour Federation established in Queensland twelve years before—had included such objectives as 'nationalisation of all sources of wealth and all means of producing and distributing wealth' and 'conducting by the State Authority of all production and all exchange'. These were soon replaced, however, by ones less likely to alarm the average voter. There was no mention of nationalisation in the first Commonwealth Labor platform, which consisted of only four planks:

1. Electoral reform, providing for one adult one vote, 2. Total exclusion of coloured and other undesirable races, 3. Old age pensions, 4. The Federal Constitution to be amended to provide for—(a) The Initiative and Referendum for the alteration of the Constitution. (b) Substitution of the National Referendum for the double dissolution for the settlement of deadlocks between the two Houses.

Labor candidates were also pledged by this platform not only to ensure the carrying out of its principles but also, on all such questions, to vote as a majority of the federal parliamentary Labor Party might decide.

The main impression conveyed by Labor candidates was one of low expectation. They did not expect to win many seats; nor did they expect to be able to do much in parliament other than bargain for concessions. Even with unexpectedly large representation, it seemed likely to them that the restrictive Braddon clause and equality of Senate membership for the smaller, more conservative states would hamper Labor's implementation of various social welfare policies at the federal level. Consequently they spoke of removing those obstacles by constitutional amendment, and in the meantime showed more inclination to side with Barton than with Reid.

It is not possible here to describe the campaign fully, but perhaps some impression of it may be conveyed at random. Jim Page, the Free Trade candidate for Maranoa, a former British artilleryman in South Africa and later a publican at Barcaldine, canvassed his huge Queensland electorate on a bicycle, sometimes travelling eighty miles in a day. Sir Malcolm McEacharn, the shipping magnate and Protectionist candidate for Melbourne, used one of the few motor cars in the country. George Reid had a buggy drawn by two horses; Lyne travelled in a luxuriously appointed railway 'boudoir car', and in Western Australia some candidates used camels. At least two candidates did not campaign in person. Colonel J. A. K. Mackay offered himself to the electors of New South Wales, for the Senate, while on active service in South Africa. John Ferguson, the Queensland M.L.A. for Rockhampton, also stood for the Senate while returning from a trip to England. His ship reached Fremantle two days before polling day.

The notorious Sydney newspaper publisher, John Norton, stood for the

Senate on a mainly jingoistic platform. At a Grand Patriotic Demonstration in the Town Hall he delivered an address entitled 'Rally Round the Mother State', and was accompanied on stage by concert performers rendering such items as 'Rule Britannia', 'Hearts of Oak' and recitations of 'A Public Man's Ambition' and 'The Charge of the Light Brigade'. A more successful mountebank was King O'Malley, an insurance agent of uncertain provenance (he claimed to be Canadian, but was more likely an American, in which case he should not have been eligible for election) who stood as a Protectionist for one of Tasmania's five seats in the lower house. O'Malley's monstrously overgrown persona seemed to be inhabited simultaneously by a spruiker from Barnum's three-ring circus, a hell and tarnation revivalist, and a four-flushing Yankee congressman. He was a moderately big man, auburn haired with watchful grey eyes and a red-brown beard, wearing a wide-brimmed felt hat, blue-grey sac suit with huge lapels and a low-cut vest, loose cravat with a diamond collar stud, and in the centre of his cream silk shirt front a large fiery opal.

'Mr O'Malley said he had lived in Hobart for a period of three years', stated a deadpan *Mercury* report that accurately reflected the snake-oil populism of O'Malley's platform manner.

> During that time he had not committed any crime, robbed a bank nor murdered anyone. Why then was he called an interloper, a foreigner or a blatherskite? He had selected the Australian colonies as the land of his adoption, and surely was as much interested in the welfare of the State as those who adversely criticised him.

In the electorate of Melbourne Sir Malcolm McEacharn came in for some rough heckling about the employment of Indian seamen on his ships, but when one interjector asked him how much the S.S. *Federal* had been insured for there were loud cries of 'That's not a fair question!' In South Melbourne the only clergyman standing for parliament—the Reverend J. B. Ronald, a Presbyterian, and Labor candidate—said that Chinese 'should be either poll-axed or poll-taxed in such a manner as would make the country too hot for them'. White Australia was a live issue in every State, but particularly so in Queensland. James Stewart, editor of a Rockhampton newspaper and Labor candidate for the Senate, went so far as to say that black men should be swept into the sea or shot down.

The first federal election was really six separate elections held more or less simultaneously—on Friday 29 March in four States, and the following day in South Australia and Queensland. Five different voting methods were used for the upper house, and five for the lower house. In fact the only point of national consistency was that in all States the list of Senate candidates was in alphabetical order. Some States used first-past-the-post voting, some used preferential voting, and Tasmania used the complex Hare-Clark proportional representation system. The latter was simple enough for voters, but so frustrating for the counters that some collapsed from nervous exhaustion. In northern Queensland many electors were temporarily disfranchised by floods which gave false promise of breaking the drought, and in Melbourne the disturbance which Wragge had named Zamoth raised such heavy dust clouds as to bring about a partial eclipse on polling day.

Voting was not compulsory, and the Commonwealth-wide turnout for the House of Representatives was only 57 per cent of enrolment. The highest for the lower house was in New South Wales (68 per cent), and the lowest was in Western Australia (36 per cent). Of the few women entitled to vote in two States, even fewer exercised that right. In South Australia there were 89 894 women of voting age; only 69 490 of those were enrolled, and only 21 418 in fact voted. The figures for Western Australia are unknown, but some women did vote there.

Results were telegraphed to the State capitals as soon as possible, and by early next week the composition of the new parliament was approximately discernible, though not yet decipherable. Barton and all his ministers were elected, but Lyne's majority was only 606 and Fysh (the hairiest man in parliament, looking rather like a Boer patriarch) did not escape from the toils of Tasmania's Hare-Clark system until six days after the poll. Free Trade triumphed predictably in New South Wales, and so did Protectionism in Victoria. South Australia and Queensland were divided between the two fiscal causes; Western Australia declared itself almost entirely for Free Trade (Sir John Forrest was the only West Australian supporter of a high tariff who secured a seat in either house); and Tasmania inclined to moderate Protection. John Norton and Colonel Mackay failed to reach the Senate; Ferguson and Stewart were successful in that regard, and so too, for the lower house, were McEacharn, O'Malley and the Labor candidates, Ronald and Page.

The House of Representatives seemed likely to have thirty-one Protectionists, twenty-eight Free Traders, fourteen Labor members, and two Independents, both from Queensland. In the Senate there would be seventeen Free Traders, eleven Protectionists and eight Labor. Apart from their agreement on certain social and industrial issues, Labor members could also be categorised fiscally as Labor/low tariff or Labor/high tariff. According to early assessments of that dichotomy, it seemed probable that the Protectionists would have a narrow majority in the House of Representatives, but would be unable to control the Senate. 'It will need all Mr Barton's tactical ability to deal with two Chambers so constituted', reported Deakin in one of his despatches to the *Morning Post*.

Mr Reid, who is far his superior in the arts of political strategy and party intrigue, is likely to make the thorns more numerous than the roses on his Parliamentary couch where certainly he cannot hope to slumber securely. It will be a hard task, too, for a man of his somewhat aristocratic tastes and associations to ingratiate himself with the uncourtly members of the working classes who have been elected. Mr Reid is sure to be on familiar terms with them in a very short time. The Prime Minister is putting on a brave face, but his heart must be inclined to sink when he looks on the material provided out of which he is required to build a new national Parliament and establish a new national policy.

In a later despatch Deakin expanded upon the difficulties facing any body of men setting out, in Barton's words at Maitland, to govern a whole continent.

There must be boundless opportunities for blundering somewhere in the endeavour to deal with so vast a territory lightly sprinkled with population along its interminable coast-line. No capital wherever situated can keep in touch with more than a fraction of its dominion, amd must be so remote from the rest as to permit the presence of but a few qualified representatives from its outlying regions. Yet its Government and Legislature must needs speak, act, and provide for the whole. Truly the Commonwealth, like an infant Hercules, will need to fight even from its cradle.

Which cradle the infant parliament would occupy was still uncertain in mid-April, with only three weeks to go before its birth. Six months earlier the Victorian parliament had passed a Commonwealth Arrangements Act empowering the Governor in Council to make arrangements for the Commonwealth parliament to use either the Exhibition Building or the Victorian Parliament House until able to meet at its own seat of government. On 10 April the Victorian Premier, Alexander Peacock, wrote to the Prime Minister offering a choice. Barton and some of his colleagues inspected both buildings three days later, and on 17 April Cabinet accepted Parliament House in Spring Street.

The Exhibition Building's western annexe was being remodelled for use by either the federal or State parliament, but would not be finished by May. Also, the building in Spring Street had an excellent library. Quite apart from these two publicly adduced reasons for the choice, however, it was easy to understand why the building in Spring Street should have been preferred. Parliament House was closer to the heart of the city, and it was the finest example of classical architecture in Australia. Designed by a Scottish-trained architect, Peter Kerr, it stood on Eastern Hill, the highest point of central Melbourne. This hill had also attracted eight churches, including St Peter's Church of England, from the steps of which Melbourne had been proclaimed a city more than half a century before, and St Patrick's Cathedral, not yet graced by its trinity of spires.

Parliament House had been built in stages, starting with the Legislative Assembly and Legislative Council chambers, which were placed on a north–south axis facing Spring Street, and ready for use when Victoria was granted responsible government in 1856. Between these two chambers, on an east–west axis, were the library (1860) and Queen's Hall and vestibule (1879). The façade—its 21 broad steps, 26 Doric columns and allegorical rooftop sculptures by Bertram Mackennal facing west across Spring Street and straight down Bourke Street—was completed in 1892. Kerr had also designed a large domed tower, reminiscent of the Capitol in Washington; but although this finishing touch often appeared prematurely in engravings of Melbourne, for reasons of economy it was never erected.

Inside, however, no expense was spared. The building consisted of a basement level; a main level at the top of the Spring Street steps, accommodating the two chambers, library and Queen's Hall; a first floor level; and a mezzanine and attic level. The floor of the vestibule was inlaid with Minton tiles in a concentric design of dolphins, arabesques, the imperial coat of arms and a biblical inscription: 'Where no counsel is, the people fall; but in the multitude of counsellors there is safety'. Beyond the vestibule was Queen's Hall, its lofty space presided over by a buff-coloured statue of Queen Victoria.

On the right and left of this hall—that is to say, the southern and northern sides—were doors leading directly into the Legislative Council and Legislative Assembly chambers, which were to be occupied by the Senate and House of Representatives respectively. Both chambers were the same size—about the area of a doubles tennis court, which was somewhat smaller than the House of Commons. Carpets and furnishings were in Westminster colours—red, the colour traditionally associated with royalty and consequently with the House of Lords, in the Legislative Council; green, the colours preferred by the lower chamber for reasons unknown, in the Legislative Assembly.

As might once have seemed appropriate for the chambers of democracy and privilege, one was content with a modicum of adornment, while the other luxuriated in baroque magnificence. Huge Corinthian monoliths of Tasmanian freestone rose from the crimson floor of the Council chamber to support a vaulted, coffered and enriched ceiling adorned at the sides by sculptures and bas-reliefs, and illumined by three large chandeliers. Over the President's Chair a pillared and carved canopy supported the royal lion, crown and unicorn.

The whole intricate structure of basalt plinths, freestone columns, marble balustrades and bronze lampstands was set in extensive grounds containing gardens, a bowling green, a lawn tennis court, stables, an ornamental ventilation tower connected by tunnel to the main buildings, and an elegant garden pavilion with stained-glass windows. Outside these grounds, Spring Street was a mixture of bureaucracy, commerce, the healing arts and entertainment. Downhill from General Gordon's statue were the Treasury buildings and other government offices, some partly occupied by the Commonwealth. On the western side of the street were seven hotels, including the Grand (later to be called the Windsor) and the Old White Hart, both directly opposite Parliament House; the Princess Theatre; a German hairdresser and Chinese laundry; six dentists, a hydropathist, oculist, aurist and medical electrician; an accordion-pleater named Mrs Gantzman, a tailor named Isidore Lipman, and two Chinese cabinet-makers named Ching and Chong.

Cabinet's choice of Spring Street must have been expected by some, for on the day before it was announced one federal M.P., King O'Malley, claimed a seat for himself in what was to be the House of Representatives. As more members arrived in Melbourne, the pinning of cards to seats became so competitive that the Victorian Premier complained to Barton. In one case, a federal member was accused of taking a Victorian M.L.A.'s papers out of a drawer and leaving them on the floor. Twenty-two members of the new parliament were no strangers to Victoria's Parliament House. Of the twenty-three Victorian members of the House of Representatives, seventeen were past members of either the Legislative Assembly or Legislative Council, and ten of these had resigned their seats in order to enter federal parliament. Five of the six Victorian senators were also former parliamentarians, and three had only lately resigned.

By the weekend of 4–5 May, visitors were flocking into Melbourne, mainly by train, at the rate of ten thousand a day more than usual. A special train packed with official guests, including Sir Samuel Griffith, left Brisbane

on Friday morning. The interstate excursion trains ran in two divisions, and a
train of seventeen cars came in from Echuca with six hundred people on
board. Sir John Forrest arrived by train from Adelaide—after a four-day voyage across the Australian Bight past the immense coastline which he had
explored thirty years before—and moved into the Grand Hotel, where some
of the other more affluent members were also staying. Like their counterparts at State level, members of the new parliament were entitled to free rail
travel, for which the Commonwealth reimbursed the various railway commissioners. The rules seem to have been rather flexible at first, but eventually members received individual gold passes, were reimbursed for ship
fares when trains were not available, and were allowed a certain amount of
free travel for their wives and other family members between home and the
seat of government.

George Reid arrived in Melbourne by train, flushed not only with Free
Trade's electoral triumph in New South Wales but also with more recent success in his forensic capacity as Reid, K.C. At Darlinghurst Criminal Court he
had been defending a certain Mrs Jane Smith, charged with having murdered a man on board the steamer *Talune, en route* from New Zealand to
Sydney, by giving him strychnine to drink in a bottle of beer.

> It was a dismal day when George Reid started his address to the jury
> [reported the *Bulletin*]. Behind the green spikes of the cage sat Mrs Smith,
> dressed in a light brown mackintosh, with a brown fur boa, a gem straw
> hat and her handkerchief covering her face, sobbing, while at the barris-
> ters' table stood George Reid battling for her life . . . He gripped the
> gloomy-looking case with both hands and buried it beneath a mountain
> of doubt. Where, he asked, was the motive? 'Gentlemen, are—you—
> going—TO HANG this woman' (the house tottered as George Reid said
> 'Hang') 'on her own thoughtless words?'

The jury could not decide, and on 28 April, while Reid was attending a com-
plimentary picnic to launch him on his federal parliamentary career, the
judge discharged it.

Just as the Commonwealth parliament had gained many leading parliamentarians from State legislatures, so it also looked in those directions for its
officers. By ministerial decision the two houses of parliament were to be
staffed in much the same Westminster fashion as the State legislatures.
Edwin Blackmore—Clerk of Parliaments in Adelaide, Clerk of the 1897–98
convention, and reader of the proclamation at Centennial Park—was
appointed Clerk of the Senate and Clerk of the Parliaments; and George H.
Jenkins, Clerk of the Legislative Council and Clerk of the Parliaments in Victoria for the previous ten years, was seconded as Clerk of the House of Representatives. Blackmore's salary (£900) was an improvement of £160 on the
salary of the Clerk of the New South Wales Legislative Council, but £300 less
than that of the Clerk of the Victorian upper house, who was also Clerk of
the Parliaments in that legislature. The salary prescribed for the Clerk of the
House of Representatives (also £900) was £60 less than for the Clerk of the
lower house in New South Wales, and £100 less than for his counterpart in
Victoria. This was of no immediate concern to Jenkins, however, because for

the time being he was on leave of absence from the Victorian Legislative Council and receiving only his higher Victorian salary. Blackmore's appointment was made by the Governor-General in Council, to take effect from 1 May; but before that date he and Jenkins collaborated with Barton in the drafting of two sets of the Standing Orders which, under the Constitution, each house of parliament could make for 'the order and conduct of its business and proceedings either separately or jointly with the other House'. The provisional Standing Orders, which the houses would be free to adopt or modify as they pleased, drew upon British and colonial examples, and particularly upon the South Australian Standing Orders, which had been used by the 1897–98 convention.

Other parliamentary officers were appointed at the same time. Perhaps compensating for the extent to which the fathers of federation had drawn on North American precedent, the ministry followed the example of State legislatures by borrowing from Westminster two ancient figures associated with parliamentary ceremony and the preservation of parliamentary order. 'Barton wants a Serjeant-at-Arms', noted Atlee Hunt earlier in the year. Whether or not it was as simple a decision as that, the Commonwealth did appoint a Serjeant-at-Arms for the House of Representatives (Thomas Woollard, formerly Usher of the Black Rod in Victoria's upper house) and an Usher of the Black Rod for the Senate (George Upward, formerly Serjeant-at-Arms in the Victorian lower house).

As in the House of Commons and the House of Lords, the Serjeant-at-Arms and the Usher of the Black Rod would attend upon the presiding officers (as provided by the Commonwealth Constitution, these officers would be a Speaker in the House of Representatives and a President in the Senate, each a member elected by his fellows to represent their House in its dealings with others, and to preside over its debates) and carry out the expressed wishes of their respective chambers. Black Rod, whose title derived from his staff of office, would play a prominent though purely symbolic role during the ceremonial opening of each parliament. On sitting days he would also conduct the President to his Chair, and during proceedings he would occupy a seat on the President's left, ready to escort any suspended senator from the chamber, or convey a message to the lower house. On ceremonial occasions he would wear court dress of long-tailed coat, knee breeches, buckled shoes, black gloves, lace jabot and cuffs, and a sword.

The Serjeant-at-Arms for his part would precede the Speaker into the chamber, bearing on his right shoulder the gilded wood and plaster Mace (a staff-sized symbol of royal authority, surmounted by crown and orb) which the Victorian Legislative Assembly had bequeathed to the House of Representatives. His other duties would be similar to those of Black Rod, and on ceremonial occasions his dress would be much the same, though he also carried a cocked hat.

The principal parliamentary reporter—B. H. Friend, previously on the New South Wales Hansard staff—was to be assisted by a staff of eight, including Ernest Scott, who later become Professor of History at the University of Melbourne. The housekeeper stayed on, as did other members of the maintenance staff rather than move with State parliament to the Exhibition

Building; but some junior employees were engaged to start their working lives with the new parliament. One of those was a 16-year-old named Thomas Pettifer, from a place called Whroo in northern Victoria. He was engaged at £1 per week to operate a small hydraulic lift, the capacity of which would soon be tested by the likes of Barton, Forrest, Kingston, O'Connor and Lyne.

Battalions of Silk Hats

The cruciform hall of the Exhibition Building which the Duke and Duchess of York entered at noon on Thursday 9 May was painted with allegorical lunettes, decked with British and Australian emblems of every imaginable kind, and crowded to capacity by twelve thousand people—many of whom, because of their positions in the nave or transept, would be unable to see or hear what was about to happen. Men and women alike were dressed sombrely out of respect for the late Queen, but occasionally the ranks of black and grey were relieved by the purple that was permitted for half-mourning and the scarlet jackets of military officers. Governors, premiers, clergy and judiciary were seated on or near the royal dais, which stood directly under the central dome facing the assembled senators of the new parliament. Members of the House of Representatives—called M.P.s rather than M.H.R.s, by Cabinet ruling—were already following the example of the House of Commons by excluding the Sovereign or his representative from their deliberations. The parliament of the Commonwealth would always be opened in the Senate rather than the lower house, and so it was too at this inaugural ceremony. The MPs were waiting in the western annexe until the Usher of the Black Rod summoned them, led by the Serjeant-at-Arms, to their places beside the Senate.

Somewhere in the galleries of the hall were two artists who had been commissioned to paint the opening scene in multitudinous detail. One of them, Tom Roberts, had been engaged by the federal government to paint in oils on a canvas measuring sixteen feet by twelve 'correct representations' of no fewer than 250 distinguished guests and parliamentarians. The other, Charles Nuttall, was under contract to a syndicate which proposed to have his canvas (12 feet by 9 feet) engraved for mass production by the famous Paris firm of Goupil. Roberts would have noticed two senators in scarlet: Lieutenant-Colonel Cyril Cameron from Tasmania, with the South African medal on his jacket; and Lieutenant-Colonel J. C. Neild, who had raised a rifle regiment in Sydney. This splash of colour would not have meant the same to Nuttall, however, for he was colour blind, and painted in mono-chrome. Both artists may also have observed, when members of the House of Representatives were led into the hall by their Serjeant-at-Arms, that one of the most important M.P.s was missing. George Reid was confined to bed at Menzies Hotel by a sudden bronchial infection, but this did not prevent him from appearing in both paintings.

The Governor-General read prayers, the Clerk of Parliaments proclaimed the Letters Patent empowering the Duke of York to open the first parliament of the Commonwealth of Australia, and His Royal Highness delivered a message from King Edward which the next morning's *Argus* would describe as 'charged with warm feeling, not packed with great thought'. In conclusion the Duke said: 'I now, in his name, and on his behalf, declare this Parliament open'. A fanfare rang out, and the Duchess touched an electric button which started a message to England declaring the object of the royal envoy's journey accomplished. Members of both houses swore their allegiance to the Crown on bibles presented to them for that purpose (or, in the sole case of King O'Malley, affirmed their allegiance) and were then advised by the Governor-General to repair to their intended places of sitting to choose a President and a Speaker. The royal party withdrew, the assembly sang the national anthem, and by carriage or on foot the new parliament proceeded to Spring Street.

The Senate assembled in its ornate red chamber for the first time at 1.10 p.m., only to adjourn five minutes later and reassemble at 2.30 p.m. What logic there was in the seating pattern owed more to parties than to States. Most New South Wales senators sat on the Opposition benches, to the right of the table, but that was because they were Free Traders. All but two of the eight Labor senators sat together, although they came from three different States.

There were three nominations for president: the South Australian Free Trader Sir Richard Baker, who because of his work at the convention was expected to command greatest support, and two Victorians, Sir Frederick Sargood and Sir William Zeal, the first a Free Trader and the other a Protectionist. The vote was to have been exhaustive, but elimination proved unnecessary as Senator Baker obtained a clear majority on the first ballot. Accompanied by fellow senators and led by Black Rod he walked some 200 yards down Spring Street to the Treasury Buildings, where he presented himself to the Governor-General in the Executive Council chamber. The little procession then retraced its steps to the Senate, which shortly afterwards adjourned until the next morning.

The House of Representatives assembled in its chamber for the first time at 2.30 p.m. on Thursday. One or two Queenslanders wore light tweeds that would have been more seasonable in their own State than during a Victorian autumn under the influence of Moloch; but most other members wore heavy three-piece suits. Except for the flamboyant O'Malley, whose hat was 'a large and remarkably aggressive looking wideawake, reminiscent of the new gold field or the cattle ranch', the benches on either side were occupied, as the *Age* reported, by 'battalions of silk hats, which according to the custom of the House of Commons, most members kept upon their heads during the sitting'. George Reid was still absent, and so also now, for reasons unknown, was the Labor Member for Coolgardie, Hugh Mahon. Ministers sat to the left of the green-covered centre table, their Protectionist supporters sat behind them, all but four of the Free Traders sat on the other side of the chamber, and Labor sat on both sides, away from the table. Clerk Jenkins and other officers including a parliamentary reporter sat at the table, and in a press gallery above the Speaker's Chair there was accommodation for thirty journalists.

The Press Gallery, as the parliamentary press corps became known, enjoyed the same kind of standing and privileges as did the Victorian

At the opening of the Federal Parliament Bulletin, *18 May 1901*

Reporters' Gallery, which, like other colonial press galleries, operated under conditions of access that had been taken over from the House of Commons. In Spring Street, as at Westminster, journalists were 'strangers', permitted and assisted to report parliamentary proceedings, but always subject to removal at the discretion of either house. Melbourne's newspapers dominated the early Commonwealth Gallery. Of the thirty-one journalists listed for 1901, eight were from the *Argus*, seven from the *Age*, three from Sydney's *Daily Telegraph*, and two from the *Sydney Morning Herald*.

There were to have been two candidates for the speakership, but Sir John Quick, the Member for Bendigo, withdrew in favour of Frederick Holder, the rightly aggrieved former Premier of South Australia, the only Premier not invited to join Barton's Ministry, and now the Honourable Member for Wakefield. And so it came about that South Australia provided not only the lion's share of the two provisionally drafted sets of Standing Orders, the President of the Senate and the Clerk of the Parliaments, but also the Speaker. Holder, a grey-bearded man of fifty-one who had been a Methodist lay preacher earlier in life, was well equipped with patience, dignity and parliamentary experience to occupy the Speaker's green leather chair. According to Deakin, he was 'thin as a paling', with 'a chest which seemed destined for consumption'. Also he was one-eyed, the other eye being virtually useless; but this did not affect his control of the house, or his impartiality.

In symbolic allusion to his British counterpart's traditional reluctance to assume the once hazardous role of 'Speaker' or spokesman in communicating resolutions of the Commons to the Sovereign, Holder was conducted to that seat by his proposer and seconder—Thomas Macdonald-Paterson (F, Brisbane Q)—and Sir Edward Braddon (F, Tasmania). The Mace, which until then had been lying under the table, was laid upon the table, as would henceforth be the practice whenever the House was sitting. After escorting Speaker Holder to meet the Governor-General, the House reassembled and attended to its first miscellaneous business.

The Speaker had only generally accepted principles and his own common sense to guide him in the conduct of debate. Two members addressed questions to the Prime Minister. The acting Leader of the Opposition—Reid's chief lieutenant, Joseph Cook (F, Parramatta, N)—asked when the provisional Standing Orders would be distributed to members for perusal, and H. B. Higgins (P, North Melbourne V), asked how soon members were to have the privileges of the library and other rooms of Parliament House, complaining that he had been refused permission to borrow a library book. To the first question Barton replied that the provisional Standing Orders would be laid on the table next day, and that a Standing Orders Committee would be elected as soon as possible to consider them. To the second question he replied that federal members were entitled to use the library, refreshment room and billiard room, but so also were the Victorian members. 'As honourable members of the State Parliament have been occupying the rooms of this building ever since its construction many years ago', he said, 'there may naturally be a little feeling of homesickness about leaving them, and one does not therefore want to press these matters too abruptly or too unkindly'.

At this point one of the Queenslanders—Charles McDonald, a watch-maker from Charters Towers, and Labor Member for Kennedy—injected some of the aggressiveness for which the political life of his State was notorious. When he rose to ask another question about Standing Orders, the Speaker informed him firmly that, as the Prime Minister had already spoken in reply, he could allow no further debate.

> Mr McDONALD.—Then, under the circumstances, I shall be compelled to move that your ruling, Sir, be disagreed with. Just now this is purely an Informal House, and under such circumstances, I must maintain my rights.
> Mr SPEAKER.—I recognise that there are some difficulties connected with our present position; but, until the Standing Orders are laid on the table, I must ask honourable members to observe such rules as are common to the procedure of every legislative body.
> Mr McDONALD.—I ask that, under these circumstances, the privileges of honorable members—
> Mr BARTON.—I must point out to my honorable friend that the absence of rules does not mean that we must have disorder, and I think it is a common rule of Parliament that when the mover of a question [That the House do now adjourn] has replied the debate is concluded.
> Mr McDONALD.—It is not so in Queensland. There we are allowed the privilege of speaking, and should have that privilege here. I intend to assert my privileges in this House, and I do not care at what cost—
> Mr SPEAKER.—I must ask the honourable gentleman to resume his seat.
> Mr McDONALD.—I am going to stand out for my rights, and I do not care what the cost may be. I claim my right to say a few words now.

McDonald was technically in the wrong; but at least his 'little scene', as an *Age* headline called it, provided parliament with a momentary baptism of fire. The Speaker stuck to his guns, and the house adjourned until next morning, when Lord Hopetoun was to deliver a speech declaring the causes for which he had called parliament together.

The opening speech, delivered to members of both chambers assembled in the Senate, mentioned various bills to be dealt with by the first parliament, though not necessarily during its first session: bills to constitute a High Court, regulate the public service, restrict Asiatic and South Sea Islands immigration, establish a federal tariff with intercolonial free trade, provide a uniform franchise for federal elections by the adoption of female as well as male suffrage, establish conciliation and arbitration machinery for the settlement of industrial disputes extending beyond any one state . . . Clearly there was plenty for parliament to do, but not immediately. The representatives returned to their own chamber where, adopting House of Commons tradition, the Attorney-General asserted their right to deliberate without reference to the immediate cause of summons by bringing up and reading for the first time a 'formal' or 'privilege' bill—on this occasion the Acts Interpretation Bill, designed to secure economy of words in all Acts. A select committee of four members was appointed to compose an Address-in-Reply to His Excellency's speech; it withdrew, and returned soon afterwards with a stylised 49-word message which would provide the excuse for a general Address-in-Reply debate at the House's next sitting. The Prime Minister laid a draft of Standing Orders on the table, and moved that it be printed. Joseph Cook addressed a question about submarine cables to the Postmaster-General, having apparently forgotten that that gentleman was a Senator; and at 11.40 a.m., twelve minutes before the Senate, the House of Representatives adjourned until 21 May.

Three days before that date the Duke and Duchess of York left Melbourne by train for Brisbane. The popular poet, George Essex Evans, likened their departure to that of the Great Southern Comet, which was then only faintly visible from the Northern Hemisphere:

> Farewell! The world with watching eyes has seen afar,
> Serene, upon the Southern skies, a Nation's star.
> It burns in rays of living light
> Against the sky line, dark and low;
> It climbs towards a loftier height
> Than we shall know.

As it happened, there was another omen still to come: on the day the royal party left Melbourne, a partial eclipse of the sun occurred between three and five o'clock. Sydney and Melbourne missed it because of cloud, but good observations were made at Newcastle, Port Darwin, Perth and Adelaide. What the poetaster of Toowoomba might have made out of that is unknown, but it is unlikely that he would have divined any relevance to the new Commonwealth or its parliament. Both were now going concerns, beyond the reach of augury.

2

A Living Organism

'Parliament began in earnest', wrote Alfred Deakin in his diary on 21 May 1901 when both houses met again. That was not altogether true, for parliamentary custom required that before undertaking any business except of a formal nature the Senate and the House of Representatives should each adopt an Address-in-Reply to the Governor-General's opening speech. But preliminary though they were, debates on such a motion had their uses. Because they allowed members to speak on almost any subject, they would later provide an opportunity for censure by way of amendments to the Address and even as early as this, before Barton's Government had done much at all to deserve criticism or praise, the Address-in-Reply debate served the useful function of introducing senators and representatives. 'We are such strangers to each other', said Senator Sir John Downer (P, SA) in his contribution to the debate, 'that we need the introduction which can only come from hearing each others' voices'.

The loudest voice belonged to Jim Page, the former Queensland Free Trader, who joined the Labor Party the day before parliament opened. Page's interjection of 'What rot!' could be heard above the loudest hubbub like the roar of his own howitzer at the battle of Majuba Hill. The highest voice belonged to George Edwards (F, South Sydney, N), a jam manufacturer who advocated conversion to decimal currency and metrication; and the fastest speakers were Deakin (P, Ballarat, V) and Paddy Glynn (F, SA). Whereas Glynn's lightning delivery was obscured by his Galway accent, Deakin's speeches were clearly enunciated, impeccably phrased and delivered in a pleasing light baritone. 'Affable Alfred', as some called the Attorney-General and Leader of the House, was never lost for the right word or gesture.

This tall, erect man with a trim black beard spoke as articulately as he wrote. W. M. Hughes (Lab, West Sydney, N), no mean speaker himself, said on one occasion that Deakin could 'sell a hotel to a prohibitionist, or persuade a timid old maid to purchase an insane dromedary as a house pet'. Some members, including Hughes, felt that his highly literate oratory was at times notable more for style than substance. And those now hearing him for the first time were—according to the *Argus* political correspondent, David Maling, who wrote under the pseudonym of Ithuriel—so surprised by 'his tendency to flippancy' that they asked whether he was really taking federation and parliament seriously. Of course he was, wrote Ithuriel:

> Those who know him are aware that the one ardent ambition of his life is realised in the Commonwealth, and the others have to learn that it is merely the light-heartedness and the joy of victory which are effervescing in him just now, and finding expression in a constant sparkle of the light and airy nothings with which his brilliant fancy enlivens the course of the debate.

Another orator of interstate renown was Senator Edward Augustine St Aubyn Harney (F, WA), a 'Demosthenes from the West' whose performance during the next three years would be judged inferior to his advance billing.

At the other end of the scale from Deakin's polished rhetoric was the Prime Minister's faculty (amounting almost to genius in Ithuriel's opinion) for saying nothing in a great many words whenever he wished to be obscure. Hansard reporters complained that each sentence of this kind had to be studied like a proposition in Euclid. If Barton found protection in ambiguity, George Reid's best weapon of defence and offence was his humour. The 'formidably comic' Leader of the Opposition (F, East Sydney, N) was an astute politician often mistaken for a clown. Such mistakes could be costly, for this 'embodiment of sleepy, lazy good humour' had a wit like a rabbit-trap. On a visit to Perth with other Commonwealth parliamentarians, he was shown over various State institutions, including the mental asylum. One of Reid's companions, a loyal Victorian, remarked that most of the asylum's staff were Victorians whereas the majority of patients came from New South Wales, 'I can explain that', said Reid. 'Any sensible man would leave Victoria, but only a lunatic would leave New South Wales.'

It is doubtful whether any cartoonist ever succeeded in exaggerating Reid's extraordinary physical appearance: his immense stomach, his stubby legs and the boots that he could button up only with the help of a long-handled button hook, his rubbery neck and many-folded chin, and his protruberant blue eyes, one of which wore a monocle. He was a caricature already. 'To a superficial eye his obesity was either repellent or else amusing', wrote his opponent Deakin, who inclined to the former opinion.

> A heavy German moustache concealed a mouth of considerable size from which there emanated a high-pitched voice rising to a shriek or sinking to a fawning, purring, persuasive orotund with a nasal tinge. To a more careful inspection he disclosed a splendid dome-like head, high and broad and indicative of intellectual power, a gleaming eye which betokened a natural gift of humour and an alertness that not even his habit of dropping

asleep at all times and places in the most ungraceful attitudes and in the most impolite manner could defeat. He never slept in a public gathering more than a moment or two, being quickly awakened by his own snore. He would sleep during the dealing of cards for a game of whist and during the play too if there was any pause, but he never forgot the state of the game or made a revoke.

Although born in Scotland, where his father was a minister of the established church, his family had emigrated to Australia when George Houston Reid (named after a local member of the House of Commons) was still only seven, and no trace of Renfrewshire remained in that orotund, nasal purr. Allan McLean (P, Gippsland, V) was even younger when he left Scotland, but he grew up among expatriate highlanders in Gippsland, and still sounded like them. Senator Gregor McGregor (Lab, S), Senator Hugh de Largie (Lab, W), and Andrew Fisher (Lab, Wide Bay, Q) were adults when they emigrated from Scotland; and the lowlands burr of the latter was said to increase with his emotions. Scotland's contribution to the first parliament was disproportionately high: sixteen members had been born there (compared with twenty-five in England, eight in Ireland and one in Wales), nine had names beginning with 'Mc' or 'Mac', and five were educated at Scotch College in Melbourne.

The members soon came to know each others' mannerisms as well as their voices. Reid used to lower his eyelids at the start of a speech, as if about to indulge in another impromptu siesta; the bearded Kingston (P, S), when excited, would push a finger across his upper lip until his moustache seemed to be growing the wrong way; Lyne (P, Hume, N), when working up an angry reply, would sometimes take a handkerchief from his pocket and put one corner of it between his teeth, biting and pulling together; and Barton, the calmest speaker in parliament, would shift his considerable weight from one foot to another, and often for no discernible reason pick up a sheet of paper from the table, and then replace it.

Sir John Forrest (P, Swan, W), who always wore a long-tailed coat, was accustomed to take one of the tails in his right hand and squeeze it while he spoke. In all probability he was doing this during the Address-in-Reply debate, when he referred to the Governor-General's non-committal remarks about the construction of a railway line to connect western and eastern Australia. 'The people in Western Australia', he said,

> will never be contented as part of the Australian Commonwealth unless we give them means of communication by a railway. In fact, I would never be content, and would use all the constitutional means in my power even to undo this federation, rather than that such an injustice should be done to the people of the great western State of it.

Some of Sir John's listeners could hardly believe their ears. Sir Edward Braddon regretted the

> unfortunate remark of the Minister for Defence because that utterance flies directly in the face of the pronouncement of the Prime Minister. Speaking at Maitland, the right honorable gentleman is reported to have said that anyone who aimed at reforming the Constitution before it had

—to the amusement of BIG JOHN FORREST.

Sir John Forrest
by David Low

had a fair trial was an enemy to federation. Perhaps the right honorable
gentleman will say that he was not correctly reported then?

Mr BARTON.—I will not be responsible for the actual words; but it was
something of that kind; and I am seriously angry with my right honorable friend the Minister for Defence for making the joke he did.

Sir EDWARD BRADDON—If we are to regard that as a joke I think it is a
very questionable one. It is not a joke that ought to come from the
mouth of a responsible Minister of the Crown.

There were no more 'jokes' about secession; but Forrest, who had once
forced his way through a Kalgoorlie picket line with an umbrella, to say
nothing of having forced his way on horseback across the Nullarbor Plain,
would always be one of parliament's stoutest fighters, in both senses of that
superlative. Other fighters of note in the first parliament were Senator Sir
Josiah Symon (F, S) and C. C. Kingston (P, S). 'Charlie' Kingston could not
harass his old enemy Symon in the Senate. Perhaps compensating for this,
he carried on a feud with Sir John Forrest, crossing swords with him in Cabinet, and infuriating the Emperor of the West by muttering 'Pork, pork!' when
passing him in Queen's Hall.

Queenslanders, particularly Labor men, soon earned the reputation of
being parliament's most persistent interjectors. Senator Anderson Dawson
(Lab, Q)—who had presided over Australia's first Labor ministry, in
Queensland, for seven days in 1899—spoke agressively, according to the
Argus, in the rough-and-tumble spirit of the diggings. It seemed that Dawson
had to 'go off', and interjections served him as a safety valve.

Another Labor interjector, in the lower house, was the 'untamed terror' of
Tasmania, O'Malley. The King's outlandish North American idiom could
unnerve even such a confident speaker as his Labor colleague, Hughes,
whose free trade views annoyed O'Malley during the Address-in-Reply
debate.

Mr HUGHES.— I ask honourable members who are protectionists to
name one economist of European and world-wide standing who
defends their theory.

Mr O'MALLEY.—Carey, of the United States.

Mr HUGHES.—I understand that there is a man named Carey, but no one
ever pays him the compliment of regarding him as an economist of
world-wide standing.

Mr O'MALLEY.—A free trader naturally reads only what suits his particular views. Carey is an e-tarnal spanker.

Mr HUGHES.—It is very easy to invent a number of supporters for one's
theories, but I still say there is no instance of a man of standing in the
economic world supporting the theory of protection.

Mr O'MALLEY.—My brother, he is the bald eagle of the Rocky
Mount-ains.

George Reid, in his Address-in-Reply speech, found a felicitous phrase for
the federal parliament. 'All the scattered energies of Australia', he said, 'have
at last been crystallized into a living national organism which will give the
fullest play to our own power and to the genius of the Australian race'. His

hopes may have been set too high, but the image was well chosen: for better or worse, the new parliament was indeed a national organism, a microcosm, a sort of amoeba or protozoon pulsing with life and regularly changing shape.

Of the thirty-six senators and seventy-five representatives, sixteen and forty-three respectively had been born in Australia, and almost all the others in the United Kingdom. With the possible exception of King O'Malley, the only member born outside the British Empire was the Leader of the parliamentary Labor Party, John Christian Watson (Lab, Bland, N). Watson was born either at Valparaiso, Chile, or on board ship between Valparaiso and New Zealand. His father's name is now believed to have been Johan Christian Tanck, and although none of this was known publicly during J. C. Watson's lifetime, it is probable that his own name was really John Christian Tanck. Perhaps his putative father's nationality, whatever it was, should have disqualified Watson from parliament, for he himself was never naturalised in New Zealand or Australia. Instead he used the British surname of his mother's second husband, and if indeed his nationality was incompatible with membership of parliament he guarded that secret as closely as perhaps O'Malley was guarding his.

Twenty-six senators and sixty representatives had previous parliamentary experience, three and ten respectively as colonial premiers, and ten and twenty as ministers, excluding the former premiers. The largest single occupational group was not surprisingly lawyers (Senate, twelve; Representatives, sixteen). In the lower house twenty members described themselves by such terms as businessmen, merchants and estate agents; twelve as farmers, graziers, pastoralists; eight miners (Fisher, de Largie and the Protectionist Thomas Glassey had all been coalminers in Scotland), compositor, rural worker, engine driver; five journalists and two newspaper proprietors.

The average age of all members at the time of their election was forty-nine in the Senate, and forty-seven in the lower house. The oldest member of the House of Representatives was W. H. Groom (P, Darling Downs, Q), a 68-year-old newspaper proprietor and veteran of the Queensland Legislative Assembly, where for thirty-eight years he had represented the electorate of Drayton and Toowoomba. William Groom was a shrewd roads-and-bridges politician known in Queensland as 'the big panjandrum of the Darling Downs Bunch'—the Bunch consisting of storekeepers and squatters rather than the wealthier Black Soil Dukes of the Darling Downs, to whom Groom's views on protection and land policy seemed rather radical.

Groom was indeed a little to the left of Queensland's centre, and in letters to his son, Littleton Ernest Groom, he wrote approvingly of the legislature to which, in spite of his earlier anti-federalism, he had now ascended.

> Dear Lit, The more I am here and sit in the House and hear the speeches of members the more I notice the enormous contrast between us and the mediocrities of Queensland and am struck with it. The tone of the House too is good. There is no class hatred or bitterness . . . Without question Victoria is profoundly democratic. It is astonishing to find so many educated men imbued with democratic principles, and who regard Conservatism as opposed to the spirit and advancement of the age.

Because of his age, Groom was chosen to move the Address-in-Reply. It is doubtful whether many of his listeners realised that this 'Father' of their House was parliament's only link with the era of convict transportation which had ended in eastern Australia fifty-one years before. At the age of thirteen, while apprenticed to a baker in Plymouth, he was convicted of stealing and sentenced to transportation for seven years. He arrived in Sydney on the convict ship *Hashemy* in 1849, was conditionally pardoned soon afterwards, but seven years later was sentenced to three years for stealing gold on the Turon fields. Pardoned again after little more than a year, he emigrated to Queensland and never looked back.

Groom's motion on the Address was seconded by R. A. Crouch (P, Corio, V), a 32-year-old lawyer and citizen soldier. Next day, when Joseph Cook referred correctly to Crouch as the House's youngest member, James McColl (P, Echuca, V) presented the Speaker with his first point of order. It was no more in order to call someone the youngest member, argued McColl, than it would be to speak of the baldest member of the House. The Speaker wasted no time in dismissing such a frivolous point, reminding the House that the Member for Corio had himself referred to his youthful distinction.

What more could be said about this national organism? In the combined chambers, 25 per cent of members had been educated to secondary level, and 36 per cent to tertiary level. But among Labor's twenty-four members there was, so far, only one university graduate, the otherwise undistinguished clergyman, James Ronald (Lab, South Melbourne, V). Hughes, encouraged by Reid and other Sydney lawyers of his acquaintance, had been reading for the Bar since 1900. He read law books during dull debates, and used to board the Sydney–Melbourne express with 'a bag of law books and a case containing a phonograph, with which he improved his hearing by carefully listening while it tinkled out the speeches of W. E. Gladstone'.

The first parliament contained only eleven Roman Catholics, four of whom were born in Ireland; and four Jews, all of whom were in the lower house. Seven members were the sons of clergymen, and at least twenty-five were active Protestant churchmen. There were twice as many Presbyterians as the next Protestant group, the Methodists.

Despite the inherent difficulties of foreign travel, some members had seen a lot of the world. Jim Page, one of the twenty members with military service, served for seven years in South Africa. Hugh Mahon (Lab, Coolgardie, W) had travelled in North America; Deakin in India; G. A. Cruickshank (P, Gwydir, N) in Europe, Africa, India and America; and Sir Edward Braddon in India.

Braddon's memoirs of his career in the Indian service (*Thirty Years of Shikar*) contained such chapters as 'Sport in Lower Bengal', 'First Joys of Pig-Sticking' and 'Murderous Propensities of the Natives'. Other authors in the first parliament were Deakin (two books about his travels in India), Forrest (journals of his exploring journeys), Bruce Smith (*Liberty and Liberalism*, a dissertation on Free Trade), Sir John Quick (*The Annotated Constitution*), George Reid (*Five Free Trade Essays*), and Senator J. C. Neild (a poem which started with the memorable words, 'Eftsoons the nocent waterspout . . .'). The list was not long, in fact authorship and wide reading were both uncommon in this parliament. Sir George Turner (P, Balaclava) and Sir William Lyne never read books, and Reid said that he read only 'sensation novels'.

The richest members of parliament were probably J. C. Manifold (P, Corangamite, V), a Victorian grazier and racehorse owner who used to complain that he was pestered by beggars as soon as he left the door of Parliament House; J. L. Bonython (P, S), proprietor of the Adelaide *Advertiser* and other newspapers; Senator Simon Fraser, who had made his fortune out of railway contracting and pastoral development; and Forrest, whose business interests permitted him to entertain lavishly in his suite at the Grand Hotel. Manifold and the New South Wales Free Trader, Sir Wiliam McMillan, preferred the Melbourne Club.

Other members lived far more modestly. Reid, who received no additional allowance as Leader of the Opposition, shared boarding house accommodation with a syndicate of fellow Free Traders. Watson and a dozen other Labor members all stayed at the one boarding house in East Melbourne.

Labor brought a more relaxed social style to the otherwise rather formal chambers in Spring Street. Whereas Barton and most of his ministers addressed one another by surname, Watson was 'Chris' to his followers. The typical Labor member wore a soft felt hat instead of the more usual hard one, and according to *Punch* he was inclined to put his feet up on the back of the bench in front of him 'like an American, and one is surprised that he does not expectorate like the Yankee in *Martin Chuzzlewit*'. Perhaps he did that, too, for Parliament House was supplied with spittoons.

Another American resemblance might have been remarked in the word 'caucus' (from an Algonquin Indian word 'caucauasu', meaning 'adviser'), which had found its way from the United States into British and colonial politics. Labor used the word to describe meetings of its federal parliamentary party. The first formal Caucus meeting, attended by twenty-two members in Parliament House on 8 May 1901, admitted two new members (Page and O'Malley) and chose Watson to lead the party in the House of Representatives. Watson was a good choice and was later confirmed as chairman of the party. Only 34 years of age, and a compositor by trade, he had already served six years in the New South Wales Legislative Assembly. He was broad-shouldered, with a neat beard, sapphire blue eyes, an even temper and the ability to get along with all kinds of men. As someone wrote, he could 'down a beer at the Wombat Hotel with Mick Loughnane with the same genuine aplomb that he could sip champagne with Bernhard Ringrose Wise at the Metropole'. By fiscal persuasion he was a Protectionist, and that gave him more affinity with Deakin than with Reid. The feeling was reciprocated.

Labor's chosen leader in the Senate, later to be confirmed as deputy chairman, was Gregor McGregor, a former builder's labourer and gardener who in his time had worked for some of Adelaide's wealthiest men, including the President of the Senate, Sir Richard Baker. Soon after his arrival in Australia, McGregor was struck in the face by a falling tree branch, and partially blinded. This did not prevent him from gardening, or from later becoming President and Secretary of the United Builders' Labourers' Association.

His eyesight continued to deteriorate, and when he visited Tom Roberts's studio to pose for the painting of parliament, he bumped straight into a table. Reading and writing became increasingly difficult for him; but Senator McGregor, a burly, heavily moustached man in dark glasses, compensated for this handicap with a capacious memory and the ability to recognise his fellow senators' voices in the chamber. He also possessed a pawky, deadpan sense of humour. Early in the Senate's life he encouraged Senator de Largie to burlesque the conservatism of many in that chamber by moving a motion condemning the *Argus* for having printed 'a foul libellous article on the memory of King James 1, referring to that monarch as a "fool and a blackleg"'. On another occasion he attempted to halt a seemingly endless speech by singing in a whining voice a song that went, 'The tears fell gently from her eyes . . . '. Called to order by the President, he denied that he had been singing, claiming that everyone knew he could not sing.

In his Address-in-Reply speech, Senator McGregor, said frankly that his party would support whichever side of the chamber seemed most likely to assist Labor in achieving its own ends. 'We are for sale', he said,

> and we will get the auctioneer when he comes, and take care that he is the right man. The bid that has been made this time is worse than use-less . . . I want to show the Government what they have to do if they intend to secure our support. Of course, that will also be an indication to the Opposition of what they will have to do, and they will have to do a lot more than they have attempted up to the present time.

Senator MILLEN (F, NSW).—That is an indication of the sort of whip you can use.

Senator McGREGOR.—Oh, yes, we are never afraid of the whip; we have been too well acquainted with bullocks for that.

Altogether the Senate spent six days debating its Address-in-Reply, and the House of Representatives spent eight. An unsuccessful attempt was made in each chamber to add a few words of regret that the proposals for legislation restricting non-white immigration had not been stronger, but in the end both Addresses were passed as originally moved. 'May it please Your Excellency:- We, the House of Representatives of the Parliament of the Commonwealth of Australia, in Parliament assembled, beg to express our loyalty to Our Most Gracious Sovereign, and to thank Your Excellency for the Gracious Speech which you have been pleased to address to Parliament'. The Senate's Address was almost identical. It may have seemed that the mountains had travailed and brought forth two mice, but it was the travail that counted. Thirty-one senators and forty-nine representatives took part in the debates, and by the time it was over they were all better acquainted.

Although federal parliament had thirty-two fewer members than the Victorian legislature, and federal ministers moved out of Parliament House to their new offices at the corner of Spring and Collins Streets early in June, the building was still crowded. This was because members from other States used its limited facilities more than their Victorian predecessors had, and because some of the Victorians continued to frequent their old haunts. Speaker Holder (who had more space than most, as he had taken over the Victorian Speaker's office and bedroom) assigned a large room on the second floor to ministerial supporters in the lower house, the room next to it to Labor members, and a large room on the first floor to the Opposition. It may be assumed that the President of the Senate made similar arrangements on the other side of Queen's Hall, though apart from the President's own chambers the only space known for certain to have been allocated in that part of the building was a Senate clubroom. Members of both houses sometimes slept in Parliament House, but whether any of them ever had rooms of their own is not known.

At times the building was dismally cold, badly ventilated and malodorous. It was not sewered (although by then much of 'Smelbourne' was), and Hughes said that the W.C.'s were disgraceful. 'I can only find anything to fully describe them', he said, 'by saying that during the height of the bubonic plague in Sydney I never experienced anything worse'. In October Senator W. G. Higgs (Lab, Q) was asking the Prime Minister to see whether there was not some means of improving, even temporarily, the ventilation of the upper house. 'One of the greatest evils a debating body can suffer from', he said, 'is that of not having fresh air . . . The air in this chamber gets vitiated very quickly. There is a kind of device for raising the hair of those who sit on the extreme back bench, but I must say that it does not seem to purify the air'.

The building was heated with only partial success by open coal fires and a combined ventilation and heating system which introduced warm air into the chambers at the top of the dados. 'The theory of this plenum system', explained J. M. Fowler (Lab, Perth, W) to the House of Representatives during winter,

> is that the floor outlets are contrived to enable the carbonic acid gas which we exhale to escape from the building. The theory proceeds on the assumption that carbonic acid gas always falls. But it has been discovered since the plenum system was put forward that the carbonic acid gas which we exhale, instead of descending, rises; so there is no advantage in attempting to get the objectionable atmosphere out of the Chamber by these lower outlets.
>
> Then, we are very apt to be misled as regards the warmth of the Chamber. When we come into it we find an agreeable warmth striking our faces. But I can assure honorable members, if they have not discovered the fact from the condition of their lower extremities, that the atmosphere about head or breast height is not by any means a criterion of the atmosphere on the floor . . . I hardly remember having suffered more physical discomfort in my life than during the two winters I have spent in this Chamber. The particular form of discomfort is a coldness of the lower extremities.
>
> I know that I shall afford an excellent opportunity for the caricaturists to depict honorable members trying to obviate cold feet with the aid of foot-warmers, hot water and mustard baths. But this has a tragic side. In my own case this personal discomfort culminated last winter in a very serious illness. Two members of this House have died, and, at least, one death may be traceable, in some degree, to the conditions under which we sit here.

The first member to die was the 'Father' of the House of Representatives. Groom had been worried about the way Melbourne's winter was affecting another elderly Queenslander, Macdonald-Paterson, and probably it had the same effect on him. He developed influenza, then pneumonia, and died at his Melbourne residence on 8 August. Both houses adjourned for the day as a mark of respect to the big panjandrum of the Darling Downs Bunch. Barton said he did not think such adjournments ought to become general practice, but when F. W. Piesse (F, T) died at his home in Hobart on 6 March 1902, aged fifty-three, the House of Representatives adjourned again. Thenceforth it was customary for single houses to adjourn whenever one of their members died while the house was sitting. Groom's son Littleton was elected with a slightly reduced majority in his father's place at the first Commonwealth by-election, on 14 September.

It was hardly surprising that relations between the federal and Victorian parliaments were sometimes less than harmonious, for one side was inclined to resent interference, and the other to resent 'eviction'. After 'striding defiantly through corridors' at Spring Street, as the *Age* reported, one State member, Thomas Bent, told the Legislative Assembly in June 1901 that 'the place has been converted into a lodging house. I do not think the people of this country have spent over a quarter of a million to allow senators to have beds made up in that place'.

At the next meeting of the House of Representatives, Jim Page asked the Prime Minister whether, in view of such expressed dissatisfaction at the Commonwealth's occupancy of the building, it would be possible for the federal parliament to hold sittings in Sydney, where no doubt it would be received in a true federal spirit. O'Malley suggested Hobart. The Prime Minister took such flippancies in good part, and went on with the business of negotiating an occupation agreement. The President of the Victorian Legislative Council wrote to the President of the Senate complaining that someone had broken into a record room at Spring Street and dispersed some of the Legislative Council documents stored there. In due course Sir Richard Baker apologised and said that the room had been restored to its original condition. When the housekeeper at Spring Street, a Victorian, was about to retire in October, the Victorian Speaker wrote to Speaker Holder intimating that he had selected the housekeeper at the Legislative Assembly to fill the vacancy. Holder, who had already chosen the principal doorkeeper for promotion, wrote back to his opposite number at the Exhibition Building: 'I shall not need to trouble you to make any appointment'.

Although Barton had stated in July that the Commonwealth would seek an occupation agreement for three to five years, the agreement signed by the Governor-General and the Governor of Victoria on 9 December had no time limit. The Commonwealth Government did not have to pay rent for Parliament House, but the agreement provided that it should meet the cost of repairs, maintenance and electricity. State members would for the time being continue to have equal access to the library, refreshment room, billiard room and gardens; one row of seats in the President's and Speaker's galleries would be reserved for State members and their guests; one room on each side of Queen's Hall would be set aside for members of the Legislative Council and Legislative Assembly; and all Victorian archives would be permitted to remain in the building.

The library was to be conducted jointly by library committees of the two parliaments for the use of their respective members, and on matters of joint interest the committees would have power to confer and act. The Parliamentary Librarian, Arthur Wadsworth, and his staff would remain officers of the Victorian Government, but the Commonwealth would reimburse Victoria for their salaries. In this ambivalent role, Wadsworth acted as librarian to the Commonwealth parliament for more than a quarter of a century without ever being officially appointed to that post.

The Victorians continued to assert their rights under the occupation agreement, but as they became more accustomed to Carlton Gardens they were seen less frequently at Spring Street. Some of them probably knew when they were not wanted. The Victorian Premier, Sir Alexander Peacock, was renowned for his remarkable laugh, a sort of kookaburra call. It was one of Melbourne's civic glories; but the federal member, Hughes, in spite of his defective hearing, declared it to be a pose and a self-advertisement. One night the famous laugh rang out disconcertingly in the federal refreshment room. Hughes picked up two plates and carefully dropped them on the floor; another peal of laughter, another crash of plates. The Premier was offended, and rarely came to dinner there again.

By agreement with the Commonwealth Government, the Victorian parliament returned *en masse* to its building for a sitting of forty days between December 1902 and April 1903, while the first federal parliament was prorogued between its first and second sessions. The reason given was that the Victorians ought not to be subjected to the inconvenience and discomfort of a summer sitting in the Exhibition Building, where during December the inside temperature was already 94 degrees Fahrenheit. During this interlude Sir Alexander Peacock would have been able to laugh to his heart's content. The experiment was not repeated, however, and for the next quarter of a century the only voices heard in the chambers at Spring Street were federal ones.

Snow-white Australia

The organism now endowed with life quickly developed a routine of its own. Both chambers usually met at 2.30 p.m., and sat into the night—the lower house usually later than the Senate, and sitting from Tuesday to Friday compared with the Senate's customary Wednesday to Friday. In both chambers the Friday sitting usually ended at 4 p.m. Proceedings began when the Speaker and the President took their chairs, each wearing a black King's Counsel gown, full-bottomed judge's wig and lace accessories. Their first duty was to satisfy themselves that a quorum was present, in each chamber at least one-third of the members. From June onwards, as a result of representations from Protestant churches, the presiding officers opened each day's proceedings by reading prayers which were almost identical in each chamber and incorporated the Lord's Prayer. Senator McGregor had spoken against this practice, which he regarded as religiosity, but was careful to dissociate his party from such a politically hazardous personal opinion.

Having read prayers, the Speaker and the President called for petitions, notices, questions without notice and the making of ministerial statements;

then called on the notices and orders of the day. Citizens of the new Commonwealth seemed to put great stock in the efficacy of signatures. During the first session of parliament the House of Representatives received 249 petitions, 176 praying that the House would take steps to see that the postal and telegraph service was not used for lotteries or other games of chance, and nineteen praying the House to pass with the least possible delay legislation extending the franchise to women. After this initial spurt, however, the number of petitions dwindled.

Everything done, as distinct from merely said, in the two houses of parliament—the wording of motions, votes on division, messages between the houses, papers tabled, members' attendance and so on—was recorded briefly but carefully in the *Journals of the Senate* and *Votes and Proceedings of the House of Representatives*, separate issues of which were published for each sitting day. What was said in parliament was reported extensively, though not completely, in *Parliamentary Debates*, a running script of both houses referred to informally as 'Hansard', after a certain Luke Hansard who had published summaries of debates in the House of Commons early in the nineteenth century.

Commonwealth *Parliamentary Debates* was first published at weekly intervals (3d per copy, and bi-weekly from 1906 onwards) and was also published cumulatively in bound volumes. In both forms the Senate appeared before the lower house, just as it was named first in the Constitution, presumably on some analogy with the House of Lords and its propinquity to the Sovereign. As the Senate did not share that privilege, the vertical dimension of 'upper' and 'lower' houses rang rather false in a federal legislature. In Volume 1 of *Parliamentary Debates* the index for the House of Representatives appeared before that of the Senate. But tradition prevailed, and from then on the States' House somewhat irrationally took precedence over the more numerous house on all occasions.

When the subject of Hansard was being discussed in the House of Representatives, Hugh Mahon suggested that shorthand writers with journalistic experience should be entrusted to condense members' speeches in order to save labour, a heavy cost in printing and much useless repetition. Fortunately this view was not widely held. The Hansard staff did take pains, however, to improve syntax where improvement was required. Interjections were recorded only when the member speaking replied to them. By long-established custom at State level, federal members were able to read the sub-edited transcript or proof of their reported words, and if necessary to make corrections. Members were expected not to alter the sense of words used in debate, or to introduce new matter, and to the extent that they complied with that expectation the Commonwealth's *Parliamentary Debates* was a close approximation of what was actually said in the two chambers.

During the second month of parliament each House established five standing committees (Standing Orders, Library, House, Printing and Elections and Qualifications committees), all of which could meet together as joint committees; the House of Representatives established its first select committee (that is, a committee to inquire into a specific matter); and each house adopted its own set of Standing Orders, or rules for the conduct of parliamentary business. The seven-member select committee on coinage, chaired by G. B. Edwards (F, South Sydney, N), inquired into whether or not the Commonwealth should issue its own silver and copper coins and adopt a decimal system of coinage. It reported affirmatively on both questions, but several years were to pass before the first course was adopted in Imperial currency, and several decades would pass before Australia converted to decimal currency.

The Senate temporarily adopted the Standing Orders of the South Australian House of Assembly, and used them until a revised code of its own came into operation two years later. The House of Representatives adopted with minor amendments the draft Standing Orders that had been prepared by Barton and Clerk Jenkins. Although adopted provisionally, these remained in use, with amendment from time to time, for almost half a century. They dealt with such matters as the sitting and adjournment of the House, notices of motion, and the process by which bills or proposed laws become acts of parliament. The latter followed long-established Westminister practice, whereby a draft bill is introduced into one house of parliament, passed by that house and agreed to by the other house, perhaps after amendment. In the originating house (usually the House of Representatives) a bill for an act passes through several stages: the first reading, which proceeds without amendment or debate; the second reading, when the bill is explained by its sponsor (usually a Minister), debated in principle and agreed to; the committee stage, when the bill is considered clause by clause and may be amended in Committee of the Whole (i.e. all the members) or, since 1978, by some other legislation committee, with restricted membership; and the third reading, when the bill as reported from committee may be debated again before finally passing the House.

It then goes to the other house to be dealt with in similar fashion and returned to the originating house, either without amendment or with messages seeking amendment. When agreed to by both houses, it is presented by the originating house to the Governor-General for the royal assent which transforms it into an act.

The earliest Standing Orders provided time limits only for speakers on an urgency motion (thirty minutes for the mover, and fifteen for other speakers). On all other occasions, members were permitted to speak as long as they wished. Both houses of the new parliament proved to be more talkative than had been expected from experience in colonial legislatures, and eventually it became necessary to employ an additional parliamentary reporter. Prolixity often defeated itself, but by the same token in the early years of parliament eloquence was capable of swaying votes to an extent that would not continue indefinitely.

As the interpreter of Standing Orders in the House of Representatives, Speaker Holder was prompt, decisive and clearly audible. He put Ithuriel in mind of Speaker Peel in the House of Commons, whose elocution was said to be so perfect that if at some dull hour he were to repeat the multiplication table up to twelve times twelve the House would quietly fill with members who would sit entranced at the rhythmic sound, strangely moved by the familiar truths. 'Mr Holder may never prove so attractive as that', wrote

Ithuriel, 'but it is pleasant to hear his sonorous tones giving out a prompt ruling, and—crowning mercy—his words reach the galleries'.

All parties acknowledged that Holder was impartial. Although he was
neither required nor expected to divorce himself entirely from party politics,
as was his prototype in the House of Commons, the first Commonwealth
Speaker's conduct of his office did approximate closely to the British ideal.
He was, after all, a veteran of the South Australian parliament which, alone
among colonial legislatures, had striven to maintain a non-partisan
Speakership. Speaker Holder was returned to parliament as an Independent,
and he remained aloof from factional manoeuvring. There was nothing in
Standing Orders to prevent him from voting in divisions in the Committee of
the Whole; but, in contradistinction to some of his successors, Holder never
did so. The Speaker cannot vote in a division in the House (as distinct from a
division in committee) unless the numbers are equal. In that event he has a
casting vote, and by tradition inherited from the House of Commons he
votes wherever possible in such a way as to enable debate to continue or to
leave a bill in its existing form.

The Speaker is assisted by a Chairman of Committees, elected from and by
members of the House, and by the permanent officers of the House—the
Clerk, Deputy Clerk, First Clerk Assistant, Clerk Assistant and Serjeant-at-
Arms. The Chairman of Committees (the first was J. M. Chanter, P, Riverina,
N) chaired meetings of the House when it was sitting as a Committee of the
Whole House to consider a bill in detail after the second reading; and when-
ever the Speaker was absent from proceedings in the House, the Chairman
presided in the Speaker's Chair as Acting or Deputy Speaker.

Among the more significant steps taken early in its life by the House of
Representatives, and to be taken routinely in future, was the resolving of
itself into two specialised forms of Committee of the Whole: the Committee
of Supply, and the Committee of Ways and Means. These followed the practice of the House of Commons. They sat in the chamber like a Committee of
the Whole, and were presided over by the Chairman of Committees, who
reported their progress to the House. The Committee of Supply was set up
early in each session of parliament to give preliminary consideration to the
Government's expenditure proposals made to parliament by way of a message from the Governor-General. Similarly, the Committee of Ways and
Means considered revenue proposals before related bills were ordered to be
brought in. As the Senate could not originate laws appropriating revenue or
moneys, the Committees of Supply and Ways and Means were peculiar to
the lower house.

The main Appropriation Bill for any year was initiated by the Governor-
General transmitting Estimates of Expenditure which were referred to the
Committee of Supply. In this Committee, on a motion that the first item be
agreed to, the Treasurer presented his Budget speech. During the ensuing
debate, the Opposition could move only one form of amendment—that the
amount of that item be reduced by a token sum. When the Budget debate
was concluded, the Supply Committee proceeded to consider all other estimates, which usually took six or seven weeks. Only after the Ways and

Means resolution had also been formally considered was the Appropriation Bill brought in to the House.

In the earliest days of the new parliament, the Prime Minister leant for advice particularly upon Deakin. At the level of parliamentary party management for debates and divisions, he depended mainly on the Government Whip, Austin Chapman (P, Eden-Monaro, N); and outside the chamber his principal public servant was the Secretary of the Department of External Affairs, Atlee Hunt. To Barton belonged most of the credit for bringing the parliamentary machine into action. For the first year of parliament's life he was Prime Minister effectively as well as nominally, but those closest to him felt that he was not ideally suited to that office. He could work with great concentration and speed, but he did so irregularly and often late at night. Barton was not a lazy man, said Hunt, but he was extravagant of time, both his own and that of others. He missed too many sittings of the House, leaving Deakin in charge, and was impatient with matters of detail.

One memory of Barton at this time, recorded by J. N. H. Hume Cook (P, Bourke, V), may tell more about the man than any of his speeches in Hansard. Soon after the House had started a morning sitting, Clerk Jenkins beckoned Cook out of the chamber and said: 'Tell Barton I've got the finest trout he ever saw in his life. Ask him what I am to do with it'. 'I immediately went to Barton, who was in charge of some bill at the table, and gave him the message', wrote Cook.

> Without turning his head, or appearing to take any notice of what I had whispered to him, he spoke out of the corner of his mouth in a slow, soft fashion: 'Thank Jenkins for me. Have him take the fish to the bar upstairs, and tell him to leave it with the attendant until I can go up myself and see it.' In a few minutes he had arranged for another minister to take his place at the table, and signalling me to join him we walked off to see the trout. It was what Barton described as 'a beauty', and his eyes glowed as he commented on its size and condition.

The chef served it in a small room behind the library for a lunch attended by Barton, Jenkins, Cook and Sir John Forrest. 'The way in which Barton carved and served that fish was an education', wrote Cook.

> There were practically no scraps and no broken bones. The skeleton almost looked as if it had been picked by ants when he had finished carving. He certainly was a master-craftsman with the fish knife and fork. As may be understood, all the etceteras including the sauce and the wine were quite in keeping and perfect.

For reasons which may have had something to do with his higher standing and salary in the Victorian parliament, Jenkins returned to the positions of Clerk of the Legislative Council and Clerk of the Parliaments in July. He was succeeded as Clerk of the House of Representatives by the Clerk Assistant in the Senate, Charles Gavan Duffy.

The first Bill enacted by parliament was the Consolidated Revenue (Supply) Act, an Act to provide out of the consolidated revenue fund, which had been growing since January thanks to Kingston's Customs Department, the sum of £491 882 to the service of the period ending 30 June. Most of the early legislation was concerned with establishing the machinery of government and parliament. For example, the Post and Telegraph Bill, introduced in the Senate, was to regulate the Commonwealth's new post and telegraph service. In his second reading speech the Postmaster-General, Senator Drake, referred in passing to the Queensland meteorologist's £12 000 worth of telegrams per annum, free of charge. It was a mistake to suppose that free business did not cost anything, said the Postmaster-General, and he had issued instructions that the amount of Mr Wragge's wires should be cut down at once by at least one-half. This mention of the ubiquitous weather prophet prompted Senator Dawson to ask whether Wragge's telegrams might breach Clause 55 (1)(c) of the Act, which prohibited use of the telegraph service 'under pretence of foretelling future events'.

Another early Act, the Commonwealth Public Service Act, established not only departments of the public service but also departments of parliament itself. Officers of the Senate, officers of the House of Representatives and officers of the Parliamentary Library were in each case deemed to constitute a department under this Act.

The first policy legislation, as distinct from legislation of a machinery or establishment nature, consisted of two complementary bills: the Immigration Restriction Bill, to place certain restrictions on immigration and provide for the removal from the Commonwealth of prohibited immigrants, and the Pacific Island Labourers Bill, to provide for the regulation, restriction and prohibition of the introduction of labourers from the Pacific Islands. In retrospect it might be wished that parliament had chosen some other subject for its first acts of policy. The debates on White Australia (for that was the subject) make dismal reading nowadays. There is a meanness of spirit about them, and from this distance it is not easy to understand the fear and prejudice which pervaded almost all speeches.

The legislation was intended to protect Australia against racial invasion, and to expel some of the racially undesirable intruders who had already slipped into the citadel. Looking back now, the figures hardly seem to have justified the concern expressed about them on the election platform and in parliament. The 1901 census showed that the Australian population of 3 782 943 included about 55 000 'coloured' aliens, of whom 34 000 were Chinese. Queensland was the most 'contaminated' State, with 9313 Chinese, 2269 Japanese, and 9327 Pacific Islanders, most of the latter being employed on low wages by the sugar industry. In the previous five years the number of Chinese in New South Wales, Victoria, Queensland, South Australia and the Northern Territory had increased by only 1307. Queensland had regulated the immigration of Japanese by treaty with Japan, and since 1898 their departures had outnumbered arrivals by 864 to 304.

Yet undeniably immigration was a live political issue. Labor candidates made much of it during the election campaign, and their electoral success, particularly in Queensland, was interpreted by the Government as a vote for White Australia. When the Labor Caucus revised its fighting platform on 20 May, the day before parliament started in earnest, White Australia took precedence ahead of adult suffrage, old-age pensions, a citizen army and com-

Victorian Parliament House in Spring Street, Melbourne, home of the Australian Parliament from 1901 to 1927

Lord Hopetoun, the first Governor-General of Australia

Sir Frederick Holder, the first Speaker of the House of Representatives

His Royal Highness the Duke of Cornwall and York opening Federal Parliament in the Exhibition Building, Melbourne, on 9 May 1901, painting by Charles Nuttall

Sir Edmund Barton

Alfred Deakin

Sir George Reid

Andrew Fisher

pulsory arbitration. The immigration legislation was brought on quickly because of its presumed popularity throughout the nation; because it would conciliate Labor members; and because there was so much wide approval in parliament for the principle of White Australia. Approval of White Australia meant opposition to Asian immigration, and the reasons advanced for that opposition ranged all the way from Asian inferiority to Asian superiority. Running through most of the arguments, devious or brutally direct, was a common thread of racism. A few Free Traders spoke up on behalf of the Chinese and Japanese, but their motives were suspect. What they were really talking about was cheap labour, not human rights.

The Immigration Restriction Bill was read a first time in the House of Representatives on 5 June, and debated and considered in its various stages during August and September. Barton and Deakin justified the exclusion of Asians with diametrically opposed arguments. 'There is a basic inequality', said Barton in the committee stage.

> These races are, in comparison with the white races—I think no one wants convincing of this fact—unequal and inferior. The doctrine of the equality of men was never intended to apply to the equality of the Englishman and the Chinaman. There is a deep-set difference, and we see no prospect of it ever being effaced. Nothing in this world can put these two races upon an equality. Nothing we can do by cultivation, by refinement, or by anything else will make some races equal to others . . .

Deakin took a superficially more respectable but really more ignominious road to the same conclusion. The Japanese, he said, should be excluded from Australia because of their high abilities. 'It is not the bad qualities but the good qualities of these alien races that make them dangerous to us. It is their inexhaustible energy, their power of applying themselves to new tasks, their endurance and low standards of living that make them such competitors'. Thus were Asian immigrants damned if they were inferior to white Australians, and damned if they were not. Watson, while admitting that Labor's objection to Asian immigration was 'tinged with considerations of an industrial nature' also emphasised racial incompatibility.

> We know that education does not eliminate the objectionable qualities of the Baboo Hindu . . . With the Oriental, as a rule, the more he is educated the worse man he is likely to be from our point of view. The more educated the more cunning he becomes, and the more able, with his peculiar ideas of social and business morality, to cope with the people here.

Successive Labor speakers combined fear of competition with unabashed racial prejudice. 'During my election tour in Queensland I saw a contract called for clearing between Bundaberg and Gladstone', said Page.

> The price offered was so low that no white man would take it. The consequence was that a sparkling subadur went up with a new shipment of Hindoos—full-blooded bucks from Bombay—who took the contract at one-twentieth of the lowest rate for which a white man could do the work. That is another reason why we desire to get rid of these aliens.

The Presbyterian clergyman, J. B. Ronald, urged his listeners to keep before them

> the noble ideal of a white Australia—a snow-white Australia if you will. Let it be pure and spotless . . . Never let us try to blend a superior with an inferior race . . . It is not Christian morals any more than it is good socialism to believe that we can blend not to our deterioration with these people.

Two of the most radical members of parliament joined in this chorus without compunction. Isaac Isaacs (P, Indi, V) reminded the House that 'when the Boer War commenced, and the Princes of India came forward, with noble fidelity, and loyally offered troops of their races to the British Government, that Government said—"No; we decline with thanks. This is a white man's war."'

'I recognise to the fullest', said Isaacs,

> that here in Australia we have a white man's war. It is a struggle for life . . . It is a white man's war that we must face, and I would not suffer any black or tinted man to come in and block the path of progress. I would resist to the utmost, if it were necessary, any murky stream from disturbing the current of Australian life.

H. B. Higgins (P, North Melbourne, V), one of the very few members to speak against Australia's participation in the Boer War, criticised efforts by Britain to influence certain terms of the Immigration Restriction Act; but he agreed with the main object. 'It is a very cheap and a very easy thing', he said,

> for the European nations to stir up matters on the east coast of Asia, because they will not feel the effects. But as soon as that great swarm of bees begin to move it will first of all move here, as this is the place of all others to which it is likely to come.

Britain's main concern about the Immigration Restriction Act was that it should not appear to discriminate against His Majesty's Indian subjects. A sop to this was provided by Clause 4 of the Bill, which prohibited immigration into the Commonwealth of any person who failed to write out a passage of fifty words dictated by an immigration officer. The Bill, as originally drafted, specified dictation in the English language, but this was amended to 'European language'. The idea of a dictation test was borrowed from the Natal Act, but it differed considerably from the test in South Africa. The Natal test was a genuine educational requirement: the passage to be dictated was scheduled to the Act, and any literate immigrant could learn it. The intention of Australia's Act, on the other hand, was to provide under the guise of an educational requirement what was really nothing less than discretion to exclude at will. Any prohibited immigrant who happened to speak English could be tested in French, German, Polish or Magyar, if necessary.

Even that was not good enough at first for the Labor Party. In the committee stage Watson moved unsuccessfully for deletion of Clause 4 and insertion of a clause excluding 'any person who is an aboriginal native of

Asia, Africa and of the islands thereof'. When the Bill reached the Senate, Senator McGregor also tried to insert a total exclusion clause; the expected support of some Free Traders failed to materialise, however, and this amendment was lost. In committee the dictation test was actually removed from the Bill on McGregor's motion. But when absolute exclusion was defeated, Labor senators supported a Government motion to restore the test.

The Bill for the Pacific Island Labourers Act also encountered some difficulty despite approval of its general principle by large majorities, including majorities of Queenslanders, in both houses. There were differences of opinion about the time required by Queensland canegrowers to adjust their operations to white labour in place of the cheaper Kanakas who were to be progressively repatriated, and about the extent to which the sugar industry should be compensated for its financial sacrifice in the cause of a snow-white Australia.

These differences were resolved, however, and the Act was assented to by the Governor-General on 17 December. The Immigration Restriction Act received assent six days later, just in time for the Commonwealth's first Christmas. It was as if the British-Australians, having loosened traditional ties at the start of the year, were now receiving the one Christmas present they wanted more than any other, a sense of racial security.

Messages from the Senate

At the end of parliament's first year—almost to the day, early in May 1902—Barton sailed for England to attend the Colonial Conference and the Coronation of King Edward VII, leaving his friend Deakin as acting Prime Minister. He was lucky still to have such a capable deputy, for only a month earlier Deakin had tendered his resignation from the Ministry. The resignation was ostensibly in protest about a proposal made in cabinet to raise a loan, which Deakin regarded as politically risky in view of the wide economic hardship still being caused by the drought, and public criticism of alleged Commonwealth extravagance. Deakin's main grievance, however, was not mentioned in his letter of resignation. It was his objection to something not publicly known: a cabinet proposal to increase parliamentary salaries.

'My dear old friend', wrote Barton, returning this unwelcome resignation to its sender.

> Don't break my heart quite. It is near that point now. How can I bear the thought of going on without you? Disappointment was hard enough, but I have long been near despair, and you have brought me face to face with it . . . Your departure now would—though you may not know it—*wreck* the Ministry. Ring me up, for I am very sore hearted.

Deakin did ring up. Barton reluctantly dropped both cabinet proposals, and then—together with Sir John Forrest, six other members of the lower house and three senators—set sail for the coronation.

With him the Prime Minister took the Government's only copy of an imperial code book, which would in any case have been available in London; Deakin had to cable him at Colombo for its return. Barton and Forrest had also gone off without making any arrangements to continue paying their shares of a salary for the vice-president of the Executive Council and Government leader in the upper house, Senator O'Connor. O'Connor was a Minister with neither portfolio nor official ministerial salary. His duties in a hostile Senate were onerous, and he was not as well off financially as the other Minister without portfolio, Sir Philip Fysh. For some months past, the seven ministers of state had been chipping in from their own ministerial salaries to provide O'Connor with an allowance for his leadership of the Senate. Now Deakin had to ensure its continuance.

Another problem left for Deakin to handle concerned a much larger allowance being claimed by the Governor-General. Lord Hopetoun had been given to understand by the Secretary of State for the Colonies that he should conduct himself officially with almost the same pomp as a Viceroy of India. He entertained lavishly, maintained the costly equipage of carriages, horses and postilions which he had brought out from England, and during the last sixteen months had spent £15 000 of his own money over and above the only reimbursement allowed him by the Constitution, a salary of £10 000. Lord Hopetoun was a wealthy man, but felt that he ought to receive a permanent allowance in addition to salary, as the Governor-General of Canada did. Barton had promised to ask parliament for an extra £8000; but parliament's response, strongly influenced by Higgins's criticism of vice-regal expenditure in those straitened times, was so unfavourable that the prospect of any permanent allowance was faint indeed.

'No allowance whatever will be given', Lord Hopetoun cabled to the Colonial Office the day before Barton left Melbourne.

> On a salary of £10,000 per annum I am expected to pay a staff, visit various States, paying all travelling expenses except railway, occupy two great Government Houses, paying lights, fuel, stationery, telegrams, postage other than official, dispense hospitality, maintain dignity of office ... The position is impossible. After grave consideration I think you had better recall me after the Coronation.

He left for England on 16 July and was replaced, in an acting capacity at first, by the Governor of South Australia—the hearty, gouty Lord Tennyson, son of the Victorian era's most admired poet, and a man who, in his efforts to secure Hopetoun's post for himself, had assured the Colonial Secretary of his own understanding that 'the Commonwealth do not want their Governor-General to keep up a great deal of State'.

For nine weeks until Lord Hopetoun departed, Deakin had the unenviable task of communicating almost daily with a man who rightly felt that the Commonwealth had treated him meanly. Hopetoun did not blame Deakin or Barton; indeed he continued to regard them both as friends. Yet it must have been some relief for Deakin to find himself addressing Tennyson instead. The changeover also enabled him to adopt a somewhat more natural form of address. Barton's practice had been to address the Governor-General in the third person, after first presenting his 'humble duty' to His Excellency. 'No, that won't do at all', said Deakin to Atlee Hunt when the time came to compose his first official letter to Lord Tennyson. 'I'm humble enough, Lord knows, but I do not present my humble duty to anyone'.

Thereafter the Prime Minister addressed the Governor-General without preamble, as 'Your Excellency'.

Greater than any of these worries, Deakin's main burden during the five months he acted as Prime Minister was the passage of legislation to establish the Commonwealth tariff. If the Commonwealth's first policy legislation had dealt with immigration restriction, the first parliament's most important and hardest fought legislation was undoubtedly that dealing with the imposition of customs and excise duties. The tariff bills were vital to the Commonwealth's existence, for they would secure its revenue. They also provided the Senate with an opportunity to test its power in relation to money bills, and that was why they eventually proved such a trial for Deakin. He took no part in the debate, appearing only for divisions; but he could not escape the fear that conflict between the houses might block the tariff altogether.

This flexing of youthful muscles by the upper house had been foreshadowed during the Address-in-Reply debate. 'At all events', said Sir John Downer, one of several senators who spoke about future relations between the chambers,

> we have the power; but whether we can exercise the power will depend, I have always said, on the personnel of the first Senate of the Commonwealth of Australia. Looking round at the honorable members I see here, I have the feeling that they are all game, and that whether Mr Barton or Mr Reid is in power, we will hold our own in the great constitutional position, and not allow our House to be subordinated to any party considerations.

He was right about the Senate being game, but wrong about it being above party considerations. Its politics were a mixture of State and party politics from the very beginning.

The tariff, however, was an issue on which most senators could feel they were properly discharging their responsibility as State representatives. Free Traders and Protectionists alike could usually identify their fiscal views with the best interests of their States, and on that issue the Labor Party allowed its members to vote as they wished. The only uniform votes required of Labor members during the tariff debates were to keep down the price of kerosene and tea. The lower house's sixteen Labor members divided fiscally into six Free Trade, five Protectionist, and five uncommitted. That produced a narrow majority for protection: 37 to 33, with five uncommitted. Of the eight Labor senators, four favoured Protection, two Free Trade, and two were uncommitted. That left the Senate with a narrow majority for Free Trade: 19 to 15, with two uncommitted. It was therefore not surprising that the details of a tariff high enough to provide necessary revenue, but not so high as to alarm Free Traders, were closely argued not only in the two chambers but also between them.

The tariff proposals were tabled by the Treasurer, Sir George Turner (P, Balaclava, V), as part of his Budget on 8 October 1901. One week later Reid moved the parliament's first censure motion, leading to a 71-hour-long debate, over a period of eleven days, which was really a curtain-raiser for the main tariff debate still to come. Reid moved that 'this House cannot accept the financial and tariff proposals submitted by the Government' because they would place the finances of the Commonwealth and the States on an unsound and extravagant basis, and because their burden was distributed unequally throughout the community. In accordance with British parliamentary practice, the upper house adjourned for the full duration of this debate, as if with bated breath, on the assumption that a censure motion might lead to the Government's resignation. Under the system of responsible government, withdrawal by the House of its confidence in a government may be shown not only by a direct vote of censure or want of confidence, but also by the rejection of a legislative measure which the government has declared to be of vital importance, or by defeat on a vote not necessarily central to government policy but accepted by the government of the day as one of confidence. But intransigence by the Opposition need not always require resignation. When Barton's Government was defeated in 1903 on important amendments to the Conciliation and Arbitration Bill and the Papua (British New Guinea) Bill, it simply dropped the Bills. No question of resignation arose from Reid's censure motion, for it was defeated 25 to 39.

The tariff came before parliament in four Bills: the Customs Bill, Excise Bill, Excise Tariff Bill and Customs Tariff Bill. The last named was the most important, and the subject of most debate. It was introduced shortly before Barton's departure by the Minister for Customs, C. C. Kingston. 'Charlie' Kingston was one-quarter Portuguese and one-quarter Scottish on his mother's side, and the rest of him was Irish—a mixture which may have explained his explosive temperament. He terrified his subordinates and insulted his colleagues. The *Age* parliamentary correspondent, George Cockerill, said that Kingston always had the gloves off, and hit hard whenever he saw a Free Trade chin. Kingston's Protectionist Ministry in South Australia had many progressive measures to its credit, including the female franchise and a conciliation and arbitration act. Along with that reputation he also possessed a certain ferocious charm, and many were cautiously fond of him.

Sometimes during dull debates, he would sit reading the New Testament. On one such occasion his friend Hume Cook, who in 1902 became probably the first member of federal parliament to marry, heard Kingston utter his familiar grunt of disapproval—'Umph!' 'Look at that!' he said, handing Cook the Testament: 'But I say unto you that whosoever looks at a woman to lust after her hath committed adultery with her already in his heart'.

'What do you think of that, umph?' asked Kingston, who, as Hume Cook knew, had twice been cited as co-respondent in a divorce case.

'Not much', replied Hume Cook.

'Not much? I should say not! I've never read anything so stupid. It's the most unsatisfactory kind of fornication I've ever heard about! Umph!'

There was more 'umph' than New Testament in Kingston's handling of the tariff bills. 'He is forcible and combative', reported Cockerill, 'and prone to silence an interjector by a sledge-hammer retort. He is clear and distinct, although his concise sentences often approach the jerky ejaculation of Mr Alfred Jingle. "There is the Minister," he said, "— control of all. Subject to him—permanent head. Subject to him—head each State"'. But for many members the tariff debates were as tedious as any that had ever driven Kingston to the Bible. 'With varying fortune', wrote Deakin eight months after Turner's tabling of the tariff, 'but with unvarying regularity, a frittering struggle over details and a shameless repetition of stock fiscal arguments has proceeded until to the public the whole debate has become a nightmare—as oppressive, mysterious and unintelligible as the last battle of Arthur in its Tennysonian version'.

Reid attended long enough to remark rashly on Barton's absence.

> That our Prime Minister should, night after night, and month after month, be within the precincts of the chamber, and yet take less interest in and less control of this most serious of all national tasks than the humblest private member, is a circumstance which I feel bound to comment upon.

This was the pot calling the kettle black with a vengeance, and when Kingston moved the second reading of the Customs Tariff Bill four days later he drew the House's attention to the absent Reid's lamentable record of attendance. Out of parliament's 164 sitting days to date, the Prime Minister had been absent for only ten and the Leader of the Opposition for eighty-seven. Reid's justification was that he could not afford to neglect his law practice in Sydney. In his absence from the House, and indeed also when he was present, the Free Trade attack on the tariff bills was led by the only businessmen in the party—the merchants, Sir William McMillan (Wentworth, N) and Dugald Thomson (North Sydney, N), and the auctioneer, Sydney Smith (Macquarie, N). Ithuriel remarked in the *Argus* that Reid had been

> taking the part of 'the coverin' ship what is lyin' dark on the weather bow.' To his lieutenants . . . he has said, 'You board the enemy on the starboard quarter, and rake them fore and aft, and shiver their timbers, and splice their main brace, and take all the other nautical measures necessary to bring down their protective shrouds and water-log their tariff.' 'Yes, but where do you come in?' 'Why, don't you see? I'll be that coverin' ship what's a-lyin' dark on the weather bow.'

On the Government side, Kingston and Turner shared the management of this Tennysonian epic. Duties were set for a schedule of 139 items, ranging from stimulants and narcotics to metals and machinery, oils and paints, and such horse-drawn vehicles as buggies, hansoms, sulkies, phaetons and broughams. The Customs Tariff Bill at first provided a form of consumer protection dear to Kingston's radical heart: the power to reduce duty where it could be shown that importers were combining to maintain excessive prices. This was negatived in the House of Representatives, however, on grounds that it would contravene Section 55 of the Constitution, the section that forbade 'tacking' a non-taxation measure on to a law imposing taxation so that the Senate could not amend it.

The Customs Tariff Bill passed its final stage in the House of Representatives on 22 April 1902, and had its first reading in the Senate next day. The Senate chamber looked like an 'upper' house. It was more ornate than the lower one, even though its three great chandeliers had now been removed by the Victorian Legislative Council, and its occupants stood on ceremony rather more than those of 'the other place'. All senators bowed to their gowned and full-wigged President when entering or leaving the chamber, as representatives did to the Speaker; but unlike Speaker Holder, President Baker returned this courtesy with a deep bow of his own.

Sir Richard Baker and his fellow senators were acutely conscious of their position *vis-à-vis* the more numerous House on the other side of Queen's Hall. During parliament's first year the President complained to the Governor-General about the precedence (or rather, lack of it) accorded to him at an official dinner. He also disputed the Speaker's sole authority over Queen's Hall. 'I must respectfully demur to your proposition that the Queen's Hall is under the exclusive jurisdiction of yourself as Presiding Officer of the House of Representatives', he wrote. 'The Hall is for the use, occupation and convenience of Members of both Houses, and I thought, and still think, that the Joint House Committee is the proper authority to control this Chamber.'

The Senate did not have to wait long for an opportunity to begin probing the extent of its power over money bills, for parliament's first enacted legislation had been the Consolidated Revenue (Supply) Act. It returned the Bill for this Act to the lower house with a 'respectful request' that the House amend it to show the items of expenditure comprised in the sums being granted to His Majesty. This was done, and when the amended Bill came back the Senate also objected to a statement in the preamble that the grant was 'made by the House of Representatives'. The House adopted instead the words 'originated in the House of Representatives', and made two other suggested amendments. The Senate was satisfied, and passed the Bill.

In that brief passage at arms, the Senate's suggestions had all been accepted by the lower house. If the House of Representatives had not been so agreeable, and had returned the Bill to the Senate without amendment, could the Senate have made the same requests again? There was much difference of opinion as to whether the Senate was entitled to 'press' requests in this way. The proof of the pudding would be in the eating, and the Customs Tariff Bill provided just such an opportunity.

After its second reading, the Senate spent thirty-three sitting days in committee considering the Bill. Senator O'Connor, always well-informed and conciliatory, had the carriage of the Bill for the Government. The Opposition had no leader in the Senate, but its members elected Senator Symon as their leader for purposes of the fiscal debate. He was a forceful debater who, according to Senator W. G. Higgs (Lab, Q) stood up 'like a Brahma Pootra rooster over a bantam, brow-beating the Chairman'. The Chairman of Committees and Deputy President was Senator Robert Best (P, V). The President, unlike the Speaker, was entitled to exercise a substantive vote, and Sir Richard Baker did so during the tariff debate.

Some of the questions raised in debate were exquisitely tedious. Horse hair was exempt from duty, but what about camel hair? Galloon, a close-woven gold braid, was exempt up to a certain width, but what width should begin to attract duty? Should mangles be exempt, like tools of trade, if used in households of persons other than washerwomen? Item by item the Bill was carefully scrutinised. On 24 July Speaker Holder announced receipt of the following message from the Senate:

> Mr Speaker, The Senate returns herewith the Bill intituled *"A Bill for an Act relating to Duties of Customs"* with amendments requested as set forth in the annexed Schedule, to which requests the Senate desires the concurrence of the House of Representatives.
>
> R. C. BAKER,
> President

There were ninety-three requests. The House made thirty-three of the requested amendments, made one in part, made ten with modifications, and did not make forty-nine. When the Bill was returned to the Senate in that form, the Senate agreed to the House's modification of eight requests, did not repeat its request to make twenty-four amendments requested earlier, modified two of its requests, and pressed twenty-six others. The accompanying message said: 'The Senate again requests the House of Representatives to make the amendments as orginally requested by the Senate . . . '.

To Deakin it seemed all too possible that the Commonwealth might be caught in this collision between two Houses intent upon asserting their respective rights. 'Constitution Corner'—that part of the lower house where Sir John Quick and Isaac Isaacs sat riffling through their constitutional authorities—was as ready to fight as Symon or anyone else in the Senate. But if the House stood on its dignity and refused to consider the pressed requests, an indefinite repetition of requests could result in deadlock, delaying the revenue without which the Commonwealth could not assert its powers with confidence.

'The other chamber has us in the toils', said W. H. Wilks (F, Dalley, N) when the House met on 3 September to consider whether it could properly receive the pressed requests, and if it could, how it should respond to them. Deakin replied: 'It has us in the toils no more than one Chamber will always have the other under its control so far as it presses upon the other a measure which in its eyes is of paramount importance'. The way out of the toils was not to put the tariff ahead of the House's constitutional rights, but to put it ahead of any final determination of what those rights might be.

Deakin moved that

> having regard to the fact that the public welfare demands the early enactment of a Federal Tariff, and pending the adoption of Joint Standing Orders [which would govern relations between the two Houses], this House refrains from the determination of its constitutional rights or obligations in respect of this Message, and resolves to receive and consider it forthwith.

With Labor support, the question was resolved in the affirmative, 36 to 9. 'A great victory for the wisest course', wrote Deakin in his diary. 'Exhausted . . . Poor night after strain'.

Next day the House amended its modification to one request, made one amendment as requested, agreed to eleven requests with modifications, insisted on its modification to one request, and did not make fourteen

requests pressed by the Senate. So ended the first major encounter between
the houses. Out of 220 consecutive sitting days, 117 had been devoted by
parliament in some way to the tariff. The lower house's message returning
the Customs Tariff Bill to the Senate, where it was agreed to, incorporated
Deakin's resolution refraining from determination of constitutional rights.
But what did the Senate care about that? It had the satisfaction of knowing
that it had pressed requests for amendments to a revenue bill, and that some
of them had been made, with and without modification. To rub that in, the
Senate passed a motion affirming 'that the action of the House of Representatives in receiving and dealing with the reiterated requests of the Senate is in
compliance with the undoubted constitutional position and rights of the
Senate'.

Barton's Government had the more practical satisfaction of knowing that
the tariff was safe. Writing for the London *Morning Post* several days later,
Deakin used Wilks's image of a bird caught in the fowler's toils. 'The country
drew a deep breath of relief', he wrote,

> simply because, at last, after months of turmoil, a tariff was passed, but
> the few onlookers who realised all the consequences of failure drew a
> deeper breath still, and felt a more profound relief as they became assured
> that the Commonwealth itself was out of the toils at last, and fast escaping
> beyond the reach of its enemies.

The first session of the first parliament ended with its prorogation by the
Governor-General on 10 October 1902. It had lasted seventeen months, and
during that period the House had sat for 220 days and the Senate for 178.
Deakin was by then close to physical collapse, and Barton, newly elevated to
knighthood in the Order of St Michael and St George, was still making his
way back to Australia, via Rome, where he and Sir John Forrest had an audience with the Pope. 'We were all very grieved to know that you were so
knocked up', Sir Edmund Barton wrote to Deakin after his return, 'and I feel
quite guilty, for having imposed on you anxieties which must have been too
much for you . . . My dear old chap, how can I ever thank you enough?'

Barton soon had further cause to thank his lieutenant. In January Deakin
was disturbed during a recuperative holiday at his favourite beach resort—
Point Lonsdale, near the entrance to Port Phillip Bay—by a letter from the
Prime Minister seeking advice about a difference which had arisen between
himself and the Governor-General. This storm in a tea cup concerned the
appointment of a secretary to the Executive Council, who would also handle
the Governor-General's official correspondence. The position was to have
been filled by Lord Tennyson's private secretary, Captain E. W. Wallington;
but when that gentleman announced his intention of returning to England,
an officer of Barton's Department of External Affairs, Captain George Stew-
ard, was appointed to it. The office of Governor-General was the official
channel of communication between the Australian and British governments,
but in his ambassadorial role the Governor-General also exchanged secret
and confidential despatches with the Secretary of State for the Colonies.
Tennyson felt strongly that an Australian public servant should not have
access to such restricted despatches, and this had aroused Barton's suspicion.

Was it possible that the Governor-General might withhold essential information from his responsible advisers in Melbourne? Of course it was. All Australian governments accepted, albeit reluctantly, that a governor was expected to warn the British Government of ministerial proposals inimical to the imperial interest, and that His Excellency would not wish such communications to be seen by his Australian ministers or their officials.

Barton wrote a letter of stern remonstrance which bewildered His Excellency, and then wrote to Deakin: 'Here are not only a Governor-General trying to take the administration for which Ministers alone have the responsibility, but Downing Street instructing him to do it. My wig! what a ruction there would be if Parliament were sitting and got hold of it all'. Tennyson also turned to Deakin for help. 'You and I have always worked so well together', he wrote.

> [I am] most anxious that you should explain to the Prime Minister that it was *never* understood that the Secretary of the Executive Council was to deal with my personal and secret correspondence with the Secretary of State—but only with the general and confidential communications through me with the Commonwealth.

With mediation by Deakin, the difficulty was overcome by using a special cypher for the Governor-General's secret despatches.

After the opening of the second session of parliament in May 1903 came another difficulty, which Deakin's diplomacy was not able to resolve. Kingston's explosive temperament blew up, and on 24 July he resigned from the Ministry. He had been clashing more frequently than usual with ministerial colleagues, particularly Forrest, and the point of resignation was reached over Cabinet's disagreement with him about a provision in the Conciliation and Arbitration Bill, which Kingston was about to introduce for the establishment of a federal arbitration court. Kingston wanted the powers of this court extended to deal with seamen on all ships engaged in the Australian coastal trade, whether they were of Australian register or not. Most of his colleagues felt it would be better to deal with seamen's wages later by way of a Navigation Act which could reserve the coastal trade to vessels that complied with acceptable conditions. Kingston would not be fobbed off with that; he felt that a bill with no application to cheap Asian crews would be 'a mockery', and in any case there was no guarantee that the Navigation Act, when it came, would deal with industrial conditions. Forrest for one, ever conscious of Western Australia's dependence on sea transport, was opposed to any restriction on the coastal trade.

'Kingston desperate', said Deakin's diary. 'Disagreement absolute ... CCK tenders resignation ... have to take up bill'. Although Kingston remained in parliament for another five years, he became a sadly diminished figure, failing in health, isolated by the death of family and friends, and making no speeches at all during his last four years in the House. 'Goodbye, old man', he said once to the journalist Cockerill. 'May God spare you from ever being alone.' But in 1903 he still had plenty of fight left in him. When Sir John Forrest spoke during an adjournment debate on the subject closest to West Australian hearts—a transcontinental railway—Kingston rose to remind honourable members that Forrest's Government had not been in favour of federation until the last moment.

> Sir JOHN FORREST.—That is very good. The right honorable gentleman
>   knows so much about Western Australia!
> Mr KINGSTON.—I do. I am sorry that the right honourable gentleman
>   can give expression to his feelings only by a series of grunts. I suggest
>   that as a Minister of the Crown he should attempt to hold his tongue,
>   and not indulge in the stupid, inane, and repeated twaddle with which
>   he is now disturbing our proceedings.

Kingston's resignation made room in Cabinet for one of the two Ministers without portfolio, Sir Philip Fysh. The other, Senator O'Connor, had a different ambition. As early as May, the first month of the second session, George Reid referred dispassionately in parliament to the likelihood that O'Connor would be appointed to the High Court, the establishment of which was the subject of a Judiciary Bill introduced by Deakin in June 1901, only to be shunted aside for the more urgent tariff legislation. After Deakin's three-and-a-half-hour second reading speech on the Judiciary Bill in March 1902 O'Connor, who listened from the gallery, sent him a note saying: '*Magnificent. The finest speech I have ever heard*'. Even listeners less closely concerned were impressed by the Attorney-General's exposition of the High Court's future role.

> The federation is constituted [he said] by distribution of powers, and it is
> this court which decides the orbit and boundary of every power . . . It is
> properly termed the "keystone of the federal arch". "The legislature", as
> [Mr Justice Marshall of the United States Supreme Court] puts it, "makes,
> the executive executes, and the judiciary declares the law". What the legis-
> lature may make, and what the executive may do, the judiciary in the last
> resort declares; so that the ties which unite the judiciary to the
> legislature—the Australian High Court to the Australian Parliament—are
> those of mutual association and dependence in the accomplishment of a
> common task. The High Court exists to protect the Constitution against
> assaults. It exists because our Constitution, although an Imperial Act, has
> a dual parentage. It proceeds from the people of the whole continent. It is
> one of the institutions which the people of Australia, when they accepted
> the Constitution, required to be established for the purpose of insuring
> that there should not be a departure from the bond into which they
> thereby entered for themselves and for posterity. This Constitution is not
> the creation of our State Parliaments only, neither is it the creation of the
> Imperial Parliament only. It draws its authority directly from the electors
> of the Commonwealth, and it is as their chosen and declared agent that
> the High Court finds its place in the Constitution which they accepted . . .
> To put this part of the case in a nutshell, I would say that our written Con-
> stitution, large and elastic as it is, is necessarily limited by the ideas and
> circumstances which obtained in the year 1900. It was necessarily precise
> in parts, as well as vague in other parts. That Constitution remains ver-
> bally unalterable except by the process of amendment . . . In the mean-
> time [it] stands and will stand on the statute-book just as in the hour in
> which it was assented to. But the nation lives, grows and expands. Its cir-

cumstances change, its needs alter, and its problems present themselves with new faces. The organ of the national life which preserving the union, is yet able from time to time to transfuse into it the fresh blood of the living present, is the Judiciary the High Court of Australia . . . It is as one of the organs of Government which enables the Constitution to grow and to be adapted to the changeful necessities and circumstances of generation after generation that the High Court operates.

The Judiciary Bill lapsed at prorogation, as all bills did automatically, and was initiated again by Deakin on the first sitting day of the second session, 26 May 1903. It did not have an easy passage. Some members suspected with good reason that Senator O'Connor was not the only federal grandee hoping to benefit from the 'fat billets bill', as the press termed it. Higgins thought the Commonwealth should make do with State courts and the British Privy Council, as in fact it had been doing so far. Glynn, who led the Opposition's attack on the Bill, wanted to 'prevent the electoral mind being offended by the play of too much, and unnecessary, machinery in the early days of the Federation'. Deakin stiffened wavering ministerialists by threatening to resign, and Labor's vote was divided. The Bill squeaked through both houses, but only after some pruning. The number of justices was reduced from five to three, and salaries were lowered to the still generous levels of £3500 for the Chief Justice and £3000 for his learned brethren. The salary of the Chief Justice of the United States Supreme Court at that time was $13 000 (£2600).

It seems only reasonable to assume that at least part of Deakin's reason for wanting the High Court established during the life of the first parliament was so that O'Connor, and more importantly Barton, could retire to it. He knew very well that Barton was tired of politics. The Prime Minister had recently been found in a state of collapse in his office. On 30 August the Governor-General urged him to take a Justiceship, and next day Barton's doctor told him in a written opinion that his expectation of life would be increased by relinquishing or diminishing the strain of political life. Paddy Glynn also recorded in his diary that for a time Barton had refrained from taking liquor, 'but the old passion seemed recently to have become his master again'.

On 21 September Cabinet approved an offer of the Chief Justiceship to Deakin's preferred candidate, who had already responded favourably to an approach by Barton: Sir Samuel Griffith. Deakin also called on his long-time patron, David Syme of the *Age*, and his diary for that day contained the cryptic but decipherable entry, 'DS says take PM'. Two days later Barton delivered his last speech in the House. He must have been preoccupied, because for the first time in his parliamentary career he was called to order by the Speaker—for addressing the House while seated, and moving an amendment upon his own motion. As he closed the adjournment debate at about 10.30 p.m., Australia's first Prime Minister doubtless derived more joy than sorrow from the probability that he would take no part in the business he was then foreshadowing for the rest of the week. His last words were: 'The more honorable members give us their co-operation in that direction, the more nearly will they approach the consummation of their desire to leave these precincts'.

Next day, 24 September 1903, Barton informed Cabinet of his intention to resign as Prime Minister, and placed himself in the hands of his colleagues. He also advised them of O'Connor's resignation. Sir William Lyne, whose inquiries had elicited the certainty that he could no more form a ministry now than he had been able to in 1900, agreed to serve under Deakin, provided he ranked immediately after him. Barton tendered his resignation to the Governor-General, who then sent for Deakin, and that afternoon the new Prime Minister announced to parliament the change of ministry and the acceptance of the Chief Justiceship by Sir Samuel Griffith and Justiceships by Sir Edmund Barton and Richard O'Connor. The 'keystone of the federal arch' held its first sitting on 6 October in the Banco Court of the Victorian judiciary buildings, standing on one of the city's few eminences about a mile west of Parliament House. Addressing those present, Chief Justice Griffith said:

> I think it will be some time before the profession and the public fully realise the extent of the power of criticism and determination that is vested in this Court with respect to the decrees of the State and Federal legislatures. Enormous and difficult questions will arise, and it is not to be expected that our decisions will meet with the views of all parties.

Glynn remarked that Barton would make a 'better judge than premier', and the *Bulletin* observed that all three justices were conservative and imperialistic. 'Griffith, Barton and O'Connor will dispense good law', said the *Bulletin*,

> will administer even justice so far as they can, but they will not, it may be safely predicted, in laying down the early precedents which will make Australian Common Law, ever fail to stretch a little towards the Tory view in local affairs, and towards the Chamberlain-Imperialistic view in external affairs.

There was not much doubt about the kind of Prime Minister Deakin would make, for he had already acted in that capacity for five and a half months, and had been in charge of parliamentary business as frequently as Barton. Deakin's critics accused him of instinctively seeking the line of least resistance everywhere. Glynn conceded 'his special ability and characteristics, but definiteness and strength of purpose [were] not among them. Still, he is, as men are, a remarkable one; even if there be at times a tepid heart beating behind his oratory'. His admirers saw a different Deakin: a liberal idealist, 'the dark-eyed gypsy of Australian politics', his bright eyes and smiling face ever watchful, his talk 'full of variety, incident, literary and personal charm'.

Now aged forty-seven, this barrister-journalist had been a politician almost continuously for the last quarter of a century. For all his social grace, it was not easy to discover what lay beneath Deakin's professional affability. The gate was kept locked at 'Llanarth'—his home in South Yarra, named after his mother's birthplace in Monmouthshire—and visitors, after being scrutinised through a peephole, might or might not be admitted. The Prime

Minister cycled at weekends, and either cycled, walked or caught a tram to the Commonwealth offices near Parliament House. In 1903 he bought seven acres of ti-tree scrub at Point Lonsdale and built there a cottage called 'Ballara', the Aboriginal word from which his electorate took its name.

The first Bench of the High Court
Chief Justice Griffith flanked by Justices Barton and O'Connor
by David Low

In that sanctuary, attended by the adoring and strong-willed women of his family, Deakin was able to nurture the cherished 'inner life' which formed such an unlikely complement to the rough and tumble of his public life in Spring Street. He was a prodigious reader (he claimed to have read everything Wordsworth ever wrote, prose as well as poetry, and on a voyage to England he read *The Brothers Karamazov* in French), and was a prolific recorder of his philosophical and spiritual reflections. He kept books of handwritten prayers, and a series of notebooks entitled 'Clues', filling the latter with 852 consecutively numbered 'clues'. Clue No. 814, written soon after he became Prime Minister, read in part: 'Death-it-must-be . . . O exquisite relief. Elysium. Then freedom . . . an ecstasy as of Heaven—no resistance—no reaction—a floating in a void and slowly a melting as of one organism into cloud . . . '. Deakin was no common or garden politician. In earlier life he had been President of the Spiritualist Association in Melbourne. He had published *A New Pilgrim's Progress* which he believed at the time had been communicated to him by some intelligence other than his own, perhaps even John Bunyan's; and throughout his life he believed in ghosts.

The second and final session of the first parliament lasted only five months. Deakin had two reasons for requesting a dissolution five and a half months before the lower house's term expired. He was naturally anxious to obtain electoral endorsement, and it would be convenient if an election for the lower chamber coincided with the first election for half the Senate, the latter of which—because senators' terms, unlike those of representatives, had been backdated to 1 January 1901—would need to be held in December 1903.

Although senators were elected for six years, Section 13 of the Constitution required the Senate as soon as possible after its first meeting to divide its members into two classes of equal number—those who would serve the full six years, and those who would retire after three years, thus making possible the continuity provided for the upper house in the Constitution. Thereafter all senators would serve six years, with half retiring every three years, until a dissolution and the election of a full new Senate, which eventually would be followed by another division into two classes. Senators were divided according to their success at the polls: the three highest-polling candidates from each of the six States were to serve six years, and the other three from each State had to vacate their seats at the end of the third year.

One three-year senator in the first parliament, Senator John Ferguson from Queensland, did not last even that long. Queensland was the only State not to have legislated against its own politicians sitting simultaneously in federal parliament, and for two and a half years Ferguson, a wealthy former builder from Rockhampton who had been elected to the Senate in spite of his absence from Australia during the campaign, was also a member of the Queensland Legislative Council. He attended fewer than half the sitting days while he remained a senator and eventually (probably because of awareness that the Commonwealth's own Electoral Act would soon put a stop to dual representation) allowed his period of non-attendance without permission to exceed the two consecutive months which, under the Constitution, would render his seat vacant. His Senate seat was declared vacant on 13 October 1903, the first and only example of such a declaration.

At about the same time, a seat in the House of Representatives was rendered vacant by the resignation of its occupant, George Reid. This was a tactical manoeuvre by the Leader of the Opposition, designed not to terminate his distinguished political career but to focus public attention on the Government's rejection of an electoral redistribution in New South Wales. As provided by the Electoral Act of 1902, commissioners had recently been appointed to redistribute the electoral divisions drawn up by four of the State Governments for the first federal election, and to create federal divisions for South Australia and Tasmania, where electors had previously voted as single electorates. The basis for distribution was to be a quota calculated by dividing the total population of each State by the number of members of the House of Representatives to be elected therein. Divisional populations could vary by as much as one-fourth more or less than the quota; and when drawing boundaries, the commissioners were obliged to bear in mind community of interest, means of communication, and physical features.

The reports of electoral commissioners were to be laid before both houses of parliament, and in the event that either house disagreed with a report the Minister for Home Affairs was empowered (but not obliged) to direct the commissioners' to try again. In 1903 only the reports for South Australia and Tasmania were accepted by parliament. As the Minister did not direct new redistributions for the remaining States, the divisions there would be the same for the coming general election as in 1901. The rejected redistribution for New South Wales would have given an extra seat to Sydney and its suburbs, where electorally the Protectionists felt themselves to be at some disadvantage. Claiming this was why the Government had rejected the work of its own appointees, Reid resigned his seat in a brief letter read by the Speaker to a startled House on 18 August. He then won it back easily at a by-election two weeks later.

The Governor-General dissolved parliament on 23 November 1903, and issued writs for an election of the lower house and half the Senate, to be held on 16 December. The historian, H. G. Turner, a former general manager of the Commercial Bank of Australia, would later refer in his book *The First Decade of the Australian Commonwealth* to 'an amount of protracted wrangling' in the first parliament 'that would have discredited an inexperienced shire council in the back-blocks'. This was hardly fair. Certainly wrangling had sometimes, and particularly in the tariff debates, been needlessly protracted. But during the lower house's 298 sitting days and the Senate's 240, much had been accomplished. Of fifty-nine statutes enacted by the first parliament (forty-seven of which had been initiated in the House of Representatives), twenty-one were appropriation and supply measures. Most of the others embodied important policy principles. One group of Acts established and regulated departments of the Commonwealth Government; a second group, including the Customs Tariff Act, established the Commonwealth's financial basis; and a third, including the Judiciary Act, dealt with legal procedure in the Commonwealth and Commonwealth–State spheres.

All members of the first parliament were later allowed, by royal consent in 1904, to use during their lifetime and within Australia the prefix 'Honourable'—a privilege otherwise accorded only to the Speaker of the House of Representatives, the President of the Senate, Executive Councillors and Privy Councillors (the latter being entitled to 'Right Honourable'), though the term was always used collectively and impersonally, as in 'Honourable Members' and 'the Honourable Member for so-and-so'. The Speaker and President used the title 'Honourable' during their periods of office, and it became customary for any who served in those offices for three years or longer to retain the title for life.

Some members of the first parliament were less deserving of their honorific than others. Farewelling them all, Ithuriel wrote: 'Experience has proved that you are what an auctioneer would describe as a mixed lot. You comprise some of the strongest, subtlest men in Australia, and others of whom the irreverent Byron would say that:

> Like the fly in amber we but stare,
> And wonder how the devil you got there'.

Some had even worse records of attendance than Senator Ferguson. Senator Harney, the Demosthenes from Western Australia, attended little more than a quarter of the sitting days and did not stand for re-election. Senator Lieutenant-Colonel Cyril St Clair Cameron (P, T) attended only 29 per cent of sittings, stood for re-election and was defeated, but later was more successful and served a full term. His brother Donald Cameron (F, T) attended only 39 per cent of lower House sittings in the first parliament, was also defeated but was re-elected at a by-election. The worst attendance record in the House of Representatives was that of F. E. McLean (F, Lang, N), who attended 29 per cent of the time and did not stand for re-election. King O'Malley and Samuel Mauger (P, Melbourne Ports, V) did not miss a single sitting day, but Ithuriel would not accept that they had been in the chamber any more than the average member: like many other members before and since, they had merely turned up at some part of every sitting in order to have their presences recorded.

Political commentators agreed that Deakin, Turner and Watson had emerged from the first parliament with reputations enhanced. Watson had thrown Labor's support on either side as it suited the party's ends; and the government, sooner than risk losing office, had granted Labor more than it expected. Reid should have done better; he had coquetted so often with Labor, and changed his views so frequently, that his followers had become too disorganised for a successful assault on the Government. Lyne had been 'dexterous enough in his own peculiar way'; Forrest had 'never taken the trouble to know much about the matter in hand'; and Fysh, although 'universally beloved' was never taken seriously.

The Senate on this maiden voyage had nailed its colours to the mast. It had insisted upon its right to press requests; had tried unsuccessfully to establish the right of ministers to address either house, an innovation which would have been quite at variance with British parliamentary tradition; and in the last weeks of parliament declined to concur in resolutions of the 'other place' that a conference be held between the two houses to consider the selection of the permanent seat of government. At such a conference, Senator Simon Fraser (P, V) reminded his colleagues, representatives would outnumber senators two to one.

> Senator FRASER.—No doubt the other House will always be unanimous in wishing to swallow up the Senate. Why should they be otherwise? They will always desire to get us to a conference. But why should we agree to a conference on this subject?
> Senator HIGGS (L , Q).—They want to get the fly into the parlour.

In his election policy speech, Deakin addressed himself to 'the men of Australia' and—as he had never needed to say in any previous campaign—'the women of Australia'. The Commonwealth Franchise Act (1902), establishing a uniform franchise for federal elections, had not extended the limited franchise exercised by Aborigines. No Aborigine could have his name placed on a Commonwealth electoral roll unless so entitled under Section 41 of the Constitution, which guaranteed the federal vote to all adults already entitled to vote at elections for the lower house of any State parliament. Very few Aborigines qualified in this way, but tens of thousands of white women in South Australia and Western Australia were entitled to vote for the lower houses of their respective States, and thus for federal parliament as well. This ensured that for the sake of electoral uniformity Barton's 1901 election promise of an adult federal franchise would be kept.

Although the vote for women was really a foregone conclusion, both sides of the unequal argument were put forward in debate. Women should have the vote on grounds of equity (so said Senators O'Connor and Glassey), because they owned property (Downer), because they earned their living (Isaacs, Wilks) and because they would improve the tone of politics (Poynton). Alternatively, but with less effect, it was argued that women should not have the vote because their God-ordained place was in the home (Knox, Senator Symon), it would reduce the standing of women (Braddon), it would favour the cities (Sawers, Senator Pulsford), there was no demand for it (Senator Gould), and it would have the effect of giving married men a double vote (Braddon).

Knox, whose main contribution to the first parliament had been to advocate the starting of each day with prayer, warned the House that in widening the franchise it was 'running counter to the intentions and to the design of the Great Creator, and . . . reversing those conditions of life to which woman was ordained'. When Isaacs asked him what he would do with the 120 000 women in Victoria who were earning their own livings, Knox replied: 'I would have them married to honourable men, so that they might become the mothers of children, and thus increase our population. The main ambition of a woman's life should be to become the wife of an honourable and honest man'.

As the right to vote for the House of Representatives had been the only obstacle to women offering themselves as candidates, the way was now entirely open, at least in theory, for their election to federal parliament. Four women entered the lists in 1903, but none came close to success. In New South Wales Mrs Nellie Martel, an elocutionist, and Mary Ann Bentley, a journalist, stood for the Senate; and Selina Anderson, an artist, stood in the Sydney electorate of Dalley. Mrs Martel was a Free Trade supporter; Miss Bentley was listed invidiously by the *Age* as an Opportunist, which meant merely that she had no party affiliation or inclination, and Miss Anderson was a Protectionist. The Senate candidates received 2.75 and 2.69 per cent of the total vote respectively, or 10.18 and 9.96 per cent of the lowest successful vote. Miss Anderson received 17.27 per cent of the total vote in Dalley, or 23.69 per cent of the winner's total (the sitting Free Trade member, W. H. Wilks, was returned). In Victoria a leader of the radical women's movement in that State, the journalist Vida Goldstein, stood as a Protectionist candidate for the Senate, assisted by the Women's Federal Political Association. She received 8.40 per cent of the total vote, and 60.38 per cent of the lowest successful vote.

Although there were now three more or less distinct political groups— liberal, labor and conservative—federal candidates still used several political labels. Deakin was usually referred to as a Liberal Protectionist ('The accredited captain of Australian Liberalism', said the *Age*), but his followers were called not only Liberal or Protectionist or both, but also National Trade, Fiscal Peace and Ministerialist. Opposition supporters were either Free Trade, Fiscal War or Conservative.

Most of the senators and representatives mentioned so far in this narrative were still in parliament after the election. Of the eighteen three-year Senators, five (including Downer, O'Connor and Ferguson) did not stand for re-election; thirteen did stand, and four of them were not re-elected. In the lower house, twelve members (including McMillan, Bonython, Manifold and the chamber's only real Independent, Alexander Paterson) did not stand again; seven who stood were unsuccessful; and out of the total seventy-five, fifty-six were re-elected.

The final effect of this election upon party strength was qualified by two successful petitions to the High Court, sitting as a Court of Disputed Returns, and the consequent by-elections; and by the transfer of a successful Free Trade candidate, Alexander Poynton (Grey, S), to the Labor Party soon after the election. Taking all this into account, the result in the House of Representatives was: Protectionists, twenty-five; Free Traders, twenty-four; Labor, twenty-five; Independent, one. In the Senate Labor now held fourteen seats, the Free Traders thirteen, and the Protectionists nine. Labor had triumphed beyond anyone's expectation, gaining nine seats in the lower house and two in the Senate. While Protectionists now had to depend mainly on Victoria, and Free Traders mainly on New South Wales, Labor had increased its strength in the less populous states of Queensland, South Australia and Western Australia. After having been a minor third party, offering itself for sale, Labor was now on equal footing with the other two parties, an eligible partner for coalition.

'Mr Deakin may well view this position before him with rueful solicitude', wrote Deakin himself six days after the election, in his clandestine role of correspondent for the *Morning Post*.

> While the fiscal question remains unsettled a coalition between Mr Deakin and [Mr Reid] is unthinkable . . . A further period of unrest, vacillation and uncertainty appears before us unless Mr Reid is able to make some arrangement with the Labor Caucus for a junction of forces. There again he has to reckon with the Government, which has precisely the same opportunity coupled with the advantages of being in office as authors of a programme some of whose proposals are very attractive to Mr Watson. Opening under such auspices it must be confessed that when the Federal Houses meet a few weeks hence the outlook is anything but satisfactory from any point of view save that of the Labor section.

3

Cut-throat Euchre

The rules of the game had changed. It was now 'a positively awful game to play', commiserated Justice Barton in a letter to Deakin soon after the election in November 1903. 'In the last Parliament, at our worst, we could defy the House on important questions—defy, I mean, the other two parties to put us out. You can scarcely do that, and it is not great comfort that nobody else can.' Deakin described the new game in cricket terms. He was no cricketer himself, but the parallel was well chosen, for Australia was then in the grip of Test fever. The second Test had been played recently on a very sticky pitch at Melbourne, and England had won by 185 runs. Later in January Deakin visited Adelaide to farewell the departing Lord Tennyson, and while he was there Australia won the third Test, thanks almost entirely to the godlike Victor Trumper, who put a double century on the Adelaide scoreboard. Deakin returned to Melbourne; greeted the new Governor-General, Lord Northcote, one time Conservative member of the House of Commons and most recently a meritorious Governor of Bombay; and, on Australia Day, attended an official luncheon of the Australian Natives' Association in the Exhibition Building.

Responding to a luncheon toast of 'The Federal and State Parliaments', Deakin compared the forthcoming second parliament to a cricket match:

Administration and legislation had always been conducted [he said] on the principle of a majority and a minority. Now, however, they had practically three equal parties, and the position was unstable. It was absolutely impossible. (Cheers.) It could not continue, and it ought not to continue. (Cheers.) What kind of a game of cricket, compared with the present game, could they play if they had three elevens instead of two—one team playing sometimes with one side, sometimes with the other and some-

times for itself? (Loud laughter and cheers.) That was a homely illus-
tration of the difficulty which the Federal Parliament had to solve.

A Voice: It's simply cut-throat euchre.(Laughter.)

The Prime Minister said that if the interjector had found 'cut-throat' a
simple game it was not his experience. (Laughter.) It was a game in which
the joker played too large a part. (Laughter.) It was absolutely essential
that as soon as possible the three parties somehow or other should be
resolved into two—either as parties or parts of parties—in order that constitutional government might be carried on. (Cheers.) . . . Someone must
give way for the benefit of the State, and which was to give way was the
delicate issue. The position was illustrated in the immortal Bab Ballads,
where the last of the two survivors of the shipwrecked crew regarded the
other with expectation as to which was to remain—

> I loved the cook as a brother, I did,
> And the cook he worshipped me;
> But we'd both be blowed if we'd be stowed
> In the other chap's hold, d'ye see.

Although 'three elevens' gained wide currency as shorthand for the prospect before parliament, 'cut-throat euchre' was the more accurate analogy.
Euchre, an American card game that had become popular in Australia, was
known as 'cut-throat' in its three-handed form, where two of the players
acted temporarily as partners against the third. The ruthless, ephemeral
quality of cut-throat euchre was well matched by the shifting alliances that
were to produce four different ministries during the first sixteen months of
the second parliament. Deakin was better able to play this game than either
Watson or Reid, for the extreme left and right wings of his party had much in
common with the other two parties. Whereas he could conceivably play with
either Labor or Free Trade, there was little liklihood that they could ever
come to such an accommodation with each other.

For several weeks before and after the second parliament was opened on 2
March 1904, Deakin explored the possibility of co-operating with Labor; but
although Watson and some of his colleagues shared common ground with
the Liberal Protectionists, no formal commitment was made. With the fatalism of one who realised that his throat might be cut at any time, Deakin went
straight ahead with the programme contained in his policy speech, regardless of possible consequences beyond his control. Among other measures, he
intended to reintroduce three bills—promised by Barton in 1901, but
allowed to lapse at prorogation—giving effect to three provisions of the
Constitution: the establishment of an Inter-State Commission with powers
of adjudication on trade and commerce within the Commonwealth, determination of a permanent seat of government, and establishment of compulsory
judicial arbitration for the prevention and settlement of industrial disputes
extending beyond any one State.

No sooner had the House of Representatives returned from hearing Lord
Northcote's opening speech than the Prime Minister introduced the Commonwealth Conciliation and Arbitration Bill. This was the latest version of
the measure initiated by Kingston in 1901 and later withdrawn, a bill whose

peaceful title was belied by its remarkable capacity for political disruption. Its chief objects were to prevent lock-outs and strikes in relation to industrial disputes; to establish a federal Court of Conciliation and Arbitration, consisting of a president appointed from among the justices of the High Court, whose task it would be to achieve amicable agreement between parties by conciliation, and to arbitrate where such agreement was not possible; to enable States to refer industrial disputes to the court; and to provide for the making and enforcement of industrial agreements between employers and employees in relation to industrial disputes.

Kingston, as we have seen, resigned from Barton's Ministry because he was not permitted to include coastal seamen in his 1903 draft Bill. Deakin initiated that Bill in Kingston's place, but the Barton Government put it aside when confronted by a strong body of opinion that the Bill should extend federal authority to cover working conditions in State government railways. Labor's intense feeling on this issue was a legacy of the short but savage Victorian railway strike of 1903. Never before had the State's employees gone on strike; the Government of W. H. Irvine treated them as mutineers, and forced them back to work with an equally unprecedented Railway Employees' Strike Suppression Act. At the height of the debate on that Victorian measure, the Labor member, Dr Maloney, had yelled across the chamber at the Premier, a chilly Melbourne barrister known to his colleagues as 'Iceberg': 'Your turn will come, my smooth beauty!' When the reintroduced Conciliation and Arbitration Bill came to its second reading on 22 March, Labor was determined to carry an amendment extending the Court's jurisdiction not only to railway men but to all State government employees. Deakin was equally determined to keep such employees out, on grounds that their inclusion would be unconstitutional and contrary to the federal spirit.

Hoping to avoid the appearance of crucial challenge, for Labor was not particularly anxious to defeat the Deakin Government, Watson delegated the moving of this contentious amendment to Andrew Fisher. Late on the night of 21 April Fisher moved his amendment in Committee of the Whole House, where the Bill had been under consideration for the past four sitting days. With help from twelve Free Traders and two Protectionists, it was carried by 38 to 29. The Committee immediately reported progress and the Prime Minister, for whom the sticking point had arrived, moved for special adjournment of the House. 'In making this motion', he said, 'in order that the Government may take the action called for by the decision of the Committee, I desire, in ceasing to discharge the duties of Prime Minister . . . to thank honorable members from my heart for the assistance I have received from every quarter of this House . . . '. Next day he tendered his resignation to Lord Northcote and advised him to send for Watson.

With the minor exception of Anderson Dawson's seven days in Queensland four years earlier, Watson's Ministry was the world's first Labor Government. A special Caucus on Saturday 23 April 1904 authorised Watson to form a government if invited to do so, and after an adjournment, during which the 37-year-old printer went to Government House and returned with his commission, the meeting debated two important questions. Should

J. C. Watson,
the first Labor Prime Minister,
by David Low

Labor follow Deakin's example, and forge single-handedly ahead with its official policy; or would it last longer with a partner, taking tricks whenever possible in the game of cut-throat euchre? Secondly, should the ministry be chosen by Caucus or the new Prime Minister? A motion that Watson approach Deakin with a view to forming a ministry with at least four paid Labor ministers was defeated, and a motion that Watson should have a free hand in the formation of his Ministry was carried unanimously.

Watson's first choices were his friends and close associates, W. M. Hughes and E. L. Batchelor (Boothby, S). Hughes was the party's only lawyer, but he had been at the Bar only a few months and for that reason preferred the port-folio of External Affairs to that of Attorney-General. He ranked second in Cabinet. Batchelor, an engineer by trade who had risen to leadership of the parliamentary Labor Party in South Australia, became Minister for Home Affairs. For an Attorney-General, Watson had to go outside the party. After seeking Deakin's advice, and receiving the latter's 'cordial approval' of such a choice, he brought into his Cabinet the Melbourne King's Counsel H. B. Higgins, a Protectionist whose views on most matters differed from those of Labor Protectionists only by being perhaps more radical. The other Ministers were Fisher (Trade and Customs), Senator Dawson (Defence), Mahon (Postmaster-General) and Senator McGregor (Vice-President of the Execu-tive Council and Government Leader in the Senate).

Like the party as a whole, Watson's Ministry was considerably younger than its predecessor (average age forty-seven, compared with fifty-six). Only Higgins and McGregor were over fifty. Although many of the thirty-nine Labor parliamentarians were amply equipped with native intelligence and the fruits of self-improvement, their level of formal education was not high. The party had only three university graduates: the clergyman Ronald and two recently elected medical practitioners, Dr W. R. N. Maloney, who defeated Sir Malcolm McEacharn in a by-election for Melbourne brought on by the Court of Disputed Returns, and Dr Millice Culpin (Brisbane).

All three party leaders were now exploring the possibilities of partnership. In the Liberal Protectionist party room Lyne, Isaacs and other radicals wanted to follow Higgins into Labor's orbit, but Forrest and others, resenting the socialists' presence in office, were advocating an alliance with Reid. Late in May Watson sent Deakin the draft terms for a Labor–Liberal alliance which had been approved, after initial hesitation, by the Labor Caucus. Deakin would have worked willingly enough with Watson, whom he trusted, but he was well aware of the anti-socialist feeling in his own party, and in any case he doubted that a programme worked out between Watson and himself would be acceptable to Labor Caucus or the Labor organisations outside parliament.

Instead he negotiated a tentative agreement with Reid, whom he did not trust, which included an undertaking not to alter the tariff or raise the fiscal issue before the next scheduled election in 1906. Isaacs and Lyne strongly opposed this, and in June the Liberal parliamentary party decided not to join any coalition for the time being. If and when it did, the chances were that party opinion would favour a combination with Reid to displace Labor. That was Deakin's feeling, and he did not relish it. As a liberal idealist, he felt that he could never tolerate the rigid discipline of Labor's party machine. Yet if Labor continued to grow, as Deakin speculated in his *Morning Post* articles, the other groups in parliament would eventually have to combine against it. Then the only place for him would be beside the conservatives.

The Watson Government's main legislative concern, like that of its predecessor, was the Conciliation and Arbitration Bill; and it too came to grief over this measure. For Watson the sticking point was preference for trade unionists. Clause 48 provided that 'as between members of organisations of employers or employees and other persons offering or desiring service or employment at the same time, preference shall be given to such members, other things being equal'. On 24 June one of the lawyers in Deakin's party, J. W. McCay (Corinella, V), successfully moved in Committee an amendment to that clause requiring applicants for preference to satisfy the Court that they represented a majority of those affected by the award. This was agreed to on division, 27–22.

Watson stressed the seriousness with which his Government regarded such a limitation on preference, and said that the Committee would be asked to reconsider the amended clause. Six weeks later he moved that the Bill be recommitted to Committee for reconsideration of ten clauses, including Clause 48. When McCay moved an amendment that Clause 48 be omitted from those to be reconsidered, Watson told the House: 'I now say distinctly that I am not prepared to remain in office and take the responsibility for a measure which, according to my conception, will not be effective, especially if this provision, which, I contend, would be absolutely unworkable, be agreed to'. On 12 August McCay's rather devious amendment was agreed to, 36–34. The Prime Minister immediately moved for special adjournment. On the next sitting day he informed the House that he had offered certain advice to the Governor-General, and, His Excellency not having seen fit to act upon it, had tendered the resignation of his Ministry.

Watson's unheeded advice had been that the Governor-General should exercise his power to dissolve the House of Representatives and call another election. The Constitution did not specify the kind of circumstances that would justify such action, and by Westminster tradition the Prime Minister was expected to show sufficient grounds for dissolution, especially if the House was nowhere near the end of its three-year term. In this case, the first of its kind in federal history, Watson's grounds were not good enough. The parliament was less than six months old. A man of Lord Northcote's political experience knew very well that the House's ministerial alternatives were not exhausted. He asked Watson to stay in office until a new administration was formed, and sent for Reid.

Deakin, although in all probability he had merely acquiesced in McCay's second amendment, was blamed by Labor for its loss of office after only four months, and blamed with a virulence that was new to parliament. In the debate preceding the fatal division, little Billy Hughes railed at him for proposing 'to strike with the stiletto of the bravo instead of coming out and fighting with the broadsword of the soldier'. 'They have inaugurated a new era', he said. 'It is the singular fortune of the honorable and learned member for Ballarat that, after having covered himself with temporary glory by resigning his position as Prime Minister when defeated upon a detail of this Bill, he should have lent himself to a base, treacherous and indefensible action.'

In reply, Deakin accused Hughes of inaugurating the new era by uttering 'a tissue of accusations, half of them malevolent and the other half false'. When Speaker Holder asked him to withdraw that unparliamentary imputation of falsehood, Deakin replied:

> Certainly, sir, if you so direct, though I thought that what I said was in order. To the speech of the Minister for External Affairs I do not propose to make any more than an indirect reply. It happens sometimes to all of us, that as we pass along the streets of the city, we meet men engaged filling drays with dirt and garbage, and unless one is discreet some of that dust and refuse may drift upon him.

He later apologised for these words, but after Hughes returned to the attack in a speech at Ballarat Deakin likened his dispossessed opponent to 'the ill-bred urchin whom one sees dragged from a tart shop kicking and screaming as he goes'. It was characteristic of the Member for Ballarat that in due course he also apologised for that inspired flash of imagery.

Although Reid came to office in partnership with Liberal Protectionists, and on the terms of fiscal truce negotiated earlier with Deakin, Deakin himself declined to join the new ministry. So also did Forrest, who rightly felt insulted by the offer of an honorary portfolio. Sir George Turner was prevented by illness from accepting Reid's offer of joint leadership, but he continued as Treasurer. The joint leader was Allan McLean, a former Premier and Chief Secretary of Victoria, who took the portfolio of Trade and Customs. Portfolios were divided equally between the parties, and McCay, a citizen soldier of some repute, became Minister for Defence.

The Reid–McLean Government's majority was sometimes as low as two in both chambers. Reid turned over a new leaf so far as attendance was concerned, not missing a single sitting day during his term of office; but what did his coalition achieve? Contemplating the fruitless manoeuvrings of the second parliament's first session, Ithuriel parodied Lewis Carroll's 'Tillers of the Sand':

> The Reidite and the McLeanite
>   Were looking round the land,
> The Reidite laughed aloud to see
>   Such quantities of sand.
> 'If we could plough it up a bit',
>   He said, 'It would be grand . . .'

Within five weeks of the new government taking office, Watson moved a want of confidence motion which was debated for fifteen full sitting days. Unlike Deakin and other Protectionists who, in spite of reservations about Reid sat behind the Ministry and voted with it, Isaacs, Lyne, Hume Cook and nine other Protectionists disapproving of the coalition took their seats on the Opposition cross benches and voted with Labor. In Watson's censure speech, Reid thought he detected the mind of Isaacs. 'When I heard my honorable friend's discreet and studied utterances this afternoon', said Reid,

'I could not help remembering—with a slight alteration—the language of old Abraham: "The voice was the voice of Esau. But the hands were the hands of Isaac"'.

The main object of Watson's censure was not Reid's neglect of the Papua (British New Guinea) Bill authorising acceptance of British New Guinea as a territory of the Commonwealth, the Fraudulent Trade Marks Bill and other measures stalled in the legislative process, though he did make that point. He was more concerned to attack Reid's general philosophical position— 'that private enterprise should be allowed full sway, and that interference on behalf of the community as a whole should be refused'. Reid stood for those, he said, who believed in marking time: for stagnation and for retrogression. This was evangelism rather than censure. The motion was lost, as it deserved to be, though only by two votes.

The one major legislative achievement during the Reid–McLean term of office—indeed during the entire first session of this arid parliament—was the passing, at long last, of the Conciliation and Arbitration Act. This measure had taken a full nine months' gestation; it had been part of the lower house's business for forty-three days, and of the Senate's for seventeen; and it had brought about the resignation of one minister and two complete ministries. McCay's narrowing of the preference for unionists was at first rejected by the Senate. The lower house would not accept the relevant amendment, however, and as the Senate did not press the matter McCay's clause became part of the Act.

Among the very few bills initiated during the Reid–McLean term was one for which that government was not responsible. The Life Assurance Companies Bill was initiated by L. E. Groom, the 37-year-old lawyer from Toowoomba who had been elected to his late father's seat in 1901. It was not the first private member's bill to be introduced (that distinction belonged to a Matrimonial Causes Bill, introduced by Senator Henry Dobson (F, T) in July 1901, to regulate divorce procedure within the Commonwealth); but it was the first to be passed, for Dobson's Bill lapsed at prorogation in 1902, and was not reintroduced. Groom's sombre little Bill was designed to permit the life assurance of children under the age of ten—so that, if necessary, parents could use the sum assured to pay for their offspring's burial. Littleton Groom took life very seriously—too seriously, felt some of his fellow Protectionists. 'Get fat', advised Thomas Ewing (Richmond, N) in a letter to him. 'Life is not worth living if you worry yourself about every little rotten thing that does not matter a two-pence the day after tomorrow.' No doubt he worried about his private member's Bill, for it seemed likely at first to disappear like Senator Dobson's. It lapsed at prorogation, but passed through all stages the following year.

In the closing days of the first session the Reid–McLean Government did something which helped to precipitate its defeat: it appointed a royal commission on the Commonwealth tariff. Parliament was prorogued on 15 December, and stayed in recess for six months. During that time Deakin became convinced that the royal commission was a breach of Reid's undertaking not to revive the tariff issue before the parliament had run its full term. Reid's recent canvassing of dissolution and the increasing stridency of his anti-socialism seemed to presage an early election; and who was to say that Reid, restored to office, would not declare fiscal war? Although he held no office in the coalition, Deakin was the broker who had helped Reid to power. 'I would like to see you throw that incubus of the Reid alliance off your back', wrote Mr Justice O'Connor to Deakin in June 1905. At the same time Watson was urging Deakin to take office in order to defend Protection if fiscal war broke out.

In a speech delivered at Ballarat on Saturday 24 June, four days before parliament reassembled, Deakin gave warning that he would reconsider his support for Reid. The warning was carefully, even mildly, worded; but as the *Age* said on Monday morning, read in any light it was 'a notice to Mr. Reid to quit'. When parliament met in the Senate chamber on 28 June the Governor-General's speech consisted of only six sentences and foreshadowed only one measure, a bill to revise electoral boundaries. The Government, realising that it had lost the support of the House, had set aside a more detailed speech. Instead, it gave the Governor-General a speech which, as Reid was to write later, 'would show that we would only stay in office to bring about an appeal to the country'. Opposition members burst into derisive laughter even before Lord Northcote left the chamber, but Reid remained affable and smiling. On the way back to the lower house, Deakin was asked by one of his friends, 'What do you think of it?' 'Well, they've asked us to put them out', he replied, 'and we'll have to do it'.

Deakin met Watson that night, and although no evidence has survived it seems likely that they discussed tactics not only for the next day's Address-in-Reply debate but also to provide some feasible alternative to dissolution, should Reid request it. Watson opened the debate, and concluded his speech with words that seemed to take Reid's fate for granted: 'I think we shall all welcome the disappearance of a Ministry that has neither achievement in the past, policy in the present, nor prospects in the future to justify its existence'. After Reid's reply—in the course of which he charged Deakin with disloyalty not only to the Free Traders but to McLean and other members of his own party who were part of the Ministry, and said that the best way to determine the Government's position would be by moving an amendment upon the Address-in-Reply—it was Deakin's turn. He dissociated himself from the *Age*'s blunt interpretation of the Ballarat speech, saying that he had been issuing a warning rather than withdrawing support; claimed that if he had foreseen the sensation his speech would cause he would have given the Prime Minister some intimation of it beforehand; and finally—giving the lie to all he had said before, it seemed to Reid—delivered the *coup de grâce*. 'But, sir, I propose to test the opinion of this House—'

Mr REID.—This is the postscript to the epistle!
Mr. DEAKIN.—By moving—That the following words be added to the Address-in-Reply:—"But are of the opinion that practical measures should be proceeded with."
Mr REID.—Here is the dagger; he had it in his pocket all the time.

After another day's debate the amendment was agreed to, 42–25. Reid sought a dissolution, was denied it, and tendered his Ministry's resignation.

On 7 July Deakin informed the House that he had accepted the Governor-General's commission to form a new administration. Forrest replaced the ailing Turner as Treasurer, Lyne was Minister for Trade and Customs, Chapman Postmaster-General, Senator Playford (S) Minister for Defence, and four other Liberal Protectionists became Ministers for the first time. They were Isaacs (Attorney-General), Groom (Home Affairs), Thomas Ewing (Richmond, N) and Senator J. H. Keating (T), the last two being honorary Ministers. Although his second Ministry was chosen only from the reunited Liberal Protectionists, Deakin could again rely upon Labor as a *de facto* partner, at least for the time being. Labor Caucus was averse to any formal coalition, but Watson was able to promise Deakin 'a cordial and generous support for this parliament', in both houses. Thanks to this informal 'Lib–Lab' alliance, the ship of state was back on an even keel. The fourth Ministry of the second parliament would see out that parliament, and most of the next one as well.

Judgement

For the next three and a half years, Australia's tripartite parliament managed to play a reasonably orthodox two-handed game with a clear-cut majority and minority. Deakin's party was supported by Labor, which shared the Liberals' interest in achieving certain social objectives, and this support more than compensated for the defection of Deakin's conservatives, who formed a 'Corner' group in the lower house. The 'squealing dozen', as they were called, refused to follow their former leader into the socialist tiger's lair, and they could not very well join Reid's anti-socialists now that the tariff was becoming a lively issue again. On non-fiscal issues they generally voted against the Government. Although both chambers made the going hard for Deakin—the lower house by stonewalling; the Senate by pressing amendments—they did no more than temporarily incommode the Government. The Government was to be thwarted, as we shall see, but not by the Opposition. It was during Deakin's second Ministry that parliament first collided with the High Court.

In its remaining eighteen months the second parliament passed several measures about which there was no major disagreement: the Papua Act, Census and Statistics Act, Copyright Act, Life Assurance Companies Act, Wireless Telegraphy Act and Meteorology Act. The last established a federal bureau to carry out the role of Australia-wide meteorologist to which Clement Wragge had once aspired. In his second reading speech Senator Keating recalled that Wragge's position had been adversely affected by the Post and Telegraph Rates Act of 1902, which made no special provision for the transmission of meteorological telegrams free of charge. At about that time Australia's 'boss weather prophet' had also lost public and state support through the failure of certain drought-breaking experiments which he conducted with six funnel-shaped cannon producing a frightful sound, but unfortunately no rain. Wragge's Brisbane weather bureau closed its doors in 1903; he moved to Auckland, and established another bureau there. He applied for the position of Commonwealth Meterorologist when it was advertised in 1907, but the job went to a younger and more orthodox candidate who had been assistant to the New South Wales Government Astronomer. Wragge continued to lecture and travel extensively until the end of his days, at Auckland, in 1922.

The bills which had the most difficult passage through parliament at this time were measures of social reform upon which the Liberal and Labor parties were agreed. Deakin could not, of course, share all Labor's enthusiasms. Watson urged him, for example, to introduce a land tax, with which Labor hoped to finance the old-age pension advocated by both parties; Deakin replied that the Liberals should not be expected to jeopardise their electoral support by moving as far to the left as that. The two parties did agree, however, on a body of bills related to what was known as 'New Protection'. 'Old Protection' consisted of duties imposed on imports in order to promote local employment, safeguard the investment of capital in existing and new industries, and stabilise conditions of labour and the standard of living. Whereas Old Protection made adequate wages and conditions merely possible, New Protection sought to ensure such benefits by linking exemption from taxation to compliance with minimal conditions of employment.

This device had been used in the United States to extend federal control over matters not directly within the range of federal power, and had been under discussion by Australian liberals since the 1890s. If an Australian manufacturer benefited financially from Protection imposed for the general economic good, why should he not be made to pass on some of that benefit to his employees? The proposition sounded reasonable, but was it constitutional? Under Australia's federal Constitution the Commonwealth had power to impose taxation, but not to regulate conditions of employment in the States. Now, in several acts of parliament, it was trying to achieve the latter by means of the former.

As early as 1902 the Excise Tariff Act had imposed a higher excise on sugar produced by non-white (which was to say, cheap) labour. The Trade Marks Act of 1905 provided for a Commonwealth trade mark signifying that goods had been produced in Australia under conditions to be determined by parliament as 'fair and reasonable'; the third Manufactures Encouragement Bill, a badly drafted measure that was rejected by the Senate in 1905, included a provision that bounties should be conditional upon wage rates conforming to a schedule; the Excise Tariff (Spirits) Act of 1906 allowed parliament to impose a penalty excise on distillers who did not pay a 'fair and reasonable' wage, or who employed more than a due proportion of boys to men; and the Excise Tariff (Agricultural Machinery) Act of 1906, the most direct form of new protection, made exemption from excise dependent upon compliance with various wage rates set out in the Act. The arbiters of this last Act were at first to be the President of the new Conciliation and Arbitration Court, and the Minister for Customs.

Taking advantage of the lack of time limit on speeches, the Opposition stonewalled against the Trade Marks Bill and other legislation with such persistence in the second half of 1905 that, according to W. G Spence (Lab, Darling, N), the Opposition Whip Wilks 'had to take to his bed seriously ill owing to the strain'. Deakin responded to these tactics by postponing debate in order to move the adoption of a Westminster-style Standing Order pro-

viding for the closure of members' speeches. Opposition members debated
Deakin's motion non-stop, except for meals, from Thursday afternoon 16
November until midnight on Saturday, and would have gone on longer, it
was said, but for Speaker Holder's sabbatarian principles. Although the new
Standing Order was not used immediately, any member could henceforth
move at any time that a member who was speaking 'be not further heard',
and the question had to be decided immediately, without amendment or
debate.

During its last session the second parliament amended the Judiciary Act to
provide for the appointment of two more judges to join Griffith, Barton and
O'Connor on the High Court. It was widely believed that one of these
appointments would go to the Attorney-General, Isaac Isaacs. Ithuriel
claimed in the *Argus* to have recognised signs of impending translation to a
higher level of existence. 'The head was carried a little further back than was
wont', he wrote of Isaacs:

> there was even more aloofness in the pose. The height from which any
> question has been regarded has been more sublime, the gracious conde-
> scension a shade more evident. In short, the mortal man, with some short-
> comings, it may be, and some fallibility, perhaps, has been gradually
> putting on the supernal judge. Such a mental adjustment has already
> been effected, and such a height of preparatory deportment attained, that
> no further ascension is necessary. Goodbye, your Honour, with great
> respect, your Honour, if your Honour pleases.

One of the new High Court seats was offered to the Chief Justice of South
Australia, Sir Samuel Way, but he declined it. Another South Australian
mentioned in this context was the Opposition Leader in the Senate, Sir
Josiah Symon. He was Leader of the Bar in South Australia, but during his
time as Reid's Attorney-General he had effectively disqualified himself from
judicial appointment by feuding bitterly with the founding judges.

The dispute—involving the exchange of more than eighty letters and telegrams, and what amounted virtually to a strike by the High Court—was
mainly about the Court's policy of sitting in other State capitals as well as
Melbourne. Although the Judiciary Act stipulated that the principal seat of
the High Court should be 'at the seat of Government', and that seat for the
time being was Melbourne, Sir Samuel Griffith and his colleagues maintained that showing the judicial flag in other cities, particularly Sydney,
would strengthen federal unity. The frequency with which they sat in part of
Sydney's criminal court building at Darlinghurst may also have been related
to the fact that all three justices now lived in that city.

Symon reminded the Chief Justice that policy-making was a matter for the
executive and parliament, not the High Court, and that it was no part of the
Court's duty to concern itself with travelling widely in the interests of federal
unity. He queried the judges' expenses (Why, he asked, had Barton and
O'Connor spent £5 and £7 10s respectively on ship fares from Sydney to
Hobart when they could have used their ex-parliamentarians' rail passes as
far as Melbourne and then taken the Bass Strait steamer?), delayed their
reimbursement, and deferred consideration of a request by the Chief Justice
for bookshelves to accommodate his law library in Sydney.

Griffith responded sternly to what he regarded as executive interference with the court's exercise of its discretionary powers. On 29 April 1905 he announced from the Bench in Sydney that a Melbourne sitting, listed to start in three days' time, would be postponed because of continuing uncertainty about travel expenses. It was all very petty and acrimonious. Symon continued to harry the judges for the remaining few weeks of the Reid–McLean Ministry. For reasons not hard to guess, the next Attorney-General, Isaacs, found greater rapport with the itinerant justices. He approved Griffith's bookshelves and settled the travel dispute to their Honours' satisfaction. In future, they were able to hear cases wherever they wished without hindrance from the Attorney-General's Department.

The other judge appointed to the enlarged High Court was Isaacs's fellow Melbourne barrister, Higgins, who had been Labor's first Attorney-General. Both were radicals, likely to find common cause on the Bench against their decidely conservative colleagues.

The third session of the second parliament was prorogued on 12 October 1906, leaving two months before a general election and a simultaneous referendum on the first proposed amendment to the Constitution—a minor and uncontentious amendment, expressed in the Constitution Alteration (Senate Elections) Bill, altering the date on which senators took office, from 1 January to 1 July. The purpose of this was to make it more likely that the half senatorial term would coincide with the life of the House of Representatives, and consequently with the life of a parliament. The Bill was approved at referendum by a majority of electors in a majority of the States, and also by a majority of all who voted, and was thus able to be presented to the Governor-General for assent. This procedure, to which future governments would have recourse sporadically but seldom with similar success, was prescribed by Section 128 of the Constitution, and in more detail by the Referendum (Constitution Alteration) Act of 1906.

Deakin's election policy contained several familiar but as yet unfulfilled promises—a transcontinental railway, bounties on iron and steel production, a Navigation Bill, and the appropriation of taxes (though not a land tax) to finance age pensions and defence. Most importantly, the fiscal truce was over: Deakin's government, if returned to office, would revise the tariff in order to create a system of 'scientific national protection'. Australian public opinion was now strongly in favour of a protective tariff. Even some members of Reid's party had come around to moderate protection, and in this election they joined forces with the conservative wing of Deakin's party, going by the name of tariff reformers. In Western Australia they were known as the Western Australian Party. Sir John Forrest assumed leadership of this party, for he shared the tariff reformers' disapproval of Deakin's co--operation with Labor; but such was his personal affection for Deakin that he declared his willingness to remain in his friend's Ministry. Forrest used to say that if Deakin had some of his pluck and he had some of Deakin's spare brains, they would both be better men.

In this election campaign Labor displayed a socialist banner which had been emblazoned at the party's 1905 federal conference. In defining the federal party's broad objectives for the first time, this conference shied away

from a blunt proposal by the Victorian executive ('The gradual nationalisation of the means of production, distribution and exchange') and adopted a
more moderately socialist objective proposed by J. C. Watson: 'The securing
of the full results of their industry to all producers by the collective ownership of monopolies and the extension of the industrial and economic functions of the State and the Municipality'.

Labor's policy for the 1906 election included proposals for a government
bank and insurance office; anti-trust legislation, or alternatively nationalisation of monopolies; an age pension; and a land tax to break up large estates
and finance the age pension. Watson, a self-professed 'state socialist', had
earlier assured parliament that his conception of socialism did 'not necessi-
tate the slightest alteration in the structure of our governing institutions'.
This did not satisfy Reid, who had been ostentatiously 'stalking the socialist
tiger' for months past. Now he flourished Labor's election policy as further
evidence of a Lib–Lab conspiracy against free enterprise. Contrary to
Deakin's earlier expectations, Reid had accepted defeat on the fiscal issue
and was preaching anti-socialism in place of free trade.

The Reidites, styling themselves Anti-Socialists or Oppositionists rather
than Free Traders, were supported during the campaign by the Women's
National League, a conservative body of women who, according to W. G.
Spence, 'probably never earned a meal in their lives, and . . . knew nothing
of the social problem except in so far as it gave them a chance to be
insultingly patronising to the poor'. But this time there were no women
candidates.

The 1906 election reduced the number of Deakinites in the House of Representatives from twenty-five to seventeen. Of the remainder, twenty-six
were Labor and thirty-two Anti-Socialist. Five of the Anti-Socialists were
tariff reformers from the Opposition 'Corner', however, and they supported
Deakin on some issues. Even with those votes Deakin would be more reliant
than ever on Labor, which again undertook informally to support him in
both chambers. In the Senate Labor now held fifteen seats, the Anti-
Socialists seventeen, and the Deakinites only four. Deakin told Watson that
he would not be able to accept 'even a check without taking it as a challenge'.
'The coming Parliament is going to repeat the history of the last Parliament
step by step', he wrote to Watson. 'This means that Reid or you will be sent
for very soon.' He was mistaken. So long as Labor continued, as Lord
Northcote put it, to enjoy 'the sweets of power without responsibility', it was
going to keep Deakin in office.

The third parliament opened on 20 February 1907, but closed its first
session the following day. This two-day session was held to comply with a
requirement of the Constitution that parliament be summoned to meet not
later than thirty days after the return of general election writs. Parliament
was then prorogued until the second session began in July. During this recess
Deakin attended the Imperial Conference in London. When he returned to
Melbourne in June his health had deteriorated, and for the first time in his
life he noticed a failure of memory that would later afflict him more severely.
'Deakin is a very sick man', wrote Hughes during the second session. 'Nervous breakdown. He ought to go away for a trip where the wire stretches not

nor does the phone tintinnabulate. But he dodges about like a fly near the paper which to him spells death but smells life.'

Hughes tended to exaggerate, but without doubt Deakin was showing the strain of cut-throat euchre. Not the least of his worries was Sir John Forrest's decision in July to leave the Deakin camp and lead the anti-socialist Corner group. In vain had Forrest urged Deakin to move away from Labor and join forces with the Corner; now he was taking his own advice, and leaving his old friend in such uncongenial company as that of Forrest's successor at Treasury, Sir William Lyne. 'I am truly sorry', wrote bluff old Forrest, 'to leave you with one who does not care for you and is playing his own game, and in the hands of the Philistines . . . '.

Lyne, who boasted of 'bullocking' all his bills through the House, became the first Treasurer to read his Budget speech. His predecessors had spoken from notes, but Lyne read from a fully prepared typescript, as would all his successors. The impudent Member for Wentworth (F, N), Willie Kelly, said that Lyne's first Budget had three faults. 'First, it was read; second, it was read badly; and third, it was not worth reading.'

The parliamentary organism seemed to be changing shape more than usual as familiar figures assumed new roles or departed from political life. Sir George Turner and Senator Sir Richard Baker retired at the end of 1906, and the latter was succeeded as President of the Senate by the New South Wales anti-socialist, Sir Albert Gould. Sir Richard Baker had zealously guarded the Senate's real or assumed prerogatives, but in spite of the vigilance which he and other senators displayed the Senate was gradually losing ground in its uneasy relationship with the 'other place'. 'In spite of themselves', wrote Deakin in one of his despatches to the *Morning Post* in 1906,

> the current of events has been too strongly against the ambitious Senators. The one assumption against which they have protested perpetually and with feverish anxiety has been that which classed them with the Legislative Councils of the States. The one thing that popular opinion tenaciously insists upon is in taking that assumption as beyond dispute . . . One has only to look at the manner in which Parliamentary business is transacted to see how in fact the Senate is subsiding into the second place instead of occupying the position which our written law . . . undoubtedly confers upon it.

The Clerk of the Senate and Clerk of Parliaments, Blackmore, went on a year's pre-retirement leave of absence in 1907, and was then succeeded as Clerk of the Senate by the former Clerk-Assistant, Charles Boydell. As senior parliamentary officer, the Clerk of the House of Representatives, Charles Gavan Duffy, contended that he should be appointed Clerk of the Parliaments. Sir Albert Gould wrote to Deakin protesting that the title had gone with the position of Clerk of the Senate since the inception of the Commonwealth and 'should not be altered without some very sufficient reason'. The Government decided, however, that no duties were attached to the Clerk of Parliaments that could not be performed by the Clerk of the Senate, and the title fell into disuse.

In the lower house C. C. Kingston, who was elected unopposed in 1906, had become a member of parliament in name only—a tragic reminder of his former self, seldom seen in the House, and, when he did attend, escorted like an invalid by his wife. He died of cerebro-vascular disease in May 1908, and Deakin went to Adelaide for his State funeral.

In October 1907 J. C. Watson retired from leadership of the Labor Party, though he continued to represent South Sydney for another three years. The ostensible reason for this premature self-effacement was ill health, but two other factors were also important: his wife, who had no interest in politics, resented his frequent absences in Melbourne; and Watson himself was chafing under the discipline imposed upon him by the New South Wales Labor machine. His 45-year-old deputy, Andrew Fisher, was elected to the leadership unanimously on the motion of Fisher's main rival in the party, Billy Hughes. The original choice of deputy to Watson had been between Fisher, the lack-lustre but 'sound' Queensland socialist, and Hughes, the party's brilliant gadfly; but such was the preference in Caucus for Scottish caution over Welsh panache that no deputy leader was elected in 1907. Fisher had plenty of hard common sense and an interest in financial matters ('The Scotch head', as he put it); he was gregarious and well-meaning, though devoid of humour; and he was a man of handsome, even distinguished appearance.

Although he seldom read a book, for fear that he might have to revise his point of view, he looked as if the last thing that point of view needed was revision. Fisher reminded one erudite political correspondent of the Lord Chancellor Thurlow, whose aspect was more solemn and imposing than that of almost any other person in public life, and of whom Fox said: 'It proved him dishonest, since no man could *be* so wise as Thurlow looked'. No one questioned Fisher's honesty—only his ability in situations requiring constant and rapid decision-making.

As party leader, Fisher travelled widely throughout eastern Australia. In the course of one four-week Queensland tour he covered 3578 miles by train, coach, buggy, horseback and railway tricycle; visited thirty-six towns; received sixty deputations, and addressed fifty-one meetings. On one tour of northern New South Wales, he complained about the hardships of parliamentary life and the physical strain imposed upon members. Turning to the Labor Member for New England, Frank Foster, he said: 'Frank, you are a new member. What do you think of it?'

'Well, Andy', replied Foster, 'it's better'n diggin' bloody post holes anyhow'.

In Fisher's case it was better than coalmining, though that experience had come very early in his life. In spite of a regulation prohibiting boys under the age of twelve from working in Scottish mines, Andrew Fisher started work in Ayrshire at the age of ten, after his father had become dusted. While still only seventeen he was elected secretary of the local branch of the Ayrshire Miners' Union, whose central secretary was the socialist Keir Hardie. Fisher emigrated to Queensland at the age of twenty-three, and worked as a manager and engine driver on the Burrum and Gympie fields. He became president of the Gympie branch of the new Labor Party, won a seat in the Queensland Legislative Assembly in 1893, and was Secretary for Railways and Public Works in Dawson's short-lived Ministry.

The strongest bond between the parliamentary Labor Party and the Liberal Protectionist Government was their common interest in Protection, both New and Old. Old Protection was signed, sealed and delivered, and the fiscal issue finally put to rest, by the tariff which Lyne introduced during the second session. The Senate took an active, not to say aggressive, part in this. It returned the Customs Tariff Bill to the House of Representatives with 238 requests for amendments which the financial nature of the Bill prevented the Senate from making itself, and later pressed some of these requests after they had been ignored by the lower chamber. As in past encounters of this kind, each chamber was careful to reserve its rights. The House, 'having regard to the fact that the public welfare [demanded] the early enactment of the tariff', refrained from determining its constitutional rights and obligations, and resolved to consider the Senate's message forthwith. The Senate for its part resolved that 'the action of the House of Representatives in receiving and dealing with the reiterated Requests of the Senate is in compliance with the undoubted constitutional position and rights of the Senate'.

Ironically, the month in which the Customs Tariff and Excise Tariff Acts received assent, June 1908, was also the month in which New Protection was ruled invalid by the High Court. The Court's judgment in *King* v. *Barger* stripped Deakin's Government of its principal achievement to date.

The chain of events leading to this historic judgment began with a general belief that the International Harvester combine was planning to eliminate Australia's agricultural implements industry by dumping North American harvesting machines on the market. Protective duties would be needed to save the local industry, and that exercise in Old Protection would provide an opportunity to ensure that the industry's three thousand workers were being paid and treated fairly by their employers.

Under the Excise Tariff (Agricultural Machinery) Act of 1906 an excise duty equivalent to the customs duty on imported machinery was imposed upon Australian-made agricultural machines, but waived when the manufacturer complied with conditions laid down either by the Arbitration Court or by wages boards which were to become the guardians of New Protection. In 1907 Mr Justice Higgins, who had succeeded his High Court colleague, Mr Justice O'Connor, as President of the Arbitration Court, delivered a judgment that rendered W. G. Barger, a manufacturer of stump-jump ploughs, liable to pay excise of £100 for non-compliance, and H. V. McKay, a larger manufacturer of harvesters, ploughs and winnowers, liable to pay £20 000 for the same reason.

This was the Harvester Judgment, in which Mr Justice Higgins set a 'fair and reasonable' standard of pay, and by this standard found Barger's and McKay's factories wanting. Higgins's excise tariff standard ranged from 7 shillings per day for unskilled labourers to 10 shillings for blacksmiths and carpenters. These rates were some improvement on the 6 shillings per day paid at McKay's factory, but it was remarkable how far they fell short of rates for other forms of employment elsewhere in the community—not least in Spring Street, Melbourne. The Parliamentary Allowances Act of 1907 had raised members' and senators' annual allowances from £400 (£7 14s per week) to £600 (£11 10s per week).

Barger and McKay refused to pay the penalties claimed, and the Common-wealth took them jointly to the High Court. If the Court had still consisted only of Griffith, Barton and O'Connor, its judgment in this case would have been unanimous. All three had been makers of the Constitution. They knew what fears and suspicions had needed to be overcome before public opinion accepted a compact between the colonies, and it was not surprising that as judicial interpreters of that Constitution they were sensitive to public appre-hension. In their concern to preserve the balance between Commonwealth and States, the founding judges took a restrictive view of the powers given to the Commonwealth by Section 51 of the Constitution. They were also influ-enced by American federal precedents, drawing out of them the doctrine of immunity of Commonwealth and State instrumentalities from each other's legislative control, and the doctrine of 'implied prohibitions'. The latter deduced from the Constitution certain limitations on the power of one gov-ernment (usually the Commonwealth) to interfere with the independence of another to an extent that might upset federal equilibrium.

The doctrine of reciprocal immunity was clearly expressed in the High Court's first judgment. In this case, *D'Emden* v. *Pedder* (1904), Griffith and his colleagues had to decide whether a Commonwealth postal employee in Tasmania should be required to pay Tasmanian stamp duty on receipts for his Commonwealth salary. They ruled unanimously that he should not, for such an impost by the State would restrict the free legislative and executive power of the Commonwealth. In *Peterswald* v. *Bartley* (1904) the question was whether the Commonwealth's exclusive power over excise duties should be extended to brewers' licence fees, which were often referred to as 'duties of excise'. The Court's negative answer established the 'implied pro-hibition' principle that constitutional grants of power to the Commonwealth should be interpreted narrowly so as not to trench upon the 'reserved' powers of the States.

The first three justices delivered judgment on an act of parliament for the first time in 1906 when, in the Railway Servants case (1906) they unanimously ruled invalid a clause of the Commonwealth Conciliation and Arbitration Act which gave the Arbitration Court jurisdiction over State industrial employees. This was the clause that had brought Deakin's first Ministry undone two years before, and now the High Court was confirming Deakin's original doubts about its constitutional propriety.

Two years later came a much more important clash between the High Court and parliament, and with it the first serious division of opinion on the Bench. By then the founding justices had become accustomed, though not reconciled, to the prickly company of Justices Isaacs and Higgins. Isaacs was a spare, dark-skinned man with incandescent eyes, protruding lips and pro-truding intellect: 'the jewling', as Barton once called him in an unguarded and unworthy moment. Higgins was icy and didactic in manner, an Irish Protestant with 'almost priggishly lofty principles'. Both men had attended the 1897–98 convention, but they were radical nationalists who would rather have seen a stronger Commonwealth than the one that emerged from those debates. As judges, they opposed their colleagues' narrow interpretation of Commonwealth powers, bending over backwards to side with parliament.

In the cases of Barger and McKay, the Court ruled against the Commonwealth by a majority of three to two. The majority opinion—delivered by Griffith, with Barton and O'Connor concurring—held that the charging of excise amounted to an attempt by the Commonwealth to regulate conditions of employment without any authority under the Constitution. Isaacs, on the other hand, began his opinion with a quotation from the United States Supreme Court:

> The power to tax is the one great power upon which the whole national fabric is based. It is as necessary to the existence and prosperity of a nation as is the air he breathes to the natural man. It is not only the power to destroy, but it is also the power to keep alive.

Higgins, in his own dissenting opinion, asked: 'Why should the Commonwealth Parliament be able to levy taxation with a view to the benefit of the manufacturers, and not be able to levy taxation with a view to the benefit of their employees?'

The High Court ruled against parliament in two more cases that year: the Union Label case, in which a majority of 3–2 held that the stamp of union approval provided for in the Trade Marks Act exceeded the meaning of 'trade marks' in Section 51 of the Constitution; and *Huddart Parker* v. *Moorehead*, in which a majority, with Isaacs dissenting, held that a section of the Australian Industries Preservation Act prohibiting monopolies among corporations exceeded the proper use of parliament's power, under Section 51, to make laws with respect to 'foreign corporations, and trading or financial corporations formed within the limits of the Commonwealth'.

These two rebuffs were of less concern to the Government than the striking down of New Protection. Deakin reiterated his Government's determination that this policy should be associated with the tariff, but how could that be done after Barger's case? During the Address-in-Reply debate when parliament reassembled in September, Fisher spoke generally of the High Court as 'a conservative body' which had 'always conserved the rights and interests of those in possession rather than initiated or opened up new interests'. On the other side of the House, W. H. Irvine, the former Victorian Premier who had been elected to the seat of Flinders in 1906, mocked the scheme for New Protection which Deakin had placed before parliament nine months before:

> . . . a Board of three omniscient archangels', he said, 'whose duty it would be to watch over the industrial interests of Australia, to see that the wage-earners got good wages, the manufacturers fair profits, and the consumers cheap wares—in other words, to bring about the industrial millenium. I do not suppose that we shall hear more of that scheme, and never regarded it as a serious political proposition.
> Mr DEAKIN.—There the honorable member is wrong.
> Mr W. H. IRVINE.—I looked upon it as a rather highly coloured balloon, sent up to amuse a House jaded with the discussion of the Tariff. It has

been punctured in a good many places since then, and is now rather flabby.

Mr DEAKIN.—If it has been punctured, it will not float.

Mr IRVINE.—It will take more gas than the united efforts of Ministers are capable of to make it float again.

Deakin's only hope, and a frail one at that, lay in a bill to amend the Constitution. But the best the law officers could do—an amendment to the Constitution permitting parliament to legislate with respect to 'the employment and remuneration of labour in any industry which, in the opinion of the [as yet non-existent] Inter-State Commission is protected by duties of Customs'—found favour with neither his own party nor Labor. With the Invalid and Old Age Pensions Act and the related Surplus Revenue Act passed, and New Protection seemingly out of reach, the Labor Party no longer had any reason to continue supporting Deakin. In July an interstate Labor conference voted against alliances with or the granting of electoral immunity to any other party, but this did not prevent Fisher and his colleagues from helping Deakin's Ministry to survive a want of confidence motion ('That the financial proposals of the Government are unsatisfactory to this House') which the leader of the Opposition moved on 20 October, after Lyne's Budget speech.

The relatively short debate on this motion was notable less for vehemence inside the chamber than for the unfamiliar intrusion of noises off. When Reid had been speaking for about an hour in support of his motion, members suddenly heard a burst of cheering. Speaker Holder leaned forward in alarm, and the Clerk and Serjeant-at-Arms hurried outside. The beautifully tiled floor of the vestibule, with its circular motto, 'Where no counsel is the people fall', was crowded with fifty or sixty noisily gesticulating men, all of whom were unemployed. They had been waiting from 2 p.m., when they had expected to be shown to places in the gallery, until 4 p.m., when they were finally refused admission. At the urging of the assistant secretary of the Socialist Party, Percy Laidler, they then tried to rush the doors into Queen's Hall, but were blocked by officers of the parliament and a handful of police.

Before they left the building there was much shouting at members who stood looking down from upper levels ('You parasites! You mongrels!'), and Laidler in an impromptu speech referred approvingly to Victor Grayson, a British Labor member who had recently been removed from the House of Commons for obstructing business. 'If the Labor members will not imitate Victor Grayson', he said,

we will do it from outside . . . We will make you members of Parliament sit up. You are loafing away your time inside there over a motion of no confidence in Deakin, while men are here who have had no breakfast and no dinner. Waste your time! We thank you for the kind reception you gave us today. We thank you for refusing us the right to sit and listen in the galleries of our own Parliament.

This was the first occasion on which the people mobbed their counsellors at work, but it was not to be the last.

On 5 November the Labor Caucus resolved that in view of the Government's unsatisfactory attitude to New Protection and other legislation 'the relations existing between the [Labor] party and the government should not continue'. The decision was binding on all Labor members. At the close of business in the House of Representatives next day the Labor leader made clear his party's position, but to everyone's surprise he moved no motion. It was as if the amiable Fisher had no stomach for executions, and Deakin would have to help him. On the next sitting day, 10 November 1908, the Prime Minister moved 'That the House at its rising adjourn until tomorrow at 3 o'clock'. It was not the sort of motion that might have been expected to bring down a government, but there was no reason why it should not serve that purpose when the die was already cast and the numbers were known. 'That proposes a difference of only half an hour in the usual time of meeting', explained Deakin, 'but it is enough for the purpose. We shall equally accept any amendment of this formal motion as a challenge to the Government'.

Fisher then moved that all words in the Prime Minister's motion after the word 'That' be left out. The House divided; Fisher's amendment was agreed to, with forty-nine Labor, Anti-Socialist and Corner members voting against thirteen Deakinites; and so fell the second Deakin Ministry. On 11 November—a date which on more than one subsequent occasion would prove to be the most inherently eventful in Australia's political calendar—Deakin tendered his resignation to a new Governor-General, Lord Dudley. His Excellency then sent for Fisher, who had Deakin's promise of much the same kind of support as Watson's Ministry had received briefly from its predecessor.

This was the end of three or four elevens and cut-throat euchre. Labor wanted office on its own, and if the non-Labor groups were to oppose Fisher's Government effectively they would have to combine. Just as the reasons for continued Liberal–Labor co-operation had vanished, so also had vanished the two greatest obstacles in the way of non-Labor combination. The fiscal issue was dead and buried, and soon after the change of government George Reid, with whom it was unlikely that Deakin could ever have collaborated, stepped down from leadership of the Anti-Socialists in favour of his deputy, Joseph Cook.

Seat of Government

One of the first measures put through parliament by Fisher's Government brought to a merciful end something which had dragged on far too long—the determination of a seat of government, to which parliament would eventually move from its 'temporary' quarters in Melbourne. The Constitution provided that parliament should select a site of at least 100 square miles within the State of New South Wales and no closer than 100 miles to Sydney. Conceivably this decision might have been made by the first parliament; the site finally chosen was among those recommended before federation, and for the first three months of 1901 the Commonwealth's Minister for Home Affairs and the Premier of New South Wales were one and the same person, Sir William Lyne. The opportunity was there, but nothing came of it. Barton's Government had other priorities, and in any case the struggle by pressure groups, not the least of which included Lyne himself, would probably have prevented speedy resolution. Before it was all over, the process of finding a site for the national capital involved seven Common- wealth governments, five New South Wales governments, two royal com- missions, nine Commonwealth Ministers for Home Affairs, four lapsed bills and three acts of Commonwealth parliament.

In 1899, after the passing of the second constitutional referendum had fixed the seat of government in New South Wales, the Lyne Government appointed a Royal Commissioner—Alexander Oliver, President of the New South Wales Land Appeal Court, and a fishing companion of the Premier—to report on the merits of sites already proposed by various Fed- eral Capital Leagues. Although Oliver was sixty-eight years old, and had lost one of his arms in a shooting accident, he showed great stamina in examin- ing twenty-three sites, at fourteen of which he held public inquiries to separ- ate truth from local boasting. Writing about this many years later, he recalled the unswerving loyalty of witnesses to their climates:

> No matter what the day temperature might be, the nights were always cool, and if the districts rejoiced in a steady sequence of seasonable frosts, the inhabitants were all the better for them . . . Where such enclosures as cemeteries existed, I was assured that nine-tenths of the occupants had been "undesirables" who came to the township as a last resort. Medical men came, looked and went away disheartened; or if they stayed, became poultry farmers, or cultivated an orchard or a vineyard. An immense pumpkin chased me round several sites. It was the silent witness for cli- mate as well as soil, and not being liable to cross-examination, did yeoman's service.

After almost a year on the job, Oliver recommended three sites: the Bombala-Eden region, an area of 1200 square miles in the extreme south- east of New South Wales, which was his first preference; the Orange region, 833 square miles in the central west; and the Yass region, an area of 930 square miles about half way on a south-westerly bearing from Sydney to the Victorian border, including the parish of Canberra and nearby Lake George.

Lyne's own preference was soon to be influenced by the narrow majority (606 votes) with which he won the federal seat of Hume, and in the years to come, with his usual lumbering shrewdness, he sought to advance the cause of Albury and Tumut in that south-western electorate against the various causes being championed by other members. The Member for Eden- Monaro, Austin Chapman, spoke up for the more elevated sites of Bombala and Dalgety in his own electorate. He won support from members who resented the crude forcefulness of Lyne's advocacy, but some New South Wales members thought Chapman's high country too cold and too close to Melbourne. Reid favoured Orange, which was dismissed from the running relatively early. Deakin, who was Prime Minister for exactly half the period of parliament's indecision, did little to settle the issue or to assuage Melbourne–Sydney rivalry.

As the minister responsible, Sir William Lyne expressed the decidedly slim hope in 1901 that parliament would meet in the 'new Washington' within three to five years. In the following year separate parties of senators and representatives visited more than a dozen sites each, the latter tour being delayed by Lyne, some said, so that Bombala and Dalgety would be seen at their wintry worst. At Dalgety, an embryonic township set on a treeless, boulder-strewn slope beside the upper Snowy River, Billy Hughes was 'quite unable to maintain [his] normal circulation when riding in a conveyance, and had to go on horseback'. 'A sergeant of police', Hughes later told parliament,

> who, from his position, was unable to express himself with that freedom that truth demands, and who was seated near a gentleman on the box seat—a gentleman who happened by coincidence to own the entire district—asked me, when I observed that it was fearfully cold, to step back a few paces, whereupon he informed me, "This is the warmest winter we have had for seventeen years."

A Royal Commission of four experts appointed at Lyne's instigation issued a final report in 1903 which ranked various sites according to criteria of accessibility, water, land cost, building cost, climate, soil and general suitability. This ranking appeared to favour two of Lyne's preferred sites, Albury and Tumut, and for that reason it probably did more harm than good to the credibility of Minister and Royal Commission alike. At Chapman's insistence, the Commission produced a supplementary report on Dalgety. Barton's only contribution on the subject before retiring to the High Court was his rather wistful proposal for a conference of both houses—an invitation which the Senate, unwilling to be outnumbered, was hardly likely to accept.

In October 1903 Lyne initiated a Seat of Government Bill, with the name of the site left out. Much of the debate in the lower chamber concerned the pros and cons of having a bush capital, which some saw as a Victorian plot. 'Who sought to put the Capital in the bush if not the Victorian people?' asked Bruce Smith (F, Parkes, N). Did the Sydney people want the Capital to be in the bush? Were the Sydney people not quite prepared to let the Federal Parliament decide as to how near to Sydney the Capital should be? The House of Representatives voted to fill the blank space in Lyne's Bill with the name of one of his own sites, Tumut; but the Senate voted for Bombala, and sent the Bill back for amendment. The lower house stuck to Tumut, and the Bill lapsed at prorogation.

Another bill, initiated in the Senate, passed through all stages under the Watson Ministry. Opinion was again divided about the bush, and not all Victorians wanted the capital there. Arthur Robinson (F, Wannon, V) thought the 'small official atmosphere . . . in a Federal Capital in the bush would make it all the more easy to cover up injustice and wickedness of every kind', and J. G. Wilson (F, Corangamite, V) said that although a bush capital 'would be somewhat lively for a short time during the Parliamentary session, it would for the rest of the year be a place of magnificent distances and deadly dullness.'

Mr Joseph COOK.—And of silent solitude.
Mr. WILSON.—The honourable member has supplied the very words I wanted. In the districts surrounding a bush capital, there will be places where melancholic lunatics could live and thrive.

In the upper house, Senator McGregor defended the bush, though somewhat facetiously. Even Victorian members would be glad to go from Melbourne, he said, because 'they will get away from the controlling influence of local opinion and parochial sentiment. They will get among the kangaroos and emus, and will have freer minds and more patriotic sentiments'. Again the Senate chose Bombala; but when the lower house voted this time for a site near Dalgety, the Senate accepted its amendment and Dalgety (little more than a court house, public school, two stores, a smithy and a public house called 'The Horse and Jockey') was incorporated in the Seat of Government Act, 1904.

This was not to say that the new Washington would be built there. The recently elected Premier of New South Wales, Joseph Carruthers, began pressing the merits of Lyndhurst, a site in his own electorate 190 miles west of Sydney. He dared the Commonwealth to drive in survey pegs at Dalgety so that New South Wales could take action in the High Court for trespass. When this challenge was declined, he transferred his attention from Lyndhurst to an area that had already found some favour with Oliver and others—the triangle formed by Goulburn, Queanbeyan and Yass. From Goulburn one railway line ran south of Lake George to Queanbeyan and Cooma, and another (the main Sydney–Melbourne line) ran west to Yass. The third side of the triangle consisted of an area formerly known as the Limestone Plains, a wide valley defined by moderately high mountains and traversed by a tributary of the Murrumbidgee called the Molonglo. The earliest name on this third part of the map was Canberra, a settlement consisting of an Anglican church, a school and several farms, one of which served as a post office.

At the suggestion of Carruthers, Sir John Forrest visited the Canberra valley in 1907, probably driving out in a buggy from Queanbeyan, which was then a town of 1260 people. Although he remained loyal to Dalgety, other federal parliamentarians who visited the area later that year were impressed by it. Some members had in fact seen these plains in the distance while inspecting Queanbeyan five years earlier. Watson, whose opinion was widely respected, turned his support from Dalgety to the site which by then was being referred to as Yass-Canberra. He was encouraged in this by the elderly Usher of the Black Rod for the New South Wales Legislative Council, Stewart Mowle, who earlier in his life had managed a property in the district, 'Yarralumla'. After visiting the Yass-Canberra district in 1907, Watson wrote to Mowle, who was one of his electors in South Sydney, saying: 'For general suitability and beauty there is none that I've seen which approaches it'.

Carruthers's successor as Premier, Charles Wade, asked Deakin to settle the matter. The Prime Minister asked Wade for all New South Wales reports on the Yass-Canberra site, and his Attorney-General, Groom, initiated a Seat of Government Bill, only to have it lapse at prorogation in June 1908. Groom then initiated yet another bill, 'to determine more definitely the Seat of Government of the Commonwealth in the neighbourhood of Dalgety', but it lapsed as well. Finally, after Labor had taken office in November, the Minister for Home Affairs, Hugh Mahon, introduced a Seat of Government Bill which lasted the distance. Although it provided that the seat of government should be in the 'district of Yass-Canberra', the location was still to be settled by voting during the debates, and the result was by no means certain.

Dalgety's cause was weakened by the illness of Austin Chapman, who had suffered a stroke. Willie Kelly, the arrogant Eton-educated Member for Wentworth, asked the House why Chapman had chosen to convalesce in Queensland instead of availing himself of the allegedly healthy climate at Dalgety. Another Sydney anti-socialist, William Johnson (Lang) said that Dalgety was a place where coaches were blown over by the wind. An attempt had once been made to rear polar bears there, he said, but they could not stand the climate.

'Is this game of bluff to go on to all eternity?' asked Reid.

The Treasurer [Lyne] is telling his friends in his large electorate, in which he has three or four Capital sites, "Austin has got the whip hand of me so far, but I shall be too much for him, I am lying dark on the weather bow. We have arranged that he shall get Dalgety twice, at intervals of four years. I am going to get my choice twice, at intervals of four years, and then I am going to have Tooma for a finish in the year 1950."

In successive ballots the House of Representatives eliminated, in order of being struck off the ballot, Lake George, Albury, Orange, Bombala, Tumut, Armidale, Lyndhurst, and Tooma, the last of which was not far from Dalgety, but in Lyne's electorate. In the final ballot Yass-Canberra beat Dalgety, 39–33. The Senate ballot papers listed six sites—Armidale, Dalgety-Tooma, Dalgety, Lyndhurst, Tumut and Yass-Canberra. The last two received eighteen votes each, the other four receiving no votes and consequently being eliminated. On the second ballot a Victorian Liberal, Senator James McColl, changed his vote from Tumut to Yass-Canberra, thus producing a narrow majority of 19–17 for the latter. When later criticised in Victoria, Senator McColl justified his change of mind by alleging that the Government had put Tumut up instead of Dalgety merely to cause disagreement between the houses so that Dalgety might be run again, successfully.

Thanks to Senator McColl the houses had not disagreed, and the Seat of Government (Yass-Canberra) Act received assent on 14 December 1908. The new capital was still almost two decades away, but its general location was now settled. Early the next year Charles Scrivener, a district surveyor borrowed by the Commonwealth from the New South Wales Government, marked out an area of more than 900 square miles, east of Yass and including the town of Queanbeyan. The New South Wales Government would not part with Queanbeyan, but agreed to almost everything else. Federal parliament passed a Seat of Government Acceptance Bill in November 1909, and the following month the New South Wales parliament passed a Seat of Government Surrender Bill. The rest of this particular story, destined to proceed in fits and starts, need not concern us yet.

4

Fusion

'Judas!'

How much simpler everything might have been in parliament for some years to come if Deakin and his dwindling band of Liberals had gone into coalition with Labor in 1908. The two groups still had many objectives in common, and together they might have formed a government of such unaccustomed stability as to break the Opposition's heart. But it was not to be. Labor had sworn off alliances and in any case Deakin, although he had once spoken hopefully of 'civilising the Labor Party', was now permanently estranged from the 'Labor Legions with their drastic discipline'. Deakin would much rather have governed through his own kind of Liberal Party: 'Liberal always, radical often and reactionary never'. As there was numerically no chance of that, he set about civilising the conservatives and making allies out of them. For the next few years Australia was to be governed alternately by Labor and Liberal-Conservative ministries, each in its turn pursuing much the same kind of policy. In a word, that policy was Deakin's.

No one would have questioned the man's integrity had he looked to the left for allies. It was a very different matter for a liberal-radical to turn right, however, and there were many who wondered about his motives. 'If you come in now', Lord Northcote wrote to him from London in April 1909, 'people may say Deakin will do anything to get back to office'. Although well aware of that, Deakin was convinced that 'fusion' with his own former right wing (Forrest's Corner group) and Joseph Cook's anti-socialists offered the only means of saving Australian liberalism. Deakin would join these uncongenial partners only if they undertook to implement the policies he regarded as vital.

The second minority Labor Ministry, which took office on 13 November 1908, did not see much of parliament, which went into a long recess four weeks later. Unlike Watson, but like all future Labor Prime Ministers, Fisher had his Ministers chosen for him by Caucus, though he was able to allocate portfolios as he wished. The Prime Minister, with his vaunted Scotch head, became Treasurer. Hughes, who had now been at the Bar for five years, was Attorney-General; Batchelor, Minister for External Affairs; Mahon, Home Affairs; Senator Pearce, Defence; Frank Tudor (Lab, Yarra, V), Trade and Customs. There were nine Ministers altogether, and most of them were from the 'small' States: three South Australians, two Western Australians and one Queenslander outnumbered the remaining two New South Welshmen and one Victorian. Labor held a minority of seats in both houses (twenty-seven in the lower chamber and fifteen in the Senate), but before the worth of Deakin's informal support could be properly tested parliament was prorogued. During the next six months all three Opposition groups busied themselves with the matter of fusion.

During February Deakin and Forrest held separate discussions with Cook. Deakin kept his distance more than Forrest, who was anxious to eliminate the hazard of triangular contests at the next election, and hopeful that if Deakin declined to lead a fusion then he, Forrest, might manage to do so. That hope was soon extinguished by Cook's blunt refusal to serve under the Emperor of the West.

Joe Cook could have told Deakin a thing or two about changing political company. Like Fisher he had started work as a boy miner, in Staffordshire, where his father was killed in a pit accident. He emigrated to Australia at the age of twenty-seven, found colliery employment in Lithgow, and in 1891 was elected President of the local Labor Electoral League and a member of the New South Wales Legislative Assembly. Although he became Leader of the parliamentary Labor Party, he later refused to sign the party's new pledge to accept Caucus direction, and consequently was returned to parliament as a Labor independent. He then accepted the Postmaster-Generalship in Reid's Ministry, and was never forgiven for it by his former Labor colleagues. By 1901, when Cook won the federal seat of Parramatta, he had become a confirmed Free Trader. Humourless but shrewd, he was a political tortoise who had beaten several hares in his time.

'Mr Deakin pursues his enigmatic methods of action', wrote Deakin himself as *Morning Post* correspondent in April 1909. 'Of Mr Deakin nothing can be prognosticated with confidence.' Among his actions was the founding of a Commonwealth Liberal Party. This party, which had neither branches nor funds, was not intended to be a vehicle for fusion; indeed some of its members assumed that at the next election it would be fighting socialists and anti-socialists alike. Such an election might not be far off, for in March Andrew Fisher had delivered in his home electorate a detailed set of proposals, published widely throughout the country, which read very much like an election policy. In addition to certain unfinished business from Deakin's Ministry—acceptance of the Northern Territory from South Australia, development of the federal capital and construction of a transcontinental railway—Fisher also outlined some proposals which Deakin could not support. Labor would seek amendment of the Constitution to enforce New Protection; it would nationalise the iron industry; and put a tax on unimproved land values.

Joseph Cook by David Low

Aware that Fisher might seek a premature dissolution when parliament reassembled, Deakin resumed discussions with Cook and Forrest. They met at Parliament House on 24 May, two days before parliament was to start its next session.

On the following day Deakin chaired a Liberal-Protectionist party meeting, of which a verbatim account was kept by the Victorian Protectionist member, Hume Cook. All but two of the nineteen Deakinites were present. Deakin began by reminding them that Fisher's Ministry was in office only because the Liberals had promised 'conditional support contingent upon that Government carrying on the policy of the Ministry it succeeded'. That position had now been changed by the Prime Minister's announcement of a policy which showed wide divergence from the Liberal programme. He would therefore seek authority from the meeting to inform Fisher that the Liberals could no longer extend support. If that authority was granted, he would explain the terms of an agreement he had already arrived at with Cook and Forrest.

Sir William Lyne, who favoured continuation of selective support for Labor, rose to his feet at once and said that he entirely disagreed with the negotiations that had taken place. Mr Deakin should have stood by his policy and have had nothing to do with Joe Cook or any others, he said. If the fusion was to come about, as he hoped to God it would not, he must then become the bitter enemy of all those present. The country was not going to be governed by conservatives. He would rather go out of politics and keep his reputation and his honour than consort with his enemies of twenty-five years' standing.

'At this stage Sir William exchanged some very angry words with Mr Crouch', recorded Hume Cook.

> He told Crouch that he was a liar and an arrant empty-headed humbug. Continuing, he said: "The Oppositionists will destroy our country. To join with them, or let them join with us, will be a piece of political treachery unequalled in the history of the southern world . . . So far as the Ministry is concerned there is no act of administration to which exception could be taken. To turn them out at this juncture will therefore be the greatest act of treachery ever perpetrated and will leave us up to our necks in mud."

Two other members spoke in similar, though less emotional vein; but when a vote was taken, withdrawal of support from Fisher's Ministry was approved by eleven to six.

Deakin then listed four points of agreement with the other two groups: no interference with the Protectionist tariff policy; New Protection through State wages boards and an Inter-State Commission, provided this could be achieved by means of a constitutional amendment that did not weaken the federal spirit; adoption of Liberal policy on defence, consisting mainly of universal training and coastal defence, with an addendum that Australia should establish contact with British naval and military authorities; and finally the planning of a more equitable basis for financial relations between the Commonwealth and the States after expiry of the Braddon clause in 1911, not merely an extension of that clause.

Again the rogue elephant of Hume went on the rampage. 'The statement is
a very pretty one', said Lyne,

> but neither Mr Deakin nor the members of this party realise the character
> of the men to whom we have been committed. They cannot be trusted. I
> would not besmirch my name by touching them . . . If the party does the
> thing contemplated we will go down, down, down as conservatives! I do
> not want to say harsh things, but I will *act*! It is impossible for me to be
> friends with "the chief" any longer for I cannot shake hands with a traitor.
> I will not say any more now for I am going to leave the room. I cannot
> longer associate with men whom I despise. I shall denounce all those who
> join the Opposition.

Deakin calmly reminded Lyne of the downfall of the first Labor ministry in
1904, when

> he aspersed me . . . almost as much as now. Yet I took no notice! We joined
> afterwards for years in another ministry. He did not then denounce me,
> whilst I chose to forget that he had ever used any hard words. Again he is
> angry, but I will not allow anything to interfere with the deep feelings of
> friendship I have for him nor with the obligations I am under for services
> rendered.

Not even Affable Alfred could soothe Sir William Lyne when his temper
was up. 'I will not join with men who will sell me', he roared, 'and I will fight
very hard and in a way that will be hard upon those who are now turning
dog on me'. With that he left the room and the party, sitting thereafter as an
Independent. The remaining Liberal-Protectionists voted for fusion by thirteen to three. Of those who felt as Lyne did, J. M. Chanter (Riverina, N) later
joined the Labor party, G. H. Wise (Gippsland, V) continued to describe himself somewhat irrelevantly as a Protectionist, and Senator W. A. Trenwith
(V) became an Independent.

Before the opening of parliament, fifteen Deakinites, thirty-eight Anti-
Socialists and twelve members of the Corner group met in the Opposition
room to choose their leader. Reid nominated Cook, but there was no seconder. Deakin was elected unanimously. The new party—at first known
simply as the Deakin-Cook Party, and later by the title of Deakin's still-born
organisation in Melbourne, the Commonwealth Liberal Party—would outnumber Labor in the lower house by forty-four to twenty-seven (plus four
Independents who usually supported Labor) and in the Senate by twenty-
one to fifteen. Fisher's end was near.

On the morning of 26 May, the day parliament was to reassemble, the
Melbourne *Herald*'s chief parliamentary reporter, Bert Cook, called on Sir
William Lyne at the Windsor Hotel. The rogue elephant was boiling over
with rage. They had a whisky, and Cook asked him what he intended to do.
'What am I going to do?' said Lyne. 'I'll tell you what I'm going to do. I am
going to point at Deakin and say, "Judas! Judas! Judas!"'

The final blow against the Government was delivered suddenly and
almost contemptuously, for the executioner was not Deakin but a junior
member of the Opposition. W. H. Kelly, a 32-year-old Eton-educated
'gentleman of independent means', had two claims to parliamentary fame:

the anathema in which he was held by Labor, and his occasional smoking of cigars in the chamber, until the Speaker put a stop to it. Hughes once said that Willie Kelly had 'as much idea of the work of the world as a butterfly has of casting an 81-ton gun'. He should also have admitted that Kelly's supercilious manner had a way of getting under Labor skins.

When the Address-in-Reply debate resumed on 27 May, Deakin uttered no more than 'Mr Speaker—' before Lyne shouted, 'Judas! Judas! Judas!' For a few seconds the House was hushed. Then Lyne cried out again: 'Judas! Judas! Judas!'

Mr. SPEAKER.—I ask the honourable member for Hume to withdraw his remark.
Sir WILLIAM LYNE.—I did not refer to any individual, personally. I have a right to say that there is a leading Judas here.
HONORABLE MEMBERS.—Shame!
Mr SPEAKER.—Order! I did not understand the honorable member for Hume to withdraw the expression.
Sir WILLIAM LYNE.—I shall always be found obeying your rulings, Mr Speaker. I withdraw.

The debate continued without further interruption until about 4 p.m., when the Prime Minister was explaining his government's intention to seek larger industrial powers for the Commonwealth by referendum. As Fisher resumed his seat, Kelly—catching the Speaker's eye before a frantically waving Lyne, who seemed to have guessed what was about to happen— proposed a motion that the debate be now adjourned. Under Standing Orders the question had to be put at once, without debate, and it was resolved in the affirmative, 39 to 30. Fisher then moved that the House adjourn, saying that he regarded the vote on Kelly's motion as one of no confidence in the Government. Before that question was resolved in the affirmative, Fisher asked whether Kelly's motion had been submitted with the concurrence of the Leader of the Opposition. 'Certainly', replied Deakin.

At the following day's sitting Fisher immediately moved for adjournment, and during the seven hours of adjournment debate Labor members elaborated on the theme of Judas. None could match Hughes for vitriol:

[The Honorable Member for Ballarat] has explained and justified the assassination of the Watson Government which he promised to loyally support. Had De Quincey lived until now he would have been able to include in his delightful essay on *Murder as a Fine Art* the methods of the honorable member for Ballarat, for no man has adopted such a variety of methods, and none has contrived to more successfully evade the consequences of his political crimes. His last assassination in some respects out-Herods Herod, but his former achievements ran it hard for first place. Then there was the assassination of the Reid Government. He made that Government, he pledged himself to support it, he destroyed it by a speech which the right honorable member for East Sydney very properly assumed was not only the beginning of the end but the end itself . . . Having perhaps exhausted all the finer possibilities of the art, or desiring to exhibit his versatility in his execrable profession he came out and bludgeoned us in the open light of day. It was then that I heard from this side of the House some mention of Judas. I do not agree with that; it is not fair—to Judas, for whom there is this to be said, that he did not gag the man whom he betrayed, nor did he fail to hang himself afterwards.

At the next sitting, 1 June, Fisher announced that he had submitted to the Governor-General a written statement of grounds for dissolution of the lower house; that when Lord Dudley had denied this request, he had tendered the Ministry's resignation; and that the Governor-General had commissioned Deakin to form a new administration. So Alfred Deakin, in his fifty-third year, embarked upon his first and last experience as Prime Minister with a clear majority. His Ministers came from all components of the fusion. Cook, who became Minister for Defence, wanted the arch-conservatives W. H. Irvine and Bruce Smith (Lib, Parkes, N) in Cabinet, but Deakin and Forrest (Treasurer) would not have them. Deakin wanted Littleton Groom as Attorney-General; but at Cook's insistence, and against his own better judgement, he gave that portfolio to the South Australian barrister, Patrick McMahon Glynn.

Deakin felt that Glynn was 'so impractical in mind, and in law so overburdened with knowledge, that his judgement is heavily handicapped'. For his part, Glynn doubted that the new Prime Minister's reputation for consistency had been enhanced by the fusion. 'Many still say that he is not to be trusted', he wrote in his diary. 'Yet his personal friends believe in his integrity. What truth can there be in history, when a leader is a puzzle to his contempories?'

In the privacy of one of his notebooks, Deakin took a very different view of his own motives. 'Not for myself O God', he wrote in one of the many prayers it was his custom to compose, 'Not for myself—for myself least and last—but for Thy purpose, for Thy will, for my country and kin first and always be my retention of official place, the extent of whatever power I have or may be given, and the use of all else attaching to me'. Yet undeniably Deakin now found himself in strange company. 'Behind me', he wrote to his sister Catherine, 'sit the whole of my opponents since Federation'.

The next few weeks of parliament were generally tedious. Fisher made a poor fist of a want of confidence motion, and some of his colleagues droned away in stonewalling speeches of remorseless duration. On 9 July, and resuming after adjournment on 13 July, William Webster (Gwydir, N), a former quarryman and builder known to his party colleagues as 'Jawbone,' set a record of 10 hours 57 minutes which—thanks to subsequent use of the closure, and the adoption of time limits three years later—was never to be broken in the lower house. The following day a fusionist, Dr J. G. Wilson (Corangamite, V), asked the Speaker for permission to lay on the table the jawbone of a bull, which he had brought into the chamber with him, 'to commemorate the great muscular effort of the honorable member for Gwydir'. Sir Frederick Holder replied that he did not think the Honorable Member for Corangamite required an answer.

This was one of Speaker Holder's last rulings. He was a man of frail constitution in his sixtieth year, and the tension of the past few weeks had affected him noticeably. Once, when hurrying to catch the Adelaide train, he became so exhausted that he could not talk for several minutes. At the sitting of 22 July the House of Representatives, still simmering with recrimination, stayed in committee all night. Although the chairman of committees was presiding, the Speaker was also present in wig and gown, having been summoned from his suite to receive the committee's report. At about 5 a.m., when Sir William Lyne was once again probing the subject of fusion, like a tongue unable to resist a sore tooth, Sir Frederick was seated at one end of the Treasury front bench talking to the Minister for Home Affairs, George Fuller (Illawarra, N). This time Lyne was belabouring the new Minister for External Affairs, Groom, whose father had died during the first year of parliament:

> Sir WILLAIM LYNE.— I am not hungering for office. I was never happier in my life than I am now, when I can kick and cuff the Government with impunity. The only thing which causes me to be unhappy is the sight of the scion of a good old man destroying his career. Surely the remains of his father must be turning in the grave.
> HONORABLE MEMBERS.—Shame!
> Sir WILLIAM LYNE.—There is no shame about the matter. All the shame rests with the man who has acted as the honorable member for Darling Downs has done.
> Mr JOSEPH COOK.—Coward.
> The CHAIRMAN.—Order! I must ask the Minister for Defence to withdraw that remark . . .

On the front bench Sir Frederick Holder muttered 'Dreadful, dreadful!' and slumped sideways, being caught before he fell to the floor. He was carried unconscious to his bedroom, where three medically qualified members (Drs Salmon, Maloney and Wilson) and a doctor from outside the House diagnosed cerebral haemorrhage. Sir Frederick did not recover consciousness, and at 4.18 p.m., as the Adelaide *Advertiser* put it, Mr Speaker received his call. A flag was immediately hoisted at half mast, signalling the death of a distinguished parliamentarian, the first death to have occurred at Parliament House during its federal tenancy. The flag would have been either the Union Jack or the Commonwealth's blue ensign, which had been gazetted six years previously. Both were used on such occasions.

The Speaker's death had a chastening effect upon the House, and less was heard in future about treachery and betrayal. Less was heard also about political neutrality in the Chair. The office became virtually a party appointment, as it was already in most State parliaments. Without consulting the Opposition, Deakin lent his support to an undistinguished but loyal personal follower, Dr Carty Salmon. Salmon was elected in his place over two other fusionists, Sir Philip Fysh (Denison, T) and Agar Wynne (Balaclava, V). Sir George Reid, newly knighted, could have had the Speakership if he wished; but he had lost interest in parliament. His attendance record slipped again, and in December he was appointed first Australian High Commissioner in the United Kingdom, a position created, not before time, by the High Commissioner Act of 1909.

Dr Salmon set a pattern for the election and conduct of his successors in the Chair. Henceforth a change of government would usually mean a change in the Speakership, and although future Speakers would be to various degrees impartial in their conduct of proceedings it would also be normal for them to attend meetings of the parties to which they owed their election. They would sometimes vote in committee, and sometimes even participate in debate.

Deakin's third Ministry had the satisfaction of seeing parliament produce what he regarded as 'the finest harvest of any session'. For Deakin himself the session was marred by poor health and more frequent lapses of memory. 'I have the testimony of a celebrated traveller', he said during the Estimates debate, '—my recent unfortunate illness affects my memory as to names—who has visited Africa, South America and Papua, and who said that . . . he regards the system in Papua as being the most severe and complete'. The name he could not recall was Beatrice Grimshaw.

Some Opposition speakers tried stonewalling again, but they were soon cut short by Standing Orders. Closure was moved for the first time in September, while 'Jawbone' Webster was on his feet, and on seventeen occasions before the end of the session. In little more than six months parliament passed thirty-one acts.

One of the session's main concerns was defence. In accordance with his undertaking to Cook about liaison with British military authorities, Deakin invited the Empire's most renowned soldier, Lord Kitchener, to visit Australia and report upon its defences. A Defence Bill initiated by Cook in August established a system of compulsory military training, but did not go as far as some of those members most outspoken about defence (particularly Hughes on the Opposition benches) would have liked.

As a culmination of the interest already shown by Fisher's Ministry and the second Deakin Ministry in establishing a navy, and of concern about Germany's growing naval power, the House of Representatives passed a resolution in November 1909 calling for the construction in Britain of a battle cruiser to become the flagship of an Australian fleet unit. Fisher and some other Labor members voted with the government for this resolution, but party policy prevented them from agreeing that the matter was sufficiently urgent to be financed by borrowing rather than by the slower means of taxation. An Inter-State Labor Conference the year before had resolved that loans for non-productive purposes imposed an unjustifiable burden on posterity. Deakin insisted on the quicker alternative. The Naval Loan Act was passed, and before the end of the year an order was placed for a cruiser that was to be known as H.M.A.S. *Australia*.

Notably absent from Deakin's legislative harvest was any revival of New Protection, even in the diluted form of his agreement with Cook and Forrest. All the Government did in this regard was ask the States to refer appropriate powers to the Commonwealth, as the Constitution permitted in the unlikely event that all States might be willing to do so. Preliminary discussion took place at a conference between Commonwealth ministers and State premiers in August 1909. The States agreed to set up wages boards, and to explore means of referring to an Inter-State Commission any cases of unfair industrial competition between the States caused by conditions of labour. An Inter-State Commission Bill was introduced in the Senate, but it lapsed at prorogation. In any case, some of the States seemed most unlikely to refer power. The whole affair was just another highly coloured balloon.

The Premiers' conference in Melbourne did reach firm agreement, however, on the urgent matter of readjusting financial arrangements between the Commonwealth and States. Under the Constitution, the Commonwealth had general taxing and borrowing powers, concurrent with those of the States. It also had exclusive powers to impose customs and excise duties, which had formerly been the main source of the States' revenue; but because of that intrusion on the State field, the Commonwealth had certain transitional liabilities. Section 87—the so-called Braddon clause, which was due to expire at the end of 1910—required the Commonwealth to pass over to the States three-quarters of its customs and excise revenue each year. Section 94 also required it to pay the States any surplus remaining after the Commonwealth had met its various commitments.

Those commitments had increased considerably with the passing of such measures as the Invalid and Old Age Pensions Act (1908), the Defence Act (1909) and the Naval Loan Act (1909). The Commonwealth had evaded the apparent intention of Section 94 by means of a Surplus Revenue Act (1908) enabling it to put revenue aside in a trust account for payment of pensions in the future, and uncharacteristically the High Court had upheld this stratagem. But something simpler and more equitable was required in place of such improvisation.

The Premiers were not overjoyed, but they agreed to accept in place of the expiring Braddon clause a system of Commonwealth grants to the States at the general rate of 25 shillings per head of population. A bill for submission to referendum, the Constitution Alteration (Finance) Bill, was introduced by Deakin in September 1909. The Opposition and some fusionists, although they might have approved the proposed grant system under other circumstances, did not want it to be enshrined in the Constitution, and without time limit. The Bill passed through committee stage in the lower house by one vote—that of J. F. G. Foxton (Brisbane), a Minister without portfolio who returned from an imperial defence conference in the nick of time. It also had an easy passage through the Senate, even though its provisions involved a substantial transfer of power from States to the Commonwealth.

By this time the 'States' House' had lost some of its former zeal for States' rights. Like the earlier Surplus Revenue Bill, which had also put the States at a disadvantage, the Constitution Alteration (Finance) Bill was passed by the upper house pretty much on party lines. The only serious resistance given to any bill by the Senate during this parliament was to the Northern Territory Acceptance Bill, from which provision for a north–south railway was very sensibly deleted. Even though the Senate sat for 27 per cent fewer days than the lower house in 1909, its attendance record left much to be desired. On 3 June, for example, no quorum of senators was present at the time appointed for a meeting. The bells were rung, and a quorum was mustered within five minutes, though fifteen senators were recorded as absent. On the previous day seventeen had been absent.

The third parliament went into recess on 8 December 1909, and expired by the effluxion of time on 20 February 1910. It was the only Commonwealth parliament ever to see out its full term, and the only parliament ever to have four sessions. At the same unhurried pace, the ensuing election campaign lasted more than eleven weeks, the longest of its kind before or since.

Time had run out not only for this parliament but for Deakin's Ministry as well. On election day, 13 April, the Liberal Party was overwhelmed by a Labor landslide, and two Bills to alter the Constitution met with a mixed reception at referendum. The Constitution Alteration (Finance) Bill was narrowly defeated, though passed in Queensland, Western Australia and Tasmania; and the Constitution Alteration (State Debts) Bill—a measure supported by both parties, enabling the Commonwealth to take over from the States all their public debts, not merely those existing at the time of federation—was passed by a majority of 55 per cent.

Apart from its half-hearted approach to New Protection and rejection of land tax, the Liberal Party's election platform was hard to distinguish from Labor's. That was perhaps one reason for the Government's ignominious defeat. Labor now seemed the more reliable of two apparently similar alternatives. It had a clearer identity than the party of fusion, it was untarnished by charges of opportunism, and it was better organised electorally. Fusionists also attributed the result to electoral apathy (only 63 per cent of electors voted) and to class-consciousness aroused by the recent prosecution and gaoling of a trade union leader, Peter Bowling, by the anti-Labor Government of New South Wales. Labor gained fourteen seats in the House of Representatives, giving it forty-one of the seventy-five seats in that chamber; and in the Senate it won all eighteen vacated seats, bringing its strength there to twenty-two out of thirty-six. Of twelve former Liberal-Protectionists who stood for re-election as fusionists, only Deakin, Salmon, Groom, Thomson and Harper (Mernda, V) survived. Lyne, who was returned as an Independent, must have rejoiced to see his enemies in such disarray. For Deakin, however, the outcome of this historic election was personally welcome. In one of his notebooks he wrote:

> O bird song! can it be
> That I, at last, am free
> This mellow autumn morning-time,
> To muse and list to thee?

A Sturdy Youth

Never before had an Australian federal government taken office with such a strong mandate for its policies as Fisher's government held when the fourth parliament assembled on 1 July 1910. For the first time since federation a government had control of both chambers—by majorities of seven in the House of Representatives, and fourteen in the Senate. The Government benches were packed with new members who were, according to the *Argus*, 'keen, bright-eyed, clever and young'. In contrast to the Labor veterans of 1901, most of whom were now grey-headed, and to the fusionists, among whom Willie Kelly was the only youthful man, the average age of the eighteen new Labor members in the House of Representatives was forty-five. Among the newcomers were such men as Frank Anstey (Bourke, V), a radical of fearsome reputation from the Victorian lower house; James Scullin (Corangamite, V), a journalist who had run unsuccessfully against Deakin in 1906; Matthew Charlton (Hunter, N), a mining union official who had spent several years in the New South Wales Assembly; and W. G. Higgs (Capricornia, Q), a former senator who now became one of the few parliamentarians to have held a seat in both houses. 'You can't block us!' called Jim Page to the Opposition. It was as if the young Commonwealth, approaching the end of its first decade, had at last decided what it wanted and how best to get it.

Those listening to the Address-in-Reply debate might have noticed, in addition to the youthfulness of new members, the marked difference between the easy-going Labor leader, now white haired, and his gnomelike, hyperactive lieutenant, W. M. Hughes. The only significant change Fisher had made to his previous Ministry was by dropping Hugh Mahon—an aloof, rather unpopular man—and giving his portfolio (Home Affairs) to King O'Malley, who by then was engaged in the difficult task of living down a reputation for incurable levity. Hughes was Attorney-General again, and in this capacity he had virtually composed the speech delivered by Lord Dudley at the opening of parliament. This presumably explained the air of aggrieved proprietorship with which Hughes listened to Deakin's criticism of the speech, mild though that criticism was. Fisher was more relaxed at the table, and occasionally indulged in the informality of addressing colleagues by their first names. When the Minister for Trade and Customs, F. G. Tudor, replied in kind to an interjection while the Prime Minister was speaking, Fisher would wave him back: 'Allow me, Frank—Frank, allow me!'

Before the end of the year, Fisher was showing signs of severe strain. Although normally good-natured, his temper became short and he could not concentrate for long at a time. 'A long effort tired his brain very much, and he would put off doing things until the last moment', wrote Malcolm Shepherd, the Prime Minister's private secretary, who became secretary of the Prime Minister's Department when that was established in 1911.

When work accumulated, the only way to get through it was to serve it up to him a little at a time. A large pile of letters put him off, and he would not read one letter under these circumstances. He used to sign away as hard as he could go, not even giving me time to mention what the letters or documents were about. Sometimes in the midst of discussion there would arise the question of the pronunciation of a word. That would be an excuse for quite a long argument. For instance, talking one day with [the secretary] of the Treasury and myself regarding the note issue, the word 'Consols' stuck Mr Fisher up, and two dictionaries had to be produced before the argument over the pronunciation of that word was settled.

Fisher took to golf, and bought himself a mansion. He paid £3000 for Oakleigh Hall, a two-storeyed porticoed residence in East St Kilda which would not have disgraced a Scottish laird. One evening—after he had shown Josiah Thomas (Barrier, N), another former miner, and Billy Hughes over the new home—Hughes presented the Prime Minister with a pocket compass, saying: 'You'll want this more than I do, Andrew, to find your way back to bed after going all round locking up'. The Honourable Member for

West Sydney might also have added that he himself had no need of a compass, for he always knew exactly where he was going.

Unlike Fisher, Hughes at this time had no settled domestic life. His first wife had died three years before, leaving him with three sons and three daughters. The children lived at a cottage in Sydney under the care of the eldest daughter, who was eighteen when her mother died. One son was then aged twenty-two, but the other children were still at school. In addition to her duties in Sydney, the eldest daughter was sometimes required to act as her father's hostess in Melbourne. Hughes's political life does not appear to have been thrown off course by his bereavement, and in 1911 he married Mary Campbell, the daughter of a New South Wales grazier. Mary Hughes provided him with a stable domestic and social life, and he had little more to do with his first family.

William Morris Hughes's own childhood had been disrupted by the death of his mother when he was six. He was born in Pimlico, near Westminster, but from the age of six to twelve he lived alternately with his Welsh father's sister at Llandudno, northern Wales, and with maternal relatives at Llansantffraid, a town more English than Welsh, although it was just inside the Welsh border. Back in London he became a pupil-teacher until, in 1884, at the age of twenty-two, he emigrated to Brisbane. During the next six years Hughes carried his swag through outback Queensland, went droving and fencing, picked grapes, bagged potatoes, and worked as striker to a blacksmith and deckhand on a coastal steamer. Although wiry in physique, and tenacious, he was not as healthy as those jobs suggested. By the time he settled in Sydney Hughes was suffering from the chronic dyspepsia which was to make him a sparing eater for the rest of his life, and also from the onset of deafness said to have been caused by sleeping in the open one wintry night near Orange.

As the father of a young family in the working-class Sydney suburb of Balmain, Hughes was at first desperately poor, eking out a living as shopkeeper, tiler, locksmith and mender of umbrellas. He also read widely and sought the company of trade union and Labor activists, among whom was another Londoner, W. A. Holman, who later in life became Premier of New South Wales. In 1890 Hughes was appointed Secretary of the Wharf Labourers' Union. Four years later he was elected to the Legislative Assembly. His political apprenticeship was long and thorough and by 1910 'that fiery particle' (as he was dubbed by the *Sydney Morning Herald*, with help from Byron) was master of the craft. Just as Deakin had dominated the first decade of federal parliament, so Hughes—more autocratic, and less parliamentary—would dominate the next decade. In the uncharitable words of Holman, watching from Sydney: 'Fisher had begun already to be, what he always remained, a conscientious and manageable puppet in the hands of abler men than himself. The leading mind in the new government was that of Mr Hughes'.

In October Fisher embarked on an official visit to South Africa, leaving Hughes as acting Prime Minister for the remaining seven weeks of the session. The change-over was welcome to both of them. Hughes pushed legislation through the lower house, and did not mind how he did it. One way was to shorten the Estimates debate, during which members discussed the statements of proposed government expenditure presented to parliament by the Treasurer as part of the Budget in August, and virtually any other subject that came to mind. 'The Estimates are a Parliamentary institution containing two fictions', said the *Argus* with healthy cynicism.

> The first is that the popular House controls the expenditure which the Ministry proposes—and this is a very wild fiction indeed. The second is that public wrongs are righted by the general debate which the Estimates provoke. Mr Hughes refused to concede any importance to any of these theories. He regarded the debate on Budget and Estimates as sheer talkativeness, so postponed it till the dying days of the session, and let it wear itself out during hours when all decent folk are asleep in their beds. Nor did he suffer the debate gladly. For the last fortnight or so he has been steadily losing the politeness he recently acquired . . .

Billy Hughes could be a charming and amusing companion, but more often his manner was cranky, mocking and overbearing. He was a small, narrow-shouldered man with big knuckled hands and a pinched seamy face which, in the days when he wore a drooping dark moustache, looked almost Oriental. If challenged in discussion, he might defer with mock courtesy. 'Let the orator speak', he would rasp, and the orator would do so at his peril. With the help of his Acousticon, a small battery-powered machine connected to an earphone which he held up to an ear or clipped over his head, Hughes could hear reasonably well—unless, of course, for tactical reasons he preferred not to hear at all. In parliament he displayed what Deakin called 'splendid guerrilla debating power', with a flair for hyperbole and bizarre similes. Joseph Cook engaging in banter, he said, was like an ichthyosaurus attempting the gavotte; a Royal Commission into the beef trust would be as effective as trying to gather the constellation Hercules into a butterfly net.

Sir John Forrest, something of an autocrat himself, was nonetheless enraged by Hughes's eager wielding of brief authority. 'I am glad to get away for a good rest', he wrote to Deakin on the eve of departing for George V's coronation. 'I want to forget that little b–- and to make myself believe I never met him.'

Even before Hughes began cracking the whip, there had been an industrious air about this session. The sittings were long, and although the closure was not applied, the new Speaker (Charles McDonald, the Labor Member for Kennedy, Q) resorted for the first time to a Standing Order which provided for suspension of a member—in this case a member of his own party, J. H. Catts (Cook, N). Catts had been named by Speaker McDonald for refusing to withdraw and apologise for having directed unparliamentary language and conduct at W. Elliot Johnson (Lib, Lang, N) and other Opposition members sitting near him:

> Mr W. ELLIOT JOHNSON.—The honorable member is sitting in my seat. *(To Mr J. H. Catts*: If you do not take your own seat I will land you one). Mr Speaker, here is the honorable member for Cook, who now comes behind me, and says, "You dirty skunks," referring to us on this

side. Is he in order in making use of an expression of that kind? If he does it again, and we are not protected, I shall be provoked into doing something that I would be sorry for afterwards.

When Catts, after having been named for disregarding the authority of the Chair, persisted in his refusal to apologise, the Speaker suspended him from the service of the House for 24 hours. The new President of the Senate (Senator Henry Turley, Lab, Q) also suspended one of his recalcitrants, but not until 1912, when he found it necessary to discipline Senator Arthur Rae (Lab, N) for refusing to withdraw an accusation of falsehood against Senator Edward Millen (Lib, N).

By dint of late hours and firm management the Fisher Government brought to completion the legislative programme of national consolidation which had been started by Barton's Government and carried on under Deakin. The legislative output of the first session was in fact richer than Deakin's last harvest, though many of the forty-three bills enacted that year had been initiated or planned by Deakin's administration. Among early measures of the fourth parliament were the Surplus Revenue Act, which established for at least ten years the system of per capita payments to the States which Deakin had failed to have incorporated in the Constitution; the Australian Notes Act, authorising the Commonwealth to take over the issue of paper money from private banks; the Land Tax Act, imposing a sliding scale of taxation on unimproved valuations above £5000; the Defence Act, requiring men to continue military training until the age of twenty-five; the Naval Defence Act, establishing the administrative machinery for an Australian navy; and the Northern Territory Acceptance Act.

Some legislative fields had, of course, been denied to parliament on constitutional grounds by the High Court. The Inter-State Labor Conference of 1908 had endorsed certain proposals for amendment of the Constitution to permit legislation on such matters, and to this task Hughes now applied himself with zeal. During the first session parliament passed two Constitution Alteration Acts, though not without opposition. The first contained four amendments to Section 51 of the Constitution, for which electors would have to vote *en bloc*: extension of Commonwealth authority to all Australian trade and commerce, not merely that of an interstate character; elucidation of the corporations power to cover creation, dissolution, regulation and control of Australian commercial and financial corporations; replacement of the arbitration power with power to control wages and conditions of employment in all industries, which would oblige the High Court to validate New Protection; and a new power to control combines and monopolies. The second Act proposed a new power to nationalise monopolies.

Hughes did not do things by halves: he was the urchin in the tart shop, wanting everything at once. Introducing the Constitution Alteration (Legislative Powers) Bill, he spoke with his accustomed eloquence and hyperbole:

we do not propose any amendment affecting the principle of Federation ... we have to fight one cry, and one only, and that is "This means Unification." The words were thought, during the last Federal campaign, to be more potent than that "blessed word Mesopotamia." They were the one answer to our every question, the one charge against all our reforms. The beast of *Revelations* was not more ghastly or terrible, and if I have dehorned this monster as I hope I have, I have done useful work . . .

This Parliament has been in existence for ten years, and has done good national work; but we cannot rest on our laurels. If we say, "Look at what we have done," instead of saying, "Look at what we are doing and intend to do," the people will have good reason to reply, "We have no use for a Parliament in which there is dignity but not power . . ."

What is our position? What can the National Parliament do? We see in section 51 of the Constitution that imposing array of powers with which we are clothed, and I am not going to say one word to belittle the very many and real opportunities for useful legislation there set forth. But when we exempt from them the powers which we have already practically exhausted by existing Commonwealth legislation—when we take away our powers with respect to Customs taxation and defence—we may well ask, "What is left?" . . . in the light of the decisions of the High Court and of our experience, we find there is little or nothing that is of national or vital moment. A National Parliament ought to deal with national matters. If our ambition aims merely at a glorified shire council uttering and re-uttering pious ejaculations concerning national sentiments about one flag and one destiny, no doubt the Constitution clothes us with more than ample power. But I take it that our desires lie in quite another direction. We desire to give legislative and administrative effect to the national aspirations of the people of the Commonwealth.

It was a good speech, but not good enough. That blessed word 'Unification' had the power to make Australians vote 'No', and Deakin invoked it earnestly during the debate and during the referendum campaign. In New South Wales Holman's Labor government also campaigned against the referenda proposals on grounds of State rights. Such support as there was for some of the *en bloc* proposals was probably diminished by the reluctance of many electors to vote willy-nilly in favour of all four. In April 1911 both Bills were rejected by overwhelming national majorities, and by negative majorities in all States except Western Australia.

In spite of that rejection by States unwilling to make further sacrifices on the altar of Moloch, the Commonwealth could now look back on a decade of substantial achievement. The tenth anniversary of federation, 1 January 1911, fell on a Sunday. It does not appear to have inspired any sermons, and was not observed with any ceremony by a Commonwealth government that was anxious to avoid the appearance of federal extravagance. The Prime Minister, recently returned from South Africa, had nothing to say about it; but the Attorney-General delivered himself of some appropriate reflections, among which was his regret that 'the constitutional instrument by which much has been achieved is yet structurally defective'.

'Men no longer speak of themselves as Victorians, New South Welshmen and so on, but really as Australians', said Hughes.

The year 1900 saw the infant Commonwealth in swaddling clothes oppressed by the politics of the parish pump—a veritable economic Tower of Babel—dependent for defence upon the motherland, and content neither to do for itself nor adequately to subsidise Great Britain to

protect it. The year 1911 finds us living in another world in all or most of
these matters. The Commonwealth is now a sturdy youth.

One indulgence the Fisher Government allowed itself in this anniversary
year was the redesigning of an amateurish coat of arms which the Commonwealth had been using since 1908. The improved version, sent to the Colonial Office for royal approval in 1911, and granted by royal warrant in
September 1912, consisted of a shield containing symbols of the six States (in
place of a rather nondescript red, white and blue design on the original
shield) and supported by a kangaroo dexter and emu sinister. The supporters
were more lifelike than in the earlier arms; the ground upon which they
stood consisted of two sprays of wattle instead of grass; and above the shield,
as before, was a seven-pointed star, the points representing the States and
the Commonwealth's territories, the latter consisting at that time of the
Northern Territory, Papua, Norfolk Island and Macquarie Island. The States
had less reason than the Commonwealth to feel satisfied with the first decade of federation. Financially they had so far been reasonably well provided
for, but under the new per capita system of revenue-sharing they would
receive in 1910–11 only about three-quarters of what the Braddon clause
had yielded them in its final year. Under Section 96 of the Constitution,
however, the Commonwealth now began granting additional financial
assistance to the two least populous States, and the loudest complainers
about federation's effect on their economies: Western Australia and
Tasmania.

The common complaint that the Commonwealth was costing more than
expected had some foundation, but this was hardly enough to justify the outcry sometimes raised. It had been said before federation that the extra annual
cost entailed by a Commonwealth government would be about £300 000, of
which £112 000 would be spent on the legislature, £14 000 on the executive,
£17 500 on the Governor-General and his staff, and £25 000 on the judiciary.
The cost per head of population, said the more optimistic federalists, would
be no more than that of a dog licence, which was then 2s 6d. In 1910 Andrew
Fisher tabled a return showing the current 'annual cost of federation' as £615
784, which was really not much more than half a crown multiplied by Australia's population as disclosed by the 1911 census—a sum that came to
£556 850.

The annual cost of parliament—£123 090 in 1901–02, and £268 226 in
1905–06—had risen to £209 678 by 1910–11, partly as a result of the 50 per
cent salary increase for members in 1907. During the decade, parliament
received 321 bills (269 of which were initiated in the lower house) and
passed 232 acts. The average number of sitting days per year was ninety-five
for the lower house and seventy-one for the Senate. The original seventy-
five members of the House of Representatives and thirty-six senators had
dwindled in number to thirty-one and thirteen respectively. Of the fifty delegates to the 1897–98 federal convention, twenty-four had been elected to
parliament, and of those only eight were left.

Before long, one of the most distinguished convention delegates and one
of the Senate's most ardent federalists, Sir Josiah Symon, would be refused

re-endorsement by the Liberal Party in South Australia and thus condemned to defeat at the next election. His offence was not neglect of South Australian rights, but defiance of his party Whip. Nothing could better have illustrated the extent to which the party system had come to dominate the intended 'States' House as well as the House of Representatives. The Senate had certainly stood up for its right to press requests for amendment of financial legislation; indeed, it had been more successful in this respect than the House of Lords, whose powers were drastically curtailed by the Parliament Act of 1911. But after that early display of self-assertion, the Senate had become what one observer in 1911, H. G. Turner, called 'merely an appendage, necessary to give statutory force to the decisions of the party which dominated the other House'.

By 1911 there was a growing air of modernity about Australia, and about its federal parliament. The nation had fully recovered from depression and drought (since 1901 the gross national product had risen from £202 million to £371 million), and was able to afford the technological changes which were taking place, particularly in transport and communications. Taxi cabs were appearing on city streets, Australia's first aeroplane flight with a passenger (a member of the wealthy Baillieu family) was made in 1911, and telephone and telegraph systems were becoming more extensive and more efficient. The Prime Minister now had an official motor car, purchased in 1910 at a cost of £831, and in the same year Hansard's staff was enlarged by the appointment of six male typists. Parliament House had at last been sewered (in 1909, long after most of central Melbourne); and in 1911, not before time, a women's toilet was installed.

As if to mark a break with the past the two chambers dispensed temporarily with wigs, buckles, ruffles and other traditional paraphernalia of the sort once characterised by Labor Senator Thomas Givens, a pugnacious Queenslander born in County Tipperary, as 'ridiculous flummery'. At the request of a majority of senators in 1910, Senator Gould had ceased wearing the President's wig and gown, and his Labor successor, Senator Turley, had followed that example. With the change of government, Black Rod and the Serjeant-at-Arms were also relieved of their ancient costumes, though not for all time. Charles McDonald dispensed with wig and gown in his first session as Speaker, and the Clerk of the lower house, Charles Gavan Duffy, wore no wig at the opening of that parliament.

At the opening of the second session, there was no sign of the Mace, either carried by the Serjeant while preceding the Speaker into the chamber, or laid upon the table while the Speaker was in his Chair. Bruce Smith, a stickler for tradition, immediately asked the Prime Minister on what authority and with what view the symbol of sovereignty had been removed from the table:

> Mr FISHER.—I am not in a position to answer the honorable member. I, too, miss it.
> Mr BRUCE SMITH.—As the Prime Minister is unable to answer my question I ask you, Mr Speaker, whether it is upon your authority that the mace has been removed.
> Mr SPEAKER.—Yes.

Another change of short duration was made during the second session of the fourth parliament, to the sale of alcohol. On the motion of W. F. Finlayson (Lab, Brisbane), a home missioner active in temperance work, the House of Representatives by a vote of 23 to 20 expressed the opinion that sale of intoxicating liquors should be prohibited in the parliamentary refreshment bar. The Senate, however, had recently negatived a similar motion by Senator Rae (Lab N). The bar continued to serve senators and their guests, among whom were many members of the other place. Some resolutions of the House are deemed to have continuing effect; others do not bind future sessions, let alone future parliaments. Finlayson's resolution was never rescinded or expunged, as it could have been on another motion, but neither does it seem to have had much binding effect. It was simply forgotten.

The second session began on 5 September 1911 after a recess of more than nine months, the longest recess to that time. The two most important national measures of this session were the Kalgoorlie to Port Augusta Railway Bill and the Commonwealth Bank Bill. Both were of close concern to King O'Malley, but for opposite reasons: he introduced the first Bill, and did not introduce the second, much as he would like to have done so, or at least to have received some credit for the institution which it brought into being. O'Malley's second reading speech on the first Bill, which provided at last for an east–west transcontinental rail link, was notable for one of the silliest flights of oratory ever heard in the House of Representatives. Speaking of the arid waste soon to be traversed by the Trans-Australian Railway, he said:

> This line will traverse territory boasting a remarkable superiority of situation on the very highway between the industrial, commercial, and financial supremacy of the east, and the pioneering, agricultural, and mineral progress of the golden West. It will open up millions of acres of soil unsurpassed in richness, possessing a fascinating, undulating beauty of surface with a health-producing climate, and capable of nurturing a powerful, generous, and healthy people, and worthy of being either the central pivot or a mighty outpost of Australian civilization. Only a few years have passed since this spacious inland empire was open only to the blackfellow and his lubra, who ran wild in the sage brush and sandalwood. I venture to predict that before many years have rolled by, after the construction of this railroad, it will draw to its spacious bosom a population larger than ever crowded within the gates of ancient Athens, when her fighting men, under Miltiades, won liberty for humanity on the field of Marathon; larger than that of Sparta when she 'bossed' Greece, and sent forth her sons quickened by the encouragement of their mothers' benediction to return with their shields, or on them; and larger, indeed, than that which crowded on the seven hills of Rome when, under her mighty rulers, she commenced that sovereign sway that afterwards embraced the whole world. I have the greatest pleasure in submitting this motion to the House.

The Commonwealth Bank Bill, which Fisher introduced without hyperbole, provided for the establishment of a trading and savings bank owned entirely by the Commonwealth Government. It was to operate under the control of a single governor, who would be responsible to parliament, and it would compete with private banks. The disastrous collapse of those private banks during the great Depression was still starkly remembered: of the sixty-four banking or quasi-banking institutions in Australia, only ten had survived the years from 1891 to 1893 without having to close or refuse payment. Most Labor party platforms came to include a state bank, but opinion varied as to what functions such a bank or banks should perform.

King O'Malley, who did more than any other Labor member to popularise the subject of banking reform outside parliament, spoke grandly of 'a financial reservoir of indestructible power' controlling the note issue, holding the gold reserves of all other banks, and sustaining credit in troubled times by rediscounting other banks' securities. In later years O'Malley also claimed to have been the true founder of the Commonwealth Bank, having organised a 'torpedo brigade' in Caucus, so he said, to force the hand of a reluctant Cabinet. This was not so. The motion to establish the bank was introduced into Caucus as a Cabinet recommendation by Fisher. Fisher initiated the Bill on 31 October 1911, and O'Malley took no part in the ensuing debate.

In a negative sense, however, O'Malley was partly responsible for the form of the new bank, because Fisher took care to allay fears aroused in the business community by the gilt-spurred rooster's earlier rhetoric. 'O'Malley pasteurised' was how one speaker, W. H. Irvine, described the Bill. The institution was to be not a central bank, but another trading bank differing from its competitors only by acting as banker to the Commonwealth Government, being supported by Government guarantee instead of by shareholders, and having a savings department. Even so, the Opposition condemned the bank's savings function as being, in Deakin's words, 'absolutely antagonistic both to Federal principles and practice'.

'Why, without any call of need', said Deakin,

> without any complaints of injustice, or cry of loss, we should enter into a sphere in which the work is being well, wisely and satisfactorily done, so as to interfere with that work, is a mystery. What demand is there upon the Commonwealth? We shall not give, for a long time, anything like as good a service as the States Savings Banks are offering. They are giving all that is required.

The Bill was before the lower house for fifteen days (its passage there was prolonged by an unsuccessful Opposition attempt to refer it to a Select Committee), and before the Senate on only three sitting days, one of which lasted until four o'clock the next morning. The Government-controlled Senate made three amendments, all of which were accepted by the lower house. One amendment was to a clause absolving the bank from all responsibility for fraudulent withdrawals, which a majority of senators, notably Senator Rae, considered unjust to depositors. Rae's leader in the Senate, Senator McGregor, later accused him of having played into the hands of 'a corrupt Opposition, which wishes to destroy the Bill'. Rae called him a liar, refused to withdraw, and stormed out of the chamber at 3.30 a.m. before the Chairman of Committees could suspend him. The Bill passed its last stage on 20 December, and the session closed next day.

The third and last session of the fourth parliament occupied the second half of 1912, and produced fifty acts, bringing that parliament's legislative output to 122 acts, compared with seventy passed by the third parliament, sixty-four by the second and fifty-eight by the first. Many of the acts amended earlier legislation, particularly the Defence and Naval Defence Acts. The Inter-State Commission Act established the tribunal that was prescribed in the Constitution for adjudication and administration on matters of trade and commerce, but was not in fact destined for great achievements. The Attorney-General also returned to the referendum offensive, preparing six Constitution Alteration Bills. These covered the same ground as his earlier two Bills, but presented the amendments separately, to be voted on at the next election.

This was Deakin's last session in parliament. Although he was no more than fifty-five years old, his memory and concentration had disintegrated to an extent unsuspected by his colleagues. For the first time in all his years of public speaking, he was now relying heavily on notes. 'I cannot keep the thread of the argument consistently', he wrote in July 1912, '—cannot pick my words even approximately—forget where I am in some sentences, and hence risk leaving them unfinished'. In September he wrote of his 'first decisive break-down in faculty and in health, in brain and digestion, in mental and physical energy all at the same time. It is now plain that only by carefully husbanding my resources can I hope to hang on till Christmas pending decisive arrangements for retirement'. By the next month alarm had turned into utter despair: 'It is plain that A.D. no longer lives as he was—Another A.D. sits among ruins picking his way carefully across the debris to the haven of complete forgetfulness that awaits me'.

Although the new A.D. had seven years still to live, the Deakin of silver tongue and flexible loyalty—undeniably the ablest politician of his day, and the principal parliamentary architect of the Commonwealth—was already dead. A specialist physician spoke of 'hyperneurasthenia', but the modern diagnosis for Deakin's condition would probably have been cerebral arteriosclerosis. His last parliamentary speech was delivered during the Estimates debate on 18 December, and Hansard's report of it disclosed no sign of his illness. He spoke about the need to extend postal and telegraph services more widely over the Australian continent.

On 20 January 1913 the Liberal Caucus elected a new leader, Joseph Cook, by a majority of only one vote over Sir John Forrest. Forrest was bitterly disappointed, particularly as his friend Deakin had voted against him and was thought also to have secured Groom's vote for Cook. 'Our paths may not again come together', wrote Forrest to Deakin.

> I can say with a clear conscience that I have done my duty to you. It is for you to find satisfaction and comfort, through the many years I hope are in store for you, in the knowledge of your *last act* towards me, your old, long tried and faithful friend.

As Deakin saw it, Cook—for all his lack of lustre—was simply the wiser choice. '[Forrest] wishes to take the post for a time having the honour and glory of retiring at leisure', he wrote. 'Greatly as I sympathise with him I acted solely in the interests of the party and its future as I see them.'

Another of Deakin's old friends, Mr Justice O'Connor, had died in

November. In the new year Hughes set about finding three new judges for the High Court: one to replace O'Connor, and two for new positions created by the Judiciary Act of 1912. One of his choices, Frank Gavan Duffy, a distinguished Victorian barrister and brother of the Clerk of the House of Representatives, was controversial. Another candidate, Charles Powers, the Commonwealth Crown Solicitor, encountered but survived a certain amount of criticism from the legal profession because he had not been admitted to the Bar. But the third, a Sydney barrister, A. B. Piddington, found himself assailed by accusations of political bias.

Although never a member of the Labor Party, Piddington was known to hold generally liberal views. Not content with that knowledge, Hughes with uncharacteristic clumsiness sent him the following cable while Piddington was at Port Said, returning from a visit to England: 'Confidential. Most important know your views Commonwealth versus State Rights. Very Urgent'. Piddington replied, 'In sympathy with supremacy of Commonwealth powers', and when his ship reached Colombo the offer of a High Court position was waiting for him. His cabled reply read in part: 'If with complete independence [as to] validity questions shall accept'.

Piddington accepted the offer formally when his ship reached Adelaide on 1 March, and almost immediately a storm of protest broke. Hughes was accused of trying to pack the Court, and although in retrospect that charge did not seem justified, it undoubtedly weakened Piddington's resolve. Shaken by the outcry from his own profession, and by the thought of Hughes's indiscreet preliminary inquiry, he concluded that he may unwittingly have been party to an improper appointment. On 24 March he resigned. His place was taken by an entirely non-political King's Counsel, George Rich.

The High Court did not affect much federal legislation during the life of the fourth parliament. It held that compulsory military service did not infringe the freedom of religion guaranteed by the Constitution, and in two notable decisions it ruled against the Commonwealth. In the Vend Case— the first, and for many more years the only prosecution against an alleged monopoly under the Australian Industries Preservation Act—Mr Justice Isaacs convicted the accused companies of illegally regulating the output and price of coal. When the defendants appealed, Griffith, Barton and O'Connor reversed their learned but radical brother's decision on the ground that the Commonwealth had not shown that the coal agreement was intended to cause public detriment.

The second case concerned a Royal Commission into the monopolistic sugar industry. The general manager of the Colonial Sugar Company refused to answer questions asked by the Commission. Parliament amended the Royal Commissions Act in an attempt to compel him, but the sugar company challenged the validity of that amendment. O'Connor had died only recently, and the remaining four judges were evenly divided. Griffith and Barton held that Colonial Sugar need not provide information about the company's internal management or its activities outside Australia; Isaacs and Higgins thought that such questions were lawful. Under the Judiciary Act, the Chief Justice's opinion prevailed.

For the first and only time in its history, the Court on this occasion granted leave to appeal to the Privy Council under Section 74 of the Constitution— the section by means of which, it will be remembered, Australian and British negotiators had in 1900 resolved the main difference between them over the Constitution Bill. Section 74 provided that only the High Court itself should have authority to grant or withhold leave to appeal from its own decisions in constitutional cases involving the relative powers of the Commonwealth and States. This was such a case, and in due course the Privy Council upheld the prevailing High Court decision.

The two remaining original members of the Court, whose conservatism prevailed so narrowly in the Royal Commission case, were to find themselves increasingly on the defensive during the next few years. Although the three new judges were neither radical nor nationalist in their cast of mind, they applied English common law principles of interpretation more literally than Griffith and Barton. This tended to bring them into concurrence with Isaacs and Higgins, often leaving the two founding judges in a minority.

Double Dissolution

After three years of parliamentary stability, the general election of 31 May 1913 produced a parliament trembling on the brink of deadlock. During the campaign, party platforms were overshadowed by Labor's second attempt to alter the Constitution by referendum, and it was probably that shadow which turned the lower house majority into a razor's edge. Although both parties advocated some measures that were beyond existing Commonwealth powers, the Liberals maintained that the Commonwealth should pursue these ends by way of co-operation with the States rather than constitutional amendment. They conjured up the spectre of Moloch, hungry for burnt offerings, and Labor suffered for it on polling day. The six referendum proposals were defeated, though all were approved in three of the smaller States (Queensland, South Australia and Western Australia), and the national margin for rejection of each proposal was not large. At the election, however, Labor lost six seats in the House of Representatives, giving the Liberals a majority of one. There was little comfort for Labor in the knowledge that its Senate majority had been enlarged to 29–7, for the crucial ratio was 37–38 in the lower house.

Labor considered trying to govern, but Hughes—according to his own account in later years—argued successfully for resignation before parliament assembled, so that the Speaker would have to come from Cook's band of thirty-eight rather than Labor's thirty-seven. When McDonald declined the new Government's invitation to continue as Speaker, the House of Representatives elected in his place the Liberal Member for Lang (N), William Elliott Johnson, who gave his occupation as 'gentleman'. When the Speaker was in his Chair, the parties each numbered thirty-seven, and in the event of a tied division the Speaker was entitled to a casting vote. Speaker Johnson saved the Cook Government several times by joining in divisions, the first such division being on 4 September, for a censure motion by amendment to the Address-in-Reply:

Mr SPEAKER.—Ayes 32, Noes 32. There being an equality of votes, as shown by the division lists, it becomes necessary for me to give the casting vote. I take this opportunity of saying that, notwithstanding anything that has appeared in the press, or elsewhere about the Speaker's casting vote, I have not been approached in any way—

Several HONORABLE MEMBERS.—Oh, oh!

Mr SPEAKER.—Order! This outburst is extremely unseemly, and I hope that it will not be repeated. I have not been approached in any way by members of the House or the press outside, or anybody else—in regard to how my vote is to go, except on one occasion, when it was done on the floor of the House . . . I give my vote with the "Noes", and declare the question resolved in the negative.

The fifth parliament opened lamely on 9 July 1913 with the Governor-General, Lord Denman, explaining that his present advisers had 'not yet been able to mature the proposals placed by them before the electors', and that consequently parliament would adjourn immediately to give them time to do so. The House of Representatives reassembled five weeks later, and stayed in session more or less continuously for the rest of the year. But the Senate, after a lapse of seven weeks broken by only one sitting day, sat irregularly for fewer than half as many days as the lower house.

Among the new members were three conspicuous departures from parliament's Anglo-Celtic norm. George Dankel (Lab, Boothby, S) and Jacob Stumm (Lib, Lilley, Q), both born in Germany, had come to Australia as children. More remarkable still, in a legislature which hitherto had no members more exotic than King O'Malley and J. C. Watson, was one of the new senators, Thomas Bakhap (Lib, T). Senator Bakhap, whose original name was presumably Bak Hap, was the son of a Chinese storekeeper and a European mother. At the age of sixteen he had been official Chinese interpreter on the Lottah tin-mining field of eastern Tasmania, and he spoke Chinese fluently for the rest of his life. No newcomer to politics, having already served four years in the Tasmanian House of Assembly, he was chosen to move the Senate's Address-in-Reply motion. Senator Bakhap's tall and portly presence was accepted with a tolerance far removed from the excesses of the Immigration Restriction Bill debate twelve years before. His features were partly obscured by a large moustache extending several inches beyond his cheeks, and although he often referred in speeches to his racial background, he did so in such a way as to disarm prejudice:

Senator BAKHAP.—I am, I suppose, looked upon with some amount of suspicion by honorable senators opposite. There are some, I believe, who conceive that I am an emissary of a foreign power in the guise of an Australian legislator. Whatever honorable senators opposite may think about me, the Tasmanian people know a great deal about me. They know that I have a claim, by virtue of blood and lineal descent, to speak feelingly in regard to fighting for the defence of the liberties of Australia. A very close maternal relative of mine was the very first man to be killed at the fight at Eureka Stockade. My uncles have all fought, and some of them have died for the British Empire. I am pleased to say that I am old enough to have known one of them who fought in the Crimean War and the Indian Mutiny.

Senator PEARCE.—(Lab, W).—Come over here.

Senator BAKHAP.—He used to get drunk twice a year—once on the anniversary of the Alma, and once on the anniversary of the battle of Inkerman.

Senator PEARCE.—No, stay where you are.

Some of the fourth parliament's most familiar figures were now missing. Deakin had not stood for re-election; Senator Sir Josiah Symon had been defeated, and so also had Sir John Quick and Sir William Lyne. Lyne had fought to the end although his health was failing rapidly, and two months after the election he died of heart disease at his home in Double Bay, Sydney, aged sixty-nine. In the *nil nisi bonum* glow of the parliamentary panegyric accorded to such events, Bill Lyne was described with genuine warmth as a hard fighter, a generous foe and a big Australian.

Before the first session of the new parliament ended, a sitting member of the lower house—E. A. Roberts (Lab, Adelaide), a Minister without portfolio in Fisher's second Ministry—fell dead in Queen's Hall. Poor Roberts was noted for his staunch imperialism, and it seemed ironic to some of his colleagues that he fell beside Queen Victoria's statue, striking his head upon its stone base and never stirring again.

Joseph Cook's Ministry consisted of five veterans from Deakin's last Cabinet, and five others including W. H. Irvine and W. H. Kelly. The party's Deputy Leader, Forrest, was Treasurer again, and Irvine (soon to be Sir William) was Attorney-General. The latter also found himself arraigned as defendant in parliament's first debate on pecuniary interest. Irvine held a general retainer from the Marconi Company, against which the Commonwealth was engaged in court action. On 9 September the Labor member for Kalgoorlie, Charles Frazer, moved that in the opinion of the House the Attorney-General's action violated rules of obligation laid down recently for the British Cabinet, and was detrimental to the best interests of the Commonwealth. Another Labor member, Dr Maloney, may well have remembered his promise to Irvine in the Victorian Assembly ten years before ('Your turn will come, my smooth beauty!'), for now he went in boots and all, accusing the Attorney-General of taking the side of a trust against his country—'a trust that leaves a slime of evilness wherever it appears'. The debate was heated, but not sufficiently so to melt an Iceberg. Irvine maintained that since a *general* retainer did not require him to accept any particular brief, his conduct did not violate the Westminster rules—which rules, as it happened, had been inspired by ministerial dabbling in Marconi's shares. The question was resolved in the negative.

Cook's statement of policy, tabled on 12 August, had not matured to much effect during the five weeks' adjournment. The only significant legislative achievements of the 1913 session were the Commonwealth Public Works Committee Act and the Committee of Public Accounts Act, establishing parliament's first joint statutory committees. These were committees established by act of parliament, as distinct from the 'domestic' committees established under Standing Orders by each new parliament for such internal purposes as printing, library and Standing Orders, and from the select committees established periodically by resolution of one or both houses to investigate such specific subjects as the old-age pension, stripper harvesters and

the tobacco monopoly. The Joint Committee on Public Accounts was modelled on practices of the New South Wales and Victorian legislatures to keep
check on public spending, and the Public Works Committee was to perform
a similar function with special reference to the Commonwealth's expanded
public works programme. Both committees consisted of six M.H.R.s and
three Senators, appointed at the start of each new parliament.

The Navigation Act of 1913, establishing a system of registration and
inspection for merchant shipping in the manner of similar British acts, had
been passed the year before. It had been reserved for the sovereign's assent,
however, because the British Board of Trade, concerned about possible conflict between some of the Act's provisions and Britain's treaty obligations,
maintained that the Commonwealth had no power to pass such legislation.
That view did not prevail, and the Act received royal assent after a delay of
ten months.

The only other events worth noting in 1913 were the introduction of several bills destined never to be enacted; and, outside parliament, the arrival of
Australia's first warships. The Government Preference Prohibition Bill,
which apart from its preamble consisted of only fifty-two words, was introduced in October for the specific purpose of provoking a disagreement
between the houses and in due course providing constitutional grounds for a
dissolution of them both. Cook had nothing to lose and possibly much to
gain from a double dissolution. So far no Governor-General had ever been
asked for such a complete re-election of parliament, but Section 57 of the
Constitution provided for double dissolution as a means of resolving
disagreement.

The Government Preference Prohibition Bill codified the existing government policy that there should be no preference or discrimination in employment by the Commonwealth on account of membership or non-membership
of any political or industrial association, which for practical purposes meant
a trade union. By no stretch of the imagination was this central to the Cook
Government's programme; but it was certain to be rejected by the Senate a
second time when re-submitted after an interval of three months. That
would give Cook his grounds for going to the Governor-General. A division
was called at every stage in the House of Representatives, and by grace of the
closure and the Speaker's casting vote the Bill was sent to the Senate. There,
however, its second reading was negatived a week before parliament was
prorogued. Round one to Cook.

With the freedom of action available to it in the Senate, the Labor Party
had initiated six bills in that chamber for the constitutional alterations which
had already been rejected twice at referendum. These bills lapsed at prorogation, but like the Government Preference Prohibition Bill, they were to
make another appearance next session.

On 4 October 1913 the first ships of the Royal Australian Navy steamed
into Sydney Harbour, setting a seal upon much work that had been done in
recent years to improve Australia's defences. The little fleet consisted of the
battle cruiser H.M.A.S. *Australia* and the light cruisers *Sydney* and *Yarra*, all
built to the Commonwealth's order in Britain; the destroyer *Warrego*,
shipped out in parts and assembled in Sydney; and the light cruiser *Encoun-*

ter, on loan from the Royal Navy. In 1913 all Royal Navy establishments in Australia were transferred to the Commonwealth. The Australian army had also been strengthened in accordance with most of Lord Kitchener's recommendations, but its role was conceived as one of national defence rather than service overseas. All young men, with provisions for exemption, were required to undergo part-time military training for seven years, and in 1911 the Royal Military College of Australia had been opened at Duntroon, the homestead of a sheep station within the area already proclaimed for the Commonwealth seat of government.

The second session, opened on 15 April 1914, was marked during its early weeks by an episode of unprecedented disorder. It was as if parliament had already begun the inevitable process of dissolution. When proceedings were resumed on 22 May after a luncheon for the new Governor-General, Sir Ronald Munro Ferguson, Speaker Johnson was informed that the Mace was missing from its customary place beneath the table, to which it had been restored, newly gilded, after the change of government. Two detectives were called to Parliament House; a search was mounted, and eventually the symbol of royal authority was found under one of the Opposition benches.

At about the same time Johnson noticed that his copy of Erskine May's treatise on parliamentary practice was also missing from its place on his desk. Late that night it was found lying open and face down in a fuel locker. In the early hours of the next morning, with a division about to take place, the attendants reported that keys had been removed from the chamber doors on either side of the Speaker's chair, preventing them from being locked during a division. Later still a coal scuttle was found outside a room in which the Treasurer was sleeping, no doubt intended to trip Sir John Forrest when he emerged.

Next day's *Argus* attributed the moving of the Mace to two Opposition members, Higgs and Webster. W. G. Higgs—sleek haired, dark suited, and rather sad of aspect—was capable of sudden outbursts of republican fury. There was an incongruity in this, said the *Argus*, as though a funeral were to bolt. He often spoke scornfully of the Governor-General, and in 1910, soon after his translation from the Senate to the House of Representatives, he had expressed the hope that the Mace would soon be placed in a museum. Higgs at first refused to confirm or deny the *Argus* report, but next sitting day he accepted full responsibility for the Mace incident.

'Acting in a spirit of frivolity', he said,

> which I admit is quite out of place in a serious-minded politician, I removed the mace. Perhaps I have not sufficient respect for the mace. These outward forms and ceremonies do not appeal to me as they do to honorable gentlemen who come from older countries, where the mace is regarded as a symbol of authority. However, I consider myself entirely to blame in the matter, and apologise . . .

His apology was accepted. A select committee was appointed to inquire into the other unseemly incidents. It held six meetings, examined twenty-four witnesses, and in the dying days of the parliament presented an interim report; before blame could be sheeted home to anyone, however, the 'committee on irregular conduct and interference' was forgotten amid matters of far greater moment.

Not since Lord Hopetoun had any Commonwealth governor-general faced problems of such urgency, and so soon after his arrival, as did Sir Ronald Munro Ferguson in mid-1914. What followed was not another vice-regal blunder of Hopetoun proportions; but to many observers at the time and later, some of the new Governor-General's actions in his first weeks of office seemed ill-advised, even improper. In retrospect this was surprising, for Munro Ferguson was probably better qualified by experience for his post than any previous governor-general, and for the rest of his long and difficult term he acquitted himself well.

Although only fifty-four when he reached Melbourne, this Scottish politician had been a Liberal member of the House of Commons for twenty-eight years, having been elected to Gladstone's old seat after graduating from Sandhurst and serving five years in the Grenadier Guards. His father and grandfather had been M.P.s before him, and his wife was the daughter of a marquess who had been Governor-General of Canada and Viceroy of India. Munro Ferguson himself had been private secretary to Lord Rosebery during Rosebery's term as Secretary of State for Foreign Affairs, and he was one of the Liberal Party Whips in the 1890s. He was a man of striking physical presence, a hard worker, and an astute judge of character.

On 28 May, only ten days after Munro Ferguson took office in Melbourne, the Senate negatived the first reading of the revived Government Preference Prohibition Bill. Cook raised the matter of double dissolution with the Governor-General soon after that, and on 3 June, having requested and obtained the Prime Minister's permission to do so, Munro Ferguson sought advice from the Chief Justice. The propriety of this informal recourse to the judiciary was to be questioned in later years, though some would conclude that it had been justified by Munro Ferguson's early lack of familiarity with the situation and the unprecedented nature of Cook's request. In any case, Sir Samuel Griffith's advice, when subsequently published, was seen to have been little more than 'Make up your own mind'. It did not follow, said Griffith, that the power of double dissolution could be regarded as an ordinary one which might properly be exercised whenever the occasion formally existed. It should, on the contrary, be regarded

as an extraordinary power, to be exercised only in cases in which the Governor-General is personally satisfied, after independent consideration of the case, either that the proposed law as to which the Houses have differed in opinion is one of such public importance that it should be referred to the electors of the Commonwealth for an immediate decision by means of a complete renewal of both Houses or that there exists such a state of practical deadlock in legislation as can only be ended in that way. As to the existence of either condition [the Governor-General] must form his own judgment.

Although he cannot act except upon the advice of Ministers, he is not bound to follow their advice, but is in the position of an independent arbiter.

The best legal opinion later came to hold that the ground of practical deadlock was self-evidently valid in 1914. Whether or not Munro Ferguson took that view, he chose to follow the principles of responsible government as they existed in the United Kingdom, where the monarch acted in all matters upon the advice of his ministers for the time being. Cook asked for a double dissolution on 4 June, and was granted it the same day.

As Cook's political opponents waited to hear whether or not there was to be an election for both houses, two members of the Press Gallery decided not to wait any longer. Parliamentary journalists were accustomed to calling on ministers in their rooms, and at their homes or hotels. On this occasion, however, Harry Peters and another representative of the Sydney *Daily Telegraph* took the liberty of going unannounced to Cook's room at the White Hart Hotel in Spring Street some time after midnight.

> They groped their way along in the semi-darkness to the Prime Minister's room [wrote one of their colleagues, B. S. B. Cook]. Their first knock was responded to by an irate "Who's there?" Peters had known Cook for years and was not deterred by his shouted terms of resentment at being disturbed. No, he had nothing to say. But the imperturbable Peters fired question after question at him . . . While the Prime Minister supplied no definite information, he spoke unguardedly and perhaps to a degree incautiously. What he said and his manner of saying it were sufficient for his acute and canny callers to justify Peters in summing up the question in the affirmative. Thus the *Daily Telegraph* had a notable scoop in announcing that His Excellency had granted Cook's request for a double dissolution.

In the Opposition's view—expressed in the form of a Senate resolution embodying an address to the Governor-General, and presented to His Excellency on 17 June by the President of the Senate, Senator Thomas Givens— such a solution violated the federal nature of responsible government in Australia. The address argued that the measure upon which the Prime Minister had based his request was not essential to the Government's programme, as the Government had already given effect to the principle contained in it; that the Senate had constitutional authority to reject the measure, and was amply justified in doing so; and that there was no real deadlock.

In support of the last assertion, the address reminded His Excellency that in 1913 the Senate had passed twenty-three bills, eighteen without amendment, and had rejected only two. This was not to say, of course, that relations between the two chambers had been harmonious. In December, for example, the Senate had placed on record its protest against a statement made by the Prime Minister that he was 'sorry to say that the language which has emanated from [the Senate] would not be heard in a pot-house'.

The address presented by President Givens asked the Governor-General to permit publication of communications between himself and his advisers, citing several precedents for such publication, and arguing that the decision to dissolve both houses simultaneously had raised matters of such grave constitutional and public interest as to justify publication of the precise reasons given by Cook in support of his request. 'The so-called "dead-lock" was deliberately created by the Government for party purposes', said the address. 'The decision of Your Excellency appears to be fatal to the principles upon which the Senate has hiterto acted, which, we submit, are in strict accordance with a truly Federal interpretation of the Constitution.'

> The Constitution deliberately created a House in which the States as such may be represented, and clothed this House with co-ordinate powers (save in the origination of Money Bills) with the Lower Chamber of the Legislature. These powers were given to the Senate in order that they might be used; but if a Senate may not reject or even amend any Bill because a Government chooses to call it a "test" Bill, although such Bill contains no vital principle or gives effect to no reform, the powers of the Senate are reduced to a nullity.

Although the Senate's function as a States' House had been greatly diminished by its own passivity, the federal argument was sound enough in theory. But it cut no ice with His Excellency. He had been advised, he said, that publication of correspondence would involve a breach of the confidential relations which should always exist in such matters between the representative of the Crown and his constitutional ministers. Furthermore, his advisers considered that to accede to the Senate's request for publication would imply recognition of a right in the Senate to make the ministry directly responsible to that chamber for advice tendered to the Governor-General, and that such recognition would not accord with the accepted principles of responsible government.

All this advice would soon be reversed by a new ministry, which would insist upon and obtain publication of Cook's grounds—grounds that proved to be no more than an assertion of a state of deadlock, epitomised by the two rejections of the Government Preference Prohibition Bill. What could not be changed was the precedent now established that sufficient cause for double dissolution could be deliberately engineered.

The Senate also added to the Governor-General's constitutional cares at this time by presenting another address praying that—in accordance with Section 128 of the Constitution, which gave His Excellency discretion to submit to referendum any proposed law for alteration of the Constitution after it had been initiated and passed by the Senate, and twice rejected or not passed by the House of Representatives—he should so submit the six Constitution Alteration Bills which had been initiated a second time in the Senate, and were now lying in the lower house. Acting on his Ministers' advice again, the Governor-General declined the Senate's request. This could be justified, for the Bills had been in the House of Representatives only one week, and at a time of constitutional crisis that hardly yet amounted to 'failure to pass'.

Both these constitutional issues, and the election campaign that was running its course to polling day on 5 September, were soon overshadowed by dissolution of another kind. The events of June and July in Europe—assassination at Sarajevo, Austria's ultimatum to Serbia, and Austrian mobilisation on the Russian frontier—did not receive the public attention they deserved in Australia, any more than they did until late July in Britain, where parliament and press were preoccupied with the issue of Home Rule for Ireland. Neither Cook nor Fisher referred to Europe in any of their campaign speeches until the very end of July. On 30 July the first official warning to Australia that war was imminent reached the Governor-General, who happened then to be in Sydney. There was some ambiguity about the deciphered cable, but next day His Excellency sent the following telegram to the Prime Minister, who was campaigning in Victoria: 'Would it not be well, in view of latest news from Europe, that ministers should meet in order that Imperial Government may know what support to expect from Australia?'

That night Cook and Fisher publicly expressed identical sentiments of loyal fatalism. The Prime Minister told a meeting at Horsham, in the Wimmera of north-western Victoria: 'Whatever happens, Australia is a part of the Empire to the full. Remember that when the Empire is at war, so is Australia at war'. At Colac, south-west of Melbourne, Fisher used words which had served much the same purpose during the Boer War: 'Should the worst happen, after everything has been done that honour will permit, Australians will stand beside [the mother country] to help and defend her to our last man and our last shilling'.

On 3 August a federal cabinet meeting in Melbourne decided to make two offers to the British Government: to place the Australian fleet under Admiralty control, and to despatch an expeditionary force overseas. 'If the Armageddon is to come', the Prime Minister told his fellow Australians, 'you and I shall be in it'. Two days later news reached the Governor-General's office in Melbourne that Britain's ultimatum over the invasion of Belgium had expired and the British Empire was automatically at war with Germany. In Australia's equally automatic, almost blithe acceptance of war, parliament was irrelevant. Not only was the institution dissolved, but the right to choose between war and neutrality was generally considered to be beyond its power. At that time the authority of the British Government and parliament in such matters was generally accepted in Australia, and no one had suggested that the Commonwealth's external affairs power could extend to declaring war and peace. In 1914 the choice was felt to lie with the Sovereign as head of the Empire, and he, or rather his British advisers, had chosen war.

Nevertheless there was some feeling in the Opposition that at this critical time parliament should somehow be revived without waiting for the election. W. M. Hughes suggested on 6 August that each party should withdraw the candidates it had put forward against sitting members. This would mean, he said, that all sitting members would be returned unopposed on nomination day, 14 August, and parliament could then meet at once. Alternatively he suggested withdrawing the formal proclamation dissolving parliament, a highly unconstitutional procedure which he felt could be validated later by an Indemnity Act from the United Kingdom parliament.

Cook's Government dismissed these inventive proposals—no doubt to its subsequent chagrin, and Labor's satisfaction. At a general election on 5 September Labor swept back into office. The new House of Representatives would have forty-two Labor members, thirty-two Liberals and one Independent, the former Protectionist, G. H. Wise; and in the Senate, Labor's majority had increased from 29–7 to 31–5. It looked as though Labor might well be in office for the duration of the war, but that appearance was deceptive.

5

Tumult and Shouting

Caesar

It was no exaggeration to say that the sturdy youth now taking up arms would thrive on war. Young Australian lives might be cruelly cut short on the other side of the world; but during the next four years the Commonwealth itself would flourish, its powers enhanced as a result of the national emergency. The same could also be said of the Attorney-General who had likened the pre-war Commonwealth to a sturdy youth, and had tried in vain to strengthen it by constitutional amendment. W. M. Hughes was by nature both combative and autocratic, and here was a fight that gave those qualities free rein. When it was all over, Australia would have sixty thousand dead, the Labor Party would be in disarray, and parliament would be in the doldrums; but the Commonwealth would be considerably stronger. Even though its emergency powers would not survive long in peacetime, the central government would be seen at the end of the Great War to have won valuable ground from its State partners in federation.

The sixth Commonwealth parliament began life on 8 October 1914. The new ministry was dominated by Fisher, Hughes and Pearce, though not necessarily in that order of importance. Hughes was Attorney-General again, and was elected by Caucus as deputy leader of the parliamentary Labor Party, a position which had remained unfilled since Fisher had succeeded Watson as leader. Labor's Leader in the Senate since 1901, Gregor McGregor, had died only three weeks before the election; but for some time past, because of failing health and failed eyesight, he had relied a good deal upon his deputy, Senator Pearce (WA), who now became Government Leader in the upper house as well as Minister for Defence. George Foster Pearce, the son of a blacksmith and himself formerly a carpenter, was endowed with the practical common sense of a good tradesman. He was calm in temperament and coolly persuasive in debate: a sound complement, in fact, for the fiery particle who would more often than not be taking Fisher's place in the lower house.

Exhausted by the Budget session, to say nothing of the political upheaval earlier in the year, Fisher departed as soon as possible for New Zealand, leaving his deputy in charge. It was not hard to discern Hughes's real motive in urging the Prime Minister to use this trip for recuperative as well as official purposes. 'You are in a land where it ought to be easy to forget everything else save the wonders of Nature', he wrote to his leader in January 1915.

> I pity the man who in the shadow of Mt Cook or perched on Malte Brun, his eye gathering in the wide flung glories of the Tasman Glacier and its majestic and awe inspiring sentinels, cannot blot out from his mind the daub of politics. Take a good holiday: don't hurry back for a week or so or more: Never mind your cursed schedule of dates . . . Store up my dear fellow, store up energy—that is store up life: For existence without energy is only another form of Death . . .

Fisher was little improved by his sea change, and in so far as anyone had charge of the parliamentary Labor Party, that one continued to be the Deputy Leader. In spite of its discipline, Caucus had always been a somewhat unpredictable group of individuals, influenced by various internal and external tensions. One tension making its presence felt at this time arose from the marked difference between attitudes held by the New South Wales and Victorian Labor Parties. The New South Wales branch—influenced by Watson, Hughes and the former Premier, J. S. T. McGowan, whose Ministry had lasted nearly three years—was pragmatic, and anxious to govern; in Victoria, where Labor had so far held office for only two weeks, the party was distinguished more by its ideological purity and its greater commitment to socialism than to gaining office.

If Hughes was the foremost exponent of New South Wales right-wing realism, his Victorian opposite was the idealistic socialist Frank Anstey, who had won the Melbourne seat of Bourke from Hume Cook in 1910. Anstey was born in Devon five months after the death of his father, and was brought up in conditions of great hardship until, at the age of eleven, he stowed away on a passenger ship bound for Australia. He worked as a bosun's boy and seaman for ten years in the Pacific trade, carried his swag in the outback, and eventually settled in Melbourne, where he became a Labor activist, president of the Tramway Employees' Association, editor of *Labor Call* and a member of the Legislative Assembly. His early life in Australia had much in common with that of Hughes, and during Anstey's first term in Spring Street the two men enjoyed a close personal association.

The war changed that almost immediately. Anstey saw Armageddon as 'a war of rival capitalists', the inevitable outcome of which would be 'the enslavement of labour', To Hughes it was nothing less than a life-and-death struggle between good and evil. On almost every wartime issue the two men were grimly at odds, and well matched. Anstey was solidly built, with a large head of wavy hair and handsome, florid features. He looked like an actor, but there was nothing contrived about the fierce abandon with which he lacerated opponents on both sides of the House. As Hughes's only equal in oratorical combat, he gathered around him several other left-wing rebels including Frank Brennan (Batman, V), the eleventh-born of one of Melbourne's best known Irish Catholic families; Dr Maloney, Australian-born and Protestant; and King O'Malley, still harbouring his grudge against Fisher and Hughes for having robbed him of the Commonwealth Bank.

On the third sitting day of the session, Fisher moved a motion that, in the opinion of the House, the sum of £100 000 should be paid from the Consolidated Revenue Fund as a grant in aid to Belgium. Although feeling in the House was overwhelmingly sympathetic to the little country which was then bravely resisting the German army, Anstey spoke strongly against the motion. He treated the House to chapter and verse on Belgium's past enormities in the Congo and ended by saying that not a penny should be voted for the relief of destitution abroad until Australia had devised a scheme for relieving misery and hunger within its own borders. Hughes spoke next, agreeing about the Congo but declaring it to be irrelevant. The question was resolved in the affirmative by 47 votes to 5.

Parliament acted quickly to arm the Commonwealth with emergency powers. The War Precautions Bill, modelled on an imperial measure, gave the Governor-General power to make regulations 'for securing the public safety and the defence of the Commonwealth'. It passed through all stages of both houses without amendment on 28 October, and was assented to the next day. A second War Precautions Bill, initiated six months later, met spirited but not very effectual opposition from Labor's left wing, on civil rights grounds. Offences against regulations under the Act were to be punishable on summary conviction. Anstey moved that nothing should be deemed a military emergency which deprived a British subject of the right of trial by jury, but the motion was lost 5–41, Anstey's only supporters being Maloney, O'Malley, Brennan and McGrath (Lab, Ballarat, V).

'I oppose every provision in this Bill', said Anstey on 29 April, the day on which parliament heard the first news of the landing on Gallipoli by Allied troops, including the Australian and New Zealand Army Corps (ANZAC), 'on the ground that there is no national emergency, and that nothing has happened to justify this interference with the civil rights of the people, and this handing over of such extensive powers to any particular section of the community'. Again Hughes spoke next:

> It appears to me that the trouble with the honorable member for Bourke and the honorable member for Batman, is that their imagination, fecund and exuberant as it is, moves only in one direction. They see the danger of civil liberty being lost. Their minds pierce the misty past, and grope with the shadowy host of reformers who have blazed the track of liberty; but they are blind to the blood-red present. They cannot see the tens of thousands of men who die every day that civil liberty may be maintained. They do not see through the mists of the abstractions in which they live the dreadful horrors of this war. They live in a little world of their own, where the sound and horrid din of war is never heard; where academic discussions about the civil rights of men take the place of action; such discussions, for instance, as the

Sansculottes and the Jacobins indulged in during the afternoon before going out next morning to behead each other . .

Mr ANSTEY.—Just a few words by way of benediction. My friend, the Attorney-General, did me the honour to say a few words about me, and to refer to my marvellous imagination. What envy! What jealousy! Never was Ananias more envious of Sapphira than is the Attorney-General of the honorable member for Bourke . . . The Attorney-General talked of the Sansculottes . . . but why did we come here if not to speak for the Sansculottes? Who constitute the nations of the world if it is not the Sansculottes? The Attorney-General was kind enough to remind honorable members . . . that the honorable member for Bourke had, at the beginning of the war, said something about the Belgian fund, the inference, of course, being that that honorable member is less English and less patriotic and less a lover of his race than is the Attorney-General.

Mr HUGHES.—I never said any of these things. That is all your—

Mr ANSTEY.—Imagination, I suppose. Do not let envy run away with you. I am saying all this to the Attorney-General in a kindly spirit.

Mr HUGHES.—You take a worm and make a sea-serpent out of it.

It was always Hughes who jousted in this way, never Fisher. While Caucus was discussing new financial proposals, including the Commonwealth's entry for the first time into the field of income tax, Anstey tried to lock horns with the 'Scotch Head' on theory of banking. Fisher merely wagged a finger at him and said solemnly, 'Ah, finance, finance, finance'. J. C. Watson—who had not contested his seat in 1910, and was now a parliamentary lobbyist and business associate of one of Australia's richest men, the Sydney wool merchant and manufacturer F. W. Hughes—heard it rumoured while visiting London in May that Fisher was going to succeed Sir George Reid as High Commissioner. Unlike earlier reports that the Prime Minister would become the first governor of the Commonwealth Bank, this one was correct.

Fisher had had about as much of the Prime Ministership as he could stand. The last straw of his frustration and humiliation consisted of being caught between pressure from the Australian Workers' Union, which wanted certain amendments to the Arbitration Act before parliament adjourned, and an undertaking which he had given to Cook that parliament would adjourn on 2 September. To satisfy the A.W.U., he had to break faith with a rightly aggrieved Opposition.

'Does the honorable member not see', asked Cook,

> that if arrangements made between parties cannot be adhered to, parliamentary government becomes impossible . . . After making this sacrifice in order to assist in clearing up the business today, we are now coolly told by the Prime Minister—although we have fulfilled our part of the bargain generously, and in full measure—that the arrangement cannot be adhered to on his side.

As soon as Cook had finished, Fisher uttered his last words in parliament. 'My words will be very brief', he said. 'The facts as stated by the honorable member for Parramatta are correct. I cannot adhere to the arrangement made, and I am very sorry.'

Soon afterwards George Pearce, entering Queen's Hall from the Senate side, met Fisher in hat and overcoat heading for the doors. Was the House up? asked Pearce. 'No, they are still sitting', Fisher replied angrily. Then, turning and shaking his fist at the eastern side of the building, he said: 'They can all go to––, George. I am not going back to that House again'. He was absent on the next three sitting days. On the fourth day, 27 October, the Speaker informed the House that Andrew Fisher had resigned his seat. The Attorney-General then announced that the Governor-General had requested him to form an administration, and that the former Prime Minister had been appointed High Commissioner in the United Kingdom. Sir George Reid's term as High Commissioner ended in January 1916, in which month he was conveniently elected unopposed to the House of Commons at a by-election for St George's, Hanover Square.

At the next Caucus meeting, 30 October, Hughes and Pearce were unanimously elected Leader and Deputy Leader of the parliamentary Labor Party. As recorded in the minutes, with occasional lapses of spelling, Hughes told the meeting that

> no matter what he may do as their cheif, without he had the same loyal support as they had accorded to Mr Fisher he could not fill the position with satisfaction to himself or the party. We had a great deal to do. Not only were we in the midst of a protracted and gastly war but had the Referenda fight in front of us which if carried would entail still more work on the party. They all knew him to be a man of strong opinions and he felt sure they would prefer him to express those opinions to the party.

Opinionated he was, indeed; but few would have been trusting enough to believe that Hughes would ever take anyone fully into his confidence. 'He has all the arts of a crab', wrote the Governor-General. 'When he does not wish to be drawn, he withdraws within the impenetrable shell of his designs, or very literally disappears into space, and apparently neither gets nor answers letters.' In spite of this, Munro Ferguson had the highest regard for Hughes—'My little man', as he sometimes called him in letters back to London. 'He is very small and nervous, very Welsh, able, active and determined . . . In some respects he is not unlike his countryman Lloyd George [Asquith's Minister for Munitions]. His judgment is better; his insight clear; his capacity for affairs great. He is highly strung and at times violent'.

In the grip of emotion, Hughes was capable of sweeping everything off his desk or hurling an ink well after some departing clerk. This was partly for theatrical effect and partly the genuine result of chronically bad health. He was a hypochondriac, and a physical fitness fanatic who exercised in the gymnasium and enjoyed horse-riding from his home at Kew, after he had settled in Melbourne, and at Sassafras, a farm which he bought in the Dandenongs. On one occasion at Kew, Hughes fell from the saddle after running into a backyard clothes line. He shouted for his chauffeur to bring an axe— not, as the chauffeur feared, to poleaxe the horse, but to vent his rage on the clothes line posts.

The only new faces in Hughes's first Ministry (the number of Ministers had been increased from seven to eight earlier that year, and was increased

*His Excellency the Right Honourable Sir Ronald Munro Ferguson
by David Low*

to nine in 1917) were those of the Mace-stealing Higgs, who became Treasurer; O'Malley, Home Affairs; and Webster, Postmaster-General. Anstey did not stand for selection. Hughes remained Attorney-General, and because of the additional burden imposed upon his department by the growing number of wartime regulations the departmental secretary, Robert Garran, was appointed to a new law office, that of Solicitor-General. In spite of the demands made on him as Prime Minister, Hughes continued to watch the law officers closely. Garran said that he seemed to have eyes all over him.

The referendums to which Hughes had referred in Caucus were the same six proposals for constitutional change that he had pushed untiringly in the past, and that were part of the platform on which Labor was returned to office. Hughes introduced them again in June 1915 with every apparent intention of going to the voters a third time. 'We were elected upon a programme which was clearly put before the people', he told the House,

> and neither the thunder of the guns nor the blood-red mists of war prevented the people from realising that they had to choose between the Liberal party and the Labor party. They chose the Labor party, one of whose fundamental planks for the last six years has been that there must be an amendment of the Constitution to protect the interests of the people. Upon that I stand, perfectly confident that the people will approve of what we propose to do.

The Bills passed through all stages, and writs were issued for a polling day in December. Well before that date, however, Hughes and some of his senior colleagues became converted to the Opposition's view that blood-red mists were not the right climate in which to canvass far-reaching changes to the Constitution. Hughes, who in any case feared that the proposals would be rejected again, was provided with a welcome alternative by the State Premiers. A conference of the Premiers, five of whom were Labor men, agreed to submit proposals to their parliaments for referral of the powers in question to the Commonwealth (as could be done under Section 51 of the Constitution) for the duration of the war and a year afterwards.

The left wing of the Labor Party felt betrayed by this submitting of its most cherished proposals to the will of the States' conservative upper chambers. 'We are about to remit these matters by agreement, to the Legislative Councils of the States', said Anstey, with a sharper edge than usual to his sarcasm

> and, of course, we may be quite sure that they will give us all the powers that we desire. Why refer these measures to the mass of the people when we do not know how they are likely to vote on them, or what we are going to get, when we can be sure as to what we are going to get from the Tory Legislative Councils of the States? I am perfectly satisfied that there could not be any better arrangement, because every honourable member opposite is agreeable to it. When I see the Leader of the Opposition agreeable to this proposal, I feel that I must be on good, safe Democratic ground.

As Anstey predicted, the States failed to legislate as required. Hughes considered recalling parliament to reinstate the lapsed referendums Bills; but there was not sufficient time before he departed for London on 20 January, leaving Senator Pearce as acting Prime Minister, and the Constitution intact. The coveted prizes of constitutional amendment had eluded the Labor Party again, but during Hughes's seven months abroad the High Court gave the Commonwealth all the power it would need in wartime. It did this primarily in the case of *Farey* v. *Burvett* in June 1916. Farey, who had been convicted on a charge of selling bread at more than the war regulation price, had challenged the validity of the relevant regulation and the War Precautions Act itself. With unaccustomed agreement, Griffith, Barton, Isaacs, Higgins and Powers upheld both instruments and gave the defence powers of Section 51 an exceedingly wide interpretation. Gavan Duffy and Rich dissented, arguing that the defence power was intended to cover only the raising, equipping and control of defence forces; economic control for war purposes, the dissenters held, was properly a State function. For the rest of the war the Commonwealth was free to fix prices, take over factories, intern aliens and censor news and opinion more or less as it pleased.

Hughes sailed for England via North America with his wife, their young daughter and a staff of four. Although Pearce acted as Prime Minister in his absence, it was as if Hughes had taken the authority of parliament with him. During the seven months he was away, parliament sat for only ten days, in May; by the end of 1916 the House of Representatives had a tally of no more than thirty sitting days, and the Senate thirty-three. In London the Prime Minister bypassed the new High Commissioner almost completely, much to Fisher's hurt surprise. Hughes relied for advice more on the 30-year-old Melbourne journalist in charge of an Australian newspaper cable service in Fleet Street, Keith Murdoch, and dealt directly with the highest levels of the British Government. He attended meetings of the full Cabinet and its war committee; became friendly with Lloyd George, though not with Asquith, whom he regarded as 'too perfectly civilised'; visited the front in France; addressed the Empire Parliamentary Association; and generally captured public imagination as a 'live wire' statesman. According to his own subsequent account, eighty-six British parliamentarians signed a request that he should stay in England and take a seat in the House of Commons; Lord Northcliffe offered to put £50 000 into a trust account for him if he would do that; and the Asquith Government dangled before him the prospect of third position in Cabinet.

Resisting these overtures, if indeed they had been made, Hughes returned home convinced by the worsening war situation that Australia would soon have to follow the lead of Britain and New Zealand by conscripting manpower for military service overseas. This was not such an unpalatable prospect for Hughes, with his long record of support for compulsory military training, as it was for many of his Labor colleagues. The main arguments for conscription were that Australia's national security depended upon Allied victory, that every Australian had a duty to defend the Commonwealth when it was endangered, and that only by compulsion could the burden of defence be shared equitably.

Trade unions were generally opposed to conscription on industrial as well as civil liberty grounds, fearing that it would be used to break down working conditions. The Melbourne and Sydney trades halls had condemned it, and annual conferences of the Political Labor Leagues in Victoria, New South Wales and Queensland had decided that any Labor members of parliament supporting conscription should be refused endorsement. Yet in May 1916 the question of a plebiscite on conscription was raised in federal parliament by the Labor Member for Grey (S), Alexander Poynton:

> Mr. POYNTON.—A referendum would settle the question.
> Mr JOSEPH COOK.—I, for one, would welcome a referendum, for my own profound conviction is that a referendum would have only one result—a triumphant vote for the application of the principle of compulsion.
> Mr TUDOR.—Would the right honorable member also, at the same time, put the questions for the alteration of the Constitution?
> Mr JOSEPH COOK.—May I suggest that that is not a question I should be asked? It would rest, I apprehend, with William the Great, when he returns home covered with honour and glory.

Hughes's first inclination was to introduce conscription by act of parliament, as Britain and New Zealand had done. The Governor-General promised him a dissolution of the lower house should that prove necessary, but it was not long before Hughes realised that the strongest opposition to such a measure would come from his own side of the House. Four days after his return, the Treasurer, Higgs, wrote him a 'Dear William' letter:

> I think I ought to tell you that during your absence public opinion amongst the trade unionists . . . appears to have become pronouncedly *anti-conscriptionist*. My view, as I think you know, is against compelling men to go abroad to fight. I think Australia has done and is doing all that can be reasonably asked of her. I think too the position is quite different to that in Europe. A conscript in Europe can return to his home within a few hours and from time to time is allowed to do so. A conscript Australian would be allowed to resume his 12,000-mile return journey only if wounded or ill . . . Conscription will, in my opinion, split the political labor party into fragments . . .

Hughes might have tried to introduce compulsory overseas service by regulation, but could he rely on the Executive Council? And would the Senate disallow such a regulation? A referendum it would have to be. On 24 August, the day Caucus began debating this crucial matter, the Government received a cable from the British Army Council—a cable now believed to have been arranged by Hughes through the commandant of A.I.F. headquarters in London, Brigadier-General R. M. Anderson—requesting, because of the exceptionally high Australian casualties at Pozières, a special draft of twenty thousand infantry in addition to normal monthly reinforcements.

Thus the stage was set for a Caucus debate that lasted four days and ended with a vote shortly before 2 a.m., endorsing the Prime Minister's proposal for a referendum, by 23 votes to 21. There was one condition, which Munro Ferguson described as 'a damaging concession . . . to the irreconcilables'. Hughes agreed that there should be one month's delay in a planned general call-up for home service (which would, of course, become overseas service in the event of a 'Yes' vote for conscription), and that if during that time enough men volunteered to meet the required number, there would be no call-up until after the referendum.

The irreconcilables were not reconciled. Hughes failed to convert the trades halls, and in the Political Labor Leagues his only substantial support came from the New South Wales Premier, Holman, and most of his ministers. On 31 August Hughes addressed a private meeting of members of both houses in the Senate club room, designed to facilitate passage of the Military Service Referendum Bill. Reporting on his visit to England, he emphasised the danger of a challenge to Australia's restrictive immigration policy after the war, and the need for Australians, if they expected Britain to help them then, to pull their weight militarily in the present emergency.

Hughes introduced the Bill on 13 September, and immediately the division within his party became apparent to all. Tudor, the Minister for Trade and Customs, resigned from the Ministry in protest, and Labor's left-wingers opposed the Bill at every stage. Their main argument against even a referendum was that military service was a matter of conscience in which a majority had no right to impose its will upon a minority.

Anstey's group mounted a root and branch attack by moving the following amendment to the question 'That the Bill be now read a second time': That after the word 'That' there should be inserted the words 'in the opinion of the House conscription of human life is inadvisable, and that the proposal of this Government, if given effect to, would be destructive of the best interest of Australia'. This was defeated by 12 votes to 49.

One of the few successful amendments, moved by the Minister for the Navy, Jens August Jensen (Bass, T), concerned a clause in the Referendum (Constitution Alteration) Act of 1906, which disqualified from voting at a referendum 'any naturalised British subject who was born in any country . . . with which Great Britain is now at war'. This would have disqualified two members of the House of Representatives—George Dankel, a former Adelaide butcher, and Jacob Stumm, proprietor of the *Gympie Times*. Dankel, who had emigrated from Germany at the age of fifteen to escape military conscription, had a son in the A.I.F.; Stumm had three. This kind of anomaly was removed by Jensen's amendment, which provided that the disqualifying clause of the earlier Act should not apply to any naturalised British subject, wherever born, who was the parent of a person who was or had been a member of Australia's military forces.

The question to be put at the referendum was: 'Are you in favour of the Government having, in this grave emergency, the same compulsory powers over citizens in regard to requiring their military service, for the term of this war, outside the Commonwealth, as it has now in regard to military service within the Commonwealth?' The campaign divided Australian society with a bitterness that was to last long after the referendum on 28 October. The anti-conscriptionists spread rumours that cheap coloured labour was being brought into Australia to replace conscripts. They in turn were smeared as cowards, traitors and sympathisers with the Industrial Workers of the World or Sinn Fein.

Ireland's troubles undoubtedly strengthened opposition to conscription from the Irish-Australian community, though an Irish name and Roman Catholic faith could not always be relied upon as indicators on this issue, and Roman Catholics volunteered in the same proportion as Protestants. Four senators and four MHRs were Irish-born, and five of them were Catholics. Of the Irish-born Catholics, two were conscriptionists: Patrick McMahon Glynn (Lib) and Senator Patrick Lynch (Lab).

On the very eve of polling day, three more ministers followed Tudor's example and resigned from Cabinet. Their disaffection began at an Executive Council meeting in Melbourne on 25 October attended by the Vice-President, Senator Albert Gardiner (N), Senator Russell (V), Higgs and Jensen, but not the Governor-General. The Solicitor-General submitted a draft regulation which he said the Prime Minister wanted them to approve but not to publish for the time being. The regulation authorised returning officers at the coming referendum to ask voters of call-up age certain questions designed to ascertain whether they had complied with the home service call-up that had been proclaimed on 29 September. Gardiner and Higgs were anti-conscriptionists. Russell, although sympathetic to Hughes, was also unwilling to approve the regulation. They refused to sign.

Next day Jensen took the night train to Sydney, where another Executive Council meeting was held on 27 October, attended by Hughes, Jensen, Webster and the Governor-General, the latter unaware that the regulation had been rejected in Melbourne. This time it was approved, and published in a special issue of the *Gazette* late that evening. Hearing of this in Melbourne almost immediately, Higgs, Gardiner and Russell telegraphed their resignations to Hughes and issued an explanatory statement to the press, which Senator Gardiner, acting Minister for Defence, was able to clear with the censor. As soon as Hughes received the telegrams, just before midnight, he telephoned the Governor-General at Admiralty House, Kirribilli, asking to see him immediately. Munro Ferguson crossed the harbour to Circular Quay, where he found a very worried Prime Minister waiting for him in a taxi. 'The poor little man asked for advice and sympathy, wrote the Governor-General to the Colonial Secretary, Bonar Law, 'saying he "had not a brainwave left!" I suggested "censoring" the announcement of the resignations until after polling day. The PM agreed and hurried off to discover it was too late . . .'.

The voters' answer next day was 'No', by a small national majority of 72 476 in a total vote of 2 308 603. Victoria, Tasmania and Western Australia voted 'Yes', but negative majorities were returned in the three other States—most strongly in New South Wales, where an important factor was the primary producers' fear that conscription would leave them short of labour. Other factors in the decisive New South Wales vote, according to Hughes, were 'the shirker vote and the Irish vote'. For Hughes the result was tantalisingly close. 'The Ides of March have come and gone and Caesar still lives!' he wrote to his London confidant, Keith Murdoch. 'But he lives as Cicero said of his dear friend Catiline on sufferance—or a least in doubt! We have lost by a head! Ah! that head. How little yet how much.'

On sufferance indeed. By 14 November, when Caucus held its next meeting, two more ministers were on the brink of resignation—Mahon (External Affairs) and O'Malley. Although Hughes had been expelled by the Political

Labor League of New South Wales he still regarded himself as a member of the Labor Party, maintaining that conscription was a federal issue, upon which neither the federal executive nor federal conference of the A.L.P. had delivered a ruling. He disliked the idea of a Deakin-style fusion, but was attracted by the possibility of forming a centre party dedicated to winning the war.

Hughes, presiding over the Caucus of sixty-four Labor members in Parliament House, said that 'the meeting had been called at the request of a number of members by requisition and he would like to hear what they had to say'. Let the orators speak! W. F. Finlayson—he who had tried to close the parliamentary bar—rose to his feet and moved, without elaboration, 'That Mr W. M. Hughes no longer possesses the confidence of this party as Leader, and that the office of Chairman of this party be, and is hereby declared vacant'. The debate that followed was the most disorderly that anyone could remember. After luncheon adjournment, J. H. Catts launched a tirade against the Prime Minister, who took it calmly enough but was smoking a cigarette, which was unusual for him. Suddenly Hughes held up his hand, silencing Catts, and said in a firm voice: 'Enough of this. Let those who think with me follow me'. Gathering up his belongings he left the room, followed by thirteen M.H.R.s and eleven senators. Pearce went ahead to unlock the Senate clubroom; when they were all seated, Hughes rose and said: 'Well, here we are!'

Where they were politically was still very much in doubt, for there had been no prior discussion with the Liberal Party. But the clubroom meeting decided at least to act as a separate party (later named the National Labor Party) and to support the Ministry which Hughes selected forthwith. Poynton replaced Higgs as Treasurer, and among other new Ministers were W. O. Archibald (Hindmarsh, S), F. W. Bamford (Herbert, Q), W. G. Spence and Senator P. J. Lynch (W). Later in the afternoon Hughes was promised 'discriminating' Liberal support so long as his Government confined itself to the war effort, and at 9.30 p.m. he took his ministers to Government House. In Munro Ferguson's opinion the strength of the Labor Ministry had been 'the hurricane force of the Prime Minister, the good character of Senator Pearce, and the trained mind of Mr Garran'. That strength would still be available. After discussion with the Governor-General, Hughes tendered his resignation and accepted a commission to form a new Government. Bibles were produced, and at a late hour His Excellency swore in the Commonwealth's twelfth Ministry.

Caesar still lived, but in the lower house his legion numbered only fifteen (Josiah Thomas, who had not attended the Caucus meeting, joined Hughes later); Labor still had twenty-four seats there, the Liberals had thirty-five, and there was one Independent. In spite of the apparent invitation to cut-throat euchre, parliament did not resume that bloodthirsty game. At a special interstate conference in December the Labor Party voted overwhelmingly to expel from its ranks all members who had supported conscription, and this was carried out with the sort of animus on both sides that precluded reconciliation. Much as Hughes disliked the idea of fusion, he and his National Labor colleagues needed the electoral organisation of an established party, and that was available only from the Liberal Party. With the help of some honest brokering by his friend Hume Cook, the Victorian Protectionist who had lost his seat in 1910, Hughes engaged in protracted negotiations with two senior Liberals—W. A. Watt (Balaclava) and Sir William Irvine, both former Premiers of Victoria—who apparently had no qualms about up-staging their parliamentary leader.

'The little devil won't listen to anything I have to say', complained Watt to Hume Cook after one of his sessions with Hughes. Sufficient common ground was nevertheless established for Hughes to parley with Joseph Cook, towards whom he usually adopted a half-amused, half-hectoring manner. On one occasion, after listening carefully to the Liberal leader for the best part of an hour, he turned off his Acousticon and said: 'It's no bloody good, Joe. You might just as well piss up against the Pyramids and imagine you're irrigating the Nile Valley'. Cook and his Victorian colleagues wanted Hughes to remain Prime Minister. Sir John Forrest, although now in his seventieth year, still yearned for leadership. He suggested a three-party wartime government, but lost what Liberal support he may have had for his ambition to lead such a coalition by arguing that conscription was properly a matter for parliament rather than a referendum, and advocating an early election on that issue. The last thing most Liberals wanted was an election race in which they would be hobbled by the 'No' vote. Labor's new leader, Frank Tudor, would not—indeed, could not—agree to coalition. The Liberals, alarmed by Forrest's talk of an election, committed themselves to a fusion led by Hughes on one main condition. This condition was that the new Government would try to extend the life of Parliament (the next election for the lower house was not due until October 1917) to October 1918 or six months after the end of the war, whichever came sooner.

Parliament reassembled on 8 February 1917, and Hughes's third Ministry was sworn in nine days later. It consisted of five National Labor Ministers and six Liberals, the latter being Joseph Cook, second in Cabinet seniority but holding the Navy portfolio; Forrest (Treasurer); Senator E. D. Millen (Vice-President of the Executive Council, and Government Leader in the Senate); Watt (Works and Railways); Glynn (Home and Territories) and Groom (Honorary Minister). Hughes's undertaking to extend the life of parliament could be carried out by referendum (a course no one wanted to take, given the electorate's recent voting record) or by amendment of the Commonwealth Constitution Act in the United Kingdom parliament. Hughes had already made arrangements with the Colonial Secretary for the second course of action to be taken should an appropriate resolution be passed by both houses of the Commonwealth parliament.

The resolution was carried in the House of Representatives on 2 March, by 34 votes to 17, but not before Anstey had spoken at length, and with apt historical allusion, about the latest Ministry:

We have in the present Fusion in Australia a repetition of the situation in 1904, when Mr Deakin took a section of his followers over to Mr Reid's side. It was, I think, on that occasion that the present Prime Minister uttered his strong denunciation . . . He wrote that "there are once or twice in a generation periods when a great party under the influence of some powerful and malignant purpose drops its principles and goes over to the enemy." The same thing is exemplified today ... Look at the line of Fusion leaders the Commonwealth has had—Sir George Reid, Mr Deakin, Mr Joseph Cook, then Mr Deakin and Mr Cook again, and now Mr William Morris Hughes. That is the line of succession of the leadership of the parties that have failed, of those who, in the history of this country, have always represented the most reactionary faction.

Words were all that the Opposition could bring to bear against Hughes in the lower house, and he was pretty well impervious to words, even those as carefully chosen as Anstey's. But how could the government have its way in the Senate, where Labor could also bring superior voting power (20–16) to bear against the proposed resolution? The answer seemed plain enough to Hughes: he would try to change the balance of power in the other place. Shortly before the resolution was introduced there, the health of three of Tasmania's four Labor senators suffered a significant decline. Senator James Long was so obviously in need of sea air that the government sent him on a trade mission to the Dutch East Indies. Senator James Guy reported by telegram from hospital in Launceston that he could not attend parliament, and soon afterwards Senator Rudolph Ready fainted at Parliament House. Ready was only thirty-eight years of age, and, as it turned out, he had another forty-one years ahead of him. The fainting spell alarmed him to such an extent, however, that two days later he tendered his resignation to President Givens, soon after 6 p.m.

What followed was likened by one observer to 'greased lightning'. It happened that the former Premier of Tasmania—John Earle, who had been expelled from the Labor Party during the recent 'Split'—was conveniently in Melbourne. That very evening he was whisked away to Government House, where he signed his resignation from the Tasmanian parliament. This was immediately telegraphed to the Governor of Tasmania together with President Givens's notification of the casual vacancy caused by Senator Ready's resignation. Normally such a vacancy would have been filled by vote of the Houses of State parliament sitting together, but as it happened the Tasmanian parliament was not in session. In such an event, the Governor of Tasmania was empowered to appoint a new senator on the advice of his Executive Council. The new Liberal Premier, W. H. Lee, who had been in touch with Hughes while visiting the mainland recently, requested an immediate meeting of the Executive Council. The Council met at 9.15 p.m., little more than three hours after Ready's resignation, and appointed Earle to the vacancy.

When the Senate met next morning, 2 March, Senator Earle was waiting in Queen's Hall to take his seat. But Hughes had not reckoned on Tasmanian pride. Two Liberal Tasmanian senators, Bakhap and Keating, considering the dignity of their State to have been struck by lightning, declared their intention of voting against the resolution. There was no longer any point in putting it to the vote. Parliament adjourned, and on 5 March Hughes advised the Governor-General to dissolve the lower house. An election for that House and half the Senate was called for 5 May.

William Morris Hughes: 'Who said Peace?'
by David Low

Hughes himself would certainly have been defeated had he tried to retain the solidly Labor seat of West Sydney. Instead he gained unanimous pre-selection as 'Win-the-War' candidate for Bendigo, a Victorian seat which Labor had won narrowly from Sir John Quick in 1913, and had held even more narrowly at a by-election in 1915. Hughes did his best to play down conscription (he denied any intention of holding another referendum on the matter 'unless Australia and the Empire were threatened with national disaster'), and concentrated on the theme embodied in the fusion's campaign slogan, which neatly implied that Labor was a 'Lose-the-war party'.

'Win-the-war' was an unbeatable slogan. The voters who had rejected conscription voted overwhelmingly for the men in both houses who had sought to introduce it. In the lower house Hughes and his supporters won fifty-three seats to Labor's twenty-two, a landslide of unprecedented extent at federal elections. In the Senate the numbers were now 'Win-the-War' (or Nationalist Party, as the fusion became known) twenty-four, Labor twelve. Hughes himself defeated the sitting Labor candidate in Bendigo by 16 272 votes to 12 091.

His *bête noire*, King O'Malley, was defeated in Darwin (T) by a 'Win-the-War' candidate, C. R. Howroyd. Doubtless it seemed only right to the King that Howroyd died before being sworn in, but that untimely death was no help to him. A better candidate—W. G. Spence, who had also left the Labor Party with Hughes, only to be defeated in May—stood at the by-election, and the 61-year-old gilt-spurred rooster did not bother to nominate. O'Malley had thirty-six more years to live, and devoted that long twilight to such tasks as running unsuccessfully for parliament on two more occasions, defending his claim to have begotten the Commonwealth Bank, and literally making his own coffin. Two other casualties of the general election were the German-born M.H.R.s, Stumm and Dankel. Both were conscriptionists, and all their sons in the A.I.F. survived the war.

Three of the candidates were women, but none of them came close to winning. The Victorian Vida Goldstein, who had run for the Senate in 1903 and 1910, did so again in 1917, perhaps just to see whether another lapse of seven years had made any difference to her chances. It had, but in a negative way: this time she received only 2.13 per cent of the lowest successful candidate's vote. Mrs Henrietta Greville, an anti-conscriptionist well known for her trade union and feminist work, stood against W. H. Kelly in Wentworth, and received 30 per cent of his vote. Mrs Eva M. Seery, an organiser of Women's Unions in New South Wales, and another anti-conscription campaigner, contested the seat of Robertson, receiving 42 per cent of the sitting Labor candidate's vote. These percentages were more or less on a par with those achieved by the few earlier women candidates for the House of Representatives—two in 1914 and three in 1913.

The seventh parliament, with Mace and wigs restored, was opened perfunctorily on 14 June, merely for the purpose of obtaining supply. The sight of the Mace and wigs elicited various satirical remarks from the Opposition, and this in turn inspired what the *Age* called 'a remarkable counter demonstration' by the ministerialists. They rose in a body, gave three hearty cheers, and sang 'God Save the King'. The last Speaker but one, William Elliot Johnson, was elected unopposed in place of Speaker McDonald, and two Supply Bills were passed through all stages. Next day members of both houses met unofficially to discuss recruiting, a matter that was to become increasingly urgent as the second half of the year unfolded. Parliament was then prorogued until 11 July, when the eighteen new senators were due to take their seats.

Hughes, still settling details of the Nationalist programme with his coalition partners, had asked the Governor-General to dispense with his traditional opening speech. For once Munro Ferguson found himself out of agreement with his 'little man': there had been no opening speech for three years past, he told Hughes, 'and this must be a record, unless in the Long

Parliament we had a rival'. Thus, when opening the second session in July, His Excellency foreshadowed a programme that was still imperfectly prepared. A parliamentary recruiting committee, consisting of members of both parties, would assist the Director-General of Recruiting in securing the seven thousand volunteers per month required to maintain Australian divisions in the field at full strength. Bills would be introduced for the taxation of wartime profits, and to increase the rate of income tax. The Commonwealth Conciliation and Arbitration Act would be amended with a view to preventing strikes and lock-outs that might affect the efficient prosecution of the war; and to show that the Government was not totally preoccupied by war, investigations would be mounted into the eradication of cattle tick, sheep blow-fly, worm nodules in beef, and prickly pear.

In response to this programme the Opposition took the unprecedented but effective course of offering no speakers for the Address-in-Reply debate. This deprived the Government of time to get its measures ready, and obliged Hughes to reveal his unpreparedness by seeking a week's adjournment. The Senate, on the other hand, occupied itself for the rest of the week with various items of business, including the re-election of President Givens, who had left the A.L.P with Hughes.

Like other combatant nations, Australia experienced widespread industrial conflict in 1917. It began at the New South Wales Government tramway workshops where a job-record system, introduced without union consultation, was perceived by employees as an attempt to make everyone measure up to the pace of the fastest. The Conciliation and Arbitration Act had not been amended to cope with strikes affecting the war effort; in any case, it would probably have taken more than that to stop the general strike of August–September from running its course. The mood of trade unions was so militant that the strike spread quickly to the railways, mines and docks, involving 95 000 workers and lasting almost three months.

The basic causes of the strike were war-weariness and dissatisfaction over the blatant differences between wages, rising prices, uncontrolled war profits and the high interest being paid on war loans. For Hughes, however, the explanation seemed more sinister. On 17 August he wrote to Lloyd George, who was by then the British Prime Minister:

> As I write we have a great strike unfolding itself. It may collapse tomorrow. On the other hand it may result in a great pitched battle, in which case I am going to see it through to the bitter end. The IWW and the Irish are mainly responsible for the trouble. In a sense it is political rather than industrial. The fact is we wiped the floor with them on May 5th and they are now trying to take the reins of Govt out of our hands . . . The Irish have captured the political machinery of the Labor organisations— assisted by the Syndicalists and IWW people ... One of their archbishops—Mannix—is a Sinn Feiner—And I am trying to make up my mind whether I should prosecute him for statements hindering recruiting or deport him.

Hughes exaggerated the significance of the Industrial Workers of the World, an international revolutionary movement which the Government had effectively suppressed in Australia after an outbreak of arson in Sydney in 1916. But his paranoia was hardly surprising, for only two days before he wrote to Lloyd George Parliament House had been besieged by an unruly crowd led by the suffragist and Labor campaigner, Adela Pankhurst. The Government had recently adopted a regulation prohibiting the holding of demonstrations within a wide area around Parliament House, but this did not deter Pankhurst, whose protest was ostensibly against the high cost of living, but also very much in sympathy with the strike. By 3 p.m. the broad steps of Parliament House were seething with a crowd of about two thousand, many of whom were women. Some five hundred police were stationed in and around the building, and fire hoses were at the ready. Pankhurst tried to address the crowd, but was snatched by the police from her screaming supporters and placed under arrest.

No sooner had the strike ended than the issue of conscription returned to divide the nation again. The war had taken a turn for the worse. In October the Bolshevik revolution removed Russia from hostilities, allowing Germany to concentrate its forces on the Western Front. Australian casualties between August and November were more than 38 000, and voluntary enlistment had fallen far below the required seven thousand per month. The October intake was in fact only 2761. America had adopted conscription when it entered the war in April, and Canada followed suit in October, by act of parliament. Why not Australia as well?

Hughes was reluctant to raise the issue again; but it was soon raised for him in public speeches by Sir William Irvine, who earlier in the year had made the extraordinary suggestion that the United Kingdom parliament should legislate for conscription in Australia. After consulting Pearce and Cook, Hughes decided that the military situation had deteriorated sufficiently to release him from his electoral promise not to hold another referendum. As parliament was then in recess, arrangements for a poll on 20 December were made by regulation under the War Precautions Act.

The second campaign reached new levels of acrimony and violence. Returned soldiers broke up 'No' meetings; pacifists heckled meetings of patriotic women; and platforms were showered with road metal and broken glass. The gaunt figure of Archbishop Daniel Mannix was more to the fore than in 1916. He accused the Government of not having 'the ordinary honesty or even decency to put a fair, straight question', and the point was well made. This time the question avoided any direct reference to compulsion. All it asked was: 'Are you in favour of the proposal of the Commonwealth Government for reinforcing the Australian Imperial Forces overseas?'

The New South Wales Premier, Holman, who had been deeply impressed by the desperate state of the war on a visit to England, agreed to support a 'Yes' vote on two conditions: that the fate of the Hughes Government should be determined by the outcome, and that the Government should not try to influence the vote by censorship. Hughes agreed, and in more than one campaign speech he rashly promised to resign if the result was 'No'.

Both Hughes's undertakings to Holman were broken. Military censors deleted material from press reports of 'No' speeches, particularly in Queensland, where the anti-conscription campaign was being led by the Labor

Premier, T. J. Ryan. The reports of Ryan's opening speech were cut so drastically that on 22 November he repeated it in parliament to secure publication by Hansard. Hughes arrived in Brisbane four days later, and at ten o'clock that night he accompanied a party of censors and soldiers to the Government Printing Office, where 3300 copies of the relevant Hansard were seized.

A special meeting of the Queensland cabinet authorised the immediate publication of an extraordinary *Commonwealth Gazette* on the incident, and some of Ryan's political associates went so far as to suggest, seriously, that the Prime Minister ought to be arrested on suspicion of being of unsound mind. Hughes nevertheless made his departure for Melbourne unimpeded, alighting *en route* at Warwick railway station, where a hostile crowd was waiting for him. In the ensuing mêlée an anti-conscriptionist named Paddy Brosnan knocked the Prime Minister's hat off with an egg. Brosnan was later arrested for interjecting during the Prime Minister's speech, but when Hughes asked the police officer in charge—another Irish-Australian, Henry Butler Kenny—to make more arrests, Kenny asked what charges were to be laid. Hughes said that he was ordering the arrests in his capacity as Attorney-General, and that the laws of the Commonwealth overrode those of Queensland. The sergeant replied that he was under instructions from the Government of Queensland. Before that issue could be resolved, the train pulled out, taking a furious Prime Minister back to Melbourne. For his intransigence, Senior Sergeant Kenny was later rewarded by Dr Mannix with a rosary and box of cigars.

The referendum decision was 'No', by more than twice the national margin of 1916; but Hughes did not relinquish office. He tendered his resignation on 8 January 1918, and later that day the Governor-General received several callers: the Labor leader Tudor; the senior Nationalists Cook, Watt and Forrest; and two other Nationalists, the former Independent G. H. Wise and the former Labor member Alexander Poynton, both of whom had been mentioned as possible leaders of a new Government. Tudor was willing to form a Ministry, but the Governor-General had no confidence in his ability to do so.

Sir John Forrest was more than willing to try, and Munro Ferguson was half inclined to let him have his chance at last. '[Forrest] denounced the Prime Minister's autocratic ways', he wrote to London, 'frequently reiterating the phrase *aut Caesar aut nihil*, his want of method in the conduct of affairs, and asserted that all real business was hung up in favour of limelight exhibitions on the platform'. After talking to Cook and Watt, however, the Governor-General concluded that Forrest would no more be able to form a workable ministry than Tudor. In a sense quite different from Cesare Borgia's motto, it was indeed a case of 'Caesar or nothing'. Two days later Hughes and all his previous ministers were sworn in again. In later and calmer judgement Hughes's continuation in office would be seen as having been justified in the circumstances; in 1918, however, there were many who could not forgive him. 'I have long known that Mr Hughes is a man whose pledged word is absolutely worthless', said his friend and associate of long ago, William Holman. '[He is] a man who has never been loyal to anybody or anything.'

Hughes had wished to drop Forrest and Glynn from his fourth Ministry, but the party would not let him. He nevertheless managed to rid himself of Sir John's hostile company by arranging a peerage for him—the first ever conferred upon an Australian. At first, to Hughes's dismay, Baron Forrest of Bunbury and Forrest (the former being his birthplace in Western Australia, and the latter his ancestral native heath in the Scottish county of Fife) proposed to hold seats in the House of Lords, the House of Representatives and Cabinet. Only his rapidly declining health prevented this. Lord Forrest was dying of a cancerous growth on the temple. He resigned from parliament on 27 March, and later in the year, accompanied by his wife and a nurse, sailed for London in the troopship *Marathon*) to take his seat in the House of Lords.

But not even the fortitude of one who had ridden twice across Western Australia, had been that colony's first Premier, and had served in seven Commonwealth ministries, could withstand the cruel adversary in his temple. He died on 3 September, soon after his seventy-first birthday, while the ship was anchored off Sierra Leone on the west coast of Africa. His body was sent ashore for burial at Freetown, a port then closed to passengers because of plague. The remains were later exhumed and reburied, to the sound of bagpipes, with Lord Forrest's sword and banner on the coffin, at Karrakatta cemetery in Perth.

Hughes easily survived a want of confidence motion by Tudor, and embarked in April on another extended visit to Britain and Europe. This time his party consisted of wife and daughter; his private secretary, Percy Deane; his messenger, Corrigan; the Solicitor-General; a publicity officer; and an abdominal specialist physician, who did what he could for Hughes's chronic dyspepsia.

Almost as if such information was immaterial, he omitted to tell the Governor-General who would be acting Prime Minister during his absence, which turned out to be an absence of seventeen months. 'Like the Chevalier Grammont who forgot to marry the Hamilton sister', wrote Munro Ferguson, 'he forgot to tell me who was to act Prime Minister and so I, not liking these little forgetfulnesses, wired to Sydney for information and wrote formally to the Cabinet pointing out that such information should have been furnished before the PM left the seat of Government'. The answer was Forrest's successor as Treasurer, W. A. Watt. Hughes made amends for his omission with 'an exceedingly nice letter', and wrote periodically to the Governor-General from London.

As it will not be possible in this narrative to deal adequately with Hughes's eventful sojourn in the Northern Hemisphere, he may be left for the time being in one of the martial poses that won him the sobriquet of 'The Little Digger'. 'I saw a great thing last week in France', he wrote to Munro Ferguson in July.

I talked to the boys who were going into the Hamel stunt just before they started: I can't tell you how splendid they were: words are poor things to describe them but as they stood there thousands of them armed cap-a-pie: helmets full kit ready for action their bayonets glistening in the sun: an enemy aeroplane overhead being attacked by our anti-aircraft guns—this

Billy Hughes and Diggers in Sydney, 1919

Charles McGrath (left) and Frank Anstey organising for the Labor Party in the backblocks of Victoria

The House of Representatives in Melbourne, c. 1909, with Speaker Salmon in the Chair and Deakin's third Ministry on the front bench

Landscaping with draught horses in front of the provisional Parliament House in Canberra, c. 1926

The Prime Minister, S. M. Bruce, welcomes Their Royal Highnesses the Duke and Duchess of York at the Duke's opening of the provisional Parliament House, Canberra, 9 May 1927.

was some 3 miles from the front of the front, I thought that with a million of such men one could conquer the world.

Khaki

Of the 330 000 Australians who served overseas during the Great War, ten were members of parliament. The figure was not disproportionately low. On the contrary, it was surprising that as many as ten members should have enlisted, at the average age of forty-three. It was also surprising that they should have retained their seats and salaries while overseas, and that in the main their electors did not seem to mind such virtual disfranchisement. Indeed a military uniform made re-election almost certain. Only one of the khaki candidates lost his seat while serving King and country, and there was a particular reason for that.

The first to enlist, immediately after the election in September 1914, were two M.H.R.s with previous military experience. Granville de Laune Ryrie had formed a troop of light horse for the Boer War, and later commanded a New South Wales Light Horse Regiment for seven years. He entered the A.I.F. as a colonel, served in Gallipoli and Palestine, was wounded twice, mentioned five times in despatches, and ended the war as Major-General Sir Granville Ryrie. During that time he was also the Honourable Member for North Sydney, receiving parliamentary salary as well as military pay and an allotment for his wife, but attending the House for only three of its 320 sitting days during the sixth and seventh parliaments. Some concern was expressed in the House that, by enlisting, Ryrie might be taking an office of profit under the Crown, which according to Section 44 of the Constitution would disqualify him from parliament. But closer reading of this section showed that receipt of pay as a member of the Commonwealth's armed forces was permitted.

Percy Phipps Abbott, the Member for New England, had been a major in the New England Light Horse, and he ended the war as a lieutenant-colonel commanding the 10th Light Horse Regiment, A.I.F. Both he and Ryrie were Liberals in safe Liberal seats. No pairing arrangements were entered into for parliament, but during the first two years of the war the Opposition was so outnumbered by Labor that the absence of Liberal votes from New England and North Sydney made no real difference.

The next to go was Senator J. V. O'Loghlin, a Labor senator who had raised and commanded an Irish Corps in South Australia before the war. Lieut-Colonel O'Loghlin spent more than a year commanding reinforcements on troopships going to Egypt, Gallipoli and England, but resumed his Senate seat when Labor's majority there was substantially reduced by the Split. The seven other members who enlisted from 1916 onwards were all M.H.R.s, and their party affiliations maintained an approximate balance that precluded any need of pairing. Two of them saw the Western Front at its worst, but the same could not be said of the other five, some of whose military careers were notable only for political controversy.

Lieutenant R. J. Burchell (Fremantle, W) had been a railway employee before entering parliament. He served as a railway transportation officer in France, and was awarded the Military Cross in 1918. Lieutenant W. M.

Fleming (Robertson, N) served in France with the Army Service Corps, and was gassed at Péronne. Both were Nationalists, Burchell having followed Hughes out of the Labor Party over conscription, and Fleming having been previously a Liberal. Warrant Officer Charles McGrath, the Labor Member for Ballarat, also served in France with the Army Service Corps from 1916 until April 1918, when he was retired medically unfit. He applied twice for service at the front; but according to the drift of a question asked in the House, his applications were denied because he was a Labor member.

Two other members who enlisted in 1916 were, like McGrath, anti-conscriptionists who remained in the Labor Party. Only that fact, it seemed, could explain the notoriety that accompanied their war service. Quartermaster Sergeant Alfred Ozanne, the member for Corio (V), was farewelled by members of both houses in May 1916, six months before the Split, at a dinner in Queen's Hall. There were toasts to the King, the Governor-General and 'Our Guest'. In response to the latter Ozanne referred to his only brother, who had enlisted in August 1914, and was one of the first to land at Gallipoli:

> He had been sent back to Lemnos to rest [said Ozanne], but had had to return to the firing line because the promised reinforcements were not forthcoming. He had been killed. The man who had hung back, and failed to make good the promise of reinforcements, was the murderer of his brother . . . He, personally, refused to stay here in comfort and security, knowing these things as he did. (Cheers) He personally was making a great sacrifice. He was leaving a wife and four children, and his brother had left a wife and three children. It was a big strain, but he realised that there were many men who were worse off than he. He had his Parliamentary salary, while many men had nothing but their 6/- a day . . . When the history of the war came to be written there would be much heart-burning and self-examination. If they asked him, 'What did you do as a legislator responsible for Australia's part in the war? Did you stay in your soft cushioned seat, drawing your salary, and asking others to give up their lives so that you might stay here in safety?' he wanted to be in a position to say, 'No; when my country asked me to do my duty I heard the call, and I went.' (Cheers.)

Ozanne was not to know that after such a warm farewell his army career, such as it was, would end in bitter political wrangling. He completed his N.C.O. training in England, but was taken ill with a serious ear infection before embarking for France. In January 1917 he clarified his political position in a cable rejecting Hughes and declaring his loyalty to the Labor Party. Although he later visited some Australian units in France, he was not destined to go on active service. The army recommended his medical discharge, and he sailed for home in April, while the general election campaign was warming up.

Ozanne was opposed in Corio by a recruiting officer named J. H. Lister, who at first had no overt connection with the Nationalist Party. The Nationalists began by paying lip service to the principle of immunity for khaki candidates; but a week before polling day, while Ozanne was still crossing the Indian Ocean, the Defence Minister, Senator Pearce, made a damaging attack on the sitting member in a speech at Corio's main centre,

Geelong. He also released to the press the text of a cable from AIF headquarters in London, sent in reply to a cable of his own, requesting details of
Ozanne's record. The unsigned cable, later said to have been sent by the
same Brigadier-General Anderson who had helped Hughes in the matter of
reinforcement figures, stated that Ozanne had been reported as absent without leave in London during the previous October. What it omitted to say was
that the Army had later found this report to be incorrect. The confusion had
arisen while he was in a private hospital receiving treatment for his ear
infection.

All the electorate heard, however, was that Ozanne had been accused of
desertion. The *Geelong Advertiser* attacked him scurrilously, and in the last
few days of the campaign the Nationalist Party endorsed Lister. After an
unexplained delay at sea, Ozanne's ship reached Fremantle the day before
the poll. A telegram from him, describing the cable as 'grossly libellous and
absolutely untrue', was read at his last election rally. 'The secret of the whole
matter', he said, 'is that I was invited to join the Nationalist Party, and
because I refused I was treated in this despicable manner'. But the damage
had been done. Lister won the seat easily, and held it against Ozanne at the
next election too. Labor later moved in the House of Representatives for a
Royal Commission into the Ozanne affair, but its motion was defeated.

The other controversial soldier-politician was Gunner George Yates, the
Labor Member for Adelaide. Enlistment was for some members a
perennially interesting subject that could be used to demonstrate one's own
patriotic fervour or, alternatively, the cold-footedness of others. Watt called
Frank Brennan 'pigeon-livered' because of his pacifist views, and said that
he himself would probably enlist before he turned forty-five. When he failed
to do so, he was taken to task by Senator M. A. Ferricks (Lab, Q), who also
recalled a similar unredeemed pledge by Senator E. J. Russell (N, V). In
Yates's case the question was slightly different, for he *had* enlisted. But why
was he still attending parliament, in khaki, several months later?

Yates had joined up, at the age of forty-five, after an interjection by the
Liberal Member for Grampians (V), Dr Salmon, which, although unrecorded
by Hansard, presumably touched him on the raw. In August 1917 the
Nationalist Member for Henty (V), James Boyd, drew the House's attention
to the fact that Gunner Yates was

> still sitting here after being seven [sic] months in khaki. If it is the fault of
> his superior officers, or of the Government, that the honourable member
> is still here when men who have enlisted for only five or six weeks have
> been already sent to the Front, I ask the government now how it is that an
> honourable member of this House can exercise influence . . . to be kept in
> Australia when men who enlisted months after [he] did are at the Front? It
> is a mighty bad advertisement for the politicians of Australia if they are
> going to enlist in the King's service and get credit for being in the Aus-
> tralian Imperial Force, and be able to come into this House seven months
> after enlisting.

Yates attributed the delay to political manoeuvring by the former Assistant
Minister for Defence, W. H. Laird Smith (N, Denison, T), and proceeded to
inquire why Laird Smith was still in civilian clothes:

Mr LAIRD SMITH.—If I had remained at the Department, you would
   have been away before now.
Mr YATES.—No doubt I would have been in Mesopotamia.
Mr LAIRD SMITH.—Exactly.
Mr YATES.—But you have not left Australia, although you are eligible.
Mr LAIRD SMITH.—I would leave tomorrow if I were your age.
Mr SPEAKER.—Order!
Mr YATES.—I will compare my age with yours at any time.
Mr SPEAKER.—Order!
Mr LAIRD SMITH.—Nobody did more to dodge going to the Front than
   you did when I was Minister.

Gunner Yates reached France in time for the big offensive of 1918, but the
particulars of his service remained the subject of political controversy for
some years. Soon after his return to Adelaide on a troopship in January 1919,
he was court-martialled. The circumstances were that many of the troops on
board were tired of remaining in quarantine within sight of home, and Gunner Yates, M.H.R., had acted as their spokesman in threatening to take possession of the boats and go ashore. He was found guilty of conduct to the
prejudice of good order and military discipline, and of having endeavoured
to persuade troops to join in a mutiny. The sentence, sixty days detention,
was not long enough to incur disqualification under Section 44 (ii) of the
Constitution, but Yates later complained of a whispering campaign about his
war service record, resulting in his defeat by 334 votes at the 1919 election.
   'The most grievous hurt of all', he told a parliamentary select committee
inquiring into the matter in 1923, 'was the misstatements of the Defence
Department to the effect that I could not have taken part in the "hop-over" at
the big offensive on the 8th August, 1918, as I was then minding a dump . . .
The suggestion was that I was not a soldier, but a tourist'. In fact, Gunner
Yates had remained a working member of his battery from May until late
August, taking part in such engagements as Villers-Bretonneux,
Morlancourt and Hamel. On 25 August he was detailed to guard a baggage
dump, but on 15 September he rejoined his battery at Feuillières.
   The select committee reported that 'ex-Gunner Yates suffered injury to his
reputation through inaccurate and misleading information being supplied
by the Department of Defence—information based on inferences drawn
from records admittedly so incomplete as to afford no justification for the
statement that ex-Gunner Yates took no part in the big offensive'. Yates was
awarded compensation of £200 for the slur on his reputation, and by that
time he also had the greater comfort of having won back Adelaide with a
handsome majority.
   The two other khaki members were Edward Heitmann, an ex-member of
the A.L.P. turned Nationalist who had taken the seat of Kalgoorlie from
Hugh Mahon, and Cornelius Wallace, a Wharf Labourers' Union official
who had taken Hughes's place in West Sydney. Both had been elected in
1917, and had enlisted in April and June 1918. If, as some suggested
uncharitably, they had joined up for the sake of a politically useful returned
serviceman's badge when the tumult and the shouting died, they were to be
disappointed by the result. In 1919 Heitmann lost the seat of Kalgoorlie to its

former occupant. Wallace stood down from West Sydney in favour of an illustrious Labor newcomer to federal politics, T. J. Ryan of Queensland, and was himself defeated by a Nationalist in another New South Wales electorate, Nepean.

Private Heitmann, M.H.R., may also have had another reason for enlisting. His father had been German by birth, and during the war that was something that took a lot of living down. The Second Clerk-Assistant of the House of Representatives, Edward Theodor Huber, was in a similar position. His father had left Germany half a century before, had married an Irish-Australian, and had died when Edward was eight years old. Edward himself had never been out of Victoria, and during the war he changed his name by deed poll to the more English-sounding Hubert. Speaker Johnson attested to Hubert's loyalty and efficiency, but this did not prevent the deferral of his salary increments and promotion from June 1915 until the end of the war.

During the war several members of parliament visited England and Europe as civilians. A party of six attended the Empire Parliamentary Congress in London during 1916, and in March 1918 Frank Anstey departed hurriedly and somewhat mysteriously, working his passage to England as a seaman. He obtained leave of absence for the remainder of the session, and in fact attended only four of the House's eighty-seven sitting days that year. The reason he gave for his absence was 'urgent private business'. He was visiting his aged mother, who was not expected to live much longer, but according to one account there was another reason as well. One of his close friends later in life, F. C. Green, said that Anstey left Australia to avoid being arrested by the small Commonwealth police force which the Hughes Government had established in the wake of the 'Warwick egg' incident.

It is not clear what charge might have been brought against him, but in speech and writing Anstey had often risked prosecution under the war precautions regulations. One of his pamphlets in 1915, *The Kingdom of Shylock*, was probably seditious as well as blatantly anti-Semitic. 'Awful is the price the workers must pay', he wrote,

> so that Shylock may get his bloody 'shentage.' He will draw blood from sweating brows and hungry mothers all the days that God gives them life. This war weakens the workers and strengthens the Money Bags. This war means misery for the toiler, and 'much monish' for the bond holder.

According to Green, Scotland Yard detained Anstey in London and cabled the Australian Government for instructions. Hughes was then on his way to England, and Watt, with whom Anstey enjoyed a relationship of mutual respect, was acting Prime Minister. Watt authorised his immediate release and made arrangements for him to accompany an Australian press delegation which was soon to visit the Western Front. The warrant for his arrest, if it really existed, appears to have been forgotten.

The Great War was not a constructive time for legislators. During those four years parliament passed a total of 181 Acts, compared with 132 in the previous four years, and 109 in the four years before that. But much of its legislative output was necessarily related to the war. Of the 138 Acts passed between 1914 and 1917, sixty-three were routine financial measures and forty were minor amendments. In spite of its high quantitative output, parliament sat for a total of only 2123 hours during the war, compared with 2591 hours in the previous four years, and 3029 hours in the four years before that. Legislatively the war was largely a time of Supply Acts, War Precautions Acts and War Loan Acts, without much need of debate. Parliament, like those of its electors in khaki, did what was required of it.

As a gesture towards wartime unity, a Federal Parliamentary War Committee was established in July 1915. This advisory body, consisting of eight M.H.R.s and four senators, half of them nominated by the ministerial party and half by the Opposition, dealt only with matters referred to it by the Government. Its main concerns were recruiting and the problems of returned soldiers.

Among parliament's few wartime measures of lasting significance were the Income Tax Assessment Act and Income Tax Act of 1915, which permitted the Commonwealth to join the various State governments in the income tax field (Commonwealth tax on an income of £456 was at first only £5 3s 1d, while concurrent New South Wales tax on the same income was £10); the Commonwealth Railways Act of 1917, establishing a permanent organisation for the transcontinental railway which was then nearing completion; and the Commonwealth Electoral Act of 1918, which consolidated earlier electoral legislation, introduced preferential voting for House of Representatives elections and reintroduced postal voting. Another Electoral Act, initiated in the Senate twelve months later, made the same provisions for elections to that chamber.

So far all federal elections had been conducted by first-past-the-post voting, with votes marked by a cross and victory going simply to the candidate who obtained the highest number of formal votes. The preferential system, used in some States since the turn of the century, was more sophisticated, and there was a particular reason for its adoption by the Commonwealth at this time. First-past-the-post was adequate for contests between two major candidates of the kind with which the Commonwealth parliament had become familiar since the fusion of 1909. It posed problems, however, in a three-cornered contest when two of the candidates shared certain common policies. In the days of 'three elevens', this had been the case with some Protectionist and A.L.P. candidates. In May 1918 it was again the case in a by-election for the outer Melbourne seat of Flinders, from which Sir William Irvine had resigned to become Chief Justice of Victoria.

Normally, Flinders would have been a safe Nationalist seat; but it was rural in character, and one of the farmers' organisations then emerging in response to wartime controls over primary production, the Victorian Farmers' Union, was running a candidate against the endorsed Nationalist, a young businessman and returned soldier, S. M. Bruce, and his Labor opponent. In a first-past-the-post contest, the danger for Bruce would be that the farmers' candidate would draw away enough of his natural support, not to win, but to let the Labor man win.

Under preferential voting, on the other hand, voters would be required to mark their ballot paper with numbers in order of preference for the candidates. Any candidate receiving an absolute majority (more than half the total votes cast for all candidates) would be declared elected; if no candidate received such an absolute majority, the candidate with the fewest first preference votes would be excluded from the count, and his votes distributed to the remaining candidates according to the second preferences indicated on them by the voters. And so the elimination would continue, if necessary, until one candidate received an absolute majority. In the case of Flinders, preferential voting would probably result in the elimination of the farmers' candidate, the distribution of most of his votes to the most popular candidate, Bruce, and Bruce's election.

What the farmers' movement wanted, and what had really inspired its candidature in Flinders more than hope of victory, was the introduction of preferential voting in time for the next general election, when it intended to put more candidates in the field. Hughes, suspicious of the farmers' movement, was not sympathetic to a new voting system which would enable it to attract first preferences away from his own party. Admittedly the system would stop Labor from slipping into a naturally conservative seat thanks to a divided conservative vote, but it would also on occasion allow the farmers' candidate to outpoll a Nationalist.

The Victorian Farmers' Union offered to withdraw its candidate from the Flinders by-election if the Government undertook to introduce preferential voting for the next general election. With Hughes conveniently overseas, Watt and his colleagues took it upon themselves to give that undertaking. It was in fact too late for the farmers' candidate to withdraw, as ballot papers had been printed. He did no more campaigning, however, and the Farmers' Union advised its supporters to vote for Bruce, who was safely elected by 14 445 votes to the Labor candidate's 7740.

Labor had mixed feelings about preferential voting when the Commonwealth Electoral Bill was introduced in October 1918. State Labor parties had tolerated the system, but at the federal level Labor had recently won a three-cornered by-election in Swan (W), and was confidently expecting a similar result in Corangamite (V) before the end of the year. The Opposition tried to have preferential voting postponed until after the return of servicemen from overseas, and in the Senate it tried unsuccessfully to stop the use of preferential voting at the forthcoming Corangamite by-election. In order to expedite the Bill, the House of Representatives adopted and used a new Standing Order for the limitation of debate. If the House agreed by an affirmative vote of not fewer than twenty-four members that a bill should 'be considered an Urgent Bill', a further motion could be introduced specifying the time allotted for all or any stages of that bill. This was the 'guillotine'. The Senate did not adopt a similar measure until 1926.

The Leader of the Opposition in the Senate, Senator Albert Gardiner (N), stonewalled against the Commonwealth Electoral Bill in a speech that lasted 12 hours and 40 minutes, from 10.03 p.m. on 13 November to 10.43 a.m. the following day, filling seventy-nine pages of Hansard. Much of the time he merely read from the Bill, which itself consisted of sixty-three pages. 'Jupp' Gardiner, well known as a former rugby footballer and cricketer, was a giant of 18 stone with a speaking style described as 'rapid in utterance, fiery in tone'. As a result of his speech, which was the longest ever delivered in parliament, the Senate in 1919 followed the lower house's earlier example and adopted rules providing that—with certain exceptions—no senator could speak in any debate for longer than one hour.

Eminently expendable though such a speech as Senator Gardiner's may have been, Hansard reproduced parliamentary debates almost in full throughout the war, in spite of routine scrutiny by military censors and the continual possibility of military censorship on grounds of national security. Most of the deletions made during the war were, as usual, authorised by the speakers themselves, without altering the substance of their remarks; and on two occasions material was deleted by direction of the Chair on authority of a resolution of the House or Senate. One of the latter concerned an affidavit read in the House by Dr Maloney, and the other a Senate debate on the War Precautions Act regulations.

Reprints of Hansard were a different matter. On the afternoon of 28 February 1918 a military officer accompanied by a detective entered Parliament House and confiscated some parcels containing copies of speeches delivered by James Catts during the want of confidence debate in January. In these two speeches Catts had repeated details of prosecutions against opponents of the Hughes Government under the War Precautions Act regulations, which he described as 'the most serious inroad made upon our liberty since the time of the Stuarts'. He himself had already been prosecuted for referring to those matters in speeches outside parliament, and had hoped to give them wider currency by means of the Hansard reprints. On 5 April the Leader of the Opposition, Tudor, moved a motion of privilege—'That the intrusion into and invasion of Parliament House by a military force for the purpose of search and seizure in defiance of the expressed objections, and without the consent of Mr Speaker, constitutes a breach of privilege of this honourable House'.

Tudor cited the current edition of Erskine May on parliamentary privilege, and asserted that there had 'never been an action like that under notice connected with this or any other Parliament'. Hughes replied coolly that Catts had already been prosecuted for making the statements in question, that Parliament House was not a sanctuary of refuge from the criminal law, and that a reprint did not have the same privileges as Hansard. Tudor's motion was resolved in the negative by 18 votes to 35.

Later in the year both chambers agreed to identical motions authorising the President and Speaker, at their discretion, to direct the omission from Hansard of any remarks made during the course of debate to which their attention may have been directed by the law officers as being calculated 'to prejudice His Majesty's relations with a foreign Power, or the successful prosecution of the war, or to imperil the safety of the Commonwealth'. In December 1918 Speaker Johnson used his discretionary power to make five deletions from Hansard after discussion with the members concerned.

Although there were few instances of censorship, Hansard's accuracy as a full transcript of words actually uttered was always open to some doubt. Few interjections were reported, and speeches were often altered to some extent before publication, either by the members who had delivered them or by Hansard reporters. A persuasive case for alteration was made in 1909 by

Hughes, who was probably less in need of such help himself than any other member. 'when *Hansard* becomes a faithful report of what honourable members actually say in this House', he said,

> there will be little short of a revolution in the country . . . Alterations in form but not in substance are properly allowed, because when an honorable member is addressing the Chamber, he is so torn by conflicting emotions, and troubled with interjections that his delicate equilibrium is disturbed, and he recovers himself only with difficulty. It is desirable, and, indeed, necessary, therefore, to present a readable report of what he would have said had he been addressing an audience having the manners to listen to him . . .

Sir William Irvine made a point of not altering his speeches, and not permitting Hansard to alter them; but that was unusual, perhaps even unique. Deakin revised his own proofs considerably, finding room for improvement in phrasing which others would have regarded as impeccable. According to one Hansard reporter, R. F. Sholl, the Labor members J. H. Catts and Hugh Mahon sometimes wrote in passages that had either been inadvertently omitted from the original speech or composed afterwards. On one occasion, wrote Sholl, Mahon wrote into his proof an attack upon another member which he had not delivered in the House. When the Hansard reporter protested about this, Speaker Holder ruled that, since under Standing Orders the word of a member must be accepted, the passage in question should be incorporated in Hansard.

Another alteration to the records of parliament during the wartime period had nothing to do with the war. It concerned an earlier suspension of Charles McGrath from the service of the House for the remainder of the session, a period of twenty days. 'Bull' McGrath was one of the A.L.P.'s most ardent Victorian radicals. Earlier in life, while a member of the Victorian Legislative Assembly, he had organised for the party all over Victoria, riding bicycles with Frank Anstey into country far from the railway lines, along the western border from the sea to the Mallee, and through Gippsland into the mining camps of the Australian Alps.

McGrath's suspension resulted from references which he made to Speaker Johnson in a speech delivered in his own electorate, and reported by the *Argus*. Mr Speaker had lost the confidence of members, said McGrath; he had deliberately altered a Hansard proof, and was proving himself to be a bitter partisan. On the next sitting day, 11 November 1913, the Prime Minister, Cook, moved for McGrath's suspension unless he retracted his remarks and apologised to the House, which he was not prepared to do. The motion was agreed to by 35 to 34, without the Speaker's casting vote.

Seventeen months later, before McGrath had enlisted, the Labor Member for Barrier (N), Josiah Thomas, moved that McGrath's suspension 'be expunged from the Journals of this House, as being subversive of the right of an honourable Member to freely address his constituents'. The question was resolved in the affirmative without a division. McGrath's suspension could not be literally expunged from Hansard and *Votes and Proceedings*, but it was deleted from the record kept by the Clerk of the House.

Josiah Thomas's successor as the Member for Barrier—Michael Patrick Considine, a young Irish-born union official from Broken Hill—could also have done with some expunging. In the course of sixteen months he became the only member of parliament ever to be suspended three times in one session. On 17 April 1918 he was suspended for twenty-four hours after refusing to withdraw the observation that there was no difference between Edward Corser (a Nationalist who had captured Fisher's old seat of Wide Bay) and a German. When the result of the division was announced, Dr Maloney rose in his place and, with mock fervour, sang the first verse of the National Anthem.

In July 1919 Considine was suspended again, for seven days, after saying that the country was being run 'by a gang of murdering thieves'. Two months later he received the maximum suspension of twenty-eight days for saying that the Hughes Government was 'supporting the champion murderer of the working classes in Russia generally, namely [the Czarist] Koltchak'. This was mild indeed for Mick Considine, who had appointed himself acting consul for the new Bolshevik government of Russia. At the time of his third suspension he was only recently out of gaol, where he had served a sentence of three weeks for remarking, in company at Melbourne's Green Room Club: 'Bugger the King, he is a bloody German bastard'. Such uncouth *lèse-majesté* would probably have received sterner punishment a few months earlier. By then, however, the war was over and the profanity of an Irishman from Broken Hill hardly seemed to merit any greater portion of the unlimited imprisonment provided in the War Precautions Act for the offence of causing disaffection among His Majesty's subjects.

After the Allied victories of October 1918 peace had seemed likely to be announced at any time. Shops did a roaring trade in red, white and blue ribbon and flags, particularly the Union Jack. The news of an armistice reached Melbourne by cable from America at about 7.20 p.m. on Monday 11 November. It was posted up outside the *Age* and *Argus* offices, and as word spread quickly to the suburbs people flocked into the city by train and tram in the greatest numbers seen since 1901, jamming Collins and Swanston Streets with impromptu processions, community singing of 'Pack up your Troubles' and other war songs, and the triumphal chairing of anyone in khaki or navy blue. Stage and picture shows were interrupted. After the first act of 'The High Cost of Loving' at the Theatre Royal, Miss Maggie Moore announced the news, and sang the Marseillaise and National Anthem. At the Paramount Picture Show, patrons gave special applause to war items in the 'Weekly Gazette'.

Next day the Senate met briefly, but not the lower house. The thirty-two senators present unanimously adopted an address to the King, congratulating His Majesty on 'the great sagacity and steadfast resolution of the statesmen of Great Britain and the Allied and Associated Powers', thanking the British and Allied forces for their patriotic sacrifices, and rendering thanks to God for the 'triumph of Righteousness over the forces of Evil'. Then, standing in their places, they sang the National Anthem and cheered the King. On the call of Senator W. J. R. Maughan (Lab, Q) they gave three more cheers for 'Our volunteer Army'; and finally, on the call of Senator

Hugh de Largie, who was no longer Labor but Nationalist, they redressed the balance with three cheers for 'The conscript armies of our Allies'.

On Wednesday afternoon the House of Representatives adopted the same form of address. The acting Prime Minister, a dark-jowled man with the voice of a cathedral organ, rose well to the occasion, though in moving the adoption he displayed more optimism than would be justified by future events. 'During the past few weeks', said Watt,

> the peoples of the world have been living amid volcanic conditions; it has been a world of falling thrones and rising republics, of dismembered Governments and of hunted monarchs. We have seen the royal families of the House of Hohenzollern and the House of Hapsburg, whose lineage stretches back to the dim records of medieval history, hunted from their high estate by an indignant and outraged people, never to return. I think that never before in the annals of man have so many fateful and stupendous events occurred in so brief a space of time . . . All this portends more than a mere military victory. Despotism has been beheaded in Europe: militarism has been burned at the roots. The ideals of the Allies have triumphed, and as a consequence this world is now, and for many a generation will remain, a safer and a happier place to live in.

The fifty-one members present (among those absent were Hughes, Cook, Anstey and five khaki members) followed the Senate's example by singing the National Anthem and giving three cheers for the King. On the call of Dr Maloney they also sang 'God Bless our Men' and gave three cheers for 'The Men'.

Later that afternoon parliament performed a sort of recessional to the terrible liturgy of the last four years. At 4 p.m., escorted by a troop of emu-plumed Light Horsemen, the Governor-General and his wife arrived by motor car and walked up a passageway through the crowd to the top of the steps at Parliament House. There, between two massive pillars, they were met by a procession of members from within the building, led by the Serjeant-at-Arms bearing the Mace, and the presiding officers. President Givens, in plain dark suit, and Speaker Johnson, in full-bottomed wig and gown, presented their loyal addresses; His Excellency, in full regalia of white cock feathers, epaulettes, sword, sash and Grand Cross of the Order of St Michael and St George, referred admiringly to the part played by Australia's sons in the mighty struggle now concluded; the Anthem and three cheers for His Majesty were heard once more; and then the viceregal party—like captains and kings departing—proceeded down Bourke Street and out of sight.

6

The Country

Between the pandemonium of Europe and an 'inferno of trouble' which he expected in Australia, Billy Hughes for once had plenty of time on his hands. For six weeks he was a passenger, travelling with other Australians who had attended the Versailles peace conference and 1200 returning soldiers, on a captured German transport, the *Friedrichsruh*. Then, for the best part of another week, he journeyed by train across the Australian continent from Perth to Melbourne. Hughes was not the most gregarious of men, nor was he a card player or a drinker; instead one may picture him on the long journey home gazing out across the ocean or the Nullarbor Plain, weighing up the glorious past and cloudy future, crablike within 'the impenetrable shell of his designs'. The *Friedrichsruh* put in for water at Freetown, from which 'God-forsaken hole', as Hughes described it, the bones of Lord Forrest had been removed five months before; took on coal at Cape Town, where Hughes began suffering from 'cold and nerves'; and at last reached Fremantle, on Saturday 23 August 1919.

On Monday afternoon—accompanied by his fellow peace delegate Joseph Cook, and W. A. Watt, who had come to meet them—the Prime Minister left Perth on what was to be a triumphal progress across the Commonwealth. At Kalgoorlie next morning he was met by half the goldfields population, including an honour guard of one hundred returned soldiers, though not the sitting Nationalist member, Heitmann. Heitmann was still being recorded in the *Votes and Proceedings* as 'On leave: absent with Australian Imperial Force', although he had been discharged from the army in London eight months before. Hughes addressed the audience on his two current themes, the danger of Bolshevism and the need to help returned men find their proper place in civilian life, and other speakers paid tribute to his championing of Australian interests, particularly the White Australia policy, at Versailles. Hughes and his companions then boarded the Trans-Australian Express, which had come into service between Kalgoorlie and Port Augusta two years before.

After crossing 250 miles of spinifex and mallee country the train stopped at Rawlinna, where the Prime Minister presented a belated D.C.M. and Bar to a veteran of the Western Front, Corporal J. Nancarrow. Then on it went through the night, across a wide plateau of saltbush, across limestone country sprinkled more and more lightly with mulga until there were no trees left at all. Here, on the Nullarbor Plain where King O'Malley had prophesied the birth of a new Athens or Rome, were a few widely spaced stations, the merest specks of settlement, used only as depots for engine water and running repairs. At some of these places a few lonely souls called out 'Where is Mr Hughes?', but the Prime Minister stayed in his sleeper. The Nullarbor stations, crouching without platforms beside a track that ran from horizon to horizon without bend, were named after Forrest and all the prime ministers up to that time. As Hughes's train passed Reid, Deakin, Hughes, Cook, Fisher and Watson, did he reflect sardonically upon the conservative company he would be keeping for generations to come on this treeless plain?

Next morning the train was in South Australia. There had been good rain recently, and the country was looking better than usual; but it was still the kind of landscape celebrated by Dorothea Mackellar in her popular poem 'My Country', a sunburnt country of beauty and terror. At Ooldea a bearded Aborigine threw a boomerang for the passengers' diversion, and three dingo skins were offered for sale. Before the next station, Tarcoola, passengers saw their first fence for 750 miles. It was the outer boundary of Wilgena Run, a sheep station of 3012 square miles. At Port Augusta Hughes was presented with an illuminated address; at Terowie a drum and pipe band of thirty school children played 'Home Sweet Home' and 'Men of Harlech'; and about 25 miles out of Adelaide a Bristol monoplane—flown by Captain H. J. Butler, son of a South Australian wheat farmer, and veteran of the Royal Flying Corps—met the train and led it into the city at roof level.

As the Trans-Australian Express steamed into Adelaide station, a group of returned soldiers jumped aboard the Prime Minister's carriage, and before it came to a halt Hughes was being carried shoulder-high through a seething crowd. The Melbourne Express later took him to the Victorian border, through mallee country that had been cleared for wheat and sheep, and finally through the electorates of Ballarat, once held by Alfred Deakin, and Corio, once held by the unfortunate Gunner Ozanne. At Melbourne's Spencer Street station, more returned men were waiting to chair the 'Little Digger' and haul his motor car through crowded streets to the Town Hall.

Looking down Collins Street [reported the *Argus*] one saw a huge swaying mass of men and women. There were no barricades, no well-ordered ranks marching in procession, no formidable force of troopers to cleave a way through the crowd. Only a single motor car with a little man perched on high, supported by a dozen enthusiastic 'diggers', and waving his hand to the mighty crowd that surged around him. And what a crowd! It swept up Collins Street like a great tide; it filled the whole width from doorway to doorway. And all the time it cheered itself hoarse for the sake of the little man in the motor car. It was a great tribute to a man who had done great things.

Writing to King George V, the Governor-General referred to this phenomenon in political terms. 'The Prime Minister', wrote Munro Ferguson,

> was received by enthusiastic crowds of "Diggers" in every City and the welcome everywhere took the form of seizing his person, draping him in flags, bonnetting him with an Anzac's hat, whirling him off to the Town Hall speechifying and handshaking all the way. It cannot have been pleasant, nor was it a dignified entry, but it certainly showed that Mr Hughes had captured the heart and its political equivalent the vote of the Returned Soldier.

But Munro Ferguson's judgement was astray. The wave of adulation that greeted Hughes was personal rather than political: it was an emotional tribute to one who had represented his country boldly on the international stage, but it was not a tribute that would necessarily be negotiable on polling day. As Hughes himself knew, his political future was far from secure. Sections of his own party distrusted him; Labor detested him; and he expected further disadvantage from the farmers' organisations which were already preparing for the next election. His only consolation—apart from the chairing and cheering, which were not likely to last much longer—was the absence of any immediate rival within the Nationalist Party. Cook was no threat; Watt, who resented Hughes's lack of communication with him during his acting Prime Ministership, was handicapped by ill health; Irvine had left parliament; and Jens Jensen (more lackey than rival) had been dismissed from the portfolio of Trade and Customs, and in effect from public life, after being mentioned unfavourably in the report of a Royal Commission on Navy and Defence Administration in December 1918.

On 10 September 1919 Hughes attended parliament for the first time in more than sixteen months. His first action there was to move that the House should approve the peace treaty with Germany, but before speaking to that motion he expressed his deep regret at the deaths of Lord Forrest and Sir George Reid during his absence. Four weeks later Alfred Deakin reached his haven of complete forgetfulness, a coffin draped in the Union Jack. At his funeral service in Queen's Hall, William Watt spoke of Deakin not as an Australian but as 'a true Britisher of the finest type'. Three months later Sir Edmund Barton died too. If one generation was giving way to another, as indeed it seemed to be, perhaps the new generation would be one in which Austral-Britons would feel more Australian than British.

After relatively short debates both houses of parliament passed motions approving of the peace treaty. In view of the fact that it had already been ratified by the British Empire, as S. M. Bruce reminded the lower house, there was 'very little that [parliament] could do to alter what had already been settled'. To be more precise, there was nothing it could do. Hughes recounted the story of his successful opposition to Japan's attempt to have embodied in the draft covenant of the League of Nations a declaration against racial discrimination, a declaration which the Australian delegation had feared would give Asian immigrants a foot in the door of White Australia. 'During the course of the long negotiations in Paris', he told the House,

> I made clear to the Japanese delegates what the real attitude of Australia towards their country was. I said that we admired the great qualities of the Japanese people . . . that we were their neighbours, we were their friends, and we hoped to remain their friends . . . I said, however, that as a self-governing nation whose citizens had fought for liberty and the right to govern themselves in their own way, we claimed the right to decide for ourselves who should be admitted within our country's gates. I believe these are the views of the citizens of Australia.

J. H. Catts spoke angrily against the mandates granted to Japan over certain former German colonies in the Pacific; but there was nothing anyone could do about that, and at least the German colony closest to Australia, New Guinea, was to be under a mandate administered by Australia itself. In the upper house, Senator Bakhap devoted his speech to the war service of some of his fellow Australian-Chinese, notably Yin Goon, who had been among the first to fall at Gallipoli. Bakhap reminded his listeners that the former First Sea Lord, Admiral Fisher, was half-Cingalese, and suggested that in the best interests of the British Empire the Prince of Wales ought to marry an Indian princess. Either the Senate had lost some of its racial intolerance, or Senator Bakhap enjoyed personal licence, for there were no interjections.

Although the seventh parliament had six more months to run, Hughes obtained an early election on grounds that his Government needed a mandate to deal with such post-war problems as inflation, profiteering and industrial unrest. The Commonwealth's wartime powers were due to expire six months after the signing of the peace treaty, but Hughes argued that the need for additional power was greater now than before the war, when, as Labor's Attorney-General, he had tried so often and without success to expand the central power by means of constitutional amendment. Much as he would have liked to present all those proposals again at a referendum with the general election, his Nationalist colleagues countenanced only two amending bills. One of these sought to extend trade, commerce and industrial powers for a maximum of three years; the other, with a similar time limit, authorised the Commonwealth to nationalise industries or businesses declared by the two houses of parliament, after inquiry by a High Court judge, to be 'the subject of a monopoly'. Both went the way of earlier referendums bills. The more conservative of Hughes's colleagues were affronted by such 'socialism', and socialists regarded the compromise bills as a fraud perpetrated by a turncoat. At referendum the bills were approved by majorities in Victoria, Queensland and Western Australia, but rejected elsewhere and in the national vote.

The election itself produced incongruous results: jeopardy for the Government in the lower house, and almost complete dominance by it in the Senate. The new House of Representatives consisted of thirty-six Nationalists, an Independent Nationalist likely to vote with the Government on most matters, and W. G. Higgs, who was expelled from the Labor Party before parliament met, and would join the Nationalist Party later; twenty-six Labor members, and one Independent Labor member who usually voted with the party; and finally ten farmers' members, beneficiaries of the new preferential voting system, who formed themselves into the Australian Country Party two days before the opening of the eighth parliament on 26 February 1920. These numbers were to change slightly, but the immediate outlook held little comfort for Hughes: thirty-seven Nationalist or quasi-Nationalist seats (of which only eight were held by former members of the Labor Party) and a potential Opposition of thirty-eight.

In the Senate, as a consequence of preferential voting for the multi-member State constituencies, the Government had an absurdly large majority. All Labor senators in the seventh parliament had reached the end of their six-year terms, leaving an all-Nationalist residue, and of nineteen Senators elected at the general election (half of the Senate plus a replacement for one casual vacancy) eighteen were Nationalists and only one was Labor. That one, the tireless Senator Albert Gardiner, found himself alone for the next three years in Opposition to thirty-five Nationalists. His only consolation was that the 1919 federal conference had voted 'Abolition of Senate' into the A.L.P.'s fighting platform. Farmers' organisations failed to win any seats in the Senate, though they had tried; but some Nationalist senators sympathised with Country Party ideals, and the new Senate was by no means as biddable as the Government's majority might have suggested.

Although it was still far from being a States' House of the kind envisaged by delegates to the constitutional conventions, the Senate at this time displayed somewhat more vigour than usual. Of the fifty-six Acts passed by parliament in 1920, a record number of fifteen originated in the upper house. The annual average number of Acts passed in the twenty years since federation was thirty-one, of which the average number coming from the Senate was seven. During 1920 the Senate held seventy-six sittings, the highest number for any year since 1908. This compared with 114 by the House of Representatives. Since federation the Senate had recorded a total of 1226 sittings, compared with 1657 by the lower house.

Despite its huge Nationalist majority, the Senate of the eighth parliament asserted itself against Government wishes on more than one occasion. In May 1920, for example, it transmitted to the House of Representatives, with a request for that House's concurrence, a resolution that the Standing Orders Committees of both houses be requested to consider the question of preparing Standing Orders which would allow Ministers in either house to attend and pilot through the other house any bills of which they had charge. This radical proposal was not even considered by the lower house, and lapsed at prorogation.

In October the Senate also rejected an Entertainments Tax Bill which had already been attacked in the House of Representatives on grounds that it discriminated unfairly in favour of theatres and cinemas as compared with other forms of entertainment. In 1921 the Senate returned the Customs Tariff Bill to the lower house with ninety-two requests for amendment (the lower house agreed to forty-eight of these, made twenty-two others with modifications, and did not make the remaining twenty-two), and returned an Appropriation Bill with two requests concerning an increase in salary for the Clerk of the Senate, and a decrease in salary for the Clerk of the House, the object being to maintain parity of salary. The House did not make the latter amendments, maintaining that the Senate should not be permitted to interfere with the lower house's control of its own officers. The Senate pressed its request relating to the Clerk of the House; the House stood firm; but the matter was later resolved by an informal conference of three members from each chamber. This conference, the first of its kind, recommended that the two Clerks should receive equal salaries.

Another difference between the houses at this time concerned the title of Clerk of the Parliaments, which had been in abeyance since Clerk Blackmore's retirement. Speaker Johnson suggested to the Prime Minister that it should be revived and bestowed upon the Clerk of the House, Walter Gale. President Givens promptly wrote to the Prime Minister, saying he was 'very much astonished to learn that Mr Speaker had taken upon himself to make such a recommendation, which concerns equally both Houses of the Parliament, without my knowledge or sanction'. If there was any reason to revive it, he said, the appointment should go to the Clerk of the Senate. So the Speaker's proposal came to nothing. The Senate remained sensitive about its standing in relation to the lower house, and during 1921, at the request of a majority of Senators, President Givens followed Speaker Johnson's example and resumed the practice, abandoned by President Gould in 1910, of wearing wig and gown.

In contrast to the Senate—where, in spite of institutional wilfulness, the Government was sure to prevail on major issues—the new House of Representatives was the most unstable of its kind since the days of 'three elevens' or 'cut-throat euchre'. The Nationalist Party was divided into ex-Liberal, pro-Country Party and ex-Labor factions, the latter sometimes finding itself in harmony with the right wing of the Labor Party. The Country Party, which now requires some introduction, also included two 'radicals' who were willing to co-operate with Labor on some issues. They were W. C. Hill, a wheat farmer and pastoralist who had entered parliament at a by-election for Echuca (V) before the general election, and Percy Stewart, another wheat farmer who had won the Victorian seat of Wimmera. In Victoria the party was more radical than in other States. It was characterised by tension between long-established farmers and newcomers with such Labor-oriented backgrounds as mining or agricultural labouring. But basically the Country Party was conservative. Its emergence as a third force likely to side with the Nationalists rather than Labor was a development of great and lasting significance.

Since 1914, candidates sponsored by farmers' organisations had won seats in the parliaments of Victoria, South Australia, Queensland and Western Australia. These and their counterparts in federal parliament represented voters in the sort of country which Hughes had seen from his train window—not only wheat growers, pastoralists and dairy farmers, but townsmen too. By giving voice to country grievances against Australia's ever-expanding cities, the Country Party had captured many country towns from the Nationalist Party. Its candidates asserted the overriding national importance of primary production, and argued that it was therefore in everyone's interest to help country regions become more productive.

By that time the predominance of metropolitan Australia was well established. The proportion of Australians living in metropolitan areas had risen from 32 per cent in 1881 to 38 per cent in 1911; and the census of 1921 would soon show that of a total Australian population numbering 5 435 000, 43 per cent were now living in metropolitan areas, and 62 per cent in towns and cities. To reverse this trend, said the Country Party, the Government should encourage more rural settlement by improving conditions of life in the country. For everyone's sake, the country should have more roads, telephones, schools and hospitals. Marketing schemes for wheat and other crops should be improved, the tariff should be reformed to lower rural costs, new States should be formed to encourage regional development, and the basis of electoral representation should be changed to give the country a stronger political voice.

Members now representing the country in federal parliament were not all men of the land, but they were all unquestionably country men. Only two were exclusively farmers or graziers; seven others combined primary production with such varied occupations as newspaper proprietor, ironmonger, contractor and insurance agent; W. J. McWilliams, who had represented the Tasmanian seat of Franklin since 1903, was a journalist and newspaper proprietor; and the new member for Cowper (N), Dr Earle Page, was a practising country doctor with interests in farming and newspaper publishing.

Although McWilliams was the only member who had been long in federal parliament, and was for that reason elected as the Country Party's first leader, the others were not without political experience. Of the seven elected for the first time in 1918 and 1919, four had served previously in State parliaments. Henry Gregory had represented Dampier (W) since 1913, and Edmund Jowett had represented Grampians (V) since 1917. They lacked cohesion at first, but only a rash opponent would have underestimated them.

Among the twenty-eight new M.H.R.s and ten new Senators were twelve returned soldiers—seven in the lower house, and five in the Senate. The highest ranking of these were Senators H. E. Elliott (Nat, V) and Sir Thomas Glasgow (Nat, Q), Brigadier-General and Major-General respectively, and D. C. Cameron (Nat, Brisbane), a lieutenant-colonel. Early in the life of the new parliament, the presiding officers decided to drop military titles from Hansard. In 1921 the new Returned Sailors' and Soldiers' Imperial League passed a resolution urging parliament to adopt the practice, in Hansard and division lists, of placing crossed swords against the names of members who had served in any war. This preposterous idea was discussed by President Givens and Speaker Johnson, and negatived. Of the sixteen returned soldiers then in parliament (four had been elected before 1919), fourteen were Nationalists.

As usual, the 1920 Address-in-Reply served to introduce new members; but some could not wait until that debate took place. The new Member for West Sydney—T. J. Ryan, who had been elected Deputy Leader of the federal parliamentary Labor Party under Tudor—surprised his new colleagues by leaping to the attack as soon as Watt had proposed that the House resolve itself into committee to consider a grant of Supply. Such a motion was usually treated routinely in the House of Representatives, but Ryan subjected it to the aggressive kind of scrutiny which it might have received in Queensland, where until recently he had been Premier. On the next sitting day, 3 March, Tudor moved as an amendment to Watt's supply motion that 'the Government be censured for (a) their failure to deal with profiteering, (b) their injudicious expenditure, (c) their control of shipping and of wheat, wool, metals and other products'.

During the debate on this want of confidence motion, another Labor member, Joel Moses Gabb, spoke for the first time. Although maiden speeches were traditionally heard in silence, Gabb, a former greengrocer and Methodist missioner who had narrowly defeated P. M. Glynn in the South Australian electorate of Angas, was heckled by one of the returned soldiers, Charles Marr, D.S.O., M.C. (Nat, Parkes, N), who seized upon the anticonscriptionist Gabb's use of the word 'sacrifice':

> Mr GABB.— . . . I say, in all seriousness, that if the way of sacrifice is not followed by all classes in Australia, there is certainly trouble ahead of us.
> Mr MARR.—Did the honorable member make sacrifices during the war?
> Mr GABB.—Yes; I made the sacrifice of standing by my wife and kiddies, so that they might not be the doormats of others and be compelled to put up with the dirty insults of the like of the honourable member. That is the sacrifice I made.
> Mr SPEAKER.—Order! I ask the honorable member to withdraw his reference to the honourable member for Parkes.
> Mr MARR.—I made a sacrifice during the war.
> Mr GABB.—In deference to you, Sir, I certainly withdraw my reference to the honorable member . . . [But] I remind the honorable member that those of us who were anti-conscriptionists could be just as sincere and could love this country just as much as those who were conscriptionists.
> Mr MARR.—By stopping at home.
> Mr GABB.—We have this satisfaction, at any rate, that the people of this country were not foolish enough to put upon themselves the curse of militarism, and yet the war has been won . . .
> Mr MARR.—Did the Hun vote put the honorable member in?
> Mr SPEAKER.—I ask honorable members generally to converse in lower tones while the honorable member for Angas is addressing the House.

Without support from Country Party members sitting together on the cross benches, Tudor's want of confidence motion was defeated by 45 votes to 22. Little though the Country Party liked Hughes, whom it regarded as the embodiment of metropolitan extravagance and socialism by stealth, it liked the Labor Party less. Although cross-voting was common in this confused period, the Country Party generally continued to support the Government's programme. Measures passed during the first session included new Customs Tariff and Excise Tariff Acts and the establishment of an administrative tribunal, the Tariff Board, which was intended to relieve parliament of detailed concern with the tariff in future; the Institute of Science and Industry Act,

bringing the Commonwealth into the field of applied scientific and industrial research by establishing an organisation from which the C.S.I.R.O. later
developed; and two Industrial Peace Acts, providing for a flexible system of
tribunals which the Government believed would be a more appropriate way
of dealing with localised industrial disputes than the Arbitration Court.
Although the Industrial Peace Acts largely remained dead letters, they had
the unforeseen effect of causing Mr Justice Higgins to declare that the Arbitration Court's usefulness had been fatally injured by them. Higgins's current term as president of that Court was about to expire. He did not seek
another term, but remained a justice of the High Court until his death nine
years later.

One measure that encountered little opposition was a Parliamentary
Allowances Bill raising members' salaries from £600 (the level fixed in 1907)
to £1000. This increase was first mooted—without public warning, but with
considerable forethought—during a grievance debate on 13 May 1920. In
accordance with the House of Commons tradition that grievances be considered before Supply was granted to the Crown, a motion that the Speaker
should leave the chair and the House go into committee of supply was used
as an opportunity for discussion and criticism of government policy. On this
occasion the father of the House, F. W. Bamford (Nat, Herbert, Q) successfully moved, as an amendment to the motion that Mr Speaker leave the
Chair, that 'this House does now resolve that the Government be requested
to increase the Parliamentary Allowance of Members to a sum not exceeding
£1,000 per annum'.

'When members are really in earnest', said the *Argus* next morning, 'they
can despatch important business very quickly'. The Parliamentary
Allowances Bill had been drafted in readiness for just such a request, providing an allowance of £1000 for members and an additional allowance (£400 in
the lower house, and £200 in the Senate) for the Leader of the Opposition,
who hitherto had received no special remuneration or been accorded any
official status. The new members' allowance of £1000 per annum was considerably higher than current allowances in the House of Commons (£400),
the New Zealand parliament (£450) and Australian State parliaments
(ranging from £250 in Tasmania to £500 in New South Wales). The Bill
passed through all stages in the House of Representatives at a sitting on 20
May which lasted until after three o'clock the next morning, the second reading being agreed to on a division by 45 votes to 12. The 'Noes' consisted of
five Country Party members; one Labor member, Moses Gabb; and six
Nationalists, including S. M. Bruce, whose reason for opposing any salary
increase was that the matter had not been raised during the recent election
campaign. The Bill passed through all stages in the Senate on 21 May, and
received assent the following day.

Although the War Precautions Acts were partly repealed, it could not have
been said that the Commonwealth was left any the weaker. On the contrary,
its power was reinforced from a quarter which earlier in the century had
seemed more intent upon restricting it: the High Court. Barton's death had
removed the last of the founding justices from the bench of that counterpoint
to parliament which sat on another hilltop within sight of Parliament House.

O'Connor had been dead for eight years, and Sir Samuel Griffith had retired in August 1919. The next Chief Justice, a former Sydney K.C., Sir Adrian Knox, was basically in agreement with arguments that had been advanced consistently by Isaacs and Higgins in their dissenting opinions—arguments against the 'Griffith' doctrines of implied immunity of instrumentalities and implied prohibitions, and against reliance upon United States precedent, by which means the High Court majority had often in the past favoured the States over the Commonwealth.

Those minority opinions came to a resounding majority climax in the 1920 judgment of *Amalgamated Society of Engineers* v. *Adelaide Steamship Co Ltd*, commonly known as the Engineers' Case. The point at issue was whether a dispute between a trade union and a State-owned sawmilling enterprise in Western Australia came within the ambit of the Commonwealth's arbitration power. The Court could have held that because sawmilling was a trading function it did not enjoy the protection against Commonwealth interference which had been established in *D'Emden* v. *Pedder* and other cases. But that would have been to dodge the issue. Instead, a majority of four (Knox, Isaacs, Rich and Mr Justice H. E. Starke, who had replaced Barton) reassessed the doctrines of implied immunity and implied prohibitions and found them wanting. The majority judgment, written by Isaacs, condemned Griffith's doctrines for having led the Court into inconsistency, and cleared the way for a more literal and wider interpretation of the powers enumerated in Section 51 of the Constitution:

> The more these ['Griffith'] decisions are examined and compared with each other and with the Constitution itself, the more evident it becomes that no clear principle can account for them . . . Some are . . . rested on implication drawn from what is called the principle of 'necessity', that being itself referable to no more definite standard than the personal opinion of the Judge who declares it . . . From its nature [the 'Griffith' doctrine] is incapable of consistent application, because 'necessity' in the sense employed—a political sense—must vary in relation to various periods and circumstances . . . Possible abuse of powers is no reason in British law for limiting the natural force of the language creating them. No Court has any right to narrow those limits by reason of any fear that the powers as actually circumscribed by the language naturally understood may be abused . . .

This was a milestone of comparable significance to the Customs Tariff Act which had saved the Commonwealth from disaster in 1902. Just as the Commonwealth had then been freed from the toils financially, so now it was out of the toils constitutionally, and fast escaping from its legal enemies. Henceforth Commonwealth powers would be given the fullest amplitude of meaning before anyone considered what powers were left to the States. This greatly enhanced the practical importance of the Commonwealth parliament, and weakened the position of States in the federal compact. To the States it would come to seem that something had indeed been sacrificed on the altar of Moloch.

Hughes's satisfaction with the Engineers' judgment was diminished by his own increasingly difficult position. He was physically unwell, and was ruling his colleagues with the heavy kind of hand they had tolerated during the war but were less willing to tolerate in peacetime. In June 1920 the Treasurer, Watt, resigned from the Ministry while overseas as Australian plenipotentiary with the Empire delegation to an international economic conference in Brussels. He gave as his reason the Prime Minister's failure to provide him with the authority and support which he regarded as necessary, claiming in a cable to Hughes that 'it would be incongruous for me to wear the garb of a plenipotentiary and the mind of a telegraph messenger'.

Watt was a popular figure, with a rather mordant sense of humour. On one occasion in the House late at night, he and other members were listening with glazed fascination to an elderly and prolix colleague who was apparently having trouble with his dentures. The member's name has not survived, but he may have been 'Jawbone' Webster, who was still in parliament at the time. Whoever he was, in desperation he finally removed his teeth, and that rendered his words almost totally incomprehensible. Another member rose to a point of order, asking the Chairman if he could inform the House what language the Honourable Member was using. 'Gum Arabic', called Watt.

Watt was also quick to take offence. Hughes described him as 'masterful and impatient', which was a perfect example of pot calling kettle black; but from the Prime Minister's explanation to parliament, fully documented with cables exchanged between the two men, it did seem that Watt was more to blame than Hughes for his resignation in the middle of an overseas mission. That, of course, did not prevent the resignation from appearing to be another nail in Hughes's political coffin. The newly knighted Sir Joseph Cook became Treasurer again, and held that portfolio until resigning his seat late the following year in order to succeed Fisher as High Commissioner in London.

On the afternoon of 14 July proceedings in the House of Representatives were disrupted in an unprecedented way by a protest against the proposed deportation of a Roman Catholic priest. Father Charles Jerger, who was of German descent, had lived in Australia from the age of sixteen; but because of remarks about conscription that he was alleged to have made during the war, he became the subject of a persistent campaign by the Protestant Federation. In 1918 he was interned as an enemy alien, and in May 1920 the Hughes Government decided to deport him, without trial, under one of the Commonwealth's remaining wartime regulations. Mass rallies of protest and support were held in Sydney and Melbourne, and on 14 July, only minutes after Speaker Johnson had taken the Chair, three women in the public gallery and another in the lower press gallery began scattering broadsheets about Jerger and shouting demands that he be given a fair trial.

This was the most blatant affront yet offered to parliament by 'strangers' within its precincts. Speaker Johnson ordered the galleries cleared, and suspended the sitting for ten minutes. Parliament had always been adequately equipped to deal with unwelcome visitors. Both chambers could exclude 'strangers' by resolution, and the Speaker or the President could effect such removal by their own authority under Standing Orders, as Speaker Johnson did in the Jerger case.

By this time the term 'strangers' included not only members of the public but also members of the Press Gallery, whose relationship with parliament was not always as free and easy as it might have been. Journalists had been officially designated 'strangers' in a 1907 ruling by Speaker Holder during debate on the printing of a report entitled 'Secret Drugs, Cures and Foods'. The report, compiled by a piano manufacturer named O. C. Beale, contained a mishmash of information about quack remedies including the use of lead to procure abortions. Arguing that abortion was not a suitable subject for the public ear, Dr Carty Salmon called the Speaker's attention to the presence of strangers. Speaker Holder then announced his intention, under Standing Orders, to put the question 'That strangers be ordered to withdraw'. Asked by a backbencher whether the term 'strangers' would include the press, the Speaker ruled that it would. Although the question was resolved in the negative, it served to clarify the Press Gallery's position in Parliament House.

Further clarification came in 1912, when F. W. Bamford (Lab, Herbert, Q) drew the attention of the House to a paragraph in the *Age* referring to an amendment which he had moved to the government's motion accepting an electoral redistribution scheme for Queensland. The paragraph appeared under the heading, 'A Political Dodge: Peculiar Division'. On Bamford's motion the House declared that, in the event of an erroneous press report reflecting injuriously upon any member, no representative of the offending newspaper would be allowed within Parliament House until the paper had published an explanation by the aggrieved member.

Parliament first used its power to exclude journalists in 1914. The 'Lousy List' affair, as it became known, began with a discovery that the Brisbane *Courier*'s representative, F. G. Samson, had been obtaining exclusive stories by the unseemly practice of concealing himself for long periods in a lavatory, where he was able to overhear conversations between ministers. In consequence of this gross invasion of members' privacy, a Joint House Committee recommended that the entire interstate press corps (though not, of course, the *Age* and *Argus*) be deprived of such parliamentary privileges as access to refreshment rooms, tennis courts, cricket pitch, billiard room and library.

Resenting this collective punishment for the misdeeds of one man, two *Sydney Morning Herald* journalists—George Goddard and Quentin Spedding—posted in the interstate reporters' room a notice headed 'The Lousy List'. It named the members of the Joint House Committee, and suggested that in future they should not be accorded any favours or 'free advertising'. This amounted to an embargo on reporting the speeches of certain members, and the President and Speaker immediately ordered the removal of all interstate journalists from Parliament House until an apology was received. The affair came to an end when the leader of the interstate press, Harry Peters of the Sydney *Daily Telegraph* , typed out an apology while sitting on the front steps, and sent it in to President Givens.

Before the end of 1920 the House of Representatives resounded with a *cause célèbre* even more notorious than the Jerger case. This was a case of parliamentary privilege which left the reputation of the Prime Minister, and indeed that of parliament as well, distinctly tarnished. In recent years the House of Representatives had been active in matters of privilege—that is to say, the rights of the houses of parliament and their members which exceed those possessed in law by other bodies and individuals. The privileges of the Senate and House of Representatives, as defined by Section 49 of the Constitution, are such as may be declared by the parliament and, until so declared, such as were possessed by the House of Commons in 1901.

In May 1918 the House of Representatives debated a privilege motion protesting against the military censorship of members' correspondence, but the motion was defeated. Also, on 24 October 1919, the presiding officers of parliament made statements of privilege to their respective chambers in relation to an Economies Royal Commission which was proposing to include certain parliamentary services in its investigation of ways and means to reduce federal expenditure. 'Once admit the right of any outside authority to supersede the authority of Parliament itself', said Speaker Johnson, 'the status of Parliament, as the supreme authority of the country, is destroyed. I do not propose, unless I am so directed by the House, whose mouth-piece I am, to sanction any inquiry of the kind which is not authorised by Parliament itself'. President Givens spoke in similar vein, and the razor gang, as it would have been called by a later generation, kept away from Parliament.

The privilege matter of 1920 was something quite different. This was parliament's first and only exercise of its power, derived from the House of Commons, to expel one of its own members. The case arose indirectly from the death of the Lord Mayor of Cork, Terence McSwiney, after a 74-day hunger strike in gaol which had aroused intense anti-British feeling in Irish communities around the world, not least in Australia, where McSwiney had relatives. On Sunday 7 November, two weeks after his death, some four thousand people attended an open-air meeting in Melbourne organised by the Irish Ireland League and chaired by Hugh Mahon, the 63-year-old M.H.R. who had recaptured his seat of Kalgoorlie from the khaki member Heitmann at the last election. Mahon, who was born in Ireland and had been a prisoner in Kilmainham gaol at the same time as Parnell during the 1880s, for inciting violence, was active in the Home Rule movement. Beside him on the platform were five other Labor M.H.R.s: Tudor, Parker Moloney, Brennan, Considine and Cunningham.

Hugh Mahon was a tall, scrawny man with steel-rimmed spectacles; a rather cold individual, according to one of his colleagues, 'into whose soul the iron had entered'. He had been passed over for the Treasurership in 1915; had at first supported Hughes on conscription, but stayed with the A.L.P.; and had two sons in the A.I.F. Cold and reserved he may have been, but on that Sunday afternoon he spoke with passionate abandon:

> They were told in the papers that Alderman McSwiney's poor widow sobbed over his coffin [read an indirect report of his speech in the *Argus*]. If there was a just God in heaven that sob would reach round the world, and one day would shake the foundations of this bloody and accursed Empire. The other day he was approached by a vinegar-faced "wowser" who said that the police in Ireland were being shot in the back. If they were shot in the back it must be because they were running away. But there were no police in Ireland. They were spies, informers and bloody cut-throats. (Applause). He read with delight that some of those murder-

ing thugs had been sent to their account, and he trusted that Ireland would not be profaned by their carcasses. Their souls were probably in hell, and their bodies should be sent to England. He would not have the sweet pastures of Ireland poisoned by their carrion clay.

At a sitting of the House four days later, on the afternoon of 11 November, Hughes moved

> That, in the opinion of this House, the honorable member for Kalgoorlie, the Hon. Hugh Mahon, having, by seditious and disloyal utterances at a public meeting on Sunday last, been guilty of conduct unfitting him to remain a member of this House, and inconsistent with the oath of allegiance which he has taken as a member of this House, be expelled this House.

Mahon was not present in the chamber, although he had received notice of the motion at his Melbourne home the previous day. He sent a letter which Hughes read to the House. In part, it said:

> My criticism, which was confined to the acts of British Ministers and their agents in Ireland, made no reference whatever to the Sovereign. I am not aware that the oath of an Australian parliamentarian binds him in allegiance to Mr Lloyd George and his associates . . . I regret that I am unable to accommodate you with a statement in person; but really do you seriously think it would make any difference? If, as reported, your Caucus has already decreed my expulsion, then if one spoke with the tongue of an angel he would not alter in one iota their clandestine decree.

Speaking in support of his motion, Hughes played down the Irish question and dealt mainly with Mahon's alleged disloyalty to the British Empire. Australia depended for its well being on the Empire, he said, and the Empire had as much right to resist self-determination by Ireland as the Northern states had to prevent secession by the South in the American Civil War, and indeed as Australia also would have if, for example, Tasmania tried to break away from the Empire or from the Commonwealth. Mahon had advocated disruption of the Empire, and that was 'treason to Australia, and [made] him unfit to sit here as a member of the Australian parliament'. Only one other Government or Country Party member spoke on general principles; he was the blind Member for Fawkner (V), G. A. Maxwell, and his conclusion was much the same as the Prime Minister's. In contrast to the 'silent and stony phalanx' on the Government and Country Party benches, fourteen of the seventeen Labor members present spoke in Mahon's defence. The last and most compelling speaker was Frank Anstey, who warned the Government dispassionately that it was setting a dangerous precedent:

> If I offend against the laws of my country the Government will, I presume, bring me before a properly constituted Court, where I shall have an opportunity of meeting my accusers before a Judge. But, because I am elected to Parliament, do I cease to enjoy the privileges of a private citizen? If I have the right of an ordinary citizen, Parliament surely has not the authority to deprive me of that right . . . This Parliament is not the judge of offences against the law; it is for the Courts of the country to judge [us]; and it is for the people who have elected us to Parliament to

judge us. You have no ethical right to do what is proposed to be done. Your only right is that of might. I do not blame you for the exercise of that might because in politics there are no ethics. You are, therefore, simply laying down a precedent, of which you may be the victim . . . It matters not that it may be a Catholic today or that it may be a Protestant tomorrow, an Irishman today or tomorrow an Englishman, a member of the Labor Party today or a member of the party opposite tomorrow. There are no morals, no ethics, in what honorable members are doing; honorable members opposite simply make an accusation, and they are themselves the accusers, the prosecutors, the judges and the executioners, driving this man out of the place into which he was sent by the people of this country.

Soon after four o'clock next morning, the debate was gagged and the motion of expulsion was passed on party lines, by 34 votes to 17. Hughes then submitted a second motion declaring the seat of Kalgoorlie vacant. The Government applied the gag a second time, and again the House divided, with the same result. In retrospect, later observers would acknowledge the legal and political difficulties in the way of prosecuting Mahon for sedition. There was no appropriate Commonwealth legislation or court, and public opinion may not have tolerated prosecution under the War Precautions regulations so long after the war. A Commonwealth official could have launched a private prosecution in a Victorian court, but this would have placed the Commonwealth at the mercy of a State Attorney-General, with power to quash such a prosecution. Furthermore, there was no certainty of success in the intricate law of sedition. Trial by parliament could be justified legally, but in this case was it a proper use of parliamentary privilege? The consensus of later opinion held that it was not. Hughes probably resorted to expulsion not out of personal malice, or even affronted patriotism, but because it offered certainty of success and a good chance that his Government would win Kalgoorlie at the consequent by-election. Sure enough, Mahon was narrowly defeated by G. J. Foley, a former Western Australian M.L.A. and part owner of a goldmine on the Kalgoorlie field. This was the first and so far the only time in the history of the Commonwealth parliament that a seat previously held by the Opposition went to the Government at a by-election. So strong is the electorate's impulse at a by-election to vote against the party in office, thus chastising the Government without dismissing it, that only the stigma of expulsion has been able to curb it.

The Country Party, uneasy about the increasing frequency with which McWilliams had been voting against the majority of his own party, elected a new leader in April 1920. There were no nominations. All ten members of the parliamentary party were regarded as candidates, but all votes except one (his own) went to the Member for Cowper, Earle Christmas Grafton Page. Dr Page was a forceful, somewhat disconcerting man who in his thirty-nine years had found time to combine a large medical practice with business interests and rural politics. His family had been involved in local government for two generations past, his paternal grandfather having been Town Clerk of Grafton for eighteen years; two paternal uncles the Mayors of

Grafton and Casino; and his father, a coachbuilder and engineer by trade, the Mayor of Grafton when that town's famous jacarandas were planted.

Earle Page was inspired to study medicine by an accident to his mother, which illustrated for him the lack of medical facilities in such a country town as Grafton, in the northern rivers region of New South Wales. Mrs Page had been struck in the eye by a flying piece of metal while using a cold chisel to remove the iron hoop from a barrel of molasses, and the treatment of her injury involved several long journeys to Sydney. After graduating from Sydney University, Dr Page set up practice at Grafton as a G.P. and surgeon in 1903. He did his rounds in the first Rover car imported to Australia, at a time when there were only about thirty cars in the entire country. After the Rover he used a 20-h.p. Itala with a special body built by his father so that the back seat could be used as an ambulance when required. No one understood the shortcomings of Australia's road system better than Page, for on several occasions he drove himself from Grafton to Melbourne and back.

Dr Page joined the Army Medical Corps in February 1916, served as a surgical specialist at Australian casualty stations in France, and was invalided home the following year because of illness. At the 1919 election, with endorsement by the Australian Farmers' Federal Organisation, he stood successfully against the Nationalist Member for Cowper, a large electorate extending down the north coast of New South Wales from the Queensland border to Port Stephens. After being elected parliamentary leader, Page introduced some semblance of organisation into his party, the membership of which had now risen to eleven through the transfer of W. M. Fleming (Robertson, N) from the Nationalist Party, or twelve if account be taken of Arnold Wienholt (Moreton, Q), who although a member of the Nationalist Party usually supported the Country Party.

Hughes regarded Dr Page as a bumbling amateur from the country, but in that he was badly mistaken. Behind the façade of Page's torrential talk punctuated by the phrase 'You see, you see', his fixed smile and nervous giggle, this solidly built man with dark curly hair and rugged features was just as tough as Hughes, and no friend of his either.

In spite of that mutual aversion, Page convinced his colleagues that they could support the Government more consistently than in the past without endangering their own independence. Shortly before the Prime Minister's departure for the Imperial Conference in April 1921, Page gave a 'qualified promise of immunity' during his absence, only to be embarrassed the following day, 14 April, when the Government was defeated 32–30 on a formal adjournment motion moved by the Country Party Member for Grampians (V), Edmund Jowett. The formal adjournment was a procedural device by which, under Standing Orders, any member could raise an urgent matter without having to give notice of motion in the usual way. All a member needed to do was rise in his place immediately before the calling on of the business of the day and propose to move the adjournment of the House 'for the purpose of discussing a definite matter of urgent public importance'. If five members rose in support, the member then formally moved 'That the House do now adjourn', and proceeded to address the chamber on the matter of urgency. It was customary for such motions to be defeated, for they were usually no more than pretexts for discussion; but the fact remained that a motion was before the House, and the possibility existed that either inadvertently or intentionally the government of the day could be defeated when it came to a vote.

Jowett moved the adjournment not to censure the Government, but to call attention to 'the excessive and crushing rates of ocean freight now being charged upon the exportable products of Australia'. The Government should have survived such a motion, even though the Country Party members voted for it, but was defeated because one of its own supporters, J. M. Fowler (Perth), voted with the 'Ayes' by mistake. Fowler was talking to a journalist in the press gallery immediately on his left. 'Whilst speaking to him', Fowler explained to the House next day,

> I was unconscious of what was taking place in the chamber, and misheard as a call of order to me what was a call for order after the House had divided. It was some little time before I realised that a division was being taken, and a little longer before I recognised its import. By that time it was too late for me to change my position . . . The situation that has been created carries considerable possibilities for me. There are members of the Ministerial party who strongly resent my vote; but I am sure that the Prime Minister is grateful to me for having afforded him an opportunity to improve his position. For the moment I cannot make up my mind whether I am likely to be expelled from the party or to be offered a portfolio.

What Fowler meant by an improvement in the Prime Minister's position was that Hughes had used the unintended taking of the House's business out of the Government's hands to extract from Dr Page a firmer undertaking of support. 'If some members of the Country party had had a little more experience', he told the House in a condescending speech, almost a lesson in parliamentary practice, which must have caused Dr Page's smile to sag a little,

> they would have known that it is almost the invariable practice to negate a motion of the character in question, and not to support it. Such motions are not moved for the actual purpose of adjourning the House. They are an interruption of the ordinary programme of work set down on the business-paper for the day, in order to discuss some matter of urgent public business.

Jowett admitted that he had not intended his motion to reflect adversely on the Government, and at the next sitting Hughes removed any lingering doubt about the Government's position by having a motion passed effectively endorsing his forthcoming attendance at the Imperial Conference. The Labor Party moved, as an amendment to the motion, the addition of the words 'and that, in the best interests of the citizens of the Commonwealth, the Prime Minister should immediately tender his resignation to the Governor-General'. The amendment was lost, 23–46; the original motion was passed, 46–23; and Hughes went on his way to London, safe for the time being.

But no sooner was he back in parliament, for the Budget session in October, than the Government came close to being defeated again. This time it was saved rather than defeated by a Nationalist who claimed he was not aware that a division had been called. The Country Party attacked Cook's Budget, arguing that its deficit could not be justified in view of the economic recession which had set in after Australia's short-lived post-war boom. On 27 October Page was confident that he had sufficient votes organised— Country Party, Labor Party and one dissident Nationalist—to amend the Treasurer's motion that the first item in the Estimates be agreed to. His amendment was that the first item ('The President, £1,100') be reduced by ten shillings, and 'that this be taken as an instruction to the Government to reconsider the Estimates for the purpose of reducing the total expenditure from revenue by the sum of £2,817,108, the amount of the anticipated deficit, in order to square the ledger'. Page's willingness to work with the Nationalists did not extend to deficit spending, even a deficit of that pristine order.

But something went wrong. While the House was in Committee of Supply, the dissident Nationalist, whose name appropriately was George Bell (Darwin, T), took a Tasmanian visitor into the Senate rooms to help him find one of the Tasmanian senators. There he was unable to hear the electric division bells rung for two minutes by the Clerk of his own House. When he returned to the chamber he found the doors were locked for a division on Page's amendment, which was defeated, 32–33.

> I know what construction may be placed on my absence', Bell told the House in a personal explanation, 'but it was well known by the Leader of the Government and, I think, by most honourable members, that I intended to vote for the amendment. I missed the division, unfortunately, through not hearing the bells ring, though I was only a short distance from the chamber. Had I heard them I would have voted for the amendment. I fear that my explanation may not be accepted by all; but I trust that those who know me will accept it. I care little what may be thought by others.

Many, including some who knew Bell, thought there was more to it than that: either the Honourable Member for Darwin had been encouraged to absent himself while the bells were ringing, or the division had been called deliberately while he was away.

Even if Bell had voted with the 'Ayes', the amendment would probably have been defeated. His vote would have produced a division of 33–33, and in that event the occupant of the Chair, who was the Chairman of Committees, would have exercised the casting vote allowed to him under Standing Orders. He would almost certainly have voted against the amendment, for—party loyalty aside—it is customary in exercising a casting vote to leave the bill as it stands. Speaker Johnson was also present in his capacity as an ordinary member, and his deliberative vote went to the Government.

Nevertheless the escape had been narrow enough to make Hughes face the necessity of taking the Country Party into his Ministry, if it would come. During his five-month absence overseas, there had been mounting criticism of the Government's failure to deal with the recession. Within the Nationalist Party, resentment of Hughes's 'socialism' (as it seemed to ex-Liberal members of the party) and dictatorial manner was also growing. Watt had voted with the Government against Page's amendment, but his palpable animosity towards Hughes left his continued loyalty in doubt.

Clearing the way for a Country Party presence in his Ministry by obtaining resignations from all his Ministers, Hughes embarked upon wary negotiations with Page in November at the home of a mutual friend. Page, hopeful of winning enough new seats at the next election to gain the balance of power and insist upon Hughes's removal from leadership of the Nationalist Party, would not agree to coalition; but he offered the Government immunity, on certain conditions, including a tighter budget, until parliament went into recess in December. If he did not know it before, Hughes now knew that he was living on sufferance.

Taking advantage of his Ministers' resignations, he reorganised the Ministry in December, dropping three Ministers, taking in four, and reshuffling portfolios. He himself exchanged the Attorney-Generalship for External Affairs. His heir apparent in the parliamentary party was the Minister for Trade and Customs, Walter Massy-Greene; but that was more apparent than real. Massy-Greene, a well-to-do dairy farmer from Lismore, had not made much of a mark in Cabinet and was viewed with suspicion by the Country Party because of his close connections with the Melbourne business community. He hoped for the Treasurership when Cook resigned, but Hughes had someone else in mind—the Member for Flinders, S. M. Bruce.

Stanley Melbourne Bruce, then in his thirty-ninth year, was an Austral-Briton more British than Australian. Frank Anstey once described him as 'an English gentleman, born in Australia—as other Englishmen are born in China, India or Timbuctoo'. His father, born in Ireland of Scottish descent, was a partner, and later the major shareholder, in the British-Australian softgoods importing firm of Paterson, Laing & Bruce, which became one of the leading businesses in Victoria. Bruce senior built a mansion at Toorak, and was co-founder of a golf club that later became the Royal Melbourne. Stanley, the youngest of five children, spent part of his early childhood in England, while his father managed the London end of the company; but most of his school days were spent in Melbourne. He went to a preparatory school in Toorak, and then to Melbourne Grammar, where he was captain of the football, cricket and rowing teams, and captain of the school in 1901.

That year the father died, and an elder brother took over management of the family company in Melbourne. Stanley spent a year working in the Melbourne warehouse; then went to Cambridge, where he won his rowing blue and graduated B.A.; read for the Bar, and in 1907 was called to the Middle Temple. He remained in England for three more years as chairman of the London board of Paterson, Laing & Bruce, for which he drew a salary of £5000 a year, practising also as a barrister, and in his spare time coaching Cambridge rowing crews, to whom he was known by the towpath nickname of 'Bruggins'. Those who knew Bruce at this time remarked upon his charm, polite arrogance, logical mind, powers of application and sense of his own importance.

He visited Australia in 1910 and 1914 to act as general manager while his brother was overseas, and between times he married Ethel Dunlop, a relative of J. C. Manifold, who was generally considered to have been the wealthiest member of the first Commonwealth parliament. The Bruces might well have been a model for the peripatetic Anglo-Australian families of that period described later in the novels of Martin Boyd. When war broke out, Stanley was still in Melbourne. Rather than enlist in the A.I.F., he returned to London, joined the Inns of Court Regiment, and was then seconded as a temporary captain to the Royal Fusiliers, with whom he landed at Gallipoli. He was wounded at Hellas; won the Military Cross at Suvla Bay for contacting and leading to safety forty men who had been cut off from their battalion; and after being wounded again, in the knee, was invalided to England. He returned to Melbourne, still a British officer on crutches, and was discharged there in 1917.

The wounded war hero who won the seat of Flinders in 1918—a tall, athletic figure with the heavy good looks of a matinee idol—was something altogether new, indeed unique, in federal politics. The *Bulletin* described him as 'the most highly-veneered politician we have yet produced'. But of course 'Bruggins' was more the product of Cambridge, Mayfair and the City than of Melbourne. He dropped his g's, and used words like 'feller' and 'bounder' in true Wodehouse style; wore Savile Row suits with spats, used polo ponies when touring his semi-rural electorate, and played royal tennis. He and his wife lived in a suite at the Oriental Hotel in Collins Street.

Or rather they lived at the Oriental when they were in Melbourne, which in 1921 was not for long. In January of that year, taking a Sunbeam car and chauffeur with them, the Bruces sailed for England, where the Member for Flinders had softgoods business to attend to. He was there for nine months, and missed seventy-seven of the eighth parliament's 207 sittings. While he was away, someone was needed to represent Australia at the second assembly of the League of Nations in Geneva. Bruce and his wife happened to be on a motoring holiday in France. Australia House tracked the Sunbeam car to a golf course in Dieppe, and Bruce went on to Geneva, where he made a good fist of the unexpected assignment.

Bruce liked to depict himself as an amateur who had come into politics more or less by accident, and was fortunate enough to have succeeded at it. But behind that nonchalance was an alert and calculating mind. After Bruce's return to Melbourne, with Sunbeam and chauffeur, Hughes offered him the portfolio of Trade and Customs, possibly just to test his reaction. Bruce pointed out the foolhardiness of giving such a portfolio to the head of Australia's largest importing firm. 'Something in that, something in that!' muttered the Prime Minister, and then offered the Treasury, which he and Bruce both knew Massy-Greene wanted. Massy-Greene had to make do with Defence, and Bruce, after only three and a half years as a backbencher, found himself ranking second to the Prime Minister.

Precarious though the Government's position may have been, the Opposition was worse off. With only one seat in the Senate and twenty-six in the lower house, Labor had also lost whatever chance it might previously have had of attracting significant support from the Country Party. Seeking to regain the support of militant unions, the A.L.P. put a much sharper point on its public ownership objective. From 1905 until 1919 the federal party had been content to aim merely at public ownership of monopolies rather than at the general collective ownership espoused by the more radical of the State branches, Victoria and Queensland. So far the Commonwealth had made only two essays at public ownership: the Commonwealth Bank which was competing to some extent with its private competitors, and the Commonwealth Shipping Line which had been established by the Hughes Government in 1916 and was still exerting a protective influence on freight rates charged by the British cartels. In 1919 the federal party adopted a policy of 'collective ownership and democratic control of the collectively used agencies of production, distribution and exchange', but this was superseded two years later by a much more resounding socialist objective.

An All-Australian Trade Union Congress summoned by the A.L.P. in 1921 recommended that the federal platform should include 'The socialisation of industry, production, distribution and exchange'. Congress also recommended that the platform should incorporate a statement of various methods by which that objective was to be attained—notably 'the nationalisation of banking and all principal industries', 'the government of nationalised industries by boards, upon which the workers in the industry and the community shall have representation', and 'the establishment of an elective Supreme Economic Council by all nationalised industries'.

Although the basic objective and methods were all adopted more or less as recommended by the Congress, some influential speakers expressed misgivings about the methods. They felt that delegates to the Congress 'had their minds saturated with ideals and dogmas that did not belong to Australia', and that a Supreme Economic Council 'would really take the place of the political Parliament'. In response to such fears, the conference later carried a declaration 'that the Party does not seek to abolish private ownership even of any of the instruments of production where such instrument is utilised in a socially useful manner and without exploitation'. There were not sufficient affirmative votes for this to be included in the platform, however, and the conference chairman ruled that it did not affect the policy already carried.

Worker control and the Supreme Economic Council were to be dropped from the platform six years later, but so far as the Country Party was concerned that scarcely made any difference. The conference of 1921 had queered Labor's pitch with the Country Party, except perhaps for one or two of that party's unpredictable Victorians. To make matters worse for the parliamentary Labor Party, it lost its Leader and Deputy Leader within six months of each other. The Deputy, T. J. Ryan, was suffering from a cold when he left Melbourne on a 2000-mile train journey to campaign at a by-election for the huge pastoral electorate of Maranoa in western Queensland, brought about by the death of the Labor veteran, Jim Page. By the time Ryan reached Maranoa from Rockhampton, his cold had turned into pneumonia. He would not call off the tour, and addressed meetings at every stop.

As his train crossed the black soil plains north of Blackall, Ryan began coughing blood. On the evening of 28 July, two days before the election, he left the train at Barcaldine, a town regarded by many, because of its importance during the shearers' strike, as having been the birthplace of Australia's labour movement. There he was taken to a private hospital, where he lost consciousness and died three days later. His untimely death at the age of forty-five was to no avail, for Maranoa was won by a Country Party candidate, J. A. J. Hunter, an accountant from Dalby who specialised in handling graziers' taxation returns.

A requiem high mass was held for Ryan at St Stephen's Cathedral in Brisbane. By chance another renowned Irish-Australian, Archbishop Mannix, arrived in the city that very day on his way back to Melbourne, via Torres Strait, after a trip to Ireland. Dr Mannix recited the offices for the dead over Ryan's coffin.

Although only Deputy Leader, Ryan had been called upon during the current session to perform many parliamentary duties for the party leader, Frank Tudor, who was badly afflicted with heart trouble. Tudor, formerly a hatter by trade, was less militant than his fellow Melburnians, Anstey, Brennan and Moloney. He was the sort of man whose colleagues called him 'cobber' and 'old sport'; his death in January 1922 saddened the party, but did not greatly weaken it. In his place Caucus elected a man of similar nature, Matthew Charlton, a former miner and union official in the Hunter Valley of New South Wales. The new Deputy Leader, more acidulous than Ryan but less well equipped for leadership, was Frank Anstey.

The second session of the eighth parliament was opened on 28 June 1922 by a new Governor-General—Lord Forster of Lepe, another ex-member of the House of Commons, the former Rt Hon. Henry William Forster. Munro Ferguson had been created first Viscount Novar at the conclusion of his successful six-year term in Australia. As a member of the House of Lords, he later became Secretary for Scotland.

Few measures of much significance emerged from this session. But one of them, the Northern Territory Representation Act, increased the number of seats in the House of Representatives from seventy-five to seventy-six. With support from three Country Party members, Labor moved to amend the Bill so as to give the Territory's M.H.R. a full vote. That amendment was defeated, however, and the representative elected at the next general election (to no one's surprise a Labor man, Harold Nelson) was entitled to speak in the House, but not to vote or be reckoned part of a quorum.

The new Treasurer at first had difficulty with Hughes in Cabinet; then, according to his later account, he simply went his own way. 'I came to the conclusion', wrote Bruce, 'that with an eccentric genius like Billy Hughes it was impossible to have any well-regulated procedure for the Cabinet. I ceased to put Treasury items on the agenda, and simply went ahead and did whatever I thought was necessary'. Bruce's Budget was little more pleasing to the Country Party than Cook's. Dr Page was now tackling the Government head on about its rural policies. Speaking at Ballarat on 21 September, he coined a phrase that touched Hughes on the raw. It was 'Drop the loot':

> In the Federal Parliament the members of the Country Party were so few that they could act merely as faithful watchdogs of country interests. Still, they could do a lot of good. Their action was frequently like switching on the electric light when the burglar was about. (Loud laughter.) That made the burglar drop the loot. (Laughter.) That had been the effect recently with regard to the Budget. In that respect the Country Party had forced the dropping of some of the loot.

The Prime Minister raised this in the House as a matter of privilege, alleging that Page had accused the Government of committing a crime. Page replied that he had been referring not to individuals but to the Government's price-fixing policy, which was 'nothing but plain, downright robbery'.

> What I said was that the general tenor of the Administration was such as to cause practical robbery of the producers of this country, and that the action of the Country Party, in continually calling attention to the state of affairs, had resulted in certain remissions. The grossly unfair and extortionate charges made upon the producer, in my opinion, completely vindicate anything I said.

Hughes did not move a resolution, and the matter was dropped, with Page the clear winner.

In the Budget debate, which the Government brought on as late as possible in the life of the parliament, Page pursued his cause of squaring the ledger. 'The appointment of the honorable member for Flinders to the position of Treasurer was hailed with very great satisfaction and high expectations by the bulk of the people', he said.

> They had hoped that "the rake's progress" of successive governments—the continual budgeting for deficits, living beyond our means, and the old wartime scale of lavish expenditure—would be brought to an end. But a close examination of the present Budget indicates that, although many of the old defects are better covered up, it is still tragically full of objectionable features, and that it is designed with an eye, not to the next generation, but merely to the next general election.

That election was imminent, for the eighth parliament had run almost its full course. Hughes extracted promises from all ministers that they would not help to form a coalition with the Country Party after the election, and Bruce declared in at least one reported campaign speech: 'If Mr Hughes is thrown out, I will go too'. The disaffected ex-Liberal wing of the Nationalist Party made no such pretence of loyalty, however, and contested several seats in Victoria and South Australia under a Liberal banner. As Hughes's seat of Bendigo had been endangered by redistribution, he transferred to North Sydney, having persuaded its occupant, Sir Granville Ryrie, to take the new and equally safe seat of Warringah. The electoral redistribution had produced five new electorates, three of which were named after distinguished former members: Barton (N), Reid (N) and Forrest (W). As none was in Victoria or South Australia, Deakin and Kingston had to wait their turn.

The 1922 election campaign was probably the dullest yet in federal history. Hughes was stabbed with a hat pin in Melbourne Town Hall; the Country Party accused him of 'fig-leaf socialism', by which it meant thinly disguised socialism; Hughes called Dr Page 'Alice in Wonderland' and the Victorian Liberals 'troglodytes'; and the voters stayed away in droves, both from election meetings and from the polls. Fewer than 60 per cent of registered electors voted, compared with more than 70 per cent at the previous general election. In Western Australia and Tasmania the turnout was less than 50 per cent.

The election resulted in no party being able to govern alone, and the Country Party holding the balance of power. In the House of Representatives the Nationalists won only twenty-six seats, and their ex-Liberal colleagues won five. The Labor Party gained three seats, giving it twenty-nine not counting the Member for the Northern Territory; and the Country Party increased its number to fourteen. There was one Independent, who usually supported the Nationalists but sometimes voted with Labor. In the Senate Labor gained eleven seats; the Nationalists eight; and the Country Party, which had fielded thirteen Senate candidates, again had none.

Among the casualties were J. H. Catts and Mick Considine, both of whom had been expelled from the A.L.P. for arcane reasons concerned with a split in the New South Wales branch; W. G. Higgs and Sir Robert Best, both of whom had served successively in the Senate and lower house almost without a break since federation; and the disappointed Massy-Greene. The ex-Labor Nationalist, Higgs, was defeated in Capricornia (Q) by a new Labor candidate, Francis Michael Forde; the ex-Liberal Nationalist, Best, was defeated in Kooyong (V) by one of the Liberal 'Hughes Must Go' candidates, John Latham; and Massy-Greene was defeated in Richmond (N) by a Country Party grazier, R. F. H. Green. Green, having lost a leg at Ypres, campaigned with the unbeatable slogan of 'Vote for the Green without an E', meaning 'without a knee'. Massy-Greene was consoled by being appointed the next year to fill a vacancy caused by the death of Senator Millen. He remained in the Senate for fifteen years, and was knighted along the way.

Hughes won North Sydney by the comfortable margin of 4600 votes, but that was less than a quarter of Ryrie's majority at the previous election. What would happen to him now, and what would happen to all those pre-election promises of solidarity? One member of the Opposition, Arthur Blakeley (Darling, N), said in the House later that Hughes 'was taken to the bathroom . . . and had his political throat cut'. It was not as brutal as that. The Country Party now had the power to insist, and eventually did insist, that there would be no coalition until Hughes resigned from the leadership of his party.

In his coalition bargaining with Bruce, Dr Page frequently withdrew to consult an adviser on whom he had come to rely—the new member for Kooyong, John Latham, a Melbourne K.C. and former intelligence officer in the Royal Australian Navy, who had conceived a strong dislike of Hughes and his *modus operandi* while serving as an adviser with Australia's delegation at the peace conference. Bruce and Senator Pearce at first urged Hughes to remain as leader, but other senior Nationalists wanted the little devil gone. On 9 February 1923 he tendered the resignation of his Ministry and advised Lord Forster to send for Bruce.

Bruce then formed a Ministry consisting of six Nationalists and five Country Party members, with Page as Treasurer, Littleton Groom as Attorney-General and Senator Pearce as Minister for Home and Territories and Government Leader in the Senate. The coalition had been inevitable, but Hughes did not go to the bathroom meekly: he went in the baleful, unforgiving spirit that was to characterise the three decades still lying ahead of him in parliament. He had been Prime Minister for seven years, three months and fourteen days. That was considerably longer than the cumulative terms of his closest rivals for length of tenure—Deakin, four years, ten months, thirteen days; and Fisher, four years, ten months, two days. Deakin and Fisher both welcomed their release when it came, but Billy Hughes was still very much the urchin resentful at having to leave the tart shop.

When Pearce was asked by Bruce to lend his ex-Labor presence to a ministry composed mainly of businessmen and farmers, he went to see Hughes at Sassafras, seeking release from his pre-election promise. 'You can do as you damn well like!' Hughes told his colleague of the past twenty-two years. Pearce was hurt by this response, and by the cold shoulder that Hughes continued to present for several years to come. As late as 1927, when the former carpenter from Perth was made a Knight Commander of the Royal Victorian Order, someone asked Hughes casually whether he knew Sir George Pearce. 'No', replied the former locksmith and umbrella mender from Balmain. 'I used to know George Pearce. I don't know Sir George.'

While the businessmen and the farmers may have stumbled into their alliance, without the benefit of any detailed treaty, there was no doubt about the basis on which the alliance rested. On the one hand Page and his farmers would accept the Nationalists' Protectionist tariff policy, both electorally and in parliament; and on the other hand Bruce and his businessmen would introduce and maintain subsidies, price supports and marketing aids designed to compensate the farmers for the cost to them of city-benefiting tariff protection. It was a marriage made in heaven.

7

Moving House

Melbourne

One of the ninth parliament's few claims to distinction, remarked upon during the Address-in-Reply debate, was that it produced the Commonwealth's first wholly Australian-born Ministry. This was a claim to difference rather than excellence, and what the difference signified was not readily apparent. Certainly it reflected rising native proportions in population and parliament alike. The locally born component of Australia's population rose from 77 per cent in 1901 to 84 per cent in 1921, and comparable figures for the first and ninth parliaments were 52 per cent and 72 per cent. Whatever the true significance of this may have been, it did provide useful material for a maiden speech delivered by the Honourable Member for Richmond, the Green without a knee, who was himself a fourth generation Australian. 'Although I am aware', he said in seconding adoption of the Address-in-Reply,

> that much has been done for Australia in the past by our forebears, it is gratifying to know that we have now got beyond the swaddling clothes stage. We have men in this country who were born, reared and educated in it, and have absorbed into their very bones the spirit of Australia. These are the men who will carry on.

Poor Green was a sitting duck for the first Labor speaker in that debate, London-born Frank Anstey. Before moving a no-confidence amendment to the Address-in-Reply, Anstey put the subject of birthplace into better perspective. 'Let me refer for a moment', he said,

> to the statement . . . that the Ministry is exclusively Australian. All credit to it, but the honourable member ignores the fact that, under our flag, we speak a common tongue, and have a common destiny, and a common faith . . . There have been Ministers within Australia who were essentially

195

and characteristically Australian, born and trained in Australia, but there have been others who, although they had their place of nativity in other parts of His Majesty's Dominions, came to this country to realise, as I and others have done, those opportunities not open to them in the land of their birth . . .

Whether they were English, Scotch, Welsh or Irish, whether they were cultured or uncultured, none of them climbed to pre-eminence without a long period of political apprenticeship, and all of them possessed that outstanding ability which enabled them to achieve success. But today we have a Government controlled by a new force, by a man who is not merely Australian, or merely English, but is a cultured Australian seeking to adapt to himself the manners, customs and fashions of Bond-street and Piccadilly. So much for place of nativity.

For Anstey, the main characteristic of the Bruce–Page Ministry was not its pure merino composition—three Ministers born in Victoria, three in New South Wales, one in South Australia and one in Queensland. Its uniqueness lay rather in the fact that it was 'a Government of "business" men, shrewd and astute, distinct from any Government that has ever held the destinies of Australia in its hands'. Bruce, the Flinders Lane importer; Page, the former country doctor with business interests, now Treasurer; Sir Austin Chapman, the country entrepreneur now Minister for Trade and Customs: these matched Anstey's description. So also, to a lesser extent, did the Postmaster-General, W. G. Gibson (C, Corangamite, V), the country storekeeper with grazing interests; the Minister for Works and Railways, P. G. Stewart (C, Wimmera, V), a wheat farmer with country newspaper interests; and the Minister for Defence, E. K. Bowden (Nat, Parramatta, N), a lawyer-cum-businessman. Only the Minister for Home and Territories, Senator Pearce, and the Attorney-General, Littleton Groom, by grace of their long service in parliament, escaped the label of 'business' which Anstey bestowed with such scorn.

The real contradiction of the present parliament, as Anstey saw it, was that a ministry composed mainly of 'shrewd and astute' businessmen should, alone of all governments since federation, be 'utterly incapable of producing a policy'. 'It knows nothing', he said in his no-confidence speech, 'and treats parliament with scorn, while regarding the general public as a thing to be played with'. Of course he was exaggerating, and overlooking earlier ministries which had taken office without much in the way of considered programmes; but even the new Prime Minister had to concede that his Ministry was the most inexperienced in federal history. Watt, who might have provided some of the ballast that was lacking, had become too much of a lone wolf for Cabinet. Instead he was elected to replace the perfectly able Sir Elliot Johnson as Speaker—a crude manoeuvre rightly characterised by one Opposition member, Blakeley, as 'the elevation of a gentleman whom they fear to a position where he cannot speak'. Speaker Watt acquitted himself well for three years until he also had to stand down for someone else.

'We're going in', Bruce wrote to Hughes, as if referring to a cricket eleven, 'but there is no one in this Government except Pearce and myself who has ever been in a government'. Bruce himself had been a minister for little more than a year, and at thirty-nine he was the youngest member of Cabinet. Because of that, or perhaps merely to emphasise the plucky amateurism of his team, he neglected to acknowledge the many portfolios held previously by Groom and Chapman. As for the rest, however, he was correct. 'It is the most amateur side that has ever taken office in any country', he wrote to Hughes.

> If we last six months it will be a miracle. And then there'll be nothing for it but that you'll have to come back. But for God's sake don't attack us too soon or you'll arouse the sporting spirit of the Australian people. They'll say you haven't given the fellers a chance.

This note was scarcely to be taken at face value. Its nonchalance, reminiscent of the Cambridge tow-path or a regimental mess, was probably intended merely to assuage a sullen and potentially dangerous former Prime Minister. Hughes had little chance of ever coming back, but he could and would make life difficult for the Government of which he was nominally a backbench supporter. The Government sent him on an extended mission to the United States, but six months later he was back again—as one Labor member said, 'the political Cerberus who sits in the corner opposite', ready to savage friends as well as foes.

Although Hughes had advised the Governor-General to send for Bruce, and had told his own Cabinet that he would support a Bruce–Page Government, he managed thereafter to convey the impression that Bruce had betrayed him. He supported the Government on most occasions, but seldom lost an opportunity of denigrating Bruce in private. Writing to his one-time departmental secretary, Malcolm Shepherd, now the official secretary at Australia House in London, he said:

> Bruce has gone to the country . . . on tour. What his idea is no man can tell. Probably he is trying to make himself known to the electors. But the less he is known the better he will do. The fact of the matter is that he is not an Australian at all, except by accident of birth. He does not appeal to the people. He is just a very conventional English Johnny.'

The Leader of the Opposition, Matthew Charlton, found Bruce 'a bumptious man, the most bumptious ever to sit in this House'. Anstey, who privately expressed admiration for the young Prime Minister's imperturbable manner, dubbed him the Viceroy. Outside the House, Bruce was not so much bumptious as aloof and urbane. 'Mr Bruce would be very glad', read a note attached to a biography sent to the press by his office, 'if the newspapers would not refer to him by his Christian name as Mr Stanley Bruce, but always as Mr S. M. Bruce'. He employed a butler and a valet, rode in his own chauffeured Rolls Royce, and whenever travelling by train he made sure that one of his people tipped the engine driver a pound note.

Conventional though he was about the trappings of wealth and class, Bruce was also a careful administrator possessed of what Anstey called 'a pelmanist brain'. Compared to his finely tuned combination of 'brains, breeding and business', Dr Page seemed rather bucolic: a country cousin full of energy and shrewdness, but not quite at home in the city. 'He used to come down from his office to mine practically every morning', said Bruce.

> He had new brainwaves every day. They were nearly always half-baked. He was bursting with energy; he was full of ideas, and to most of them you had to say: "My dear Page, for God's sake go away and have your head read". But if you had the patience to listen to Page, he'd come up with a helluva good idea now and then . . . I was the bird that had got to have the judgment to know which notion was worth a sick headache and which was no good at all.

There were no brainwaves in the Governor-General's speech at the opening of parliament on 28 February 1923, and precious few in Bruce's first speech as Prime Minister the following day. Lord Forster said that in view of the recent assumption of office by his advisers, time was required for the preparation of measures to give effect to their policy. Bruce's speech dealt in general terms with the need to improve transport and communications; the Government's belief (shared by State governments, though for different reasons) that financial relations between the Commonwealth and the States should be placed on a new footing; and the construction of a federal capital, including a new Parliament House, on the site 220 miles south-west of Sydney, by that time officially known as Canberra.

Canberra's halting progress since its selection as the capital site in 1908 will be described later in this chapter. For the moment it is enough to say, as Bruce said in the Address-in-Reply debate, that plans for a monumental capital had been interrupted by the war; planning and development were proceeding gradually, so as not to strain financial resources, and as yet there was no target date for moving parliament to the new seat of government.

After Address-in-Reply debates of four days in the lower house and one day in the Senate, in the course of which Anstey's no confidence amendment was defeated by 32 votes to 20, parliament was prorogued until June. That gave the Government time to prepare the unspecified measures referred to by the Governor-General, and arrange a conference of State Premiers in Melbourne devoted mainly to financial relations between the federal partners. Since 1910, when it ceased returning surplus customs and excise revenue to the States in accordance with the Braddon formula, the Commonwealth had been paying annually to each State 25 shillings per head of population from its national revenues. The system had become unsatisfactory to both parties. As the Commonwealth took more initiatives, particularly in the fields of social service and defence, it supplemented indirect revenue by using its taxation powers concurrently with the States— first land tax, then taxes on income, deceased estates and entertainment. After the outbreak of war it also entered the loan market alongside the States. The Commonwealth did not relish collecting taxes on behalf of the States. Nor did the States welcome the central Government's competition in revenue and loan raising, for during and after the war they were sometimes in deficit.

At the conference in June 1923, State Premiers (all non-Labor except Ryan's redoubtable successor in Queensland, E. G. Theodore) suggested that the Commonwealth should end the per capita system and leave the field of income tax to the States. The Commonwealth was not willing to forgo that source of revenue, but one subject on which the two sides agreed was the need to co-ordinate loan-raising by the various governments to their common advantage. This led to the establishment of a Loan Council on a voluntary basis.

In 1923 the Commonwealth also made its first 'earmarked' grants to the States, under Section 96 of the Constitution. Before the war parliament had made special assistance grants, unconditionally, to the least populous States, Tasmania and Western Australia, for whom per capita payment was not always enough. Section 96 permits parliament to grant assistance on such terms and conditions as it thinks fit, and in 1923 it thought fit to earmark the assistance exclusively for main road development. This was welcome news to many country electorates, but in some capital cities it was seen as an erosion of State autonomy.

The Country Party also had other causes for satisfaction with the legislative programme rammed through parliament in the first period of the second session, which lasted only from mid-June to late August. Among the thirty-six measures passed during these ten weeks were a Wheat Pool Advances Act to finance schemes for wheat marketing, an Advances to Settlers Act for the supply of wire netting to settlers, and a Meat Export Bounties Act. Cerberus in his corner might well have muttered: 'Drop the loot!' And the Leader of the Opposition spoke wryly about rural socialism:

> When the Prime Minister (Mr Bruce) and other members of theGovernment state that their policy is, 'No interference with business, which should be allowed to run in its natural channel,' and yet do something along socialistic lines every week, one wonders why so much condemnation is heaped upon the Labor Party for its Socialistic policy. Last week a wheat guarantee was proposed. That was a very proper thing, and I take no exception to it. This week the proposal is for a bounty to meat producers. I take no exception to that either, but again I recall the statement made by the Prime Minister [in reponse to a deputation asking him to regulate the coal trade 'because men in one portion of the industry were in a state of semi-starvation' that] it was not his duty, nor was it the policy of his Government, to interfere in any way with the ordinary channels of trade.

Bruce wanted to expedite the Government's legislative programme so that parliament need not sit while he attended the Imperial Conference in October. To that end he used the closure more often than any of his predecessors. Labor responded with want of confidence motions, and with one of the few other tactics available to a gagged Opposition—ritualised disruption by divisions on every question. The result was one of the rowdiest periods in the House of Representatives since federation. Press coverage of this sporadic uproar included the first photograph ever published of the House of Representatives in session. It was taken by the Melbourne *Herald* from the press gallery, without permission, and showed Dr Maloney 'pressing home a point . . . in Labor's verbal attack on the Bruce–Page Government'. A print was shown to the Speaker, and he agreed to its publication provided that the figure of one recumbent member was left out.

In June the Opposition moved want of confidence four times, to no avail; and while a Supply Bill was being gagged through an all-night sitting on 27–28 June, there were no fewer than thirty closures and sixty-eight divisions. The tedium of such a sitting is hard to imagine. Bruce, knowing that his Government had a safe margin of about ten members, would move that the question be now put without further debate. The Opposition would then exercise its right to demand a division, though it had no chance of outvoting the Government. Each division—with the ringing of bells, and tellers calling the names to be marked on the voting sheet—would take about seven minutes. The question would be resolved in the affirmative, and Bruce would move on to the next question (e.g. 'That the Vote, "The Attorney-General's Department, £21,445," be agreed to'), the next closure and the next division. 'Listen to the phonograph!' yelled Labor members as Bruce went remorselessly through this ritual. When interjections lapsed, they also sang 'The Red Flag', 'Solidarity for Ever' and 'Bollocky Bill the Sailor'. There were six divisions before 11.55 on Wednesday night, at which time the House went into Committee of Ways and Means. Between midnight and 10.06 on Thursday morning, when the House adjourned until 3 p.m., there were another sixty-three divisions.

The *Age* was scandalised by this 'very poorly simulated stage fury', which it saw as nothing other than the Opposition's malicious determination to 'place every obstacle in the way of the reasonable despatch of public business before the date on which the Prime Minister must leave for London'. Certainly the fury was simulated; but most parliamentarians would have agreed that if there was a place for the closure in parliamentary proceedings there was also a place for time-wasting disruption. As one Speaker of a later generation would remark: 'If the ministerial managers will not give time to debate an issue the Opposition can register its disapproval and non-cooperation by calling for divisions. The "waste of time" is the Opposition's only weapon and usually restores the process of consultation and accommodation, but only after disruption'.

The abominable night of 27–28 June was followed immediately by a motion that promised new surroundings, perhaps even the turning over of a new leaf. Like a breath of fresh country air, the Labor member, W. G. Mahony (Dalley, N), moved on Thursday afternoon that the Governor-General be 'requested to summon the first meeting of the Tenth Parliament at the Federal Capital, Canberra'. After five hours of debate the motion was carried by 37 votes to 12, the minority (Country Party, 5; Nationalists, 4; Labor, 3) including six Victorians and no New South Welshmen. Thus, if the ninth parliament was to run its full course, the Canberra Day about which newspapers were now speculating would be early in 1926.

As part of Bruce's determined effort to close parliament behind him, Page introduced his first Budget earlier than usual, on 26 July. Like other former apostles of the squared ledger, he found as Treasurer that it was harder to live within one's income than he had believed. Hughes took sour pleasure—'as one who must take the greater share of responsibility for the finances of this country during the last seven or eight years'—in declaring that Page's Budget was not as frugal as it pretended to be. It was not a deficit Budget; but, as Hughes pointed out, in order to conceal the possibility of deficits, Page had indulged in the same kind of surplus-hoarding as some of his predecessors:

> The honorable gentleman claims to be doing two things: First, he says he is effecting a big saving on last year's expenditure; and, second, that he is living within his estimated income. As a matter of fact he is doing neither. I should be the last to condemn a man who was not doing either of these things, if he but stated his position plainly. I do not condemn him because he is spending more than his income, but for pretending to be that which he is not . . . The Treasurer posed as a champion of economy, and told us that he would clean out this Augean stable. Now he says, "I have not done anything; I am unable to do it". Previously he said, "What we want is a reduction of our national debt". He has increased it. He said, "What we want is a thorough overhauling of departmental expenditure". Now that he is in office he says, "I see that this cannot be done". Last year he said, "What we want is a plain, honest statement of accounts". Now he says, "I see very clearly that if I were to give such a statement I should show a deficit, and, as I must not show a deficit, candour and honesty must be thrown to one side so that I can give you the Budget that is on the table". That is the way the honorable gentleman sees his duty today.

Shortly before midnight on 16 August the Opposition, at almost full strength, took control of the lower house's business from the poorly represented Government—first by defeating Bruce's motion for adjournment, 27 to 18, and then by moving successfully, 27 to 19, that Mr Speaker leave the Chair. Next morning Charlton asked the Prime Minister whether, in view of the events, he would tender his resignation to the Governor-General. The question was little more than rhetorical, for everyone knew that the Opposition had merely taken advantage of a poorly attended sitting. 'I can assure him', replied Bruce, 'that if, last night, the control of the business was taken out of the hands of the Government, the Government will very soon take it back into its own hands today'. And so it did, beginning another late sitting with the suspension of an Opposition member, D. C. McGrath.

During Question Time McGrath had raised the matter of High Court judges refusing to conduct a certain commission of inquiry, and asked the Prime Minister whether he was 'prepared to allow the Justices of the High Court to go on strike, and refuse to do the work for which the country pays them'. Speaker Watt called upon the Honourable Member for Ballarat to withdraw that reflection upon the judiciary; he refused, and was named for disregarding the authority of the Chair. Bruce moved that he be suspended from the service of the House. A division was called for, but when the Opposition refused to provide tellers for the 'Noes' ('We are on strike like the Judges', shouted Scullin) Mr Speaker declared the 'Ayes' had it. McGrath was then escorted from the chamber by the Serjeant-at-Arms, as he had been once before, in 1913. This time his suspension was not expunged.

On 25 August, after sitting for thirty hours, both chambers of parliament adjourned until dates to be fixed by their presiding officers. Bruce boarded the *Orvieto* for London, accompanied by his wife, the Solicitor-General, Sir Robert Garran, and Lady Garran, and the Comptroller-General of Customs and his wife as well. Earle Page became acting Prime Minister, and parliament remained in recess for the next seven months. For all the flurry of activity between June and August, the lower house held only fifty-two sittings in 1923, and the Senate thirty-five.

Parliament was more orderly after the long recess, but some Oppositionists were still capable of creating what the next morning's papers would call 'disorderly exhibitions'. On the night of 25 June 1924, for example, ex-Gunner Yates (Adelaide) came close to another mutiny while a Supply Bill was being considered in committee. First he spoke about the need for censorship of films such as 'Flaming Youth', a silent picture then being advertised as presenting 'the bold facts, the truth about modern society, with its gay life, its petting parties, its flapper dances, its jazz':

> What is the censorship for [he asked] if it cannot rule out a picture that is disgusting? You find a girl escaping out of her bedroom. She puts on one of her sister's dresses and pulls it down in front and at the back so that she may be as bare as those she saw down below. Then she climbs out of the window, falls into the arms of a drunken young libertine, and after being well squeezed is taken into a ballroom. The mother dies a little later, and when the girl goes to tell her father he is seen sitting at a piano in a drunken condition playing "Yes, we have no bananas." In the face of such pictures, can it be said that this Parliament, in supporting a censor who passes stuff like that for the edification and amusement of the public of Australia, is standing up to its responsibilities?

Prompted perhaps by his distaste for 'Yes, we have no bananas', which he said small boys were whistling everywhere, the Honourable Member for Adelaide launched into another subject, the need for an Australian national anthem. He suggested 'The Song of Australia', and despite repeated calls of order from the Chair proceeded to sing the first verse, beginning 'There is a land where summer skies . . . '. When the Prime Minister moved the adjournment a few minutes later, he read Yates a lecture and appealed to members to refrain from doing anything which would lower the dignity and prestige of parliament in the eyes of the people.

Film censorship was not the only sign of modernity during the life of the ninth parliament. Wireless broadcasting licences were issued for Sydney, Melbourne and Perth; and the Air Force Act carried out the separate organisation of the Royal Australian Air Force. In October 1924 Bruce became the first Australian Prime Minister to travel by air on official business. While on a tour of western Queensland by rail and car, he and his entourage flew in two De Havilland aircraft belonging to Queensland and Northern Territory Aerial Services Ltd (QANTAS) from Longreach to Winton and back, a distance of 214 miles.

In 1924 Parliament produced another crop of measures inspired by the Country Party: the Canned Fruit Bounty Act, Cattle Export Bounty Act, Dried Fruit Advances Act, Meat Industry Encouragement Act, and Hop Pool Agreement Act. It also amended the Commonwealth Bank Act with two main intentions: the eventual development of central banking functions by the Commonwealth Bank, and an immediate change of the bank's top management. Far from becoming the 'people's bank' of Labor rhetoric, the Commonwealth Bank was now to be a 'banker's bank' controlled by a board consisting of the bank's governor, who was also to be its chief executive officer, and seven directors, six of whom had been actively engaged in agriculture, commerce, finance or industry. The policy of such a board would almost certainly be not to compete actively with private banks for general banking business. Labor opposed the measure resolutely, but to no avail against closure and guillotine. 'We expected that it would become a national bank, truly a people's bank', said Charlton. 'To do that it would have to come into competition with the existing banks, but it has not come into keen competition with them ... The Bill is nothing less than an attempt to kill the Bank.'

Reacting to the poor turnout of voters at the previous general election, parliament legislated for compulsory voting. Although this was a logical corollary of compulsory electoral registration, which had been introduced in 1913, compulsory voting was still relatively untried elsewhere in the world. Queensland had pioneered it for the British Empire in 1915, and was still the only Australian electorate with compulsion. The Bruce–Page Government was itself unwilling to take such an initiative for federal elections, but was not averse to a private member doing so. The Commonwealth Electoral Bill was introduced in the upper house by Senator H. J. M. Payne (Nat, T), and sponsored in the House of Representatives by Edward Mann (Nat, Perth). It was only the third private member's bill passed into law since 1901, the others having been Groom's Life Assurance Companies Bill (1904) and an amending Conciliation and Arbitration Bill (1909) initiated by Senator Edward Needham (Lab, W). Future elections would not show that compulsory voting helped one party rather than another. In one observer's opinion, however, it did seem to magnify electoral feeling: that is, it helped popular governments and worked against unpopular ones.

The main industrial issue of 1925, conflict in the maritime industry, mounted in crescendo as the ninth parliament approached its end. For several years past the Seamen's Union had been delaying departure of ships and negotiating settlement of the disputed issues, often quite trivial ones, in such a way as to bypass the normal arbitration machinery. When the union was deregistered by the Arbitration Court, interstate ship owners refused to sign an agreement confirming award conditions, and the union called a strike that was to last for seven weeks.

The Government then proceeded to bang the disputants' heads together, with noticeably more antipathy towards the seamen. In one sitting of parliament that lasted from 3 p.m. on 15 July to 7.25 a.m. on 17 July two draconian measures were guillotined through all stages. The first was an amendment to the Immigration Act establishing a three-man board with power to recommend the deportation of any foreign-born person obstructing the transport of goods, or whose presence the board deemed to be 'injurious to the peace, order and good government of the Commonwealth'. The second measure was a Navigation Bill permitting the Government to counter maritime strikes by introducing into the coastal trade British and foreign vessels on which Australian wages and conditions did not apply.

When the Government attempted to initiate proceedings against two maritime leaders in New South Wales—Tom Walsh, an Irishman and a Communist, and Jacob Johnson, who was born in Sweden—the militant Labor Premier of that State, J. T. Lang, refused to provide police assistance. Bruce responded with a Peace Officers Bill establishing a uniformed Commonwealth police force in place of the wartime plain-clothes service, which had been disbanded four years earlier.

In this bellicose atmosphere parliament was dissolved and writs were issued for a general election on 14 November 1925. The Government parties campaigned on law and order, with posters showing Tom Walsh trampling on the Union Jack. Six days after the election Walsh and Johnson were arrested in accordance with a recommendation by the deportation board. They applied for writs of habeas corpus, and in December the High Court decided in their favour by a majority of three to two.

Two years earlier the same Court had ruled that the Commonwealth had ample power to deport immigrants—in that case, two Irish citizens visiting Australia to advance the cause of Irish republicanism. But were Walsh and Johnson immigrants? Walsh, who was the father of seven children by Adela Pankhurst, had been in Australia for thirty-two years, and Johnson for fifteen years. The Court's majority judgment held that a person ceased to be an immigrant, and so passed beyond reach of the Commonwealth's immigration power, when he had 'merged' with the Australian community. It did not lay down any test of 'merging', but effectively put an end to the Bruce–Page Government's propensity for deporting its industrial troubles.

Although they thwarted the Government in court, Walsh and Johnson, together with the 'Red' scare that was promoted out of their activities, undoubtedly contributed to the Government's success at the election. So too did an electoral pact between the coalition partners. The Nationalist and Country Parties had agreed to exchange preferences, and not to oppose each other in seats that might fall to Labor. Only two seats were deemed safe in that regard: Wannon (V), where the sitting Nationalist defeated a Country Party candidate; and Richmond (N), where the sitting Country Party member, Green without a knee, beat candidates confusingly named Harry Green and J. B. Greene. The Liberal dissidents in Victoria and South Australia, having achieved their 'Out Billy' objective, were no longer a distracting electoral force. The ablest of them, J. G. Latham, contested this election as an endorsed Nationalist.

The Government was returned with a majority of twenty-nine, which was an improvement of twelve on its previous position. Although that improvement in the House of Representatives was all on the Nationalists' side (the Country Party's representation had actually dropped from thirteen to twelve), they were still unable to govern without Country Party support; and so the coalition continued. Labor now held twenty-three seats, and there were two Independents likely to favour the Government—William Watson (Fremantle, W); and P. G. Stewart (Wimmera, V), who had left the Country Party in protest over the election pact. In the Senate the Country Party increased its strength from one to four. The combined Government forces in that chamber numbered twenty-nine, leaving only seven Labor senators.

The tenth parliament did not hold its first meeting in Canberra as planned;

but constructional and other works at the new seat of government, although behind schedule, were nonetheless well advanced. In May 1926 the Prime Minister announced that parliament would meet there for the first time on 9 May 1927, the twenty-sixth anniversary of its first meeting. The twenty-fifth anniversaries of federation and parliament had been allowed to pass almost unremarked by a Commonwealth never anxious to draw the attention of its federal partners to the magnitude it had assumed. The Treasurer announced that the cost of federation, excluding money outlaid by the central Government in place of the State governments, had increased from 1s 3d per head of population in 1901 to 3s 2d per head in 1925—still not much more than the proverbial dog licence, if one allowed for wartime inflation.

The last parliament to sit in Melbourne was opened on 13 January 1926 by a new Governor-General, Lord Stonehaven, another former member of the House of Commons. His speech, delivered as always to the assembled members of both chambers in the Senate, promised further financial discussion between the Commonwealth and States, special assistance to Western Australia and perhaps also Tasmania, and improvement in the position of primary producers through more efficient marketing and more lending by the Rural Credits Branch of the Commonwealth Bank.

Back in their own chamber the members of the House of Representatives elected a new Speaker, Sir Littleton Groom. Watt had made it known during the election that he did not wish to continue in that post, but there was good reason for believing that he left it reluctantly nonetheless. He served four more years in parliament, but was by then a spent force politically.

Just as Watt had made known his intention before the necessity for it became apparent, so Groom had asked to be relieved of the Attorney-Generalship on medical grounds (and on condition that he receive support for the Speakership) before the High Court delivered judgment in the case of Walsh and Johnson. Nevertheless it appeared, even before this judgment, so at variance with Groom's expectation, that Bruce had become dissatisfied with the quality of his Attorney-General's advice. There would be grounds later for thinking that the Honourable Member for Darling Downs resented his sudden transformation into wig and gown.

The new Attorney-General was J. G. Latham—a cold, hard-minded lawyer described by one Melbourne newspaper as 'the disembodied brain'. For the rest of his Prime Ministership Bruce relied heavily upon Latham in pursuit of his increasingly hazardous preoccupation with industrial relations. Early in the parliament the Government succeeded in amending the Crimes Act to provide wider powers of response to industrial extremism. The Conciliation and Arbitration Acts already prohibited strikes and lock-outs by organisations registered under those Acts, but the Crimes Act of 1926 applied in similar fashion whether workers were organised unions or not. In a provision aimed especially at the Australian Communist Party, which by then had been in existence for six years, the Act also declared revolutionary and seditious associations to be unlawful.

Like others before it, the Bruce–Page Government also tried to find some constitutional path through the 'Serbonian bog' (as Mr Justice Higgins called it) of divided Commonwealth and State industrial powers. In September

1926 two proposals for extending the Commonwealth's industrial power were submitted to referendum. The first proposal was to extend the Commonwealth's powers with respect to corporations, trusts and combinations, and to extend its conciliation and arbitration power beyond Section 51's limited application to *interstate* disputes. The second was to add the power of 'Protecting the interests of the public in case of actual or probable interruption of any essential service'. Both proposals met industrial and State rights opposition, and were defeated.

The Federal Aid Roads Act organised on a ten-year basis the Commonwealth's funding of road construction by the States, and the Science and Industry Research Act placed the existing government research institution under the control of a Council for Scientific and Industrial Research (C.S.I.R.). But the principal legislative achievement of this parliament was the States Grants Act, a crucial element in the reorganisation of financial relations between the central and State governments. At a Premiers' Conference in May 1926, Page proposed that the Commonwealth abolish its per capita payments to the States, and in return abandon the fields of land, estate and entertainment tax, and reduce the rates of federal income tax. The Premiers rejected this offer, for they were not satisfied that moving into fields vacated by the Commonwealth would compensate them fully for the loss of per capita assistance.

The States Grants Bill, introduced in the following month, was nothing less than an ultimatum from the Commonwealth to its federal partners. It proposed an end to the per capita system forthwith, thus putting pressure on the States to accept Page's terms. In the face of strong protests from Labor and coalition dissentients that the Commonwealth was adopting a stand-and-deliver attitude toward the States, the Government held the Bill over until March 1927. By then Bruce was more conciliatory, but the Bill encountered stiff opposition nevertheless. Acknowledging that 'a deplorable spirit of antagonism' had come about, Bruce proposed that the per capita payments should continue throughout 1927–28, and that in the meantime the federal partners should meet again to consider a scheme for associating abolition of the per capita payments with the Commonwealth's taking over of responsibility for State debts.

'I recognise', said Bruce in his second reading speech on 2 March,

> that today there is a considerable body of opinion in this country to the effect that the present Government desires to aggrandize the Commonwealth at the expense of the States, that we wish to bring the States into some form of financial tutelage, and desire to invade realms that legitimately and properly belong to them. I give my assurance to the House and to the people of Australia that Ministers have no such desire.

In spite of the concessions, Bruce's assurance was not taken at face value by everyone. Scullin, who later in the year would replace Anstey as Deputy Leader of the parliamentary Labor Party, likened the Government's approach to 'chopping a man's head off and proposing then to discuss with him the state of his liver'. Six Nationalists, including Hughes and Watt, voted with the Opposition, and the Bill was carried in the House of Representatives by only nine votes. The Senate passed it by a majority of eight, but not without recrimination from a handful of senators who reminded their colleagues of the chamber's originally-intended role as a bulwark for State rights. Senator Edward Needham (Lab, W) recalled the words of Sir John Quick in 1910: 'I think that the leaders of parties in the Federal Parliament should set a good example, and should not sanction anything like a war against the States, because the State Parliaments, as well as the Federal Parliament, are representatives of the Commonwealth'.

> I desire to emphasise the words "a war against the States" [said Senator Needham]. Despite the assurances of the Prime Minister and the Leader of the Government in this chamber, this bill is a war against the States . . .
> Senator OGDEN (Lab, T).—I am afraid the Government has the numbers.
> Senator NEEDHAM.—I echo Senator Ogden's fear. If honorable senators were true to their principles, the bill would be defeated; but the party whip has been cracked and—
> Senator PEARCE.—Has it not been cracked in the Labour Party room?
> Senator NEEDHAM.—No; the Opposition is not in charge of this bill. I repeat that, if it were a question of principle and not of party, the bill would be defeated. It is unfortunate that honorable senators should be more concerned about party than about principle.

Senator Sir Henry Barwell (Nat), a former Premier of South Australia, said that the Senate was being asked to sign a blank cheque. 'It will be only the beginning of the end of federation, as we know it, if the Senate agrees to this bill', he said. 'It will mean the financial strangulation of the States . . . The Senate has to face the position. There is no doubt that the people of Australia are looking to the Senate—the chamber specially constituted to safeguard the interests of the States—to see that their rights are not in any way infringed.' If the people really were watching, they were to be disappointed. Without resort to the Standing Order for limitation of debate (the 'guillotine'), which had been adopted by the Senate in 1912, the Bill was returned to the lower house without amendment. Of the eleven Senators who voted unavailingly against it at the second and third reading stages, five were Labor and six Nationalists; three were from South Australia, three from Western Australia, two from New South Wales, two from Victoria and one from Tasmania.

Two days after the passage of this Bill, on 24 March 1927, parliament met for the last time in the building which it had occupied five times longer than originally envisaged. The day was cool and cloudy, but a distinct improvement on that day in 1901 when an Antarctic disturbance named Moloch had whistled between the pillars of this graceful old building on Melbourne's Eastern Hill. In the House of Representatives the Prime Minister moved the incorporation into Hansard of a report of proceedings at the new Parliament House in Canberra five months previously, when visitors from the United Kingdom Branch of the Empire Parliamentary Association had presented a gift from members of the House of Lords and House of Commons. The gift was a Speaker's Chair, an intricately carved replica of that in the House of

Commons, canopied with pinnacles, pendants and the British coat of arms, made partly of oak taken from the roof of Westminster Hall and Nelson's flagship at Trafalgar, H.M.S. *Victory*.

The House also agreed to Bruce's motion for a gift of £50 000 to the Victorian parliament in addition to £30 000 which the Commonwealth had recently spent on repairs and renovations before returning the building to its owners. It was expected, on the Commonwealth's part, that the Victorians would use the gift to erect a memorial of some kind in connection with the Commonwealth parliament's long occupation of their building. To the disapproval of some federal members, however, the Victorians eventually spent this sum, not on marble or bronze, but on a well appointed refreshment room in the building to which they had returned. After putting up with inferior accommodation at the Exhibition Building for more than a quarter of a century, they deserved it.

The building in Spring Street had been a comfortable home, though still cold in winter and poorly ventilated, and the prevailing mood on 24 March was nostalgic. Only three of those who had been sworn in on the first day were still in parliament: Senator George Pearce, W. M. Hughes and David Watkins (Lab, Newcastle). Pearce was absent, but Hughes and Watkins each spoke at the last sitting. Hughes, although the best qualified to pronounce valediction, confined himself to speaking in support of an Opposition motion that the House adjourn to discuss a definite matter of urgent public importance—'The case of Robert Denholm, formerly employed in Parliament House'. It was a tragic case. Denholm, aged thirty-four, had been a lift driver and waiter at Parliament House since before the war. Now he was unemployable because of a spinal condition known as syringomyelia. According to some doctors, the condition had developed as a result of meningeal irritation caused by an influenza inoculation which Denholm had been obliged to undergo, in the course of his employment as a public servant, during the influenza epidemic of 1919.

As a parliamentary employee, he was not covered by workers' compensation. He received the invalid pension, such as it was then, and the Government had also made him an *ex gratia* payment of £50. The question now was whether he should be given a compassionate allowance. Hughes took up his cause either out of human sympathy or because he thought he had found a chink in the Government's armour. 'If I had to deal with this case', he said,

> I would put this man in the position of being sure at least of the ordinary comforts of life. It is true that he was only a humble attendant and not a member of the Parliament; but, nevertheless, we met him every day and he was one of our number . . . He was stricken down while doing his duty. Surely we are not obliged in such circumstances to examine with microscopic exactness into the precise causes of his trouble. Let us treat the case as human beings, and give the man something. We have been in occupation of these buildings for 26 years; let us on the eve of our departure do at least one just and generous act.

Dr Page, who had carriage of the matter for the Government, reminded members that Denholm was receiving the invalid pension, and cast doubt upon the connection between his spinal condition and the earlier meningitis. 'I suggest', he said, 'that the Commonwealth cannot make itself responsible for the permanent medical treatment of any of its employees, the cause of whose illness has not been definitely traced to employment in the Commonwealth Service'. The question was resolved in the negative, and was never raised in parliament again.

The other survivor from May 1901, David Watkins, contributed briefly to the valedictory remarks after other business was concluded. Perhaps predictably, he said that members of the first parliament were political giants, and that political fights then had been keener than in the present parliament. Dr Maloney, whose Van Dyke beard was greying, recalled how he had held the dying Speaker Holder in his arms, and had stood in sorrow beside the lifeless form of Ernest Roberts after his collapse at the foot of Queen Victoria's statue.

As the dinner hour approached it fell to Speaker Groom, whose father had delivered the first speech in the House of Representatives, to conclude that chamber's proceedings in Melbourne. He thanked the Press Gallery for its 'spirit of co-operation and friendship', and the Hansard staff for making 'every effort on our behalf to keep, in Spenser's phrase, the "well of English undefyled"'. The adjournment was agreed to, and at 6.04 p.m. Mr Speaker said: 'The House stands adjourned at its rising to Canberra, and will meet at such time on Monday, the 9th of May next, as shall be fixed by me, and notified to each member by telegram or letter'. Members then joined hands and sang 'Auld Lang Syne'.

Canberra

The site to which parliament stood adjourned was certainly a bush capital, with all the inconvenience which that entailed; but it was by no means the howling wilderness pictured by some of its detractors. More than a century had passed since Europeans first reached the Limestone or Canberra Plains, and in that time the land formerly occupied by people called Ngarrugu and Ngunawal had been transformed into rural countryside by three generations of sheep and wheat farmers.

The first explorers, a party of three led by Dr Charles Throsby, a pioneer in the Moss Vale district, rode past Lake Bathurst and Lake George in March 1821. 'I continued to follow the [Queanbeyan and Molonglo] rivers down', wrote Throsby, 'which had now become very considerable and rapid, extensive plains and good grazing country on each side, with a considerable portion of rich meadow land on the banks of the rivers, the water still going to the westward'. He followed the Molonglo across almost treeless grassland, flanked by hillsides covered with bluegum, stringy bark and outcrops of limestone, to within a mile or two of its junction with a new river, the Murrumbidgee. Although Throsby did not see the junction, he reached the Murrumbidgee itself a few miles upstream, and was credited with its discovery. In this early stage of its roundabout journey to the River Murray and the Southern Ocean, the Murrumbidgee flows north beside the wall of the Brindabella Range. The Limestone Plains, affording a clear view of this range, were inhabited by some four hundred Aborigines, and by abundant wild life, the most evident species being the grey kangaroo, wallaby, emu and brolga.

In the path of the explorers came stockmen with flocks of sheep. The earliest pioneers, employed by Joshua Moore, who was then clerk to the Judge Advocate in Sydney, took up land on the north-western side of the Molonglo in 1823. Moore, who never lived there himself, already occupied land near Goulburn, and the Limestone Plains venture was at first merely an out-station of that property, run by an overseer and some convict stockmen.

The Aborigines in whose vicinity they settled were called, in various forms of European spelling, Canberry, Kamberra, Kembery or Nganbra. This name was also applied to land at the foot of one of the tallest mountains on the northern side of the valley (later named Black Mountain), bounded on the west by a creek entering the Molonglo River from the north (known at first as Canberry Creek and later Sullivan's Creek) and extending eastward on the northern side of the river.

When Moore applied to buy 1000 acres of this land in 1826, he described it as 'situate at Canberry, on the E. bank [but still north side] of the river which waters Limestone Plains, above its junction with the Murrumbeeja, adjoining the grant of Mr Robert Campbell, Snr'. Moore's property was known as 'Canberry'. A later owner renamed it 'Acton', after his family's village of origin in England; but the name 'Canberry', converted to the permanent form of 'Canberra' by an entry in the diocesan register in 1856, survived as the name of the little community, scarcely a village, of which 'Acton' was a large part.

The adjoining property referred to by Moore had been granted in 1825 to Robert Campbell, an enterprising Sydney merchant who pioneered trade between New South Wales and India, as compensation for the loss of one of his ships while under charter to the Government. Campbell's land was taken up on his behalf, after Moore's, by Robert Ainslie, a former trooper of the Scots Greys, who was prone to violent behaviour, supposedly because of a head wound received at the battle of Waterloo, but was otherwise a reliable stockman. Ainslie brought 700 sheep from Bathurst to Campbell's grant, upstream from 'Canberry' on the same side of the river. Campbell's property was at first called 'Limestone'; then 'Pialligo', the name of another local Aboriginal group; and finally 'Duntroon', after a castle in Argyll with Campbell connections.

In 1834 the Polish botanist, Dr John Lhotsky, visited 'Limestone' and the 'Kembery Plains' on his way south to the Australian Alps. Of the Kembery (Canberry) and Pialligo people he wrote with chilling brevity, 'They are now no more'. As for the country of which they had been dispossessed, he made this prophecy:

> Limestone is also one of the most important spots as far as the political economy of the colony is concerned. The Plains themselves must contain at least 20,000 acres of good, compact, arable land, besides which they form a point where three principal roads, the great road from Sydney, that to Yass Plains, and that to Menero [Monaro] Downs—will eventually converge. At Limestone, therefore, at no distant period, a fine town will exist . . .

The plains and adjacent pastures were soon parcelled out, usually at five shillings per acre, which Lhotsky regarded as 'far too much for primary grants to Emigrants or well behaved freed men, but far too little for those already possessing large property, who in that way might now purchase entire Dukedoms'. The Campbells extended their holdings south of the river, the Murray family settled at 'Yarralumla', and the interstices between such dukedoms were taken up by smaller farmers. A steepled Anglican church of sandstone and granite—St John the Baptist, standing between Canberra and Duntroon—was consecrated in 1845. That year a 33-year-old woman named Sarah Webb died giving birth to her tenth child at Uriarra, in the foothills of the Brindabella Range. Her tombstone at St John's was inscribed with a text from Hebrews that would later seem no less remarkable than Lhotsky's prophecy: 'For here we have no continuing city, but we seek one to come'.

The choice of this site for a federal capital territory was formalised, as has been recounted in an earlier chapter, by the Seat of Government Acceptance Act in 1909. What the Commonwealth accepted from the State of New South Wales was an area of not less than 900 square miles in the district of Yass–Canberra. Its boundaries were drawn, after an arduous topographical survey by Charles Scrivener who was later appointed Director of Commonwealth Lands and Surveys.

The Federal Capital Territory, as it was first known, became vested in the Commonwealth on 1 January 1911. It consisted of 910 square miles, measuring 57 miles from north to south, and 32 miles at the widest. Four years later New South Wales also transferred a separate area of 28 square miles, at Jervis Bay on the south coast. The Jervis Bay territory was intended as a port for the Commonwealth, but was later used only as a naval base and training college. The Federal Capital Territory, about 80 miles inland, did not include the nearby towns of Queanbeyan and Yass. It contained a population of 1714 people, among whom there was not a single full-blood Aborigine. The last such inhabitant, 'Queen Nelly', died at Queanbeyan during the 1860s.

Scrivener's detailed map, naming paddocks as well as topographical features, conveyed some feeling of the pastures which then supported almost a quarter of a million sheep and several thousand cattle: 'Crow and Magpie Paddock', 'Clump of Trees Paddock', 'Woolshed Paddock', 'Thistle Paddock' and 'Red Hill Paddock'. West and south of the plains respectively were the Brindabellas, rising more than 6000 feet above sea-level, and a sub-alpine region which the Aborigines had called Namadji. Both were flecked with snow in winter-time, shrouded by haze or bushfire smoke in the scorching heat of mid-summer, and perennially haunted by the music of magpies and currawongs.

Ordinances proclaimed by the Governor-General under the Seat of Government Acceptance Act and Seat of Government (Administration) Act laid down certain rules for provisional government. The Territory would be subject to the same laws as New South Wales, but almost all revenue received within its boundaries would be retained by the Commonwealth, and residents would not be entitled to vote at State or federal elections. Privately owned land would be acquired for Commonwealth purposes, and no licences would be issued for the sale of alcohol. There had been much lobby-ing by temperance groups, and the first Minister for Home Affairs with responsibility for the Territory, King O'Malley, was himself an abstainer. On one occasion he said that having a bar in parliament was like having a tiger snake in your bedroom.

The first portions of the Territory put to permanent Commonwealth use were Duntroon and Mt Stromlo. On 27 June 1911 Duntroon homestead and environs assumed a new role as the Royal Military College of Australia, just in time to have seven of its first graduates killed at Gallipoli four years later. Mt Stromlo, a narrow ridge rising high above the surrounding country south-west of the river, became a Commonwealth observatory, dedicated initially to solar observation. Its first telescope came into operation in 1911.

In April 1911 the Commonwealth Government announced a world-wide design competition for the urban site surveyed by Scrivener, a site overlap-ping the land taken up by Moore and Campbell almost a century before. Topographical models were sent overseas where they could be viewed by competitors, and information sent directly to competitors included two cycloramic paintings, one done from Mt Vernon (later named City Hill) on the northern side of the river, and the other from Camp Hill on the southern side.

There were 137 entries, and they were submitted to three judges anony-mously. Two judges—John Kirkpatrick, an architect; and James Smith, an engineer—wanted to award the first prize (£1750) to an American architect, Walter Burley Griffin; second prize (£750) to Eliel Saarinen of Finland; and third prize (£500) to Professor D. Alfred Agache of France. But the chairman, a surveyor named John Coane, did not favour any of these. His first choice was an entry by three Australian architects—W. S. Griffiths, R. C. Coulter and C. H. Caswell. On 23 May 1912 the Minister for Home Affairs, acting as adjudicator, supported the majority decision.

This was the best decision King O'Malley ever made, for the design by Griffin, a 36-year-old former associate of the renowned Frank Lloyd Wright, was head and shoulders above the rest. His strongly symmetrical design, incorporating radial and concentric street patterns, was influenced to some extent, but not to the exclusion of originality, by design ideas which he had absorbed at the Chicago Fair, the 1801 plan for Washington, and the 'City Beautiful' movement in America. The design he submitted for Australia's capital city placed the functions of parliament, government, education, busi-ness and recreation along two axes: a north–south land axis, containing gov-ernment buildings, running from Mt Ainslie (midway between Duntroon and Moore's original property) to an eminence south of the river which Scrivener named Kurrajong Hill and Griffin renamed Capital Hill; and a west–east water axis, running from Black Mountain along a string of lakes to be formed by damming the Molonglo. There was to be a recreational casino near Mt Ainslie; a 'Capitol', or 'people's building' used for public gatherings and national archives, on Capital Hill; a parliament house and executive buildings below Capital Hill, where in Griffin's view they would be rightly subordinate to the somehow more democratic Capitol; and a university below Black Mountain.

The design was well received professionally, but there was some political criticism of it on grounds of extravagance. In response to that, O'Malley referred the winning designs to an interdepartmental board under the chairmanship of Colonel David Miller, head of the Department of Home Affairs and resident administrator of the Federal Capital Territory. Seeing little merit in Griffin's ideas, the board recommended instead a pastiche of its own inexpert concoction. One member of parliament, Dr Maloney, referred to this as 'the efforts of a few good little Australian artists to repaint pictures of Tintoretto or Raphael'. Although the departmental plan was also characterised by Britain's leading town planner as a 'third-rate Luna Park', the Government gave Miller permission to proceed with it.

On 20 February 1913 O'Malley drove a symbolic first peg into the north–south survey line. Three weeks later, on 12 March, another ceremony was held on Camp Hill, a northern spur of Capital Hill, to name the proposed city and mark its commencement. The name was a closely kept secret until the Governor-General's wife, Lady Denman, announced it on Camp Hill. Parliament had no opportunity to determine the matter, as it had done in the case of the federal site, and in view of certain bizarre suggestions then being canvassed there was concern in both chambers. Austin Chapman, who had campaigned unsuccessfully for the site of Dalgety, was again unsuccessful in trying to have the choice of name debated in the last few days of the fourth parliament:

> Mr CHAPMAN.—Then what name is to be given to the Capital? I understand that the Minister proposes to call it Shakespeare or Captain Cook. If he does, Parliament and the people will censure him.
>
> Mr CHANTER.—Parliament will have something to say about the naming of the Capital.
>
> Mr CHAPMAN.—The Minister will name it during the next recess.
>
> Mr WISE.—What does it matter?
>
> Mr PARKER MOLONEY.—Would the honorable member suggest a name?
>
> Mr MAHON.—Radiance would be a good name.
>
> Mr CHAPMAN.—I think we should call it "Austral", to signify that it is the Capital of Australia. The Minister's proposed name is an absurd one.
>
> Mr O'MALLEY.—Would you like Federalia?

Eight days later, on 20 December 1912, Senator T. D. Chataway (F, Q) asked Senator Pearce, representing the Minister for Home Affairs, when the Government would give parliament an opportunity to discuss the proposed name of the capital. 'I am informed by my colleague that the matter is still under consideration', replied Pearce, 'but he hopes to be able to make an announcement very shortly as to the procedure he proposes shall be adopted'. That was in fact the last sitting of parliament for the next seven months, and, as O'Malley well knew, the name would have to be decided before the commencement ceremony in three months' time. The decision was taken by Cabinet, which had before it a list of suggestions that was in large part either ridiculous or pretentious. The most popular source of inspiration was the imperial connection: New London, Britalia, Georgetown,

Kingstown, Royalton and Empire City, to name only a few. There were also nationalist suggestions (Homestead, Austral-Eden, Waratah), personal ones (Wentworth, Dampier, Bartonsburgh), abstract ones (Concordia, Democratia, Utopia) and White Australian ones (Alba, Albania and Aryan City).

Common sense prevailed, and when Lady Denman opened a gold cigarette case and read the decision aloud, Cabinet was found to have chosen the name by which this site, or part of it, had probably been known for untold generations. 'I name the capital of Australia, Canberra', she said, and a 21-gun artillery salute echoed over the plains and hills of the Federal Territory. The Prime Minister later explained that the name was spelt with two r's, and should be pronounced, as Lady Denman had pronounced it, with accent on the first syllable (*Can'*bra). Some were led to speculate wistfully that perhaps the word was a corruption of 'Canburgh', and so had some connection with respectable Celtic-Saxon stock, like 'Edinburgh' or 'Farnborough'. But the more usual reaction was a willing acceptance of this indigenous word, which might well have been older than 'Edinburgh', and relief that no generally unpopular selection had been made. The only name ever suggested in its place afterwards was inspired by wartime patriotism. In May 1916 Senator P. J. Lynch (Lab, W) moved that in the opinion of the Senate the capital should be re-christened 'Anzac'. Debate was adjourned, and six months later the motion was discharged.

At the ceremony on Camp Hill Lord Denman, Fisher and O'Malley each used golden trowels to lay three foundation stones for a proposed Commencement Column. This uninspired monument was meant to consist of a central monolith representing the Commonwealth, buttressed at the base by six granite blocks symbolic of the States. Fortunately it was never built, and neither was the departmentally designed city which Lord Denman thought he was inaugurating with his golden trowel.

Walter Burley Griffin, understandably enraged by the change of design, offered to come to Australia. The Cook Government, which had taken office only three months after the ceremony on Camp Hill, was already disturbed by criticism of the departmental plan from British and Australian architects. Cook suspended that plan, and invited Griffin to visit Canberra. He arrived in August 1913, and was immediately captivated by the site which until then he had known only from the topographical model, cycloramic paintings and contour maps. 'The morning and evening lights at Canberra are wonderful', said Griffin.

> The shadows of the clouds and the mists as they cross the mountains are very beautiful indeed. It is a grand site for a city . . . Australians do not paint their country as they should. They give it a sombre appearance both in literature and in art, but what I have seen of it is anything but sombre . . . The gum tree instead of being one continual monotony has strongly appealed to me. It is a poet's tree, and ought to have a more dignified name. Gum tree! It does not fit it at all.

Griffin's enthusiasm and proficiency won the day. The new Minister for Home Affairs, W. H. Kelly, abolished the interdepartmental board, and in its place appointed Griffin as Federal Capital Director of Design and Construction for three years. In that capacity the American proceeded to implement his design as quickly as meagre funds allowed, but the going was not easy. From selection of the federal site to the opening of Parliament House in Canberra, a period of nineteen years, eight ministries held office and no fewer than twelve ministers had responsibility for Home Affairs. This was conducive to changes in direction, the forming of grudges and the settling of old scores. Colonel Miller and his departmental allies did not forgive Griffin for their humbling in 1913. They found a friend in W. O. Archibald, Minister for Home Affairs in Fisher's third Government, and it was not until O'Malley regained this portfolio in 1915 that Griffin was able to hold his own against their deliberate obstruction.

This time, to his credit, O'Malley supported Griffin inside parliament and out. In 1916 Cabinet renewed Griffin's appointment for another three years and appointed a Royal Commissioner to inquire into his relations with the Departments of Home Affairs and Works. The Royal Commissioner, Wilfred Blacket, reported that there was 'a combination, including Archibald and certain officers, hostile to Griffin and to his design for the Capital City'.

One of Griffin's early steps, in 1914, had been to arrange another international design competition, for a Parliament House. At first there was to have been one judge, in London; then there were to be five—one architect each from Australia, Britain, France, the United States and Germany, until the outbreak of war made it necessary to replace the German with a Finn, Eliel Saarinen. Entries were due in January 1917, but three months before that date the current Minister for Home Affairs informed parliament that because of the war the competition had been postponed indefinitely. It was never revived, and some competitors later received compensation for their wasted effort.

Griffin persevered with his work, in an atmosphere that was still hostile, until his second term of engagement expired in 1919. During that time he directed the layout of the city's basic services, completed his plan, and began construction of some of the main avenues and the planting of forest reserves and parks. But his departmental enemies defeated him in the end. In 1920 Cabinet decided that Griffin lacked some of the qualities (notably willingness to compromise) which it considered would be needed if the project was to be carried forward economically as well as efficiently. The Prime Minister, Hughes, informed Griffin that his appointment would not be renewed, and that from January 1921 design and construction authority would be vested in a Federal Capital Advisory Committee under the chairmanship of the Sydney architect Sir John Sulman.

Griffin declined to serve on this committee, on grounds that it would have no executive power, and that consequently the design and construction of Canberra would in fact be controlled by the Works Department, which the Blacket Commission had found to be 'consistently hostile to myself, my plan and my procedure'. With those bitter words, Griffin returned to private practice. His fears for the future of Canberra were only partly justified. Certainly his design would be modified considerably during the years to come; but enough of it would remain intact for Walter Burley Griffin to be rightly acclaimed as the creator of Canberra.

Although parliament had had nothing to do with the choice of design or the naming of Canberra, it did debate fully the timing of its move to the new capital and, in general terms, what kind of building should be erected for it there. In June and July 1923 the House of Representatives debated and agreed to W. G. Mahony's motion that the Governor-General be requested to summon the first meeting of the tenth parliament at Canberra. That would require construction of a new Parliament House in less than three years. Three years earlier the Prince of Wales had laid yet another foundation stone, on Capital Hill; but this had been for the chimerical Capitol, not Parliament House. Speakers in the debate on Mahony's motion were divided as to whether Parliament House ought to be a provisional building (something more than temporary and less than permanent, estimated to cost £220 000, and intended to last about fifty years) or the nucleus of a permanent and monumental building, costing £350 000 for the nucleus alone. Those who had visited Canberra, like John Latham, stressed the rigours of travel and the inadvisability of moving there prematurely:

> I returned yesterday from a visit to Canberra. I considered it right to see the place for myself, rather than accept my information about it at second hand. I am prepared to say at the outset that, so far as I am able to judge, Canberra is a beautiful site for a beautiful city. [But] transportation to Canberra, at present, is one of the most awful things that an Australian citizen could be asked to endure in the course of a normal life. In July there is really no pleasure, even though one sees beautiful snow-covered mountains on the horizon, in getting up at 5 o'clock in the morning at Yass and travelling 46 miles by motor car, over indifferent roads for a considerable distance, to arrive at Canberra for breakfast. To return to Melbourne you leave Canberra at night, and drive 11 miles to Queanbeyan, over only middling roads. You then travel from Queanbeyan to Goulburn. The night on which I did the journey was cold and wet. At Goulburn you enter a train already occupied by persons who are asleep, and who do not wish to be disturbed. You arrive at Melbourne at 2 or 3 o'clock the next afternoon. It is a miserable and wretched journey both ways.

What came as a rude shock to the barrister from Kooyong was nothing particularly new to members representing such distant electorates as Maranoa, Kalgoorlie or Barrier. For Melburnians, Canberra was certainly less accessible than Spring Street; but for many other members the journey was little harder than usual, and sometimes easier. Since 1914 there had been a railway freight service between Queanbeyan and the part of Canberra known as Kingston, and in October 1923 this line was opened for passenger traffic as well. The Government also considered building a railway line from Canberra to Yass. This never materialised, however, and train travellers from Canberra to Melbourne first had to undertake a preliminary journey either by rail to Queanbeyan and Goulburn, or motor vehicle to Yass.

Latham and others spoke of the danger that temporary buildings would become permanent. But the Federal Capital Advisory Committee had recommended construction of a provisional Parliament House on the slope of Camp Hill, and on 26 July 1923 the Minister for Works and Railways, P. G.

Stewart (C, Wimmera, V), moved that this be proceeded with. The Government wanted to avoid the charges of extravagance that a monumental building would probably provoke, and a provisional building seemed to offer more chance of keeping to the tight construction schedule.

Stewart's motion was agreed to in the House of Representatives, but four weeks later the Senate expressed objection to a provisional building. Senator J. F. Guthrie (Nat, V) moved as an amendment to a Loan Bill 'that the item "Works, Services and Acquisition of Land in Federal Capital Territory, £165,000" be reduced by £1' as an instruction to the Government not to proceed with the building of a provisional Parliament House. Some senators cited the cost of Canada's new Parliament House ($10 million, and still rising) as dire warning of what the construction of a permanent building might involve. The majority, however, agreed with Senator Guthrie's view that money the Government was so anxious to spend on a provisional building would be better spent on the nucleus of a permanent one, and if the project took longer then so be it.

The amendment was agreed to, 19–13, the 'Ayes' consisting of eleven Labor senators and nine Nationalists. This had no effect on the lower house. Next morning Bruce repeated the arguments of time and economy, and moved successfully that the Senate's amendment be disagreed to. From then on, construction of the city and its provisional Parliament House moved ahead with remarkable speed, though not quite fast enough to keep the appointment with the tenth parliament.

There was no time, or inclination on the government's part, for another competition. Probably this was just as well, for the Parliament House then designed by the Chief Commonwealth architect, John Smith Murdoch, suited its purpose admirably. Admittedly it was a far cry from the grand edifice that had been designed for Spring Street by another Scottish-born architect seventy years ago. Murdoch strove for a building of simple, utilitarian lines—'decorous', as he wrote, 'and embellished internally with restraint'. Yet this white stuccoed brick building, soon to become a household image on commemorative postage stamps and florins, was by no means lacking in dignity.

Murdoch's design derived mainly from the late Classical Revival, a style which had been applied to government buildings in Washington by American architects who were influenced by the Ecole des Beaux Arts in France. It was characterised by careful composition, strict symmetry and absence of excessive ornament. Not for Canberra the pillars, balustrades, cornices, cherubs and dolphins of the two chambers in Melbourne!

The new building's wide two-storey range of balconied suites and offices, slightly projecting bays with arched bronze windows, and steps leading to a portico at its centre, was decorated only with eight small roundels and, at roof level, two bas-relief coats of arms—lion and unicorn on the left, kangaroo and emu on the right. Behind this façade, which faced north towards the willow-fringed Molonglo River, and shone with the intensity of a white-trunked scribbly gum, could be seen the balancing roofs of two legislative chambers: the House of Representatives on the eastern, or lion and unicorn side; and the Senate on the western, or kangaroo and emu side. Between the chambers was a spacious colonnaded hall, King's Hall rather than Queen's Hall.

From the turning of the first sod below Camp Hill on 28 August 1923 Parliament House took just over three years to complete. Building materials were brought to the site on two temporary railway lines, one from the station at Kingston and the other from a brickworks at Yarralumla. A third temporary line was built from the site across the river to Civic Centre, where offices and shops were being built near City Hill.

During this period, the Government encouraged members of parliament to see for themselves what Canberra would be like. They were accommodated at the old Yarralumla homestead, built by the Murray family, later owned by the Campbells, and lately acquired by the Commonwealth as the Governor-General's future residence. The object of the visits was to overcome any lingering misgiving about the idea of a 'bush capital'. Dusty roads and bush flies may sometimes have had the opposite effect, but according to Earle Page at least one antagonist, J. H. Prowse (C, Swan, W), was won over to Canberra when he caught three large trout.

On 30 January 1924 Cabinet held its first Canberra meeting in the writing room at Yarralumla, with Page presiding in the Prime Minister's absence overseas. All other ministers were present, and the agenda included conditions of land sale in the Territory. Federal land would be disposed of at public auction, it was decided, and private land would be held on 99-year leases rather than freehold title.

Later that year the Federal Capital Advisory Committee was replaced by a more powerful Federal Capital Commission, under the Chief Commissionership of J. H. (later Sir John) Butters, an engineer. Parliament also made provision for Griffin's city plan to be published in the *Commonwealth Gazette*, the effect of which was to protect it from any variation without the proposed change being tabled in both houses of parliament and open to a motion of disallowance. The plan as gazetted in November 1925 consisted mainly of streets and avenues, making no provision for the lakes and monumental buildings envisaged by Griffin. Those would be determined by a later generation. The first stage of Canberra's development consisted of parliament, attended by such departmental officers as would be required to work closely with their ministers, and of such auxiliary works as power, water, roads and housing.

The Prime Minister announced in May 1926 that the seat of government would be moved to Canberra in twelve months' time. All parliamentary staff, numbering eighty-four, would be transferred to the new Parliament House; the Prime Minister's Department would send its central administrative staff, numbering fifty-four; the office of the Governor-General's official secretary, seven; the central administrative staff of the Attorney-General's Department, thirty-three; Treasury, sixty; Home and Territories, fifty; Works and Railways, ninety-six; and Trade and Customs, eighty-five. Altogether 539 public servants would move in the first wave, and for the time being the rest of the public service would stay where it was, mainly in Melbourne.

'Members of the Public Service have naturally felt some apprehension about the move to Canberra', said Bruce in his statement to parliament, 'but I am confident that, when they have had an opportunity of seeing the future Capital city, and have learned how much assistance will be given to them in establishing homes there, they will realise that they will be able to live there happily and contentedly'. Many were not reassured, and one public service trade union leader referred to the impending move as a sword of Damocles.

Those who arrived before the opening of Parliament House found a scattered community which, although provided with essential services, lacked many metropolitan advantages. At the end of 1926 Canberra had 5915 residents (6913 in the capital territory as a whole), 1 500 000 planted trees, and thirty miles of kerbed and guttered road, much of it still unsealed. Water came from the Cotter River dam, thirteen miles away, and electricity from a generating plant at Kingston. There was an automatic telephone service; a weekly newspaper (the *Canberra Times*, founded in 1926 and soon to become a morning daily); and by 1927 the city and suburbs, such as they were, were sewered. The Molonglo was crossed by three bridges, the largest of which was in Commonwealth Avenue, the main north–south thoroughfare running from Civic Centre to the base of Capital Hill.

Accommodation was available at hotels which, because of prohibition, were really hostels. These were the Hotels Canberra (£5 per week for single room), Kurrajong and Acton (£3 15s), and Wellington (£3 5s). The Canberra and Kurrajong—designed by the Commonwealth Architect's office in the horizontal Prairie style of Frank Lloyd Wright, popularised in Australia by Burley Griffin—were early examples of a federal architectural tradition.

Some houses had been built, but as yet these were only in two areas: Ainslie, north of the river, and Blandfordia, on the southern side. The latter soon changed its unwieldy name (the botanical term for Christmas Bells) to Forrest and Deakin. Between these rudimentary suburbs were paddocks with sheep and cattle in them. There were hire cars, but no taxis and not enough buses. Often the best means of getting around was on foot or bicycle. One young man who came to work at the Commonwealth Observatory in 1926, Clabon W. Allen, found that he could walk the seven miles from Mt Stromlo to the Hotel Canberra in an hour and 45 minutes. On another walk into the bush beyond the Cotter River he came face to face with a dingo. He used to swim in the Molonglo, attend gymnastic classes and concerts by the Stromberra Quintet, listen in to Melbourne wireless stations, go to dances, and play the mouth organ. Such were the innocent pastimes of early federal Canberra.

By May 1927 Commonwealth expenditure on the capital amounted to £7 million, of which £644 600 (£424 600 more than originally estimated) had been spent on building Parliament House, and £250 000 on furnishing it. Cabinet held its first meeting in the new house on 11 October 1926, and after the final Melbourne adjournment on 24 March 1927 parliamentary files and other belongings were transferred by rail to the new building. The Victorian Legislative Assembly allowed the House of Representatives to take the Victorian Mace, which the House had been using since 1901, but not to take a Victorian sand glass, which the Assembly wished to keep. Although the new Speaker's chair was ready for the first sitting in Canberra, the President of the Senate had to make do with temporary furniture until the arrival of his Chair, a gift promised by the Canadian Government. Another chair was also still to be installed. This was the Throne, a high-backed chair surmounted by a crown, which would be used only by the Sovereign, the Governor-General or his substitutes at openings of parliament.

The Commonwealth parliamentary library suffered to some extent, but not seriously or more than temporarily, by separation from its Victorian counterpart. Its share of the holdings in Spring Street had been considerably enlarged in 1909 by donation of the great Petherick collection of Australiana, intended as the nucleus of a future national library. The subsequent growth of this nucleus was fostered particularly by Kenneth Binns, who joined the Commonwealth parliamentary library as a cataloguer with responsibility for the Australian collection in 1911. Unlike his superior, Arthur Wadsworth, Binns was a trained librarian. He built on Petherick's foundation to the extent that funds allowed, and when the transfer to Canberra approached, he obtained £3000 from parliament to replace much of the reference material which would have to be left in the Victorian parliamentary library.

Altogether 100 000 volumes were transferred to the new library at the rear of King's Hall. The move took place by rail over a period of twelve months, and not a single book was lost or even damaged. Wadsworth retired, and Binns was appointed parliamentary librarian from 1 January 1928.

King's Hall was less spacious vertically than Queen's Hall in Melbourne, but its parquetry floor of jarrah and silver ash was larger and more inviting than the hall over which Queen Victoria's statue presided. On a marble pedestal stood a bronze statue of 'George V Rex Imperator' by Sir Bertram Mackennal, and fixed to some of the columns in the hall were plaques bearing the likenesses of such federal champions as Parkes, Griffith, Barton and Deakin. Elsewhere in the building were a large and well equipped dining room and kitchen; billiard and card rooms, lounges and clubrooms; rest rooms, complete with arm chairs and wall beds, for the Prime Minister, the Leader of the Opposition, the Speaker and the President of the Senate; and finally (something noticed by most visitors, and taken by them to mean that perhaps Canberra would not remain dry indefinitely) a room with a brass rail, obviously a bar. As master of its own house, parliament could have provided itself with an alcoholic oasis in the otherwise dry federal territory. But the outcome of a debate on this matter in 1926 had been, firstly, that the question of the sale of liquor in the territory should be submitted to a local option poll of residents, and, secondly, that until the poll was taken no liquor should be offered for sale in Parliament House.

Parliament House was to be opened on Monday 9 May 1927 by the Duke of York—the future George VI, whose father, as Duke of Cornwall and York, had opened the first Commonwealth parliament twenty-six years before. The main part of the ceremony would take place at the top of the steps before a crowd assembled on several acres of lawn planted in front of the building and bordered at a distance by sawn-off pine trees, up to forty feet high, which had been planted rootless for the occasion. An address of welcome would be read to the Duke; His Royal Highness would respond, and would then turn a gilt key to open the bronze and plate glass doors leading into King's Hall.

For reasons unrecorded, the Prime Minister considered the voices of the Clerk of the House of Representatives, Walter Gale, and the Clerk of the Senate, George Monahan, 'utterly unsuitable' for reading the address of welcome, an assignment traditionally performed by some such officer of the parliament. It may have been that their voices did not carry sufficiently well in the open air, or that the Prime Minister thought Australian accents would be out of place on such an exalted occasion. Whatever the reason, Bruce decided that he should welcome the Duke himself, in the accent of Cambridge and Mayfair. To those concerned about such niceties, this seemed an unwarranted intrusion by the executive between parliament and the King's deputy. Not only would the Duke be welcomed by the leader of the executive, but his Royal Highness, after unlocking the doors, would hand the key to the Prime Minister rather than the Speaker or the President. After seeing an advance copy of the programme for the opening ceremony, the former Speaker, Johnson, wrote to his successor, Speaker Groom, protesting that the Duke should hand the key directly to the Speaker or President as custodians of the respective houses. 'As it is', he wrote, 'both offices have been by the proposed procedure subordinated to that of the head of the Government'. If Johnson had expected Groom to make an issue of this, he was disappointed.

After a cold night that left a carpet of frost on the Limestone Plains, Monday was a day of perfect autumn sunshine, with hardly a breath of wind to stir the city's flags. Distance and uncertainty of accommodation kept the number of visitors much lower than expected. By 9.30 a.m., however, fifteen thousand invited guests were assembled in two viewing stands— parliamentarians and their wives, premiers, judges, bishops, lord mayors and soldiers: almost everyone who might have been expected, including Walter Burley Griffin. Elsewhere in front of the building a roughly equal number of spectators took up positions wherever they could. One who stood out in this crowd was a bare-foot and grey-bearded Aborigine from Gundagai, known by the name of Marvellous because of his fondness for that exclamatory word in conversation. Marvellous was said to walk at least 1000 miles every year, doing the rounds of country shows, and he was the only Aborigine present at the opening ceremony in Canberra. Two inspectors and a sergeant of police suggested that he move away. A clergyman standing near by called out that the Aborigine had more right than anyone else to be at the ceremony; other voices offered encouragement, and the old man was allowed to stay. According to the *Argus*, people in the crowd showered him with coins amounting to thirty or forty shillings.

The Duke and Duchess of York were driven from Government House at Yarralumla by car, but at the Prime Minister's residence—'The Lodge', a two-storey white stucco mansion in Deakin—they changed into an open horse-drawn coach with costumed postilions. Preceded by the viceregal couple, Lord and Lady Stonehaven, and by an escort of mounted police and Light Horsemen, the royal party drove around National Circuit past the

Hotel Kurrajong and East Block secretariat building to the red-carpeted steps of Parliament House. The ensuing tableau, as depicted in a painting by H. Septimus Power and a short cine-newsreel, was a vivid composition of blue sky, white stucco, red Australian ensigns and Union Jacks, gold braid, top hats and slouch hats, full-bottomed wigs, women in cloche hats and long dresses, and scarlet coated aides-de-camp topped with lofty bearskins.

The Duke, wearing the dress uniform of an admiral, inspected a guard of honour from the three Australian armed services and reached the portico at 10.45 a.m. As Dame Nellie Melba stepped forward to sing the National Anthem, an R.A.A.F. squadron flew low overhead, drowning out most of the diva's performance. The Prime Minister made himself heard, but when the planes passed over a second time, the Duke's reply was all but lost. 'Within these portals', he said,

> will be framed those laws which will mould the destiny of a people. May those who enter this open door govern with justice, reason, and equal favour to all. May they do so in humility and without self-interest. May they think and act nationally. May they speak with the voice of those who sent them here—the voice of the people.

Sharp at 11 o'clock His Royal Highness opened the door, and a religious service of dedication began. Accompanied by massed bands, the audience sang 'O God our Help in Ages Past', the President-General of the Methodist Church read Psalm 145, the Moderator-General of the Presbyterian Church delivered a dedicatory prayer, and the acting Primate of the Church of England pronounced the benediction. The Roman Catholic Church held fast to its policy of not taking part in interdenominational services.

Entering the building at the head of the royal party, the Duke unveiled the statue of his father and proceeded to the Senate chamber, where, in the presence of the members of both chambers, the Governor-General and five State Governors, the Clerk of the Senate read out the King's Commission authorising the Duke to proclaim the inauguration of meetings of parliament at Canberra. The Duke, who was seated with the Duchess on a dais at the head of the Senate table, made reference in his speech to the 1926 Imperial Conference which had reached certain major decisions about future relations between the United Kingdom and such self-governing dominions as Australia. 'It is perhaps peculiarly fitting', he said,

> that we should celebrate the birth of this new capital city just after the close of an Imperial Conference, which represents the beginning of another chapter in our Empire story . . . .We turn today a new page of history. May it be a page glorious for Australia and the whole Empire.

With duty done, the royal visitors attended luncheon in the parliamentary dining room. One of the guests, C. L. A. Abbott (C, Gwydir, N), found himself sitting next to the great Melba, who complained to him that she felt a little slighted by the manner in which she had been received at Parliament House that morning. To make conversation he asked whether she remembered singing in the church at Mandurama, a small town in his electorate. 'I don't remember anything about it', she replied tartly. Feeling slighted himself, Abbott turned away, only to be startled a few seconds later by a sharp pinch on the leg. 'I'm sorry', said Melba. 'Tell me about it.'

Another guest who was out of sorts, Lady Stonehaven, later wrote in her diary that the luncheon was 'ghastly'. As no wine was served, the loyal toast was drunk in fruit cup. Later the Duke and Duchess watched a military review near Parliament House, during which an air force plane crashed in full view of the spectators, fatally injuring its pilot.

The Senate and House of Representatives reassembled shortly after 5 p.m. to approve addresses to the Duke of York, then went into an adjournment which was to last for almost five months. Cleaning up after a day of unexpectedly low attendance, the caterers found themselves left with more than four tons of meat pies and sausage rolls, 1900 lbs of cooked prawns and 1700 lbs of fish. Unable to refrigerate them, they buried the lot at Queanbeyan garbage tip.

As members began journeying back to their electorates next morning, the *Age* and the *Argus* expressed strikingly different opinions about the legislature which had now departed from their city. 'In the new city', said the more hopeful *Age*, 'members of Governments and of Parliaments might appropriately adopt a new sense of responsibility; the Australian people might coincidentally indulge in a new and more radiant vision of their national destiny'.

The *Argus* editorial took a more realistic view. 'A new Federal Capital confers no additional power on the people of Australia', it said.

> The fact that the Parliament has been sitting for years in one place and will for the future sit in another leaves every person in Australia much the same as he was before. The old men will assemble in the new house: they will be 'National' or 'Provincial' as they were before, and will continue to believe that the last opinion which they expressed was wiser than an earlier one. The old problems will not be nearer solution because they have been carried many hundreds of miles in portfolios and in files of papers, or in the less definite but highly diversified forums in which they flit through the minds of those who toy with them. Life has to be taken up at the point at which it was abandoned. Parliamentary warfare is not likely to undergo a change in the new surroundings. There will be misrepresentation, conscious or unconscious; satire, ponderous and pointed; argument, close to and wide of the mark; facts which look like fiction, and fiction dressed to look like facts.

Although parliament had gone into adjournment after only one brief sitting, almost as though it wanted nothing further to do with Canberra, the seat of government was now there to stay. Public servants continued to arrive, construction of the city went ahead, and the parliamentarians who had fled so abruptly would be returning in September. As a coda to the first part of this narrative, however, it should be mentioned that on 16 June 1927 the six State Premiers, who were also the six State Treasurers, attended a climactic financial conference with the Prime Minister, Treasurer and Attorney-General of the Commonwealth—not at Canberra, but in the old Senate chamber in Spring Street, Melbourne.

This was the conference called by the Commonwealth to negotiate a financial agreement between the federal partners. 'Negotiate' was hardly the right word, for in spite of assurances that the Commonwealth would deal justly and generously with the States, the Premiers regarded the States Grants Act as something of a gun on the table. They could argue and protest as did two Labor Premiers in particular, Jack Lang (New South Wales) and Philip Collier (Western Australia); but in the end they would have to accept the Commonwealth's terms.

Those terms, admittedly more conciliatory than before, included a Commonwealth contribution to the payment of State loan interest, which would probably prove to be more generous than the soon-to-be-abandoned per capita payments; a fifty-fifty contribution towards sinking funds for new State debts; and creation of a constitutionally entrenched Loan Council in place of the voluntary one that had been operating for the last four years. In the kind of rhetoric that was becoming stylised at Premiers' Conferences, Lang told Bruce:

> You have put us in a position where, no matter how we desire to meet your wishes, we cannot do it. We have been cribbed, cabined and confined in our taxation powers, while you are free to roam as you will. The Commonwealth should not ask the sovereign States to abandon all their rights, and to hand themselves shackled to a Loan Council, in which the Commonwealth will be the controlling influence . . . Am I to hand to some outside body the power to say whether the works deemed necessary by the people of New South Wales should be executed or not? If so, I would be surrendering the sovereign rights of the State, which I am not prepared to do for an instant.

Collier spoke of unequal sacrifices.

> Although Mr Bruce claims that the Commonwealth, as well as the States, sacrifices certain of its sovereign rights, the Commonwealth is better off because it will receive one-fifth of loan money raised and have three votes on the Loan Council. The effect of the operation of the Loan Council would be to restrict borrowing, and a permanent Loan Council on the lines proposed would be the greatest step towards unification since the inception of the Commonwealth.

How much of this was rhetoric alone, and how much the genuine fear of sovereign States scenting smoke from the altar, can only be surmised. It seems fair to say, however, that some sacrifice was made and the Commonwealth's role, if not that of Moloch, was certainly that of priest rather than burnt offering. The Premiers consoled themselves with the generous fine print of the financial agreement, and on 14 December 1927 Bruce moved the second reading of a Financial Agreement Bill, describing it as 'the most important financial measure that has ever been submitted to this Parliament'.

The Labor Opposition, although by no means averse to a stronger Commonwealth, wanted the per capita system continued until, as it hoped, the Constitution could be generally overhauled. A royal commission had been appointed recently to report on the Constitution. The Opposition was supported in its view by a few government backbenchers who held that the new agreement would give the Commonwealth too much power over State financial policy, but even so the numbers were insufficient. Labor motions to postpone the Bill until after reform of the Constitution were defeated in the House of Representatives by 34 votes to 19, and in the Senate by 25 to 5. Senator Lynch (Lab, W) reminded his colleagues of their duty 'to see that the interests of each State are preserved . . . and that the States as a whole receive fair play as between them and the central government'. But that kind of speech belonged to a past era, and the so-called States' House voted more solidly for the Bill than the lower house did. In the following year a referendum was held on a proposed constitutional amendment to remove any doubt about the Commonwealth's power to make agreements with the States about their public debts. For a change the answer was 'Yes', by a large majority in every State, and Section 105A was inserted in the Constitution. Again it could be said, in Alfred Deakin's words a quarter of a century before, that the Commonwealth was out of the toils and fast escaping beyond the reach not only of its enemies, but of its friends as well.

Part Two

Canberra 1927–1949

8

Buried in the Bush

Mace and Sword

No comet or squall attended the transfer of parliament, but anyone remembering those inaugural omens from 1901 might have noticed signs even more ominous in Canberra. On the opening day a young pilot had crashed to his death in front of Parliament House. Three months later, with parliament in recess and snow lying thick on Mt Ainslie, the Clerk of the House of Representatives, Walter Augustus Gale, was reminiscing about his Western Australian childhood with a lifelong friend who had called to see him in his new office. Suddenly he complained of feeling unwell. Remarking that the room was too hot, the visitor went to open a window. When he turned around, Gale was dead from a heart attack.

At parliament's next sitting, on the afternoon of 28 September, Prime Minister Bruce moved a motion of condolence upon the Clerk's death. The new Clerk at the head of the Table was John Robert McGregor, a New South Welshman who had been promoted from the position of Second Clerk-Assistant because the Clerk-Assistant was due to retire. That afternoon, while in the act of handing the Speaker a document concerning his predecessor, Clerk McGregor himself collapsed with cerebral haemorrhage, unable to move or speak. One of four doctors in the House, Sir Neville Howse (Nat, Calare, N), had him carried out to the ministerial lobby and then taken to Canberra's only hospital, a cluster of weatherboard buildings on the northern side of the Molonglo River.

After the dinner adjournment the Speaker, Sir Littleton Groom, announced that word had been received of McGregor's death, whereupon the Prime Minister moved for another adjournment. 'Words cannot express our feelings', he said.

229

> Earlier in this sitting we carried a resolution of sympathy with the rela-
> tives of Mr Gale, the late Clerk of the House, and expressed our great
> regret at his demise. A few minutes afterwards we heard the announce-
> ment from the Chair that a new Clerk had been appointed. Now we are
> faced with the tragic fact that that Clerk, too, has passed away.

The only other speaker on the adjournment motion was the Leader of the
Opposition, Matthew Charlton. 'Fate appears to have followed us to our new
home', he said.

> Only today we carried a resolution of condolence with the wife and rela-
> tives of our late beloved Clerk, Mr Gale, and now his successor, after a few
> short moments of office, has also been called away. These tragedies indi-
> cate that the officials of the House have heavy and exacting tasks to per-
> form, and we should do our best to ease their positions.

Gale and McGregor were buried, as the dead pilot had been, in the pine-
shaded graveyard of St John's Church, directly across the river from Parliament House. Perhaps it was not too fanciful to imagine that by these burials
parliament was symbolically taking root in the unfamiliar limestone plains
to which, for better or worse, it was now committed. Whether or not the
Clerks' lives had been shortened by the move to the bush capital, a heavy
task in which both had taken a leading part, it did seem that fate had followed parliament to its new home. As the *Argus* had warned mockingly, parliamentary life would be resumed in Canberra precisely where it had been
suspended in Melbourne: human nature would not be altered, nor would old
problems be brought any closer to solution by being transported hundreds of
miles. On the contrary, one of parliament's most enduring problems—its
relationship with the executive—was destined to take a turn for the worse in
the new surroundings.

To some private members it seemed sadly appropriate that the Duke of
York had presented the key of Parliament House not to the Speaker or the
President, but to the Prime Minister. Parliament may still have been master
of its own house; but the executive, in the form of Cabinet, now had its foot
firmly in the legislative door. At Parliament House in Melbourne, executive
accommodation had originally been limited to one room on the ground
floor, which was made available to the Prime Minister. Cabinet was accustomed to meeting in the Commonwealth Offices, but after the Bruce–Page
Ministry took office it met sometimes in Parliament House as well.

The new Parliament House in Canberra provided accommodation for the
Prime Minister and the Leader of the Government in the Senate, seven
single rooms for ministers, and a Cabinet room for emergency meetings.
Ministerial accommodation was necessary in Parliament House for the time
being because most government departments could not move from Melbourne until adequate administrative office space was built in Canberra.
Cabinet's weekly meetings were intended to be held usually at the Prime
Minister's Department in No. 2 Secretariat (West Block), some little distance
from Parliament House. And in the main they were, at least for the first two
and a half years. From mid-1927 to late 1929, Cabinet held ninety-seven

meetings in West Block, twenty-six in Parliament House while parliament was sitting, and only three in Parliament House while parliament was not sitting.

Cabinet minutes for the following two years did not specify place of meeting, but by the early 1930s Cabinet had taken permanent and exclusive residence in its room at Parliament House. Some said later that ministers had been discomforted by the heat of the afternoon sun in West Block, but the more likely explanation was that Parliament House, where all ministers had their own rooms, was simply more convenient. And so, by 1932 at the latest, the executive had physically invaded the legislative sphere to an extent that somewhat blunted the Constitution's sharp distinction between legislative, executive and judicial powers.

This was a time of increasing concern by parliamentarians, and more particularly by lawyers, about a certain tendency that had developed in the Westminster style of executive. The fashionable term for it was 'new despotism', from the title of a book published in 1929 by Lord Hewart, the Lord Chief Justice of England. Hewart and other writers on the subject warned against the effects of delegated legislation under which, in the name of efficient government, an executive could make its own rules, regulations and by-laws. 'It is manifestly easy', wrote Hewart,

> to point a superficial contrast between what was done or attempted in the days of our least wise kings, and what is being done or attempted today. In those days the method was to defy Parliament—and it failed. In these days the method is to cajole, to coerce and to use Parliament—and it is strangely successful. The old despotism, which was defeated, offered Parliament a challenge. The new despotism, which is not yet defeated, gives Parliament an anaesthetic. The strategy is different, but the goal is the same. It is to subordinate Parliament, to evade the Courts, and to render the will, or the caprice, of the Executive unfettered or supreme.

Writing on the same topic in 1930, a future Commonwealth Solicitor-General, Professor K. H. Bailey, assessed the incidence of new despotism in Australia, where the High Court early in its career had sustained parliament's right to grant rule-making power to the executive. That kind of delegation had taken two main forms: power to make an order or issue a proclamation applying the will of parliament in particular cases that were provided for only generally or by implication in an act; and, more usually, power to make rules, regulations or by-laws prescribing all matters required or convenient for giving effect to such an act.

Rule-making power had been exercised to such an extent in the Commonwealth that in quantitative terms the body of statutory rules far exceeded acts of parliament. 'A consolidated edition fills 3600 closely printed pages', wrote Bailey.

> It is a commonplace that at present members are quite unable to keep up with the mass of regulations and orders emanating from the executive. They cannot even read them all, let alone form opinions on them . . . More and more, in fact, modern legislation comes to be, and must be, a declaration of principles whose application is left to be worked out by the administration.

Professor Bailey took comfort from the power vested in each house of federal parliament (by the Acts Interpretation Act) to disallow regulations made under delegated legislation, and also from the general absence in Australia of any provisions, such as the Imperial parliament had employed, that rules or orders made under an act should have effect as if enacted in the act itself. But he also drew attention to the paucity of motions for disallowance of regulations, and to certain examples of legislation conferring power on the Governor-General to vary the act itself. An amending Navigation Act, for instance, empowered the Governor-General to suspend provisions of the act should he 'think it expedient in the public interest'. This, Bailey remarked, was a power as wide as that which cost James II his throne, and there was no provision for any parliamentary review of His Excellency's decision. 'Such instances are almost enough to indicate a tendency', he wrote,

> and one that demands careful attention . . . The vital point is that Parliament should be kept thoroughly informed of what is being done in the purported exercise of its will, and should have reasonable facilities for ensuring that nothing is done which if laid before Parliament directly in the form of a Bill would have been rejected.

The parliament which reassembled in its new home for the 1927 Budget session was a generation removed from the first parliament in Melbourne. Only three M.H.R.s and one senator had served continuously since 1901 (Hughes, Groom, Watkins and Senator Pearce), but thirty M.H.R.s and thirteen senators had been in federal parliament for ten years or more. Thirty-seven members of both houses had also served in State or colonial parliaments (compared with eighty-six in 1901), and two had been Premiers (as against thirteen). The latter were Senator Sir Henry Barwell from South Australia and E. G. Theodore, the former Premier of Queensland who had been elected earlier in the year from the Sydney seat of Dalley. The largest occupational group was no longer lawyers (fifteen, as against twenty-eight) or businessmen (thirteen, as against twelve), but farmers, graziers and pastoralists (twenty-nine, as against twelve). There were six miners, six journalists and four teachers.

The average age of members at the time of their election was fifty-six in the Senate (as against forty-nine in 1901) and fifty-two in the lower house (fifty-four). The oldest member was a 76-year-old plumber, John West (Lab, East Sydney), and the youngest was 32-year-old Roland Green. The 'Green without an E', it may be remembered, had lost one of his legs in the war. Another disabled M.H.R., George Maxwell (Nat, Fawkner, V), had been blind for the past twenty-six years but was nevertheless an active debater and criminal barrister.

As for place of birth, eighty-three Senators and M.H.R.s had been born in Australia, compared with only fifty-nine in 1901, and all other members had been born either in the United Kingdom or New Zealand. There was no O'Malley or Watson among them to impart even the faintest exotic tinge. Of the native-born members, more than half came from the south-eastern States: twenty-nine from Victoria and twenty-one from New South Wales. Thirty per cent of members had been educated to secondary level (as against

25 per cent in 1901) and surprisingly only 22 per cent to tertiary level (36 per cent). The parliament now contained fifteen Roman Catholics, as against eleven a generation before. Fourteen made no declaration of religion.

One member of the tenth parliament was probably a murderer, and if he had not become a murderer yet, he certainly became one later in life. Thomas John Ley (Nat, Barton, N), a former New South Wales Minister for Justice, entered federal parliament under the illusion that he was destined one day to lead the Nationalist Party in place of Stanley Bruce. He was a formidably bulky lawyer with glossy black hair, a resonant voice and unctuous manner. During a particularly nasty campaign, the sitting Labor Member for Barton, Frederick McDonald, had publicly accused Ley of attempting to bribe him into failing to lodge his nomination. Ley promptly sued for slander, and after the election McDonald presented a petition to the Court of Disputed Returns, praying that Ley's election be declared void on grounds of bribery. Shortly before the petition was listed for hearing, poor Fred McDonald vanished, never to be seen again.

This was not the first time that someone in Ley's vicinity had vanished without apparent reason. No one had yet put two and two together, but the reputation which preceded him to Canberra was nonetheless distinctly unsavoury. Bruce passed over him for the ministry, and Ley found himself largely ignored by his fellow members. After a maiden speech devoted to the film industry, he seldom spoke in the House. Defeated at the next election, he emigrated to England where, in 1947, he was found guilty of murdering a man out of sexual jealousy. He was sentenced to death, declared insane, and confined to Broadmoor Criminal Lunatic Asylum, where he died within a matter of months. Of all federal parliamentarians, T. J. Ley was probably the most grotesque.

The Treasurer, Dr Earle Page, brought down his fifth consecutive Budget only minutes after the stricken Clerk McGregor had been carried from the chamber. This brown-panelled and green-furnished chamber, like its red counterpart on the western side of King's Hall, was somewhat larger (4090 square feet) than the Victorian Legislative Assembly (2842 square feet), and its ceiling was about the same height (thirty feet). It was comfortable and visually pleasing; but the acoustics were far from ideal, the cooling plant gave cause for complaint, and sometimes the roof leaked. The building and its land belonged to the Commonwealth, not parliament, but in line with House of Commons precedent the two houses and their presiding officers, the President and Speaker, had exclusive jurisdiction to keep order and decorum within the building and its curtilages.

Page's Budget was a complacent one, reflecting the readjustment that had taken place between the Commonwealth and the States, but failing to take account of some ominous economic signs. Drawing on an accumulated surplus, and estimating a further rise in customs revenue, he was able to reduce rates of income and land tax. Unfortunately a downward turn in the economy that year led to a fall in customs and income tax revenue, leaving Page with his first deficit. One Government speaker in the 1927 Budget debate— Henry Gullett (Nat, Henty, V), a former journalist and war historian— criticised Page's optimism and in the process saddled him with an enduring nickname. 'I make that statement as a Nationalist member sitting behind the Treasurer', said Gullett, 'whom I do not recognize as my leader, but merely as the leader of the Country Party. I have made it clear that I am opposed to the Treasurer's policy, root and branch. I regard him as the most tragic Treasurer that Australia has ever known'.

The burden of Gullett's speech was that Page's policy was one of helping weak rural industries with assistance drawn from the few industries that were self-supporting, mainly wool and wheat, and from a series of London loans. 'I am old enough to remember the crisis of the early nineties', he said,

> when scores of thousands of men, down on the breadline and below it, were out of work. Knowing the seasonal uncertainties, and the variations in prices that have occurred in my lifetime, and will, no doubt, be experienced again, in the wool and wheat industries, those two supports cannot be regarded as irremovable. They may fail us at any time. If they do, we shall assuredly see an era of human suffering that we have never known before.
>
> Mr WEST.—Do not be so downhearted about it.
>
> Mr GULLETT.—We should face the issue. We cannot bury our heads in the sand.

Before the Budget debate had talked itself out, the Leader of the Opposition moved want of confidence in the Government for its decision to sell the Commonwealth Shipping Line which Hughes had established during the war. The Senate—on a rather dubious argument advanced by the Government leader, Senator Pearce, that the censure was not a motion of no confidence—refrained from its usual practice of adjourning while the lower house debated Charlton's motion. It was defeated 23–40, and the shipping line was sold during the following year without any consultation of parliament by the executive.

During December 1927 the Attorney-General, Latham, resumed the Government's offensive against militant unions by introducing another Commonwealth Conciliation and Arbitration Bill for debate later in the session. This was intended to discipline unions which had been pursuing industrial ends through strike action rather than arbitration, and to control wage levels. On the first score, it contained provisions empowering the Arbitration Court to order secret ballots and deregister organisations which failed to take adequate steps to prevent their members from engaging in lock-outs or strikes; union funds were to be made liable for penalties in relation to strikes, and penalties were prescribed for using violence, threats or abuse in an attempt to prevent anyone from working in accordance with the terms of an award. With regard to wages, the Court would be required, before making any award, to take into account the award's probable economic effect on the community. The measure was provocative, and was viewed with alarm by the Opposition and by the recently established Australasian Council of Trade Unions.

The Christmas adjournment seemed to sever parliament's last links with Melbourne, and although federal members' offices were maintained there and in Sydney, many of the members returning in February 1928 had their first clear appreciation of the reality that Canberra, for all its isolation, was indeed the seat of government. As if to emphasise this, the most famous Australian of the day, Bert Hinkler, the first pilot to fly a light aeroplane solo from England to Australia, landed his little Avro Avian in March on the grassy review ground near the Hotel Kurrajong. Canberra went wild about Hinkler. The Prime Minister presented him with a cheque for £2000 at a ceremony on the steps of Parliament House; the Governor-General received him at Yarralumla; the Returned Sailors', Soldiers' and Airmens' Imperial League of Australia held a reception; the Government honoured Hinkler again at an all-male parliamentary dinner while ministers' wives entertained his mother and sister elsewhere; the Bruces had him to dinner at The Lodge, Duntroon held a reception; and finally the Senate and House of Representatives admitted him to a seat on the floors of their chambers. Bert Hinkler was the thirty-second distinguished visitor to have been honoured in this way, and among his predecessors were the Prince of Wales, Admiral Lord Jellicoe and ten State or colonial governors.

Hinkler's 15-day journey from London to Darwin was the world's first long solo flight since Lindberg's crossing of the Atlantic ten months before. The flight was certainly comparable to Lindberg's; but even so, Canberra's reaction to it was more enthusiastic than could be explained in terms only of Hinkler's achievement. Perhaps this also had something to do with the rudimentary city's sense of being buried in the bush half way between Melbourne and Sydney. Hinkler's Avro Avian, the first aeroplane to land there, was a tentative link with the wider world and an earnest of closer links to come.

In the meantime, Canberra did what it could to foster its own identity. Tree planting and building continued apace, the *Canberra Times* spoke up for local interests, residents asserted their independence by voting 2218 to 2161 in favour of legalising the sale of liquor on licensed premises, dances were held in the new Albert Hall, and the Federal Capital Commission invited designs for a civic coat of arms. One Sydney newspaper suggested a civil servant rampant on a field of red dust, but Canberra's dust was not red, and there were more traditional symbols at hand.

The armorial bearings of the City of Canberra, granted in 1928 by the College of Arms, London, were based on a design by C. R. Wylie of Sydney. The arms consisted of a triple-towered castle borrowed from the arms of various other cities, a crossed mace and sword symbolising parliament and the executive respectively, a crown for imperial sovereignty, and a white rose of York commemorating the Duke's inaugural role. The crest consisted of the portcullis associated with the City of Westminster and the House of Commons, a gum tree for obvious reasons, and another imperial crown for good measure. The motto, was *Pro Rege Lege et Grege*, borrowed from the City of Perth in Scotland, and meaning 'For the King, the Law and the People'. The supporters were an unexpected pair of swans: dexter sable, symbolising Australia in its native state, and sinister white, symbolising European settlement. If only Wylie had been more familiar with the Canberra region, he might have preferred its most abundant and distinctive bird, and incidentally one whose plumage combined black and white—the magpie.

In March 1928 Matthew Charlton, one of the few survivors of Labor's last term in federal office eleven years before, resigned from the parliamentary party's leadership. It was time for him to go. Although Labor ministries now held office in all States except South Australia, the Bruce–Page Government remained comparatively untroubled by Charlton and his numerically weak party. It was being said privately that Matt was too stodgy, that the party could never hope to win under his leadership. The recently elected Deputy Leader (Anstey had resigned, apparently because of ill health) was a strait-laced but well regarded Victorian, James Scullin. He became acting Leader, and two other members—E. G. Theodore and George Yates—were believed to have stood against him when the leadership was contested one month later. 'Gunner' Yates had no real chance, and Theodore, although never an opponent to be treated lightly, was disadvantaged by the recent and some-what murky nature of his translation to the federal sphere.

To the discomfiture of New South Wales Premier Jack Lang, who recog-nised a political rival when he saw one, Theodore was endorsed for the fed-eral seat of Dalley, without any preselection, after a convenient resignation by the sitting Member, W. G. Mahony. Allegations were made that Mahony had been recompensed for this, and the federal Government set up a royal commission which duly concluded that monetary inducement of £5000 had caused Mahony to resign his seat, that all financial benefit had been in the interest of Theodore, but that the source of the benefit was unknown. Although Theodore admitted having made a present of £200 to Mahony, the commission was unable to say whether that had been part of the induce-ment. When the commissioner's non-committal report was eventually tabled in the House of Representatives it passed almost without notice.

Scullin was elected Leader by a substantial but undisclosed majority, and in the ballot for Deputy Leadership Arthur Blakeley, a shearer who had rep-resented Darling for ten years, defeated Theodore by only one vote. In the years ahead, however, Theodore would play a much larger part than Blakeley in the party's affairs. He and Scullin were both Roman Catholics with Australian Workers' Union connections, but in temperament and per-sonality they were chalk and cheese.

James Henry Scullin was born in 1876 of Irish parentage at Trawalla, a railway siding near Ballarat. His father had been a farmer in County Derry, a miner at Ballarat, a railway labourer and finally a railway pensioner. There were eight children. Leaving school in his thirteenth year, Jim Scullin worked at odd jobs until, at the age of twenty-four, he opened a grocer's shop in Ballarat, which he ran for the next ten years. He attended night school, became president of the Ballarat branch of the Catholic Young Men's Society, competed for oratory prizes at Ballarat's renowned South Street competitions, and joined the Political Labor Council.

In 1906 he stood, with predictable lack of success, against the local federal member—who happened to be the Prime Minister, Alfred Deakin. Next he became a part-time organiser for the A.W.U., driving himself through the country districts of Victoria by horse and buggy, and in 1910 he was elected to the federal seat of Corangamite. Defeated at the next election, he became managing director and editor of the Ballarat *Evening Echo*, which soon afterwards was taken over by the A.W.U. Scullin campaigned for Home Rule in Ireland and against conscription during the war. As a member of the Victorian A.L.P. State executive, and later president of the State branch, he was a strong albeit patient supporter of the party's socialist objective—even if it took '1000 years' to achieve. In 1922 he beat a strong field of candidates for preselection to one of the safest Labor seats in Australia, Yarra, an industrial Melbourne seat rendered vacant by the death of the parliamentary party leader, Frank Tudor.

Returned to parliament that year, Scullin took a special interest in taxation and impressed members on both sides with his debating power and respect for parliamentary tradition. Some said he was influenced by Dr Mannix, but his speeches contained no evidence of any particularly Roman Catholic approach to social issues. He used to say that he had once gone to St Patrick's Cathedral in Ballarat, asking someone to explain Pope Leo XIII's *Rerum Novarum*, the encyclical applying moral theology to conditions created by the industrial revolution. But no one could help him.

Nor was there any evidence that Labor's new leader was helped or influenced by John Wren, the shady Melbourne power broker who was one of Scullin's electors and did appear to influence Frank Anstey in the nearby electorate of Bourke. Scullin was an unassuming, diligent man, a non-smoker and non-drinker, a man of less than average physique, with a long but kindly face surmounted by a crest of thick greying hair. Although he had no artistic pretensions, it did seem in character that he played the violin.

Edward Granville Theodore was more ruthless than Scullin, and physically much more robust. If he had played any instrument, it would have been brass of some kind. His father was a Rumanian, the son of a Greek Orthodox priest named Teodorescu, and the family traced its history back to a migration organised by the Emperor Trajan. One of Ted Theodore's uncles was named Trajan, and Theodore himself—a big man with dark hair and Roman gravitas—could easily have passed for a young emperor.

The father came to Australia as first mate on a ship, married one of the passengers, an English migrant, changed his name to Theodore, and worked as a stevedore in Port Adelaide. Ted was born there in 1884. He left school at twelve, worked as a casual gardener and log-cutter, and at the age of sixteen joined the gold rush to Western Australia. During the next few years he worked as a labourer on the Murchison field, shovelled guano on the Abrolhos Islands, drilled for gold at Kalgoorlie, prospected for copper at Leigh Creek, worked at Broken Hill and prospected for tin at Chillagoe in northern Queensland. It was nothing for him to walk with his swag for two or three hundred miles.

'Red Ted', as he became known, was a political prodigy. At the age of twenty-three, he played the main part in founding a militant union in northern Queensland, which soon amalgamated with the A.W.U. Two years later he was elected to Queensland's Legislative Assembly from the seat of Woothakatta (later renamed Chillagoe), and in 1913, at the age of twenty-nine, he was elected unopposed as President of the A.W.U. When Labor won office under T. J. Ryan in 1915 he became Treasurer and Secretary for Public Works. After Ryan's entry into federal politics, Theodore was Premier and

Chief Secretary for six years, and Treasurer for five of those years before resigning from the Queensland parliament.

Still in his early forties, Theodore was a match physically and temperamentally for Stanley Bruce. 'They were big, masterly men with the same orderly manner of delivery and the same confidence in their superiority to the worms around them', wrote a close observer of both men, Frank Anstey.

> They were co-experts in the art of self-suppression, because—to gentlemen as to gangsters—even a flush on the face is a sign of weakness. Their only visible differences were that Theodore had more bulbous lips, more hair on the back of his hands, more on his head, and indulged at times in a cold, calculated vituperation the other would scorn ... Both were pipe smokers, solitude thinkers, planners, plotters ... They worked with ease—like motors with abundant power—and no task put them to exertion.

Theodore's arrival coincided with the parliamentary party's loss of confidence in its leader. There was nothing overt to connect him with any anti-Charlton conspiracy. He sat at his table in the party room, reading the latest economic reports, writing, smoking, affable to any who addressed him, but never obtruding himself upon the party's attention. 'Yet whenever the party met', wrote Anstey, 'one of his admirers would rise to dig a spur into Charlton and another would pour caustic on the wound'. Theodore's narrow defeat for the deputy leadership was generally regarded as a penalty for his presumed conspiring against Charlton.

Early in May 1928 the House of Representatives resumed debate on the consequences of the Imperial Conference of 1926. This was a subject which parliament had considered fourteen months earlier, and to which it would return later without much enthusiasm. One of the speakers on this occasion—E. A. Mann (Nat, Perth, W), later more widely known as a radio commentator called 'The Watchman'—remarked that the subject had been in cold storage for so long that to thaw it now would not restore anything like its former interest. It reminded him of Lewis Carroll's 'Hunting of the Snark':

> Under the leadership of one of the cleverest word-spinners of the British Empire, it was sought to gloss over a difficulty by expressions and phrases which really amounted to very little, and, as in that famous poem, I venture to say that when the formula was found it was very much like the old "Snark" because it turned out to be a "Boojum" after all.

What he meant was that the Imperial Conference had formally defined dominion sovereignty, but the British Commonwealth turned out to be a British Empire after all. The conference recognised certain changes that had already taken place in dominion status, and began a process of further legal change which would lead to the passing of the Statute of Westminster by the imperial government in 1931. The Balfour Report which provided the basic formula for dominion sovereignty declared that the United Kingdom and the dominions were 'autonomous Communities within the British Empire, equal in status, in no way subordinate one to another in any aspect of their domestic or external affairs, though united by a common allegiance to the Crown, and freely associated as members of the British Commonwealth of Nations'.

Although the Snark may have looked remarkably like a Boojum, one corollary of the formula was a significant change in the role of dominion governors-general. Australia and South Africa had often previously urged that the governor-general should be relieved of his ambassadorial functions: that he should represent only the Sovereign, and not His Majesty's government. This argument was given irresistible force in 1926 by the Canadian Governor-General's rejection of advice from his Prime Minister to dissolve the Canadian House of Commons. Instead the Governor-General, Lord Byng, accepted Mackenzie King's resignation and commissioned the Leader of the Opposition, Arthur Meighen, to form a government. No more able to control the chamber than his predecessor, Meighen in turn asked for a dissolution, and was granted it. At the ensuing election King was returned with a comfortable majority. Lord Byng had acted with constitutional propriety, but it was generally agreed that he had also displayed political unwisdom.

The 1926 conference resolved that the governor-general was no longer 'the representative of His Majesty's Government in Great Britain', and that it was therefore no longer constitutionally appropriate for him to remain the official channel of communication between a dominion and Great Britain. Communication in future would be directly from government to government, leaving the governor-general as 'the representative of the Crown, holding in all essential respects the same position in relation to the administration of public affairs in the Dominion as is held by . . . the King in Great Britain'. A United Kingdom High Commissioner would take over the ambassadorial function, and the first such appointment was made in 1931. Responsibility for the coding and decoding of offical correspondence, previously carried by the governor-general's official secretary, was assumed by the Prime Minister's department.

Australia's incumbent Governor-General, Lord Stonehaven, felt that the new emphasis on dominion autonomy would heighten the symbolic importance of his post. 'The idea that there is need for a man to pretend he is the King in an ultra-democratic British community 12,000 miles away certainly has something gloriously illogical and British about it', he wrote, 'but it is a curious job and rather nerve-racking because you never know when you make a false step and even a little one is not forgiven lightly'. Writing to his predecessor, Lord Forster, he speculated on the kind of appointment which might be made after his own term:

> Since the Governor-General represents the King only and not the British Government, it would seem right and natural that the King's views should predominate. It would be obviously unwise to stretch that theory too far, but I think it would be safe and desirable to make it justify the exclusion from the list of candidates all men whose chief recommendation is service to a political party at home. When some of the other Princes are married, there will doubtless be a request for their appointment; in the meantime I feel that the best man would be either a peer of good standing and experience though not necessarily distinguished in political life, or an elder son like Hartington.

For the time being, however, Stonehaven himself managed to present a fair likeness of someone pretending to be the King. He and Lady Stonehaven had arrived in 1925 bringing with them two Daimler cars and, among their other effects, twenty-five cases of port wine, five bottles of quinine, a case of cigars and a case of saddlery. After their move to Canberra, the Stonehavens came to regard Yarralumla with as much affection as a British sovereign might have felt for Balmoral. 'This place is so delightful in the spring . . . and the autumn', wrote the Governor-General, 'that there is undoubtedly a temptation to sit down here and lead a quiet country life, especially if one is fond of polo, which we play now twice a week, and trout fishing'. Stonehaven nonetheless travelled widely throughout the Commonwealth, often by air and at considerable expense. 'The essence of the position, as I see it', he wrote, 'is that the Representative of the King should live on a different footing and in a different atmosphere from other people, as the King does at home: and whatever may be said to the contrary, I believe that that is what Australians expect'. In spite of some criticism about extravagance, Stonehaven remained on good personal terms with the Prime Minister and the Leader of the Opposition. Bruce he considered to be 'an outstanding example of what can be done by a combination of an Australian Public School and a British University'; Scullin, who had enjoyed the advantage of neither, was nonetheless 'a very decent little fellow'.

The closing months of the tenth parliament were characterised by the industrial offensive which Latham had foreshadowed before Christmas, conveniently providing the government with a law and order overture to the next general election. The Opposition attacked this measure strongly, and so also did Billy Hughes, who had begun to stir from his sullen quiescence of the last few years. At least one Nationalist, John Perkins (Eden-Monaro, N), considered Hughes still capable of revenge. 'I felt confident', he wrote, 'that the policy of constantly cold shouldering him and slapping him in the face was bound sooner or later to bring a bitter aftermath'. Speaking during the second reading debate on the Conciliation and Arbitration Bill in May 1928, Hughes asserted that by permitting legalised lock-outs the measure would create conditions for industrial civil war. 'Admittedly it is easier to put out a small fire than a large one', he said, trying another metaphor.

> In many parts of our bush one can read notices prohibiting the use of wax matches, and the lighting of fires except in places set apart for the purpose, because when a fire gets a good hold, the whole countryside is imperilled. Yet it is here proposed to fan a small fire into a great one, in order that we may extinguish the small one.

He nevertheless voted obediently, and the Bill passed both houses on party lines.

Four months later the waterfront provided another example of the kind of strike at which the new Act was aimed. As part of an attempt to reorganise Australia's waterfront, Mr Justice Beeby had introduced into the Waterside Workers' Federation award a requirement for attendance at pickups twice a day. Some ports went on strike over this, but not others, and although the union was opposed to the change it was undecided as to whether it should dare the disciplinary sections of the Act by calling an official strike. The Government did not hesitate. It had already drafted a bill permitting non-unionists to work on the wharves under protection, and at the urging of the Government Leader in the Senate, Sir George Pearce, Bruce decided to rush it through before parliament expired and the election campaign began. Many years later he told his biographer that he 'suspended Standing Orders to shove it through, and blasted it through both Houses'.

The Transport Workers Bill, soon dubbed the 'Dog-Collar Act' by wharf labourers because it required them to be licensed, was introduced on parliament's third last sitting day, Thursday 20 September. While the Bill received its second reading on Friday afternoon, Melbourne shipowners were enrolling five hundred non-union labourers at a building directly opposite Bourke Street police station. Union stevedores tried to intimidate them, but were driven back by the police. When the volunteers worked four overseas vessels on Saturday, stones were hurled at them, and the Waterside Workers' Federation was later fined £1000 for having encouraged a strike against the terms of an award. In the House of Representatives, the Opposition directed its strongest criticism at the crux of the Bill, Clause 3, which Frank Brennan described as a blank cheque for the executive. It empowered the Governor-General to 'make regulations, which, notwithstanding anything in any other Act, shall have the force of law, with respect to the employment of transport workers'. The Attorney-General reminded members that under the Acts Interpretation Act such regulations had to be laid before both houses of parliament within thirty days or, if parliament was not sitting, within thirty days of its next meeting. But, as Brennan pointed out, the Governor-General would have a free hand in this case, for parliament would soon be adjourning for at least two months. Here was a clear case of the sword proving sharper than the mace.

> this inspiration has occurred to the Prime Minister only in the closing hours of a dying Parliament [said Brennan]. Now, I do not say that there is nothing novel in this bill, or that it is modelled on lines already covered by the laws of the Commonwealth. I suggest that it is an audacious proposal, utterly unprecedented in our Commonwealth legislation, and that it has not been adequately defended by the Attorney-General because it is indefensible from every point of view
> The Attorney-General suggested that the regulations proposed to be passed under this bill, under which these drastic powers to cope with the present pressing situation are to operate, ought to be laid on the table of this House and reviewed by the next Parliament when it meets.
> Mr PARSONS (N, Angas, S).—Is the honorable member not confident that he will be here then?
> Mr BRENNAN.—I may not be here, and the honorable member may not be here then. Does he think that the industrial trouble with which this emergency legislation proposes to deal will still be in existence?
> Mr PARSONS.—No, it will be all over by then.
> Mr BRENNAN.—It will. Does the honorable member suggest that these regulations will not be operative in the meantime? Does he know anything of what will be contained in them? We are asked to respect our Position as members of this House, responsible to the people of the

> country. I remind the Attorney-General that honorable members on
> this side have too much respect for our position to hand over our
> responsibilities to the Executive Government to enable it to operate
> under the authority of a blank cheque when we are not here ... I
> suggest that similar words [to Clause 3] will not be found in any other
> Act that has been passed by the Commonwealth Government.

In the last few minutes of the committee stage, Bruce moved an amendment to Clause 3, inserting the words 'but subject to the Acts Interpretation
Act'. This merely acknowledged what would have applied in any case, and
the fact remained that the executive was to receive a blank cheque. The Bill
was read a third time at 5.40 a.m. on Saturday and was promptly sent to the
Senate, where Standing and Sessional Orders were suspended to let it pass
through all stages without delay. The Bill was through by 5 p.m., less than
two hours before the Senate followed the House of Representatives into
indefinite adjournment, and on Monday morning it received royal assent.
Regulations were made within the spirit of the Act to license waterside
workers, but beyond that the executive treated its blank cheque with
discretion.

Licensed non-unionists continued to work the Melbourne wharves under
police protection, and violence erupted again. On the morning of 2 November, fifteen days before the election, several hundred unionists broke
through a cordon of twenty-three constables on Prince's Pier. The police,
finding themselves assailed on both sides, and with two of their number
injured by pieces of flying road metal, fired warning shots into the harbour.
As this had no effect, the sub-inspector in charge ordered his men to fire at
the mob. One stevedore was shot through the neck, and died from his
wound. Three others were wounded less seriously.

This sort of incident was a nightmare for governments as well as individuals. The Victorian Government was responsible for the action of its police,
but not for the larger industrial issues which led to the bloodshed on Prince's
Pier. Section 51 (xxxv) of the Constitution gave federal parliament power to
make laws with respect to conciliation and arbitration for the prevention and
settlement of industrial disputes extending beyond the limits of any one
State. Although many disputes remained within the State sphere, and were
exclusively within the State's competence, the waterfront dispute had
spread to other States and so into the Commonwealth's sphere.

In spite of unreconciled tensions on the waterfront and in other industries,
the general election of 1928 was one of the dullest on record. Predictably the
Government campaigned on law and order, but not as effectively as might
have been expected. It promised further strengthening of the arbitration system, and a cut-back on foreign migration because of rising unemployment,
the rate of which had reached 11 per cent of the working population. Labor
emphasised the need for higher tariff protection, promised to extend the
trading business of the Commonwealth Bank, and warned that the sale of
the Commonwealth shipping line to British interests would mean higher
freight charges. Both sides urged a 'Yes' vote at the referendum on the
Commonwealth's power to take over State debts, which was to be held on
polling day.

Although the coalition regained office, and retained an overwhelming majority in the Senate (27–9), it lost valuable ground in the House of Representatives. The new House consisted of forty-two Government members; thirty-one Labor, including such impressive new members as J. B. Chifley (Macquarie, N), John Curtin (Fremantle, W) and J. A. Beasley (West Sydney, N); and two rural Independents, P. G. Stewart (Wimmera, V) and W. J. McWilliams (Franklin, T). Labor had increased its representation by eight seats: six formerly held by Nationalists, one by the Country Party, and one by an Independent. The Victorian seat of Indi, which the Country Party could not have failed to hold in the normal run of events, fell to Labor purely by chance. At 3 p.m. on the day that nominations closed, the retiring Country Party member, Robert Cook, reached the divisional electoral office at Beechworth with a nomination form in his pocket, believing the closing time to be 5 p.m. In fact nominations had closed at noon, and the unopposed Labor candidate had already been declared elected.

The coalition could ill afford such an accident, for in addition to other seats lost it could no longer count upon the loyalty of all its own members in the lower house. Hughes was now further embittered by the Government's appointment of an undeserving Sir Granville Ryrie to the High Commissionership in London, a post which Hughes would have welcomed, and one hitherto reserved for ex-Prime Ministers like himself. This indestructible veteran of political catastrophe still regarded himself as an alternative leader of the Nationalist Party, and it was not impossible that other malcontents might also come to see him in that light. In the first week of the new parliament, Latham wrote to his wife: 'Personally I think we will stay in for a time—but Hughes and one or two others of "ours" are burning to put us out'. Before long, indeed, Hughes would be saying of the Bruce–Page Ministry: 'For the greater part of the last parliament I had other fish to fry, but now I am quite free, and given decent health I will make our friends Janus and Co sit up'.

The Serbonian Bog

In the very year that Stanley Bruce put the final touch to his greatest achievement as Prime Minister—a simultaneous strengthening of the Commonwealth's financial position, and improvement of its relationship with the States—he also, to the astonishment of colleagues and opponents alike, proposed to weaken the Commonwealth's industrial power. It seemed paradoxical, but Bruce was desperate. His Government was floundering in what the second president of the Arbitration Court, Mr Justice Higgins, had once called the Serbonian bog of divided Commonwealth and State industrial powers. Whole ministries had disappeared in Section 51 (xxxv) of the Constitution, and in 1929, as industrial matters went from bad to worse, Bruce began to think that his best course might be to take the Commonwealth right out of that morass.

No hint of this was contained, however, in the Governor-General's speech at the opening of the eleventh parliament on 6 February. Lord Stonehaven, who arrived at Parliament House in a state carriage, accompanied by mounted escort and greeted by an artillery salute, expressed the pious hope that a conference then taking place between representatives of those engaged in industry might reach an agreement for co-operation to solve the industrial and economic problems confronting the nation. Such a solution was badly needed, for in January the timber workers had gone on strike against an award which confirmed labour's worst suspicions about the new Conciliation and Arbitration Act by reducing wages and restoring a 48-hour week. This strike soon matched the turmoil on the waterfront. Volunteers were bashed, guns were used, and sawmills set on fire.

So far as the economy was concerned, Lord Stonehaven hoped for the best in spite of indications to the contrary. 'Owing to unfavourable seasonal conditions, and other temporary factors', he said,

> there has been a period of diminished activity in the commercial and industrial life of certain parts of the Commonwealth. Notwithstanding these adverse circumstances, which have necessarily affected public revenues, the financial position of the Commonwealth is sound. Conditions have already improved, and there are encouraging indications that the coming year will witness a return to normal prosperity.

The Leader of the Opposition, who took a more serious view of the economy, and in each of the two previous years had warned the Government about the extent of Australia's overseas borrowing and trade deficit, found nothing in the Governor-General's speech worth discussing in the Address-in-Reply debate. After only six minutes, Scullin ended his speech abruptly: 'I do not propose to assist in a futile discussion. If the Government has business to do, if it proposes to carry out those works which it promised to the people of Australia, let it drop this obsolete procedure and begin immediately upon the real problems of the country'.

In the first week of parliament Bruce introduced the Financial Agreement Validation Bill, which, thanks to the referendum result, would remove any lingering doubts about the agreement. He also narrowly escaped defeat on the floor of the House over an industrial issue. On 13 February a Labor member, Percy Coleman (Reid, N), took the unusual course of moving that a recent award by a public service arbitrator should be printed. Regulations embodying such awards were automatically laid before each house of parliament for scrutiny and possible veto. Coleman's motion, if passed, would have amounted to approval; the Government, however, was anxious that the award should not be approved, for it granted some public servants a special Canberra allowance which might have had a wider impact on wage levels. Bruce moved that Coleman be no longer heard, and the motion was carried by only two votes, with one Nationalist, Mann, and two Independents voting with the Opposition.

Scullin then made the point that while the Government was condemning unionists all over Australia for failing to observe awards of the Arbitration Court, here it too was endeavouring to defeat an award given by a public service arbitrator. Bruce replied that the Canberra allowance had been provided for public servants transferred there compulsorily, and that now public servants were coming to the capital in the normal course of promotion. To pay them a special allowance would be unfair to those who were transferred to other parts of Australia where the cost of living was just as high as in Canberra.

In this debate Hughes spoke forcefully against his own side, maintaining that the principle of arbitration was at stake. If the award was to be disallowed, he added, it should be disallowed not by the Senate (as the Government apparently intended, for there was already a motion for disallowance on the Senate's business paper), but by the House of Representatives. Hughes argued that the present members of the Senate had not been elected by a recent vote of the people, for those elected in November would not take their seats until June 1929. He suggested that the Opposition withdraw its motion, and that the House be given an opportunity to debate a motion for disallowance. If that was done, he said, he would vote with the Government; if not, he would vote against it.

Scullin agreed to withdraw Coleman's motion, but the Government was not prepared to follow the rest of Hughes's prescription and the question was put forthwith. The House divided 35–35, with Hughes, Mann and the two Independents joining the 'Ayes'. Only the Speaker's casting vote could save the government, and Sir Littleton Groom obliged. 'The numbers being equal', he said,

> the decision of the question rests with me, and I desire to give my reasons for the course I propose to take. If this were merely a motion for the printing of a paper, the matter would be easy to determine; but as it is intended to obtain a vote of the House upon a different issue, I shall follow the practice of my predecessors in this chair, and to give an opportunity to deal with that issue on a specific motion, cast my vote with the noes.

But of course the issue was dealt with in the other place, where the Government could safely rely on numbers not being equal. On 21 February the Senate disapproved the award by 23 votes to 6.

That same day the Nationalist Party unanimously passed a resolution of confidence in Bruce's leadership. As the Prime Minister himself sardonically remarked, 'to have a vote of confidence passed in one is a certain indication that there is some lack of it'. Indeed it was well known outside the party room that Hughes and Mann had abstained from voting. Before the vote was taken, Hughes attacked the Government for securing disallowance of the public service award in the Senate rather than the lower house, and according to the *Argus* he went as far as to remind his party colleagues that retirement from office by Bruce and his Ministry need not necessarily mean the succession of a Labor Ministry. 'If Mr Bruce decided to resign', he was reported as saying, 'it would be his duty not to advise His Excellency the Governor-General to send for Mr Scullin, but for "Mr Jones, of the Nationalist Party"'. The Welsh choice of anonym would not have been lost on Hughes's audience.

Now that Billy had shown his colours he turned his baleful attention to the coalition's junior partner. On 15 March, while Dr Page was absent from the chamber, Hughes used the Supply debate to belittle the Country Party's performance as protector of the man on the land, and to offer his own services in that role.

They came in to advance the interests of the man on the land. I have always stood for his interests; I have been waiting long—and in vain—to follow them, in the almost forlorn hope that something might be done for a fast vanishing race. It is my fortune to represent a constituency where agriculture cannot be said to flourish, but what ... [the Country Party] needs is a new banner bearer, and I offer it my services. I have said very little, by comparison with them, about new States, but if I had been for six years where they have been, I would have had States sprinkled as thickly over this great continent as potatoes in a paddock, or I would have disembowelled the Ministry. This, I say in order to commend myself to their favour when in their more sober moments they turn over the offer that I have made.

The offer was bizarre, coming as it did from the big smoke of North Sydney, and from someone more adept at disembowelling ministries than planting potatoes. Earle Page gave it short shrift at the next sitting. 'His purpose', he said,

is to disrupt the alliance between the Nationalist and Country parties ... There is an ugly name given to soldiers who enlist in one camp, yet poison the wells of their own forces and give ammunition, even though it be dud ammunition, to the enemy. The right honorable gentleman, who has lost the leadership of two other parties, said that he now aspired to the leadership of the Country Party and offered himself as a banner bearer and a new leader. The political treachery of his attacks of the last few months against the Government he was elected to support is sufficient to disqualify him permanently from the leadership of any party.

Another veteran of earlier parliaments, King O'Malley, wrote in characteristic vein to Page, as if warming himself at the glowing coals of old enmity:

I desire to congratulate you on at last turning on that vicious little mugwump—Billy Hughes. "Mugwump" means a politician who has been in all parties, but belongs to none. In my opinion he has reached the saturation point in egotism and self-constituted importance ... In fact, he is so poisonous and vicious in his hatred for all thinking human beings that he is in my opinion a mental and moral political derelict, capable of separating a cripple from his crutches.

As if the waterfront and timber industry were not causing troubles enough, in early March some twelve thousand miners were dismissed from their jobs on the northern coalfields of New South Wales after refusing to accept a reduction of one shilling per ton in the award rate for hewing coal. The employer mainly responsible for this lock-out was John Brown, a legendary coal baron who might have been invented by Galsworthy or Sinclair Lewis. Although reputed to have secretly paid some of his employees' food bills during an earlier closure, Brown was better known as a hard negotiator and a successful racehorse owner. According to the new Member for Hunter—Rowley James, a former miner himself—John Brown had told his locked-out employees: 'You cows, I will see you eat grass'. Brown, for his part, justified the lock-out on grounds of the depressed price for coal and the greatly diminished export trade: he could not afford to keep the mines open. Although it may have been irrelevant to the argument, those seeking to denigrate Brown pointed out that he owned 240 brood mares and seven stallions, and in the last few years had won about £100 000 in racing stakes.

On 22 March, the last sitting day before parliament adjourned for five months, the Attorney-General announced that the Government would prosecute Brown in connection with the lock-out, under provisions of the Industrial Peace Act and the Conciliation and Arbitration Act. Anything could happen in a recess, however, and two weeks later the Prime Minister, while opening a peace conference between colliery owners and mining unions, announced that the prosecution against Brown had been withdrawn in the hope (vain, as it was to turn out) of establishing a more conciliatory atmosphere in the industry. More unexpected still, on 28 May, the first day of a Premiers' Conference in Canberra, the Prime Minister sent all Government members the following telegram:

> Am making important announcement in opening premiers' conference today with regard to industrial matters and desire to advise you of government's attitude before making public. After very careful consideration government has come to the conclusion that dual control of industrial matters by commonwealth and states has produced a situation which in the interests of industry and the community cannot be allowed to continue. States or commonwealth may be able to deal with the problem but it is impossible for both to do so at the same time. Accordingly the government is proposing to states that either they immediately give full powers to commonwealth or that commonwealth repeals its industrial legislation.

Such perfunctory warning could not have done much to lessen the amazement with which members read in the following day's newspapers that Bruce had indeed proposed something never formally discussed with either of the Government parties, and not so much as hinted at during the recent election campaign. George Maxwell, whose blindness prevented him from even reading the newspapers, said the news came like a bolt from the blue. All premiers stated immediately and more or less definitely that they regarded industrial matters as primarily a concern of the States, and could therefore not agree to give the Commonwealth exclusive powers. Accepting this decision, Bruce told the premiers that his Ministry would ask parliament to abolish the Arbitration Court, retaining under Commonwealth control only the shipping and waterside industries, over which parliament already had sufficiently complete powers under the Trade and Commerce subsection of Section 51.

Some additional justifications were advanced by others for this remarkable decision. Perhaps Bruce was trying to bluff the States into transferring their industrial powers. He was also said to be concerned that worsening economic conditions might impose a greater need for wage reduction, and was anxious to transfer the onus for that on to State tribunals. Certainly there was no legal obstacle to what Bruce was proposing. As the *Sydney Morning Herald* reminded its readers, the fathers of the Constitution had given the Commonwealth power to make laws with respect to disputes extending beyond the limits of any one State, but had not *compelled* it to do so. 'Even those who espoused [Section 51 xxxv] most warmly', it said, 'did so with the reservation that whether it was used or not was entirely a matter for the Parliament'. The insertion of an industrial power had been first proposed at the Adelaide federal convention, but there it was defeated. At the Melbourne convention H. B. Higgins, whose life had ended only four months before Bruce issued his ultimatum to the premiers, raised the matter again. This time sub-section xxxv was adopted, by 22 votes to 19. It was carried only because several delegates who had voted against it in Adelaide changed their minds in Melbourne, perhaps as a result of Higgins's eloquence. 'I do not ask the committee to say that arbitration shall be compulsory', he said, 'or even that any steps shall be taken to secure the settlement of industrial disputes; I simply wish to give the Federal Parliament power to legislate on the subject'. Another influential delegate, Sir William Zeal, remarked: 'There is no harm in it, but there will be great difficulty in giving effect to it under certain circumstances'.

That prediction was borne out by the frequency with which parliament found reason to amend the Conciliation and Arbitration Act after its first enactment in 1904—a series of twelve amending acts, or an average of one every two years. 'There has never been anything but dissatisfaction in one quarter or another with the Act', said the *Sydney Morning Herald*,

> passed in the first instance as a compromise after months of shameful political wrangling and lobbying . . . Actual or technical 'extension of disputes' [beyond the limits of any one State] has been the method used by trade unions to enlarge the field of Federal jurisdiction . . . in order to create the widest possible choice of what the late Mr Justice Higgins called 'rival shops'. The Federal Court finally broke down the resistance of the States against its interference in purely State domain to an extent which has made serious inroads on the sovereign powers of the States. The conflict has become so serious that, under the latest Federal amending Act, where a State award or a State law is at variance with a decision of the Federal Arbitration Court the latter shall prevail. The consequences are profoundly disturbing to both industry and politics in the States.

Bruce's proposal made some sense, then, on grounds of federalism as well as the supposed advantage of undivided industrial power and (from the Commonwealth's point of view) the passing of an increasingly difficult buck to the States. The Royal Commission appointed two years earlier to inquire into the working of the Constitution was by this time reaching a conclusion similar to Bruce's, but it would not be unanimous, and in any case its report was still six months away. 'In our opinion', a majority of the seven Commissioners would eventually report, recommending deletion of sub-section xxxv, 'industrial legislation should be regarded as a function of the States . . . We do not think that it would be for the good of Australia that the Commonwealth Parliament should be occupied with industrial questions or that Federal elections should turn on industrial issues'. A minority of three held a different view. 'If the [industrial] power is removed from the Commonwealth', they reported, 'and vested in the States, an intolerable condition of unfair competition between manufacturers in different states owing to varying rates of pay and conditions of employment will be created. One of the benefits of a central government is that it can remove danger of this character'. This dissenting opinion was of only academic interest, for the Royal Commission's report was destined to sink without trace.

Far more significant expressions of disapproval, which Bruce had sadly underestimated, were those of the Opposition, the dissident Nationalists and the electorate at large. Whatever justifications might be contrived for Bruce's proposal, many Australians were deeply suspicious of it. One hundred and forty-nine trade unions with some seven hundred thousand members were bound by awards of the Commonwealth Arbitration Court. In the main they were satisfied with the judicial treatment they received, and suspicious that any other system would mean lower wages. If Bruce's proposal went through, federal unions would find themselves having to deal with as many as six different State tribunals. To the Opposition, Bruce's proposal seemed to promise victory; to Hughes it promised revenge.

The immediate outlook for Bruce was stormier than he could have expected, for when parliament reassembled on 14 August 1929 the Bruce–Page coalition had little more than a month left to it. On the second sitting day, the Opposition moved want of confidence in the Government on grounds that, by withdrawing the lock-out prosecution against a millionaire like John Brown, after its vigorous prosecution of trade unionists, it was unjustly discriminating between the rich and the poor. In the absence of Scullin, who was ill with influenza and pleurisy, the new Deputy Leader, Theodore (Blakeley had stepped down to make way for him after the 1928 election), led the attack. He widened the case to embrace three other millionaires for whose welfare the Government had also been solicitous—the Abrahams brothers, who had been allowed to leave the country in spite of alleged tax frauds amounting to £500 000; and the cattle king, Sir Sidney Kidman, who had successfully evaded the payment of land tax. After an all-nighter on 21–22 August, the motion was defeated by 28 votes to 32, with Hughes and Mann paired against the Government, the Independent McWilliams voting with Labor, and the Independent Stewart absent from the chamber when the vote was taken.

The narrowness of this escape seemed to inspire Bruce with a greater sense of urgency about arbitration. After Question Time that afternoon, he sought leave to bring in a Maritime Industries Bill, by means of which the Commonwealth was to be hauled out of the industrial bog. This was an eventful day. The Bill was read a first time, and the second reading was made an order of the day for the next sitting. Dr Page then brought down his seventh consecutive Budget, and some time before midnight the Nationalist Party also found time to rid itself of Hughes and Mann. 'We have been asked by the Prime Minister', wrote the Nationalist Whip to the two offenders,

to inform you that in view of your general attitude towards the Government, and particularly of your speech and vote in the House on the recent censure motion, he does not propose in future to regard you as a supporter of the Government, and that in future no invitations to attend party meetings will be issued to you.

The tone of Page's Budget speech was distinctly less confident than in 1928, when he had invoked 'the wonderful recuperative powers of the Commonwealth'. The Tragic Treasurer now had an accumulated deficit of £5 million, which he hoped to reduce to £3.5 million by various means including a super-tax on incomes of more than £2000 per annum and a new amusement tax of 5 per cent on total receipts. He warned, however, that Australia faced two main difficulties: a decline in the value of its production, caused by falling prices of staple commodities, and the danger of an actual diminution in production, caused by industrial disturbances.

Before Page's Budget could be debated, the House turned its attention to the Maritime Industries Bill. This measure, as Bruce explained in his second reading speech, would provide machinery to establish the industrial regulation of the shipping and waterside industries by a new type of tribunal, one created not under Section 51 (xxxv), as the Arbitration Court had been, but under Section 51 (i), the Trade and Commerce power. The title of the Bill implied that the new tribunal was its only concern. But in fact the most important clauses were those repealing the Conciliation and Arbitration Acts and Industrial Peace Acts and thereby abandoning industrial regulation to the States, except for regulation of the maritime industries and Commonwealth employees.

Once again Theodore led the Opposition's attack in place of a leader who was ill in bed. 'One man is proposing to undo the work of a generation of men', he said in a well reasoned and forceful speech. He showed that Australia had fewer industrial disputes than many other countries, including Britain and the United States, and that the federal system of awards and agreements did not conflict or overlap to any great extent with State laws. On the other hand, abolition of that system would produce overlap and conflict between various State tribunals. 'The action which the Government proposes', he concluded,

> involves a weakening of the Federal spirit. The Government is proposing weakly to surrender the authority of the Commonwealth and retire from the field of industrial legislation, one of the most important functions entrusted to its care and administration by the Constitution without any excuse dating further back than a couple of months. The Opposition will do all that is permissible under the Standing Orders to prevent the Government from effecting its unworthy purpose by means of this proposed legislation.

As the second reading debate continued into September, the excommunicated Nationalists Hughes and Mann declared themselves unequivocally against the Bill.

> Mr MANN.—A quaint local custom of one of the old Greek States was, that any one desiring to bring into the State a new law should appear before an assembly of the citizens to propound that law with a halter round his neck, so that should the law not meet with the approval of the Assembly, or not be considered necessary for the requirements of the State, the halter might properly be used to strangle him.
> Mr HUGHES.—Oh, that those days might come back again!

Mr MANN.—In the position in which we find ourselves today, we have a
counterpart of that custom, because the Ministry is standing before this
House with a bill for which it asks the approval of the House. If the
House rejects it, there is little doubt but that politically execution will
properly be administered to the Government.

Mann declared that he would vote against the second reading motion, and
so did Maxwell, whose Nationalist loyalty was being eroded by a mixture of
what Latham later described as 'genuine idealism, personal vanity, and dislike of Bruce'. On 5 September Hughes brought to the debate not only his
scalding rhetoric but also a perspective that took in all of parliament's
twenty-nine years. 'From the inception of federation', he said,

until this ill-omened day the watchword of the National Parliament has
been "Advance Australia". The Leaders of parties, whether in office or in
opposition, have striven zealously to develop and exercise the authority
vested in this Parliament by the framers of the Constitution. Checked in
one direction by decisions of the High Court, they have striven along
other lines; but their advance has never halted . . . It has remained for this
Government to sound the trumpet for a general and shameful retreat from
a difficult but vitally important strategic position.
    The system of Commonwealth industrial arbitration has serious
defects, but the purpose of this bill is not to remedy them; not to improve
the system, but to destroy it. At one fell stroke it wipes out all industrial
laws passed during the last 25 years . . . It leaves not one stone standing
upon another of that temple of industrial legislation slowly and painfully
reared by successive governments. And it does this in the name of industrial peace!

Hughes said that he hoped the second reading would be defeated, but added
that, if it were not, he would move in committee an amendment to the effect
that the measure should not be proclaimed until it had been submitted to the
people either at a referendum or a general election. According to Latham,
who advised his colleagues that the Government had no constitutional
power to hold a referendum of this kind, Hughes had specified a referendum
solely to bolster the courage of those of his potential supporters for whom an
early election held no attraction.

The second reading was carried on 7 September by a majority of only four.
Hughes, Mann, Maxwell and Stewart voted against it; but McWilliams, in
spite of an ominous speech, voted with the Government. So did the
Nationalist, Walter Marks, although he too was known to be out of sorts with
the Government. Marks was a fitting successor to the previous Member for
Sydney's upper-crust electorate of Wentworth, Willie Kelly. He was a
wealthy clubman, belonging to no fewer than forty-two clubs, and had substantial investments in the coal industry and real estate. In 1921 Marks had
surprised his parliamentary colleagues by delivering an earnest speech,
replete with biblical authority, about the coming Armageddon, which he
expected in 1934. Nonethless he was a successful businessman with a keen
interest in motion pictures. He was an amateur cinematographer, went
religiously to the pictures three times a week, and chaired a royal commission on the moving picture industry in Australia. One cause of his party

disaffection was that his royal commission report in 1928 had been ignored by the Government. Another was the Government's failure to consult him about the entertainment tax, which was going to bear onerously on film exhibitors.

When parliament met again at 3 p.m. on 10 September, Bruce moved that the Maritime Industries Bill be considered an urgent bill, so that guillotine time limits could be applied. The Bill was declared urgent, again with a majority of four. Marks was still among the 'Ayes', but the Government had reason to believe that when Hughes moved his foreshadowed amendment, requiring approval by the electorate, Marks would vote for it. The House went into committee and Hughes moved his amendment at 3.55 p.m. Bruce accepted the challenge, saying that if it was passed his Government would go to the people. This was intended to stiffen the resolve of Government members in the vote that would soon be taken, and the resolve most in need of stiffening was that of Walter Marks. The Chairman of Committees avoided giving Marks the call to speak before he suspended the sitting for dinner, and during the adjournment Government emissaries looked in vain for him, hoping to ascertain and if necessary alter his intention. He was later said to have been playing billiards with Billy Hughes.

Marks spoke immediately after dinner, expressing cautious approval of the Bill, but also supporting Hughes's amendment. 'I regret to have to do it', he concluded, 'but my conscience compels me to vote for the amendment'. It now seemed likely, but still not certain, that the Bruce–Page Government would be defeated 35–34 on an issue which the Prime Minister had accepted as one of confidence. The Chairman of Committees, James Bayley (Oxley, Q), was a loyal Nationalist, but as Chairman he could not cast a deliberative vote. Only if the numbers were equal could he decide the outcome with his casting vote. The forgetful Robert Cook could have saved the day, if only he had remembered to lodge his nomination in time. There was still, however, one potential voter who could in theory produce a tie which would then be converted into a negative decision by the Chairman's casting vote. This was the Speaker, who was entitled to a deliberative vote in Committee as well as a casting vote in the House. But would Sir Littleton Groom oblige?

Earlier that year Groom had used his casting vote to save the Government from embarrassment over the public service award; and in the Commonwealth parliament, unlike the House of Commons, there were precedents for a Speaker voting deliberatively in committee. Speaker McDonald had once saved a Labor Government by that means, and Speaker Johnson had rendered a similar service to the Cook Ministry. On this occasion, Speaker Groom, a mild and somewhat pedantic man, once likened to the president of a ladies' seminary, had already decided to follow the House of Commons practice of not voting during proceedings.

The *Sydney Morning Herald* had reported as much that morning, without comment, but the possible implication of such a decision was obvious to the Prime Minister. Bruce must have been expecting the worst for, according to a letter dated 10 September, he and Latham visited the Governor-General that afternoon, presumably before parliament sat. After completing their undisclosed business with Lord Stonehaven, they drove to The Lodge, where—

again according to the letter, written some time that day by Latham to his wife—'Bruce offered to retire in my favour and to give me strong and warm support as Prime Minister. I refused'. He also confided to Bruce that some days earlier a journalist claiming to speak with authority from the Opposition had come to him with a proposal that, if he would replace Bruce as Leader of the Nationalist Party, and postpone the arbitration proposal for a year, Labor would guarantee him that period as prime minister. He declined the offer, if a genuine offer it was.

Late that afternoon the Prime Minister went to the Speaker's suite, to see what he could do about Groom. 'Just before the House rose for dinner', Groom wrote to his wife in Toowoomba,

> Bruce came to see me. It was about the time Walter Marks wanted to speak. They must have known what he was going to do. Bruce asked me to come in to the House. I told him I had thought it all over. I reminded him that our party had always stood for British traditions and that the absolute impartiality of the office of Speaker was the most sacred. He argued that the damage to the office of Speaker was small compared to the damage of the Government going out of office. We talked for a while on the subject and he made further appeals. I told him I had studied the matter carefully from every aspect and could not see my way to do it. At about 9 o'clock the division bell sounded. I did not go in.

It must be suspected that Sir Littleton's stern adherence to impartiality was sweetened with at least a certain amount of vengeance. The Prime Minister who had been appealing to him so urgently was the same person who had moved him from the Attorney-Generalship to make way for Latham, and who had subsequently tried, though unsuccessfully, to replace him as Speaker with the more compliant Bayley.

While Sir Littleton remained in his room, the committee divided, with every member present or paired: 'Ayes', 35; 'Noes', 34. Hughes, Mann, Marks, Maxwell, McWilliams and Stewart had all voted with the Opposition, and so the question (which was not so much that the Maritime Industries Bill be referred to referendum or election, as that yet another ministry should fall victim to industrial arbitration) was resolved in the affirmative. The House resumed, and the Chairman formally reported what had happened in committee. Using the conventional parlance of defeat on the floor of the House, Bruce announced that in consequence of the vote that had just been taken the Government desired an opportunity to consider its position. He then moved the adjournment until three the following afternoon.

Next day's sitting lasted only two minutes, during which Bruce told the House he had tendered certain advice to the Governor-General at an interview that morning. The possibilities being canvassed by the press were for a reconstructed Nationalist Government, led by Latham; a Labor Government, led by Scullin and supported by the Hughes group; and even more improbably, a Hughes Government supported by Labor. But in fact, as Bruce informed parliament on 12 September, he had advised the Governor-General to grant a dissolution of the House of Representatives, and although the eleventh parliament was only seven months old His Excellency had accepted that advice. With the salutary memory of Lord Byng so fresh in his mind, how could Lord Stonehaven have done otherwise?

Dr Page then introduced a bill for supply to carry on the public services of the Commonwealth until after a general election. This took only nine minutes to pass through all stages of the lower house, and five minutes in the Senate. Bruce went out with characteristic style, lounging at ease while others spoke, and somehow managing, when the time came to move the adjournment, to congratulate Mr Speaker on the manner in which he had conducted the business of the House. As the House adjourned, Bruce hurried across the chamber calling, as Bruggins might have called along the towpath at Cambridge, 'Scullin! Scullin! Let's shake hands. We are going into the ring, and I think it's usual for opponents to do that'.

Both Bruce and Scullin campaigned almost exclusively on the arbitration issue, though Bruce could not resist the pleasure of also attacking Sir Littleton Groom in his electorate on the issue of the Speaker's vote. In a letter to all Darling Downs electors, he invited support for the Nationalist candidate standing against Groom, who styled himself as Independent Nationalist. 'A vote for Sir Littleton', he told them, 'is a vote for Mr Theodore and the Labor Party against the Government'. Hughes, Mann and Maxwell also stood as Independent Nationalists. They too were opposed by endorsed Nationalists, but were granted electoral immunity by Labor, as also were McWilliams and Stewart.

Apart from arbitration and the fear that a state-regulated arbitration system would mean lower wages ('Not a penny off the pay', went one Labor slogan, 'nor a minute on the day'), the only issues remarked on by the press were the northern coalfields lock-out, the withdrawal of prosecution against John Brown, and the amusement tax. Scullin managed to avoid committing himself about the lock-out, but Theodore was less prudent. To his leader's annoyance he told a meeting in the Hunter Valley that if Labor was elected to office the mines would be reopened on the men's terms within a fortnight. The worsening international economic situation, which would later be regarded in retrospect as a backdrop of impending cataclysm, was referred to by some of the players in this electoral drama; but no one conveyed any real sense of crisis, and some Labor members even spoke of recovery. Also unforeseen was the resounding nature of the verdict soon to be delivered by an enigmatic electorate.

The result of the election on 12 October was the greatest landslide since the Nationalist victory of 1917, and Hughes, despite the disappointment of his vain hopes for another Prime Ministership, must have relished it almost as keenly as that earlier confounding of his enemies. Labor won forty-six of the seventy-five seats; Nationalists, fourteen; Country Party, ten; and Independents, five. But this election had been only for the lower house, and whereas the victors of 1917 had won all eighteen seats in the half-Senate election as well as fifty-three seats in the House of Representatives, the victors of 1929 would still face an implacably hostile Senate.

No fewer than five outgoing ministers lost their seats, including Bruce himself—the first and only Prime Minister ever defeated in his own seat. In humiliating contrast to his 12 000 majority at the previous election, Bruce lost the seat of Flinders by 305 votes to the president and general secretary of Melbourne Trades Hall Council, E. J. Holloway. Of the rebels who had brought about his downfall, Hughes, Marks and Maxwell were returned with their majorities relatively unchanged. Stewart and McWilliams were also returned, though the latter died before parliament was summoned, and the consequent by-election resulted in another victory for Labor. Mann was badly defeated in Perth by a Nationalist, W. M. Nairn; and in Darling Downs, Sir Littleton Groom paid the penalty for his ambivalent impartiality. On the first count he was 9948 votes behind the Nationalist, A. C. Morgan, who won the seat after distribution of preferences.

Bruce could at least savour the thought that Groom's trouncing had been worse than his own. 'The satisfactory feature of the election', he wrote to a friend, 'was that little Groom was dealt with. He really behaved extraordinarily badly and deserved all that he got'. This was small consolation compared to the extent of his own ministerial and personal defeat. Yet he took it with his usual sang-froid and on 14 October returned to the quiet of Canberra, there to clear up his departmental work and perhaps reflect upon the fickleness of the electors who had now buried their first ministry along with Gale and McGregor in the bush. Such reflection should have given rise to satisfaction as well as regret, for Bruce had been an effective Prime Minister even if his judgement had failed him badly near the end. He had held office for six years and eight months. This was longer than any other Ministry since federation, longer than the combined Ministries of Deakin or Fisher, and not far short of the seven-and-a-quarter years of Hughes's four Ministries.

While Bruce was in Canberra a newly elected member from South Australia, Charles Hawker, wrote offering to stand down from his seat, Wakefield, so that Bruce might contest it at a by-election. Bruce declined the offer, saying it was 'possibly as well that I should be out of the running for a little time, because the people have had me for many years now, and probably a relief from constantly hearing of me will strengthen my position and the party's'. Soon afterwards he sailed for England—to see the university boat race, as he told the newspapers, and to tend the affairs of Paterson, Laing & Bruce. The latter would keep him busier than he knew, for the approaching cataclysm would be no respecter of families or their businesses.

9

Serpent's Eggs

As the train carrying the next prime minister pulled into Canberra station on Monday morning, 21 October 1929, the Canberra City Band, with unwitting irony, played 'See the Conquering Hero Comes'. Many public servants had stopped work in order to welcome Mr and Mrs Scullin. Lord Stonehaven, who had arrived by viceregal carriage on the same train, passed almost unnoticed through the cheering crowd of about six hundred on the platform, though his aide-de-camp, Captain J. M. Blakiston-Houston of the 11th Hussars, was chiacked while clearing a way for His Excellency through the side gate. Addressing the crowd with his usual lack of pretension, James Scullin said that Labor had made no lavish promises. It had promised an ordered system of work to assist progress and prosperity, and would redeem that promise. 'When our time ends', he said, 'we hope to leave behind a better state of affairs than our predecessors have left for us'. The Scullins then drove to the Hotel Canberra, which for reasons of public economy they had chosen as their residence in preference to The Lodge. Later Scullin's wife Sarah visited Canberra Hospital to donate the many bouquets she had received on the way from Melbourne, and Scullin went to the Prime Minister's room in Parliament House, where he talked with Theodore and waited for the Governor-General's summons.

Most Labor members stayed at the non-licensed Kurrajong Hotel, and that evening in the hotel's recreation room there was a rowdy sing-song culminating, to the annoyance of outnumbered Nationalist guests, in a loud rendition of 'The Red Flag'. High spirits were understandable on the eve of a Caucus meeting to elect Labor's first federal ministry since 1916. But although the new Opposition raised the matter at the earliest opportunity in the Senate, 'The Red Flag' was no more reliable a forecast than 'See the Conquering Hero Comes'. For all his merits, Scullin was not made of heroes' stuff. He and his party may have conquered the Bruce–Page coalition, but now they faced difficulties that would have dismayed anyone.

Scullin was taking office with the largest one-party majority ever achieved in the House of Representatives, but in the Senate his Government would still have only seven votes compared to the Nationalist Party's twenty-four and the Country Party's five. Frank Anstey, borrowing aptly from *Julius Caesar*, wrote in his memoirs that on coming to power the Scullin Government found itself 'sitting on the eggs of the serpent'—eggs which, in Brutus's words, should be killed in the shell lest, being hatched, they follow their nature and grow mischievous. The Senate was an egg that could be crushed, in the event of disagreement between the houses, if the Government had sufficient resolve to seek a double dissolution which might give it control of both houses. Anstey himself advocated such a course, but few of his colleagues fancied the idea. After thirteen years in Opposition most of them were looking forward to office, with or without power, and were not in the least anxious to play double or quits. By the same token the Senate majority was in no hurry to meet the people either, and so the main questions of the twelfth Parliament would be how far the Government was prepared to restrain its demands on the hostile Senate, and how much the Senate was prepared to give the Government—a delicate balancing act performed in the mutual interest of avoiding premature election.

Some of the serpent's eggs were even harder to crush than the Senate, and Labor could do little more than fearfully watch them hatch. The most immediate problem bequeathed by the previous Government was the coalfields lock-out, which Theodore had rashly undertaken to settle within a fortnight. Scullin presided over a fruitless peace conference in November, and the dispute dragged on miserably. More disturbing still was the looming economic catastrophe which revealed itself symbolically during the week Scullin's Ministry was sworn into office. Already the economy was in an acutely vulnerable position. For the last four years Australia had been importing far more than it exported, and borrowing heavily to pay for its continuing programme of urban industrialisation. The Commonwealth Bank had been exporting gold to narrow the trade deficit; but there were limits to the gold reserve, and to make matters worse prices for Australia's two main exports had fallen steeply during 1929—the price of wool by 30 per cent, and of wheat by 10 per cent.

Before Scullin took office, he received an unexpected invitation from the chairman of the Commonwealth Bank, Sir Robert Gibson. 'I saw him in his own rooms in Melbourne', Scullin recalled several years later,

in company with the Governor of the bank, and he placed before me the figures regarding Australia's financial position in London. I was staggered . . . The overseas debt had increased by £53 000 000, and a similar sum, or a little more, had been borrowed by the six State governments . . . These obligations had to be met at a time when prices had tumbled and the volume of exports had fallen.

And worse was to come. Two days after Scullin's Ministry took office, the

New York Stock Exchange collapsed. The events of that 'Black Thursday' were reported in Saturday's *Canberra Times* under the headlines: 'New York Bears Cause Collapse/Worst Break in History/Wild Scenes on 'Change/ Millions of Shares Sold'.

To make matters still worse for Scullin, his Cabinet was relatively inexperienced, and his party ill-disciplined. Only two ministers had extensive Cabinet experience, and that at the State level. They had both been premiers: Theodore, who now became Treasurer; and the newly elected Tasmanian, J. A. Lyons (Wilmot), who received less than he expected when Scullin made him Postmaster-General. The Attorney-General was Frank Brennan, and the Minister for Defence was A. E. ('Texas') Green. Although newcomers to Cabinet, Brennan and Green—like Scullin, Blakeley (Home Affairs), James Fenton (Trade and Customs) and Parker Maloney (Markets and Transport) —had considerable parliamentary and committee experience to their credit.

It was said that although Cabinet included eight Roman Catholics, mostly of Irish descent like Scullin and Lyons, its only rebel was an Englishman: Frank Anstey, the Minister for Health and Repatriation. But this overlooked two of the Catholics—Theodore, whose capacity for independent thought and action was never in doubt, and Jack Beasley, the young radical from Sydney Trades Hall who squeezed into Cabinet as an honorary minister. Scullin's majority in the lower house was too big for comfort, permitting backbenchers and even ministers to pursue their own ends in a way the party would not have tolerated in a more evenly divided chamber. Anstey was never backward in telling his Caucus and Cabinet colleagues where they were wrong, or drowning political sorrows in company with his long-time protégé, John Curtin. Curtin, a former editor of the *West Australian Worker*, enjoyed Anstey's bibulous but stimulating conversation. 'Lend us a fiver', he would ask one of his friends in the Press Gallery. 'Frank Anstey and I want to go on the scoot.' Theodore also had subversive allies, and was counted an enemy by Beasley and other federal parts of the Lang machine in New South Wales.

On the Opposition side, Latham had succeeded to leadership of the Nationalist Party, with Gullett as deputy. Page still led the Country Party, while Billy Hughes had to make do with leadership of a newly formed splinter group, the Australian Party. Hughes's only followers were Marks and Maxwell in the lower house and Senator W. L. Duncan (N). The Australian Party was never officially recognised in parliament, and before long it vanished altogether.

The twelfth parliament was opened on 20 November, and in fourteen sitting days before Christmas it performed certain obvious tasks. In place of the defeated Speaker, the House of Representatives elected a Methodist lay preacher from South Australia, Norman Makin (Lab, Hindmarsh). Speaker Makin discontinued the use of the Mace, which he pronounced 'a relic of barbarism', and dispensed with 'fancy dress', wearing instead a black suit and black bow tie.

The deficit left by the previous Government had not diminished, as Page had hoped; on the contrary, it had grown to £6 500 000, and so the new Treasurer had to supplement the Budget as soon as possible. Before

Christmas he also saw through all stages a Commonwealth Bank Act which in effect removed Australia from the gold standard. This was a storm precaution by means of which the Commonwealth Bank could require all holders of gold coin and bullion to exchange them for notes, and could also prohibit the export of gold. Similar action had recently been taken in many other countries, including the United Kingdom. The Senate agreed to the Bill with several amendments, but when the lower house disagreed to some of these amendments the Senate did not insist upon them.

If Scullin needed any evidence of backbench waywardness, it was thrust before him by the member of Caucus most keenly aware of the continuing coalfields lock-out, Rowley James. At a Caucus meeting on 3 December, shortly before the House of Representatives sat at 3 p.m., Scullin drew attention to the fact that James intended moving the adjournment of the House for a debate on the coal situation. He went on to warn that before any member could take such a step it was necessary for him to secure the consent of the party. In spite of that, James immediately followed certain procedural advice which, unknown to the party, he had obtained from the ever-helpful Billy Hughes. He went straight from Caucus into the chamber and, before the business of the day was called on, rose to propose moving the adjournment for the purpose of discussing 'a definite matter of urgent public importance', which he would be permitted to do under Standing Orders if five other members supported him by also rising in their places. He was supported by only two Labor men, David Watkins (Newcastle) and H. P. Lazzarini (Werriwa, N), but there was no shortage of support from the other side. James, who had learnt his oratory at pit top meetings, then proceeded to butt his party in the midriff:

> I called Mr Bruce and his followers the greatest traitors Australia has produced. But they were not. They at least were true to the class that sent them here. They did what they were asked to do. This Government, on the other hand, has failed to carry out its promises. We cannot get away from that fact. The suffering people whom I represent have been used as a political football, and have been kicked by both sides . . .

Scullin was in a cleft stick. How could he deny James's angry charges of inaction? The Government had flinched from the only feasible way of ending the lock-out on union terms, which would have involved sending troops to take over the mines, and had not even revived the prosecution against John Brown. All Scullin could do was excuse James's insubordination and hope that it was not infectious. 'I disregard [his] charges, to some extent', he said,

> and also excuse the honorable member, in a certain degree, for the tone in which some of his statements were uttered. I realize that the honorable member feels his position keenly, because he represents a constituency that has suffered for eight or nine months through the situation in the coal industry.

Never was cheek turned more deftly. The debate continued for its permitted two hours, and then the business of the day was called on. At the next

Caucus meeting James was gently taken to task, but replied that he had no regrets to offer the party for his action.

The initiative in the coal dispute was left to a conservative New South Wales Government, which provided police protection for the reopening of Rothbury colliery with non-union labour. At 5.30 a.m. on 16 December several thousand miners broke down the fence at Rothbury and invaded the colliery grounds. The police made a baton charge. Three revolver shots were allegedly fired by miners, without hitting anyone, and the police then opened their own revolver fire, killing one miner and wounding seven others. By that time parliament was scattered all over the Commonwealth in an adjournment that lasted for three months.

When parliament resumed on 12 March the Government's legislative programme included an amending Commonwealth Conciliation and Arbitration Bill, the Central Reserve Bank Bill, the Wheat Marketing Bill, and three bills proposing amendments to the Constitution. One way or another, in part or in whole, all these ultimately fell foul of the Senate. The first measure substantially modifed the penalties against strikes and lock-outs contained in the Bruce–Page Act, and the Opposition conceded that the Government had a mandate to do this. The Bill also gave conciliation commissioners the same general powers as judges, including the power to make awards; and provided for a new system of conciliation committees, formed by representatives of parties to a dispute, and competent to make majority decisions having the effect of awards. This Bill passed its second reading in the Senate without division, but did not fare so well in committee. It was returned to the lower house with thirty amendments.

To the regret of its more radical supporters, the Government adopted a conciliatory approach in this disagreement by calling parliament's first formal conference between the houses, as provided for in both sets of Standing Orders. Five managers, including Latham and Page from the Opposition, were appointed by the lower house, and five by the Senate. They met in the Senate committee room at 12.30 a.m. on 8 August 1930, and after lengthy discussion the lower house managers reported back to their colleagues that the Senate insisted upon nineteen of its amendments, would drop four, and would accept modification to seven. The compromise which was then quickly passed by both houses was a victory for the Senate, though the Government did have the satisfaction of substantially saving the Bill's main principles. Another managers' conference was held four months later on amendments to the Northern Territory (Administration) Bill, insisted upon by the Senate, and again the Senate came off best.

The Central Reserve Bank Bill would have brought to fruition those central banking functions foreshadowed in the Commonwealth Bank Act of 1924 by establishing a separate Reserve Bank to hold the trading banks' reserves and government accounts. This was a relatively orthodox proposal. It was supported by some Opposition members, and would undoubtedly have strengthened Australia's banking system during the Depression that was then developing. But the Senate demurred, referring the Bill to a select committee which eventually submitted an adverse report. Much the same fate befell the Wheat Marketing Bill, which was the Scullin Government's main attempt to help wheat growers who had been grievously affected by the collapse of world prices. The Bill offered a guaranteed price in conjunction with compulsory wheat pools to be authorised by State legislation. Everyone favoured a guaranteed price, but part of the Country Party and all Nationalists regarded compulsory pooling as the next worst thing to socialism. The Bill was rejected by the Senate in July. Scullin could have used this rejection to force a double dissolution, but was unwilling to coerce his financially straitened party into what would have been a third election in three years.

Three other measures defeated on their second reading in the Senate were the Constitution Alteration (Industrial Powers) Bill, the Constitution Alteration (Power of Amendment) Bill and the Constitution Alteration (Trade and Commerce) Bill. The first of these was the very antithesis of Bruce's ill-judged attempt to take the Commonwealth out of industrial arbitration. If passed, it would have led to a referendum on the question of replacing Section 51 (xxxv) with a power to legislate directly on all industrial matters, regardless of whether or not disputes extended beyond the limits of any one State. Similarly a Trade and Commerce referendum, if passed, would have widened Section 51(i) by removing the limiting words 'with other countries and among the States', thus empowering the Commonwealth to legislate on both interstate and intra-State trade and commerce, except for State railways.

Neither of those referendums would have been necessary if a referendum envisaged by the third Bill had been submitted to the people and approved. Here the Government was shooting for the moon: it wanted to alter the Constitution by conferring upon parliament absolute power to amend the Constitution. No more would parliament have to pass a bill for a referendum, at which the vote would almost always be negative. Instead the proposal was that the Constitution could be amended at any time by simple act of parliament. Not surprisingly the Opposition regarded all three constitution alteration Bills—and particularly the third one, which in any case was itself constitutionally dubious—as too far-reaching. After the defeat of these measures in the Senate the Government proceeded no further with them.

No fewer than fourteen Government bills were defeated in that chamber during the life of the twelfth parliament. The role of executioner sat strangely on a Senate which for more than two-thirds of the Commonwealth's three decades had been controlled by the same political forces as the House of Representatives, and in consequence had usually been far more inclined to meet the wishes of that place than otherwise. Having long since exchanged the role of States' House for that of lower house's rubber stamp, the Senate was sometimes referred to by outsiders as the morgue, a term possibly inspired by Lord Sherbourne's description of the House of Lords after making his maiden speech there. Asked how he had felt, Sherbourne replied: 'It was like addressing a lot of corpses by candlelight in a charnel house'.

The Senate was rarely as moribund as that, but there was a rather stuffy clublike atmosphere in the red chamber that was not discernible in the green. Although the thirty-six senators had long been voting on party lines, they did not face each other on opposing sides of the chamber but sat together sociably, friends beside foes. The Senate did not sit as frequently as the House of Representatives, but the difference between the two chambers in this regard had altered little in the last ten years as compared with the previous decade. The average number of sitting days per year in 1920–29 was sixty-nine for the House of Representatives and fifty-two for the Senate, as compared with sixty-seven and fifty respectively during 1910–19.

Unlike Speaker Makin, the President of the Senate—Senator Walter Kingsmill (Nat, W), who had succeeded Sir John Newlands (Nat, S) during the previous parliament—remained staunchly loyal to wig and gown. The Usher of the Black Rod, R. A. Broinowski, was also more of a stickler about formality and propriety than was the Serjeant-at-Arms in the other chamber. This may have been simply his nature, which was a quirky amalgam of sophistication, erudition and severity; but 'Bruno' Broinowski must have suited the Senate, for he went on to become its Clerk. He wrote verse, delivered ABC radio talks on such subjects as Marco Polo and Hannibal, and established the rose garden on the Senate side of Parliament House. Broinowski ran the Senate side of the building sternly, and did not shrink from such unpopular decisions as banning poppy-sellers from the precincts on Remembrance Day, and stopping parliamentary staff from playing ping-pong. The latter edict inspired five stanzas by C. J. Dennis, including the following:

> Oh, his brows were wreathed with thunder
> as he gazed in stupid wonder,
> As he heard the sinful pinging and the
> sacrilegious pong.
> And he said, 'henceforth I ban it. If I
> knew who 'twas began it
> I would have him drawn and quartered,
> for 'tis obviously wrong.'
> Then back adown the corridors, unbending
> as a god,
> Went the adamantine Usher of the Big
> Black Rod.

This rather Gilbertian image had to be revised considerably in light of the Senate's unaccustomed power, and a consequent revival of interest by senators in playing a more responsible role in the business of parliament. On the first sitting day Senator P. J. Lynch (Nat, W) asked the Government Leader, Senator J. J. Daly (Lab, S) whether Cabinet would continue to be represented in the Senate by only two ministers, or whether that number would be increased 'to give this chamber a reasonable opportunity to handle the same volume of business that is undertaken in another place'. With the obvious intention of reminding the Opposition of the risk entailed in disagreement, Senator Daly replied curtly: 'The answer to the honorable senator's question depends upon whether or not we have a double dissolution'. Yet that possibility did not deter the Senate Opposition from exploring the safe limits of its power, and to some extent reassessing the nature of the Senate's role.

In December 1929 Senator R. C. D. Elliott (C, V), a country press and radio proprietor, successfully proposed the establishment of a select committee to report on the advisability of establishing Senate standing committees on statutory rules and ordinances, international relations, finance and private members' bills. 'My purpose in moving this motion tonight', he said with engaging candour, 'is to make this august chamber interesting . . . Those honorable senators who wish the Senate to be something more than a nozzle through which the legislation of the lower chamber passes almost automatically . . . will vote for it'.

The select committee recommended establishment of a Standing Committee on Regulations and Ordinances, but not on other subjects. Limited though the results may have been, this was the first thorough investigation of the constitutional possibilities of a system of standing committees in the Senate. In 1931 the Senate resolved to establish a Standing Committee on Regulations and Ordinances. Lord Hewart would have approved of this Standing Committee, to which all ordinances laid on the table of the Senate were to be referred for consideration and report. The 'Regs and Ords' Committee, which became a very useful adjunct of the Senate, was also charged with responsibility for ensuring that clauses of bills conferring power to make regulations did not confer legislative power of a character which ought to be exercised by parliament itself.

By mid-1930 the Scullin Government, assailed by the worsening Depression and other difficulties, was being driven increasingly on to the defensive. Caucus meetings were more fractious than usual, and in May Scullin moved in the House that Government business should take precedence over general business. Latham deplored the fact that for the rest of the session members would in effect have no right to introduce private business, but he bowed to the inevitable and did not oppose the motion. Members could still make themselves heard, however, and the pages of Hansard afforded many a bleak glimpse of Australia's plight. 'Last weekend I was at the South Coast', said Bert Lazzarini in an adjournment debate during May, 'and I saw there persons actually scraping holes in the sand and covering them with pieces of wood for sleeping purposes. There are dozens of such cases. In addition many families are camping in the bush'. In June the Hunter Valley miners at last admitted defeat and went back to work on the proprietors' terms. But before they could earn their first full pay after the 16-month lock-out, most of the collieries were laid idle by flood.

The percentage of trade unionists unemployed in Australia rose from 10 per cent in mid-1929 to 18.5 per cent in mid-1930, and by mid-1931 the figure would be 27.6 per cent. The severe liquidity crisis resulting from depletion of London funds was now, half way through 1930, compounded by a more fundamental balance of payments problem, and this demanded severe reduction of imports if Australia was to avoid default. In Canberra the Royal Military College was transferred as an economy measure to Victoria Barracks, Sydney; major construction was suspended for the same reason; and only a few minor projects were kept going to provide work for some of the growing legion of unemployed. On 8 May some two hundred unemployed men, most of whom had been dismissed by the Federal Capital Commission, demonstrated outside Parliament House. Disfranchised by residence in the Federal Capital Territory, they had no member of their own to call upon. Instead they were addressed from the steps by the geographically most appropriate person, the Labor Member for Eden-Monaro, J. J. Cusack, who delivered a rousing call for the conscription of wealth as a means of dealing with the Depression. Later that day, addressing the House during a Supply debate, Cusack expanded on his theme. 'Why', he asked, 'does not the Government demand from the rich men of this country a loan of £10,000,000 or £20,000,000 free of interest, with which to relieve unemployment, and to give succour to the needy?'

At a more sophisticated level than Cusack's rural populism, three alternative approaches to crisis management were being canvassed in Australia. The first—favoured by Scullin and other moderate members of his party, including Theodore for the time being—was that of mild deficit expansion. A moderate extension of central bank credit, it was argued, should be used to alleviate the effect of unemployment, but not to the extent of causing dangerous inflation. Secondly, the radical wing of the A.L.P. advocated unilateral default. By repudiating external interest commitments, argued such members as Anstey and Beasley, the Commonwealth and State Governments would be able to spend more on the relief of distress. Thirdly, conservatives in the financial community and parliament urged the stern policy of cutting costs. Only by contracting expenditure, declared men like Sir Robert Gibson and Latham, could budgets be balanced quickly without producing chronic inflation. These traditionalists, and also indeed the Labor moderates, rejected default out of deeply held conviction that such a policy would harm Australia's long-term borrowing prospects and would in any case be morally wrong, even un-British.

As Chairman of the Commonwealth Bank, Sir Robert Gibson was not the remote figure-head envisaged by the 1924 Act. The governor of the bank was meant to be its chief executive, but the occupant of that post, E. C. Riddle, was a professional banker with little taste for the high-level financial politicking now called for more urgently than usual. In consequence, Gibson took over full tactical responsibility for the bank's policy. This slightly built, sharply bearded industrialist did not know a great deal about banking, but he knew his own mind, and knew how to impose it on others. Having emigrated from Scotland at the age of twenty-seven, he made his fortune in Melbourne as a manufacturer of fuel stoves and baths, then ventured boldly on to paths of public power.

With restless energy undiminished by failing health, and an imperious manner which inspired fear as well as respect, Gibson dominated the bank board and turned a stony countenance to Scullin when the latter presumed to broach the matter of credit expansion. Although Scullin professed the greatest admiration for Gibson, he seemed to be as much under his thumb as Riddle was. At one Cabinet meeting he attended, Gibson responded to another request for credit expansion with the words: 'Mr Prime Minister and members of the cabinet, I bloody well won't'.

Gibson insisted that Australia could stabilise the value of its currency only if governments balanced their budgets. At his urging, Scullin and Theodore, without reference to Cabinet or Caucus, invited the Bank of England to send a representative to Australia to help prepare a plan for rapid budget-balancing. The next federal Budget was due to be introduced on 9 July 1929 by Theodore, who had already established himself in the opinion of many as probably the Commonwealth's ablest Treasurer yet. He was the first Keynesian in Australian public life, and was said to have a firmer grasp of the economic situation than anyone at Treasury.

Imagine, then, the dismay with which Scullin learned on 4 July that a Queensland Royal Commission had found Theodore deeply implicated in the 'fraud and dishonesty' of what was known as the Mungana affair. The Mungana silver-lead mines, near Theodore's old electorate of Chillagoe, had been sold to the Queensland Government several years before, while he was Premier. It was widely believed that Theodore had held shares in the mines, and that the government paid an overly generous price for them. No inquiry was held by the Labor Government, but a royal commission was appointed as soon as the Ministry changed.

Scullin saw no option but to ask for his colleague's resignation from the Ministry and to be sworn in as Treasurer himself. Announcing this in parliament on 8 July, he spoke generously of Theodore's loyalty, courage, 'immense industry and great intellectual capacity'. For his part, Theodore said that he had no alternative but to resign and await an opportunity to clear his character of what he insisted was a grave injustice. Thereafter he had more time for fishing along the Molonglo, as he liked doing with J. B. Chifley, and more time for organising the numbers in Caucus.

In his Budget speech next day, Scullin firmly rejected any notion of default and introduced a range of taxes to close the gap between projected revenue and expenditure, a gap which otherwise seemed likely to produce a deficit of £14 million. 'I regard the national debt as I would a personal debt', he said. 'There will be no repudiation of our obligations by this government.' The left-wing view was put by Frank Anstey, under goading by a senior Nationalist, Archdale Parkhill (Warringah, N), who used to attack Government speakers 'like a bull ant':

Mr ARCHDALE PARKHILL.—Would the Minister prefer to repudiate the payment of the interest on loans?
Mr JAMES.—I certainly would.
Mr ANSTEY.—The honorable member for Warringah has no doubt asked me this question confidentially, and, as between the two of us, with no one else listening, I say to him that if I had to choose between the repudiating of the responsibility for making provision for the men, women and children of this country to earn sufficient to provide themselves with bread and butter and clothing, and to maintain themselves in decent habitations, and the repudiating of the payment of these interest charges, I know which I should prefer.
Mr ARCHDALE PARKHILL.—And so do I know which I would prefer; but the Minister has answered my question.

In addition to widening differences within Caucus, Theodore's resignation, the Senate and the Depression, Scullin had another problem. He now had to leave Australia with two of his ministers, Brennan and Moloney, on one of those pilgrimages to the Imperial Conference in London which consumed such a disproportionate amount of Australian politicians' time.

Anstey scoffed about the trip, Beasley begged Scullin not to go, and a Melbourne *Herald* cartoon depicted the captain deserting his sinking ship. Later, however, it would seem fairer to say that Scullin's absence from Australia at such a critical time was regrettable yet unavoidable.

As well as attending the Imperial Conference with other dominion prime ministers, Scullin felt that he had to reassure the British financial community about the essential soundness of Australia's economy. He also wanted to conclude negotiations, initiated earlier in the year and not at all well received by London, for the unprecedented appointment of an Australian as the next Governor-General. In the event of trouble at Canberra during his six-months absence, at least he would be able to communicate readily with his lieutenants, for a radio-telephone link had been opened between Britain and Australia only four months previously.

The last few days before his departure were for Scullin a feverish combination of decision-making and illness. Without prior reference to Caucus, he obtained Cabinet approval to extend Sir Robert Gibson's appointment, due to expire soon, for another seven years. On the following day he chaired a meeting of the Loan Council, which was addressed by the Bank of England's newly arrived emissary, Sir Otto Niemeyer, and on 18 August a special Premiers' Conference opened in Melbourne to consider recommendations by Niemeyer and Gibson for much more substantial cuts in expenditure than were contemplated in Scullin's Budget. As Scullin was in bed with a heavy bronchial cold at his home in Richmond, the Commonwealth was represented at this conference by the two ministers who would be acting as Prime Minister and Treasurer respectively during Scullin's absence—James Fenton and J. A. Lyons. According to the uncharitable Niemeyer, Fenton and Lyons were out of their depth, 'like a couple of rabbits popping their heads occasionally out of the hole'.

Although running a temperature of 103 degrees, Scullin attended the third day's proceedings. He then returned to his sick-bed, from which he presided over a hastily convened Cabinet meeting, with Sir Robert Gibson in attendance. After hearing Gibson explain once again that governments must reduce expenditure because the limits of bank credit would soon be reached, Cabinet decided that the Commonwealth should join the State Premiers in adopting the Niemeyer-Gibson policy.

Scullin, still feverish, took the transcontinental train to Perth, and from Fremantle, on 26 August, he and his wife set sail for England. At about this time Jack Beasley was talking to a journalist from the Press Gallery. 'Well', he said, 'Scullin is leaving his government behind him; he may not find it here when he returns'.

Caucus

With health restored by the voyage, Scullin disembarked at Toulon, travelled by train to Geneva, where he addressed the armaments reduction committee of the League of Nations, and reached London on 24 September. There he moved into a suite at the Savoy, overlooking the Thames. A state limousine was placed at his disposal and between public engagements, before the Imperial Conference began, he and his wife did some sightseeing.

One day they visited Thomas Gray's burial place, the church at Stoke Poges, Buckinghamshire, which had inspired Scullin's favourite poem, Gray's 'Elegy Written in a Country Churchyard'. And who could blame this modest, tormented man for seeking out such a place, 'far from the madding crowd's ignoble strife', perhaps to ponder the obscure fate of village Hampdens and mute, inglorious Miltons?

The Imperial Conference opened on 1 October, and at its third session the delegation leaders discussed a subject of particular interest to Scullin—the appointment of governors-general. A successor to Lord Stonehaven would soon have to be appointed, and this time the process of selection had been rendered more difficult than usual by the new nature of the post and the change of government in Australia. Now that governors-general represented the King rather than the British Government, King George maintained that the choice should be his alone. In this His Majesty was also influenced by concern to avoid any repetition of his recent brush with the South African Prime Minister, who had insisted on selecting Lord Clarendon against royal preference.

Scullin's Government felt equally strongly that the only viceregal difference since 1926 was that governors-general would in future be appointed not by His Majesty's ministers in Britain but by His Majesty's ministers in Australia. The Government was also determined that the next Governor-General of Australia should be Sir Isaac Isaacs, the judge and former parliamentarian who had recently been appointed Chief Justice of the High Court on the resignation of Sir Adrian Knox. The only other candidate considered by Cabinet for the Governor-Generalship was the outstanding Australian soldier of his generation, Sir John Monash. Both men were equally distinguished in their own fields, and both as it happened were Jews. Monash's health was not equal to the task, however, and Cabinet settled wholeheartedly on Isaacs. Since the death of Higgins, Sir Isaac had been the only surviving member of the five convention delegates who shaped the Commonwealth's constitutional jurisprudence. He was seventy-seven years old, but as fit as a fiddle.

In February 1930 the King's private secretary had advised the Dominions Office of His Majesty's view that 'it would be a grave mistake to give [Scullin] an opportunity of naming the next Governor-General'. Nevertheless Scullin's official recommendation was conveyed five weeks later through Lord Stonehaven, and in April the press correctly identified Isaacs as the nominee. At the King's request, the matter was then stood over until Scullin came to London.

During discussion at the Imperial Conference, Britain's Labour Prime Minister, Ramsay MacDonald, and the Secretary of State for the Dominions, James Thomas, remarked pointedly that the governor-general was now the personal representative of the King only. In an *aide-mémoire* prepared by Scullin soon afterwards, he wrote, 'I was asked [at the conference]: Did I deny the King's prerogative? My answer was: No, but the King exercised his prerogative on the advice of his responsible Ministers and, in the case of the appointment of an Australian Governor-General his responsible Ministers were the Australian Ministers'. At a meeting with Scullin on 11 November the King's private secretary, Lord Stamfordham, said that Australia had 'put a pistol to the King's head in that [it] had nominated one man, and one man only, thus giving the King no choice whatever in the matter'. Scullin stood firm and cited two precedents: South Africa's recent insistence, and the appointment of an Irishman as Governor-General of the Irish Free State.

'Do not talk to me about Ireland', said Lord Stamfordham to his Irish-Australian and Roman Catholic visitor. 'That is a country of rebels and the man nominated for the position of Governor-General was himself a rebel.'

'You appointed [him] on the recommendation of the Irish Free State Government', replied Scullin.

> Am I to draw the inference that you accept the recommendation of a Government of rebels and the appointment of a rebel amongst themselves, but if a country is loyal, such as Australia undoubtedly is, you refuse to accept the nomination from the government of a loyal country and the appointment of an Australian born citizen whose loyalty has not been questioned?'
> 'I thought you would say that.'
> 'Was it not obvious?'

Scullin then asked what objection the palace had to Isaacs.

'We have nothing against Sir Isaac Isaacs personally', replied Stamfordham, 'but the King's representative must be entirely free from politics'.

'Then that makes my position very easy because Sir Isaac Isaacs has been dissociated from politics for a quarter of a century . . . and even when he was in politics, he did not belong to the party which I lead in parliament today.'

Lord Stamfordham replied that all men were politicians.

'Well then', answered Scullin, 'none is fit to be a Governor-General according to that dictum'.

'Oh no, it is only local politics which matters.'

'Then it comes back to the original protest: your objection is because our recommendation is a local man, an Australian.'

Soon afterwards Scullin went to Ireland, rebel south and loyal north. While visiting his father's birthplace in County Derry, he received a message from Lord Stamfordham that the King would like him to consider another possible candidate—the English soldier who had commanded ANZAC at Gallipoli, Field Marshal Sir William Birdwood. But Scullin remained firm. On 29 November he met the King at Buckingham Palace. 'Perhaps before you say anything I might express my views', said His Majesty. 'It is now 30 years since I opened the Commonwealth parliament in Australia. Since then we have sent many Governors, Commonwealth and State, and I hope they have not all been failures.' Scullin assured him that they had not all been failures, and explained why the Government wanted Isaacs.

The King replied that he and his British advisers had the highest regard personally for Sir Isaac, that the last thing he wanted was controversy of the kind which would accompany a referendum on the subject, which Stamfordham had suggested earlier. His Majesty then concluded the forty-five minutes of discussion by saying: 'I have been for 20 years a monarch and

I hope I have always been a constitutional one, and being a constitutional monarch I must, Mr Scullin, accept your advice'. He didn't like it, though, and the official announcement, when it came from the palace, said 'The King . . . has appointed' instead of the usual 'The King . . . has been pleased to appoint'. To ensure that the point was not lost upon His Majesty's Australian ministers, Lord Stamfordham asked the Solicitor-General, Sir Robert Garran, to show the exact wording to Scullin.

The retiring Governor-General did not like it either; nor did Latham and his colleagues on the Opposition benches. Isaacs was a far cry from one of the aristocratic elder sons whom Lord Stonehaven had suggested, and in private correspondence his lordship referred to his successor as 'a septuagenarian Jew'. Latham was careful to avoid any personal criticism. Speaking on the adjournment in December, he confined his disapproval to breach of a general principle that judges should have nothing to hope for and nothing to fear from governments, and the peremptory form of Scullin's recommendation. As the appointment was an act of the Australian Government rather than the King, it was open to parliamentary and other criticism, like any other act of the Government of the day. This, said Latham, would unfortunately tend to diminish the prestige of the office.

On the contrary, however, Sir Isaac and Lady Isaacs were accorded a warmly enthusiastic welcome by several thousand people when they arrived by state carriage at Victoria's Parliament House on 22 January 1931 for a swearing-in ceremony performed by the new Chief Justice of the High Court, Sir Frank Gavan Duffy. Sir Isaac wore the court dress of a Privy Councillor, and for the first time in federal history the King's Commission was signed not by a British Secretary of State but by an Australian Prime Minister. The Bible on which Sir Isaac took his oaths of allegiance and office had been presented to him when he first entered this same building as a member of federal parliament thirty years before.

While Scullin had been holding a pistol to the King's head, dining at Chequers, and talking up the Australian economy, his parliamentary following in Canberra came more and more to display the madding crowd's ignoble strife. Caucus, in the words of one onlooker, became a bag of spilt marbles. Earlier in the year Scullin had tried to ensure privacy by soundproofing the party room. Thick double doors, heavily baized and close fitting, were installed inside the existing doors, but not even these could confine the uproar which broke out between various factions during the Prime Minister's absence. When Caucus was meeting, journalists upstairs could feel the vibration.

As chairman, Fenton dealt ineffectively with such disruptive forces as the Langites and Victorian radicals. Although he was acting Prime Minister, the *locum tenens* partnership was usually referred to as Lyons and Fenton rather than the other way round, for the acting Treasurer was much the abler man. At the age of fifty-one, Joseph Aloysius Lyons had been a parliamentarian for more than twenty years, a party leader for thirteen years, Treasurer of Tasmania for seven years and Premier for five years. The only obvious weakness in his background was the big difference in political pace between Hobart and Canberra. He realised the need to acclimatise himself politically, but nonetheless resented Scullin's failure to give him a more senior portfolio than Postmaster-General.

Joe Lyons was a warm, kindly man with features which reminded cartoonists of a large koala bear; the adjectives he applied to himself most frequently were 'plain' and 'blunt'. One extraordinary thing about him, however, was his family. He first met his wife, Enid, when he was a 29-year-old teacher and she was eleven years old. They married six years later, by which time he was Minister for Education and she a junior teacher. Enid Lyons embraced her husband's religion (she had already embraced his politics, for her Methodist mother had brought her up in the labour movement) and during the next twenty years she gave birth to twelve children, of whom eleven survived.

When the marbles began to spill in earnest, Lyons wrote to his wife saying how 'heavenly' it would be if he could return to Tasmania for good. Perhaps he suspected how much worse the situation would become. Caucus's first meeting without Scullin, the main subject of which was to be long-term economic policy, did not begin until 27 October, two days after J. T. Lang's triumphant return to office in New South Wales. The four Langites—Beasley, Eldridge (Martin), Lazzarini and James—were basking in the glory reflected from that truculent Labor demagogue whose enemies were later to call him 'greater than Lenin'. Few though the Langites were in federal Caucus, they operated with the same disciplined pragmatism as the 'Big Fella' in Sydney, and interpreted his victory as proof that their own electors did not want Niemeyer's stern prescription for recovery. On the second day of Caucus Lazzarini moved that the government immediately instruct the Commonwealth Bank directors to take up, either by credit expansion or note issue, a £27 million conversion loan falling due in December. Lyons tried to reconcile that mood with his own and Fenton's determination to implement the Niemeyer–Gibson contractionary policy. He moved as an amendment 'that the policy of the party should be as follows: (1) Free exchange rates. (2) Stabilisation of internal prices by monetary control. (3) Reduction of interest rates. (4) Provision of credits for Industry, and that every effort shall be made by the Government to induce the Commonwealth Bank to carry out such policy'. Another amendment, much closer to the original motion than to Lyons's amendment, was then moved by George Gibbons (Calare, N), a man generally regarded as cat's-paw for Theodore. His amendment required the Commonwealth Bank to provide £20 million for public works, and to finance the federal government's requirements for all services covered by parliamentary appropriations.

Lazzarini withdrew his motion in favour of Gibbon's amendment, Lyons's amendment was lost, and that of Gibbons, submitted as a motion on the morning of 30 October, was carried by 26 votes to 14. Those who saw Theodore's hand in all of this realised that in his banishment 'Red Ted' had deserted Scullin's moderate group and joined the inflationary left. Lyons managed to obtain approval for reductions of parliamentary and ministerial salaries, but otherwise he was left to face parliament that afternoon without a financial policy. Humiliated, he requested a special adjournment so that he could prepare legislation acceptable to Caucus, and when the Government

See the conquering hero comes! The Scullins at Canberra railway station, 21 October 1929

Lord Stonehaven, the eighth British Governor-General of Australia

Sir Isaac Isaacs, the first Australian Governor-General, after taking the oath of office at Parliament House, Melbourne, 22 January 1931

R. G. Menzies and P. C. Spender, c. 1940

Dr Earle Page

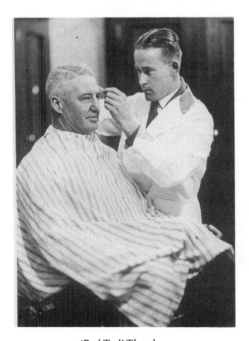

'Red Ted' Theodore

'Stabber Jack' Beasley

moved for closure of the adjournment debate, to gag Opposition speakers with whom Lyons had some sympathy, he showed his anger by voting with the 'Noes'.

Scullin was kept advised of these developments by cable and radio-telephone. One night a journalist returning late to the Hotel Kurrajong heard a ring from the telephone booth. Picking up the receiver, he heard the Prime Minister's voice, twelve thousand miles away, asking: 'Is that you, Jim?' The journalist then went upstairs to fetch Fenton in pyjamas and slippers.

When Caucus met again on 6 November Fenton read a cable from Scullin supporting the minority vote on Gibbons's motion and opposing any further expansion of credit or attempt to coerce the Commonwealth Bank.. This was not debated, but Lyons made his own position clear by proposing that the Loan Council should convert the loan falling due in December, and that the Gibbons–Theodore plan should be submitted to the Commonwealth Bank board by the whole Cabinet rather than by himself alone. A motion by R. A. Crouch (Corio, V) embodying those proposals was substantially amended by Curtin and Anstey, and when the meeting resumed angrily that evening it voted on the following motion:

> That the Cabinet as a whole meet the Directors of the Commonwealth Bank prior to the meeting of the Loan Council, and require the Directors to meet the loan due on 15th December 1930, and in anticipation of the Directors failing to do this, that a bill be at once prepared, and presented to Parliament, renewing for a period of twelve months the £27,000,000 loans falling due between this and the end of December.

The motion was carried by 22 votes to 16. Fenton reminded the meeting that thirteen members of the parliamentary party were absent, including the three ministers in London, and said, like a leader defeated in the House, that in view of the vote he and Lyons would consider their position. Although the House was to sit that evening and next day, Lyons went straight from the party room to catch the evening train for Goulburn and Melbourne. His departure had been arranged some days before, but ministers who were not aware of this concluded that Lyons might now be intent upon resigning. 'Texas' Green followed him to the railway station and was ever afterwards remembered as having called while the train pulled out: 'For God's sake, Joe, don't do it!'

What Lyons did do the next day, on his way home to Devonport, was send a cable to Scullin, saying in part:

> . . . This is absolute repudiation. I immediately notified the party I would not be prepared to carry out their decision, but would communicate with you and ask you, if you approved their action, to relieve me of my position in the Cabinet and appoint a successor to submit the necessary legislation, which will inevitably crash credit of Australia. Pending your decision I propose to carry out my previous decision to recommend [£27 million] loan to meeting Loan Council . . .

Scullin replied:

I do not approve and will not support resolution of party, which, I agree, is repudiation, which is dishonest and disastrous. Brennan and Moloney concur. We agree that you are right in recommending to Loan Council issue of loans, as party's resolution has demoralised Australian stocks here, and unless rescinded will render renewal of bills here, as well as conversions in Australia, impossible . . .

At the next meeting of Caucus, on 12 November, Yates and Lazzarini moved that the party reaffirm its decision of the previous week. But after Fenton had read Scullin's cables to the meeting it was agreed that the matter should stand adjourned until the Prime Minister's return early in January. Although Lyons remained in Cabinet, and still attended Caucus, he kept himself at some distance from the party, took part in a successful public campaign for conversion of the loan, and waited anxiously for Scullin. Another Caucus meeting on 10 December produced angry exchanges between Lyons and two of his fellow ministers, Anstey and Beasley. A committee was appointed to formulate a public statement on financial and economic policy, and Lyons refused to serve on it. This meeting also discussed an offer made the previous day by the Leader of the Opposition. Speaking in the House on the need for emergency measures on a non-party basis, Latham proposed an alternative to the present method of government—not a coalition, he insisted, but a council comprising members of the Government and Opposition, State representatives on the Loan Council, and representatives of the banks. Needless to say, the idea did not commend itself to Caucus, but the next *Labor Daily* carried a grossly distorted report from Canberra under the headlines: 'Lyons Wants To Jettison Federal Labor/Proposes Coalition Government/Caucus Howls Lyons Down/Angry Party Meeting/Sinister Move'. It might well have been written by Beasley or Lazzarini. In the House that afternoon Lyons denounced the report as a downright lie, saying that he had used the word 'coalition' only once during the Caucus discussion in order to make it plain that Latham had not proposed one.

Caucus had another surprise in store for Fenton and Lyons, concerning the High Court. The numerical strength of that bench had been reduced from seven to five by resignations of Mr Justice Powers and the Chief Justice, Sir Adrian Knox. Sir Adrian's resignation on April Fool's Day, 1930, followed fast upon his inheritance of a fortune from John Brown, whose death had occurred on 5 March. This was the same coal magnate whom two federal governments had failed to prosecute. Twice during the lock-out, colliery proprietors had recourse to the High Court, and twice they were successful.

Isaacs was appointed Chief Justice, but in view of the need for economy, and the not overly crowded state of the court lists, Scullin and his Attorney-General, Brennan, decided to leave the vacancies unfilled for the time being, and eventually to reduce the number of judicial posts to six. During the absence of Scullin and Brennan, however, the acting Attorney-General, Senator Daly, began canvassing the claims of two Labor politicians for elevation to the High Court: H. V. Evatt, a distinguished constitutional lawyer who was by that time Member for Balmain in the New South Wales Legislative Assembly; and E. A. McTiernan, the federal Member for Parkes who, although less learned in the law than Dr Evatt, was a former New South Wales Attorney-General.

When Daly advised Brennan in London that steps were being taken to appoint two justices, Scullin cabled to Fenton: 'It is a reversal of Cabinet decision, and means that Cabinet accepts political direction on appointments to the High Court judiciary. Political interference removing this matter from Cabinet responsibility strikes fatally at the authority of the Court. Attorney-General and I will be no party to that . . . '. To Lyons he cabled: 'I would go out of office if under the circumstances appointments were rushed through during our absence'.

In spite of Scullin's proclaimed attitude, Daly was able to tap a strong feeling in Caucus that Labor was entitled to influence the general outlook of the court by appointing men of different background from those normally chosen by non-Labor governments. In the words of one legal historian, Geoffrey Sawer, 'parties of the right habitually appoint social conservatives to such positions, but need make no parade of it since most eminent lawyers are social conservatives'. The case for filling the two vacancies quickly, and filling them with justices who would not be likely to inherit fortunes from coal magnates, was strengthened early in December by the announcement of Sir Isaac Isaacs's appointment as Governor-General, and by the High Court's judgment in the case of *Australian Railways Union* v. *Victorian Railways Commissioners and Others*.

Although the High Court had not followed parliament to Canberra, preferring to continue sitting only in State capitals, its writ could still at any time thwart the intention of federal legislators. In the A.R.U. case the Railways Commissioners of Victoria and three other States had applied to the Arbitration Court for a reduction in wages because of the financial crisis. The federal Government sought to delay this application by appointing a conciliation committee under Section 34 of the newly amended Conciliation and Arbitration Act. The Commissioners argued that this type of committee, empowered to make awards by the majority decision of nominated members, did not amount to either conciliation or arbitration, and was therefore in breach of Section 51 (xxxv) of the Constitution, which conferred industrial power for those two purposes only. A majority of four justices accepted this argument, with Isaacs dissenting, and Section 34 was held void.

Ten days after this judgment Caucus rejected a recommendation by Cabinet to defer the judicial appointments until Scullin's return, and instructed Cabinet to fill the vacancies. By that time Scullin had already embarked on his return voyage. Learning of Caucus's decision in a cable from Fenton, he replied on 19 December: 'Attorney-General and I hold views which we want to express, and cannot agree any appointment coming into force until our return. Grave principle involved'.

By the time this arrived, Cabinet had appointed Evatt and McTiernan, and the latter had resigned his seat. Lyons, who was not present at the Cabinet meeting, cabled apologetically to his leader, somewhere in the Indian Ocean: 'Consider only course now possible is to stand by Cabinet decision'.

At a by-election in January, the week after Scullin returned, McTiernan's seat was won by the Nationalist Party.

Opposition

The worst decision of Scullin's hag-ridden Prime Ministership, which he revealed when he met his party again on 26 January 1931, was to reinstate Theodore as Treasurer. Admittedly, as Scullin reminded Caucus, Theodore was technically the best man for the job. On the other hand, he was still entangled in the Mungana affair, with criminal charges pending against him; he had abandoned financial moderation, and in Scullin's absence had connived against such loyalists as Lyons and Fenton. Lyons, who might reasonably have expected confirmation of the Treasurership in addition to Scullin's thanks for his loyalty, could hardly believe his ears. He moved that all Cabinet positions be declared vacant, but then withdrew the motion. Debate continued throughout the day and into the evening, with all factions split, but in the end Scullin had his way. A motion for reinstatement was carried by 24 votes to 19, with Lyons and Fenton voting against reinstatement until the Mungana difficulty was resolved. Theodore was also elected Deputy Leader again.

The external effects of this volte-face were not so damaging to the Scullin Government as effects inside the party. Queensland continued to delay criminal proceedings, perhaps out of concern that Theodore might be acquitted; but a civil suit came to court in July, putting the Mungana allegations in issue, and ending with a verdict that exonerated Theodore. The shadow of Mungana would continue to haunt him, but would never materialise.

The internal effects began with defection by Joel Gabb, the rather eccentric South Australian who had been returned to parliament by the landslide, and was known to his colleagues as the 'Gawler Bunyip'. In a letter of resignation to Scullin on 27 January Gabb declared: 'I have lost faith in your judgment as a leader and in your possession of gratitude'. Of the same mind, and with more reason, Lyons stayed in the party for the time being but avoided most of his colleagues, keeping company with Fenton and two fellow Tasmanians—J. A. Guy (Bass) and C. W. Frost (Franklin). Together they spent most of 28 January driving and walking around Queanbeyan, and left for Melbourne that night. Next day Fenton and Lyons resigned from Cabinet.

With Scullin's full endorsement, Theodore set about preparing a three-year financial plan for presentation at a Premiers' conference due to start in Canberra on 6 February. The 'Theodore Plan' derived essentially from the Gibbons–Theodore resolution by Caucus, and assumed that the Commonwealth Bank could be persuaded to advance further substantial credits. Theodore presented it to the Premiers on Saturday 7 February, but when the conference resumed on Monday Jack Lang put forward a very different plan of his own. A by-election was soon to be held for the federal seat of East Sydney, and over the weekend Lang had become convinced that he could improve the chances of his candidate, E. J. Ward, by sponsoring a financial policy more radical than Theodore's.

The 'Lang Plan' proposed that Australian governments should pay no further interest to British bondholders until Britain had dealt with Australia's debt in terms comparable to those which she had obtained for her own debt to the United States; that interest on all Government borrowings in Australia should be reduced to 3 per cent; and finally that the federal Government should abandon the gold standard in favour of a currency based somehow on the 'wealth of Australia'. The third point was mumbo-jumbo, for Australia had effectively been off the gold standard for more than a year; the other two points were unequivocal and unashamed expressions of repudiation.

The Commonwealth eventually prevailed, using its casting vote to secure endorsement of Theodore's expansionary but non-repudiatory plan. Lang nevertheless derived some benefit from the aggressive stance he had adopted. In spite of the A.L.P. federal executive's ruling that members of Caucus must accept the Theodore plan, Ward espoused Lang's plan in his successful campaign for East Sydney. Ned Ward did not accept direction easily. Born in the slums of East Sydney, and a member of the Surry Hills A.L.P. branch since the age of sixteen, he was largely self-educated. A tight-mouthed puritan full of class hatred, he boxed well and ran with the Redfern and Botany Harriers.

At the first Caucus attended by Ward, on 12 March, Scullin ruled that any member elected on a policy other than that of the federal A.L.P. could not be a member of the Federal Parliamentary Labor Party, and that consequently the new Member for East Sydney could not take part in business of the parliamentary party. Beasley said that if Ward was to be excluded from Caucus, other New South Wales members who had supported his candidature should be dealt with similarly. When claims were made in the course of debate that Ward was prepared to abide by the majority decision of Caucus, Scullin asked him whether that was true. The glowering Member for East Sydney made no reply, and in fact said nothing throughout the meeting. Scullin's ruling was upheld by 34 votes to 3. The seven Langites—Beasley, Eldridge, Lazzarini, James, Ward and Senators Dunn and Rae—then left the meeting and formed a separate Lang Labor group. In the House of Representatives they sat on the Government cross benches, in the curve between the two sides of the chamber.

Scullin saw the mischief that Beasley and Lyons could do, but it was too late to kill them in the shell; the eggs had hatched. Beasley and his followers held the balance of power. They could vote the Government out of office if they wished, but only by joining forces with the Nationalists and the Country Party. The Nationalist Whip sounded them out about that, but no agreement was reached. Beasley kept his options open, just as he always used an office with a back door, so that when necessary he could leave without being seen. For the time being, the Langites left Scullin alone; but they were an ever-present and vigilant force, never far from the chamber whenever parliament was sitting. Their enmity was offically recognised on 28 March when a special federal conference of the A.L.P. expelled the New South Wales (Lang) Branch and established a separate federal party in that State.

Lyons, distressed by the thought of leaving his party, was at first uncertain about the future. But before long the future came looking for him. Certain influential figures in Melbourne's financial and conservative political circles were anxious to find a new federal leader of the Nationalist Party in place of Latham, who for all his worthy attributes had proved a disappointing successor to Bruce. One of these kingmakers—the stockbroker Staniforth Ricketson, senior partner of J. B. Were and Sons—felt that Lyons was their man. He had met Lyons long ago in Tasmania, and more recently helped him during the loan conversion campaign. Early in February, when according to Ricketson Lyons was 'at his wits' end to know where to turn and what was the true course to follow', Ricketson arranged a meeting in Melbourne between Lyons, himself and five others: C. A. Norris, the general manager of the National Mutual Life Association; Sir John Higgins, a former chairman of the British and Australian Wool Realisation Association; R. G. Menzies, a prominent young Melbourne barrister and new member of the Victorian Legislative Assembly; Kingsley Henderson, a Melbourne architect with extensive business and political connections; and Ambrose Pratt, a journalist and author with connections similar to those of Henderson.

'The Group', as Ricketson and his friends called themselves, proposed to Lyons that he leave the Labor Party, bringing enough of his colleagues with him to defeat the Government. In return, they promised to help him become the leader of an alternative government combining all anti-Scullin forces. Only a change of government, they said, could prevent collapse of the Australian economy and possibly civil strife. This offer was made without consulting either the Nationalist Party or its fund-raising body, the National Union. Lyons returned to Tasmania without committing himself. His wife urged him to take the plunge, but another month was to pass before he did that. In some moods he considered leaving politics altogether; then, at Caucus meetings on 18 and 19 February, he cautiously broached the subject of defection with those he thought most likely to leave the party with him.

For its part, the Group set about opening doors in the Nationalist Party. The President of the Nationalist Union, Robert Knox, approved the plan and discussed it tentatively with Latham, who agreed to co-operate. Latham did not undertake to step down for Lyons, but the enthusiasm with which the Melbourne *Herald* was promoting the latter as 'Honest Joe' must have given him ample warning that such a course might be required of him. Lyons did not attend the next meeting of Caucus, held on 2 March, two days before parliament reassembled after the Christmas adjournment, and informed the Group that he and Allan Guy had decided to leave the Labor Party. This was announced in the Melbourne *Herald* of that afternoon, and on 3 March Guy said that he would vote for any motion censuring the Government for the reinstatement of Theodore. Encouraged by the news of at least two defections, Latham prepared to move such a motion at the earliest opportunity.

In Caucus Theodore explained the Government's three-year financial plan, which included funding the short-term London debt of £38 million by exporting gold reserves, and issuing fiduciary currency to the extent of £28 million in lieu of creating bank credit. The latter would provide bounties for the hard-pressed wheat farmers, and £1 million per month for Commonwealth works to absorb unemployed workers. This meeting of Caucus also conducted a spill of all Cabinet positions by secret ballot. Scullin and

Theodore were re-elected Leader and Deputy Leader without difficulty. Chifley was elected on the second-last ballot, and appointed Minister for Defence. Beasley, Senator Daly and Anstey all paid the penalty for dissidence by being dropped from the Ministry.

Anstey took his rejection stoically, telling the press that 'when a group of honest men like that permits me to escape with my life I am very thankful'. But in fact his long parliamentary career was now descending steeply towards final disillusionment. His friend John Curtin was to have been a candidate in the last ministerial ballot, but Curtin withdrew; the odds against a drinking mate of Frank Anstey were too great. Although Curtin was regarded as one of the finest speakers in parliament, he had also acquired a reputation for heavy and sometimes tearful drinking, and that weighed heavily against him in the estimation of a teetotaller like Scullin.

When parliament reassembled at 3 p.m. on 4 March it seemed reluctant to get down to business. Scullin announced the recent deaths of the Princess Royal, Dame Nellie Melba, a former M.H.R. and one sitting member. As a mark of respect to the latter, John West (East Sydney), and in keeping with past practice, he then moved the adjournment. George Maxwell protested at the folly of adjourning the House at a time of unparalleled need for parliamentary action. 'We have been summoned from all parts of the Commonwealth to tackle a very difficult job', he said, 'and the sooner we get to work the better. Surely, by standing in our places as we did, and then getting on with our job, we shall pay respect in the fullest measure to the memory of our late colleagues, and at the same time conserve the interests of those who sent us here.' But because of tradition, and perhaps also the Government's unreadiness to face parliament, the House adjourned after having sat for no more than thirty-five minutes.

The next day's sitting was even shorter. To shouts of 'Privilege!' and 'Shame!' from the Opposition, Theodore rose to perform the first parliamentary duty of his second Treasurership, giving notice of a motion for leave to bring in a bill relating to the issue of fiduciary currency. Four months earlier the Opposition had moved as a matter of privilege that Theodore be suspended from the service of the House while he was the subject of a royal commission; the Speaker ruled this out of order, however, on grounds that the matter was not one of privilege.

As Theodore went through the brief formality of giving notice for the Fiduciary Notes Bill, which was to be the mainstay of the Government's financial plan, H. S. Gullett moved that he be not further heard. The Speaker ruled that Theodore had already resumed his seat before Gullett had completed his motion. Gullett moved that Mr Speaker's ruling be disagreed with, and that motion was placed on the notice paper for subsequent defeat. Latham then gave notice that on the following day he would move want of confidence in the Government, and Scullin again moved the adjournment. Gregory (C, Swan, W) protested as Maxwell had done the previous day, but tradition was followed again and the House adjourned, having sat for only nineteen minutes.

In the course of debate on Latham's want of confidence motion, which lasted four days, it became apparent that only two more Labor members would expel themselves by joining Lyons, Guy and Gabb in voting with the

Opposition. They were Fenton and J. L. Price (Boothby, S). Lyons's speech on the last day of the debate was to have been one written by Ambrose Pratt, but as it did not arrive in time he had to speak more or less off the cuff. Some thought it the greatest speech of his career. 'It may be', he said,

> that in spite of my own inclination I may be separated, not only politically, but also to some extent personally, from my friends; but that will not be of my volition, because, whatever comes or goes in the future, I can never have other than the highest respect for those men with whom I have been so long associated . . . [But] I believe that the policy of this Government means an increase of unemployment, misery and destitution. I see these things in our midst today, and this is why by my vote, voice and action, I want to enter my vote against that policy in an endeavour to have it changed.

The next speaker, Brennan, removed any doubt about the kind of personal relationship which would exist henceforth between Lyons and members of the party he was deserting. Brennan called him 'traitor', but in future the more usual Labor term would be 'rat'. The Langites were still biding their time, and so Latham's motion was negatived by 33 votes to 38. Lyons and his four companions moved on to the Opposition benches, and were joined there two days later by one more Labor defector, D. C. McGrath.

Lyons's little band had at least three choices: to remain independent of the disunited Opposition; to merge with the Nationalist Party, which was the official Opposition; or to seek support from such extra-parliamentary groups as the All For Australia League in New South Wales and the Citizens' League of South Australia. These latter movements were products of disillusionment with the established parties and with parliament itself. The times were singularly unstable, and the Group now influencing Lyons's course of action had not been exaggerating when it warned of civil strife. Dictatorship was in the air. At a meeting of the Western Australian section of the Flying Corps Association in March 1931, it was suggested that five thousand returned soldiers should take Canberra, turn out the Government, and install General Sir John Monash as dictator. Crack-brained it may have been, but only a few weeks earlier Sir John, soon to leave for India as Australia's official representative at the opening of New Delhi, had been obliged to rebuke one respectable proponent of just such a *coup d'état*.

'Your name is on the lips of every sane man in this State', wrote a New South Wales businessman, C. Barclay Smith. 'For God's sake, Sir John, abandon all idea of leaving your country when it needs you most.' Monash replied: 'What do you and your friends want me to do? To lead a movement to upset the Constitution, oust the jurisdiction of Parliament, and usurp the government power? If so, I have no ambition to embark on High Treason, which any such action would amount to.'

The Anglican Bishop of Willochra in South Australia, Dr Richard Thomas, called for the dissolution of all Australian parliaments and the appointment of Lord Irwin, a former Viceroy of India, to rule the Commonwealth with a free hand. In Sydney the paramilitary New Guard was being organised by Sydney businessmen, most of whom were returned soldiers; and, in Melbourne, returned men of the same kidney had formed a clandestine White

Army. Who would have been surprised, looking out from Parliament House at the Limestone Plains, if suddenly there had appeared a distant motorcade? The only question would have been whether it was the New Guard, the White Army or something proletarian. Some of the unemployed presented a vaguely military appearance because, as Chifley informed the House, the Department of Defence had issued that ragged army with 20 965 greatcoats, 69 850 khaki jackets, 17 579 pairs of boots and 10 750 hats. Within a stone's throw of Parliament House, like a standing reproof of what was happening all over the Commonwealth, travelling unemployed were accommodated and fed in what had formerly been a sewerage workers' camp.

In this restive political atmosphere Lyons found himself moving, and to some extent being guided towards the formation of a new parliamentary party. The Group, describing itself as his 'special bodyguard', was also Latham's burial party. 'I have ... had about enough of my Melbourne "friends"', wrote Latham to his wife on 15 April, 'who have, I know now, been engaged in direct negotiations with Lyons which I plainly should have conducted'. At a Nationalist Party meeting two days later Latham tendered his resignation as parliamentary leader and nominated Lyons in his place. Elected unanimously, Lyons quickly reached agreement with the Group to try to form a new federal organisation, the United Australia Movement, by amalgamating the Nationalist Party with the All For Australia League and other similar bodies.

The Country Party was at first unwilling to form part of even a loosely united Opposition, its leader protesting that 'the mob behind the Lyons–Nationalist coalition are all big Melbourne manufacturers and stockbrokers, and would have no more mercy on us than on Latham, whom they have buried alive'. Page had second thoughts, however, and when Lyons notified the Speaker and the House on 7 May that he had been elected Leader of the Opposition, with Latham as his deputy, the Opposition was a fully co-operative though not formally integrated front consisting of the new United Australia Party (twenty-three members, including Hughes), the Country Party (ten) and two Independents, Marks and Stewart: thirty-five in all. The official Labor Party also numbered thirty-five, of whom one was the Speaker, and thus the balance of power was more clearly than ever held by the Lang Labor group of five.

The United Australia Party (U.A.P.) was ideologically the mixture as before. One Labor M.H.R., Crouch, told the House that it reminded him of a time in his boyhood when he spent all his pennies making repeated visits to a raree-show in which a shark was being exhibited. 'Some time later', he said,

> another shark was exhibited, this time a blue one. It was no easier for me to get pennies this time than before; but I scraped together all I could, and approached the man who was running the show. The man drew me aside, and told me, as I had been such a good customer, not to spend my money looking at this shark; it was only the old shark painted blue. That is the position of the United party today. It is the old Nationalist Party painted a different colour.

But at least for Lyons and other Labor defectors the new blue party had the charm of novelty. 'Lyons told me that his followers were astonished by the character of the proceedings', wrote Latham after the first U.A.P. meeting at Parliament House on 7 May.

> even when the meeting passed on to the discussion of controversial questions the debate was decent and friendly. Lyons told me it was a revelation to 'his mates' to be treated like gentlemen. They were accustomed, in the Labor Party room, to vile abuse—to violent language—and to threats of physical violence. He gave me the impression that his people were saying 'Farver, is this 'eaven?'

When Lyons moved a want of confidence motion against the Government on 8 May, he was greeted by his former colleagues with such terms as 'Urish Heep', 'the humble servant of pelf', and the representative of 'boodle instead of the people'. 'The scene in the House was the worst to date', wrote Latham; 'Scullin, Brennan, Maloney, Blakeley and Beasley all showed their anger and resentment in a most childish manner—Scullin and Brennan particularly—they quite lost control of themselves'. This was less than fair to Scullin, who did acknowledge the calibre of his new opponent—a man 'who has virtues and fighting qualities which neither [Latham] or anyone else on that side can lay claim to'. The want of confidence debate lasted little more than two hours, and with Lang Labor's help the Government survived again, by two votes.

The Senate was an even more hostile environment. In filling a Senate vacancy in April 1931, the South Australian parliament ignored any suggestion that casual vacancies should be filled by nominees from the same party as the deceased. A Labor senator, Henry Kneebone, replaced a Country Party senator, but the difference he made to the imbalance of power was infinitesimal: the Nationalist/U.A.P. senators still numbered twenty-four; their Country Party allies, four; A.L.P., six; and Lang Labor, two. There was nothing Scullin could do about such odds. The Opposition would now have welcomed an election for both Houses; but the Government, eschewing grounds for double dissolution, pressed on doggedly with Theodore's financial measures, which it must have realised had no hope of being allowed through by a Senate Opposition solidly at one with the Commonwealth Bank Board and the Bank of England on financial policy. By hanging on to office, even at the price of legislative humiliation, Labor was at least postponing the attack on living standards which a conservative ministry was certain to launch.

It was in this mood of fatalism that Theodore introduced the Bills embodying his financial plan: the Fiduciary Notes Bill, authorising the printing of up to £18 million in unredeemable Treasury notes; the Bank Interest Bill, authorising the Treasurer to vary bank interest rates; and the Wheat Bill, an enabling measure for distribution of fiduciary assistance to the wheat industry. The first two met strong resistance in the lower house during March on grounds that they would allow political control of banking and currency, and produce inflation.

Theodore and a few others strove to maintain a respectable level of debate, but many speakers were either out of their depth or more concerned with personal issues than economic ones. The Gawler Bunyip moved that the word 'Fiduciary' in the title of the Bill be replaced by the word 'Reduciary' because, he said, the measure would reduce confidence in the currency. When the chairman of committees ruled Gabb's amendment out of order because the word was not to be found in any standard dictionary, T. W. White (U, Balaclava, V) moved that 'Reductionary' be used. That in turn was rejected by the chairman, as also was Charles Hawker's suggestion of 'Inflationary'. Cusack dubbed the proposed new notes 'Federal Fidos', and Gullett said that the Government should ensure that the full value of the notes was properly appreciated by printing the Treasurer's photograph on the front, and the findings of the Mungana royal commission on the back.

The second reading of the Fiduciary Notes Bill was negatived in the Senate on 17 April, and the Government then withdrew the other two Bills. In reply to Opposition demands for an election, Scullin said that he would seek a double dissolution if the Senate again rejected the Fiduciary Notes Bill after the interval of three months provided for in Section 57 of the Constitution. This was only talk, however, and the Bill was not re-submitted.

Another component of Theodore's doomed financial plan, the Common-wealth Bank Bill (No. 2), was an emergency measure to meet impending obligations by raiding the gold reserve. Five million pounds worth of Aus-tralian Treasury bills were falling due in London on 30 June. As the federal Government did not have funds to redeem them, and there seemed no hope of a reissue, the Commonwealth Bank Bill (No. 2) was introduced to author-ise shipment of Australia's remaining gold reserves at the Treasurer's dis-cretion. The Bill passed its second reading in the lower house on 23 April by a majority of four votes. In the Senate, however, the Opposition leader, Sir George Pearce, moved that the chairman of the Commonwealth Bank Board be called to the Bar to give evidence on the Bill.

This was the first calling of a witness to the Bar of either chamber, but there were precedents for such action in colonial and State parliaments. Usually such rare events had involved parliamentary privilege, and the witness had appeared in the role of accused. Sir Robert Gibson, on the other hand, was a willing and welcome witness. Indeed his summoning was almost certainly a collusive arrangement with the Opposition majority to bring pressure upon the Government not to export gold. At 3.15 p.m. on 6 May Sir Robert was led by the Usher of the Black Rod to the Bar, a gate of Tasmanian blackwood at the perimeter of the Senate's central aisle, where the Clerk administered the oath to him. He was then given a seat at the far end of the table, but insisted on standing up to answer each question. In addition to the general public, some forty M.H.R.s were present in the gallery, making it difficult for the lower house to maintain a quorum.

For the next hour and a half the Opposition tried to show that the Com-monwealth Bank disapproved of the Government's financial policy, the Government tried to minimise the evidence of such disapproval, and Gibson tried not to involve the bank in political controversy while at the same time expressing its aversion from any currency not substantially based on gold. Gibson agreed with the new Government Leader, Senator John Barnes (V), that there was danger of default overseas unless special steps were taken to meet the situation, and that default would be very serious for Australia. Later, under questioning by Sir William Glasgow (Nat, Q), he said there was another alternative to the export of gold—obviously meaning, though he diplomatically refrained from being explicit, a policy of deflation and cost-cutting. 'If I were to tell honorable senators how this [exporting of gold] could be avoided', he said, 'I should certainly be accused of entering into politics, and I would, no doubt, get another of those nice little admonitions informing me that I am overstepping my position as Chairman of the Commonwealth Bank Board and am seeking to dictate the policy of governments'. In the heat of all this, one of the Lang Labor Senators, 'Digger' Dunn, lost his temper:

> Senator DUNN.— . . . The questions submitted by the Opposition are a frame-up, purely and simply, against the Government of the day.
> The PRESIDENT.—Order!
> Senator DUNN.—I denounce the Opposition for having brought Sir Robert Gibson—
> The PRESIDENT.—Order!
> Senator DUNN.—to the chamber—
> The PRESIDENT.—Order!
> Senator DUNN.—in order to get his evidence to use as political propaganda against this Government.
> The PRESIDENT.—Order!

Senator Dunn refused to apologise, and when Senator Barnes moved that he be suspended he left the chamber. Senator Barnes might just as well have gone with him, for all the good his Government could hope to do in the Senate.

Another suspension, of a different kind, was still in force at this time on the Representatives' side of Parliament House. During March the Melbourne *Herald* correspondent, J. A. Alexander, scored one of the most interesting scoops in the history of the Press Gallery. From someone—probably Lyons, in view of the latter's special relationship with the Murdoch press—he obtained copies of the cables which had passed between Scullin, Lyons and Fenton during the Caucus crises over financial policy and High Court appointments. Joe Alexander was an experienced correspondent, not only well supplied with sources but also reputedly able to read upside down while talking across a politician's desk, and even to read the lips of members in close conversation in King's Hall. Unfortunately for him, the cables story, which he sent to Melbourne on a Saturday for publication in Monday's *Herald*, was also supplied to Alan Reid of the Sydney *Sun* for syndicated publication on the same day. The editor of the *Sunday Sun* happened to see it, cleared his front page, and stole the Melbourne *Herald*'s thunder.

The Government nonetheless held Alexander responsible for its embarrassment, and on 23 April Speaker Makin invited him to explain why he should not be banned from the precincts of Parliament House. Alexander's reply, of which a verbatim note was taken in the Speaker's office, concluded as follows:

> [Because] the documents were not documents of Parliament in any form . . . I do not see how Parliament or the Speaker comes into this matter at

all. Parliament of course would obviously have full authority to expel by carrying a motion to that effect but I do not see how in the absence of any precise authority of Parliament the Speaker has any right to intervene . . . For the Speaker to act as an instrument of the Executive Government in awarding punishment for an offence, or alleged offence, of which he has no personal or official cognisance is, I submit with the greatest possible respect, completely violating all the principal foundations of the Speakership.

This argument was presented more concisely next day in a motion by the former chairman of committees, Bayley. He moved that the expulsion of a journalist from the precincts of the House was 'a question for the House to decide, and not a matter for decision by the Speaker, acting either on his own authority or at the suggestion of the Ministry'. The vote on this was tied at 23–23, but the Speaker upheld his own authority by giving his casting vote to the 'Noes'. He then wrote to Alexander notifying him that henceforth he would not be admitted within the precincts of the House of Representatives. Makin was otherwise a model Speaker, but in this case most observers agreed that he should not have become involved in a dispute between the Government and the press.

The Senate, unwilling to be bound by the Speaker's edict, made it known that Alexander would be welcome to report proceedings on the western side of Parliament House. For several days he took advantage of this hospitality, venturing as far as an imaginary centre line in King's Hall, from where perhaps he still managed to read a few lips on the other side. Then Keith Murdoch recalled him to Melbourne. After four months the Australian Journalists' Association reached a compromise with the government whereby Alexander was allowed to return on his assurance that he had come by the text of the cables in the ordinary course of his work as a journalist.

The Press Gallery at this time consisted of only six permanent correspondents, representing the *Sydney Morning Herald*, Sydney *Sun*, Melbourne *Argus* and Melbourne *Herald*, plus the country and interstate news service, Australian United Press. These men (there were as yet no women in the Press Gallery) made their homes in Canberra, and enjoyed a close, symbiotic relationship with their professional hosts, the members of parliament. During parliamentary sessions the Gallery strength more than trebled. Journalists played cards with members on long train journeys, shared hotels with them, went fishing and picnicking together along the Molonglo and the Murrumbidgee, and mingled freely at Parliament House, particularly on the verandas overlooking the garden courts behind the two chambers.

Some newspaper reports were sent by train to Melbourne and Sydney, but urgent copy was transmitted either by telegraph, from Canberra post office, or, less frequently, by telephone. When Theodore brought down the 1931–32 Budget prematurely at 9.45 p.m. on 10 July, the Press Gallery had to take most of it verbatim from the Treasurer's speech in the House. Between 10 p.m. and midnight the telegraphists transmitted more than 100 000 words.

In this Budget Scullin's Government, bowing to the *force majeure* of banks and Senate, implemented measures which were anathema to most members of the Labor Party. It had no option. The accumulated deficit had risen to £21 million, revenue had continued to fall below the previous year's estimates and unemployment had reached 28 per cent. In addition, the Commonwealth had to meet United Kingdom interest payments on which the Lang Government had defaulted. Theodore's budgetary response to these conditions was dictated essentially by a stringent economic plan to which the Commonwealth had reluctantly but resolutely subscribed at a three-week-long Premiers' Conference in May and June. The Premiers' Plan, as it became known, was an agreement by all governments to effect a 20 per cent reduction in expenditure by such means as cutting pensions, civil service and parliamentary salaries, and bounties; reducing interest on internal public debt; and increasing taxation. Most of the Commonwealth's obligations under the Premiers' Plan, including a reduction of members' own salaries from £1000 to £800, were authorised by Financial Emergency Acts in July and September.

As part of the Premiers' Plan, the Commonwealth Bank Board approved the export of £5 million worth of gold to meet Australia's urgent need in London, and the Bill for this encountered no difficulty in a suddenly acquiescent Senate. The Senate could afford to be magnanimous now. It felt sure of its power, and when Senator Dunn in accordance with the A.L.P. platform moved quixotically for the Senate's abolition, it scarcely bothered to defend itself. Dunn's motion, proposing a referendum for an amendment of the Constitution to abolish the Senate, was debated on 12 November for barely half an hour, and neither the Government nor Opposition leaders bothered to attend. Senator Dunn himself spoke for only one minute, saying that as a Labor man, albeit Lang Labor, he was pledged to work for abolition of the upper house. His fellow Langite, Senator Rae, seconded the motion, though he would rather have abolished the House of Representatives, he said, and increased the number of senators. Only one Opposition senator, Paddy Lynch, deigned to speak against the motion. It was resolved in the negative, by 5 votes to 14.

In this period the Senate permitted itself the rare experience of acting as a true States' House. The Opposition had tried unsuccessfully in the lower house to amend the Federal Aid Roads Bill, in order to give country roads priority over metropolitan ones. The State Governments wanted metropolitan priority, and when the Bill came to the Senate in August it was passed without division.

One other assertion of upper house independence was less successful. In May 1931 the Senate presented an address to the Governor-General protesting against the Government's recent practice of making regulations which were substantially the same as regulations already disallowed by the Senate, and asking His Excellency to refuse approval when such second attempts were presented to the Executive Council. Sir Isaac Isaacs's message in reply, reading remarkably like a High Court judgment, concluded that he could only follow the path defined by the Acts Interpretation Act, and that if a regulation was legal then it must be approved.

Unlike his predecessor, Sir Isaac lived exclusively at Government House,

Yarralumla, for the Scullin Government had economised by cancelling the leases of Government House in Melbourne and Admiralty House in Sydney. At first it had seemed to some, perhaps hoping to find their expectations fulfilled, that the first Australian Governor-General was uneasy in his new role. 'He is rather a pathetic figure, poor little man', wrote the Governor of South Australia, Sir Alexander Hore-Ruthven, to Lord Stonehaven in England, 'and appears to be wondering who is going to kick him next'. This impression was mistaken. Sir Isaac performed his duties with as much dignity and wisdom as anyone could have wished, and the Governor of New South Wales, Sir Philip Game, gave him a good report after staying at Yarralumla in 1931.

To Scullin, working at his office in Parliament House during November, and dining with his wife at the Hotel Canberra, it must have seemed that Senator Rae had somehow succeeded in his peculiar notion of turning parliament into one big Senate. Although the House of Representatives had gone into adjournment at the end of October, the Senate remained in session, appropriating King's Hall and the Hotel Canberra, and filling the pages of Hansard exclusively with its own proceedings. Its main task, day after day, was a debate on the Customs Tariff Bill, during which the Opposition busily reduced many of the import duties which had been imposed in the lower house. Disappointing as this was to Labor protectionists, Scullin now had even more to fear from his own chamber. Since embracing financial orthodoxy, the Government had been losing the sufferance of Beasley's Lang Labor group on which it depended for survival. No longer did the Langites care whether the House was controlled by Labor or the U.A.P., for to them the financial policies of both these parties were almost indistinguishable and equally obnoxious. This left the Langites free to pursue without inhibition their long-standing feud with the official A.L.P., and particularly with Theodore.

In the first half of November Scullin thought he discerned signs of returning prosperity, and on that fragile premise he launched a campaign to restore public confidence. The deficit was falling, the stock market was marginally up, and prices of wheat and wool were starting to rise again. In a radio talk from Canberra on 8 November Scullin urged employers to undertake new work, and announced that the federal Government would spend £250 000 on unemployment relief works before Christmas. On 21 November he told an audience in Melbourne that he believed Australia was at last emerging from the Depression. 'For the first time since I have been prime minister', he said, 'I can see daylight ahead in Government finances'. Whereupon one of his listeners shouted: 'You must have very good eyesight!'

What Scullin must have seen with greater clarity by then was the closer prospect of serious trouble for the Government at the next sitting of the House of Representatives. During a Senate adjournment debate on 19 November Senator Dunn asked how the federal Government was distributing its Christmas grant of £250 000 for unemployment relief works—a matter of particular interest to the Lang faction which suspected the operation of a pork-barrel designed to benefit the A.L.P. *vis-à-vis* Lang Labor at the next

federal election. To Senator Dunn it seemed that a disproportionate part of
the grant was going to Cockatoo Island Dockyard, in the Treasurer's own
electorate of Dalley:

> We regard [Theodore's] action in connexion with the distribution of the
> New South Wales share of the Commonwealth grant as neither more nor
> less than political high-jacking, something that one would expect from a
> Yankee four-flusher ... My group has the numbers, and the consti-
> tutional power to move the adjournment of another place next
> Wednesday, and then the Government will be challenged to a showdown
> as to the allotment of this money.

That was not all that happened when the House reassembled at 3 p.m. on
Wednesday 25 November, with more visitors than usual in the public gallery. Immediately after Question Time, Beasley moved the adjournment of
the House for the purpose of discussing a definite matter of urgent public
importance: the method used to select recipients of employment provided by
the federal grant. Whether he realised that he was about to earn the nickname of 'Stabber Jack' is uncertain. He must have recognised the possibility,
but according to Jack Lang he thought it unlikely. At a Lang Labor meeting in
Sydney two days earlier, one of Lang's lieutenants said to Beasley: 'Jack, do
you know what you intend doing with that motion? Have you considered
the fact that Scullin and Theodore . . . may be looking for a way out and you
may be faced with an election?' 'Don't worry', Beasley is said to have replied,
'they wouldn't be game to take such a risk'.

But they were, and Lyons was ready to seize the opportunity created for
him by Beasley. Beasley demanded a select committee into the Cockatoo
Island affair. Theodore denied any impropriety, and Scullin refused an
inquiry, warning the House that he would regard the carrying of Beasley's
adjournment as a matter of confidence. Ignoring the warning, or egged on by
it, Lang Labor moved the closure and the House divided. Beasley and his
four colleagues sat incongruously with the Opposition: Ned Ward from
Surry Hills beside Thomas White, the son-in-law of Alfred Deakin, from
South Yarra; Rowley James, the champion of locked-out coalminers, beside
a Tasmanian grazier, George Bell. Thus Beasley's motion was carried by 37
votes to 32, and the House adjourned.

The Governor-General was making an official visit to Wangaratta, in
north-eastern Victoria, but at Scullin's urgent request he caught the night
express to Goulburn and motored from there, reaching Government House
on Thursday morning. Scullin arrived soon afterwards and formally advised
Sir Isaac to dissolve the House of Representatives. In a written reply Sir Isaac
cited a recent interpretation of the 1926 resolution on the post of governor-
general, by Professor Berriedale Keith, to the effect that governors-general
were not deprived of all authority to reject ministerial advice, but should
accept such advice, save only in extreme crises. This was not such a crisis,
and Sir Isaac accepted the Prime Minister's advice.

When parliament met that afternoon Scullin announced the dissolution,
saying also that an election for half the Senate, due in any case, would
coincide with one for the lower house on 19 December. His last parliamen-

tary action as Prime Minister was to table a copy of the proposed Statute of Westminster, then under consideration by the United Kingdom parliament. The Statute, abolishing remnants of the imperial parliament's power to legislate for such dominions as Australia, was enacted at Westminster on 11 December but the Bruce–Page Government had insisted on a clause requiring adoption by act of the Commonwealth parliament before the Statute's key clauses would apply to Australia; it remained for the next Labor Party Government to take that step in 1942.

Many Australians still thought it more important to preserve ties with the United Kingdom than to sever them, and the U.A.P.'s election campaign made good use of that sentiment. Lyons's main slogan, 'Tune in with Britain', referred to imperial loyalty and the popularity of wireless sets among those who could afford them. Political broadcasts came into their own at this election, with Scullin and Lyons both using radio to assert their claims to credit for the Premiers' Plan.

In New South Wales the U.A.P. invited voters to 'Smash the Empire Wreckers' and 'Smash the Soviet Repudiationists'. Every effort was made to associate Labor, and particularly the Lang faction, with Communism. In most New South Wales electorates where the A.L.P. had any chance, the Lang machine also ran its own candidates. Nowhere was this internecine rivalry more pronounced than in Dalley, where the Lang candidate was a militant ex-timberworker, J. S. Rosevear, who had managed Theodore's campaign there in 1929. Supporters of Rosevear invaded A.L.P. meetings singing 'Yes, we have no Munganas', and the Theodore camp had an anthem of its own, beginning:

> The Beasley, Lang and Trades Hall gang
>   Are rats and nothing more;
> Not true men, like you men,
>   And true blue Theodore.

Unfortunately for Theodore, Dalley was a true blue Trades Hall seat. Rosevear received more than two-thirds of the split Labor vote, and easily defeated the U.A.P. candidate. Theodore then turned his back on politics. He became a successful newspaper proprietor in partnership with the Packer family, and—appropriate for a former Treasurer—managing director of three productive goldmines in Fiji. Among the other election casualties were Chifley, who also had to contend with Lang Labor as well as the U.A.P., and Curtin, who was beaten by an Independent, William Watson.

Scullin held his own seat with a much reduced though still substantial margin, but his party was defeated almost as ignominiously as the Nationalists had been two years before. 'The people are fickle and irresponsible', wrote Theodore. 'They reward the political treachery of Lyons, Fenton, McGrath, Price, Gabb and Guy (what a crop of rats this time!) and they turn out Parker Maloney, Cunningham, Brennan, Chifley, four good and sterling men whose defeat leaves the Labor Party poor indeed.' The U.A.P. won thirty-four seats in the House of Representatives, including Flinders, recaptured by Bruce. Groom was re-elected as an Independent from Darling Downs, and was later admitted to the U.A.P. The Country Party won sixteen seats; A.L.P., fourteen; Lang Labor, four; and Emergency Committee (a South Australian group whose members were sympathetic to, and later joined either the U.A.P. or the Country Party), six.

Scullin's hair had turned completely white during the last two years, and those who knew him later in life said that he never fully recovered his spirit or health. Depression, Senate and Caucus had all been too much for him, and it was no wonder that he accepted defeat gracefully, even gratefully. He presided over his last Cabinet meeting in Canberra on 5 January 1932, and next day met Lyons for the transfer of power. While catching his train back to Melbourne that evening, Scullin told a reporter: 'I feel like a school kid going on holidays'.

The worst that may be said of Scullin is not that he was weak or wrong-headed, as some of his contemporaries believed, but merely that he was overwhelmed. He made one egregious mistake: the reinstatement of Theodore, which split his parliamentary party and invited the wrath of Lang. Otherwise, as his biographer, J. R. Robertson, was to conclude a generation later, 'he was simply unlucky to be caught by events which would have blasted any man's reputation'.

10

The Hat Trick

Recovery

While Joseph Lyons was a boy growing up in northern Tasmania, he happened to see something so shockingly unexpected that it haunted him for the rest of his life. Near the town of Stanley stood a huge basalt outcrop surmounted by a plateau of pasture ending in sheer cliffs about 300 feet high. Walking around the bottom of these cliffs one day, the boy approached an object which for a moment he could not identify. It was the burst carcass of a cow that had fallen from the top only minutes before, leaving a dreadful splash of milk and blood on the path ahead of him. According to an account written long afterwards by Enid Lyons, the boy was so deeply affected by this experience that for several days he could not bring himself to eat. 'Milk revolted him; he could never again bear the sight of blood and never again could he see pain of any kind unmoved. He had sympathy for every living creature.'

Even allowing for the bias of a devoted wife, there was some truth in this. Australia's tenth Prime Minister was the very model of a sympathetic family man. When the mother of a crying baby went to leave one of his election meetings he said: 'Don't go; I'm used to that at home'. And so he was, still only fifty-three years old, with ten children aged from one to sixteen. 'Honest Joe' Lyons was the sort of common man with whom average Australian voters could identify. 'I am no orator', he told them during the 1931 campaign. 'I am just a plain blunt man with a simple straightforward story to tell of what seems to me to be the position in Australia today.'

That position was still perilous, in spite of the remedial steps which had finally been taken by the previous government. The hopeful rise in wheat and wool prices had petered out, and unemployment had risen to 30 per cent. Of twenty-six amateur players in the Canberra City Band which

289

greeted the Governor-General's car at the opening of the thirteenth parliament on 17 February 1932, only six were fully employed. The New Guard and militant trade unionists were said to be arming against each other in Sydney, and the Lang Government had recently advised Lyons of its intention to default again on overseas interest payments. By no means was it impossible that Australia would yet end on the rocks, an ugly mess of wheat, wool, milk and blood.

In his speech to parliament the Governor-General relayed a warning from his advisers that return of prosperous conditions depended upon the recovery of world commodity prices, and that so far there were no indications of such a recovery. While waiting for improvement in world prices, he said, most Australian governments were adhering to the Premiers' Plan of financial and economic rehabilitation by adjusting their expenditure to available means. There were, however, three exceptions: the States of Western Australia and Tasmania, whose economic circumstances required special financial consideration; and the New South Wales Government, whose deficit spending had placed it beyond the financial pale.

'My Ministers . . . deem it their duty', said the Governor-General,

> to emphasize that the deficit in the accounts of the Government of . . . [New South Wales] gravely affects the whole budgetary position of Australia. Unless definite action is taken the whole Commonwealth may be involved in a financial collapse . . . My Ministers also view with the utmost concern the failure of the Government of the State of New South Wales to meet its public obligations . . . While unhesitatingly condemning the policy that has led to public default . . . my advisers have felt impelled, in the interests of the credit of the nation as a whole, to honour the obligations of that Government. My Ministers will take steps to compel the repayment of these moneys to the Commonwealth by the Government of the State.

In spite of the U.A.P.'s electoral success, it lacked an absolute majority in the lower house. Its expected strength of thirty-nine (after reinforcement by five South Australian members of the Emergency Committee) was soon reduced to thirty-eight, when a new Liberal and Country League member from South Australia who had been expected to join the U.A.P., A. G. Cameron (Barker), chose to sit with the Country Party instead; and then to thirty-seven, when a U.A.P. candidate, who had defeated E. J. Ward in East Sydney, died before taking his seat. Ward regained the seat at a by-election, bringing Lang Labor's strength to five. Thus, after providing a new Speaker—George Mackay (Lilley, Q)—the Government party could theoretically be defeated by two votes.

Coalition was out of the question for the time being. Shortly before Christmas Lyons managed to get a message through to Dr Page, who was holidaying on the north coast of New South Wales. The U.A.P. was not interested in forming a composite government, said Lyons, but he had allocated three portfolios for Country Party members: Postmaster-General, Markets and Honorary Minister. Page was not that easily bought. At a meeting in Melbourne after Christmas he demanded Trade and Customs, and some assurance about downward tariff revision. Lyons declined, and a joint statement was issued to the effect that the Country Party would co-operate as far as possible with the new Government, but not in Cabinet. That undertaking was worthless, and for the next three years the Lyons Government was continually harassed by those who should have been its political allies. The only consolation for the Government was that Page and his followers were unlikely to combine with Labor.

Parliament had seen less than usual of Dr Page lately, for during the Scullin Government's term in office he spent a good deal of time developing 'Boolneringbar', a property on the upper Clarence River which he had taken up as a joint venture with some friends. At about this time he also suffered two severe personal blows. In 1931 he almost died of acute appendicitis, and in 1932 his eldest son, Earle junior, was struck by lightning. The boy and one of his brothers were mustering cattle at 'Boolneringbar', on opposite sides of a creek, when an exceptionally violent thunderstorm began. Earle reined his horse under the shelter of a tree, and in a flash was killed instantly.

When Dr Page broke the news to his wife, she suffered a stroke affecting the movement of her hands. 'Ever afterwards', he wrote,

> until her death 25 years later, she could not hold a cup of water or tea but was obliged to drink from a glass tube . . . This terrible family blow affected us all in many ways. I proposed to relinquish my responsibilities as Country Party leader and even contemplated resigning from the Parliament itself. But the party refused to consider my proposals, appointed Tom Paterson acting leader and gave me extended leave of absence to recuperate from the personal aftermath and straighten out my business affairs.

After a few months Page was his old giggling self again, back in Canberra and making more mischief for the Government. The Prime Minister, writing to Enid Lyons in Devonport, relayed a vivid description by one of the Government Whips, Senator H. S. Foll (Q): 'The Country Party are like copulating cats, getting all they want and crying out all the time'.

The U.A.P. ministry left much to be desired, at least in the stern judgement of Bruce, who pronounced it 'tragically weak'. The Prime Minister was his own Treasurer; Latham, the Government's main strength, was Attorney-General, Minister for External Affairs and Minister for Industry; Pearce took Defence; Gullett, Trade and Customs; Parkhill, Home Affairs and Transport; Hawker, Markets; and Bruce, Honorary Minister assisting the Treasurer. The rest were, in Bruce's words, 'complete and absolute passengers'. Even Lyons was found wanting by his hypercritical assistant. 'For this job', said Bruce to Enid Lyons after the election, 'a man really needs three things, or some of them anyhow: a hide like a rhinoceros, an overpowering ambition, and a mighty good conceit of himself. And your poor husband has none of them'. That was the tactful way of putting it. After a few weeks of the new parliament, Bruce reported more candidly to Latham that although 'the stress and strain was nothing like what it is going to be the PM [showed] clear and unmistakable signs that it was telling on him . . . He has had several attacks where for a short space of time he is completely knocked out'. The doctor had found nothing seriously wrong, but Bruce wondered whether Lyons's health would stand the strain of confronting Lang over repudiation.

That confrontation lasted three months, and with Bruce's assistance Lyons was equal to the demands of this extraordinary period. Never before had the Commonwealth waged financial war against one of its partners in federation. At one level the Commonwealth was seeking to recover money which it had spent in servicing the loans on which New South Wales had defaulted. But its tactics were also designed to force the New South Wales Government to an election over Lang's bellicose economic policies, particularly a Mortgages Taxation Bill which threatened banks and insurance companies with a 10 per cent tax on mortgages. This Bill had passed all stages, and was awaiting royal assent.

The federal Government's main legislative weapons against Lang were the Financial Agreements (Commonwealth Liability) Act, designed to remove any doubts about the Commonwealth's legal duty to pay repudiated State debts incurred under the Financial Agreement of 1928–29; several Financial Agreements Enforcement Acts, establishing garnishee procedure by which the Commonwealth could apply to the High Court for a judgment to recover liabilities of this kind from State funds held by trading banks; and finally the Financial Emergency (State Legislation) Act, designed to frustrate the intention of Lang's Mortgages Taxation Bill. The latter federal measure— 'for the peace, order and good government of the Commonwealth'—was no less extraordinary than the times that provoked it. First, it purported to negate any State law imposing a tax on mortgages if the federal Commissioner for Taxation certified that payment of such a levy would unduly impair ability to pay federal taxation; furthermore, it provided that the Governor-General might relieve insurance and banking businesses of the obligation to pay such a capital levy if the two houses of federal parliament resolved that the levy would endanger the financial and economic stability of the Commonwealth.

Against strong opposition from the Lang Labor group, some A.L.P. members and even some U.A.P. and Country Party defenders of State rights, the Government guillotined its garnishee and State Legislation measures through all stages. Unlike the first garnishee Act, which the High Court upheld against a challenge by the Lang Government, the Financial Emergency (State Legislation) Act was almost certainly unconstitutional. It was never tested in court, however, because it never had to be used. The Bill for this Act passed its final stage in the House of Representatives at about 2 p.m. on 13 May 1932. Two hours later Lang received a letter from the Governor of New South Wales, Sir Philip Game, dismissing him from office on grounds that his efforts to evade the federal garnishee process were unlawful. Although this was the first dismissal of its kind in Australian history, it occasioned no great controversy. Lang went quietly, probably thankful to have been released from the toils of his own making, and the Leader of the U.A.P., Bertram Stevens, formed a coalition Ministry with the Country Party. Stevens then obtained a dissolution, won the election, and brought New South Wales into step with the Premiers' Plan.

This plan was formally approved at a Premiers' conference in April, but most of its principles as they affected the Commonwealth had already been applied in Scullin's last Budget. Those estimates were working so success-fully that there was little adjustment for Lyons to make in his September Budget. Revenue had been £4 million more than expected, an American moratorium on war debts had saved a similar amount, and for these and other reasons the year 1931–32 had ended with a current accounts surplus of £1 300 000 instead of an expected deficit of £2 million. The total deficit of all Australian Governments was less than half an expected £40 million, and the external balance of trade showed a credit of £31 million compared with the previous year's debit of £33 million. Things were looking up, although nearly one-third of the work-force was still unemployed.

In accordance with the Premiers' Plan, members of parliament voted themselves a second salary reduction—from £800 to £750. The member for Angas, J. M. Gabb, moved an amendment for a larger reduction, to £600, and in so doing caused the resignation of one of Cabinet's better Ministers, and its only rural expert, Charles Hawker. This young South Australian, who had suffered terrible wounds in the war, was regarded by Lyons as 'the only other brain in the cabinet' besides Latham and Bruce. As a 21-year-old lieutenant in the Somerset Light Infantry (he had been at Cambridge when war broke out), Hawker was wounded twice at Ypres. After recuperating from fourteen operations, but now blind in one eye, he returned to the front only to be wounded even more severely, being temporarily paralysed from the waist down. After more operations he managed to walk again, but for the rest of his life he had to wear surgical leg irons. This did not prevent him from working one of his family's properties in the Flinders Ranges, often on horseback. He studied wool-classing, forestry and botany, and travelled overseas to further his knowledge of rural marketing.

Hawker possessed great personal charm, but was also endowed with cer-tain rigid ideals that were not well suited to political life. Having told his electors that he would vote for the greatest possible reduction in members' salaries, he felt himself bound to support Gabb's grandstanding amendment rather than the level of £750, to which Cabinet was collectively committed. And having joined Gabb and six others in a fruitless vote for the amendment, he felt obliged to resign from Cabinet, to which he never returned.

As another economy measure, requested by the government, the presid-ing officers asked the Public Service Board to examine the five departments of parliament—Senate, House of Representatives, Parliamentary Reporting Staff, Parliamentary Library and Joint House—and report upon ways, if any, in which their combined expenditure, amounting to about £60 000 per year, might be reduced for the sake of the Premiers' Plan. This was an unpre-cedented concession to the executive, and when the Public Service Com-missioner, J. T. Pinner, presented his report in 1933 the new President of the Senate, Senator P. J. Lynch (W), felt constrained to justify the invitation that had been extended by his predecessor and the Speaker. 'Had I then been President of the Senate', he said,

I believe that I would have acted as Senator Kingsmill did, although I realise how dangerous and unprecedented it is to permit an outside body to inquire into the exercise by Parliament, or by those appointed to give effect to the authority of Parliament, of the time honoured, traditional and exclusive powers of this august body. But the conditions then prevailing made it incumbent upon the presiding officers to give that authority, because the request of the Government could not be interpreted as an attempt on the part of the Crown to encroach upon the preserves of Parliament.

It was one thing to receive recommendations, however, and another to implement them. The Pinner Report was never tabled, and so the public remained unaware that in its author's opinion the Senate staff of twelve could have been reduced to seven, and the staff in the lower house from eighteen to ten. The President and the Speaker informed their respective chambers that some of Pinner's recommendations would be adopted (for example, secondment of Hansard reporters to the Attorney-General's Department during parliamentary recess, a practice which continued until 1949), but that others, likely to 'disorganise the work of Parliament, and inconvenience its members', would not be adopted.

The thirteenth parliament passed two Wheat Relief Acts, providing grants for farmers impoverished by Depression prices for their crops. It also spent ten weeks of sitting time on the first complete tariff revision since 1922. The tariff schedule that finally reached the Senate in June 1933 contained 1800 items. Most of these were designed to give local manufacturers an advantage over imports, and the consequent expansion of secondary industry became a significant factor in Australia's economic recovery. The Senate returned forty-seven tariff items to the lower house, all accompanied by requests for less protection or free entry; the House made thirty-three of the requested amendments, made another seven with modifications, and did not make the remaining seven.

Both houses then played the contentious game of pressed requests. The Senate decided to press three of the seven rejected requests, concerning rabbit traps, dates and spray pumps. In spite of the other chamber's doubts about the Senate's constitutional right to do this, the procedure was now well established. One member of the Opposition, Senator J. V. MacDonald (Q), nevertheless scandalised his colleagues by siding with the House of Representatives—not over rabbit-traps, dates and spray pumps, but over the right to press requests.

> Senator MACDONALD.—We should not quarrel with the House of Representatives over details. Rabbit traps, dates and spray pumps are not of sufficient importance to justify a major disagreement between the two branches of the legislature. I have had a good deal to do with words and their meanings, and it is plain that while the Senate has the power to make a request on this measure, it has not the right to persist in that request.
> Senator O'HALLORAN (L, S).—Undoubtedly it has.
> Senator MACDONALD.—Well, if words mean anything, it has not, and to keep on requesting would be ridiculous. If we persist in our request, we shall be practically insisting that we have power to amend a money bill.

But the Senate did persist, and the House of Representatives responded in accordance with the unwritten rules of the game. After resolving that public interest demanded early enactment of the tariff, and carefully refraining 'from the determination of its constitutional rights or obligations', the House agreed to the pressed requests, with modifications. On receipt of this message the Senate resolved that the House's dealing with its reiterated requests was 'in compliance with the undoubted constitutional position and rights of the Senate', and agreed to the Bill as amended.

Australia's financial position was substantially improved during 1932–33 by the conversion of several British loans. This was supervised in London by Bruce, who remained a member of parliament while acting unofficially in the post of High Commissioner, vacated recently by Sir Granville Ryrie. There was some suggestion that Bruce should continue in both capacities, but this proved to be constitutionally impossible. He therefore resigned his seat in October 1933, was appointed High Commissioner, and held that post with distinction for twelve years.

After Bruce's appointment to London, the Prime Minister relied more heavily on Latham; but Latham's days in parliament were numbered, for he was expected sooner or later to succeed Sir Frank Gavan Duffy as Chief Justice of the High Court. As early as 1933 Lyons sounded out a member of his 'special bodyguard' in Melbourne—the constitutional lawyer and Victorian M.L.A., R. G. Menzies—about entering federal parliament and becoming the next Attorney-General. 'Menzies is rather tickled with the prospect', wrote R. G. Casey to Bruce, in whose place he was now Minister assisting the Treasurer, '—but has apparently not made up his mind'.

Although Lyons was not a very good organiser of executive or parliamentary business, and may sometimes have welcomed a guiding hand from Bruce or Latham, as a national figure he inspired confidence in the gradual economic recovery that was now under way. His socialism, which in Tasmania had never prevented him from finding common cause with the Nationalists in joint approaches to the Commonwealth, was now completely transformed into a conservatism which some felt had always been part of his character. 'Disraeli was a conservative by tradition and romance', wrote Hawker, 'Lord Salisbury of the land, Bonar Law of successful industry. Lyons is a conservative of the man with small savings and a home of their [sic] own. It is in his bones and is genuine but independent of isms and dogmas and als and ives'.

Somehow it seemed reassuring that The Lodge, after having been closed during Scullin's two desperate years, was now occupied from time to time by numerous members of the Lyons family. And as if to express confidence in the future, Enid Lyons gave birth to her twelfth surviving child and sixth daughter, in October 1933. This was the first child born to the wife of an Australian Prime Minister in office.

Another expression of confidence at about this time was contained in the Financial Relief Act of October 1933. Late on the night of Thursday 19 October a meeting of the Government party decided to recommit the Financial Relief Bill so that the parliamentary salary could be raised from its reduced level of £750 to £825. Next morning the House carried an amendment to that effect by 44 votes to 16, the 'Noes' consisting of eleven U.A.P. members (Hawker was paired as a 'No'), three Country Party and two Independents, including Gabb. Two days later Sydney's *Sunday Sun* devoted the upper part of its front page to a predictably censorious editorial entitled 'Salary Grab came as Thief in the Night'.

> 'Cometh as a thief in the night'—the midnight meeting of private members of the Federal Parliament, to jockey the public for a £75 rise in their salaries, by a swift and shameless Parliamentary vote next day. At the very same hour on the very same day, the Arbitration Commission cut away 2s a week from the basic wage of £3 8s 6d, reducing it to £3 6s 6d on the ground that 'cost of living' is reduced since April.
>
> Poor devils on the basic wage—labourers, struggling to maintain home and wife on £3 6s 6d a week—must bow to the Law; and the 2s loss from their wages is what the Law prescribes.
>
> But there is no law to control Honourable Members, who vote £75 a year extra to their Honourable selves . . . 'So are they all, all Honourable Men.' But why did they creep together at midnight to arrange their salary grab in the furtive fashion of sneaks?
>
> You may hear the Honourable Men defend themselves by saying that once on a time they had £1000 a year, and even now are taking only £825.
>
> This may serve to make the act of rapacity more cowardly, but not less contemptible.

In privilege debates during the next three weeks, the House decided, first, that the printer and publisher of the *Sunday Sun* were guilty of contempt, and, second, that they should be called to the Bar of the House for it. By the time the second motion was agreed to, however, the Prime Minister had received a letter of qualified regret from the chairman of the board of Associated Newspapers Ltd, Sir Hugh Denison. The board agreed with the policy expressed in the *Sunday Sun's* editorial, said Sir Hugh, but it acknowledged with regret that the editorial was 'garnished with somewhat highly coloured phrases' which might have been construed as imputations against the personal honesty of members, and it assured the Prime Minister that no such imputations had been intended. This was close enough to an apology for the House to resolve that no further action be taken.

Recovery and confidence were still notably absent in one State, Western Australia. Indeed the Depression had fomented long-standing grievances in this vast but underdeveloped region to such a point that there was wide popular support for a movement to secede from the Commonwealth. No one contemplated the use of force, but many Western Australians were prepared to go almost any distance short of that in putting the first and still the only case ever seriously made for secession from what the campaigners for federation had called 'One Flag, One People, One Destiny'. Western Australia's main grievances closely resembled the fears expressed a generation before by those who predicted that federation would become a Moloch upon whose altar the welfare of smaller States would be sacrificed. Western Australia, said the secessionists, had been reduced to a subservient position through whittling down of the essential federal principle of the Constitution by High Court decisions and direct amendment; it had been deprived of adequate revenues by the Commonwealth's entry into the fields of direct taxation; its primary industries were burdened by a federal policy of Protection designed to foster manufacturing in the more industrialised eastern States; and its representation in federal parliament was too small to influence the policy of Commonwealth governments, invariably dictated by the more populous States. The Loan Council, referred to by Perth newspapers as 'The Beggar's Opera', had been making special grants to Western Australia since 1910; and the Commonwealth Grants Commission, established in 1933 to help the claimant States of Western Australia, South Australia and Tasmania, recommended generous annual grants to the first of these States in view of its great size and scattered population.

Before the Grants Commission came into being, however, the Western Australian parliament legislated for a referendum on secession. Lyons and Senator Pearce took part in the campaign, as Tasmanian and Western Australian federalists respectively, and so did Billy Hughes. Pearce stayed in Perth after his colleagues had returned east, and on polling day, 8 April 1933, he telegraphed to Lyons in Canberra: 'In view of feeling excited by the secession campaign I have arranged certain precautionary measures in respect of principal Commonwealth buildings. Have also arranged that any urgent and secret communications from the heads of Departments here shall go through'. It sounded like sandbags and barbed wire around the G.P.O., but in fact the referendum was quite orderly, though it resulted in a decisive vote for secession, by 138 653 to 70 706.

This prompted a Senate adjournment debate with faint overtones of Fort Sumter. Senator Dunn demanded to know whether Senator Pearce, the Minister for Defence, intended to submit the names of Western Australian rebels to the Attorney-General for action under the Crimes Act, and Senator T. C. Brennan (Lab, V) told Senator E. B. Johnston (C, W) and the five other federal parliamentarians from Western Australia who supported secession that he found it 'hard to draw a distinction between those who would break this indissoluble Commonwealth into which we have entered, and straight out rebels'.

In reality nothing short of amendment of the Constitution by a plebiscite of all Australian electors, or the unthinkable alternative of civil war, could have enabled Western Australia to withdraw from the Commonwealth. But the secessionists mistakenly believed that there was another way: appeal to the United Kingdom parliament by whose enactment the Commonwealth of Australia had been constituted. To this end the state government prepared a 600-page *Case of the People of Western Australia in support of their desire to withdraw from the Commonwealth of Australia . . . and that Western Australia be restored to its former status as a separate self-governing colony in the British Empire*. The federal Government replied by appointing a committee under the chairmanship of Sir Robert Garran, which produced a short but trenchant *Case for Union*, closing with this admonitory question from English history: 'What shall we say of them who, being in the common-wealth, feeling a sore greevous unto them, and easie to be amended, sought not the remedie, but have increased the griefe?'

In 1934 an official delegation led by the former Western Australian Premier and senator, Sir Hal Colebatch, presented a petition for secession to the imperial parliament, where eventually it met with the response expected by most federalists, and by those conversant with the Statute of Westminster. Although the Statute had yet to be adopted by federal parliament, it amounted to a formal declaration that the imperial parliament would exercise no supervisory powers over the legislation of self-governing dominions. A select committee of the House of Commons and House of Lords rejected Western Australia's petition in May 1935 on the legal ground that even to receive it would have been against constitutional practice in relation to dominion affairs. That stopped the secession movement in its tracks. The western 'rebels' had achieved what was probably their principal purpose, simply the drawing of Commonwealth attention to the State's economic and financial problems. But they had to face the facts that they were Australians first and Western Australians second, and that, in the contemporary aphorism, amputation was not the only cure for prickly heat. Other cures, or at least palliatives, were to be found in recovery from the Depression and the annual ministrations of the Grants Commission.

Lyons had already promised larger grants to the States for unemployment relief and rural subsidies in his policy speech for the general election of 15 September 1934. The U.A.P. campaigned mainly on a continuation of existing economic and financial measures; Labor promised banking and monetary reform, more tariff protection for industry, and restoration of the remaining cuts made in wages, salaries and social services under the Premiers' Plan; and the Country Party cried out like tom cats for less protection of secondary industry and more help for the man on the land.

This election produced a second victory for Lyons, although there was a small swing towards the two Labor groups. Membership of the House of Representatives had been reduced by redistribution from seventy-five full-voting members to seventy-four, plus the Member for the Northern Territory. The missing electorate was Angas (S), and with it into political extinction went the Gawler Bunyip. In the new House, the U.A.P. had thirty-two members; Country Party, fifteen; A.L.P., eighteen; and the New South Wales Labor Party (Lang), nine. Lyons lost his two ex-Labor colleagues, Fenton and Guy; and also his mentor, Latham, who retired from Kooyong and was appointed Chief Justice of the High Court in October 1935. Robert Gordon Menzies took over Kooyong with a reduced but still very comfortable majority, and was duly appointed Attorney-General.

The swing to Labor returned John Curtin from Fremantle. During the last three years Curtin had continued to read Hansard from cover to cover, and had earned his living first as a sporting journalist on the *Westralian Worker* and later as chairman of a board appointed by the State Government to prepare Western Australia's first case before the Commonwealth Grants Commission. His friend Anstey had hoped that Curtin might succeed him in the safe Melbourne seat of Bourke—'a kind of family succession', as he put it—but that preselection went to a radical Melbourne lawyer, Maurice Blackburn. Anstey had displayed rather cynical disregard for his electors during the thirteenth parliament. 'I've finished with [parliament]', he wrote to Curtin, 'and I had been sick of it for years'. In those three years, which he treated as 'long service furlough prior to retirement', he attended parliament for only thirty-one out of 123 sitting days. In a letter written to his friend the Clerk-Assistant, Frank Green, soon after his own retirement, Anstey passed harsh judgement on the parliament which he had adorned for so long. 'The night I was leaving Canberra for ever', he wrote, 'the past rose before me like a dream . . . Now, what is left? That awful Dead House, that habitation of decayed souls. That glorious old ranter Ezekiel bellowed—"I will take out of you your hearts of dung and give you hearts of flesh." He is wanted now'.

External Affairs

The fourteenth parliament was notable for a sinking of differences on both sides: the two non-Labor parties formed a governing coalition, and Labor regained its former unity. Lyons had to be prodded by the Country Party, however, before he recognised the necessity for coalition. 'He hates the idea of having to live in the same house as Page etc', wrote Casey to Bruce in the second week of the parliament, 'but even he [now] recognises the urgent necessity of it—and the inevitability of it—if we are to have 3 years of more or less stable government'.

Lyons had met the new parliament for the first time on 23 October 1934 with an exclusively U.A.P. Ministry, but that evening he was pulled up suddenly by the Country Party's unexpected opposition to his motion for a special adjournment until the following Wednesday. The Duke of Gloucester was then visiting Australia for Melbourne's centenary, and various Commonwealth dignitaries, from the Governor-General and the Prime Minister down, were expected to attend functions in His Royal Highness's honour. One of these functions was the Melbourne Cup, and in his remarks on the adjournment Dr Page managed to sound properly disapproving of a motion concerned in part with the desire of members of parliament to attend a horse race. 'The people of Australia', he said,

> and particularly those resident in country districts, are looking forward with a great deal of hope to the work of this Parliament, and they would be cheered by the knowledge that we were to remain at work rather then to adjourn over the period suggested. I ask the Prime Minister to look further into this matter.

What the Honourable Member for Cowper was really after was the Deputy Prime Ministership and Commerce portfolio for himself, one other full portfolio for the Country Party, and two assistant ministerships. During the next twenty minutes Lyons agreed, and the special adjournment was carried. The following Tuesday the Duke of Gloucester, suitably attended by Commonwealth representatives, watched Darby Munro ride Peter Pan to its second Melbourne Cup win. This was the twenty-third consecutive year in which federal parliament, for one reason or another, had not been sitting on Melbourne Cup Day.

Four U.A.P. Ministers made way for Country Party replacements, and in 1935 the membership of Cabinet was increased from nine to ten. The Prime Minister remained Treasurer; Page became *de facto* Deputy Prime Minister and *de jure* Minister for Commerce; his party deputy, Thomas Paterson

(Gippsland, V), became Minister for the Interior, and two other Country Party members became assistant ministers. Pearce took External Affairs; Menzies, Attorney-General and Industry; and Parkhill, Defence. Hughes, restored to grace after eleven years on the back benches, became Vice-President of the Executive Council and Minister for Health and Repatriation; and Casey was again Minister assisting the Treasurer.

Although Menzies was appointed Deputy Leader of the U.A.P. in 1935, there was no generally accepted line of succession after Lyons. Menzies was well aware of rivalry in this regard from the Minister for Defence, Sir Archdale Parkhill, around whom the party's arch-conservatives gathered. Archie Parkhill wore spats and pince-nez, and carried a silver-topped walking stick. For twenty-five years he had been general secretary of the Liberal and Nationalist parties in New South Wales, and he was said to control the purse-strings of the U.A.P. In parliament Parkhill was something of a fire-eater, a formidable politician but inclined to pomposity. Menzies for his part attracted some of the party's liberals, but was also rather adept at losing friends. Many years later he would look back critically at himself during the 1930s. 'I was still in that state of mind', he wrote, 'in which to be logical is to be right, and to be right is its own justification. I had yet to acquire the common touch . . . to realise that all-black and all-white are not the only hues in the spectrum'.

The young Menzies was undeniably majestic, still in his early forties, tall, slightly corpulent, resonant in tone and magisterial in features, grave when it suited him but also quick of eye and tongue. Often too quick. Some said that his superior, combative manner was a shield for inner nervousness, but many found this hard to believe. Stories told about him were seldom to his credit. One evening at the Hotel Canberra, for example, he was accosted in friendly enough fashion by a senator for whom he had no high regard. After complimenting Menzies on his performance in the House, the Senator rashly added: 'Your great trouble, Bob, is that you don't suffer fools gladly'. Menzies replied: 'And what, pray, do you think I am doing now?' Another story told against him at this time was that his justification for not having enlisted during the war was that he had had 'no intention of robbing Australia of a future Prime Minister'.

By and large the coalition was harmonious enough. 'The composite U.A.P.-CP Cabinet is working quite well', wrote Casey to Bruce,

—although Page is inclined to jump on his horse and dash off in all directions—particularly in the absence of a strong leading rein such as you were well able to provide . . . I can get on well enough with Page—but Harry Gullett [assistant minister] and Tom White [Trade and Customs] are inclined to fight with him . . . I don't know how long Lyons is going to last as PM. The lack of leadership is very apparent—both in Parliament and in Cabinet and in the general direction of affairs. We amble along as a collection of individuals doing the obvious things that come to our hand—but doing no forward thinking—and generally managing to avoid or side step the difficult problems until they are on our doorstep—then we make a snap line-of-least-resistance decision which is usually costly, and in which we nearly always sacrifice principle. Heaven knows how we have kept out of real trouble—probably only because the opposition, although stronger than in the last Parliament, is really rather ineffective.

That advantage was soon to cease. Partly because of health, but also because he and others believed the party could be reunited more effectively under a leader who had not been in the forefront of the 1931 split, Scullin resigned as Leader of the parliamentary A.L.P. on 1 October 1935. At that day's meeting of Caucus, John Curtin was elected in his place, defeating the Deputy Leader, Frank Forde, by one vote. The group organising for Curtin, led by the Victorian, Holloway, had first obtained his assurance that he had overcome his drinking problem; and so indeed he had. It is not clear whether he had yet given up drink; but alcohol was no longer the problem it had once been for Curtin, who was now fifty years old, and at some time after his return to parliament he stopped drinking altogether. According to one account, while returning to Perth on the transcontinental he threw a glass of whisky from the window, saying, 'Damn it, I'll never have another one of them'.

The crucial vote in Curtin's election was that of Maurice Blackburn, who seemed to resent Curtin's aspiration to the seat of Bourke as much as Curtin resented his occupation of it. 'I do not regard Blackburn as a Messiah of the Latter Day', Curtin had written to Anstey in 1934. 'He is a blancmange—clever, perhaps; a man without sin, he is really destitute of virtue. He is personally too good to be politically worth a damn.' When one of Holloway's men, Arthur Drakeford (Maribyrnong, V), sounded Blackburn out, Blackburn said he could never vote for Curtin, but neither could he bring himself to vote for Forde. He would therefore not vote at all. At the last minute, however, he sent Drakeford his proxy to use, if Drakeford wished, for Curtin.

John Joseph Ambrose Curtin, as he was baptised, was a Labor leader in the mould more of Scullin than Theodore. He was born in the Victorian mining town of Creswick, where his Irish father was police constable. His mother was of Irish ancestry, and the family was Roman Catholic. Jack Curtin, as he was known early in life, was educated at church and state schools until at fourteen he started work as a copy boy on the *Age*. He left the church for reasons unknown, joined the Political Labor League and Victorian Socialist Party, and in those circles formed his close friendship with the older Frank Anstey. Reserved and studious by nature, he nonetheless became secretary of the Victorian Timber Workers' Union and, during the war, organiser of the national executive of the Trade Union Anti-Conscription Congress in Melbourne.

In 1916 he was sentenced to three months' imprisonment for failing to enrol under provisions of the military service proclamation. He served three and a half days of this sentence in a Melbourne gaol, but was released as a consequence of the 'No' vote in the first conscription referendum. This was one of Curtin's worst years for drinking. The measure of his immoderation may be gathered from a letter written by Anstey to Curtin in a private hospital which he had entered for treatment. 'Don't hate yourself, despise yourself, or be ashamed of yourself, or ashamed to face others', said Anstey.

There is no redemption that way. John drunk was a damn nuisance, but he was even in that state a better man than thousands sober, and John sober is the Nestor of them all . . . And when you come out be 'John' to the world—let 'Jack' go with the booze. John will speak or write or lecture to the future.

As 'John' Curtin, leader of the parliamentary Labor Party, he travelled widely throughout the Commonwealth, fighting by-elections and striving to bring the Langites back into the official party. 'My aim is to revive the spirit and unity of the Labor movement', he said in one speech soon after becoming leader, 'to renew and to vitalise its sobriety and commonsense so that it may once again serve the needs of Australia in an era in which the portents of evil are grave and numerous'. The Langites had done well at the election, increasing their number from five to nine. This was too big a schism to be tolerated unnecessarily, and in February 1936 the A.L.P. federal conference rescinded its 1931 resolution expelling the New South Wales branch. Lang retained control of the party in New South Wales for five more years, but Beasley and his followers in federal parliament returned to Caucus forthwith.

Labor's confidence and growing sense of unity were strengthened by a lengthy parliamentary debate late in 1935 on the Government's proposal that Australia should follow Britain's example by supporting economic sanctions against Italy, organised in the League of Nations to deter that power from its invasion of Abyssinia. The Lang Labor group was at first inclined to support sanctions, but then joined forces with the A.L.P., which it was soon to rejoin officially, in opposing the government's policy mainly on the isolationist ground that Australia should not become involved in something which could conceivably lead to another European war. That view was also taken by one U.A.P. Minister, Hughes, in a book which he published on the subject, *Australia and War Today*. Ministerial solidarity required Hughes's resignation, but three months later, after Australia sided with the League of Nations, he was back in Cabinet.

As the mists of Depression gradually dissolved, it seemed that Australians were becoming more aware of the world beyond their shores. The other side of Labor's concern with avoiding embroilment in foreign wars was its concern, given strong expression in the September 1936 Estimates debate, that Australia should achieve a greater degree of self-reliance in defence. Curtin questioned the impregnability of Britain's base at Singapore, and asked whether a British government involved in European war would be able to spare sufficient naval force to deny the western Pacific to an aggressor in those waters. Like Latham some four years earlier, he cautiously but unequivocally identified Japan as a potential aggressor.

Mr CURTIN.—. . . The dependence of Australia upon the competence, let alone the readiness of British statesmen to send forces to our aid is too dangerous a hazard upon which to found Australia's defence policy.

Mr LANE (U, Barton, N).—Great Britain has never failed us.

Mr CURTIN.—History has had no experience of the situation I am visualizing.

Prime Minister Bruce welcomes the aviator, Captain Bert Hinkler, outside Parliament House, 14 March 1928, with Duntroon cadets in the foreground.

Clerk of the House of Representatives (1917–1927), W. A. Gale

Clerk of the Senate (1939–1942), R. A. Broinowski

The Lyons family at The Lodge

The first meeting of Federal Cabinet in Canberra, held at Yarralumla House on 30 January 1924 and attended by (back row, left to right): Senator T. W. Crawford, Honorary Minister; E. K. Bowden, Minister for Defence; A. Chapman, Trade and Customs; L. E. Groom, Attorney-General; Dr E. Page, Treasurer and acting Prime Minister; (front row, left to right): L. Atkinson, Vice-President of the Executive Council; W. G. Gibson, Postmaster-General; P. G. Stewart, Works and Railways; and Senator G. Pearce, Home and Territories

Mr LANE.—It is imagination.

Mr CURTIN.—No, it represents a reasonable examination of the possibilities of the situation. Great wars in which Australia's security is to be imperilled will not be European wars. They will be wars in the South Pacific. The delay in despatching the British fleet to our aid would be bound to be prolonged. This delay would provide an enemy the opportunity to capture or damage the Singapore base . . . Singapore is well placed for the defence of India and the trade routes of the Indian Ocean, but it is nearly 3,000 miles west off a direct line from Japan to the eastern coast of Australia as far as Gibraltar is across the Atlantic from New York . . . That a naval unit based on Singapore which would obviously be weak in relation to Japan's naval strength would be a real deterrent to any hostile overseas intentions on Australia is contrary to all naval history. From my reading of naval history there is nothing so inferior as an inferior fleet. If a nation has a fleet that cannot conquer it would be better off without one.

On this ground, Curtin argued that the government should not be seeking to spend such a large proportion of the proposed defence vote on naval works, and should spend more on an air force capable of attacking hostile aircraft carriers. He also advocated closer links with the United States. 'We should look upon the people of the United States of America', he said, 'our neighbours across the Pacific Ocean, with a degree of fraternity, disregarding altogether the direct trade relations which their circumstances and ours have produced, as men and women who speak our language and who are of the same common origin'.

On 9 December 1936, only five days after parliament had risen for a recess that had been expected to last until March, Lyons recalled it for a debate on the constitutional crisis arising from the desire of King Edward VIII to marry a twice-divorced American commoner, Mrs Wallis Simpson. Lyons merely informed the House that the Commonwealth Government concurred in a decision by the British Government not to legislate for something in the nature of a morganatic marriage, which would have denied the status of Queen to the King's wife and thus perhaps have permitted him to remain on the throne. With that hope now gone, Edward would have to choose between the throne and Mrs Simpson. 'In a state of affairs so delicate', said Lyons, reverently tuning in with Britain, 'so fraught with possibilities of good or ill for the future of all of us, a respectful and sympathetic silence in Parliament is the best contribution we can offer to a happy solution. May God strengthen His Majesty, and guide his decision aright'.

King Edward's decision the next day was to renounce the throne. The United Kingdom Government had prepared a Bill for an Act giving effect to his Instrument of Abdication and to succession by his younger brother, the Duke of York. This was an 'alteration in the law touching the succession to the throne', and, as stated in the Statute of Westminister, any such alteration required assent by the dominion parliaments as well as the United Kingdom parliament. Although the statute had not yet been adopted in Australia, federal parliament on 11 December debated a motion by Lyons assenting to the alteration.

The only discordant voices were those of the Langites— particularly Ward and the new Member for Cook, J. S. Garden, who, although now members of Caucus, still sometimes took the bit between their teeth. Jock Garden—a former Baptist clergyman, secretary of the New South Wales Labor Council, foundation member of the Australian Communist Party, and coiner of the phrase 'Lang is greater than Lenin'—advanced the implausible proposition that King Edward had been deposed because of his sympathy with the working class. 'I desire to be assured', he said,

> that the offence for which the King is now being subjected to an iniquitous inquisition is not the articulation of his spiritual ardour, which dared to condemn all that tended to brutalize and destroy that greatest of God's creation, the mammal Man, to arrest the development of man and desecrate the glories of progress with retrogression.

Curtin had no patience with this kind of nonsense. He rebuked Garden and Ward for claiming, by way of interjection during his own speech, that Lyons had been less than frank with the House, and he strongly supported Lyons's motion. It was carried without division.

Parliament had recently been discussing another personal relationship with political implications of a less exalted kind. This was a romantic attachment between a young English divorcee, Mrs Mabel Magdalene Freer, and an Australian army officer, Lieutenant Robert Dewar, a married man, who had met Mrs Freer while visiting India. After Dewar returned to Australia, and instituted proceedings for divorce, Mrs Freer followed him. For reasons never fully explained, but probably connected with representations by Mrs Dewar or her relatives, the Minister for the Interior, Thomas Paterson, authorised customs officials to prevent her from landing in Australia. When the liner *Maloja* reached Sydney, Mrs Freer was required to take one of the Commonwealth's notoriously difficult dictation tests, which under the Immigration Act could be conducted in any modern European language. This one was in Italian. Mrs Freer stopped her ears rather than listen to it, was deemed to have failed, and had to extend her voyage to New Zealand, where no exception was taken to her arrival.

On 12 November 1936 Jock Garden moved the adjournment for the purpose of discussing a definite matter of urgent public importance, 'The exclusion from Australia of Mrs Freer'. The ensuing debate achieved nothing more than permitting the Minister to make a fool of himself. The only reason he advanced for his extraordinary action was that 'the presence of this woman would have wholly and irreparably encompassed the wreckage of an Australian home'.

> although that is, of course, not the prime motive for the exclusion of Mrs Freer [he said] he would be a callous man indeed who would dismiss it as a factor to be entirely disregarded. What amazes me in this matter is the superabundance of misplaced sympathy for an adventuress and the apparent total absence of a thought of compassion for a wife and child, whose domestic world is tumbling about their ears.

The new U.A.P. Member for Fawkner (V), Harold Holt, declared the exclusion to be another undesirable exercise of New Despotism. Other

U.A.P. members were privately embarrassed by Paterson's blunder, but at the Country Party's insistence the Government supported him, and the adjournment motion was negatived without division. Mrs Freer was excluded by the Italian test again, when she tried to land from New Zealand in December, and the High Court upheld the legality of this. Soon afterwards Paterson lifted the ban without explanation, and in July 1937 Mrs Freer was at last admitted to Australia, where she eventually married not Lieutenant Dewar but a Sydney fish merchant named Cusack.

This was not the first time Paterson had attempted to protect the Commonwealth from outsiders ludicrously misjudged as undesirable. In 1934 the Czechoslovakian left-wing writer, Egon Kisch, was prevented from landing on the basis of a declaration that he was undesirable, issued by the Minister in accordance with Section 3 of the Immigration Act. Kisch, an ex-Communist, was to have been the main speaker at a united front anti-war conference in Melbourne, organised by the Congress Against War and Fascism, which was generally regarded as a Communist Party front.

Speaking on his own motion for adjournment on 14 November, Frank Brennan (Lab, Batman, V) said that the 'government, and especially the Attorney-General, [had] bungled the matter inexcusably, the Attorney-General sacrificing accuracy and a sense of responsibility to his insatiable hunger for notoriety and the applause of his press claqueurs'. This was Menzies's first real brush with the Opposition on the floor of the House, and he came off second best, resorting to vague charges about the Congress Against War and Fascism, and invoking national security as a reason for refusing to specify grounds for the action against Kisch:

> Mr MENZIES.— . . . I take leave to doubt the sincerity of those emissaries who pronounce their love of peace, and their hatred of fascism in Australia, while all the time they are in direct communication with, and in receipt of instructions from, those who are boasting to inhabitants of Russia of the increased military power of that country.
> Mr MAKIN.—What has this to do with the Kisch case?
> Mr MENZIES.—It has everything to do with it, because Herr Kisch is directly connected with the international Communist organisation.
> Mr MAKIN.—He has repudiated it.
> Mr MENZIES.—Of course, and this country contains more than one person who has repudiated communism, but we are not bound to accept all such repudiations at their face value. Above all, the Government, which necessarily has access to confidential and secret sources of information, is not bound to take these protestations at their face value.
> Mr MAKIN.—Can the Attorney-General produce proof?
> Mr MENZIES.—The honorable member knows that it is not consistent with the practice of government, or with the security of the community, to disclose the sources of such information as I have referred to.

Three days later, in the High Court, Mr Justice Evatt ordered Kisch's release from the liner *Strathaird*, then berthed in Sydney, on the ground that no evidence had been produced, as was required by Section 3 of the Act, to show that the ministerial declaration of undesirability was based upon information received through official channels from another government. Kisch, who had earlier broken his right leg by jumping from the ship, was carried down the gangway and immediately taken to central police station for a dictation test in Gaelic. Although he was reputed to speak eleven languages, Gaelic was not one of them, and Kisch was detained as a prohibited immigrant. Once more he appealed to the High Court, which upheld his objection that Gaelic was not a modern European language within the meaning of the Immigration Act. At this point the Commonwealth gave up, agreeing to pay Kisch's costs if he left the country voluntarily, which he did in March 1935.

In a book which he wrote about the incident, Egon Kisch presented Australia as a rather provincial society, and he was not the only visitor to form that impression during the 1930s. The United States Consul-General, a professional diplomat named Jay Pierrepont Moffat, kept a personal diary. He was based in Sydney, but made periodic motor trips to Canberra, which he recorded as if they were made by covered wagon. 'For miles and miles there wouldn't be a human habitation visible', he wrote in 1935,

> just hillsides or valleys dotted with gum-trees . . . then, over the divide, we came upon country so like portions of our own West that if it were not for the ubiquitous gum tree and the incredibly brilliant hued wild parrots I should have believed myself in Wyoming or Montana.
>
> Then Canberra. It is a lovely place, only it is not a city; it is not even a town. The whole impression is that of a nice summer resort, with parliament buildings instead of a *Kursaal* with the [Hotel Canberra] built in a series of pavilions surrounding a central portion reached via open air colonnades. In the middle distance, a mile or two away, are a series of villages with red-roofed bungalows. That is all and that is Canberra.

The permanent residents, he said, were 'lonely and bored, and rather uncomfortable', and parliamentarians spent as little of their time there as they could manage. At one dinner party he was diverted by Menzies, 'a first class raconteur', and White, who had 'a fund of adventures on which to draw'. The wartime adventures of Lieutenant-Colonel White included crash-landing his Royal Flying Corps biplane near Baghdad, being captured by Arab irregulars, and eventually escaping from Turkish captivity. His book about this, *Guests of the Unspeakable*, was sometimes referred to by Opposition members as *Jests of the Unspeakable*.

'[Menzies and White] hate Canberra', wrote the Consul-General, 'stay there the minimum time possible, never bring their wives or families, and count the hours till they can get back to Melbourne. It is only when parliament is in session, or when special cabinets are called, that they come here at all'. Development of Canberra was still restrained by financial exigency, but in 1938 the city and surrounding federal territory acquired a legal name for the first time. Although commonly referred to as the Federal Capital Territory, or more cumbersomely the Territory for the Seat of Government, this federal enclave had never been given any statutory title. By amendment to the Seat of Government Acceptance Act, it became the Australian Capital Territory, also known by the suitably legislative acronym of ACT.

Although this parliament's legislative harvest was not bountiful, the Country Party did well for its constituents with such measures as the Wheat

Growers' Relief Act, Wheat Bounty Act, Apple and Pear Bounty Act and Orange Bounty Act. Two bills of 1936 contained proposals for amendment of the Constitution, but these were no more successful than past experience would have led anyone to expect. One of them was intended to protect marketing laws from the influence of Section 92, guaranteeing freedom of interstate trade. Until recently it had been assumed that the Commonwealth possessed power to control interstate movement of produce for the purpose of marketing schemes, but the Privy Council had upset that notion by ruling against federal control of the interstate movement of dried fruit. The amending bill proposed merely to restore the situation as it had been thought to exist before the Privy Council's judgment, but concern for States' rights ensured its defeat in all States at the referendum.

The other referendum was prompted by another judicial decision, the High Court's ruling that in matters of intra-State aviation the Commonwealth could legislate only under its external affairs power. This meant that it could legislate in terms of the Paris convention on air navigation, but not on matters outside that convention, such as standards of airworthiness. The proposal to add 'air navigation and aircraft' to the powers enumerated in Section 51 was opposed by most State Governments and defeated in a majority of the States.

Flying was no longer the novelty it had been in the 1920s. A weekly air service between Australia and London by Queensland and Northern Territory Aerial Services (QANTAS) and a British company, Imperial Airways, had been operating since 1934, and the first scheduled Melbourne–Canberra–Sydney service was started in October 1935 by Holyman Airways (later Australian National Airways). Federal parliamentarians were slow to use air transport, for which their gold passes were not valid. But a few of the more adventurous and affluent, like White and Hawker, patronised the Holyman service, and two members even flew themselves to parliament.

Canberra aerodrome was a paddock leased for that purpose near Duntroon, and it was used regularly during parliamentary sessions by Major J. V. Fairbairn (U, Flinders, V). In 1934 the Department of the Interior wrote to Fairbairn asking whether he would like the area cleared of sheep each time he arrived and departed. He replied that, as he always ran sheep on the landing ground at his property, Mt Elephant, he did not anticipate any trouble. The other parliamentary pilot was R. G. Casey. During sessions, he and his wife lived in the Duntroon Commandant's house, which had been left vacant when the Royal Military College moved to Sydney. Both the Caseys were licensed pilots, and they often flew to Canberra from Victoria in their own Percival Vega Gull.

According to Consul-General Moffat, who dined with the Caseys at Duntroon, they were 'the worldly members of Cabinet'. Richard Gardiner Casey was a British-Australian in the style of his friend and patron, Stanley Bruce. Born into a wealthy pastoral and mining family, he was a product of Melbourne Grammar; Cambridge, where he graduated with honours in mechanical science; the war, from which he returned as an A.I.F. brigade major with Military Cross; and the Department of External Affairs, whose liaison officer he had been in London. He looked and sounded like an

Englishman, perhaps a Guards' Officer in well cut mufti; rather aloof most of the time, but affable when he chose to be. He had travelled widely in Europe and North America, spoke good French and some German, and had the knack of impressing people in high places. Bruce, when Prime Minister, referred to him as 'our Richard'.

Although nominally only Minister assisting the Treasurer, Casey had in fact introduced the 1935 Budget. Soon afterwards he was appointed Treasurer in Lyons's place, and he presided over two more Budgets in that parliament. Each year the economy improved, but it could hardly be said that either Treasury or Cabinet was to any great extent responsible for such good news. According to a later generation of economic opinion, deliberate policy measures were comparatively unimportant in affecting the speed of Australian recovery. For the most part, government policy merely followed the market.

As commodity prices rose, the balance of payments improved and unemployment returned to pre-Depression levels, Casey was able to restore the cuts which had been made to public service salaries and pensions. The Budget which he introduced in August 1937 did not reduce taxation, but in other respects it was well calculated to help the Government at the approaching general election. It restored the maximum pension to a pre-Depression level of £1 per week, it made provision for the initial costs of a proposed national insurance scheme, it raised defence expenditure from £8 800 000 to £11 500 000—and what was more, it balanced.

This was the third time Lyons had led the U.A.P. at a general election, and if there was one thing he knew better than another it was how to campaign. He travelled 5000 miles by train, aeroplane and car, sometimes accompanied by his wife, the newly honoured Dame Enid Lyons, who was just as popular a public figure as the Prime Minister. Enid Lyons had received her Dame Grand Cross of the Order of the British Empire while she and her husband were attending the Coronation of King George VI. The main issue of the campaign was defence. Lyons claimed credit for a steady increase in defence spending over the last five years, and emphasised the danger of Labor's anti-British attitude. Singapore was impregnable, he said, and air power would be useless against battleships. Curtin, who delivered his policy speech by radio from Perth, advocated greater expenditure on local manufacture of munitions and aircraft, warned against Australian involvement in another European war, and suggested that in the event of war a conservative government would probably introduce conscription.

The result of the election on 23 October was another victory for Lyons, who thus became the first Australian Prime Minister to win three consecutive general elections. This time, however, the win was less substantial. In the House of Representatives the coalition won forty-three seats to Labor's twenty-nine, and there were two Independents, both conservatively inclined. Within the coalition, the Country Party did relatively better than the U.A.P., increasing its strength from fifteen to sixteen. The U.A.P. lost four seats, including Warringah, where the Minister for Defence was unexpectedly defeated by an Independent, P. C. Spender, who ran on a strong defence platform and received many A.L.P. second preferences.

Casey told Bruce in London that there had been a revolt against Parkhill for personal reasons. 'Much as I have always distrusted Abraham Lincoln's dictum that the masses of the people in [the] end always decided right', he wrote, 'I am rather coming round to the essential wisdom of it'.

In the upper house, where all non-retiring senators belonged to the coalition parties, there was a strong swing to Labor, though not strong enough to gain control (20–16). The Labor Party hedged its bets in New South Wales by choosing candidates whose names all began with the letter 'A', thus ensuring first place on the ballot paper and a helping hand from the donkey vote. Amour, Armstrong, Arthur and Ashley were all elected. Labor would probably have swept the Senate board in New South Wales even without resorting to this shabby trick, for the party was now united and receiving considerable underdog sympathy.

In Western Australia Labor also benefited from secessionist bitterness towards Senators Pearce and Lynch, both of whom were swept out of parliament more peremptorily than their long and distinguished careers deserved. Sir George Pearce ascribed this partly to lack of interest in the election, claiming that thousands of votes had been recorded haphazardly. Paddy Lynch merely remarked that some voters had 'the brains of a sandfly'.

Leadership

To some observers it seemed as if the match in which Lyons had performed the hat trick was being played between the executive and parliament. Whatever his third consecutive term may have signified electorally, it also served to emphasise the Government's ascendancy not only over the Opposition but over parliament as well. In 1937 the House of Representatives sat for twenty-nine days, a shorter period than during any previous year; and the Senate sat for twenty-seven days, a period surpassed for brevity in that chamber only by twenty-two sitting days three years before. By way of contrast, the average annual number of sitting days since federation had previously been seventy-six for the House and fifty-six for the Senate.

According to some of the defenders of parliament whose protests were heard during the next two years, these figures were evidence of an increasing tendency by the executive to bypass parliament whenever possible. In June 1938 a young barrister who was later to become parliament's foremost historian, Geoffrey Sawer, told the annual meeting of the Council of Civil Liberties that Cabinet had discovered that one of the most effective ways of keeping parliament quiet was by not having it in session. 'Apparently it is of no importance', he said,

> that private members might have matters they wish to discuss. Parliament has no say, except in approving Mr Lyons's own proposals. A weakening in the system is [also] being caused by the delegation of legislative powers to administrative bodies. When Parliament met this year it had before it 87 sets of executive regulations made under 49 acts. The excuse is often given that Parliament has no time to give attention to all these regulations, but that argument is blown to pieces by the few sitting days.

Others making similar protests included John Curtin and no less a champion than Sir Isaac Isaacs. 'Sooner or later', wrote Curtin in the *Australian Quarterly*,

> unless the march towards that position is arrested, we shall see the Commonwealth Parliament merely a register for Cabinet's views and decisions to go out to the people though the press and radio, and then, in due time, to be given effect to (should the reaction be favourable) by legislative processes which, in themselves, are rapidly becoming mechanised.

Sir Isaac Isaacs, who joined this protest the following year, had retired as Governor-General in 1936, leaving behind him a reputation for decorum that was marred only slightly by one curious incident. In November 1934 he addressed a letter of rebuke to his successor as Chief Justice, Sir Frank Gavan Duffy, over what he alleged was 'a public breach of duty to the Governor-General'. The occasion was a reception held in King's Hall for the Duke of Gloucester by the Governor-General.

Not to put too fine a point on it, Sir Isaac accused Sir Frank of snubbing him. 'Closely following the presentation of several other distinguished persons', wrote Isaacs,

> . . . who, as they passed by the group, duly paid respect both to His Royal Highness and to the Governor-General, the Chief Justice, on his name being announced, advanced. After an inclination of the head towards His Royal Highness, the Chief Justice distinctly and conspicuously turned his head so as to look straight before him, and passed on in front of the Governor-General quite ignoring the presence of the King's principal Representative in Australia. Several days have been allowed by the Governor-General to elapse in the hope that some voluntary communication from the Chief Justice would render the present action unnecessary. It is now the paramount duty of the Governor-General to invite from the Chief Justice a reply adequately relieving the situation from its present aspect of a public breach of duty to the Governor-General as His Majesty's Representative.

Whatever the truth of the matter, or the real feelings existing between the two men, there could be only one response to such a letter. 'The Chief Justice deeply regrets the incident to which his attention has been drawn by His Excellency the Governor-General', replied Sir Frank. 'Until he received that communication, he was not aware that he had been guilty of any discourtesy towards His Excellency, and he now sincerely apologises for his delinquency.'

Sir Isaac was just as touchy about parliament as he was about the Crown or his personal dignity. In a pamphlet published in March 1939 he criticised the government for having failed to summon parliament during a recent national crisis in which maritime unions had attempted by strike action to prevent the export of scrap and pig iron to Japan, on the ground that such exports were of military value to a potential enemy. It was in this crisis that Menzies, as Minister for Industry arguing the case against unnecessary provocation of Japan, received the nickname 'Pig-Iron Bob'.

Sir Isaac's pamphlet, *Australian Democracy and Our Constitutional System*, reminded readers that the people were supposed to be present in parliament to make their laws, and generally to watch over and direct their national affairs. 'Why, in a time of crisis, must Parliament be silent?' he asked.

> Why should it consent to be deaf, dumb, blind, and impotent at the will of its own administrative officers and so reverse the relative positions the Constitution intends them to occupy? It is a breach of a fundamental right . . . How long will Australians stand by and see their National Parliament function like a Trilby to sleep, wake, sing, or be silent, at the dictation of whatever Svengali happens to be in control for the time being?

The last few years had afforded many examples of parliament in the role of Trilby, but perhaps the most striking had been the all-nighter of 9–10 April 1935. Between 9 p.m. and the following 5 p.m. the Government moved forty-one closures in the House of Representatives and there were eighty-three divisions, thus outdoing the worst Bruce–Page excesses of 1923. The division bells rang for more than four hours altogether, and not one speech was completed before the gag was applied and another division taken.

The Government was mainly to blame. First, it forced through a Supply Bill providing £6 704 400 for the first three months of the next financial year. Then, shortly before midnight, it began applying the same tactics to several Customs Tariff Validation Bills, designed to validate that year's tariff schedules without debate. By that time, as the *Canberra Times* reported, parliament had taken on the appearance of a mad house. Langites shouted abuse at ministers who were applying the gag; there were cat-calls, shrieks, and choruses of 'Hallelujah, I'm a Bum' and 'How Dry We Are'. It may well have been the worst performance parliament ever staged. Next day, both adjourned for five months.

To such critics as Isaacs, Curtin and Sawer, it may have seemed that protests had not been altogether in vain, for the fifteenth parliament met more frequently than might have been expected. During 1938 the lower house sat for sixty-six days, and the Senate for forty-six; the corresponding figures for 1939 were fifty-one and thirty-three. Probably, however, this statistical improvement owed more to the pressure of events than to any change of heart by the executive. The fifteenth parliament was characterised by rapid political change, both internationally and within Australia's governing coalition. For Joe Lyons it was also marred by failing health and a further decline in his powers of leadership.

Parliament was opened on 30 November 1937 by Sir Isaac Isaacs's successor, the former Sir Alexander Hore-Ruthven, who had been successively Governor of South Australia and New South Wales. Lyons had not troubled the King for another Australian Governor-General, preferring in this matter, as in others, to tune in with Britain. Failing to find a suitable candidate there, he settled on Hore-Ruthven, who was not only 'both suitable and available', but already in Australia. 'Sandy' Hore-Ruthven, or the Earl of Gowrie as he now became, was a distinguished soldier who had adapted successfully to viceregal service. He had won the Victoria Cross in the Sudan, been severely wounded at Gallipoli, commanded the Brigade of Guards, and proved a popular Governor in Adelaide and Sydney. At the time of his first appointment, Casey reported from London to Bruce that he was 'not too intellectual nor too sporting, nor too anything else, and an easy and pleasant fellow to talk to'.

Lord Gowrie's opening speech in the Senate chamber emphasised his advisers' intention to press on with further strengthening of Australian defences. It also contained more than the usual run of good intentions that would not in fact be fulfilled in the life of this parliament. For example, the Inter-State Commission was to be re-established. A bill for this purpose passed the Senate, where it had been introduced, but was abandoned in the lower house mainly on the ground that many of the functions proposed for the Inter-State Commission were already being dealt with by the Grants Commission and the Tariff Board. Another bill was to have provided for the Commonwealth's adoption of relevant sections of the Statute of Westminster, but it was not introduced. The Governor-General also announced that his ministers would immediately proceed to frame appropriate legislation and establish suitable administration for national health and pensions insurance. In this he was only partly correct.

The National Health and Pensions Insurance Bill, which was the most contentious measure of this parliament, had been mooted for many years. A similar measure based upon the findings of a Royal Commission, the National Insurance Bill, had been introduced by Page in 1928, but it perished with the Bruce–Page Government. Nothing further was done until 1937, when the Lyons Government invited two British experts on national insurance to come to Australia as advisers. The Bill, introduced by Casey in May 1938 and debated during the next eight weeks, provided for a system of compulsory insurance for all employed persons on a basis of contributions from consolidated revenue, employers and employees. 'This bill embodies one of the most far-reaching schemes of social reform that has been presented to the federal Parliament', said Casey.

> It brings directly within its scope . . . a total of no less than 3,600,000 persons, or about 52 per cent of the people of Australia. It applies to the breadwinners, the sick, the aged, and to the wives, the widows and the orphans of the workers, and it affects persons in nearly every walk of life.

These bold intentions were weakened by numerous amendments in committee. Although there was enthusiasm on the Government side for the scheme's partly contributory nature, which was intended to minimise the cost to taxpayers, some Country Party members remained apprehensive about the scheme's likely effect on income tax. Labor, on the other hand, opposed the contributory principle for pensions, but not for health insurance. The measure, which passed its final stage on 30 June, and received royal assent on 21 September, nonetheless embodied useful reforms. But as later events were to show, the future of national insurance was by no means fully ensured.

Although the Lyons Government was 'pressing on' with defence measures, a growing body of opinion held that it was not pressing hard enough. And as this opinion spread in 1938 it emboldened those in U.A.P. circles who, for one reason or another, were dissatisfied with Lyons's leadership. Sir Henry Gullett, temporarily out of Cabinet for reasons of health and probably also disaffection, wrote editorials for Sir Keith Murdoch's Melbourne *Herald*, accusing the Government of indecision and failure to make Australians sufficiently aware of the danger they would face if the German-Japanese-Italian grouping became an aggressive military alliance. The *Herald* called the Government's defence policy 'ineffective and wasteful', advocated compulsory military training, but did not yet single out Lyons himself for attack. With Parkhill gone, the main alternatives to Lyons within the U.A.P. seemed to be Menzies and Casey, though others also carried batons in their knapsacks. Lyons sometimes spoke of Casey as a possible successor who would command wider party support than Menzies; but Casey himself did not seem ambitious enough to put up the fight which any direct challenge to Menzies would almost certainly entail. As Casey wrote later in life: 'I wasn't going to kick anyone to death to do the job'.

Menzies, on the other hand, was looking for an opportunity to canvass the leadership question publicly, and in October 1938 he found one. After the strain of the Munich crisis in September, Lyons went to Devonport for a rest, and during his absence from the mainland a rumour began to circulate that ill health might cause him to retire. This was followed closely, soon after his return to Canberra, by the rejection of proposals for defence and national development which he advanced at a Premiers' conference on 21 October. In a speech delivered three days later to the Constitutional Association in Sydney, Menzies made certain remarks about leadership which, although he refrained from naming Lyons, were widely regarded as an attack on his leader.

After referring to recent events in Austria and Sudetenland, Menzies said that democracies could not maintain their place in the world unless they were provided with leadership as inspiring as that of the dictator countries. Australians were a good-natured, easygoing people who did not want to be troubled with uncomfortable facts; but when they were told the facts, and believed them, they had an unrivalled capacity to face those facts and act accordingly. 'The first lesson for the governments of Australia', he said, 'is that in these times of emergency we must not hesitate to take the people fully into our confidence and give them leadership along well-defined lines'.

Lyons did not believe that he had been attacked, but his wife did. Over breakfast at The Lodge next morning she asked him if he had read the newspaper reports of Menzies's speech.

> 'Yes, why?' he replied.
> 'Why! Can't you see that he's attacking you?'
> 'No, it's merely the way it's been reported, to give that appearance, but Bob wouldn't be guilty of such a thing.'
> 'Don't be a fool. He makes a speech like that, he knows perfectly well how it will be taken . . . He knows that, he's not an idiot.'

Later that day Menzies called on Lyons in his office at Parliament House. 'Joe, I hope you didn't think that that was taking a hit at you', he said. And Lyons replied: 'Well, you needn't even have mentioned it to me, Bob. I know perfectly well that there was no malice in that'.

Sir Keith Murdoch knew better. The Melbourne *Herald* redoubled its attack with editorials suggesting that Lyons was unable to control Cabinet or adequately handle policy difficulties, and other newspapers also endorsed the message which they had read between the lines of Menzies's speech. At a meeting of businessmen in Melbourne, Murdoch boasted that, having put Lyons in, he would now put him out.

Had it not been for one of the air disasters which bedevilled commercial aviation during the 1930s, Menzies's attack on Lyons would have been followed two days later by a motion of no confidence from the Leader of the Opposition. On 25 October Curtin gave notice of his intention to move the following day that, 'because of its lamentable lack of leadership in regard to urgent national problems, the government has forfeited the confidence of this House'. Before the adjournment which followed this notice, the Prime Minister announced that an Australian National Airways DC2, the *Kyeema*, had crashed on Mt Dandenong, near Melbourne, killing at least six of those on board. Soon after parliament adjourned, further news was received: all eighteen on board had perished, and among them had been a member of parliament, the maimed war hero Charles Hawker.

Although this indomitable South Australian had still been regarded by some of his colleagues as a potential prime minister, Lyons had never invited him back into Cabinet, an omission attributed by Hawker to personal antipathy on the Prime Minister's part. This effectively freed him from party restrictions, and although continuing to support the Government on crucial votes he became something of a freelance in debates on trade and defence. Much of his spare time was spent studying the American civil war from the Confederate point of view, for he was trying to visualise the kind of war which a small Australian army might one day be called upon to fight against a Japanese invader.

No one could have guessed from Lyons's eulogy on 26 October that he and Hawker had been anything but the best of friends. Curtin and Page paid similar tributes, and the House adjourned for a week. Curtin's motion was debated on 2 November, and negatived by 26–34 on party lines.

The Victorian and New South Wales branches of the U.A.P. continued to support Lyons, urging him to remain in office at least until the next election; but inside Cabinet, divisions were deepening. At a Cabinet meeting on 1 November, the first anyone could recall ever having been held on a Melbourne Cup Day, the issue of compulsory military training almost led Colonel White to resign. After Hughes had declared against it, White passed him a note asking if he had seen an article about universal training in the ex-servicemen's journal *Mufti*, and warning him that he could lose his seat by backsliding on the very issue he had once championed.

'[Hughes] snarled and shouted', wrote White in his diary,

> and I told him he could read [the note] out to Cabinet if he liked, which he did, and there were high words between us both . . . the Prime Minister [who was also opposed to universal training] intervened on Hughes's behalf, so I told him that I had already made up my mind that I could not remain in a Cabinet that could not support universal service and that I had thought it over well and intended to withdraw, and I left the room.

Casey and Page hurried after him, arguing that his resignation on the eve of a censure motion would probably mean an election, and sullenly he returned. Two days later the Postmaster-General, Senator A. J. McLachlan (S), tendered his resignation from Cabinet for quite another reason: pecuniary interest. The Opposition had given notice of a question relating to McLachlan's directorates in companies which had been awarded contracts by the postal department, and the Senator's ministerial colleagues did not fancy his chances of surviving untarnished.

On 7 November Lyons responded to criticism in and out of parliament by reconstructing the Cabinet, which by amendment of the Ministers of State Act was again enlarged, this time to accommodate eleven full ministers. The main object was to move the Minister for Defence, H. V. Thorby (C, Calare, N), to a new portfolio of Works and Civil Aviation, and give Defence to a new minister, G. A. Street (U, Corangamite, V). Menzies, Casey, the newly knighted Sir Earle Page (Commerce) and Hughes (Senator Pearce's successor at External Affairs) retained their portfolios. White was to have kept Trade and Customs, but on the day the new Cabinet was to be sworn in he carried out his threat to resign. His main reasons, expressed in a letter to the Prime Minister which White read to the House, were Lyons's decision to form an inner policy group of Cabinet, from which White was to have been omitted, and disagreement over defence policy.

In the few weeks remaining before parliament went into recess for Christmas and the following four months, the Government tried to allay further criticism over defence. Street announced that aggregate expenditure on the current three-year defence programme would be increased from £44 500 000 to £63 000 000, and both the Prime Minister and Dame Enid broadcast Australia-wide appeals for volunteers to raise the strength of the militia from thirty-five thousand to seventy thousand.

The rising of parliament on 8 December 1938 was accompanied by rumours that priority for defence spending might require postponement of the national insurance scheme, and that Menzies and Casey were considering resignation on this score. The prospect of national insurance was indeed rapidly receding, for reasons both of defence and reluctance by the medical profession to co-operate on health insurance. For all practical purposes the embryonic scheme finally disappeared at a Cabinet meeting on 14 March 1939, which decided to repeal the provisions of the Act relating to old age, widows' and orphans' pensions, and to substitute for the remainder of the Act a new medical scheme, no details of which had yet been worked out. There were tears in Lyons's eyes when he left the Cabinet room. 'It's finished, is it, Joe?' asked a journalist from the Sydney *Sun*.

'It's gone', replied Lyons, 'it's wrecked, it's finished'.

Menzies, concurring in that judgement, immediately tendered his resignation as Attorney-General, Minister for Industry and Deputy Leader of the U.A.P. In his letter to Lyons, he quoted from another letter which he had sent to the electors of Kooyong a few weeks before: 'Let me say quite categorically that I stand by National Insurance, and that a defeat in defending it would, in my opinion, be an honourable one'. 'I frankly do not think', he told Lyons, we can expect to be taken seriously if we start off again with conferences and drafting committees at a time when we have already so notoriously failed to go on with an Act which represents two years labour, a vast amount of organisation, and a considerable expenditure of public and private funds.

Although this had some appearance of being a matter of principle, many of Menzies's colleagues regarded it as being also, and predominantly, a matter of ambition. Page in particular believed that Menzies was deliberately freeing himself of Cabinet and party responsibilities in order to raise the question of leadership again, and he remonstrated with him for doing so at a time of international crisis. On 15 March German troops occupied the western provinces of Czechoslovakia. In conversation with Menzies that day, Page said Australia could be at war by evening, and that it was unthinkable for the third-ranking man in the ministry to have resigned at such a time.

If Menzies had expected others to follow his example, he was disappointed. His fellow Victorians Gullett, Holt and Fairbairn openly supported him, but there were no more resignations. The press was generally approving of his action, but only the Melbourne *Herald* declared it 'welcome proof of his fitness for leadership in national affairs'. The State branches of the U.A.P. considered him unpopular with the electorate and were still hoping that Lyons would see them through one more election. Lyons, however, was desperate to retire. With Menzies challenging him, Casey *hors de combat*, and Page disqualified politically, the only feasible successor, and not very feasible at that, was someone not even in parliament—Stanley Bruce. For some months past there had been talk of the High Commissioner re-entering Australian politics, and as it happened he was then visiting Australia. Lyons met him late in March, said that he could stand the strain no longer, and asked Bruce to replace him. Bruce suggested certain conditions, including the formation of an emergency all-party government, but when the possibility of such a national government was canvassed in the press Curtin immediately rejected it.

At a second meeting, in Canberra on 27 March, Bruce agreed to do as he was asked, but only on rather unrealistic terms. He stipulated that Lyons must inform the Governor-General next day that he was reluctantly compelled to return his commission on grounds of health, advise His Excellency to send for Bruce, and at the same time express his willingness to serve under Bruce in a less responsible office. Bruce would then become Prime Minister without a seat in parliament, but under Section 64 of the Constitution he would have three months to make good that deficiency. Lyons accepted these conditions, but changed his mind overnight, telling Bruce next day that they were not politically feasible. Three days later Bruce embarked on the *Mariposa* for Los Angeles, on his way back to London.

On the weekend of 1–2 April Lyons and his wife met U.A.P. officials in Melbourne, and reluctantly agreed that he should not retire. Dame Enid returned to Devonport, and although the parliamentary recess had two more weeks to run, her husband caught the night train to Canberra for a Cabinet meeting. On Tuesday night he left Canberra by car for Sydney, where he was to open the Royal Easter Show, and on the way he had a heart attack.

In Sydney he entered St Vincent's private hospital for observation. His wife was flown from Devonport to Melbourne by a Broken Hill Proprietary Ltd aircraft, and caught the train to Sydney. After seeming to recover at first, Lyons quickly suffered four more heart attacks, the last of which ended his life at 10.40 a.m. on Good Friday, 7 April 1939.

As Lyons was the first Australian Prime Minister to die in office, there was no precedent for a situation in which a Prime Minister was not able to advise the Governor-General on the commissioning of a successor, let alone a situation such as this, in which the major coalition party no longer had any Deputy Leader. Sir Earle Page—as next in ministerial rank, and occasional acting (though not officially Deputy) Prime Minister—called a Cabinet meeting at midday, attended by nine ministers who were in Sydney. Hughes, now Attorney-General for the fourth time, suggested that Lord Gowrie be advised to commission Page to form an interim government. This was agreed to unanimously, and during the afternoon Page was sworn in at Admiralty House as the Commonwealth's eleventh prime minister. As he told his colleagues, however, he made two provisos: as soon as the U.A.P. chose a new parliamentary leader, he would have no wish to continue as Prime Minister; and if that leader should be Menzies, Page would not serve in any Cabinet of his. Many years later Page said of the second proviso that he had not been willing to place his party 'in pawn with a Prime Minister who ... would not achieve that stability in government necessary for an effective approach to the pressing problems of approaching war'.

The body of the dead Prime Minister lay in state at St Mary's Cathedral, where it was viewed by forty-five thousand people. Public tributes to him dwelt on his personal qualities, and were expressed with affection as well as respect. For some years, said the Leader of the Opposition, Lyons had borne a strain probably greater than any of his predecessors. If he had lived another sixteen days he would have exceeded even the cumulative four ministries of the indestructible Billy Hughes, and Lyons had been patently destructible.

Casey, who was probably closer to Lyons at the end of his life than any of his colleagues, said he had been 'a man in whom the average man and woman felt—and felt rightly—that they had a friend who would look after them'. That was more or less the way Joe Lyons had thought of himself. Shortly before his death, he had written to his wife: 'Think of the homes that are happy because of what we did, and realise that no home is *un*happy because of anything we did'. Admittedly he had failed to provide those homes with national insurance, and no one could be certain how much or how little his Government's actions had influenced the course of the Depression. Yet Lyons had undoubtedly inspired a much needed sense of confidence during the 1930s, and the cow had not fallen over the cliff.

On Tuesday 11 April Lyons's coffin, draped in a blue Australian ensign, was taken by gun-carriage through the crowded but silent streets of Sydney to a destroyer, H.M.A.S. *Vendetta*, for his last journey to Tasmania. Two days later he was buried at the Church of Our Lady of Lourdes in Devonport. As mourners were leaving the graveside, Curtin told Page that he would support his government for the remainder of the fifteenth parliament, which still had eighteen months to run, providing Page made no attempt to introduce conscription. When Page said that he was instinctively averse to being head of a government without its own majority in parliament, Curtin remarked that the only thing worse than a government of two parties was a government of three.

11

Time of War

Crippled

In the confused period immediately ahead, from 1939 to 1941, parliament could have produced something even worse than a government of three parties: namely, a government of three disunited parties. Whether such a national government would really have been worse than anything else was of course a matter of opinion. The U.A.P. and the Country Party—both troubled by internal dissension, and each at odds with the other—regarded national government as some *deus ex machina*, creaking and unwieldy, but perhaps capable of miraculously settling all political differences in the nick of time. Labor, also temporarily divided once again, was not so sanguine; its natural instinct was to wait for the chance of governing alone. Thus the next two and a half years were notable for fruitless yearning on one side of the House, and stern denial on the other.

During his brief Prime Ministership, Sir Earle Page pursued the rather fanciful objective of a national government led by Stanley Bruce. Committed as he was to resigning when the U.A.P. chose its new leader, and determined to take his party out of the governing coalition if that leader was Menzies, Page had nothing to lose, and perhaps the euchring of Menzies to gain, by reviving this old partnership. The High Commissioner was by then in Los Angeles on his way back to London. On the morning of 18 April 1939, one day before parliament resumed after the Christmas adjournment, Page and Casey held a three-way radio-telephone conversation with him at the Biltmore Hotel. Bruce agreed to return and enter parliament, on the understanding that he would not belong to any party and would try to form a national government of all parties.

That afternoon Page reported to a meeting of the Country Party, which unanimously approved the idea of an all-party government led by Bruce. It

319

also resolved unanimously that the Country Party would be unable to co-operate in, or give any undertaking of support to, a government led by Menzies. This was known to the U.A.P. when it also met in Parliament House later the same day. Casey reported Bruce's response, but the meeting was not deflected from its intention of electing a new leader from among those present. There were four nominations: Menzies, Hughes, Casey and White. Menzies was elected, but only by a narrow margin and on a third ballot. Casey and White dropped out early; Hughes who became Deputy Leader, was supported by a majority of the party's M.H.R.s; and Menzies owed his success to a majority of the party's senators.

When Page told Bruce next morning how little the U.A.P. party room had been swayed by his offer, Bruce said: 'Then the attitude of Menzies and Hughes was really "Oh, to hell with this"?' 'No', replied Page,

> I think Hughes might possibly be right on this, but there is no question about Menzies's end. But the position now is that Menzies has been elected, although he has not got a majority support in the party. It took him three ballots to win, and there is no question in my mind that he will lead everyone to political suicide. The feeling of my fellows is that they must take to the raft at once rather than sink in the same boat with him.

Sir Earle himself had more than survival in mind: in the act of abandoning ship, he also aimed a murderous shot at the new captain. Some Country Party members, knowing the strength of his antagonism towards Menzies, whom he held partly responsible for Lyons's death, urged him to be careful. But there was no stopping him. His resignation speech on 20 April contained one of the most vicious and ill-judged attacks ever made in the House by one member upon another. After moving a special adjournment for the purpose of forming a new government, preferably one consisting of all parties, Page said that he had been forced to consider whether Menzies possessed 'the three essential qualities of courage, loyalty and judgement' which would be required for the leadership of such a national government.

> I had to ask myself whether his public record was such as to inspire the people of Australia to the maximum unstinted effort in a time of national emergency. Because of that I was reminded of three incidents in the public career of the newly elected leader of the United Australia Party. The first of the three happened only 24 days previously, when honorable members will remember, the right honorable gentleman tendered his resignation as Attorney-General in the Lyons administration . . . At this time, when all our efforts were being strained to put the defences of this country in order, the right honorable gentleman insisted on resigning from the government because he differed from its attitude towards national insurance . . . The second incident is this: Some 24 weeks ago he went to Sydney, where he made a speech on leadership; that pronouncement was regarded by the public and the press of Australia as an attack upon his own leader. I do not say that it was; I merely say that it was construed in that way.

Mr JOHN LAWSON (U, Macquarie, N).—His leader did not regard it as such.

Sir EARLE PAGE.—I spoke to Mr Lyons and he was very distressed about the matter.

Sir FREDERICK STEWART (U, Parramatta, N.).—At least six members of this House had an assurance from Mr Lyons that he did not so regard it.

Mr SPEAKER.—Order! The Chair must insist that the Prime Minister be heard.

Sir EARLE PAGE.—I come now to the third incident: Some 24 years ago the right honorable member for Kooyong was a member of the Australian Military Forces and held the King's Commission. In 1915, after having been in the military forces for some years, he resigned his Commission and did not go overseas.

Mr JAMES (L, Hunter, N).—That is dirt!

Page then referred briefly to Bruce as a national leader under whom the Country Party would be willing to co-operate, and concluded by saying he would resign his commission that afternoon. The House was still bemused by the bizarre symmetry of 24 days, 24 weeks and 24 years. Menzies, his arm in a black sling because of a fall the previous day, received the Speaker's call immediately. With well controlled disdain he defended himself quite effectively against what he termed 'the most remarkable attack that I have ever heard in the whole of my public career'. The resignation, he said, had been unavoidable because of a specific pledge to his electors, and his remarks about leadership, 'a homily which I was addressing to myself and every other person in Australia who occupied any public position involving leadership of the people', had been taken out of context. As for the third incident,

> [The Prime Minister] said, with all its deadly implication, that I resigned a military commission a year after the Great War broke out. If he had investigated a little further, he would have discovered that I, in common with other young men of my age, was a trainee under the then existing system of compulsory training . . . When my period of universal training expired, my activity in connection with the system also expired. I did not resign anything. I served the ordinary term of a compulsory trainee. I was in exactly the same position as any other person who at that time had to answer the extremely important questions—is it my duty to go to the war, or is it my duty not to go? The answers to those questions cannot be made on the public platforms. Those questions relate to a man's intimate, personal and family affairs, and in consequence, I, facing those problems, problems of intense difficulty, found myself, for reasons which were and are compelling, unable to join my two brothers in the infantry of the Australian Imperial Force.

The three Menzies brothers of enlistment age had decided among themselves that, for their parents' sake, the youngest should not volunteer. Robert, who was nineteen when the war began, served out his compulsory military training in the Melbourne University Rifles and rose to the rank of lieutenant. As he said later in life, the lot of a young part-time soldier was not easy during the Great War. In 1918 his fiancée, grief-stricken by the death of her brother, one of Menzies's university contemporaries who had been on active service with the A.I.F., ended their engagement.

The only other speaker on Page's special adjournment motion was the Leader of the Opposition. Curtin steered well clear of personal controversy, and rejected Page's proposal for a national government in much the same words as he had used at Lyons's funeral. 'If there could be anything worse than a government consisting of two parties', he said,

> it would be a government consisting of three parties. Such a combination would not be a government, it would be a society of disputation and debate; decisions would never be reached ... I say to Australia quite seriously, that however good a government may be, it will be all the better if it is composed of men who subscribe to the one set of political principles ... For myself and my party, I say that either in peace or war we are pre-pared to take the responsibility of governing this country on the basis of our own programme [when] the people of Australia give us a majority in this House.

Page's philippic damaged its deliverer rather than the intended victim. Two Queensland members of the Country Party—Arthur Fadden (Darling Downs) and B. H. Corser (Wide Bay)—immediately dissociated themselves from the speech and adopted Independent status. Their example was later followed by T. J. Collins (C, Hume, N) and A. O. Badman (C, Grey, S). Menzies's wife, who heard Page's speech from the gallery, never forgave him for it, and never spoke to him again. She should rather have been grate-ful, for the speech had aroused more sympathy for Menzies than his natural demeanour would normally have inspired. Page himself was unrepentant, and sceptical of the U.A.P.'s chances of governing alone. Speaking to the itinerant High Commissioner on 21 April, one day after Menzies was invited by the Governor-General to form a ministry, Page said:

> It seems to me that the elements of trouble will be tremendous. I would not like to be in his position because the U.A.P. have only twenty-six members, one more than a quorum.
> BRUCE: What is Mr Casey doing?
> PAGE: He is just sitting back ... I have a personal regard for Menzies. I felt it had to be done and the only straight and courageous thing to do was to put it beyond any dispute ... Menzies says that he will co-operate with the Country Party despite my speech.
> BRUCE: Was my name dragged into it at all?
> PAGE: I just mentioned that the offer had been made by me but you were not discussed at all.
> BRUCE: I will go on to Washington and then to London.

The U.A.P. Ministry sworn in on 3 May was indeed in a precarious pos-ition, depending for its survival on the discriminating support of a party that could combine with Labor at any time, particularly on the sensitive issue of wheat. Page's party wanted to establish a guaranteed price for wheat; Labor was keenly aware of the wheat farmers' plight, and their vote; but the U.A.P. was generally against a guaranteed price. Menzies could have sought a dis-solution, but an early election would have been hard to justify in the existing international crisis, and, perhaps more to the point, it would have been very hard for him to win. In the circumstances, all he could do was persevere.

Australia's twelfth Prime Minister had no more affection for the Country Party than most of its members had for him. Menzies came from an actively political family, three members of which, all Nationalists, had come off second best against the Country Party: an uncle on his mother's side was defeated in the federal seat of Wimmera, his father-in-law in the federal seat of Indi, and his father, James Menzies, in the seat of Lowan for the Victorian Legislative Assembly. James Menzies, a second-generation Scottish-Australian, started work as a coach painter in Ballarat, where he had the distinction of painting H. V. McKay's first 'Sunshine' harvester. He married Kate Sampson, whose Cornish-born father was a co-founder of the Australian Miners' Union. In 1893 the family moved to Jeparit, a dusty little town in the shire of Dimboola, north-western Victoria, where James became a storekeeper and Robert Gordon Menzies was born on 20 December 1894. After some primary education at Jeparit, Bob Menzies went to live with his paternal grandmother at Ballarat, attending a state school there and, at the age of thirteen, topping the State in Victoria's scholarship examination. He was exceptionally bright, and further scholarships were his for the taking. From Grenville College, Ballarat, he went to Melbourne's Methodist Wesley College, where he passed the senior public examination with honours in history and English, winning a scholarship in the faculty of law at Melbourne University, and an exhibition as a non-resident student at the Presbyterian Ormond College. He graduated in 1916, LL.B. with first class honours and the Bowen Prize for an essay entitled 'The Rule of Law During the War', but continued to take an active interest in the Law Students' Society and the Students' Representative Council as well as the University Rifles. He also taught Bible class, and once delivered a sermon at his local Presbyterian church.

Menzies's legal career could scarcely have begun under better auspices. After being admitted to the Bar in 1918 he entered the chambers of a rising constitutional lawyer, Owen Dixon, and two years later was briefed to appear before the High Court for the Amalgamated Society of Engineers. This was the landmark Engineers' case, in which the Court had to decide whether a dispute between a trade union and a state-owned enterprise came within the scope of the federal arbitration power. Menzies argued that it did, and counsel for various States, including Latham and Evatt, argued to the contrary. Menzies prevailed, and at the age of only twenty-six his reputation was made. He took Silk in 1929; followed his father into the Legislative Assembly, where he served for two years as Attorney-General; and was a trusted member of the group which captured Lyons from the A.L.P. and helped him to form the U.A.P.

By the time he became Prime Minister, at the age of forty-five, he gave every appearance of having been in that office for years. There is a photograph of him leaving the Dominions Office dressed in a plushy double-breasted suit of dark striped cloth, walking stick in hand and a soft felt hat set at just the correct angle above his enormous eyebrows and an expression of lordliness that even Stanley Bruce might have envied. His wife once said that she had to send his suits for dry cleaning after every major speech because they were soaked with perspiration. No one could have guessed as much, and deduced from it that in fact the man was nervous. He looked and sounded impregnable.

One way of avoiding attack was to see as little of parliament as was compatible with the gravity of world events. The new Ministry met parliament for the first time on 3 May. Menzies was Treasurer; Casey took the newly created portfolio of Supply and Development; Hughes, Attorney-General; G. A. Street, Defence; Gullett, External Affairs; and Fairbairn, naturally enough, Air and Civil Aviation. Holt and Spender (the latter having now joined the U.A.P.) were Ministers without Portfolio, assisting Casey and Menzies respectively. In the twenty-five days on which parliament sat during May and June, before adjourning indefinitely, it dealt with several matters relating to defence preparedness. The main measures passed were a Supply and Development Act, establishing a department for the procurement and manufacture of war equipment; a National Security Act, giving the Executive Council power to make regulations for the public safety and defence of the Commonwealth; and the National Registration Act, authorising a census of males between the ages of eighteen and sixty-five, and a census of property, as a basis for mobilisation in the event of war.

Labor voted against national registration, out of suspicion that it would be a step towards conscription, and the Government was obliged to use the guillotine in both chambers. Curtin, although keenly aware of the conscription issue's power to split his party again, nevertheless insisted upon respect for the national register once it became law. While the Bill was still before parliament, an A.C.T.U. committee had requested that all federal Labor members pledge themselves, as part of a national boycott, not to supply personal information required under the Act. 'I told the committee', Curtin informed Caucus, 'that it was treading dangerous soil to lay down a policy of revolt to a law . . . I would not allow the bankers or the Chamber of Manufactures to disobey the law were a Labor Government in power'. With deft diplomacy, Curtin made sure that there was no boycott.

Another measure, the National Health and Pensions Act, cancelled proclamations already issued in connection with the emasculated insurance system, and provided that the system should not be re-established except by resolution of both Houses. The Prime Minister, who had so recently resigned from Lyons's Cabinet in defence of national insurance, proposed a select committee to re-examine the original Act. The motion for this was defeated, however, and national insurance was finally laid to rest. The only pensions act passed by this parliament was the Special Annuities Act, providing a pension of £500 per annum for Dame Enid Lyons and a further £500 per annum for the maintenance, education and benefit of the Lyons children.

During the long adjournment the Country Party made plans to defeat Menzies on the wheat issue when parliament resumed. At a meeting of all State and federal organisations in Melbourne on 1 September it seemed at first that all federal parliamentary members would be instructed to vote against the Government. But at afternoon tea time the delegates saw a late edition of the Melbourne *Herald* with the headline 'HITLER BOMBS WARSAW'. Page said to John McEwen (C, Indi, V): 'There will be a coalition by midnight'. He was wrong about that, but certainly the German blitzkrieg ruled out any immediate challenge to the Government on a domestic issue. The presiding officers, acting on the Prime Minister's instructions, had summoned members of parliament three weeks previously to reassemble on 6 September. Before most of them had started on their way back to Canberra, the Prime Minister announced that Australians were again involved willy-nilly in a European war. Speaking over all wireless stations at 9.15 p.m. on Sunday 3 September, he said: 'It is my melancholy duty to inform you officially that, in consequence of a persistence by Germany in her invasion of Poland, Great Britain has declared war upon her, and that, as a result, Australia is also at war'.

Later the same night the *Commonwealth Gazette* published a proclamation by Lord Gowrie, approved by the Executive Council, drawing attention to the existence of war and thus marking the beginning of what the Defence Act defined as 'Time of War'. This was as close as Australia came to declaring war against Germany, though the Commonwealth was nonetheless fully committed to such a state of hostility. As in the Great War, no formal declaration was considered necessary. Menzies firmly believed that a declaration of war by Britain automatically involved Australia as well, and even such an anti-imperialist as Maurice Blackburn considered it legally impossible for Australia to remain in the British Commonwealth at a state of peace once the King had declared war.

When parliament met on 6 September Menzies merely referred to the Governor-General's proclamation, and tabled a white paper containing relevant documents exchanged between the British and German governments. Curtin then read a statement of policy formulated by Caucus the day before. The A.L.P., while doing its utmost to maintain the integrity of the British Commonwealth, would nonetheless continue to preserve its separate entity in parliament. It would support measures for the welfare and safety of the Australian people. These should include immediate Government control of all essential raw materials, resumption of factories required for war production, and control of prices and rents to prevent profiteering. There should be as little interference as possible with civil liberties, and parliament should remain in session.

The latter was asking rather too much of an executive already resolved to impose its will upon parliament more arbitrarily than in time of peace. There were only eight sitting days in September, none in October, eight in November, and four in December before parliament adjourned and was later prorogued, with no sittings for nearly five months. During those relatively few sittings, parliament did very much what it was told. This was particularly true of the Senate, which became little more than a rubber stamp near the end of the session. On 7 December the Senate passed no fewer than fourteen bills; and on 8 December, the last day of the session, it passed seventeen. Paradoxically, however, this period of parliamentary automatism produced two examples of that rarity, the private member's bill. Both introduced by Curtin, they passed through all stages in September. One was the Supply and Development Act (No. 2), protecting industrial awards and agreements against interference under the original Act. The other was the Defence Act (No. 2), widening the grounds for conscientious objection.

Before the year ended, the executive had partly adapted to time of war. In September Menzies formed a War Cabinet consisting of himself, Hughes, Casey, Street, Gullett and Senator George McLeay, the Minister for Commerce. Menzies, after bringing down the 1939–40 Budget in September, had transferred the Treasurership to Spender. Full Cabinet remained responsible for general policy; but the War Cabinet, which was a standing committee of Cabinet, charged with detailed prosecution of the war, soon began to initiate general policy in that rapidly expanding area. Consciously following British example, the War Cabinet established its own secretariat headed by the Secretary of the Department of Defence, F. G. Shedden, who attended all meetings. This was an important innovation for Cabinet, which had never previously developed a secretariat, nor recorded its decisions in full and systematic minutes. Another standing committee, the Economic Cabinet, was established in December. A new Ministry for Information was placed under Gullett, and Defence was split into three separate departments—Army, Navy and Air.

During parliamentary recess the U.A.P. and Country Party managed to achieve what had seemed impossible only a few months earlier: a two-party coalition. Soon after the war began, the Country Party offered to sink its differences with Menzies if a new ministry could be selected by arrangement between himself and Sir Earle Page. When Menzies rejected this because 'it would appear to involve [Page's] own entry into the Cabinet', Page offered to 'place [himself] in the hands of [his] party, so there is no longer room for argument on the personal aspect'. He resigned as party leader on 13 September, and the position was contested by John McEwen and A. G. Cameron.

The wrong man won. Archie Galbraith Cameron, a dairy farmer from the Adelaide Hills and a major in the militia forces, was temperamentally unsuited for leadership. He was a martinet given to eccentric posturing. Although a church-going Catholic and strict Rechabite, he always refused to take the oath of allegiance after elections, preferring to make an affirmation by affidavit because he felt that a man's word should suffice, without religious emphasis. In 1938, while acting Minister for Commerce in Lyons's Cabinet, he became the first Minister of the Crown to be named and suspended from the Australian parliament. His offence—calling the Victorian Independent, Alex Wilson, a 'clean-skin', meaning 'unbranded'—hardly deserved rebuke; but when Speaker Bell called upon Cameron to withdraw, he stubbornly refused. That was his style.

Archie Cameron renewed the party's demand for an equal say in choice of ministers, Menzies again refused, and the prospect of coalition lapsed for the time being. Within days of assuming the leadership, Cameron also managed to prolong the estrangement of Fadden and the three other deserters from the Country Party. On 21 September he angrily attacked the good faith of those, including some members of his own party, who had voted for Curtin's conscientious objection bill. McEwen, who had been among the 'Ayes', described his leader's remarks as 'outside the scope of recognised parliamentary behaviour', and Fadden took the opportunity to declare that neither he, Corser, Collins nor Badman regarded Cameron as their leader.

But not even Cameron's clumsy belligerence could stop the two conservative parties resuming their normal working relationship once the Prime Minister realised that he needed a *modus vivendi* at any price. This was made clear to him at a by-election on 2 March 1940 for the seat of Corio, left vacant by Casey who had resigned from parliament in order to become Australia's first Minister to the United States. Menzies's undoubted satisfaction at this opportune departure by his main U.A.P. rival was quickly overshadowed by the loss of Corio to a Labor candidate, J. J. Dedman. Eleven days later Menzies offered the Country Party five portfolios, to be selected by mutual agreement, and a composite government was formed on 14 March. The Country Party Ministers were Cameron, Deputy Prime Minister, Commerce and Navy; McEwen, External Affairs; Thorby, Postmaster-General and Health; Fadden, who by then had returned to the fold, and H. K. Nock (Riverina, N), both assistant ministers.

Having gone that far, Menzies extended an attractive invitation to the Labor Party in June to join a national government, with Curtin as Prime Minister. It was rejected without hesitation. Curtin was having enough trouble controlling one party, let alone three. Faction fighting had recently broken out again in New South Wales, producing three Labor parties there: one recognised by the federal party; one controlled by Lang, without federal recognition; and one closely connected with the Australian Communist Party, which in June was banned as a subversive organisation by regulation issued under the National Security Act. Beasley was again leading a pro-Lang group outside federal Caucus, called the Australian Labor Party (Non-Communist). This time he had only four followers: Rosevear, Mulcahy, Gander, and Tom Sheehan, the latter of whom had obtained preselection for Garden's seat after Garden had fallen out with Lang. Ward, James, Lazzarini and Clark remained in Caucus, a blessing that Curtin would sometimes willingly have done without.

The second session of the fifteenth parliament, starting on 17 April, had six months to run before the full term expired. During this time parliament sat for only thirty days, but passed fifty-eight statutes. One of these, the Commonwealth Electoral Act, responded to the farce of Labor's 'four As' by providing that in future the order in which candidates' names were grouped on Senate ballot papers should be determined by lot rather than alphabet, and that the groups should be printed horizontally rather than vertically. Another, the Judiciary Act, enabled Sir John Latham to remain Chief Justice while serving as Australian Minister Plenipotentiary in Japan, a post for which his early career fitted him well. During his residence in Tokyo, Mr Justice Rich was acting Chief Justice.

The session's most controversial measure was the Motor Vehicles Agreement Bill, the original intention of which was to establish a motor vehicle industry by conferring a monopoly on Australian Consolidated Industries Ltd, which already enjoyed one monopoly, over the manufacture of glass bottles. The Country Party was firmly against this proposal, and under the coalition agreement its members were to be permitted a free vote on the Bill. The U.A.P. and A.L.P. were both divided on the issue, which had already cost the Government one of its ministers. In February 1940 it had become known that the Minister for Trade and Customs, J. N. Lawson (U, Macquarie,

N), had leased a racehorse from W. J. Smith, the managing director of Australian Consolidated Industries, with whom Lawson was negotiating the motor vehicle agreement. Although professing not to doubt Lawson's honesty or integrity, the Prime Minister nevertheless accepted his resignation for this *faux pas*. The Act was passed with an amendment by Curtin omitting the monopoly provision, and for this reason as well as wartime difficulties the agreement never came into effect.

In spite of the advantage which Menzies gained from coalition, it could not be said that his fortunes had changed for the better. Ahead of him lay a disastrous personal as well as political blow, followed soon afterwards by electoral disappointment. Between the infrequent parliamentary sittings he often returned to Melbourne for War Cabinet meetings at army headquarters in St Kilda Road. After sitting up all night in the train on Friday 9 August, and attending War Cabinet right through that weekend, he planned to leave for Canberra again on Sunday night. His private secretary, learning that three other ministers would be flying from Melbourne to Canberra by R.A.A.F. Lockheed Hudson on the morning of Tuesday 13 August, suggested this as a possible alternative to another uncomfortable night in the train. But the Prime Minister insisted on the Sunday night departure. On Tuesday morning, while Menzies was at work in his parliamentary office, someone came in to tell him that an aeroplane had crashed almost within sight of Parliament House. It was the same Lockheed Hudson with ten people on board, including the Cabinet Ministers, Street, Gullett and Fairbairn, and the Chief of the General Staff, Lieutenant-General Sir Cyril Brudenell White. After circling Canberra's runway, the bomber had flown towards Queanbeyan to make another landing approach; on the return it stalled and crashed on to a hillside one and a half miles from the aerodrome. It caught fire immediately, and there were no survivors.

No fewer than fourteen members of the parliamentary U.A.P. were said to be either openly or covertly hostile towards their leader, but the dead ministers had not been among them. 'On that dreadful day', wrote Menzies, 'I was sad beyond the powers of description; some of my greatest friends had gone'. Although the Government was now 'crippled', as the Prime Minister said, it could at least hope for some improvement in its position after the coming general election. Cabinet had considered postponing this election if parliament agreed that the war situation warranted such an unprecedented course. The Opposition also felt that parliament could suspend the Constitution, sit as a constituent assembly, and later ratify what it had done in that extra-Constitutional capacity—but only if the circumstances were sufficiently desperate. They were not, and on 7 August Labor Caucus decided against extending the life of parliament. Two weeks later Menzies announced that a general election would be held on 21 September.

Campaign speeches dealt mainly with the war. U.A.P. candidates presented Menzies as an Australian Churchill, but in Labor rhetoric he bore more resemblance to Chamberlain. Menzies and Cameron advocated a national war government along Churchill–Attlee lines. Curtin ignored that subject, and placed his main emphasis on the importance of air defence. The outcome of the election was a bitter disappointment to Menzies, for it produced a parliament that was almost unworkable. Both houses were virtually deadlocked. In the Senate the Government parties held nineteen seats and Labor held seventeen. In the House of Representatives the U.A.P. held twenty-three seats (four fewer than at the previous general election); the Country Party, thirteen (three down); A.L.P., thirty-two (five up); Langites, four (one down); and Independents, two.

Thus in the chamber where governments were made and broken the coalition held thirty-six seats, Labor and the Non-Communist Labor Party held thirty-six, and the balance of power resided with two Victorian Independents. One of the Independents was the 'clean-skin', Alex Wilson; the other was A. W. Coles, the managing director and co-founder of the retail chain G. J. Coles, who had not been opposed by the U.A.P. in the late Sir Henry Gullett's seat of Henty. The other dead ministers' seats, Corangamite and Flinders, were retained by the U.A.P., the latter being won by Richard Casey's brother-in-law, Rupert Ryan.

Among the new Labor members were A. A. Calwell, who succeeded the late Dr Maloney in Melbourne; J. B. Chifley, who recaptured his old seat of Macquarie from the imprudent racehorse lessee, Lawson, after reconciliation between the federal and New South Wales Labor parties had enabled him to win preselection there; and the former Mr Justice Evatt, who resigned from the High Court to contest the New South Wales seat of Barton. During Chifley's nine years out of parliament, he had led an active public life in Bathurst despite difficulties placed in his way by the vindictive Lang machine. Lang's influence deprived him of his union ticket, but perhaps that was all to the good. Instead of returning to his old livelihood of locomotive engine-driving, he earned his living, such as it was, by means which tended to sharpen his financial acumen. He became a director of the *National Advocate* newspaper, and an adviser on business and property dealings.

Chifley had unsuccessfully challenged Lang's man in Macquarie at the 1934 federal election, and at the following year's State election he quixotically opposed the 'Big Fella' himself in the stronghold of Auburn. He became President of Abercrombie Shire Council, and in 1936–37, at the invitation of the Federal Treasurer, Casey, he served on a royal commission into Australia's monetary and banking systems, which the Lyons Government had appointed in response to public interest in Douglas Credit, and to Country Party criticism of the way in which many farmers had been treated by their banks during the Depression.

The royal commission was an invaluable learning experience for Chifley, who of necessity became an apt pupil of one of his fellow commissioners, the Sydney University economist, Professor R. C. Mills. In his minority report Chifley had advocated the complete nationalisation of banking. The majority report was more cautious, but the Lyons Government had made no effective use of it, let alone of Chifley's radical proposals.

The other prominent new Labor member in 1940, Dr Evatt, had served five years in State parliament before his elevation to the High Court at the exceptionally early age of thirty-seven. He had known Curtin and Forde for many years, and shared a mutual sense of rivalry with Menzies, dating back to their days at the Bar. Herbert Vere Evatt was a big, rather shaggy man with a profound intellect, towering ambition and sometimes erratic judgement. His father had been a publican in the Hunter Valley, and his mother, although born an Irish Catholic, had brought her children up in the Protestant faith. Bert was as brilliant a student as Menzies, who was his exact contemporary, and like Menzies he could not be bothered stooping, or even feigning, to conquer. On the High Court he bickered frequently with his crustier colleagues, and in the Labor Party he seldom bothered to conceal his belief that Curtin was not pushing hard enough to gain office. He himself was avid for power. Several months before the election he sounded out Percy Spender, whom he had known since school days at Fort Street, about the possibility of a national government, and whether, if the A.L.P. reconciled itself to that, he (Evatt) would be acceptable to the U.A.P. as a national leader. Whatever reply Spender may have given at the time, he later wrote that only a man of Evatt's 'insatiable aspirations and vanity could have thought it feasible'.

As it happened, Curtin came perilously close to losing his own seat in the 1940 election. He had neglected Fremantle for the sake of campaigning longer in the eastern States, and on the basis of early counting the press assumed that he would be defeated by his U.A.P. opponent. Because of this likelihood, he asked the deputy leader, Forde, to speak on behalf of the party. The *Sydney Morning Herald* reported that if Curtin was indeed defeated Dr Evatt would almost certainly be elected leader, but that was a dubious assertion. In any case, after a nerve-racking week the arrival of soldiers' votes from overseas saved Curtin, by the narrow margin of 1025.

The situation of near-deadlock facing parliament gave new life to the proposal for national government which the coalition parties had advanced during the campaign. Although many Labor members were still opposed to the idea, sufficient interest had been shown, not least by Curtin and Evatt, for the Opposition to take part in discussions arranged by the Government before the sixteenth parliament was opened in November. At three meetings held in the Cabinet room at Parliament House, Menzies put forward a number of points upon which agreement might be sought to achieve full co--operation, and Curtin suggested the establishment of an Advisory War Council instead of full national government. On 23 October Labor Caucus voted in favour of partial co-operation through an Advisory War Council, but nothing more than that. Menzies expressed his regret, and accepted the lesser proposal.

The Advisory War Council, established on 28 October under National Security regulations, was a creation of the executive, not of parliament. Its eight members (four from the Government and four from the Opposition) considered matters of great importance which for reasons of security could not be raised openly in parliament, but they held no executive responsibility. Apart from the War Council's use in helping parliament to function under difficult circumstances, it also had more specific value on both sides of the house. For Curtin it was something with which to appease the Langites, and one of the Opposition's seats on the Council went to Beasley. For Menzies it helped to secure Opposition sufferance during a long visit to Britain which he intended to make during the first half of 1941. He undertook to keep the Advisory War Council informed of his activities in London, and Curtin indicated informally that he would not take advantage of the Prime Minister's absence. The first War Council consisted of Menzies, Fadden, Hughes, Spender, Curtin, Beasley, Forde and Makin. Evatt and McEwen were added the next year.

The Country Party was now under new and more capable leadership. At its first meeting after the election Cameron, finding himself opposed by Page and McEwen, left the party room in a huff. He was persuaded to return, which he did 'like a glowing coal', but would take no part in the ensuing ballot. In three consecutive ballots, the two candidates received eight votes each. To break this deadlock Arthur Fadden agreed to serve temporarily as acting Leader if nominated and seconded by Page and McEwen, and elected unanimously; and so he was.

Although he represented Darling Downs, and was an accountant by profession, Arthur William Fadden was essentially a North Queenslander who had come up the hard way. His Irish-born Presbyterian father was a police constable at Ingham, and his mother was Irish-Australian. Artie, as everyone called him, was the eldest of ten children. He started work on the canefields; put on a white collar to become a sugar mill office boy and later the assistant town clerk at Mackay; established an accountancy practice in Townsville, specialising in taxation; and later represented part of Townsville in the Legislative Assembly before entering federal politics. He was a shrewdie, but a tubby, rollicking one who made friends as easily as Archie Cameron had made enemies, and regaled them with an endless fund of *risqué* stories.

For the sake of party harmony, Fadden went to see Cameron and offered him a place in the new coalition Ministry. Archie spat the full length of his office, pulled off one of his elastic-sided boots and hurled it against the wall, saying that he 'would not be found dead with the Country Party mob'. Thereafter he sat with the U.A.P., a glowing coal ready to inflict third-degree burns at the slightest provocation.

Menzies's third Ministry, which met parliament for the first time on 20 November, included Fadden as Treasurer; Hughes, Attorney-General and Navy, and again Deputy Leader of the U.A.P.; Spender, Army; Holt, a new portfolio of Labor and National Service; E. J. Harrison (U, Wentworth, N), Trade and Customs; McEwen, Air; and Page, now tolerated by Menzies if not forgiven, Commerce. Parliament sat for only twelve days before adjourning for Christmas and the following two months. In this short time, thanks to Curtin's obliging acquiescence, Fadden was able to bring down the first full-scale war Budget, estimating war expenditure of £186 million for 1940–41.

On the last sitting day before Christmas, 13 December, the House of Representatives held parliament's only 'secret sitting' of the war. Soon after midnight, while the House was dealing with defence estimates in the committee of supply, the Prime Minister and Leader of the Opposition agreed that members should discuss in secrecy a matter that had been raised by Cameron concerning the Minister for the Army, Percy Spender. The House agreed to a motion for the withdrawal of strangers, but accepted the Prime Minister's qualification that senators, although 'strange', were not 'strangers'. All occupants of the galleries except senators, of whom there were some in the senators' gallery, then left the chamber, and all doors were locked. The Clerk, F. C. Green, the Clerk-Assistant, Sydney Chubb, and the Serjeant-at-Arms, Harry Dodd, remained in their places. Although no record of proceedings was kept by Hansard from 12.32 a.m. until members returned to the defence vote at 3.30 a.m., the general nature of Cameron's attack on Spender became known outside parliament soon enough, and will be referred to later in this chapter.

There were no external attempts to censor Hansard during World War II, such as had occasionally happened in the previous war. The presiding officers did make deletions for security reasons, but this was done only with the approval of members concerned. For example, the Hansard report of Cameron's remarks shortly before the withdrawal of strangers on 13 December was interrupted by several asterisks, indicating an excision by the Speaker. What Cameron had said, in part, was this: 'If an enemy vessel were to sail up Spencer Gulf, it could do enormous damage in half an hour's target practice at Whyalla or Port Pirie. It need not go near Sydney or Newcastle or Port Phillip, or any other defended place'.

Secret assembly was the most extreme form of self-censorship, but was resorted to only occasionally. During the next two years there were six secret meetings of the two houses, held in the lower chamber following an adjournment or suspension of a sitting. These were not sittings of the House, but rather 'joint secret meetings', comparable to the one meeting of members and senators held in the Senate clubroom during World War I, and their main purpose was to heighten parliament's sense of involvement in the war. Whether members always observed the strict secrecy expected of them was open to some doubt. At one meeting Chifley noticed that the new Member for Riverina—an old hotel keeper named Joe Langtry, best known for his recitations of Robert Service's frontier ballads—was taking notes. When asked why, he said that it would be something interesting to tell the people at Barellan.

Wrecked

Menzies knew that he was taking a political risk by leaving Australia while parliament was so evenly divided, but he may not have realised just how very risky his four-months trip would be. 'If you feel you must go', his wife Pattie told him, 'you will go. But you will be out of office within six weeks of your return'. Unlike the Prime Ministers of Canada and South Africa, Menzies did feel a compelling need to visit London in 1941, primarily, he said later, to discuss the danger of Japan entering the war, and to urge the strengthening of British defences at Singapore. In addition, he was irresistibly attracted by the prospect of being close to, perhaps even part of, imperial decision-making at this crucial hour in British history. 'Why do we regard history as of the past', he wrote in his diary of this trip, 'and forget that we are making it?' While he was making history in London, however, others could be making trouble in Canberra, Sydney and Melbourne. Curtin had struck some kind of truce, but who could vouch for Menzies's own colleagues?

The last leisurely official voyage to London by sea had been made by Page in 1938. Now that journey could be made quickly and comfortably by air.

Leaving Fadden as acting Prime Minister, Menzies departed from Sydney on 21 January by Qantas Empire flying boat, accompanied by F. G. Shedden, secretary to the War Cabinet and Advisory War Council, and John Storey, an industrial engineer who had been placed in charge of military aircraft production. For a British-Australian of Menzies's ilk, the flight from Sydney to the Middle East was a deeply impressive reconnaissance of the British Commonwealth—or rather the British Empire, as such a loyal subject as Menzies still thought of it. The flying boat passed over or splashed down at Singapore, Penang, Rangoon, Karachi, Dubai and the Sea of Galilee. 'Wherever the aeroplane came down', he said later in a BBC broadcast,

> we found some young or youngish Englishman waiting to receive and instruct us. Sometimes he was a Governor, sometimes a Commissioner, sometimes a Resident, sometimes a Law Adviser. But whatever his description, he always turned out to be fresh-faced, cultivated, alert, composed about his job and, though I suppose this to be mere coincidence, incredibly good-looking. The words of George Santayana frequently came into my mind: 'Never since the heroic days of Greece has the world had such a sweet, just, boyish master. It will be a black day for the human race when scientific blackguards, conspirators, churls, and fanatics manage to supplant him'.

It was in this mood of imperial fervour that Menzies, after visiting Australian troops in Palestine, Egypt and Libya, landed at Poole, in Dorset, on 20 February. He had been 'home' twice before, but one of his fellow passengers—the British politician and diarist Henry Channon—remarked on the Australian Prime Minister's 'touching excitement' as the flying boat approached England. Channon, who saw something of Menzies in Egypt, found him 'jolly, rubicund, witty . . . with a rapier-like intelligence . . . He says he does not intend to be blitzed by Winston but he will be'. Menzies's first impression of Churchill in wartime was pretty much as Channon had predicted. 'What a tempestuous creature he is', he wrote in his diary at Chequers on 22 February, 'pacing up and down the room, always as if about to dart out of it, and then suddenly returning. Oratorical even in conversation . . . But there's no doubt about it; he's a holy terror—I went to bed tired!'

Next day there was a 'momentous discussion' with Churchill about the defence of Greece, largely with Australian and New Zealand troops. 'This kind of decision, which may mean thousands of lives, is not easy', wrote Menzies. 'Why does a peaceable man become a Prime Minister?' On 24 February Menzies attended a meeting of the War Cabinet at Downing Street, which decided to use Australian troops in Greece—'subject of course to consent of Australian cabinet'.

> Procedure interesting [read Menzies's diary entry for that day] . . . Greek affair called on. 'You have read your file, gentlemen, and report of the Chief of Staff Committee. The arguments are clear on each side. I favour the project.' And then around the table. Nobody more than three or four sentences. Does this denote great clarity and directness of mind in *all* these ministers, or has Winston taken *charge* of them, as the one man whom the public regard as indispensable? There may be a good deal in

this business of building yourself up by base arts so that you can really control a cabinet . . . I was the only one to put questions, and feel like a new boy who, in the first week at school, commits the solecism of speaking to the captain of the school.

By April his references to the school captain had become less reverent.

Winston is a dictator; he cannot be over-ruled, and his colleagues fear him. The people have set him up as something a little less than God, and his power is therefore terrific. Today I have decided to remain for a couple of weeks, for grave decisions will have to be taken about [the Middle East], chiefly Australian forces, and I am not content to have them solved by 'unilateral rhetoric'.

Menzies was not 'blitzed' by Churchill, or anyone else. He argued strongly against what he perceived as the Foreign Office's policy of 'drift' in relation to the Japanese danger, and pressed as hard as he could for the reinforcement of Singapore. Far from being some colonial puppet, as his detractors would later claim, he was at this time an 'independent Australian Briton' who kept sight of Australia's interests and when necessary, with valuable assistance from High Commissioner Bruce, took issue with British War policy.

And how he relished it all! War Cabinet, dinner *à trois* with the King and Queen at Windsor Castle, lunch with Noel Coward, compliments from *The Times*, banter with Lady Astor in the air raid shelter at Cliveden, and an ovation in the House of Commons. 'Some of these fellows would not mind my defeat at Canberra', he wrote after addressing the Empire Parliamentary Association at Westminister, 'if they could get me into the Commons. *Omnis ignotus pro magnifico*'. The tag from Tacitus affected a modesty that did not ring quite true: 'Everything unknown is thought to be wonderful'.

The thought of defeat in Canberra jarred like a skeleton at the feast, reminding Menzies of his political mortality. Letters from Australia at first hinted discreetly and then warned bluntly that trouble was brewing in Cabinet and the party room. Fadden, whose leadership of the Country Party had been confirmed in March, was said to be enjoying his surrogate Prime Ministership, and becoming too popular with the press and Opposition. Hughes had been heard to say in King's Hall that Menzies could not lead a flock of homing pigeons; and even Spender, earlier esteemed by Menzies as his 'faithful Achates', came under some suspicion. Spender was sounded out by one of Menzies's backbench foes, W. V. McCall, (U, Martin, N); but by his own account, Spender's only offence was to warn Menzies against Fadden after seeing what purported to be an official letter from Country Party headquarters. The letter, presumably placed by mistake in an envelope addressed to the New South Wales President of the U.A.P., Sir Sydney Snow, said in effect that Menzies would have to be replaced by a Country Party man if the coalition was to be preserved. In a letter relaying all this, Spender warned Menzies that 'his political grave was being dug'.

If the Minister for the Army did not regard himself as a potential successor to Menzies, others apparently did, and were anxious to cruel his chances. The *Sydney Morning Herald*'s Canberra correspondent, Ross Gollan, was skilfully promoting Fadden as a permanent alternative to Menzies, and one way to improve Fadden's chances was to damage Spender's. This he did by ridiculing some ill-considered remarks made by Spender after visiting Australian headquarters in the Middle East. 'My outstanding experience, of course, relates to Bardia', said Spender in a broadcast. 'Sir Thomas Blamey, of the Australian Army Corps, and his staff officers, discussed with me at length the plans to take Bardia. The attack was fixed to begin at dawn two days later.' By the time Gollan had finished with the hapless minister, whom he dubbed 'the Baron of Bardia', Spender stood convicted of what the *Herald*'s headlines called 'Mr Spender's Lapses/The Limelight's Lure/Errors in Publicity'.

Spender also came under fire on 2 April, this time from Archie Cameron, who was temporarily in Army Intelligence. The attack was ˙similar to Cameron's speech at the secret sitting in December, but to the annoyance of many in the chamber he stopped short of revealing publicly what the fuss was all about. After moving that the Minister for the Army had lost the House's confidence 'because of his handling of the internment, trial and release from internment of certain enemy aliens', Cameron confined himself to specious and jingoistic generalities. 'The kid glove, pansy method of handling aliens may eventually have awkward consequences', he said.

> Certain Jewish refugees also have been interned, and a lot of hot air is being talked about them. I have heard talk of friendly aliens. I do not know what a friendly alien is. I know that when my country is engaged in a life and death struggle with Germany and Italy any man of German or Italian birth is an enemy alien.

The motion lapsed for want of a seconder, and the acting Prime Minister declared that Cameron had been wasting the House's time when it should have been dealing with more important business. Two months later the remorseless Eddie Ward, like a jackal snapping up carrion dropped by some other scavenger, raised the matter directly at Question Time. Was it a fact, he asked the Minister for the Army, that at the outbreak of war a warrant had been issued for the arrest of Phillip Raoul Hentze, and that Hentze was permitted to retain his liberty on the personal guarantee of the Minister? Had Hentze come to Australia from Germany as a wool-buyer? Had the Minister recommended Hentze for a position with the communications censor? And finally, was Hentze in any way related to the Minister?

> Mr SPENDER.—The man Hentze to whom the honorable member referred is married to my wife's sister. He is not a German. He is the son of a Belgian. His mother was a daughter of Sir Graham Berry, who is very well known in this country. He was born in Germany while his father was on an assignment there. He was educated in this country and has lived here for practically the whole of his life. I at no time made any representations whatever to have him placed upon the censorship staff . . .

Ward kept returning to 'the Case of Mr P. R. Hentze' until August, but got nowhere. It was indeed a waste of time, considering that the House sat for a mere twenty-four days in the first eight months of the year. During these sittings parliament passed, in addition to another batch of war measures, the

Ministers of State Act, enlarging the ministry to a maximum of nineteen; and the Child Endowment Act, a measure more to have been expected from a Labor government than from the coalition. The latter provided, without means test, a weekly payment of five shillings for each child maintained in excess of one.

At last Menzies returned, on 24 May. Having visited President Roosevelt in Washington and Mackenzie King in Ottawa, he crossed the Pacific by Pan-American clipper to Auckland. There he contemplated his imminent homecoming in a mood far removed from the excitement of his arrival in England. 'A sick feeling of repugnance and apprehension grows in me as I near Australia', he wrote in his diary. 'If only I could creep in quietly into the bosom of the family, and rest there.'

Fadden met the Prime Minister at Rose Bay flying base, and to his amazement was treated with a coolness verging on rudeness. Two nights later, in a speech at Sydney Town Hall, Menzies gave further evidence of the frame of mind in which he had returned from matters of global importance to domestic politics. 'It is a diabolical thing', he said in a phrase quoted later by his critics, 'that anybody should have to come back and play politics, however clean and however friendly, at a time like this'. What else were politicians for, even in time of war, if not to engage in politics? And was the game any more diabolical on one side than the other?

The speech was nonetheless well received by his audience, and at a reception held later in the Lord Mayor's suite Menzies shouldered his way through the convivial crowd to where Spender and his wife were standing somewhat apart, sardonically discussing one of the themes of Menzies's speech, the loyalty shown by his Cabinet colleagues during the last few months. 'Well Percy', he asked, 'where is this grave you wrote about?'

'It's been dug all right, Bob', replied Spender, 'it is only waiting for you to be pushed into it'.

Menzies took three weeks to announce a 'prospectus of unlimited war effort', and when he did so in another speech on 17 June it failed to silence criticism from the Opposition, now formally reunited by readmission of the Lang faction to Caucus; from the press, particularly the *Sydney Morning Herald*, which was still sounding Fadden's praises at every opportunity; and indeed from some members of his own party. There were to be five new departments—Aircraft Production, Transport, War Organisation of Industry, Home Security and External Territories—bringing the ministry to its full permitted strength. In July Menzies also moved successfully for the establishment of Joint Parliamentary Committees on Broadcasting, Profits, Rural Industries, Social Security and War Expenditure. These were comparable to the long-standing Joint Statutory Committees on Public Accounts and Public Works, and were intended to involve members in executive war responsibility. Government and Opposition were equally represented on them, but the chairmen, who exercised a casting vote, were nominated by the Government.

To Archie Cameron, this seemed 'not an attempt to secure better administration of the war effort, but an attempt to secure the acquiescence of a majority of members of Parliament in the perpetuation of a system which will not get this country out of its troubles'. Some Labor members also feared that the new committees would be used to muzzle parliamentary debate, but Menzies came closer to the truth when explaining the system. 'Having regard to the fact that in war-time a considerable transfer of power to the Executive had been found necessary', he said,

> and to the further consequential fact that Parliament meets for comparatively brief periods, it seemed to me of the first importance that in order to preserve the continuity of parliamentary influence, and the continuous responsibility of members of parliament, they should be given some continuous function in relation to administrative affairs. This committee system does that.

Menzies's prospectus for unlimited war was sound enough, but his critics maintained that he was failing to convert it into administrative action. Sir Earle Page defended him in parliament, saying that 'no one could have done more than he has done at the heart of the Empire to uphold the interests of all sections of the Australian people'; but this was rightly perceived as no more than a ceremonial burying of the hatchet. Others wielded their hatchets with a will. McCall, who was generally regarded as Hughes's hatchet-man, and another U.A.P. backbencher, W. J. Hutchinson (Indi, V), publicly demanded a party meeting on the question of leadership.

When Menzies called a meeting on 28 July, thirteen of the forty nominal U.A.P. members of parliament failed to attend. No vote was taken, and Menzies announced that he would shortly visit South Australia, Western Australia and Queensland. This could have been the prelude to an early general election, but Menzies had travelled no further than South Australia when reports of party unrest obliged him to make what the press described as a 'retreat from Adelaide'. The malcontents had now been joined publicly by Sir Charles Marr (U, Parkes, N), who accused Menzies of pandering to the interests of monopolies, and Colonel White, who was alarmed, as others were, by Japan's increasingly aggressive behaviour.

In the last few days Japanese troops had landed in French Indo-China, and the British Government had advised Australia that Churchill and Roosevelt were about to meet in the Western Atlantic. On the day the Atlantic Charter was signed, 11 August, a full Cabinet meeting was held in Melbourne to discuss the imminent danger of a Japanese invasion of Thailand. This meeting decided that the Prime Minister should return to London and try to ensure that Australia's interests were taken fully into account in the event of Japan joining the Axis powers. In a cable to Bruce, Menzies said that the Australian point of view must be pressed in British War Cabinet:

> As you know I sent my views on Dominion representation to British War Cabinet to Mackenzie King and Smuts but neither of them is interested in it, Smuts going so far as to say . . . that we Dominion Prime Ministers should mind our own business and leave Churchill to mind his. This completely overlooks the fact that many matters dealt with by British Cabinet and Foreign Secretary are our business as well as Britain's and that present Cabinet set up excludes us from a real voice at the right time.

Some sections of the press suggested that Menzies should resign the Prime Ministership and go to London as a private member; but he, perhaps suspecting that *primus* was an even more important qualification than *ignotus* in Downing Street, insisted that only a Prime Minister could adequately represent Australia in the British War Cabinet. When Cabinet's decision was made known to the Advisory War Council, Forde and Evatt opposed it, the latter dismissing the proposed journey as no more than a political ruse to save Menzies from being pushed out of the leadership. Curtin was ambivalent. On the one hand, he said, the Prime Minister's place at this critical time was in Australia; but on the other hand, Australia should have a representative of high standing in London.

Curtin was in a state of indecision generally. Although reluctant to fight for office, he was being urged to do so by some of his colleagues, particularly Evatt, Forde, Beasley and Calwell. His reluctance was caused mainly by doubt about his own capacity: he was diffident, and quite nervous at the thought of becoming Prime Minister. Evatt said privately at this time that Curtin was 'woefully timid' and 'merely going to endorse everything the government did'. Another cause of Curtin's reluctance was his deep distaste, dating back to the Scullin Government, for the idea of having to govern with a hostile Senate. Although the Government held nineteen seats in the Senate and the Opposition seventeen, the President and Chairman of Committees were both Labor men. This was merely the luck of the draw. Two Government senators had been absent when the election for president was held— Senator K. C. Wilson (S), who was in the Middle East with the A.I.F.; and Senator A. N. MacDonald (W), in hospital with gallstones—and in each of two consecutive ballots between the retiring president, Senator J. B. Hayes (U, T), and Senator James Cunningham (Lab, W) the result was 17–17. The Senate then proceeded to decide the question by drawing a name out of a box. This was the first time such a draw had been necessary, and when one senator inquired how it would be conducted the Opposition candidate for Chairman of Committees, Senator Gordon Brown (Q), said: 'The Senator who stops in is in, and the Senator who comes out is out'. Cunningham and Brown stopped in.

The Senate at this time bore little resemblance to the brave hopes expressed for it at the federal conventions. Political parties had tightened their hold on senators, particularly since the introduction of preferential voting, and it was fair to say that the calibre of senators had deteriorated. 'With a few exceptions', wrote one observer, 'it was a chamber of ageing party hacks and superannuated servicemen from World War I. It had a high proportion of heavy drinkers'. In 1941 the Senate was again functioning as a rubber stamp. 'Fifteen bills have been hurled at honorable senators since 4 o'clock this afternoon', protested Senator R. V. Keane (L, V) at one sitting. 'The manner in which Ministers are handling the business of this chamber is an outrage.' As Curtin well knew, however, a tame Senate could easily become a hostile one if the lower house came under different management.

In the few remaining days before parliament reassembled on 20 August, Forde and Evatt said publicly that the time had come for Labor to take office. Despite Curtin's continuing caution, this was hardly the sort of climate in which Menzies could expect another truce from the Opposition. On 20 August, after delivering a statement on international affairs, he informed parliament that Cabinet had asked him to return to London. 'Having regard to the balance of parties in Parliament', he said, 'I have indicated that it would not be practicable for me to go abroad at present, except with the approval of all parties'. The sitting was then suspended from 3.55 p.m. to 10 p.m. so that members and senators could discuss the matters raised by the Prime Minister at a joint secret meeting in the chamber.

Next morning the Labor Caucus passed a motion declaring that it was essential for the Prime Minister to remain in Australia to direct the organisation of a total war effort, and that some other arrangement should be made to ensure that Australia's point of view was kept before the British War Cabinet. The debate on international affairs in both chambers later that day left Menzies in no doubt that if he went to London himself there would be no truce. On 22 August he again invited the A.L.P. to join a national government, in which Labor and the non-Labor parties would share portfolios equally, and in which Menzies himself would be willing to serve under Curtin or any other person selected as Prime Minister. On his way back to Melbourne after parliament had adjourned, Menzies encountered Mrs Jean Spender in the railway kiosk at Albury, where passengers had to change trains. To her consternation, he said grimly: 'Give me the dagger, Lady Macbeth!'

On 26 August Curtin rejected Menzies's final offer. The crux of his reply was that Menzies could no longer give Australia stable government, but that the Opposition, if it received the same measure of co-operation in parliament as Labor had hitherto been extending to the Government, could certainly do so. 'I consider', he concluded, 'that in view of your statement that you cannot secure . . . a workable Parliament you should return your Commission to the Governor-General and advise him of the purport of this communication'.

At the next meeting of Caucus, shortly before parliament met on 28 August, Calwell moved an amendment designed to bring about an immediate challenge to the Government on the floor of the House. According to Calwell's subsequent account, he did this at the solicitation of Dr Evatt; but after Curtin had spoken against the amendment, arguing for a want of confidence motion later on the Budget, Evatt joined the majority in voting against the amendment which he himself had inspired.

Speaking on the adjournment at about 5 p.m., Menzies announced that the Government had decided that a minister, other than the Prime Minister, should be sent to London as soon as practicable. Cabinet met that evening, and after some discussion the Country Party Ministers withdrew, leaving their U.A.P. colleagues to private deliberation. At 9 p.m. Menzies informed a meeting of the parliamentary U.A.P. that he had decided to resign so that another Prime Minister could be chosen. The meeting was at times emotional, and one member—Arthur Coles, who had temporarily abandoned his Independent status—walked out in disgust. The impulsive Coles had spent some time with Menzies in London, and had been so impressed by the Prime Minister's achievements there, and by the Sydney Town Hall speech, that he joined the U.A.P. Now he became a clean-skin once again in protest at what he regarded as a forced resignation. 'It was something so unclean', he later told the press, 'that it will never be erased from my memory—it was nothing but a public lynching'.

At 10.30 p.m. Country Party members joined the U.A.P. meeting. Hutchinson moved and Marr seconded that Fadden should become Prime Minister-elect. There were no other nominations, and the vote was unanimous. Menzies, now committed to becoming the first and so far the only Australian Prime Minister ever to resign from office—comported himself with dignity throughout what he later referred to as a 'stroke of doom' and 'humiliation'. After leaving the joint meeting with tears in his eyes, he wryly quoted to his private secretary, Cecil Looker, two lines from an old Scottish ballad, 'Sir Andrew Barton':

> Ile lay mee downe and bleed a while
> And then Ile rise and fight againe.

Menzies seemed to have armed himself against humiliation with recondite literary allusions. The Gallery correspondents were waiting for him on the way to his office, and to them he offered a fragment from the *Odyssey* about Ulysses being wrecked on the island of Phaeacia.

> . . . a monstrous wave upbore
> The chief, and dash'd him on the craggy shore.

On 29 August Menzies returned his commission and the Governor-General invited Fadden to form a ministry. That evening Menzies and his wife were walking along a corridor in Parliament House when they encountered the Spenders approaching them. 'Bob and Pat passed us, going in the opposite direction', wrote Mrs Spender.

> One wanted to say something. They both looked at us coldly and passed us by. Pat was always such a warm person. Why should she look at us coldly? There was no doubt in my mind that Percy was considered the nigger in the woodpile. I was sorry, for it was so untrue. Wherever their information had come from, they had been misinformed.

The new Prime Minister retained his former office of Treasurer; Menzies, who remained Leader of the U.A.P., was appointed Minister for Defence Co-ordination; and the minister chosen to represent Australia in British War Cabinet was none other than Sir Earle Page. Fadden's term of office, like the deluge in Genesis, lasted exactly forty days and forty nights. It came close to being even shorter, for in September, before Fadden opened his Budget, the Government found itself embroiled in something which could well have provided the Opposition with sufficient ammunition for a want of confidence motion. Joseph Winkler, a journalist employed in the Prime Minister's Department, had given Curtin a memorandum about payments made by the Attorney-General, Hughes, to a union official as part of a clandestine campaign to combat industrial unrest. Curtin, suspecting a trap, would have preferred to ignore it; but when he realised that the memorandum was a carbon copy, and that other copies might have been given to some of the hotspurs in Caucus, he raised the matter with Fadden and

Menzies. A royal commission was appointed, and its report eventually exonerated those concerned.

The Opposition sensibly preferred to attack the Government on Fadden's Budget. On 30 September Caucus resolved that the proposed budgetary methods were 'contrary to true equality and sacrifice' and should be 'recast to ensure a more equitable distribution of the national burden'. The substance of this was used by Curtin when, in the Committee of Supply on 1 October, he moved that the first item in the Estimates be reduced by £1. At last the battle lines were being drawn, 36–36, and the Opposition had good reason to expect support from the two Independents. Coles's alienation from the Government had been aggravated by Fadden's failure to find a place for him in the new Ministry; and Wilson, a Wimmera farmer, unexpectedly found himself being cultivated by Dr Evatt.

On the day the House was expected to vote on Curtin's amendment, 3 October 1941, Curtin called at Fadden's office on his way to lunch. 'Well, boy', he said, 'have you got the numbers? I hope you have, but I don't think you have'.

Fadden replied, 'No, John, I haven't got them. I have heard that Wilson spent the weekend at Evatt's home, and I can't rely on Coles'.

'Well, there it is', said Curtin. 'Politics is a funny game.'

Soon after the luncheon adjournment, when time expired for H. L. Anthony (C, Richmond, N), Coles and Wilson stood simultaneously to catch the eye of the Chairman of Committees, J. H. Prowse (C, Swan, W). Prowse gave the call to Wilson, the less assertive of the two, and Wilson waved it to Coles. 'I have decided to vote against the government on the amendment moved by the Leader of the Opposition', said Coles. 'In the only . . . interview that I have had with [the Prime Minister] I told him frankly that he could not regard me as a government supporter.'

> Mr FADDEN.—Unless I put the honorable member in the Cabinet.
> Mr COLES.—I challenge the Prime Minister to say that on oath, because it is a deliberate untruth.
> Mr FADDEN.—It is no such thing.
> Mr COLES.—I told the Prime Minister in his own office that he could not regard me as a supporter of the Government.
> Mr FADDEN.—Unless I put the honorable member in the Cabinet.
> Mr COLES.—That is a lie. What I said was, "Unless I am satisfied with the policy of your Government and the membership of your Cabinet. I am not seeking any preferment for myself".

Holt spoke next, and then Wilson. Wilson uttered only three words— 'During this debate . . . '—before Eric Harrison interjected: 'The honourable member is now only a pricked bubble'. And so he was, for it had been generally assumed that he would follow Coles's lead, whatever that might be. The vote was taken at about 4 p.m. with all members present or paired. The chairman could not vote deliberatively, but the Speaker, W. M. Nairn (U, Perth, W), voted with the Government. That was not enough, however, and the question was resolved in the affirmative, 36–33. This was the eighth occasion since 1901, and the last such occasion to date, on which defeat on the floor of the House obliged a government either to resign or advise a dis-

solution. Later that day Fadden submitted the resignation of his Government, and Lord Gowrie commissioned John Curtin to form the first Labor
Ministry for almost ten years. Only the day before, Caucus had passed a
motion congratulating Curtin on the sixth anniversary of his election as
party leader, and members had sung, 'For He is a Jolly Good Fellow'. Now,
when he called at the party room to say that he was on his way to Government House, someone remarked: 'You'll be Prime Minister against your
will'.

Curtin's nineteen-strong Ministry was sworn in on 7 October. He was
Minister for Defence Co-ordination; Forde was Minister for the Army;
Chifley, Treasurer; Evatt, Attorney-General and External Affairs; Beasley,
Supply and Development; and Ward, Labour and National Service. Fadden
remained Leader of the Country Party, and in the absence of anyone more
acceptable to both non-Labor parties, he became Leader of the Opposition.
Menzies resigned from leadership of the U.A.P., and was succeeded by
Hughes, then in his fortieth year as a federal member. Menzies remained an
Opposition member of the Advisory War Council, but this was a poor substi-
tute for British War Cabinet. Two days after the change of government Lord
Gowrie sent a 'Secret and Personal' cable to the Secretary of State for the
Dominions, Lord Cranborne, presumably with Menzies's knowledge:

> Under present conditions it is evident that Menzies's remarkable gifts
> cannot be fully utilised here. This seems deplorable waste of valuable
> material at these times. Do you think seat could be found for him in House
> of Commons if he went home . . . If invitation to stand could emanate
> from your political organisation it would facilitate his severance from
> Australian politics. Grateful for your private and personal views.

The reply dashed Ulysses back upon the craggy shore. 'I have spoken to
Prime Minister with regard to your suggestion', cabled Cranborne.

> He feels strongly that from imperial points it would be unwise of Menzies
> to leave Australia at present time . . . With his outstanding abilities and
> experience, he will be able to speak in Australian parliament with a voice
> of combined authority and independence which no-one else could com-
> mand. In this time he may play a far greater part in moulding future than
> would be possible for a newcomer to political life here.

Menzies might indeed have played such a part in Australia during the rest of
the war if he had not resigned from leadership. If instead he had resigned
himself to the disappointment of not returning to London as an Australian
Prime Minister sitting in the British War Cabinet, Coles and Wilson would
probably have stood by him. If he had stuck it out for just a few more weeks,
he would have seen the war escalate to such an extent that he could well
have remained in office for its duration.

12

Victory

Flames

Within five weeks of taking office, Australia's reluctant Prime Minister found himself extolling the Anzac tradition. Such rhetoric did not come naturally from an old pacifist and anti-militarist like Curtin, but in the circumstances it rang true enough. The occasion was an official opening of the Australian War Memorial on 11 November 1941. Erected during the previous seven years, the War Memorial crouched below Mt Ainslie like a sphinx, its copper-domed head and pale sandstone paws facing south along Burley Griffin's land axis to Parliament House two miles away. It was both temple and museum, replete with memorabilia of Gallipoli, the *Emden* and the Somme; and by good fortune it was being opened at a grimly opportune time. Tunes of glory serve a purpose, like whistling in the dark.

Led by the Eastern Command band and a detachment of seventeen Victoria Cross winners from all Australian States, a procession of service units and ex-servicemen marched up Peronne Crescent and Flanders Avenue to a terrace in front of the Memorial, where more than five thousand people had assembled. Among them were the Governor-General and Lady Gowrie, whose only son was serving with a British Rifle Brigade in North Africa; General Sir Thomas Blamey, General Officer Commanding the A.I.F., back from the Middle East for consultation with the new Government; General Sir Harry Chauvel, who had commanded the Desert Mounted Corps in the Great War which had ended on this day twenty-three years before; R. G. Menzies, who filmed part of the ceremony with a cine-camera he had bought in England; and Dr C. E. W. Bean, the official war historian, who had done more than any other individual to create the Australian War Memorial and its animating spirit.

Three buglers sounded 'The Last Post', two minutes' silence was observed

343

at the eleventh hour, and 'Reveille' signalled the opening of the Memorial's portals. Wreaths were then placed upon a Stone of Remembrance in the Court of Honour by the Governor-General, the Prime Minister, the presiding officers of parliament and—among many others—the American and Japanese Ministers, Nelson T. Johnson and Tatsuo Kawai. Lord Gowrie said in his speech that the Memorial would honour heroic deeds of the present generation as well as the last, and the Prime Minister referred to the symbolic alignment of this 'treasure house' of the Anzac tradition with Parliament House on the other side of the Molonglo River. 'The parliament of a free people deliberating day by day', said Curtin, 'cannot but be inspired and strengthened in the performance of its great duties by the ever-present opportunity to contemplate the story that has gone before—the story . . . which links the ordered ways of a free people with that matchless courage that inspires their sons to maintain it'.

Four weeks later—between 2.40 a.m. and 8.27 a.m., Monday 8 December, Eastern Australian Time—Japan attacked Malaya, Thailand, Hawaii, Singapore and Guam. The Prime Minister had left Canberra intending to return to Perth for Christmas; but after attending a meeting of War Cabinet on Friday 5 December, and receiving the latest reports of Japanese naval movements, he decided to spend the weekend at the Victoria Palace, a temperance hotel which he usually patronised when in Melbourne. On Monday morning Curtin was wakened by his press secretary, Don Rodgers, who had heard about the Japanese attack from the Department of Information's 24-hour short-wave monitoring service. The War Cabinet met again later that day and, after discussion with the military chiefs of staff, came to the obvious conclusion that Australia must consider itself involved in a state of war with Japan. 'Men and women of Australia', said Curtin in a national broadcast that evening. 'We are at war with Japan. That has happened because, in the first instance, Japanese naval and air forces launched an unprovoked attack on British and United States territory; because our vital interests are imperilled and because the rights of free people in the whole Pacific are assailed.'

This time, in contradistinction from its passive acceptance of war against Germany and Italy in 1939, the Australian Government made a formal declaration of its own—indeed, four declarations. In October the Soviet Union had asked the United Kingdom to declare war on Finland, Hungary and Rumania, all of which were fighting against it. The new Attorney-General, Dr Evatt, felt strongly that Australia should exercise its full dominion rights by acting independently in that matter; but whereas the Governors-General of Canada and South Africa had power delegated by the King to declare war, and had exercised it on behalf of their dominions in 1939, the Australian Governor-General had no such power. Parliament could undoubtedly have enacted declarations of war, but at present it was not 'deliberating day by day' in the ideal manner described by Curtin at the War Memorial. The only alternative was to obtain an express delegation of power from the King to the Governor-General, via the High Commission in London. This procedure was already being followed for the rather academic declarations against Finland, Hungary and Rumania, and now it was also applied to the enemy much closer at hand. Proclamation of the existence of a state of war with Japan, as from 5 p.m. on 8 December, was gazetted on 9 December.

In keeping with an undertaking given by Curtin to recall parliament if the situation in the Pacific deteriorated, both houses reassembled on the afternoon of 16 December. By that time there was nothing for them to do but approve the action already taken and pledge themselves to defend the Commonwealth and achieve final victory over its enemies. It was a time for memorable words, and the Prime Minister provided them. Curtin was a parliamentary speaker of the old school, and almost a match for Scullin or Anstey. He still habitually wore the kind of stiff collar he had been advised to wear when practising public speaking as a young man: put your head back, he was told, until you feel your neck on the collar, and that will automatically throw your voice to the back of any hall. His only weakness was a passion for Latin abstract nouns. As Menzies once remarked, Curtin would never say 'war' or 'battlefield' if he could get away with 'theatre of disputation'. But on the afternoon of 16 December, there was no beating around the bush:

> I, like each of you, have seen this country at work, engaged in pleasure, and experiencing adversity; I have seen it face good times and evil times, but I have never known a time in which the inherent quality of Australia has to be used so unstintedly as at this hour. I know not what the fortunes of Australia will be in the weeks, months and years that lie ahead, but I am confident that the political machinery and administrative services, the fighting forces and the labouring classes of this country today stand united in order that not one of us may, through any act of commission or omission, help those who seek to destroy the nation.

After one more sitting parliament adjourned, leaving Australia's political conduct of the war to its rightful executants, the War Cabinet and Advisory War Council. The next few months, which Curtin rightly termed Australia's 'gravest hour', brought a dramatic change in the scope and urgency of Australia's war effort: existing military forces were to be re-deployed, and all services enlarged; a Manpower Directorate was established to ensure efficient organisation of labour; and an Allied Works Council, under the chairmanship of E. G. Theodore, began construction of such essential facilities as roads and airfields.

Curtin spent Christmas 1941 in Canberra, working at his office, and once visiting Lord Gowrie, with whom he had become friendly. His much-loved wife, Elsie, seldom made the journey from Perth, and his only regular company at The Lodge was his driver and partner at billiards, Ray Tracey. During this holiday period Curtin inadvertently made headlines around the world, and was as much surprised as anyone else by the response they provoked. The Melbourne *Herald* had invited him to write a New Year's message for its readers. It was published on 27 December, under the following lines from Bernard O'Dowd:

> That reddish veil which o'er the face
> Of night-hag East is drawn . . .
> Flames new disaster for the race?
> Or can it be the Dawn?

After that sibylline introduction, Curtin summarised Australia's situation and warned that the nation must quickly be placed on a war footing. He also gave clear expression to something which, although obvious enough to many of his countrymen, would nevertheless be remembered by posterity as one of the most crucial remarks ever made by an Australian Prime Minister. 'Without any inhibitions of any kind', he wrote, 'I make it quite clear that Australia looks to America, free of any pangs as to our traditional links or kinship with the United Kingdom'. This statement was reproduced by other Australian newspapers, and cabled overseas. Casey was embarrassed by it in Washington, where some officials thought that Australia was changing loyalty out of panic. The *Sydney Morning Herald* found it 'not without value', but regretted Curtin's unnecessary reflections on 'Britain's effort in this world-wide struggle and the value of our traditional relationship to her— reflections bound to give offence, as they have given offence, to great numbers of people here and elsewhere'. As events were soon to show, however, the Prime Minister was the right man for his time—not an 'independent Australian Briton' like Menzies or Deakin, but simply a pragmatic Australian.

Curtin settled into the role of wartime Prime Minister with an ease and apparent confidence that belied his earlier misgivings and somewhat reserved manner. He was an ordinary-looking man of mild, bespectacled appearance, with a cast in one eye, which he blamed on early years of study by candlelight. Although introspective, and given to spells of melancholy, he commanded deep friendship and loyalty from many of those around him. His favourite word was 'mateship'.

His best mate and principal lieutenant was Ben Chifley, whose sound common sense and wide range of contact with the trade union movement were a constant source of comfort and help to Curtin. For about an hour every afternoon the Prime Minister would stretch out on the couch in his office—not sleeping, but gazing at the ceiling with a cigarette holder jutting upwards from his mouth, mulling over some problem or other. Later he would compare notes with Chifley, whose office was only two doors away. The office between them was occupied by James Scullin. Although not in Cabinet, Scullin still had great influence with Curtin, but not as much as Chifley had.

Chifley used to say in his gravelly voice that he was luckier than the Prime Minister: he could go to bed at the Kurrajong, read a Western and drop off to sleep, whereas Curtin would lie awake worrying at The Lodge. Late one night, for example, the Treasurer arrived after a long drive over bad roads from Bathurst, to find a note from Curtin saying: 'Come over, I'm spiritually bankrupt'.

Early in 1942, as the reddish veil of flames spread south, Curtin had good reason for insomnia. On 10 February War Cabinet announced an economic plan for total war mobilisation, involving government control of all prices, profits, investments, manpower and materials. Five days later Singapore surrendered, leaving Australia like a tethered goat in a tiger's path. On 17 February Curtin addressed an urgent cable to Churchill, asking that the 6th and 7th A.I.F. Divisions, then proceeding in convoy from the Middle East to the Netherlands East Indies, be redirected to Australia, and that the 9th Division also be recalled as soon as possible. That request, soon to become a demand, was made on the advice of the Australian chiefs of staff, and confirmed the next day by the Australian War Cabinet. The first responses to it came from Australia's representative in the British War Cabinet, Sir Earle Page, and the High Commissioner in London, Bruce. Both recounted British reasons for wanting to divert the 7th Division—not to Australia, but to Burma. Burma was the greatest danger at present, they said, and only the 7th Division, then steaming south from Colombo, could reach Rangoon in time to stem the Japanese tide. The Americans, anxious to keep open their access to China through Burma and India, felt that the 6th and 9th Divisions should also go to Rangoon, and America would more than compensate for that by sending troops of its own to Australia.

On 21 February Churchill and Roosevelt addressed personal messages to Curtin. Nothing else in the world could fill this gap, said Churchill, and there would be very serious consequences in Washington if Australia refused to let its troops step into a breach so close to the convoy's course. Roosevelt—arguing that although Japanese forces were moving rapidly, no vital interests of Australia were in immediate danger—asked Curtin to reconsider his decision for the sake of the whole war effort in the Far East. The Australian War Cabinet held to its original decision. Curtin's answer to Churchill, on 22 February, concluded:

We assure you, and desire you to so inform the President, who knows fully what we have done to help the common cause, that, if it were possible to divert our troops to Burma and India without imperilling our security in the judgment of our advisers, we should be pleased to agree to the diversion.

President Roosevelt accepted this philosophically, saying, according to Casey, 'Well, if they have made their mind up, that's the way it is'. Churchill made one more attempt. The convoy had already been diverted north into the Bay of Bengal, he told Curtin on 22 February, 'because we could not contemplate that you would refuse our request'. When Bruce saw a copy of this message he sent a cable of his own to Curtin: 'I am appalled by it and its possible repercussions. It is arrogant and offensive and contradicts the assurances given to Page that the convoy was not being diverted'. Curtin replied to Churchill that, with Malaya, Singapore and Java fallen or falling, Australia could not possibly reverse a decision that had been taken carefully, affirmed and reaffirmed. He said also that Churchill would be held responsible if the convoy came to any harm as a result of its temporary diversion. Churchill immediately ordered the convoy back to Colombo to refuel and resume its voyage to Australia. The 7th Division reached Port Adelaide three weeks later.

During that crisis Curtin's driver, Tracey, confided in the Clerk of the House, Frank Green, that the Prime Minister was spending much of each night walking about the grounds of The Lodge. On his way home, well after midnight, Green entered the unfenced grounds and soon came face to face with Curtin. 'I asked him what was the matter', he wrote, 'but he did not answer me. We stood in silence in the darkness for some minutes, and then he said: "How can I sleep with our men in the Indian Ocean among enemy submarines"'. This 'little touch of Harry in the night' might seem too melodramatic for anything short of Agincourt, but Green was not the only witness to Curtin's distress. During an overnight train journey at this time, the journalist Alan Reid found him walking restlessly in a jolting corridor. Reid was one of several Press Gallery correspondents who followed the Prime Minister everywhere, and to whom Curtin, a former journalist himself, often spoke trustingly off the record. He had confided to them about the 6th and 7th Divisions, and in the corridor of the train that night he told Reid that he had just had a nightmare of troopships being torpedoed. 'When he was talking to me', Reid recalled many years later, 'his hands were trembling, and the sweat was pouring out of him . . . He couldn't sleep and I remember we woke a couple of others and for the rest of the night we played bridge'.

Despite Curtin's earlier advocacy of more sittings by parliament, there was no improvement in that regard during 1942. The House of Representatives held forty-three sittings in 1940, fifty in 1941, and forty-five in 1942. If the war was to blame for this, it did not have the same effect on other legislatures. Comparable figures for the House of Commons were 129, 119 and 114; for the United States House of Representatives, 199, 209 and 205; and for the Canadian House of Commons, 83, 83 and 124. No matter how infrequently the Australian parliament met, however, it remained a useful stage for ceremony and a rostrum from which the executive could impart information.

The most important ceremonial use of parliament during the war was General Douglas MacArthur's visit to the House of Representatives on 26 March 1942. The General had arrived in Australia from the Philippines only nine days before. Curtin was informed of his arrival the next day, and was advised by one of the General's subordinates that President Roosevelt would welcome his nomination of MacArthur as Supreme Allied Commander in the South-West Pacific Area. The Prime Minister eagerly complied, and the appointment was announced immediately. General MacArthur, wearing his usual neat but informal uniform, was greeted on the steps of Parliament House by the Minister for the Army, Forde, and taken to the Prime Minister's suite. At this first meeting, MacArthur put his arms around Curtin's shoulders and said: 'Mr Prime Minister, we two, you and I, will see this thing through together. We can do it and we will do it. You take care of the rear and I will handle the front'. Then came a meeting of the Advisory War Council which, according to the minutes, consisted entirely of a confident briefing by the General:

> It is doubtful whether the Japanese would undertake an invasion of Australia as the spoils here are not sufficient to warrant the risk. From a strategic point of view, invasion of Australia would be a blunder, but the Japanese might try to overrun Australia in order to demonstrate their superiority over the white races. He inclined to the opinion that our main danger is from raids. He thought that the Japanese would also attempt to secure air bases in Australia . . . The vast number of [Japan's] common soldiers were only one degree removed from savages, but they were very

effective as an organised fighting machine. The Japanese, however, has his weaknesses. His tactical concept is based on the frailty of his opponents. He could be described as a 'front runner' and was dangerous as such, but when he is opposed and fought by well organised and determined troops, he can be beaten.

At one point, as if to demonstrate good organisation and determination, one of MacArthur's aides delivered a message to him. 'Pardon me, Mr Prime Minister, while I attend to this matter', said the General. He then dictated a signal. 'Read it back', he ordered, and when that was done he said, 'Despatch!' 'We all remained silent, gazing at him', wrote the Baron of Bardia, Percy Spender. 'This was MacArthur drama.'

After dinner in the parliamentary dining room, and a speech in which MacArthur declared 'We shall win or we shall die', the House resumed its debate on an Opposition motion for disallowance of a National Security Regulation governing employment on the waterfront. Amid applause, Macarthur was escorted by the Serjeant-at-Arms to a seat on the floor of the House beside the Speaker. When the Minister for Labor, Eddie Ward, rose to speak, his colleague Rowley James called out like a larrikin: 'You will enjoy this, Doug!' It seemed that the General may not have done so, for soon afterwards he left the chamber and retired to bed at Government House.

Curtin and MacArthur were to work harmoniously together for the next two and a half years, but only because Curtin looked after the rear, as he had been told, and left the front to the General. It was no exaggeration to say, as MacArthur himself said privately, that Curtin was completely in his hands on military matters. On 18 April the Prime Minister informed the Australian service commanders that they were to regard orders from MacArthur as coming from the Commonwealth Government. General MacArthur held meetings with Curtin and his chief defence adviser, Sir Frederick Shedden, but these were rather like a strong government's dealings with a weak parliament.

One of the few times parliament enjoyed the illusion of participating in great wartime events was when Curtin announced, on the afternoon of 8 May 1942, that the battle of the Coral Sea had been joined. For most of that day the House had been in committee with an amending Invalid and Old Age Pensions Bill. Progress was reported shortly before 4 p.m., and then Curtin moved the adjournment. 'I have received a communiqué from the Commander-in-Chief of the Allied Forces in the South-West Pacific Area', he told the House,

stating that a great naval battle is proceeding in the south-west Pacific zone . . . nobody can tell what the result of the engagement may be. If it should go advantageously, we shall have cause for great gratitude and our position will then be somewhat clearer. But if we should not have the advantages from this battle for which we hope, all that confronts us is a sterner ordeal and a greater and graver responsibility . . . I ask the people of Australia, having regard to the grave consequences implicit in this engagement, to make a sober and realistic estimate of their duty to the nation . . . The front line needs the maximum support of every man and

woman in the Commonwealth . . . Men are fighting for Australia today;
those who are not fighting have no excuse for not working.

Alan Reid, who had been dozing in the press gallery, jerked awake during
this announcement, and ever afterwards remembered it as Curtin's most
stirring wartime speech. But such a moment soon passed. The House
adjourned, and when it reassembled five days later the marginally favourable outcome was known to all: Admiral Nimitz's task force and a Japanese
carrier force assisting the planned invasion of Port Moresby had both suffered severely. Tactically both sides emerged more or less even, but the Japanese had been stopped for the first time in the war, and the danger of attack
on northern Australia had been averted. A matter of greater concern to parliament by then was the stoppage of work to which Curtin had alluded
obliquely in his Coral Sea speech. That appeal had not persuaded Hunter
Valley coalminers to end their strike against the terms of an award, and now
the Government came under attack from one of its least reliable supporters,
the truculent parliamentary spokesman for the Miners' Federation, Rowley
James.

Fortunately for the Government, Curtin was a patient and resourceful parliamentary tactician—perhaps, it has been said, the best manager of an
evenly divided parliament since Alfred Deakin. The fate of his Government
still depended upon support from the two Independents, Coles and Wilson,
as well as such dissidents as James, and the Independent Labor member
Blackburn, who had been expelled from the A.L.P. in 1941 for refusing to
observe the Victorian central executive's rule that members should not participate in activities of the Australia–Soviet Friendship League. In these circumstances Labor chose to leave two Opposition members in the
Speakership and Chairmanship of Committees. Speaker Nairn (U) and
Chairman Prowse (C) could be relied upon to use their casting votes
judiciously, and while they were willing to remain in those posts the Government conserved its full floor strength. Nairn's only departure from tradition was to move an amendment to the Australian Broadcasting Bill. This
was the first time a Speaker had moved an amendment, although at the time
the House was in Committee and he was not in his Chair. In June 1943 the
U.A.P. and Country Party prevailed upon Nairn and Prowse to resign, thus
returning their 'fighting' votes to the Opposition benches for a
no-confidence motion that was soon to be moved, and obliging Labor to provide new presiding officers—the former Langite J. S. Rosevear as Speaker,
and W. J. Riordan (Kennedy, Q) as Chairman of Committees. The Government could still survive, but only just.

The most far-reaching legislative measures of the sixteenth parliament
were undoubtedly those designed to secure adequate revenue for the
national war effort by depriving the States of their income tax powers and
giving the Commonwealth a monopoly in that field. Only in such a grave
emergency as that of mid-1942—with flames over the Coral Sea and Midway, and enemy submarines in Sydney Harbour—could the Commonwealth have done such a thing and been upheld by the High Court.

The uniform tax scheme was embodied in four Bills: one acquiring State income tax departments for the Commonwealth; one imposing Commonwealth income tax at levels higher than all existing Commonwealth and State income taxes combined; one giving the Commonwealth priority in payment of income taxes; and finally one authorising compensatory grants to the States equivalent to the revenue they would lose by ceasing to impose income tax, on condition that they did so cease. All parties were divided on the wisdom and validity of such a fundamental alteration to the balance of federal partnership; but the Bills were passed in less than three weeks of May and June. Naturally enough the erstwhile 'States' House' showed greater reluctance than the House of Representatives, but even there the 'Ayes' formed a majority of twenty to twelve.

South Australia, Victoria, Queensland and Western Australia immediately challenged the constitutional validity of these Acts in the High Court before a bench of only five Justices, Dixon J. being absent on leave as Australian Minister to Washington. The Court, by majority, upheld the validity of the Acts and dismissed the State challenge. Three justices held all four Acts valid. Latham C.J. and Starke J. dissented as to the acquisition of State tax departments, and Starke also dissented as to the compensatory grants. The acquisition measure was held valid only under the expanded 'hot war' defence power, and might have been invalid if Dixon J. had been sitting. The other Acts were held valid on tax, grants and incidental powers so as to be potentially valid in peacetime as well. This shift of fiscal power greatly strengthened the Commonwealth component of the federal partnership. It seemed that the flames of war had rekindled the altar of Moloch, and once again State rights had been sacrificed for the common weal.

State rights of a particular kind were defended by the Senate at this time, but the issue was so bizarre that it did little to restore that chamber's diminished reputation as a States' House. On 13 May the Senate disallowed a National Security regulation overriding Victorian legislation in order to permit the sale of beef cattle from a State-operated farm at Werribee. The Victorian Health Act prohibited such sales, purportedly because the pasture at Werribee was fertilised with sewage. After a long debate, during which Country Party senators expatiated on the horrors of beef measles and tapeworms, and Labor senators asserted that the State ban had been imposed solely to support the graziers' market for fat cattle in Melbourne, a motion for disallowance was passed by 17 votes to 16. This prompted the Canberra correspondent of the *Sunday Telegraph* in Sydney, Richard Hughes, to write an article entitled 'Those Meddlesome Old Men of the Senate':

> Cackling an old man's foolish laugh, the Senate jabbed a long darning-needle into the war-wearied rump of the Government this week.
>
> The old boys of the Upper House pulled down their woollen stomachers, and, with weak, arthritic wrists and wheezing voices, threw out a regulation that could have released to the Commonwealth supplies of urgently needed prime beef.
>
> Don't ask why they did it. Most of those who voted against the measure wouldn't know.
>
> [Some] who knew that the regulation was designed to kill a rotten Victorian Country Party racket at the expense of the Werribee Farm, a once-

flourishing public asset, persisted in voting against their own convictions and the advice of governmental experts because they felt—God help us all!—that State rights were being sacrificed to the Commonwealth.

It's difficult to know what to do about the Senate.

It was intended to be a responsible, non-Party chamber of review, modelled on the American pattern. It has become, instead, a comfortable Home for Old Men, to which election can be lubricated if your surname begins with 'A' . . .

The 'old men', whose average age was in fact fifty-nine, were furious. President Cunningham called upon the *Sunday Telegraph* to publish an apology for 'statements calculated to discredit the Senate and to bring it into contempt'. When the paper refused, he issued instructions that representatives of the *Sunday Telegraph* and all other Consolidated Press publications should be excluded from the precincts of the Senate. Speaker Nairn took similar action, effectively banning Hughes and five colleagues from Parliament House. The matter was resolved three months later when the general manager of Consolidated Press wrote to the President, advancing the dubious but acceptable proposition that Hughes's article was not intended as a personal attack on individual senators or a disparagement of parliament.

More gratifying to the Senate was its successful pressing for the amendment of a money bill which, under the Constitution, the Senate itself could not amend. This dispute between the houses concerned Clause 2 of the Income Tax Bill of March 1943, referring to the National Welfare Fund Act. The Government proposed to establish a National Welfare Fund from which payments would be made for unemployment, health, family and other welfare services, but the Bill for this Act had not yet reached the Senate. A majority of senators, regarding this as the 'tacking' of an amendable bill to an unamendable one (a practice not unknown in past British parliaments, and forbidden by Section 55 of the Australian Constitution), requested the lower house to omit the clause. 'We have before us a case of tacking in one of its worst forms', said Senator A. J. McLachlan (U, S). If this was indeed a case of tacking, it was the first in the Commonwealth's parliamentary history. In the House of Representatives Curtin tabled legal opinions to the effect that Clause 2 was not contrary to Section 55 of the Constitution, and the Bill was returned to the Senate with some requested amendments made, but not the request concerning Clause 2. The Senate then sent the Bill back a second time with the same request.

In spite of the Government's legal opinions, there was considerable support in the lower house for the Senate's persistence. 'I do not think that [Clause 2] was inserted simply for the purpose of coercing the Senate', said Maurice Blackburn.

It was more likely to have been put there in order to influence certain honorable members of this House. But the Senate properly resented its inclusion and properly asked that it should be left out. I do not think that the question which we have been considering is one of pure law. No courts could have decided it; the two Houses of Parliament alone could decide it.

After passing the customary resolution preserving its constitutional rights, the House of Representatives deleted Clause 2 as requested and returned the Bill to the Senate, where the third reading was promptly agreed to.

During this session parliament at last availed itself fully of legislative advantages inherent in the Statute of Westminster. It did so by adopting five sections of the Statute which did not apply automatically to the Commonwealth, but required Australian as well as British enactment. The Statute, it will be remembered, had been enacted by the United Kingdom parliament in 1931. Since that time, the Commonwealth had remained subject to certain restrictions upon its legislative competence which could be removed only by adoption of Sections 2 to 6 of the Statute, of which 2 and 3 were the more significant. Section 2 would exempt acts of the Commonwealth parliament (though not of State parliaments) from the inhibiting influence of the Colonial Laws Validity Act, an Act of the imperial parliament under which colonial or dominion statutes inconsistent with an imperial statute applying to that colony or dominion were, to the extent of the inconsistency, invalid. Section 3 provided that the Commonwealth parliament had full power to make laws having extra-territorial operation.

The Lyons Government had tried to have these sections enacted in 1937, but its efforts were frustrated by opposition arising from fears by some States that adoption would disturb the federal system to their disadvantage, and from a feeling that enactment would amount to cutting the painter with Britain. Archie Cameron, never one to shrink from hyperbole, characterised the Adoption Bill as 'one of the most dangerous measures ever introduced into this parliament'. The inconvenience caused by failure to adopt became more obvious in wartime, for the Commonwealth needed extensive control over shipping and other extra-territorial activities. Dr Evatt therefore introduced a Statute of Westminster Adoption Bill in October 1942, providing for the adoption of all five sections. Opposition imperialists criticised the Bill because in their view it was likely to weaken relations with Britain. Dr Evatt dealt effectively with these arguments, and the measure was passed with second reading majorities of 47–7 in the Representatives and 19–10 in the Senate.

On 24 December 1942 Curtin addressed a seasonal note to Robert Menzies who, although no longer Parliamentary Leader of the U.A.P., was obviously better fitted for that position than its present occupant, the ancient and ineffectual Billy Hughes. There had been talk of Menzies resigning his seat in order to become British Minister of State in South-East Asia. Churchill had also suggested that perhaps Menzies could replace Casey in Washington when the latter was appointed Minister of State in the Middle East. Nothing came of these tentative overtures, however, and Menzies was making the best of his parliamentary lot. He was a member of the Advisory War Council, spoke frequently in the House, and was a prized guest at dinner parties in Melbourne.

'Dear Bob', wrote Curtin, who was working in Canberra for the second Christmas in succession, 'You know well how I regard you ... As to my health—it is only fair. The aches have gone, but I've got a skin bother which is not nice. At times I think I am Job II'. As well as boils, if his skin trouble was the same as Job's, the Prime Minister was afflicted with more trouble than usual in his party room. Although Curtin managed to keep the threat of invasion alive for several months after it had, in General MacArthur's view, been removed by American victory at Midway, some of his parliamentary colleagues found it all but impossible to take the war as seriously as he did. At a Caucus meeting in September 1942, when Curtin gave a résumé of the war position in New Guinea, where Australian troops had recently begun a counter-offensive on the Kokoda Trail, Rowley James moved a motion to suspend Standing Orders to discuss beer supplies. Malcontents like Ward, Calwell and Brennan were rebellious at the best of times, and at worst they drove Curtin to tears. This, of course, was part and parcel of Caucus life. When someone remarked disapprovingly to Scullin about one of Ward's merciless onslaughts, Scullin said, 'Oh, I don't know; Curtin did that to me every day in the depression'.

But in 1942 the more restive members of the party had taken up a singularly divisive issue: an issue which had split the A.L.P. a generation before, and conceivably could now do the same again. It was the old bogy of conscription. This issue was first raised in parliament by the Leader of the Opposition. Speaking in a debate on international affairs on 1 May, Fadden said: 'It is all-important that there shall be for the defence of the Commonwealth an Australian army which the Government can employ anywhere without statutory limitation of any kind'. In effect there were two Australian armies—the volunteer A.I.F., which could serve anywhere in the world; and the Citizen Military Forces, or Militia, which were conscripted and could serve only in Australia or Australian territories, including Papua and the Trust Territory of New Guinea. If these were to be amalgamated for service under one command, as General MacArthur was urging, Australia would be sending conscripts to fight beyond Australian limits, and that was something which a majority of Australians, including Curtin himself, had refused to sanction at two referendums during the previous war. Curtin recognised the strategic value of 'one army under one command', but dreaded the thought that conscription might undo the party's hard-won unity. 'The paramount thing', he had said in a speech delivered in November 1939,

> is that, however the war ends, its termination must see in Australia a united, well-organised, clear-thinking labour movement, so that the trophies of victory won't just be for non-workers . . . War might smash this party again—conscription would tear us apart as before—we may get our political opportunity and wedges will be driven in our ranks by every militant, every militarist, every politician, every opportunist.

Now that the danger was at hand, Curtin set himself to persuade the A.L.P. to modify its traditional policy without disruption. An ardent minority, mainly Victorian, tried to evoke the pure anti-conscription spirit of 1916 and 1917, but as one of them put it, the old spirit failed to flourish in a new season. The South-West Pacific was not France, and in any case what Curtin wanted was only a limited form of conscription for service in a prescribed geographical area. On 17 November 1942 he asked an A.L.P. Interstate Conference for authority to extend the territorial liability of the Militia for service under the Defence Act, but discussion was adjourned pending consideration of the matter by State executives. At a meeting of Caucus on 9 December Arthur Calwell moved that [the parliamentary party] was 'opposed to any proposals for the conscription of Australian manhood for overseas service as being fundamentally the same as those which the Labor Movement rejected in 1916'. Curtin ruled this out of order because the matter was under consideration by State executives, and a further motion by Calwell, that Curtin's ruling be disagreed with, was defeated.

In parliament the next day, during debate on a statement of the war situation by Curtin, Maurice Blackburn moved an amendment which, if carried, would have amounted to a resolution against 'the imposition of any form of compulsory service outside Australia and the Territories of the Commonwealth'. Blackburn professed his belief that the community had no moral right 'to compel persons to go abroad from this land to fight'; Calwell said he was still as much an anti-conscriptionist as he had been in 1917, and whether compulsion was for the Pacific or for Europe, it was still military conscription; and Brennan disapproved of the 'pleasant felicitations exchanged between "Jack" and "Artie"'. When a Government member moved adjournment of this embarrassing debate, Blackburn and Coles voted with the Opposition to prolong it. The division was 34–34, but Speaker Nairn very properly gave his casting vote in favour of 'obtaining a determination of the question during the present sittings of Parliament', and declared the motion lost. Blackburn's amendment was also lost, without a division.

So much for the anti-conscription cause. On 4 January 1943 another A.L.P. interstate conference adopted Curtin's proposal to extend use of the Militia to any area of the South-West Pacific Zone proclaimed by the Governor-General as being necessary for the defence of Australia. The Defence (Citizen Military Forces) Bill, introduced on 29 January, defined the South-West Pacific Zone as being bounded on the west by the one hundred and tenth meridian, on the east by the one hundred and fifty-ninth meridian, and on the north by the Equator. This enlarged the Militia's potential war zone by the addition of only Netherlands New Guinea, Timor, Amboina, and parts of Java, Borneo and the Celebes.

Curtin said this was all that General MacArthur required, but to many members of the Opposition who were advocating unrestricted deployment of the Militia, the Bill was an anticlimax. 'With all the alarms and all the excitement in the press', said Menzies in the second reading debate, 'everybody was waiting for the storm clouds to burst, but what did the clouds produce? Did they produce a really dynamic flash or a real crash? Not at all. The result was merely like the toot of a tin whistle'. His party leader, the would-be conscriptionist of 1915–16, supported the Bill and took malicious pleasure in reminding Curtin that conscription was now being imposed for the first time in Australia's history, and 'imposed by a man who all his life has bitterly opposed it'. Amendments by Blackburn on the one hand and advocates of wider deployment on the other were comfortably defeated.

One day before the Defence Bill reached the upper house, a majority of senators wanting more than the toot of a tin whistle tried to take matters into their own hands. The Opposition Leader, Senator George McLeay (U, S), introduced a bill to amend the National Security Act by removing a section which prohibited compulsory military service beyond the limits of Australia and its territories. The way would then be clear, it was said, to introduce unlimited conscription by regulation. This backdoor Bill was passed by the Senate and sent to the lower chamber, where it was quickly rejected. In the meantime the Defence (Citizen Military Forces) Bill had also been received from the Senate, without amendment. It received assent on 24 February, and the conscription debate was over.

Oddly enough, Labor came through this controversy better than the U.A.P. Admittedly, Curtin remained on bad terms with the few anti-conscriptionists. At a Caucus meeting on 24 March he referred angrily to Calwell as 'the hero of 100 sham fights'. 'It's all very well for you to say that', replied Calwell, 'but the way you're going, you'll finish up on the other side, leading a National Government'. Curtin immediately retired from the meeting and composed a letter inviting the party either to dissociate itself from Calwell's accusation or appoint another leader. When Forde read the letter to the meeting, Calwell withdrew his statement and apologised.

In spite of this incident, and the usual chivvying by Ward and a few others, the A.L.P. was a paragon of unity compared with the main Opposition party. The 23-strong U.A.P. had been badly split by disagreement about the extent to which the Militia should be used outside Australian limits. Menzies, Spender and Harrison resigned from the joint Opposition executive, and on 1 April Menzies and sixteen other members advised Hughes that they were forming a National Service Group to organise a more vigorous U.A.P., and would no longer attend party meetings.

Not the least of the demoralised Opposition's troubles was a sustained one-man attack upon it by the Minister for Labour and National Service. From October 1942 onwards, Ward contended at every opportunity that the Menzies and Fadden Governments had approved a defence plan—the so-called 'Brisbane Line'—which, in the event of invasion, would have meant abandoning a large part of Australia to the Japanese. The 'Brisbane Lie', as the Opposition dubbed it, was by Ward's account a defeatist plan approved by the traitorous coalition, but cancelled by the patriotic Labor government once it took office. Menzies called it a figment of Ward's 'exuberant imagination', and Hughes said it was 'a wicked invention'. And they were right. The Prime Minister complained at one of his off-the-record press briefings that Ward was 'a bloody ratbag', but for the time being Curtin did nothing to quash this useful furphy. The 'Brisbane Lie' was one of several grounds for a want of confidence motion by Fadden on 22 June 1943, others being Labor's unwillingness to participate in a national government and its failure to prevent strikes, particularly on the coalfields.

During the no-confidence debate, which lasted almost continuously for more than thirty-eight hours, Curtin conceded that when he became Prime Minister he was not aware of any such defence plan as had been described by Ward. The nearest thing to a 'Brisbane Line' was in fact a plan, intended only as a last resort, which had been discussed by the War Advisory Council in

February 1942, after Labor came to office. Ward took that in his stride, however, by simply asserting that a document must be missing from the files.

The want of confidence motion was defeated at about 6 a.m. on 24 June by 27 votes to 26, with Coles supporting the Government. When the House resumed that afternoon Curtin announced that he and the Army Minister had conferred with Ward, who now accepted their assurances that no document was missing. Not even that deterred Ward from his efforts to promote the 'Brisbane Line' into an election issue. Speaking immediately after Curtin, he said: 'I unreservedly accept that assurance, and I am satisfied that the document to which I was referring on Tuesday night is still in existence. The real issue is whether my charges against the former Prime Ministers are, or are not, true. Those charges still stand'. Fadden then gave notice of his intention to submit a motion seeking a royal commission into the matter, but the Prime Minister beat him to it. After the dinner adjournment and further discussion with Ward, Curtin told the House that he was ready to constitute a royal commission and had adopted the normal procedure of relieving Ward of administrative duties until the commission tabled its report. The commissioner reported four months later that there was no missing document, but he was unable to make any finding as to the basis of Ward's belief because that honourable member, invoking parliamentary privilege, had refused to answer any questions concerning his parliamentary activities.

The sixteenth parliament was dissolved on 7 July, and a general election called for 21 August. Curtin's policy speech was the first ever delivered from Canberra by the leader of any political party. Speaking over a national radio hook-up, he compared his own government's conduct of the war effort with that by the coalition ministries, and promised a comprehensive programme of post-war reconstruction, including expansion of social services, full employment, and the re-establishment of ex-servicemen in civil life. Although he did not mention the 'Brisbane Line', the tone of his references to the Menzies and Fadden Ministries was such as to jog the memory of any electors who may have forgotten Ward's charges. Fadden's policy speech for the joint Opposition matched Curtin's post-war plans, and also promised a post-war refund amounting to one-third of all income tax collected under the Uniform Tax Scheme.

Although the National Service Group had resumed its normal U.A.P. stance for the election campaign, Menzies now said publicly that a one-third refund was more than the country would be able to afford. Fadden denounced this as another in the series of stabs in the back 'for which Menzies [had] become notorious'. Menzies denied any treachery, on grounds that he had taken no part in preparing the joint policy, but he must have known that such a show of disunity would hurt the Opposition.

Curtin also detected a whiff of treachery in his own ranks, and quickly put a stopper on it. While the Prime Minister was campaigning in Adelaide, Dr Evatt said in Sydney that if the Curtin Government should be defeated, Heaven forbid, he would be willing to join a national government. The Sydney journalist, Alan Reid, travelling with the Prime Minister's party, learned of this from his editor, who said that Evatt was not available for comment because he was in bed sick. Reid went to Curtin's press secretary, Don Rodgers, who agreed with him that Evatt seemed to be having 'a bob each way'. Rodgers alerted the Prime Minister, and an urgent telegram was sent to Sydney. When Reid himself reached the Prime Minister, Curtin said: 'You'd better get your comment from the Doc'.

'I can't', replied Reid. 'He's in bed sick'.

'Yes you can', said Curtin. 'I think you'll find he's had a miraculous recovery'.

Another danger nipped in the bud by Curtin was an allegation made during the campaign that Labor intended taking advantage of the war to attain some part of its long-standing socialisation objective. Speaking in Perth three days before the election, he said: 'My government will not during the war socialise any industry'. Voters thus had little to fear from Labor, and much to approve in its conduct of the war.

The result was a spectacular two-chamber victory, including the greatest landslide ever to have occurred in the House of Representatives. Labor won forty-nine seats (an increase of seventeen); U.A.P., fourteen (down by nine); Country Party, nine (down four); and Independents, two. In the Senate, Labor gained its first majority since 1914: twenty-two seats, as against twelve for the U.A.P. and two for the Country Party. The A.L.P. lost only two sitting members, and was not greatly distressed by the defeat of the Independent Labor member, Maurice Blackburn. Among its seventeen new members were a farmer and rural expert, Nelson Lemmon (Forrest, W); A. D. Fraser (Eden-Monaro, N); L. S. Haylen (Parkes, N); and F. M. Daly (Martin, N).

Apart from the former Speaker and Chairman of Committees, Nairn and Prowse, the Opposition casualties had not greatly distinguished themselves in parliament; but several of their more prominent colleagues came within a hair's breadth of defeat. 'This is the first election in which my return has not been a foregone conclusion', wrote Hughes to the defeated Member for Eden-Monaro, J. A. Perkins.

> We've been struck by a cyclone—even Spender lost thousands—while Harrison although quite confident of winning may quite easily lose to Jessie Street. Just imagine—26,000 votes for a pro-Russian Labor candidate. Wentworth—the original I mean—would turn in his grave if he knew how things have gone.

Eric Harrison managed to retain the seat of Wentworth against Mrs Street, the wife of a Justice and future Chief Justice of the New South Wales Supreme Court; but he did so only on a fourth count, by 2335 votes. Two other male incumbents were less successful against female opponents, and now, for the first time in parliament's forty-two years of existence, the Senate and House of Representatives would each have one woman among their members. Little has so far been said in this narrative about women candidates, for, until the impetus of World War II was reflected in politics as well as other fields, there were remarkably few of them.

It was not until 1921 that the first woman was elected to any Australian parliament. She was Edith Cowan, elected as a Nationalist to the West Australian Legislative Assembly. In the years from then until 1943 seven other women were elected to State lower houses, and two were appointed to the upper house of New South Wales. At the federal level only three women stood for parliament during the 1920s, and five during the 1930s. In 1943, however, there were no fewer than twenty-one women candidates for the Senate and House of Representatives. The two successful candidates were Senator Dorothy Tangney, a 32-year-old teacher and Labor activist from Perth; and the 46-year-old Dame Enid Lyons, who won the Tasmanian seat of Darwin on a sixth count, by 816 votes, and was the only new member elected for the U.A.P.

In an editorial typical of favourable press comment on the entry of women into federal parliament, the *Sydney Morning Herald* said: 'In the days when women have taken their place in the armed Forces, on lathe and loom and assembly line, and in transport and communications, it is natural that they should bid also for seats in the national Parliament'. Candidature had also been encouraged by a 'Women for Canberra' movement, modelled on the feminist 'Women for Westminster'. Yet it was doubtful whether the war and feminism together would have been sufficient to overcome the electoral prejudice which hitherto had kept Australian women out of federal parliament. Miss Tangney and Dame Enid were not feminist candidates, and the wartime mood was not the only reason for their success. One was swept into the Senate by her party's landslide, and the other was probably the best known and most widely respected woman in Australia.

Plans

By the time Lord Gowrie opened the new parliament on 23 September 1943, the war was in its fifth year. Parliament was of course preoccupied by that baleful drama and its effects upon Australian life; but despite the presence of a Dutch squadron of Mitchell bombers at the aerodrome, and the use of a new community hospital by the United States Army, Canberra was not so obviously at war as Australia's coastal cities. No convoys rumbled through its streets, no troop trains whistled at the station, and no searchlights practised on the night sky.

The city was usually blacked out at night, and a few members injured themselves while groping their way down the steps of Parliament House and along footpaths marked with white paint to their darkened hotels. Blacking-out was not always as efficient as it should have been, however, and in October 1942 the Government Leader in the Senate, Senator J. S. Collings (Q), complained that the front of Parliament House was 'a blaze of light inviting the enemy if he chose to bomb the place to come here and do it'. In such an event members were advised to take shelter in the main corridors of the ground floor. There were also slit trenches on the lawn in front of Parliament House, but no one ever needed them.

All the same, parliamentary life was affected in many ways by the war. In the overwrought atmosphere of emergency and austerity it did not seem strange that Moral Rearmament should stage a performance of its morale-building revue, 'Battle for Australia', at Parliament House. After seeing the revue in Sydney, the Prime Minister asked its cast of thirty to perform in the members' dining room on 25 February 1943. Although Curtin had long since exchanged religion for rationalism, he must have felt that there was some practical value in the quasi-religious inspirational theatre of Moral Rearmament. Before an audience that included the Governor-General, Cabinet ministers and members of both houses, the cast presented such songs as:

> For the new world we're wanting we'll certainly find
> In the heart of the ordinary man.
> When we leave all our greed and our grousing behind,
>   and listen to God for his plan.

According to the new Labor member, Fred Daly, no one liked to play tennis or cricket for fear of being thought flippant about the war. Daly himself had so little exercise during his first year in Canberra that his collar size expanded from 13½ to 16½. Private members spent much of their time attending to letters from their electorates about food and clothes rationing, shortages of tobacco and beer, and anomalies of the call-up system for military service.

Only three members of parliament served overseas with the armed forces, compared with ten in the previous war; but seven others served for various periods in Australia. All remained members of parliament during their terms of service, and received parliamentary salary as well as military pay. As in the Great War, jingoes challenged their younger colleagues to enlist, and some of the less blatantly patriotic members questioned the motives of those who wore military uniform in the chamber. Ward, for example, complained that Captain Eric Harrison was 'strutting about in military uniform and wearing ribbons of the Coronation and Jubilee Medals to try to make out to the public that he had seen service with the fighting services at the front'. The Honourable Member for Wentworth did not deny this, but said that he bore on his body a wound sustained in the last war.

In spite of wartime restrictions, the Government found sufficient labour and building materials to enlarge Parliament House. The only previous extension had been to the parliamentary library, in 1939, and the building was now unable to meet demands being made upon it by the proliferating executive. According to the Clerk of the House, Frank Green, the head of one department advised his Minister early in the war to try to obtain the Speaker's suite for his ministerial use. When this was put to Speaker Nairn, it was of course vehemently rejected. 'If you Ministers had your way', said the Speaker, 'I would be in a tent on the bank of the Molonglo'.

It did not come to anything like that. The additions, completed by the end of 1943 at a cost of £12 000, consisted of two double-storey wings, one on the Representatives side and another on the Senate side, enclosing the courtyards behind the two chambers. The new wings provided forty-six more rooms, many of which were placed at the disposal of ministers when the new parliament opened.

The seventeenth parliament opened in a mood of optimism about the progress of the war and planning for peace. Lord Gowrie—whose son, Major Patrick Hore-Ruthven, had been killed in Libya a few months before—referred in his opening speech to the recent improvements in every theatre of war. Australian and American forces had captured Salamaua and Lae in New Guinea, Italy had surrendered, the air offensive against Germany was continuing on an ever-increasing scale, and the German army had suffered its first serious reverses on the Russian front. 'My advisers', said the Governor-General, 'confident in the ultimate victory of the Allies, are preparing plans for the organisation and development of the resources of Australia in peace. Already preliminary surveys have been made upon which those plans may be brought to fruition'.

Curtin was lying ill in bed at The Lodge, and his place at the opening was taken by the Deputy Prime Minister, Frank Forde. All but one of Curtin's nineteen ministers were re-elected by Caucus, and that one (George Lawson, Brisbane) was replaced by Arthur Calwell. Curtin and Chifley worked hard against Ward, but could not keep him out of the ministry. Curtin retaliated by giving him the unwelcome portfolios of Transport and External Territories, remarking as he did so that both were in the hands of the Army anyway. His other main irritant, Calwell, was appointed Minister for Information, in which capacity he soon became too busy fighting the press over censorship to play the stormy petrel in Caucus with his customary vigour. Chifley retained Treasury and the increasingly important portfolio of Post-war Reconstruction, the latter department being run by a brilliant protégé of his, Dr H. C. Coombs.

The two Opposition parties resumed their separate identities, and the Advisory War Council was reconstructed accordingly. Fadden continued to lead the Country Party, but Hughes did not defend his leadership of the U.A.P. There were four candidates to succeed him (Menzies, Spender, White and A. M. McDonald), and the outcome was as expected: an easy win for Menzies, who also, as leader of the larger non-Labor party, became Leader of the Opposition. Spender had somehow gained the impression from Menzies that he could rely on his support for the Deputy Leadership. Not surprisingly this proved to be wrong, and Hughes was elected Deputy.

The first women to sit in parliament were welcomed with every sign of good will by members of the other sex. 'We do not any longer sit here as men', said Curtin, 'nor does the honourable member for Darwin attempt to suggest that she sits here as a woman: we all sit here as persons upon whom our fellow citizens have imposed a duty by preferring us to others who offered at the polls'. Even Major Cameron, who had asserted during the campaign that women ought to remain in the kitchen, had the grace to say: 'I welcome the honourable member and will give her any assistance that such a rough diamond of the male sex as myself may be able to give her'.

Senator Tangney, moving the Address-in-Reply, delivered a speech of no discernible gender, concerned only with the war and post-war plans. Dame Enid, on the other hand, devoted much of her maiden speech to home and motherhood. 'I believe very sincerely', she said,

> that any woman entering the public arena must be prepared to work as men work . . . she must attack the same problems, and be prepared to shoulder the same burdens. But because I am a woman, and cannot divest myself of those qualities that are inherent in my sex . . . honorable mem-

bers will have to become accustomed to the application of the homely
metaphors of the kitchen rather than those of the operating theatre, the
work shop or the farm.

Few would have been misled, however, into thinking that Joe Lyons's
widow had lost any of her political acumen.

Parliament's most immediate concern was Chifley's Budget for 1943–44,
providing for expenditure of £715 million (£45 million more than in the previous year), of which £569 million was war expenditure. The Opposition
acknowledged that the Government had an electoral mandate for its financial policy, and the necessary appropriation bills were passed without delay.
Parliament rose on 15 October, but compensated for such an early adjournment by reassembling on 9 February. The number of bills placed before this
parliament was not particularly great, but such was the innovatory importance of many of them that parliament sat more often than usual—forty-three
and fifty-seven sitting days for the Senate and House of Representatives
respectively in 1944; fifty-one and ninety in 1945. With firm control of both
houses, and Allied victory in sight, Labor started turning planks into acts of
parliament. Not since Deakin's 'finest harvest' of 1909 had any parliament
broken so much new ground. Constrained only by Curtin's 'no socialisation'
promise, the Government secured the passage of forty-nine important acts,
many of which strained federal power to the utmost. Two of them in fact
went too far for the High Court's liking, and were ruled invalid.

The Government tried unsuccessfully to secure a temporary addition of
constitutional power to facilitate the task of post-war reconstruction. Dr
Evatt had prepared a draft Bill for this purpose as early as October 1942. A
conference of federal and State Governments decided to try to avoid the
inconvenience of a referendum, by State reference of powers to the Commonwealth; but in the next few months only the parliaments of New South
Wales and Queensland passed the amending Bill as drafted. A referendum it
had to be, and on 19 August 1944 Australians voted to decide whether or not
the Constitution should be amended to accommodate Section 51A, containing fourteen new powers including reinstatement and advancement of
returned servicemen, employment, organised marketing, companies, monopolies, profiteering and prices, control of overseas exchange and investment, national health, uniformity of rail gauges, and people of the
Aboriginal race.

These headings of power had been approved by the 1942 A.L.P. federal
conference, and they were intended to last for only five years. But Australia's
political climate had altered drastically in the last two years. Both Opposition
parties feared that the Government now controlling both houses so decisively would use any further constitutional power for socialist ends. They
campaigned against the Bill, and it was defeated in all States except South
Australia and Western Australia. Thus the transition from war to peace
would have to be made within the ambit of existing Commonwealth power.

Although none of the new measures exactly breached Curtin's undertaking not to 'socialise any industry' during the war, several of them bore the
hallmark of socialist planning. The Pharmaceutical Benefits Act, intended as

the beginning of a comprehensive health scheme, established a system under which chemists would supply patients with prescribed medicines free of charge, and be reimbursed by the Commonwealth. For reasons of cost, but also with the intention of rationalising the pharmaceutical industry, this Act limited the list of medicines from which doctors could prescribe. The Australian National Airlines Act, which Menzies described as 'contrary to the whole spirit of the people's verdict at the referendum', established an Airlines Commission with power to control interstate civil aviation, and to establish a Government airline, Trans-Australia Airlines. The Aluminium Industry Act established a joint Commonwealth–State authority to smelt aluminium in Tasmania, the Education Act established a Commonwealth Office of Education and a Universities Commission, and the Commonwealth and State Housing Agreement Act emphasised the building of public housing for rental rather than purchase.

The Minister responsible for the latter measure was John Dedman, a dour Scottish soldier and farmer who had come to the A.L.P. by way of the Victorian Country Party. As Minister for War Organisation of Industry, he had become notorious for having killed Santa Claus and trimmed shirt tails in the name of austerity. Dedman was an avowed socialist, and in the course of introducing the housing Bill he could not refrain from saying: 'The Commonwealth Government is concerned to provide adequate and good housing for the workers; it is not concerned with making the workers into little capitalists'. The Opposition demanded retraction, and under prodding from Major Cameron the Minister sourly paid lip service to the private ownership of homes.

In January 1945 Chifley obtained Cabinet approval for a series of banking reforms which, although stopping short of the nationalisation he had recommended before the war, were in his view at that time adequate to prevent any repetition of the banking collapse in the 1890s or the Commonwealth Bank's refusal to co-operate with the Scullin Government during the Depression. What he proposed was the passing of wartime banking regulations into permanent statute law, and a reconstitution of the Commonwealth Bank. The main purposes, embodied in the Banking Bill and Commonwealth Bank Bill, of 1945, were to strengthen the central banking functions of the Commonwealth Bank by providing for the co-ordination of banking policy under its central direction, control of the volume of credit in circulation through the special account system, and central control of bank interest rates and advance policy. All banking business of governments and governmental authorities would be reserved to publicly owned and controlled banks. The Commonwealth Bank Board was to be abolished, and management of the bank entrusted to the Governor, assisted by an advisory council of Commonwealth Bank and Commonwealth Government officers, all being responsible to the Commonwealth Government (in practice, the Treasurer) rather than to parliament. No longer would a hostile Senate be able to call some latter-day Sir Robert Gibson before it, and meddle in banking policy.

For some Labor members this was not enough. At a Caucus meeting on 20 February, after Chifley had explained his Bills and moved that they be introduced in the House, Tom Burke (Perth) moved as an amendment that 'the present Bills be withdrawn and a Bill introduced giving the Government power to acquire the business and assets of the private trading banks as a going concern'. Burke referred to a speech on bank nationalisation which he had heard Curtin deliver at Fremantle in 1931. That speech had led him to join the Labor Party, he said, and now Curtin's Cabinet was bringing down this half-baked proposal. Curtin interrupted him: 'Tom, that was a good speech in 1931, but how did I go in the election?' He had been defeated, of course. Burke's amendment was lost, and Chifley's Bills were approved.

Both Bills were strongly opposed by the trading banks, some sections of the business community, and the Opposition parties. It was said that they would hand over the banking system to political control and open the way to general socialisation of industry by indirect means. The parliamentary debate extended over five months. Chifley would not accept any significant amendments, and where necessary the guillotine was applied. 'The adoption of this [guillotine] procedure is absolutely undemocratic', protested T. W. White, in terms which were to become increasingly popular on the Opposition benches,

> but because the Government has the support of a certain number of trade unionists, the socialists in the community, and the "Commos", it seems to think that it is justified . . . But the time is coming when honourable gentlemen opposite will be swept from the Treasury benches and when their socialistic legislation will be removed from the statute-book.

For the time being, however, the Labor Government could regard the banking Acts—assented to on 29 August 1945—as safe and sound.

The same could no longer be said of two important measures passed earlier in the life of this parliament—the Pharmaceutical Benefits Act and the Australian National Airlines Act. Both were then under appeal in the High Court. In the former case the Victorian Attorney-General, acting on behalf of certain medical practitioners, challenged the free medicine scheme of the Pharmaceutical Benefits Act. His first main ground of appeal was that the measure was not merely an Appropriation Act, as the Commonwealth contended, but an Act with respect to medical and pharmaceutical services, and therefore not within any of the heads of power under Section 51 of the Constitution. Five of the six justices upheld this argument, and that alone was enough to invalidate the legislation. Secondly, the appellants argued that even if the measure was an Appropriation Act it would still be invalid because the federal spending power was limited to matters about which the Commonwealth could legitimately make laws. In view of its other decision, the Court did not feel obliged to rule on this point; but remarks by three of the justices suggested that they took a restrictive view of the spending power.

In the Airways case non-Government airlines argued firstly that Section 51(i), conferring power to make laws with respect to 'trade and commerce . . . among the States', authorised regulation of such trade, but not government participation in it. This was rejected unanimously. A second ground of appeal was that certain provisions of the Act placed the interstate operations of private airlines at the discretion of the Government, which would consequently be able to drive them out of business if it wished; and this was said to infringe the absolute freedom of trade among the States enshrined in Section 92 of the Constitution. The High Court agreed unanimously. As a result there could be no socialisation of air transport by the back door, only competition between Government and private carriers.

Other significant measures passed in 1944 and 1945 were the Income Tax Assessment Act, introducing the 'pay as you earn' system of tax collection at source; the Matrimonial Causes Act, authorising State courts to deal with failed wartime marriages when the husband was no longer domiciled in Australia; the Charter of the United Nations Act, approving that charter; and the Re-establishment and Employment Act, providing rights and preference for returned servicemen.

By 1944 the new Speaker, J. S. Rosevear, had shown himself to be temperamentally unsuited for that office. Sol Rosevear was elected to the Speaker's Chair as consolation for not having been made a minister. There had been room for only two Langites in Curtin's Cabinet, and Rosevear, unforgiving and unforgiven, was passed over in favour of Beasley and Lazzarini. As Speaker, he was less orthodox and more unpopular with both sides of the House than any of his predecessors. In best Labor tradition, he refused to wear wig and gown. He also continued to hold the position of Controller of Leather and Footwear (an earlier sop to his ministerial ambition), and spent a good deal of time assisting Beasley with the portfolio of Supply. In the Chair he was often overbearing and blatantly partisan. His Labor predecessor in the office, Makin, had to admit that Rosevear was 'somewhat less than "without fear or favour": he certainly had no fears, but in other respects he possibly looked too consistently one way'.

Disapproval of Speaker Rosevear's conduct boiled over on 28 September 1944. Two days earlier the Minister for Transport, Ward, had announced that prosecutions would be launched against four Geelong Grammar boys who had travelled from Geelong to Sydney for the school holidays in a plane specially provided for them by Australian National Airlines, contrary to wartime transport regulations. One of the boys was the son of an A.N.A. director, Captain Ivan Holyman, and another was a son of the Governor of New South Wales, Lord Wakehurst. In his eagerness to bring this matter to light Ward had apparently forgotten that authority to authorise prosecutions was vested solely in the Attorney-General, and Dr Evatt later announced that in view of the boys' ages he had decided not to proceed. At Question Time on 28 September the Opposition tried to take advantage of Ward's embarrassment, but was sternly rebuffed by the Speaker. A question by Larry Anthony (C, Richmond, N) was ruled out of order before he finished asking it, and when Anthony protested and refused to apologise, he was named and suspended. 'All this is just to save the face of a larrikin Minister', said Sir Frederick Stewart (U, Parramatta, N). He was suspended too.

Fadden tried to move an urgency motion on the denial to members of the right to discuss public and national affairs. When that was ruled out of order, he took the unprecedented step of moving suspension of Standing Orders so that he could move a motion of no confidence in the Speaker and have it debated immediately. This roundabout approach was necessary because Standing Order 287 provided that any objection to a Speaker's decision had to be moved and seconded immediately, but could not be debated until the next sitting day. Fadden wanted to avoid the intended cooling-off period, but his motion for suspension of Standing Orders was defeated on party lines. By next day tempers had indeed cooled off, and the matter was taken no further.

In spite of the resentment he provoked in the Chair, Speaker Rosevear helped to improve facilities for members of parliament by securing the appointment of a committee of inquiry on accommodation, clerical assistance and other related matters. This committee's report in 1944 led to provision of more office space in Parliament House, secretarial assistance for members, and a travelling allowance of £1 2s per day. Members' rights were also protected at this time by the establishment of a Standing Committee of Privileges. On 25 February 1944 Major Cameron rose to a question of privilege and said that his mail was being censored. This must have been particularly galling to a former operative of Army Intelligence. It appeared that a registered airmail letter from one of the Major's electors had taken seventeen days to reach him, and had been opened *en route* by the military censor. Cameron moved that this was a breach of parliamentary privilege.

His motion was debated, amended and eventually withdrawn after agreement that a committee be established by Standing Order to consider the matter. The committee concluded that censoring of letters to members was not a breach of any existing privilege of the House, and that there was no evidence of Cameron's mail having been singled out for special censorial attention. Thenceforth a similar committee of nine members was appointed at the start of each parliament, to assist the House whenever necessary in examining issues of privilege. The Senate eventually followed this example, but not until 1966.

White's prediction of defeat for the Government was hardly likely to be fulfilled in the near future, but under Menzies's leadership the Opposition was working at it. On resuming the leadership of his party, Menzies had insisted that he should have *carte blanche* to weld various non-Labor forces—including the U.A.P., but not the Country Party—into a new political organisation. The political landscape was littered with such conservative vehicles as the New South Wales Liberal Democratic Party, the Nationalist Party of Victoria, the Queensland People's Party, the South Australian Liberal and Country League, the United Ex-service Men and Women's Political Association and the Middle Class Organisation—all going their own way, if in fact they were going anywhere at all. 'The picture thus presented', wrote Menzies,

> is one of many thousands of people all desperately anxious to travel in the same political direction but divided into various sects and bodies with no Federal structure, with no central executive . . . and, above all, with no clearly accepted political doctrine or faith to serve as a banner under which all may fight.

Soon after his return to the leadership, Menzies circulated a confidential

'Mr Prime Minister, we two, you and I, will see this thing through together'; General Douglas MacArthur and John Curtin in Parliament House, 26 March 1942

Curtin lying in state, King's Hall, 6 July 1945

The Prime Minister, Ben Chifley, walking to Parliament House from his room at the Hotel Kurrajong

memorandum emphasising the urgent need for a new party. 'The wreck produced by the election gives us a great opportunity if we are ready to seize it', he wrote.

> The name United Australia Party has fallen into complete disregard. It no longer means anything. Many of my own strongest supporters in my own electorate decline to have anything to do with the Party as such . . . To establish a new party under a new name, it is I think essential to recognise that the new groups and movements which sprang up in the six months before the election were all expressions of dissatisfaction with the existing set-up . . . The time between now and the next election is already beginning to run out!

Only a few weeks before, Menzies had been the Opposition's Hamlet, a man seemingly unwilling to face dangerous issues, in a world out of joint. Now he took the role of Fortinbras, acting decisively both in and out of parliament. Convinced that he would have more freedom in parliament without the constraints imposed by membership of the Advisory War Council, he resigned from that body in February 1944, giving as his reason the continued presence of E. J. Ward in Cabinet. Hughes did likewise, but the only other U.A.P. member, Spender, retained his membership and was consequently expelled from the party. The two Country Party members, Fadden and McEwen, stayed on the War Council, and Page joined them in one of the two vacant U.A.P. seats. The other seat was soon resumed by its previous occupant, Hughes, who reversed his earlier decision and was expelled like Spender.

In 1944 Menzies moved three want-of-confidence motions against the Government, and campaigned with notable success against the 'Fourteen powers' referendum. The referendum campaign—concerned as it was with the fear of socialisation, and conversely the defence of private enterprise—made an excellent testing ground for the kind of doctrine Menzies wanted as a banner. Between sittings of parliament he worked tirelessly at promoting interest in a new party. He dined with Sir Keith Murdoch, Frank Packer of Australian Consolidated Press, and Rupert Henderson of the *Sydney Morning Herald*; discussed funding with W. S. Robinson and other influential businessmen; and organised a conference of eighteen political groups from all States, held at Canberra on 13–16 October. The Canberra conference approved Menzies's preferred name for the new organisation—'The Liberal Party of Australia', replete with overtones of freedom, Gladstone, Asquith and Deakin—appointed a provisional executive, and agreed to hold another conference at Albury on 15–17 December.

Both conferences were dominated by Menzies. 'His initiative, leadership, hard work and persuasiveness have brought [the party] to its present stage', reported the *Argus*'s political correspondent, Crayton Burns, from Albury.

> Physically he stood head and shoulders above most of the delegates, and intellectually he undoubtedly did. He put all his talents into the job at Albury, and when he was opposed, as he was on two or three organisational aspects, he agreed in the end to let the critics have his own way. And he did it charmingly. Though greyed and falling to flesh, he was

still the best-groomed and handsomest man present, a tribute at once to his tailor, his barber, his valet (if any), his laundry and his cook. His draftsmanship runs all through the documents, and the more they are studied, the more the new party is seen to be the Menzies party . . .

Menzies anticipated that after the war Australia would have to choose between a continuation of Government controls, leading to socialism and perhaps eventually to Communism, and on the other hand a society based upon 'free and encouraged private enterprise'. He and his party would stand for the latter. 'In a vision of the future', he said in his opening speech at Albury,

> I see the individual and his encouragement and recognition as the prime motive force for the building of a better world. Socialism means high costs, inefficiency, the constant intrusion of political considerations, the damping down of enterprise, the overlordship of routine. None of these elements can produce progress, and without progress security will turn out to be a delusion. It thus appears that private enterprise and the State are both engaged in a task in which the people will prosper best if the individual and the State each perform his or its proper function . . . Australia looks to us for a lead, a lead back from the abyss.

To those of a different political persuasion, as for example the *Argus* correspondent, there was nothing essentially new about the policy presented at Albury. 'Though expressed with more conciseness and precision', reported Burns,

> it is in general the same policy as that espoused by the Bruce–Page, Lyons and Menzies administrations of the past, and more aggressively put forward by Mr Menzies and his gallant little band in Opposition in Canberra more recently. It is the policy of the *status quo* adjusted to meet changing physical circumstances . . . There is nothing revolutionary about it; indeed it is directed to oppose anything at all revolutionary.
>
> The new party begins its life with traditional disapproval of the socialistic objective, which has lain almost dormant on the Labor Party platform for about half a century in Australia, but which the Liberals now fear is to be brought into effect against airlines, banks, commercial radio stations, newspapers and goodness knows what next. They abhor communism in all its manifestations, and share Mr Menzies's alarm at the spread of it through the trades unions, in universities and among intellectual groups . . . The choice which the Liberals propose to put to the people of Australia is one between liberalism and communism. Labor supporters, they predict, will eventually be forced one way or the other.

When parliament resumed on 21 February 1945 Menzies formally embarked on what he would soon be calling 'this magnificent voyage of ours', by informing the House that those sitting with him desired to be known in future as members of the Liberal Party. They numbered only twelve, for Hughes and Spender were still disqualified by membership of the Advisory War Council. E. J. Harrison, who had replaced Hughes as Deputy Leader of the U.A.P., was Deputy Leader of the Liberal Party and the Opposition. Another twelve Liberals in the Senate were led by Senator George McLeay of South Australia.

In a fourth want-of-confidence motion, on 31 May, Menzies moved that the Government was deserving of censure for, among other things, its refusal to permit discussion in parliament of matters under consideration at the United Nations conference in San Francisco, and its use of the forms of the House to stifle full debate on important legislative proposals. The guillotine was being used to hasten the passage of the Re-establishment and Employment Bill, and only two days previously Menzies had protested strenuously, but to no avail, about that Bill's disregard for the responsible authority of parliament. Clause 135(2) stated that regulations could repeal, amend or add to any provisions in the Act. 'If that provision is to be written into the statute', said Menzies, 'then the Parliament might just as well close its doors; because, if this is to become a precedent, we shall occupy months in this place hammering out legislation, and, under this most extraordinary power, the Executive will then proceed to do exactly what it likes about it'. The chief executive defendant on this occasion was not Curtin but Chifley, who for reasons to be explained later was acting Prime Minister. Replying to the censure motion, Chifley made no apologies for either Clause 135(2) or the guillotine. 'I regard a good deal of this debate as taking up time that could be better used', he said. 'It is strange to hear the Opposition condemning the use of the "guillotine". In the first session of the Fourteenth Parliament, the Lyons Government, of which some of the present Opposition members were supporters, applied the "guillotine" no less than fourteen times.' The Opposition had no hope of carrying its censure motion, which also charged the Government with failing to deal adequately with industrial lawlessness, and encouraging Communist activities in Australia. The motion was defeated, but at least Menzies had scored some useful points for the new party.

By this time Chifley was well accustomed to acting on Curtin's behalf, and sometimes replacing him altogether, in parliament and party room as the need arose. Forde, the Deputy Prime Minister, was normally the replacement when one was required by reason of Curtin's absence or illness; but sometimes Forde was absent too, and in any case, whether formally Acting or not, Chifley was consistently the Prime Minister's main source of support in government and parliament. 'You handle it, Ben', Curtin would say, and Chifley would organise a timetable for the House, or preside over a meeting of Caucus.

In April and May 1944 he replaced the Prime Minister on the Advisory War Council (by his own wish, Chifley was not a permanent member) while Curtin visited the United States and Britain. Curtin and his party, including Mrs Curtin, Sir Frederick Shedden and Don Rodgers, crossed the Pacific on the Matson ship, *Lurline*. After meetings with President Roosevelt and the Secretary of State, Cordell Hull, he flew to London for the Commonwealth Prime Ministers' Conference. This was his first trip 'home', and it was a disappointment. Not for him the excitement that Menzies would have felt at being in England now that April was there, and on the very eve of D-Day. Curtin kept mainly to his hotel room. Although he had a civil enough discussion with Churchill about the possibility of British troops eventually taking part in a final assault on Japan, Curtin resisted attempts made to see him by several other British public figures, including the socialist, Sir Stafford Cripps. One night he said moodily to Rodgers: 'Let's go out and find a bloody Australian'.

At the Prime Ministers' Conference Curtin failed to arouse much interest in proposals which he made for closer co-operation between members of the British Commonwealth. It must have seemed to him, in fact, that his visit to London was hardly necessary. There was not even any need to discuss the appointment of a new governor-general, for that long-standing matter had been settled before Curtin left Australia. During the last year of Lyons's Prime Ministership the King's youngest brother, the Duke of Kent, was appointed to succeed Lord Gowrie when the latter relinquished his post, as he planned to do, in November 1939. With the outbreak of war, Gowrie agreed to remain in office indefinitely. By the time he made known his wish to return to England, because of his son's death, the Duke of Kent had also been killed on active service, in the crash of an R.A.F. Sunderland flying from Scotland to Iceland.

Curtin first offered the Governor-Generalship to Scullin, who declined. Churchill suggested the British Commander-in-Chief in India, Lord Wavell, but Curtin resented that intrusion and successfully resisted it. Nevertheless it would seem that an acceptable name—that of another royal brother, the Duke of Gloucester—emanated from Britain rather than Australia. On 6 October 1943 Lord Gowrie said in a telegram to the King's private secretary: 'Have discussed question with Curtin he is very honoured and gratified with idea'. Curtin consulted those ministers who happened to be in Canberra, but others were left to learn of his decision from the press. At the next full Cabinet meeting, on 23 November, Ward protested at the Prime Minister's failure to advise all ministers of a selection in such stark contrast to the last Labor-nominated Governor-General, Sir Isaac Isaacs. Curtin spoke forcefully in defence of his decision. He had not been able to settle upon an Australian with the necessary attributes, who was not also associated with the military or some sectional interest. The Duke would be 'a symbol in Australia of the whole Empire', and furthermore his presence might be expected to influence the despatch of British forces to the Pacific after conclusion of the European war. The latter consideration seemed to have weighed heavily with Curtin. Cabinet endorsed the choice, and the Duke of Gloucester began his unexceptionable but also undistinguished term of office on 30 January 1945.

Curtin, according to those around him, was never the same man after his return from London. The strain of his first two years in office had affected his health, which at the best of times was prone to aches and pains. Early in November 1944 he suffered a coronary occlusion, and spent the rest of the year in a Melbourne hospital. He returned to The Lodge in January, recovered sufficiently to attend the opening of the third session of parliament by the Duke of Gloucester, and took part in the Address-in-Reply debate on 28 February 1945. His speech dealt mainly with the forthcoming United Nations conference, and particularly the membership of Australia's delegation. 'Surely it is not suggested', he said, 'that I, as the head of the government should have persons chosen for me to represent Australia at a conference of this nature! The primary responsibility most certainly is mine, and the collective security is that of the Government'.

Mr SPENDER.—The responsibility is that of this parliament.
Mr CURTIN.—I am responsible to the Parliament. The Parliament can dismiss me if I fail to do the right thing. Until it does so, I propose to carry out the functions of government as I see them.

That was Curtin's last major speech. He attended parliament only briefly on most of its few sitting days during the next two months. Late in April he returned to hospital with congestion of the lungs, which affected his heart condition; then back to The Lodge for another vain attempt at convalescence. As Forde was leading the Australian delegation to the United Nations Conference in San Francisco, Chifley became acting Prime Minister on 1 May. Victory was obviously close in Europe, but no one could tell how much longer the Pacific war would last. At 3 p.m. on 8 May Chifley informed the House that German forces had surrendered. The sitting was suspended from 10.50 p.m. to 11.10 p.m. so that members could listen to a short-wave broadcast by Churchill announcing the official cessation of hostilities in Europe. Chifley then repeated the announcement in parliament, saying that his pleasure in making it was tempered with regret that the Prime Minister, who had contributed so much to the war effort, was unable to make the announcement himself because of illness.

Curtin's condition deteriorated rapidly. 'I'm not worth two bob', he told Ray Tracey. By this time Elsie Curtin was with him. On 2 July a medical bulletin expressed concern about his condition. A local Roman Catholic priest called to see him, but was turned away at the door. At about 10 p.m. on Wednesday 4 July Tracey went in to the Prime Minister's bedroom, where a nurse was on duty. 'Who won the match?' asked Curtin. Tracey told him that Fitzroy had won, and he said: 'Well that's good, isn't it. That's good'. Around midnight Curtin and his wife had a cup of tea together. Mrs Curtin went to an adjoining bedroom. She lay awake there until someone came to tell her, soon after 4 a.m., that her husband had just died in his sleep.

The House resumed at half past two that afternoon. Forde, who had taken over from Chifley as acting Prime Minister only three days before, moved a motion of regret and sympathy, followed soon after by adjournment. In a statement repeated half an hour later in the Senate, Forde said that the Australian nation offered to

this common man, this son of the people, a tribute of affection, gratitude and honour, which has been offered rarely, even to kings. For this man [he said] was truly one with the masses who populate our country. He had striven and struggled among them, and when he came to the highest place in the land he was still one of them . . . John Curtin is as one to-day with those fighting men of our race who have given their lives that we might live . . . the captain has been stricken in sight of the shore. His memorial stands around us—a free land, a free people . . .

This was as true as such tributes ever can be. No Australian could be said to have played a truly decisive role in keeping his land and people free, for that sort of credit belonged elsewhere. Undoubtedly, however, Curtin was the most distinguished of Australia's wartime casualties. He had worked as hard as Hughes did in the previous war, and had been less able to bear the strain. Scullin, who had nearly killed himself the same way, said of his friend's death: 'It is not hard work, either mental or physical, that kills a man. It is anxiety and worry'.

On Friday morning Curtin's coffin was carried into King's Hall and placed below King George V's statue, with the lid open to show his face. Led by Forde, who later that day was sworn in as Prime Minister by the Duke of Gloucester, members of both Houses filed past the coffin in solemn farewell. At 2 p.m., in the presence of the Governor-General and members of the Curtin family, and with hundreds of people crowding the hall and the approaches to Parliament House, a memorial service was conducted by a local Presbyterian minister, the Reverend Hector Harrison, with whom Curtin had been friendly. The coffin was then taken in funeral procession, preceded by an R.A.A.F. band and motor cycle escort, through several Canberra suburbs to Fairbairn airport.

There it was placed on board an air force Dakota for the journey to Perth. Six Boomerang fighters and six Kittyhawks circled the airport, and escorted the Dakota out of the A.C.T. It landed for the night at Adelaide, and next morning flew on across the Nullarbor Plain. At Cunderdin, north-east of Perth, it was overtaken by the Duke of Gloucester's Avro York, carrying among others Mrs Curtin, Tracey and Rodgers. The burial took place on Sunday afternoon, at Karrakatta cemetery, where Lord Forrest's West African remains had been reinterred a generation before.

General MacArthur was prevented by his duties from attending the funeral, but he sent Mrs Curtin a cable couched in idiosyncratic vein: 'The death of your husband is the loss of one of the earth's great sons'. Chifley did not go to Perth, or even Fairbairn airport. 'I couldn't go', he said. 'I simply couldn't go.' Grief would have been sufficient reason for this, but perhaps there was another reason too. Politics does not stop for death, and the election of a new party leader would have been preoccupying Chifley as well as others. Scullin had persuaded him to stand, if in fact he needed persuading, and no one understood better than Chifley the arithmetic of power. 'In parliament or in Caucus', he once said, 'if you have the numbers you can do what you think ought to be done . . . And if you have not got the numbers you are a fool to pull on a fight'.

During Curtin's illness, the Australian Public Opinion Polls, a national organisation which had been using the Gallup method of opinion sampling since 1941, asked Labor voters who they thought best fitted to lead the Government. Fifty-eight per cent said Curtin; 20 per cent, Evatt; 5 per cent, Chifley; 4 per cent, Ward; and 3 per cent, Forde. Dr Evatt, unfortunately for him, was somewhere in the Pacific, returning from the United Nations Conference on a ship observing radio silence because of Japanese submarines. A message was dropped by air on to the ship's deck, informing him of the political situation in Canberra, but there was nothing he could do personally so far as numbers were concerned.

The nominations were Forde, Chifley, Makin and Evatt; and a motion that the election be postponed until Evatt's return lapsed for want of a seconder.

Chifley was elected on the first ballot with an absolute majority of forty-five. Forde was reported to have received fifteen or sixteen votes; Makin, seven or eight; and Evatt, one or two. In the vote for Deputy Leader, Forde received sixty-eight, and Evatt one or two. So much for public opinion polls. Forde took his leadership defeat gracefully, and Chifley was sworn in as Prime Minister on 13 July.

The final victory, which Curtin had only glimpsed in the distance, arrived suddenly in August. Parliament was in adjournment when the atomic bombs were dropped on Japan, and when the Japanese Government accepted allied surrender terms on 10 August. At the next sitting, on 29 August, Chifley informed the House formally of these events and moved two similar yet oddly contrasting motions. One was an expression of gratitude to 'the King's Most Excellent Majesty' from his 'dutiful and loyal subjects' in the House of Representatives for the outcome of the war; the other was a more realistic expression of thanks to General MacArthur. The latter motion extended warmest congratulations amd recalled with deep gratitude MacArthur's 'outstanding contribution to the victory in the Pacific and to the defence of Australia during the most critical period of our history'.

The incomprehensible new weapon that had precipitated the end of the war did not occasion much parliamentary discussion. Larry Anthony asked whether the Prime Minister would consider sending Australian scientists to Hiroshima and Nagasaki so that they could recommend to the Government protective measures against atomic bombs. Chifley thought not. The only other reference to the bomb at this time was contained in a Dorothy Dix question by T. F. Williams (Lab, Robertson, N), who asked whether the Government had taken any steps to control the mining and export of uranium and its compounds. Dedman replied that the Attorney-General's Department was investigating whether such action could be taken under the Commonwealth's defence power.

With a long Christmas adjournment ahead of it, parliament attended to the year's loose ends at a continuous sitting from 3 p.m. on 2 October to 4.05 p.m. on 5 October—a total of nearly forty-six hours for the lower house, excluding suspensions for meals. On the last day of the sitting the Minister for the Army, Forde, made an unusual statement by leave concerning the Page family. Although leaving much unsaid, this was a vivid reminder of the price that some had paid for victory. Forde informed the House that two members of Sir Earle Page's family were missing. His brother Harold had been Government Secretary at Rabaul when the Japanese landed there, and Harold Page's son, Captain Robert Page, had been awarded the Distinguished Service Order for reasons not then publicly disclosed. As later became known, both men were dead. Harold Page was killed with other prisoners of war when an American submarine torpedoed a ship taking them to Japan, and his son, one of the Australian commandos who paddled canoes into Singapore harbour to destroy shipping there, was captured and beheaded by the Japanese.

Of the three members of parliament who served overseas with Australian forces during the war, one came close to sharing the Pages' fate. He was the Country Party Member for the Northern Territory, Adair Macalister Blain, an outback surveyor who had been wounded and gassed in the first world war, and was elected to parliament in 1934. 'Chil' Blain, as his colleagues called him, was best known for his exposition of conventional Territorian attitudes toward the Aborigines—or 'Abori *gines*', as Blain always pronounced it. He spoke in defence of flogging, yet claimed to have the interest of Aborigines at heart. 'When the true story comes to be told', he said in 1938, 'the fact will be realised that no person had endeavoured to soften the pillow of their passing more than I'.

After enlisting in the 2nd A.I.F., at the age of forty-six, Sergeant Blain went into captivity with the 8th Division at Singapore. He was bashed by Japanese military police during interrogation about the smuggling of letters through Japanese lines, and his weight dropped to seven stone. All this time he was still a member of parliament, having been re-elected *in absentia* in 1943. On 26 September 1945 he resumed his seat in the House of Representatives, virtually straight from Changi. 'I realise that honourable members do not expect to hear a speech from me', he said in reply to a welcome from the Prime Minister, 'but I shall say a few words, if only so that I may get my mind, shall I say, out of the splints in which it has been bound during the last three and a half years'. He went on to thank Archie Cameron for looking after the interests of his electorate—'that vast electorate', he said, 'where men have on their brows the mark of those who gaze at distant horizons'.

Two years later the memory of Sergeant Blain's captivity was revived in regrettable circumstances by the Labor Member for Lang, Dan Mulcahy. On 6 November 1947 Mulcahy referred in the House to a victim of the Depression who was 'a one-legged digger'. 'Where is the digger now?' interjected Blain:

Mr MULCAHY.—I hope he is in heaven.
Mr BLAIN.—The honorable member ought to be ashamed of himself.
Mr MULCAHY.—This man, who went away to fight for his country, became a member of [New South Wales] Parliament; but, unlike the honorable member for the Northern Territory (Mr Blain), he did not show his gold pass to the Japanese in order to get special treatment.

The matter was referred to the Standing Committee of Privileges. Blain gave evidence that in connection with plans to escape he had sometimes given his gold pass, as an indication of authenticity, to Chinese messengers carrying letters out of the prison camp. Mulcahy could not substantiate his statement, and the Standing Committee reported that the Honourable Member for the Northern Territory had not wrongfully used either his gold pass or his parliamentary privilege. The whole unsavoury affair ricocheted like a last stray bullet, briefly reminding parliament of the chapter in its story which by then was mercifully closed.

13

The Second Battle

One of the few flourishes in Ben Chifley's otherwise plain vocabulary was an occasional reference to 'the tides' of parliament. For him, this was more than a figure of speech. Chifley had been left stranded by the tide that carried Scullin's Government away; and unlike another notable casualty of the 1931 election, Curtin, he had not floated back into parliament on the incoming tide. If he had been returned in 1934, he might well have won the party leadership when Scullin stood down a year later, and so have become wartime Prime Minister. Instead, he became Prime Minister at the turning of another tide, from war to peace. Never had the prospect been so bright for Labor as it was when parliament resumed in February 1946. The party was united, and in control of both houses for the first time since Andrew Fisher's heyday. Now that the war was over Australia needed orderly transition, so why not include some Labor objectives in the process? As always, however, there was the High Court to be reckoned with. Chifley's two Ministries, running from 1945 to 1949, were remarkable for the quantity and controversy of the bills they put through parliament, and for the adverse judicial tide that flowed so strongly against some of those measures.

Not least among the Government's advantages at this propitious time was Joseph Benedict Chifley himself. In spite of all that he had in common with Curtin's background, Chifley was a markedly different man, and in some ways better suited for party leadership. Both were born in country towns in 1885 to Roman Catholic parents of Irish birth or descent. Chifley's paternal grandparents had emigrated from Ireland, and settled in the goldmining district of Bathurst; his father became a blacksmith in the town, and married a newly arrived immigrant from County Fermanagh. Because of poverty during the Depression of the 1890s, Ben was sent to live from the age of five to fourteen with his grandparents in their wattle and daub hut at Limekilns, outside Bathurst.

Bathurst was a railway town, and at the age of twenty-seven Chifley received his locomotive driver's licence. For the next five years he drove goods and passenger trains on the western mountain lines, out of the rail depot at south Bathurst. Like Curtin he became active in the affairs of his union—in his case the Locomotive Enginedrivers' Firemen's and Cleaners' Association, which later became the Australian Federated Union of Locomotive Engineers—and, again like Curtin, married a Protestant, the daughter of a fellow unionist, outside the church of his own family and schooling. But whereas Curtin left the church completely, Chifley attended mass regularly all his life, and derived genuine satisfaction from the Bible, which he was reputed to have read at least a dozen times.

Like Curtin, he campaigned against conscription at the referendums of 1916 and 1917. He went out with his union in the general strike, and paid for it, as hundreds of other railwaymen did, by temporary dismissal and loss of seniority—a form of victimisation which left, as Chifley said, 'a legacy of bitterness and a trail of hate'. In the long aftermath of that strike he made a name for himself as a capable union negotiator, appearing as an advocate before industrial tribunals and serving as a State delegate at federal conferences of the Australian Federated Union of Locomotive Enginemen. He stood successfully for parliament in 1928, the same year as Curtin, and impressed Caucus sufficiently to become one of Scullin's ministers in the reshuffle of 1931, eight months before the tide went out. At this time he seemed older than Curtin, and certainly more reliable. 'There can be no fireworks with him', said the Bathurst *National Advocate*, reporting one of his speeches.

> His appeal is to sanity and commonsense; in fact to plain downright Australianism . . . as his speech progresses the sense of his power grows steadily. He speaks in homely phrases and paints word pictures that all can understand [with] just the rugged sincerity that comes to those who interpret the plain man's thoughts in his own plain language . . . A man's man, Mr Chifley has been gifted with a deep, pleasant, resonant voice.

By 1946 a further fifteen years of public speaking had hoarsened that resonance into what Chifley himself described as 'a lot of rusty old chains knocking together'. It sounded as though something was pathologically wrong with his voice, but the best available medical advice was simply that he had overworked his vocal cords. Apart from this, he seemed to have withstood the strain of political life remarkably well. The thing most often remarked about him was that he was never in a hurry. Always a good listener, puffing reflectively on his pipe while others talked, he was also firm in response. 'Chif' was tougher than Curtin, and better at handling people. Far from having trouble with the Honourable Member for East Sydney, he had Ward fairly eating out of his hand. The same went for Calwell and Evatt. Curtin had always kept Evatt at a distance, but Chif had a much closer relationship with him, calling him 'my learned friend', 'the Doc' or, with amiable mockery, 'Ivan the Terrible'. Evatt, a man of great compassion for people collectively, but ruthless and insensitive with individuals, was nonetheless devoted to the new Prime Minister.

Chifley was certainly a man's man, but he could also charm an angry deputation of Liberal ladies without the least apparent effort. Dame Enid Lyons said he reminded her of a Great Dane. His wife Elizabeth was a semi-invalid, and seldom if ever came to Canberra. For that reason, but also because of his strong affinity for Bathurst generally, Chifley usually went home every other weekend, often driving himself by the shorter back road route. Even as Prime Minister he remained an Abercrombie Shire councillor, and liked nothing better than 'going round', by which he meant driving and yarning his way through Oberon, Carcoar, Rocklea and other parts of his shire and electorate. In Canberra he continued to live at the Hotel Kurrajong, walking to and from Parliament House. The Lodge was used only to accommodate distinguished visitors.

Chifley's first Ministry was not greatly different from Curtin's last—or from Forde's, which had lasted only seven days. Beasley took Curtin's place as Minister for Defence, and Senator W. P. Ashley (N) took over Beasley's portfolio of Supply and Shipping. Chifley remained Treasurer, and Calwell became Minister for Immigration as well as Information. In his new role Calwell presided successfully over a programme of mass migration which presented a striking contrast to earlier Labor suspicions of migration, either planned or unplanned.

The Government's main post-war objectives were transition to a peace-time economy, economic growth, and extension of social welfare—but not at the cost of unemployment or inflation. It therefore sought to maintain full employment, by orderly transfer of manpower from the armed services and defence industry (and, later, the orderly intake of migrant labour); and to prevent inflation, by maintaining such wartime measures as rationing, price control and high taxation, and, no less importantly, by exercising the central control of credit provided for in the Banking Act of 1945.

In pursuit of its post-war objectives, the Government also tried to obtain additional powers by amendment of the Constitution. In 1946 it brought down three amending Bills for approval by referendum at the next general election, due before the end of the year. One of these proposed a Common-wealth power to make laws concerning organised marketing unhampered by Section 92's guarantee that trade, commerce and intercourse among the States should be absolutely free. Another proposed a power to make laws about 'terms and conditions of employment in industry', but contained a proviso that such power would not extend to '[authorising] any form of industrial conscription'. The third proposal, embodied in a Constitution Alteration (Social Services) Bill, was for power to make laws concerning the provision of maternity allowances, widows' pensions, child endowment, pharmaceutical, sickness and hospital benefits, medical and dental services (but not so as to authorise any form of civil conscription), benefits to students and family allowances.

This third Bill was intended to remove certain doubts cast upon Common-wealth spending power in the social service field by the High Court's ruling in the 1945 Pharmaceutical Benefits case. The Opposition generally sup-

ported the Bill, but Menzies, scenting socialised medicine, persuaded the
Attorney-General, Dr Evatt, to incorporate in it a guarantee against civil conscription almost identical with that contained in the industrial referendum
Bill. 'It is perfectly true', said Evatt after Menzies had moved this
amendment,

> that [the Leader of the Opposition] has borrowed certain words from the
> bill dealing with industrial matters, but the Government had previously
> borrowed the same set of words from the National Security Bill intro-
> duced by the right honorable gentleman when he was Attorney-General.
> I believe that one good turn deserves another, and that if industrial
> workers are entitled to be protected against conscription members of the
> medical and dental professions are entitled to similar protection. I, there-
> fore, have pleasure in accepting the amendment.

This was a pleasure Chifley's learned friend would later regret.

Among other measures passed in 1946 were an amending National Security Act, the first in a series of such measures extending the operation of wartime regulations under that Act for a year at a time; the Australian National
University Act, establishing a university in the Australian Capital Territory;
the Atomic Energy (Control of Materials) Act, making good Dedman's
undertaking of the previous year; the Overseas Telecommunications Act,
establishing an Overseas Telecommunications Commission with responsibility for Australia's part in a British Commonwealth telecommunications
service; the Coal Industry Act, establishing a Joint Coal Board (empowered
jointly by Commonwealth and New South Wales law) to control and mod-
ernise the New South Wales coal industry after the expected contraction of
the Commonwealth defence power, on which power similar wartime
measures had relied; an amending Judiciary Act, restoring the number of
High Court justices to seven; and the Parliamentary Proceedings Broadcasting Act, requiring the Australian Broadcasting Commission to broadcast
debates and other proceedings from both houses of parliament.

Parliamentary broadcasting had been adopted in New Zealand ten years
previously, mainly as a Labor government's response to what it regarded as
inadequate and often tendentious reporting of parliament by an overwhelmingly conservative press. For much the same reason the Curtin Government
had requested the joint Parliamentary Standing Committee on Broadcasting
to report on whether parliamentary broadcasting was desirable, and if so,
how it should be undertaken. After consulting party leaders, the ABC, and
New Zealand opinion, the committee reported in September 1945 that the
innovation should be made as soon as circumstances permitted. 'We share
the views', it said, 'of those who have expressed the opinion that the result
would be to raise the standard of debates, enhance the prestige of parliament, and contribute to a better informed judgment throughout the community on matters affecting the common good and the public interest,
nationally and internationally'.

The resulting Act required the ABC to broadcast parliamentary
proceedings initially over a national station in the capital city of each State,
and in Newcastle. It also provided for a Joint Committee on the Broadcasting

of Parliamentary Proceedings—to consist of six members of parliament, three appointed by each chamber—which would allocate broadcasting time between the Senate and House of Representatives according to its assessment of the importance of debates and the public interest in them. The ABC made a studio out of the Press Gallery's common-room, previously used for card games, and installed standing microphones in both chambers, where the only other microphones were those of an extension speaker from the parliamentary table down to the Records and Papers Office, and Billy Hughes's latest Acousticon.

Parliament made its wireless debut on 10 July 1946, when proceedings in the House of Representatives were broadcast from 2.55 p.m. until 6 p.m., and 7.55 p.m. to 11 p.m. Speaker Rosevear's strident voice was heard first, reading the prayers and calling for petitions. He was followed by Arthur Calwell, giving notice of two motions to do with immigration; W. J. F. Riordan (Lab, Kennedy, Q), asking a Dorothy Dixer about the reported inflationary trend in America; and the Prime Minister, answering Riordan with a brief dissertation on the dangers of inflation. Those who had not heard Calwell's and Chifley's voices before were surprised at their harshness. The *Sydney Morning Herald* reported next morning that the Prime Minister had a bad radio voice, 'harsh and uninflected, and inclined to grate on the ear'. The best ministerial voice, according to the *Herald*, was that of Frank Forde—'clear and unaccented ... if a trifle reminiscent of prunes and prisms'. Dame Enid Lyons's delivery and enunciation were also found to be in agreeable contrast to those of many of her male colleagues.

Prunes and prisms soon gave way to the more natural rough and tumble of parliamentary debate. This came as a shock to many listeners, and whenever the House fell into uproar letters of protest poured in to the Speaker's office, usually criticising Mr Speaker himself, the Opposition and the Government, in that order. Clearly broadcasting would not always enhance the prestige of parliament. On one occasion soon after it began, Rowley James paused in mid-speech to address his dentist in Sydney. 'Milton, get my teeth ready this weekend', he said. 'If you're listening it's a cheap way of getting a telegram.'

The advent of parliamentary broadcasting was of little immediate electoral use to members, for parliament was dissolved after only twelve broadcast sittings, with polling day still seven weeks away. Chifley made few campaign promises other than continuation of the post-war policy, establishment of a missile-testing range at Woomera in South Australia, and certain promises that presupposed favourable referendums results. If the appropriate powers were granted, the arbitration system would be reformed, and a comprehensive national health service would be established. Although the federal Labor Party was completely united, in New South Wales the Lang machine fielded twelve candidates, including the 'Big Fella' himself. The Liberal Party was also united, Spender and Hughes having been permitted to join it after dissolution of the Advisory War Council, and the party enjoyed some electoral co-operation with the Country Party. Menzies criticised the Government for its failure to prevent coal strikes that were causing gas and electricity shortages, drew invidious comparisons between socialist regulation and free enterprise, and promised child endowment for the first child, not merely for subsequent children as was currently the case.

The election held on 28 September reduced Labor's strength in the House of Representatives from forty-nine to forty-three, leaving it still firmly in control of that chamber nonetheless, and increased its Senate majority from twenty-two to a massive thirty-three. The only Oppositionists in the new Senate were three Queenslanders: Senators Neil O'Sullivan and Annabelle Rankin, both Liberals, and Senator W. J. Cooper of the Country Party. In the lower house, the Liberals numbered seventeen, compared with the U.A.P.'s fourteen after the last election, and the Country Party numbered twelve, compared with nine. Chifley could fairly regard this as a decisive vote of confidence in his Prime Ministership and a mandate to continue on the present post-war course. Unfortunately for the Government, there would be no substantial addition to the Commonwealth's constitutional power, for only one of the three proposed amendments, Social Services, was approved at referendum. At least, however, the Government would now be able to have a second try at free medicine.

The eighteenth parliament, opened by the Duke of Gloucester on 6 November 1946, was the most stable in terms of party cohesion and leadership since Fisher's Labor Ministry in the fourth parliament of 1910–13. It also produced more legislation in quantitative terms, and more important legislation, than any previous federal parliament. In the three full years it was to run, this parliament passed 299 Acts, of which 106 (as compared with sixty-seven in the previous parliament) were neither routine financial measures nor minor amendments.

Among members missing from the new parliament were Forde, who had been defeated in Capricornia by a Country Party candidate, C. W. Davidson; Beasley and Makin, who had resigned in order to accept diplomatic appointments, the former incongruously but ably replacing Bruce as High Commissioner in London, and the latter becoming Australia's first Ambassador to the United States; and the two Independents, Coles and Wilson, both of whom resigned before the election. The most notable newcomers were two Independent Labor members: Mrs Doris Blackburn, widow of Maurice Blackburn, and the malevolent J. T. Lang. Mrs Blackburn had virtually inherited the seat of Bourke from her husband and, with Senator Annabelle Rankin's help, she brought the number of women in parliament to four. Jack Lang had defeated the sitting Labor Member for Reid (N), Charles Morgan, who was perhaps best known during his two terms of parliament for having been called 'a bloody bastard' by John Dedman during a debate on wartime building restrictions.

Lang, still fighting fit in his seventy-first year, was determined to discomfit the Government, and particularly its leader. He stayed at the Hotel Canberra, then favoured almost exclusively by the Opposition, and was ostracised by most Labor members. Soon after his arrival, he passed Chifley in a corridor of Parliament House. 'Good day, Mr Lang', said the Prime Minister. Lang did not acknowledge the greeting (some said he had not heard it), and that was the extent of their social contact.

In three years Lang missed only seven consecutive sitting days. At every other sitting he was in his place, beside Mrs Blackburn, listening grimly and finding fault with members on both sides of the House. Menzies, according to Lang, spent most of his time in the chamber either 'doodling or apparently writing poetry'. The Leader of the Opposition was indeed a better than average parodist, as is shown by the following fragment from the eighteenth parliament, inspired by Pope's 'Rape of the Lock':

> All hail, great Chifley, whom six States obey,
> > Who sometimes baccy takes and sometimes tea.
> How are the boys, my placid Benedict?
> > Is it true that Jack Lang has them tricked?

In his maiden speech, Lang did his best to open old wounds. Holding a pack of small typed cards, which he flipped expertly but seldom needed to read, he spoke in a remorseless staccato:

> After 33 years as a member of the Labour party in the Parliament of New South Wales I find myself, on entering this chamber, looking for the Labour party in this Parliament. The Labour party has always been a party of high ideals. It stands for improved conditions of living. It stands for better conditions for the aged. But what do we find in this Parliament? We have a government that calls itself a Labour government . . . If this government persists in its present attitude, then [the] fight of 1931 must be repeated. The vital spark that gave birth to the Australian Labour Party is not dead. The present state of compromise and appeasement cannot last. When the inevitable clash of fundamentals takes place, as it must, members on the government benches will have to decide whether they will continue to follow the line of right-wing conservatism or whether they will take the democratic trail and return to the Labour party platform and aspirations.

This was more than Speaker Rosevear could stand, although he had once belonged to the Lang faction himself. On 26 November, while the House was in committee of supply under chairmanship of the Deputy Speaker, J. J. Clark (Lab, Darling, N), he rose to speak in his capacity as the Honourable Member for Dalley. His vicious counter-attack on Lang put another Labor member, Les Haylen, in mind of 'the hungry huskies in the Arctic Circle eating their fallen comrade in the traces so that the remainder could survive'. Rosevear began by recalling how Lang, who now spoke glibly of abolishing the means test, had appointed ninety dole inspectors during the Depression. 'I know', he said, 'because I was among the unemployed at that time'.

> Those inspectors went into the people's homes first thing in the morning to count the beds in order to see how many beds were slept in the previous night and to determine whether the father of the family was collecting too much dole or getting extra food to feed his family. Those are truths. I know that they are truths because I was there amongst it. I tell the honorable member for Reid that when he comes here talking about treading on corns *ad lib* and treads on my corns and tells me that I am not as good a Labour man as he, by God, he is looking for trouble, and is going to get it . . . The honorable member for Reid was my friend. He would still be my friend politically if he was still in the Labour movement, but he is now

no more a friend of mine politically than the right honorable member for
North Sydney (Mr Hughes) who ratted on the Labour party in 1916. I say
pointedly to the honorable member for Reid that on a thousand occasions
I have heard him proclaim from the public platform . . . that if ever the day
came when the press of this country lauded him and featured him and the
Opposition applauded him, he would no longer be a Labour man. I ask
him to look around at his newfound friends.

Lang listened impassively to this remarkable speech and did not bother to
reply. Never before had a Speaker taken such an overtly political part in the
proceedings of the House, but the House was by this time well accustomed,
though not by any means reconciled, to unconventional and sometimes partisan behaviour by both the Speaker and Deputy Speaker. Only four months
earlier, Menzies had moved want of confidence in the Speaker, citing among
other grievances Rosevear's repeated refusal to let Harold Holt state a point
of order to the Chair. That was the last occasion on which the Opposition
took formal action against him, but in 1949 want of confidence was moved in
the Deputy Speaker, to no avail of course. In that debate the Deputy Leader
of the Country Party, McEwen, alleged that Deputy Speaker Clark had been
winking at Government supporters whenever he scored a point.

It was not clear which alleged failings by the Chifley Government Lang
had been impugning, but in any case the events of the next few months put
the Government's Labor credentials beyond even his reproach. For one
thing, Chifley returned to Labor orthodoxy in the appointment of governors-
general by recommending, and of course obtaining, the appointment of an
Australian to succeed the Duke of Gloucester, who was returning to London
after a term of little more than two years. His choice was the Labor Premier of
New South Wales, W. J. McKell, who had recently decided to retire from
politics.

The Opposition protested about this in a censure motion also directed at
'political jobbery in public appointments' (the Beasley and Makin appointments), industrial strife, and high taxation. In moving this censure on 20 February 1947, Menzies stressed that the essence of the Opposition's aversion to
McKell's appointment was not that he was an Australian, or that he was a
Labor man. 'It is recognised', he said,

> that Governors-General in the past have had their own private political
> beliefs. The real essence of our attack lies in this: that Mr McKell was, at
> the moment when his appointment was announced, Premier of an Aus-
> tralian State, and actively engaged as a partisan leader in Australian pol-
> itical affairs. That is a grave disqualification. It strikes at the very
> foundation of the office of the Governor-Generalship, because that office
> in Australia should be as far removed from party politics as is the Crown
> itself in Great Britain.

Chifley, knowing that he had the numbers, made no attempt to answer that
point; almost contemptuously, he merely defended the appointment of an
Australian, which, since Isaacs's immaculate term, required no defence.

'I . . . accept full responsibility for the nomination of Mr McKell', he said, and I offer no apologies for having made it. I am completely confident that as time goes on I shall have no reason to regret my action . . . Let me remind honorable members that a South African, a man who was also a politician, was appointed Governor-General on the recommendation of a government with which Field Marshal Smuts was associated. Speaking later on the subject, Field Marshal Smuts declared that the appointment of a citizen of South Africa as Governor-General in no way weakened the ties linking that Dominion to the Mother Country. I maintain that the position is the same in Australia. Any Australian citizen of sufficient ability, reputation and integrity of character is entitled to occupy the position of Governor-General.

McKell, a one-time Sydney boilermaker, and assistant secretary of the Boilermakers' Union, assumed office on 11 March. Over the next six years he showed that Menzies's fears had been groundless.

Later in 1947 the Chifley Government proved beyond all possible doubt that it took the A.L.P. platform seriously. For twenty-eight years the platform had included 'nationalisation of banking'. The Banking Bill of 1945 had moved in that direction, but only part of the way. Now, with a zeal born of the banking Royal Commission and the Scullin Government's anguish, Chifley went the whole hog. As Haylen put it with his usual flair, Chifley 'took the holy ikon of Socialism off the walls of Caucus and marched with it into the House'.

Strangely enough, banking had not been one of the election issues. The private banks had seemed willing to put up with the restraints of Chifley's 1945 legislation, although the Chairman of the National Bank, Leslie McConnan, did seek legal opinion about it from the leading constitutional silk of the day, Garfield Barwick. Barwick thought that a High Court challenge could be mounted, particularly against Section 48 of the Banking Act, which prohibited private banks from accepting banking business for 'a State, or for any authority of a State, including a local government authority'. No action was taken on this advice until, in May 1947, the Treasury began warning local government authorities that from 1 August they would be obliged to conform to the requirements of Section 48, if necessary by transferring their banking business to the Commonwealth Bank. One of these authorities which happened to be a customer of the National Bank, Melbourne City Council, then briefed Barwick to challenge Section 48 and sections of the Banking Act which required private banks to maintain special deposits with the Commonwealth Bank. At the last minute, however, it was decided to confine the challenge to Section 48; the special deposit power was crucial to the Government's plan to ward off inflation by controlling liquidity, and some private banks feared that any challenge to that part of the Act might invite nationalisation.

As other governments had found often enough in the past, High Court deliberations were seldom a matter of weighing given circumstances to determine with Olympian exactitude whether or not they conformed to the precise requirements of the Constitution. For one thing, the Constitution was not always precise; for another, its learned interpreters were often more human than Olympian, and just as likely as governors-general to have their

own private political beliefs. Given the conservative nature of the legal profession, those political beliefs were more likely to be conservative than not.
In 1948, for example, the Chief Justice, Sir John Latham, received the following letter from R. G. Casey, who at that time was federal president of the Liberal party:

> My dear Jack, I enclose copy of roneographed letter that I have written to
> the President of each State Division of the Liberal Party—on the subject of
> canvassing on certain definite lines. I mentioned this to you this morning.
> With best wishes, I am, Yours sincerely, Dick.

This seems to show that the one-time leader of the parliamentary U.A.P.
had not left his political convictions in Parliament House when he ascended
to the High Court bench. The same could doubtless be said of McTiernan J.,
but his ounce of Labor loyalty was far outweighed by conservatism in the
scales of private High Court political belief. None of the five justices apart
from McTiernan and Latham had been politicians, but all of those except the
new justice, Sir William Webb (a former Chief Justice of Queensland, who
was on leave of absence from the High Court to serve as President of an
International Military Tribunal trying Japanese war criminals), had been
appointed by non-Labor governments. No one could say whether private
political belief ever found its way into judgment; but neither could anyone
deny that on occasions it probably did. Where the Constitution was
imprecise, judges tended to make their own doctrine. As Menzies, the victor
of the Engineers' case, once remarked: 'There is no question that what we
call constitutional law is only half law and half philosophy—political
philosophy'.

In its judgment on *City of Melbourne* v. *Commonwealth* (The State Banking
Case), the High Court reverted to the doctrine of intergovernmental immunity which it had developed in the early years of federation by implication
from American principles and the assumed requirements of the federal system. This doctrine, asserting that Commonwealth and States should not
interfere with one another's essential functions, had been overturned by
Isaacs J. and others in the Engineers' judgment of 1920. Now it was in vogue
again.

Five of the justices held Section 48 of the Banking Act invalid, with only
McTiernan J. dissenting. Latham C.J. held it to be invalid, not on any general
principle of reciprocal immunities, but on the simpler ground that a law discriminating against the States and their authorities, by telling them where to
bank, was not a law with respect to banking but a law with respect to State
functions, and thus beyond Commonwealth power. The other four justices
held that although Section 48 was in their opinion a law with respect to
banking, it was nonetheless invalid because it interfered with an essential
function of State government, the depositing of State revenues where the
State or its local authorities wished to deposit them.

This judgment, delivered on Thursday 13 August 1947, opened the way
for challenge to sections of the Banking Act dealing with special deposits. At
any rate that was Chifley's assessment, and he decided to take the initiative.
It may even have seemed to him that the High Court was daring him to go

the whole hog, for Justice Dixon's judgment read in part: 'If there be a monopoly in banking lawfully established by the Commonwealth, the State must put up with it'.

At a meeting of Cabinet on the following Saturday Chifley raised the question of nationalising the banks, discussed the electoral risks involved, and then went around the table asking his ministers for their views. After all had spoken in support of nationalisation, R. T. Pollard (Ballarat, V) asked with mock seriousness: 'What about you, Chif? Where do you stand?' 'With you and the boys Reggie', he replied. 'To the last ditch.'

And so the die was cast. When the Cabinet meeting ended, Chifley remarked drily to waiting journalists that his press secretary, Don Rodgers, might have something interesting for them. The press statement from the Prime Minister consisted of only forty-two words: 'Cabinet today authorised the Attorney-General and myself to prepare legislation for submission to the Federal Labor parliamentary party for the nationalisation of banking, other than State banks, with proper protection for the shareholders, depositors, borrowers and staffs of private banks'. One journalist was said to have been so affected by this announcement that he bit through the stem of his pipe.

By the time Caucus unanimously endorsed the proposed measure on 16 September, Dr Evatt was on his way to the United Nations, where he was to chair a committee on Palestine. From the ship he sent a cable to Chifley saying that if the High Court overturned nationalisation he was confident of a successful appeal to the Privy Council. On 15 October Chifley introduced the Banking Bill, the purpose of which was 'to empower the Commonwealth Bank to take over the banking business at present conducted in Australia by private banks'. The business, assets and shares of private banks, valued at about £100 million, would be acquired voluntarily or compulsorily, and compensation would be paid for all property or shares compulsorily acquired. State banks and savings banks would not be affected, and private bank officers would be guaranteed continuance of employment, salaries and conditions. At that time the number of private banks had been reduced by amalgamation to nine, and according to Chifley they had let the country down.

> The Labour party [he said in his second reading speech] has maintained for many years that, since the influence of money is so great, the entire monetary and banking system should be controlled by public authorities responsible through the Government and Parliament to the nation. On this principle the Labour party has held further that since private banks are conducted primarily for profit and therefore follow policies which in important respects run counter to the public interest, their business should be transferred to public ownership.
>
> For this view the strongest reasons can be stated. In the absence of control, private banks can expand or contract the volume of their lending and so vary within wide limits the supply of money available to the public . . . Whatever regard they may claim to pay to the wider concerns of the nation, their policies are dictated in the last resort by the desire to make profits and to secure the value of their own assets . . .
>
> Time and again the policies of the private banks have run counter to

national needs for steady growth and high levels of employment. To go some years back it is correct to say that the banks fed the boom and promoted unsound development in the 'twenties. When the depression came the banks as a whole restricted new lending and called in advances . . . The effect of this was to accentuate the contraction of business and the unemployment of those years. They helped but little in recovery during the 'thirties, waiting rather for improvement to come from other sources instead of taking the initiative and helping to promote recovery. They followed these courses because it seemed best and safest from the standpoint of their own interests.

Labour policy on banking has envisaged that, together with the elimination of private banking, the Commonwealth Bank would be strengthened to give it adequate control of monetary and credit conditions within Australia and its services would be extended to meet the needs of all sections of the people.

Eight days later Menzies delivered a powerful rejoinder, defending the private banks and also addressing the wider issue of free enterprise versus state control. 'I rise to speak tonight with a heavy sense of responsibility', he said.

It is my duty, and, I do not mind saying, my pride, to open the debate against the most far-reaching, revolutionary, unwarranted and un-Australian measure introduced in the history of this Parliament. Beyond question, the Banking Bill is the most important measure of a domestic kind ever to come before us, or before our predecessors, in this House . . . It will wantonly destroy the system of trading banking which has been intimately associated with the whole of the economic development of Australian business and production. It will create in the hands of the ruling political party a financial monopoly, with unchecked power to grant or withhold banking facilities or bank accommodation in the case of every individual citizen . . .

This bill goes far beyond banking . . . This bill will be a tremendous step towards the servile State, because it will set aside normal liberty of choice, and that is what competition means, and will forward the idea of the special supremacy of government. That is the antithesis of democracy . . .

Let nobody suppose that these aspiring dictators will rest content with the destruction of the banks. That is merely the first giant stride towards complete socialization, which is to come partly by the ruthless exercise of such powers as the Commonwealth possesses and partly by close collaboration with socialist governments in the States, producing interlocking legislation and the establishment of government trading corporations with monopolistic powers . . .

This debate, we passionately believe, begins a second battle for Australia, a battle in which victory will go to those who are not only brave, but alert and vigilant. As the great John Milton said, in his essay on *The Second Defence of the People of England*—'Unless that liberty, which is such a kind as arms can neither procure nor take away . . . shall have taken deep root in your minds and hearts, there will not long be wanting one who will snatch from you by treachery what you have acquired by arms.

The second battle for Australia had been joined not only in Parliament House, where the result was a foregone conclusion, but thoughout the Commonwealth at large, where the numbers were larger, and less predictable.

The private banks briefed counsel, under Barwick's leadership, to prepare for a legal challenge as soon as the Bill became law. Ninety-two petitions against the proposal were presented to the House, and four to the Senate. Newspapers were unanimously and vociferously opposed to the Bill, and their pages bulged with anti-nationalisation advertisements inserted by the banks, chambers of commerce and manufactures, the Institute of Public Affairs, and the United Bank Officers' Association. Hundreds of bank officers were seconded from their usual jobs to campaign against the Bill while it was going through parliament, and the Bank of New South Wales stationed a man in the public gallery night and day during the 17-day debate to report progress in hourly telephone calls to Sydney. The Opposition sought a referendum on bank nationalisation; but the Government, ignoring the precedent of the conscription referendums, maintained that there was no constitutional basis for a referendum on any subject other than alteration of the Constitution itself. The next best thing to a referendum was a straw poll, and this was provided in Victoria by the conservative Legislative Council, which brought about an election by withholding supply. Although Victoria's Labor Government was in no way responsible for the Banking Bill, bank nationalisation was very much at issue during the campaign, and on 8 November the Government was routed.

All but three members of the House of Representatives and six senators spoke during the debates. The only notable absentees were Scullin and Dr Evatt. Scullin's health had failed, and he had already announced that he would be resigning his seat before the next election. Evatt was still in New York.

One of the most zealous opponents of the Bill was Sir Earle Page, who was reported to have said in his electorate that before the issue was settled blood would flow more freely in Australia than in the partition riots then raging in India. In parliament the Right Honourable Member for Cowper chose his words more carefully, but was still definitely up in arms. 'I do not know what the position is in the cities', said Page,

> but I am acquainted with the feeling in the country. There, people of all shades of political opinion, not merely those who support the Australian Country party or the Liberal party, but also those who support the Labour party, are up in arms, and feel outraged and disturbed. They have given notice, and we endorse it, that the Communists will not be allowed to put a thing like this across. We shall fight this communist ramp against individual freedom by every means in our power—political, legal, constitutional and, if need be, physical. The people in the country are descended from British ancestors who for a thousand years fought along those lines.

'Physical'? If the word meant what the Opposition took it to mean, this was probably the first time a member of federal parliament, and a former Prime Minister at that, had advocated violence on the floor of the House. The Minister for Commerce and Agriculture, Reg Pollard, linked this to a comment made in his own electorate by Menzies, to the effect that a letter which Pollard had written to a bank manager in Ballarat, criticising the private banks' treatment of their employees, 'would justify assault and battery by the man who received it'. He went on to say that after Menzies's speech a Ballarat bank officer had been beaten up by three men while on his way home. 'Does the Leader of the Opposition not notice a connection between his advocacy of violence and that happening?' he asked.

> These are the things that are going on in the community. Had the statements [by Menzies and Page] been made by any member of the Labor party, the press of Australia would have carried black headlines proclaiming a trend towards communism or revolutionary socialism, but no such headings were used in connection with these statements.

For all the passions that were inflamed by the banking issue, blood was not really about to stain the wattle of Ballarat or Cowper. Sir Earle's volatility had to be taken into account, and one Government speaker, Les Haylen, adopted just the right tone to bring him down to earth:

> the right honorable member for Cowper . . . boiled the British blood in our ears when he spoke of bloodshed in this country . . . [He] comports himself in this House as a roaring lion, but behaves outside it as a most amiable and likeable fellow. He is a split personality—Dr. Page and Mr. Rage. He jogs merrily up and down the country with his colleagues, the honorable members for New England (Mr. Abbott) and Richmond (Mr. Anthony), and they have become known as the "Three Black Crows". Those "Three Black Crows" of the north of New South Wales are really a political farce. None of them has, in the whole course of the time he has spent in the north of New South Wales, seen anything but smiling fields and flowing rivers, nor mingled with anyone but successful pastoralists, dairy farmers and banana-growers. Yet, they are the greatest calamity howlers in this House. The wheel is always broken in New England, and it is never going to rain any more in Richmond. They bring a melancholy story from a smiling and fertile land, the blight is upon Cowper, and the worm is in the rose.

The House agreed to the Senate's amendments to the Banking Bill at about 10 p.m. on 26 November, and when the House rose for the night, with members of both parties milling around the parliamentary table, the Liberal Member for Flinders, Rupert Ryan, said to Haylen: 'You are a Communist bastard'. Ryan, a brother-in-law of R. G. Casey, was known as the 'Ancient Briton' for the imperial loyalty that distinguished most of his speeches. Later, in the parliamentary bar, he apologised to Haylen for the way he had expressed himself in the heat of the moment.

The Governor-General, McKell, gave assent to the Bill next afternoon, and on the following day the banks obtained an injunction restraining the Government from taking action under the new Act until the High Court heard an appeal against it. The case began in Melbourne on 8 February 1948, with Dr Evatt leading for the Commonwealth, and Barwick for the banks.

Evatt, still holding two portfolios, and now President-elect for the coming session of the United Nations General Assembly, was not the uniquely equipped defender that he imagined himself to be. Brilliant though he was, he had not argued before a court for seventeen years, and his former brethren on the High Court bench remembered him without affection—some of them, indeed, with distinct animosity. As if to put even more weight in his saddle, Chifley's learned friend objected at the first day's hearing that Mr Justice Starke's wife owned shares in the National Bank, and that Mr Justice Williams held shares jointly with his sister in two other banks. If Evatt expected either of them to stand down he was disappointed, for the Chief Justice ordered the case to proceed.

The hearing was the longest in the High Court's history, running in Melbourne and Sydney until 15 April. The private banks had been joined in their challenge by three States, the latter arguing that nationalisation infringed the doctrine of intergovernmental immunity just as much as the invalid Section 48 of the 1945 Banking Act had done. That argument was quickly rejected, however, on the ground that bank nationalisation was not a *direct* interference with State governmental functions. Thus the real battle was joined by Barwick and Evatt, the main point at issue between them being Section 46 of the new Act, which prohibited private banks from carrying on banking business in Australia and provided a penalty of £10 000 for each day of contravention.

Barwick argued that this infringed the guarantee of free trade, commerce and intercourse among the States provided by Section 92 of the Constitution. 'Section 92 is infringed', he said,

> whenever an individual or a corporation is engaged in interstate trade, commerce or intercourse and, either by direct prohibition, or by acquisition with the object . . . of affecting such a prohibition, the carrying on of such a business by him is forbidden. It is the individual's freedom to . . . conduct his business across State lines that is protected or guaranteed by Section 92.

Evatt, who spoke for eighteen days compared with only seven by Barwick, argued that the banking power in Section 51 of the Constitution was wide enough for prohibition of private banking (a proposition which Barwick had been at pains to demolish), and contradicted his opponent's interpretation of Section 92. The purpose of that section, said Evatt, was not to guarantee the interstate rights of every individual or corporation, but to see that trade and commerce themselves remained free; nationalisation would not impair the activity of banking, only the right of private banks to take part in that activity.

The Court spent four months preparing judgment, and when it was delivered, on 11 August, there was champagne for everyone at the Bankers' Club. Four of the six justices held a large part of the Act invalid, with Latham C.J. and McTiernan J. dissenting. There were several factors in the majority judgment, but only one that parliament could not have overcome by amending the Act. That was the majority's agreement with Barwick that Section 46 of the Act infringed Section 92 of the Constitution, and this alone was enough to thwart nationalisation. Latham's dissent, a salutary reminder that legal judgment need not always correspond with political belief, was based mainly on the view, held also by McTiernan, that banking was not 'trade and commerce', and that consequently the Act did not infringe Section 92.

Casey cabled the news to Menzies, who was visiting London, and fol-

Aloft and Alow
cartoon by Heth in the Bulletin, 3 September 1947

lowed that up with a letter saying: 'Like cool waters to a thirsty soul is good news from a far country'. Dr Evatt was naturally very disappointed, but according to Chifley he had expected the going to be hard and the most he had hoped for was a photo-finish. But he was still confident of ultimate success, and two days after the judgment Cabinet decided to go against Labor instinct and take the case to London. The Judicial Committee of the Privy Council granted the Commonwealth leave to appeal on the issue of the validity of Section 46 of the Act. Such an appeal was apparently possible without a certificate from the High Court, because the issue did not involve an *inter se* (between themselves) question of the type defined in Section 74 of the Constitution—a question as to 'the limits *inter se* of the Constitutional powers of the Commonwealth and those of any State'. But that appearance, as it turned out, was deceptive.

The case proper began on 14 March 1949 in the small Judicial Chamber of the Privy Council, Downing Street, before seven Lords of Appeal. Again the battle was between Evatt and Barwick, supported by twelve other King's Counsel. The hearing spread over thirty-six sitting days, with Evatt speaking first for fourteen days, then crossing the Atlantic to preside over the General Assembly, and returning to London in May for six more days in reply. Barwick spoke for only six days altogether. Two of their lordships died during the hearing, but the other five lasted the distance. Their judgment, delivered without reasons on 26 July, dismissed the appeal. When reasons were released three months later it became clear that their lordships had expressed an opinion on Section 46 rather than delivered judgment on it; but the effect was the same. They took the view that the Privy Council had no jurisdiction to hear the matter without a certificate from the High Court because, although the matter itself was not *inter se*, it could not be dealt with in isolation from other matters which did involve *inter se* questions.

Nevertheless, their lordships thought it right to state their views upon the sole ground of appeal, and those views accorded with Barwick's argument for individual freedom. This would be the answer if the Commonwealth cared to obtain a certificate from the High Court and argue the matter all over again in Downing Street; and if the High Court declined to issue such a certificate, that would end the matter. Either way, bank nationalisation was a dead letter. Dr Evatt may have cut a brilliant figure in New York, but he had not been much of a legal counsel.

Wrath

Not surprisingly, relations between the Commonwealth's legislature and judiciary were rather strained during the late 1940s. One Sunday afternoon, after a High Court decision, the Speaker of the House of Representatives got up in the Sydney Domain and said that 'the government and the people had been knocked back by seven incompetent septuagenarians'. The justices, whose average age was then only sixty-six, ignored Rosevear's defamation; but one of them, Sir Owen Dixon, later gave tit for tat to federal politicians generally. Addressing the English-Speaking Union in March 1949, he said that with one exception the 'Canberra orchestra' could be divided into two categories—'those who played the fool, and those who blew their own trumpets'. The exception was R. G. Menzies, who had never belonged to either category.

Certainly some members of the eighteenth parliament had been playing the fool, or otherwise laying themselves open to censure. In 1947 Senator Stan Amour, one of the four As from New South Wales, became involved in a fracas on board an airliner at San Francisco while on his way back to Australia from an International Labour Organisation conference at Geneva. According to a version recounted in the House by one of the three black crows, J. P. Abbott, who had it from an eyewitness, Senator Amour became drunk at the airport, refused to let another passenger sit beside him, and kicked him on the leg. When the captain remonstrated with him, the Senator swung a haymaker, and had to be removed from the aircraft by police. Senator Amour's own version differed substantially in detail. He told the Senate that without thinking he had struck a match to light a cigarette, something which was not permitted during take-off, and that another passenger had become excited and told him to put the match out. 'I said, "Do not get excited old man", and he charged at me. I put my arm up, and pushed him back, as any other Australian would do.' The captain ordered him to leave, and he complied without intervention by the police.

In September 1948 the Labor Member for Watson, Max Falstein, was fined £320 for understating the value of some wrist watches he had imported into Australia. He appealed unsuccessfully against this conviction, and was subsequently expelled from the A.L.P. This was not the first time Falstein had been in trouble. During the war he had joined the R.A.A.F. while still a member of parliament, and retained his seat despite having been court-martialled for a minor offence. Falstein had been a dutiful member since the war, but as an Independent he had no chance of holding his seat, and was defeated at the next election.

One other contretemps of this parliament concerned the Minister for Territories. Ward—that 'searching hungry political puma', as his friend Haylen once described him—was not used to being hunted himself, but he proved to be an elusive quarry. In 1947 the Opposition moved unsuccessfully for the appointment of a joint select committee to inquire into administration of the territory of New Guinea, which was Ward's ministerial responsibility. There was ample ground for criticism, even suspicion of corrupt practice; and in December 1947 the Minister himself initiated criminal proceedings against several people, including his former campaign director, the ex-member for Cook, Jock Garden. During subsequent court proceedings, in which Garden was sentenced to three years' imprisonment for fraud over the handling of timber leases in New Guinea, allegations were made that Ward had also been involved. Being cautious as well as searching and hungry, the Minister had kept every cheque book he had used since entering parliament, and these he made available to a Royal Commission appointed at his own request. The Royal Commission's report, tabled on 24 June 1949, cleared him of all suspicion. When the House adjourned, Menzies came around behind the Speaker's Chair and said to Ward: 'Congratulations, old man. We disagree on many things, but I never thought your integrity was in question'.

Ward, who must have been taken aback by such an unexpected testimonial, replied: 'Thank you very much'.

Egregious though the Banking Act may have been, it was only one of a flock of measures passed by the eighteenth parliament, most of which, unlike the Banking Act, escaped judicial culling. The Wheat Industry Stabilisation Act (1948) repealed an earlier and ineffectual measure, and established a stabilisation scheme that was ratified by wheat growers. Reasonably enough the Government expected some electoral thanks from the marginal wheat seats, but when the time came it was sadly disappointed in that regard.

The Snowy Mountains Hydro-Electric Power Act (1949) established a Snowy Mountains Authority, consisting of a single Commonwealth commissioner, to organise the harnessing of hydro-electric power in the Australian Alps. The legal basis for this ambitious undertaking was the defence power of the Constitution (it could be argued that additional electric power would be required in time of war) and the Seat of Government Acceptance Act, which permitted the Commonwealth to use Snowy water for the production of power for the Australian Capital Territory. No one could deny the value of such a project, but the Opposition argued for State representation on the Authority. 'Why should the Commonwealth', asked Menzies,

> knowing perfectly well . . . that its demands upon the current that is generated will be very small compared with the demands for ordinary civil purposes in New South Wales and Victoria, insist upon keeping those States out of the project . . . Is the Commonwealth to co-operate in a spirit of goodwill with the States on matters that require joint action . . . or is the Commonwealth to say: 'We are not going to bother about the States. We will label this project "Defence", or we will even label it "Supplying something to the Australian Capital Territory," and then we will smash our way through. Who is going to prevent us? Then, when we have done the work it will be ours, and you can come along like anybody else and be our customers".

Sir Earle Page moved an amendment that the Commissioner be assisted by three Associate Commissioners, appointed by New South Wales, Victoria and South Australia; but it had no chance of being accepted.

The Whaling Industry Act (1949) established an Australian Whaling Commission to conduct whaling operations; the Qantas Empire Airways Act of 1948 completed the Commonwealth purchase of Australia's overseas airline; three amending Commonwealth Conciliation and Arbitration Bills (one of which incorporated the only amendment moved successfully by the Opposition during this parliament added to the principal Act many of the principles established by National Security Regulations during the war; and the Shipping Act (1949) established a Government line for the first time since the Bruce–Page Government had sold off Hughes's 1916 creation. There was more than a hint of State ownership or control in most of these measures, and the Opposition sounded the anti-socialist alarm at every opportunity.

This was very much the case with the Pharmaceutical Benefits Act (1949), a measure intended to establish a free medicine scheme similar in most respects to that which had been held invalid by the High Court four years earlier. Dr Evatt was confident that the 1946 social services referendum had removed all obstacles, but in fact it had not. In 1949 the Government's second try for a free medicine scheme was ruled invalid by the High Court in the British Medical Association case. By a majority of four to two, the Court held that compulsory use of Commonwealth prescription forms amounted to the 'civil conscription' which Menzies had prevailed upon Evatt to proscribe in his social services referendum Bill, which added Section 51 (xxiiiA) to the Constitution.

The Parliamentary Allowances Act (1947) increased from £1000 to £1500 per annum the basic member's salary, which, apart from the Depression cut and its subsequent restoration, had been unchanged for twenty-seven years. In the meantime, the average weekly male wage had increased by 53 per cent, from £4 10s to £6 18s. Lang moved unsuccessfully that the increase be postponed until the Government's deflationary wage-pegging regulations were repealed; and Menzies, with equal lack of success, moved that the Bill be withdrawn and redrafted after the whole question of allowances had been investigated by an all-party committee of both houses. Both must have realised that the measure would almost certainly be passed without amendment, and so it was.

Two other measures should be mentioned in this context. The Parliamentary Retiring Allowances Act (1948) established a contributory system of retirement allowances for members, and benefits for their dependants in the case of death while in office or while receiving the retirement allowance. A second Parliamentary Allowances Act (1947) also authorised a special allowance for the leaders of parties of ten or more members—the intended beneficiary being the leader of the Country Party, Fadden, who, unlike the Prime Minister and the Leader of the Opposition, had not previously received any more than his member's allowance.

Another group of measures affected in various ways the procedure by which parliament would be elected in future, starting with the next general election, before the end of 1949. An amending Commonwealth Electoral Act (1949) extended the federal vote to Aborigines who were enfranchised in their State of residence, or had served in the armed forces. To parliament's collective shame, this was the first change of any kind to the very limited vote provided for Aborigines in the Franchise Act of 1902. That measure had merely confirmed the franchise exercised by a few Aborigines under Section 41 of the Constitution, which guaranteed the federal vote to adults already entitled to vote at elections for the lower house of any State parliament; but Aborigines who subsequently qualified for a State vote were not enfranchised federally. The new Act belatedly rectified that anomaly, but said nothing about Aborigines who might qualify for a State vote in future. It also acknowledged that Aborigines who had fought for the Commonwealth should also be able to vote for its parliament, something that had not required acknowledgement after World War I, since Aborigines were not officially supposed to have been in the first A.I.F.

During the first reading debate Harold Holt confessed to 'a feeling of uneasiness at the way in which we, as a people, have treated the aborigines who are the true natives of the Australian continent'. Arthur Calwell said that parliament was 'now admitting some of [its] obligations to the descendants of Neanderthal man, whether he be full-blood, half-caste or three-quarter-caste'. When the Bill reached the upper chamber, Senator Frederick Katz (Lab, V) told his colleagues that 'the Australian aboriginal, given equal educational opportunities, can hold his own with the white man in almost every walk of life, including even the arts'.

The Australian Capital Territory Representation Act (1949) provided for the A.C.T.'s representation in the House of Representatives on the same restricted basis as the Northern Territory—that is by one member entitled to vote only on motions to disallow A.C.T. ordinances. Two other measures, the Representation Act and Commonwealth Electoral Act of 1948, made more substantial changes.

So far, the only major changes to the electoral structure of parliament had been the adoption of preferential voting for both chambers, starting at the 1919 general election. Now, for reasons to be explained, parliament would soon be greatly enlarged, and the method of electing senators would be changed from preferential voting to proportional representation. Under the Constitution, parliament could increase or diminish the number of members in each house, but in doing so it had to ensure that the number of representatives remained, as nearly as practicable, twice the number of the senators. More representatives would mean more electorates, and consequently electorates containing fewer voters. There was a strong case for reducing the number of voters per electorate, because that figure had more than doubled since the first general election. The national population had risen from 3 765 339 to 7 580 820, and the average number of voters per electorate from 25 247 to 64 599. But the number of representatives could be increased only by proportionately increasing the number of senators at the same time.

In May 1947, on a motion by George Lawson, Caucus recommended to Cabinet that steps be taken to increase the membership of parliament before the next redistribution of electorates. A Cabinet sub-committee for this purpose consisted of the Minister for the Interior, Victor Johnson (Kalgoorlie, W); the Minister for Health and Social Services, Senator N. E. McKenna (T); and the Minister for Information and Immigration, Arthur Calwell. Calwell was the dominant member; he was mainly responsible for the Committee's recommendations, and it was he who sold them to Caucus. First, the number of senators for each State was to be increased from six to ten, enlarging the Senate from thirty-six to sixty; the number of Representatives would be increased from seventy-four to 121, not counting the two territorial members; and the Senate would be elected by proportional representation.

Explaining these proposals in his second reading speeches on 16 April 1948, the Attorney-General justified enlargement solely on grounds that local-member work had become too onerous. As for the method of electing senators from their State-wide electorates, Dr Evatt said that proportional representation, a system used in Eire and Tasmania, was fairer than the preferential block majority system currently in use, and more likely to enhance the status of the Senate. The preferential system had the advantage of usually producing a clear-cut majority; but unless there was a nearly equal and opposite swing at successive elections, the majority could be inordinately large and so unrepresentative of the national electorate as to make a mockery of serious debate. Since 1946, for example, three non-Labor senators had been opposing a Government majority of thirty-three.

Under proportional representation, voters would continue to mark their ballot papers preferentially, but votes would be counted by a complicated quota system which reflected electoral feeling more accurately than preferential voting. Gross imbalance would be avoided, it was claimed, but there was also the possibility of another extreme: a chamber too evenly divided could well become deadlocked.

Although both proposals had much to commend them, the Opposition reasonably enough asked why they were being introduced at this particular time. The question was rhetorical, of course, for Menzies knew the answer. 'The thing "which sticks out a mile"', he said,

> is that the scheme now before us has been devised for a particular purpose at a particular time in the history of this Parliament. This scheme has been devised to deliver individual Labour members of this House from the wrath to come. It is also designed to secure to the Australian Labour Party, irrespective of the popular will as it will express itself at the general elections next year, power to resist and obstruct its opponents, and to accomplish everything short of a double dissolution in the Senate until 1953.

This was not far from the mark. Calwell, in lobbying for his proposals, had assured M.H.R.s that enlargement would guarantee their own tenure because they could count on keeping the 'safe' part of their divided electorates at preselections after the next redistribution. He also told the eighteen senators due to retire in 1949 that proportional representation would have the effect of guaranteeing their re-election so long as they retained party preselection. The package was attractive, and in spite of Cassandra-like predictions by Rosevear that it was a 'gold brick scheme' which would eventually damage the parliamentary Labor Party, Caucus adopted it and parliament passed it.

No electorate was left unchanged, some being parcelled out to help make as many as five, six and even seven new divisions. The choosing of new names provided an opportunity to honour a few distinguished former members (Curtin, Fisher, Kingston, Lyne, Ryan, Higgins and Isaacs); a few earlier historical figures, mainly explorers (Blaxland, Lawson, Burke, Wills, Cunningham, Leichhardt, Mitchell, Sturt, Shortland, Phillip and Banks); and, not before time, an Aboriginal (Bennelong). Deakin had already been added to this roll in 1936.

The Commissioners' proposals had an easy passage through parliament, and most sitting members stepped adroitly into the safest parts of their old seats. One who missed out was Fred Daly, the Labor Member for Martin. His seat was strengthened, from Labor's point of view, by the addition of Balmain and Rozelle, and the sitting Labor Member for West Sydney (to which those suburbs had previously belonged), W. P. O'Connor, decided to contest preselection for Martin because he lived in Rozelle. Chifley would not hear of such a squabble between sitting colleagues, and told Daly that he would have to contest one of the new Sydney divisions. Daly set his cap at Grayndler, a working-class division running from Newtown to Marrickville, and won that preselection.

In readiness for the seventy-one new members, a third storey was built on each of the rear wings which had been added to Parliament House in 1943. The lower ground and main floor were also extended, and additional accommodation for the press was provided on the upper floor adjacent to the chambers. This was done in 1948 and 1949 at a cost of £65 000.

The confidence with which Menzies had spoken of 'the wrath to come' was inspired mainly by the High Court's invalidation of the 1945 Banking Act, the Government's consequent attempt to nationalise the private banks, and the intense public opposition to that attempt. The High Court had yet to deliver judgment in the bank nationalisation case, but the banks' campaign against the nationalisation Bill had kept the issue of free enterprise versus state control well and truly alive. It also assured the Liberal Party of ample funding from the banks and other business sources.

Further encouragement lay in store for the free enterprise crusaders, and not only from the High Court and Privy Council judgments on bank nationalisation. First, the Government failed to secure permanent power to control rents and prices. Uncertain as to how much longer the contracting defence power would allow continuation of the price control which it regarded as an essential weapon against inflation, and failing to obtain reference of a substitute power from the States, the Commonwealth Government brought down a Bill to alter the Constitution by empowering parliament to legislate on prices and rents. The referendum Bill was badly timed, for it came on the heels of the acrimonious debate on bank nationalisation. It passed all parliamentary stages, of course; but the Opposition raised such an uproar in and out of parliament, claiming that the proposed power would be used to destroy free enterprise, that the referendum, held in May 1948, was defeated in all States.

Two other issues, which came to a head during the election year of 1949, were Communism and petrol rationing. By this time Australia was well and truly embroiled in the widest 'second battle' of all, the cold war between the world's two super-powers. Chifley's Government had already taken some anti-Communist measures. The Approved Defence Projects Protection Act tightened security against Communist trade union officials at such defence centres as Woomera; an amending Conciliation and Arbitration Act was intended to help anti-Communist majorities in trade unions to vote Communist officials out of office; in March 1949 the Australian Security Intelligence Organisation was established by executive action, without reference to parliament; and the Government successfully prosecuted two leading members of the Australian Communist Party for sedition.

One of these officials was the party's general secretary, L. L. Sharkey. His offence was to have said, in answering a question put to him by a journalist: 'If Soviet forces in pursuit of aggressors entered Australia, Australian workers would welcome Soviet forces pursuing aggressors as the workers welcomed them throughout Europe when the Red troops liberated the people from the power of the Nazis'. Sharkey was sentenced to three years' gaol, but the term was later reduced to eighteen months.

Such actions were not sufficient, however, to satisfy the zealots of the Opposition, particularly those in the Country Party. Fadden had stated his party's position on Communism as early as 1946, when he said in his election policy speech: 'The Country Party regards the Australian Communist in the same category as a venomous snake—to be killed before it kills. Therefore, it stands foursquare for declaring the Communist Party an illegal organisation'. The parliamentary Liberal Party, after first taking the view that banning would merely drive Communists underground or make martyrs of them, decided in March 1948 that the Australian Communist Party, and all organisations controlled by it except trade unions, should be banned.

Chifley resisted pressure to follow suit, arguing that the Communist Party should be opposed politically, in particular by changing the social conditions in which it was able to attract support. This exposed Chifley to charges of weakness over Communism and security, despite a certain amount of evidence to the contrary. The Government was criticised for failure to prevent embargoes on Dutch shipping in Australian ports, imposed by the Communist-controlled Waterside Workers' Federation at the request of Indonesian trade unions. It was also accused by Fadden of being regarded as a security risk by the United States.

During a Budget debate in October 1948, while Menzies was in London, Fadden quoted from what seemed to be a confidential government record of statements made by Chifley to a meeting of British Cabinet earlier in the year, and by Dedman to the executive committee of the C.S.I.R.O. Both statements were to the effect that the United States was wary of sharing certain types of defence information with its Australian ally. The Opposition had made similar claims before, and now Fadden apparently had the proof. Chifley responded by sending two detective inspectors of the Commonwealth Investigation Service (the organisation soon to be replaced by A.S.I.O.), to question Fadden in his parliamentary office about the provenance of his confidential documents, which it was reasonable to assume had been either stolen, illegally copied or forged.

When Fadden refused to answer questions unless members of the Press Gallery were present, the security men withdrew. At the next sitting of parliament, on 7 October, Fadden raised the attempted interrogation as a matter of privilege. 'I make it plain to the Prime Minister', he said,

> and to the community in general that, no matter what the consequences may be, I shall not be interrogated by any secret gestapo of this Government. Long ago, as far back as the seventeenth century, when our democratic institutions were being cradled, it was provided by the 9th Article of the Bill of Rights that any Prime Minister, regardless of his political persuasion, should, if he were at all democratic, uphold the principle—and I quote the exact words of the article—"That the freedom of speech and debates of proceedings in Parliament should not be impeached in any court, or place, out of Parliament." I take my stand upon that principle.

The deep organ tones of the Convention Parliament of William and Mary

Dr H. V. Evatt

J. S. Rosevear, Speaker of the House of Representatives (1943–1950)

E. J. Ward

Arthur Calwell

Sir William McKell, former Labor Premier of New South Wales and twelfth Governor-General of Australia

Sir John Latham, Chief Justice of the High Court from 1935 to 1952, shown here when he was Leader of the Opposition, c. 1930

Senator Dorothy Tangney, one of the first two women elected to parliament, in 1943

Les Haylen electioneering in Campsie, New South Wales, 1946

came incongruously from the Leader of the Australian Country Party, but Artie Fadden was pulling out every stop nonetheless. He moved that it was a breach of privilege that security police should have sought to interrogate him, at the instigation of the Prime Minister and Government, in his official room 'in respect of matters occurring in, and arising out of, the discharge of his public duties in this national Parliament'. As the motion was defeated, the basic question of whether police were entitled to question a member about one of his speeches in parliament remained unanswered.

At its most extreme, the Opposition's tactical use of anti-Communism against the Government included attempts of the most melodramatic kind to link Labor with the Communist Party, and socialisation with Communism. Sir Earle Page, for example, successfully moved the adjournment for discussion of a definite matter of urgent public importance, namely 'the extent to which the Commonwealth Literary Fund [was] being used to subsidise ·Communists, and former Communists in the production of Australian literature'. It mattered not to Sir Earle that expenditure on the Fund, established by the Deakin Government in 1908, was so miserly (it had awarded twenty-nine fellowships and published twenty-three books since 1908) that even if every penny had gone to help Communists past or present the ideological content of Australian literature would not have been greatly affected. As it was, Sir Earle had only one allegation to make—that the Commonwealth Literary Fund had awarded one of its fellowships to an alleged publicist for the Communist Party, J. N. Rawling, to write a biography of Charles Harpur, whose poetry the Right Honourable Member for Cowper admired. The short answer, provided smugly by Dr Evatt, was that Rawling had left the Communist Party in 1940 and had actively opposed it ever since.

Even more bizarre, but also more damaging to the Government, was a series of radio broadcasts by the Liberal Party, entitled 'John Henry Austral'. Written and produced by the Goldberg Advertising Agency in Sydney, these featured tendentious dramatisations of purported historical events, often with Russian accents and snatches of 'The Red Flag'. In the finale of one episode entitled 'Mission *from* Moscow', in which Comrade Kolarof, general secretary of the Communist International, had been discussing the possibility of '[bringing] together all the militant elements within and without the Australian Labor Party under the banner of the Communist Party', the commonsensical voice of John Henry Austral said:

> Communism has fastened itself on Australian Labor as a tick fastens itself to the skin of a dog. Now I am no politician. I speak under the present auspices tonight only because I see in rapid trend towards complete socialisation a dark and dangerous threat to the people and the future of this country. As I have shown you, sensational current events are but the fruit of years of Communist infiltration. It is for you to decide whether the men and the forms of government which have aided or tolerated such infiltration can be allowed, politically, to survive.

Certainly the Communist Party had gained much influence, amounting at times to ascendancy, in some of Australia's most important trade unions. Yet Labor had not been as apathetic as John Henry Austral would have his listeners believe. In 1945 the New South Wales branch of the A.L.P. formed 'industrial groups' to oppose Communist influence in the trade unions. The 'Groupers', as these right-wing activists were known, extended their activities to other States, particularly Victoria. Two-thirds of them were Roman Catholics, and of those about half were associated with 'The Movement', a clandestine organisation of Catholic laymen dedicated to opposing Communism. Led by B. A. Santamaria, a zealous young Catholic intellectual, and confidant of the ancient Archbishop of Melbourne, Dr Mannix—'The Movement' exerted strong influence on the A.L.P. Groups, which in turn held considerable power on some State A.L.P. executives. The Groupers were certainly effective, but they were also divisive. Indeed some Labor moderates wondered whether their vaccine might be more dangerous than the risk of Communist infection.

Although Chifley's Government at first left the industrial fight against Communism mainly to the Groups, it was now playing a vigorous part as well. By mid-1949 it was engaged in a decisive confrontation with the Communist Party's main industrial ally, the Miners' Federation. The High Court's rejection of bank nationalisation convinced the Communist Party that the holy ikon of socialism had been returned to the Caucus room for good. 'The rejection of bank nationalisation means that the Labor Party's economic policy is in ruins', wrote Sharkey, 'shattered by the dictatorship of the bourgeoisie, who have once more shown their power to defeat and destroy both reforms unpalatable to them and the Government that proposes such reforms'.

Disillusioned with A.L.P. reformism, the Communist Party went all out for hegemony of the working-class movement, no matter how much that might embarrass or damage Chifley's Government. The showdown was a seven-week-long strike on the coalfields of New South Wales, called by the Miners' Federation while the Coal Industry Tribunal still had a miners' log of claims before it. In spite of strong and ultimately successful Government action, this devastating strike caused widespread power shortages and unemployment during the winter of an election year. A National Emergency Coal Strike Act, which received assent on the third day of the strike, permitted the Commonwealth to freeze the funds of unions engaged in the strike, and prohibited federal unions from making or receiving any payments in support of the strikers. The New South Wales Labor Government assumed similar powers, and union officials convicted of concealing funds illegally were gaoled for contempt of court.

At the cost of bruising many a Labor conscience (not least that of the one-time striking engine driver who was now Prime Minister), the Government ordered troops to begin working open-cut mines on 1 August. Two weeks later mass meetings of the striking miners voted by a majority of three to one, against the recommendation of their leaders, to return to work. The Communist Party never recovered from this setback, but that did not invalidate Communism as an election issue.

Another issue of relevance to the free enterprise–state control battle was petrol rationing, an irritating vestige of those wartime controls to which, so the Opposition claimed, Chifley's Government was needlessly attached.

The Government, while intending to remove petrol rationing at the earliest opportunity, maintained that it could not do so yet without seriously depleting the sterling area's dollar reserves. In June 1949 the High Court ruled that the Commonwealth's defence power could no longer support petrol rationing. Although rationing was lifted forthwith the Government persuaded the States to refer powers necessary for its reimposition. Legislation for this purpose, the Liquid Fuel (Rationing) Bill, passed its final stage on the last sitting day of the eighteenth parliament, 27 October 1949. Victoria and South Australia passed their own rationing Acts, and shortly before the general election petrol rationing resumed in all States except Tasmania, whose upper house refused to pass the necessary Bill.

It was as if Chifley knew that the tide had turned, and could not be bothered swimming against it. Only five months earlier, before the Privy Council's decision on bank nationalisation, he had spoken of Labor's great objective: 'the light on the hill, which we aim to reach by working for the betterment of mankind'. But now, after three consecutive Labor terms, perhaps the light had dimmed. The Australian Public Opinion Polls showed that the percentage of respondents willing to vote for Labor had dropped from 51 per cent before the coal strike to 46 per cent afterwards.

In spite of warnings from Beasley and others that he could not expect to get away a second time with standing on his record, Chifley in his policy speech offered 'no glittering promises'. He invited electors to judge the Government 'on [its] record and on [its] ability to go on with the job of building Australia into the nation we all want it to be'. His only reference to banking was that the Government could not go beyond its constitutional powers to acquire the trading banks, and consequently would 'proceed with its policy of expanding the services of the Commonwealth Bank to provide an efficient and comprehensive system of banking'.

But nothing he said could possibly persuade his opponents to drop the issue of socialisation during the 74-day-long election campaign, the longest since 1910. On the second last sitting day of parliament, newspaper advertisements inserted by the Institute of Public Affairs declared that 'All Labor candidates are pledged to the socialisation of every undertaking—even the corner store in your suburb'. That morning, in answer to a Dorothy Dix question, Chifley did his best to damp down the issue. 'No Australian government', he said,

> regardless of its party political complexion, would have the power under the Constitution to do any of the things that the advertisement implies that a Labour government would do . . . If public utilities are not being used in the best interests of the people, or if they are being used to exploit the community, they should be socialized. However . . . even that statement must be qualified in so far as the Australian Government's power to introduce any form of socialization is extremely limited under the Constitution.

If anything, this merely served to strengthen the chorus of advertisements, pamphlets, door-knocks and campaign speeches asserting that Labor would press on towards full socialisation, if necessary by packing the High Court and abolishing appeal to the Privy Council. Menzies, in his joint Liberal–Country Party policy speech on 10 November, promised a constitutional amendment to prevent 'socialist legislation such as bank nationalisation' being passed without the people's approval at a referendum. He was in superbly orotund form, speaking almost twice as long as Chifley, with 'a fervour and intensity often previously lacking', to quote the grudging praise of the *Sydney Morning Herald*. Glittering promises abounded. A Liberal–Country Party Government would pay five shillings a week endowment for the first child of a family (excluded from endowment under the Curtin–Chifley Act); it would outlaw the Communist Party, or any new form into which that party changed itself; repeal the bank nationalisation Act; import enough petrol to remove rationing once and for all; introduce peacetime military training; and defeat inflation, or, as the campaign slogan said, 'Put Value Back in the Pound'.

'The best years of my life have been given to what I deeply believe is a struggle for freedom', said Menzies in a masterly peroration to the speech. 'That struggle has reached its climax. Victory is in front of us. We can fail to achieve it only by indolence, or indifference, or a failure to realise that on December 10 we will be deciding the future of our country. It is in your hands, Australia!'

Fadden and his party co-operated fully with the Liberals, contributing to the campaign their own particularly ardent brand of anti-socialism. 'If you choose the Labor Party', said Fadden, 'then your ballot paper will truly be your last will and testament, disposing in your own lifetime of your liberties and your property and condemning your children and your children's children to the living death of socialist regimentation'. In this context Fadden used to speak about 'The Seven Dwarfs', by which he meant certain of the Prime Minister's senior public service advisers (for example, Dr H. C. Coombs, former Director-General of the Department of Postwar Reconstruction, and currently Governor of the Commonwealth Bank), all of whom happened to be men of short stature, sharp intellect and socialist or centralist persuasion.

The daily press linked Communism with socialism, and socialism with the A.L.P.—thus, as Chifley remarked, 'creating a fear complex in the minds of a percentage of the middle class vote'. Roman Catholic opinion had been divided on the issue of bank nationalisation, and was still divided on the wider issue of socialism. During the election campaign a pamphlet written by the associate editor of the *Catholic Weekly*, Brian Doyle, reminded voters that a statement on social justice by the Roman Catholic bishops of Australia had pronounced the A.L.P.'s socialist objective to have 'a Marxist basis repugnant to Christian social principles'.

One of the few weapons missing from the anti-Labor armoury was a bombshell of personal scandal, and in the last week of the campaign Jack Lang detonated that as well. In a national broadcast on 6 December he alleged that between 1930 and 1942 Chifley and his wife had lent a total of £15 000 on mortgage at interest rates of up to 9 per cent. The details came from records of the New South Wales Registrar-General.

Was the mortal enemy of private banking a usurer himself? The answer was no, but there was precious little time left to repair the damage done by 'Lang the Wrecker'. Speaking in Lang's electorate the following night, Chifley said that with one small exception the transactions referred to had involved money entrusted to him for investment; he had made no personal profit from them. Back in his own electorate on the last night of the campaign, he spoke with uncharacteristic bitterness:

> There is one matter I think I should refer to, and that is a Labor rat in this country. I dealt with him at Auburn last night. He is a Labor rat. I am not pursuing any further a Labor rat into the sewer.

It was hard to say what effect Lang's bombshell had on the outcome of the election, for so many other factors were also working to the same end. Chifley was safely returned (while Lang was routed by an A.L.P. candidate, E. J. Harrison), but four of his ministers and seven other colleagues were defeated. The result was in fact a landslide for the coalition—not as great a landslide as those of 1943, 1925 or 1917, but a landslide just the same. The Liberal Party won fifty-five seats and the Country Party won nineteen (the latter being about the same proportionately as in the smaller House), making a coalition strength of seventy-four in a House of 121, with a Labor opposition of forty-seven. Chifley's only consolation was the defeat of Lang and the other Labor Independent, Mrs Blackburn.

Calwell's promises of re-election had not saved the ministers Dedman, Lemmon, H. C. Barnard (Bass, T) and W. J. Scully (Gwydir, N) from the wrath predicted by Menzies. But in the Senate, proportional representation had lived up to its billing. All retiring Labor senators were re-elected. Labor won nineteen seats, and the coalition parties won twenty-three. Counting half the members of the old Senate who had not been due for re-election, this left Labor safely in control of the enlarged chamber, by thirty-four to twenty-six.

Chifley was mainly to blame for the outcome in the lower house. By his own reckoning the main causes of that débâcle had been petrol rationing and the 'fear complex' engendered in the middle class by the sudden apparition of the holy ikon. The reimposition of petrol rationing and the attempt to nationalise the banks had both been primarily his doing, and he had badly miscalculated the feeling of middle Australia, particularly in the latter case.

By the same token, credit for the coalition victory belonged largely to Menzies. He had judged the middle class correctly, and had brought it flocking to his banner. 'Dear Bob', wrote his ally since U.A.P. days, the Melbourne stockbroker Staniforth Ricketson, in a brief note of congratulation. 'How grand!' Another old U.A.P. associate—now Viscount Bruce of Melbourne, the first Australian peer since Lord Forrest—wrote more cautiously from the House of Lords. 'Notwithstanding the appalling job of work that lies ahead of you', said Lord Bruce,

> it must be a great satisfaction to have pulled off such a triumph . . . Now that I have seen the figures my comment to you would be that I think you have rather overdone it. To keep the Country Party lads and your own boys in order with as big a margin as you have got will be fairly difficult.

After almost half a century of federal existence, and eighteen individual parliaments in Melbourne and Canberra, the tide had turned with a vengeance, like a king tide, sweeping out of office one party laden with many honourable achievements and a few bad mistakes, and launching another party on what its founder fully expected to be a 'magnificent voyage'. Out went disillusionment and frustration; in came high hopes and good intentions. Yet campaign rhetoric was not always to be taken seriously. It remained to be seen how much of the outgoing Government's work the new one would attempt to undo, and just what that new Government would accomplish in its own right.

Part Three

Canberra 1950–1988

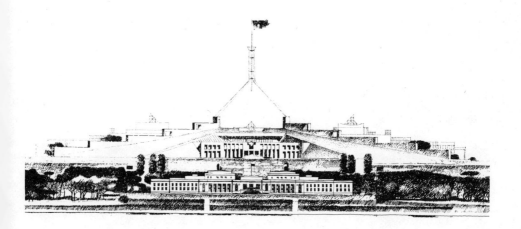

14

Lord Protector

It was generally agreed that the opening of the nineteenth parliament on Wednesday 22 February 1950 was Canberra's most splendid occasion since the Duke of York had officially opened the provisional Parliament House in 1927. But few members were able to make this comparison from their own experience. The first generation of Commonwealth parliamentarians had all but vanished, and even the second generation was now outnumbered, at least in the House of Representatives, by the host of new members swept into an enlarged parliament at the recent general election. Of the 123 M.H.R.s, no fewer than sixty-four were taking seats for the first time. Only four members (and no senators) had been there for the royal opening. They were Billy Hughes, in his eighty-eighth year, and representing yet another seat; Sir Earle Page; Josiah Francis, the Liberal Member for Moreton (Q); and a newly elected Independent, Dr Lewis Nott, who, although now the inaugural member for the Australian Capital Territory, had also represented Herbert (Q) as a Nationalist in the 1920s. The Clerks of the two chambers would also have remembered the earlier ceremony, for John Edwards had spent most of his working life in the Senate, and in 1927 Frank Green had been Clerk of Records. Another participant in both ceremonies was the Chief Justice, one-time Attorney-General and Leader of the Opposition, Sir John Latham. On Wednesday morning, in his capacity as deputy for the Governor-General, Sir John administered the oath or affirmation of allegiance to the members of the nineteenth parliament in their respective chambers. The new Prime Minister, most of his Cabinet and a number of Government backbenchers wore black coats and striped trousers. A few attired even more formally, with cutaway coats and toppers, were crudely ribbed by some of the Opposition members in plain lounge suits. But what

407

did they and the other black coats care? After all the years of Depression, war and post-war austerity, morning dress was back in vogue. It seemed as though a new day had dawned.

After members had been sworn, the House proceeded to elect a new Speaker. There was only one nomination—Archie Galbraith Cameron— and in his speech of acceptance that prickly individual showed the eccentric cut of his jib. First he warned the House that it would find him, 'as King Charles I found Montrose, a rather proud servant'. He was reminded, he said, of the parable of the trees in the Book of Judges. The trees, when they assembled together to select a leader, first chose the olive; but the olive refused to give up its fatness and preside over them. In like fashion the fig declined to give up its sweetness, and the vine to forsake its spirit. And so the post was offered to the bramble, which accepted it with these words: 'If in truth ye anoint me king over you, then come and put your trust in my shadow; and if not, let fire come out of the bramble, and devour the cedars of Lebanon'.

Speaker Cameron then declared that henceforth he would not take part in debate or attend meetings of the parliamentary Liberal Party. That, of course, had probably been his colleagues' main purpose in electing him. As the retiring Speaker told Cameron, it would be safer for the Prime Minister 'to have you in the chair rather than on his flank'. When Rosevear went on to question Cameron's past interpretation of Standing Orders, Prime Minister Menzies turned from the table to the ministers behind him and remarked: 'Sheer bad taste!'

At 2.30 p.m. the plain-suited and as yet unknighted Governor-General, W. J. McKell, arrived at Parliament House preceded by a motor cycle escort, was saluted by a guard of honour from Duntroon and a battery of 25-pounder guns, and applauded by several hundred spectators. He was then escorted into the parliamentary library to greet the new Speaker and members of the House of Representatives, all of whom had gone there in procession behind the Serjeant-at-Arms bearing the Mace. Speaker Bramble, scorning his predecessor's mufti, wore the traditional full-bottomed wig and robes, a lace cravat, lace cuffs, and buckled shoes in place of his accustomed elastic-sided boots.

By 3 p.m. the Senate chamber was crowded more than ever before with the members of both enlarged houses, the full diplomatic corps and other guests in ecclesiastical and judicial robes, bemedalled military uniforms, black coats and summer dresses—all waiting for the Usher of the Black Rod to announce His Excellency's approach. Some in this red chamber were reminded of W. B. McInnes's painting in King's Hall, which showed the Duke of York reading his address on a similar occasion. The only element missing from the present tableau was royalty, and perhaps it is not too fanci-ful to think that the closest substitute for that heady crimson essence was not the Commonwealth's plebeian Governor-General but its decidedly imperial Prime Minister.

Three years after the birth of Robert Gordon Menzies, a history of Clan Menzies was published in Edinburgh. Whether that book eventually reached such an obscure branch of the clan as Menzies of Jeparit is not known, but if it did one may be sure that it was devoured by a child whose reading included Jane Porter's historical novel, *The Scottish Chiefs*, and the works of Sir Walter Scott. On its title page Bob Menzies would have found this prefatory note: 'The Gaelic of the name is Meinnrigh, which signifies of a Majestic Countenance, or having a Royal-mien, or Regal-bearing'. Surely no Menzies ever justified that derivation more amply than the new Prime Minister of Australia. In the eight years since Menzies's first tenure of the office his powers had reached plenitude. Still only fifty-five, he was a most imposing figure, yet not austere, and rarely pompous, for his *gravitas* could be lightened on the instant by dextrous wit and charm.

The man's height and girth, his monumental head and vibrantly penetrating voice put some in mind of a Roman emperor, or even, according to one flight of fancy, Louis Quatorze the Sun King. Before long Menzies would become widely known by the nickname of Ming, a pun on both the Gaelic pronunciation of his surname ('Mingies') and 'Ming the Merciless', an interplanetary despot in the comic strip *Speed Gordon*. No less extravagant a parallel than any of these, but somewhat more useful, would be that of the parliamentarian who three centuries earlier had become King of England in everything but name. Oliver Cromwell was Lord Protector of the Commonwealth, and, although the analogy has obvious limitations, that title would have suited Menzies very well. In the years of office that lay ahead of him—many more years than might have been expected—Menzies would make much out of protecting the Commonwealth. Australia was assailed during the 1950s by many real and imaginary dangers: Communism, espionage, sectarianism, the yellow peril and inflation. Middle-class Australians were slow to recover from the fear complex which had been engendered by the prospect of nationalisation, but the Lord Protector was now there to comfort them. And some of his opponents believed that when fear subsided he was not averse to conjuring another bogy from the dark.

For a start, as the Governor-General announced in his opening speech, the new Government would fulfil its election promise 'to protect the community against the activities of subversive organisations and individuals . . . in particular the Communist Party and its members'. It would repeal the Banking Act of 1947, and amend the Commonwealth Bank Act of 1945–48 to provide that institution with a board of directors chaired by the governor of the bank and controlled by the parliament. A bill would also be introduced proposing alteration of the Constitution 'to ensure that, in future, no measure giving to the Government or its instrumentalities, to the exclusion of others, monopolistic rights to engage in commerce or industry can become law unless it has first been submitted to and approved by the people at a referendum'. A new ministry of National Development would be established, and the Snowy Mountains hydro-electric scheme, initiated by the previous Government, would be carried to completion; taxation laws and the machinery for conciliation and arbitration would be reviewed; immigration would continue on a large scale; and child endowment would be extended, as promised, to the first or only child in every family.

The parliament which heard these and other measures outlined by the Governor-General was a discernibly different organism from that which had assembled before the Duke of York a generation earlier. There were differences of age (the average was now fifty-four for senators and fifty for representatives, compared with fifty-six and fifty-two in 1927), birthplace (91 per cent of all parliamentarians were Australian born, compared with an earlier figure of 74 per cent), religion (27 per cent were now Roman Catholics, compared with only 13 per cent), education (37 per cent to tertiary level, compared with 22 per cent) and occupation. Many members were still primary producers of one kind or another (22 per cent, as compared with 26 per cent in 1927), but the largest categories were those described as 'business and commercial' (30 per cent) and 'professionals' (25 per cent). The largest professional sub-group was that of lawyers (11 per cent of all members, compared with 27 per cent in 1901). Eleven senators and forty-nine representatives were ex-servicemen, and of these only seven were A.L.P. Among the coalition's 'fortyniners' were six former prisoners of war, five of whom had endured years of Japanese captivity. One Labor senator from Tasmania, Justin O'Byrne, had spent three and a half years behind wire in Germany.

'There do not appear to be any striking personalities amongst the new members', wrote Ben Chifley to an acquaintance overseas. This was hardly fair to such Liberals as R. G. Casey, who was embarking upon his second parliamentary career in the Victorian seat of La Trobe, P. M. C. Hasluck (Curtin, W), William McMahon (Lowe, N), A. R. Downer (Angas, S), Allen Fairhall (Paterson, N), A. G. Townley (Denison, T), W. S. Kent Hughes (Chisholm, V), W. C. Wentworth (Mackellar, N), and a new Victorian senator, J. G. Gorton. Even in his own sorely depleted party Chifley was overlooking such newcomers as Clyde Cameron (Hindmarsh, S), yet another member bearing parliament's most common surname, but not related to the Speaker; and a group of abrasive Victorians including S. M. Keon (Yarra), W. M. Bourke (Fawkner) and J. M. Mullens (Gellibrand).

'The Victorians', as these particular Victorians were loosely known in Caucus, numbered eight in all, of whom six (including Keon, Bourke and Mullens) were Roman Catholics associated with the anti-Communist Industrial Groups. They were younger and better educated than most of their Labor colleagues, and although about 60 per cent of the parliamentary party was Catholic at that time, 'the Victorians' formed a suspicious and rather suspect enclave within Caucus. It was no wonder that Chifley failed to mention them.

Among the 183 parliamentarians were five women, where there had been four in the previous parliament and none a generation before. Nine women stood for the Senate in 1949, and two of them—Agnes Robertson, a Western Australian teacher, and Ivy Wedgwood, a Victorian housewife, both Liberals—succeeded in joining Senators Tangney and Rankin in that otherwise male chamber. Of twelve women who stood for the lower house, only one was elected, or rather re-elected. Doris Blackburn was defeated, as an independent Labor candidate in the redrawn electorate of Burke, by one of 'the Victorians', E. W. Peters; but Dame Enid Lyons was returned comfortably for the third time. Dame Enid now became the first woman to join a federal ministry, as Vice-President of the Executive Council.

Menzies's first Ministry consisted of fourteen Liberals and five members of the Country Party. His chief lieutenant, Eric Harrison, took Defence and Post-war Reconstruction; Casey, National Development, and Works and Housing; Spender, External Affairs and External Territories; Holt, Labour and National Service, and Immigration; Senator Neil O'Sullivan (Q), who was Government Leader in the hostile upper house, Trade and Customs; and Senator J. A. Spicer (V), Attorney-General. Fadden was Treasurer once again, and his deputy McEwen was Minister for Commerce and Agriculture.

The new Government quickly abolished rationing of petrol, butter and tea by executive action, without need of parliament, and made peace with those public service brahmins whose ideological bias it had criticised while in opposition. 'Don't take any notice of all that bullshit I was talking during the election', said Fadden on the telephone to the foremost of The Seven Dwarfs, 'Nugget' Coombs. 'We'll be needing you, you know.' And not only Coombs. In short order other Dwarfs were appointed to posts of the highest responsibility: Allen Brown became secretary of the Prime Minister's Department; J. G. Crawford, secretary of the Department of Commerce and Agriculture; H. A. Bland, secretary of the Department of Labor and National Service; and Roland Wilson, secretary to the Treasury.

Dr Coombs himself was to become Chairman of the new Commonwealth Bank board, but first the Government had to get its 'desocialising' Commonwealth Bank Bill past a Senate still controlled by defenders of the 'people's bank'. Although the A.L.P. platform called for abolition of the Senate, the tactical value of the upper house was undeniable at times like the present. But careful judgement was required as to how that advantage could be used against the Government without provoking a double dissolution election at which Labor was likely to be savaged again. Some unpalatable measures would therefore be allowed through the Senate; but during the Address-in-Reply debate, Chifley had warned the Government that Labor would oppose any move to reconstitute the Commonwealth Bank board, if necessary by blocking it in the Senate. The sword of inter-house disagreement was hanging over the nineteenth parliament on a very tenuous thread.

Fadden introduced his Bill to repeal the 1947 Banking Act and re-establish the bank board on 16 March. During the second reading debate Chifley reaffirmed his party's opposition to a bank board, accusing the coalition of wanting thereby to cripple the bank and impede its progress—'the worst service that the Government of this country could ever perform'. Although the Bill easily passed all readings in the lower house without amendment, it was a different story in the other place. The Senate agreed to the Bill with amendments which the lower house would not accept. In October the Senate insisted on its amendments, and the House insisted on disagreeing. A second identical Bill was rushed through the lower house, but the Senate did not return it.

An equally contentious measure, the Communist Party Dissolution Bill, encountered less opposition in the Senate. The idea of outlawing an unpopular and allegedly subversive political party in peacetime had first been proposed by the Country Party during the wave of post-war strikes. Menzies had resisted the idea at first, but came around to it eventually: 'it will be without avail', he said in his second reading speech on 27 April, for any honorable member to point out . . . that for some years I and other persons resisted the idea of a Communist ban on the ground that, in time of peace, doubts ought to be resolved in favour of free speech. True, that was my view after the war, and it was the view of many others. But events have moved. We are not at peace today, except in a technical sense. The Soviet Union—and I say this with profound regret—has made perfect the technique of the "cold-war".

The preamble of this Bill, after citing the defence power of the Constitution, asserted that 'the Australian Communist Party, in accordance with the basic theory of communism, as expounded by Marx and Lenin, engages in activities or operations designed to assist or accelerate the coming of a revolutionary situation, in which [that party], acting as a revolutionary minority, would be able to seize power and establish a dictatorship of the proletariat'; that industries such as coal, iron and steel, transport and power were vital to Australia's security and defence; and, finally, that activities of the Australian Communist Party were designed to cause, by strikes or stoppages, disruption of those industries. For those reasons, stated the Bill, it was necessary, for the security and defence of the Commonwealth, that the Australian Communist Party and bodies affiliated with it should be declared illegal and dissolved, and that their members be disqualified from Commonwealth employment and from holding office in any trade union with substantial membership in a vital industry.

Sections 9 and 10 of the Bill provided for the declaration and disqualification of such persons, placing the onus of proof not on the Commonwealth but on the person so 'declared'. The danger of this was all too well demonstrated by Menzies himself, for during his second reading speech, he read out a list of fifty-three 'Communists in high union office'. The Prime Minister's list was wrong in five particulars, and he was subsequently obliged to make correction.

Labor had difficulty in making up its collective mind about this Bill. Some members, including the 'Victorians', favoured active and unqualified support for the Bill; but a more substantial group, including Chifley and Evatt, preferred passive and qualified support, including amendment to the 'onus of proof' clause and provision of the right of appeal to State Supreme Courts as well as the High Court. The latter became Caucus policy, and appropriate amendments were made when the Bill reached the Senate. The Government refused to accept these, and on 23 June the Bill was laid aside. Two days later the Korean war began, lending sudden credence to the Bill's preamble, and when parliament reassembled in September the Bill was reintroduced.

Speaking to the motion for a second reading, the Leader of the Opposition again attacked the 'onus of proof' clause (which Rowley James insisted on calling 'anus of proof') and made a rare public reference to his own Irish ancestry. 'I am the descendant of a race', said Chifley,

> that fought a long and bitter fight against perjurers, pimps and liars and I should be very ashamed to stand for any principle that did not give the ordinary men and women of the community the right to know what they are charged with, the right to defend themselves and the right to have their case heard in public.

As events were to turn out, he and other like-minded Opposition members had to bear that shame. While the second debate was proceeding in the lower house, the Catholic-influenced Western Australian branch of the A.L.P. joined forces with the right-wing groupers in Victoria to argue that the parliamentary party's attitude to the Bill should be reconsidered by the Federal Executive. When Tom Burke rang Chifley with this news, Chifley told him: 'You couldn't have done a worse thing to the party . . . Oh well, boy, this is the end'. To a visitor in his office at the time, Chifley said of the party's pro-Bill faction: 'We could beat them yet by getting the Executive to refer the question to Caucus, but you'd have a first-class split and all those mad buggers would know Caucus couldn't really give a binding decision'. Federal Executive passed a so-called 'chicken resolution' directing the parliamentary party to let the measure pass without amendment, and reluctantly Chifley brought his senators to heel. The Bill received the Governor-General's assent on 20 October, but the fight against it was renewed in the High Court. The Communist Party and various trade unions quickly obtained an injunction restraining the Government from making use of the Act until its validity could be decided. To everyone's surprise and the Government's delight, Dr Evatt, despite his record of anti-Communism, accepted a brief in these proceedings for the Communist-controlled Waterside Workers' Federation. 'Rightly or wrongly', gloated Harold Holt in parliament, 'the people of Australia will read into the appearance of the right honourable gentleman a sympathy and support for the cause which he seeks to defend'.

A third measure which disturbed Labor senators was a bill to amend the Constitution—not in order to forestall future exercises in nationalisation, as had been foreshadowed in the Governor-General's speech, but to avoid Senate deadlocks after double dissolutions. Proportional representation had solved the problem of lopsided senates, but in doing so it had created the new danger of senates that were too evenly balanced. Unless some change was made, said Menzies when introducing the Constitution Alteration (Avoidance of Double Dissolution Deadlocks) Bill on 4 May, it was next door to a stone certainty' that the Senate would be divided 30–30 after a double dissolution election. On the basis of votes cast at the last election, it would be necessary for one side or the other to win 55 per cent of formal votes in order to win six out of the ten Senate seats in each state—and that, as everyone conceded, was virtually impossible in the present political climate. Thus, if the Government obtained a double dissolution, as was by no means unlikely, each side would probably win five seats in each of the six States. 'What would happen then?' asked Menzies.

> Mr WARD.—The right honorable gentleman could declare a couple of the Labour senators.
> Mr MENZIES.—I am obliged to the honorable member for the suggestion. I can think of at least one Labour senator whom it would be easy to declare.
> Mr WARD.—The Führer has spoken.
> Mr MENZIES.—I can think of one member of this House who might escape only by the skin of his teeth.

Mr CHIFLEY.—The right honorable member is on dangerous ground.
Mr MENZIES.—I agree—on dangerous ground . . .
Mr WARD.—Heil Menzies.

Menzies conceded the Opposition's point that bills whose twofold rejection had occasioned a double dissolution could then be made the subject of a joint sitting of both houses, at which the Government's will would be sure to prevail. 'But thereafter', he said, 'there is no provision for a joint sitting at all. In relation to every other bill on the government's programme for the rest of the term of Parliament, there would be no means at all of getting a joint sitting'. The proposed solution was that, in the event of a dissolution of the Senate, the ten vacancies in each State should be filled by the election of two odd-numbered groups of candidates at concurrent ballots—five senators for a six-year term, and five for three years. 'In each group', said Menzies, 'one side or the other in politics must secure a majority. I agree with the person who said that there is luck in odd numbers. We are going to have odd numbers and I anticipate the luck'.

This 'crossword puzzle business', as Chifley dubbed it, required approval by referendum; but the Senate saved Australia's voters the trouble of rejecting it, as they would surely have done, by not returning the bill to the lower house. Menzies said on one occasion that to get an affirmative vote from the Australian people on a referendum proposal was one of the labours of Hercules, and his Government did not attempt that kind of feat again in the life of this parliament. No bill was introduced to forestall nationalisation, and nothing ever came of a mooted referendum bill for the establishment of national contributory insurance against sickness, widowhood, unemployment and old age. The latter was a plan of the kind whose earlier false start had prompted the younger Menzies to resign from Lyons's Ministry. According to one unidentified minister, it would replace the entire range of social services and make the Snowy Mountains hydro-electric scheme 'look like peanuts'. But in this regard Menzies did even less than Lyons.

Discussion of international affairs by this parliament, starting with a debate in March on a white paper by Spender, showed an increasing awareness of Asia's importance to Australia. This was hardly surprising, considering the events of World War II and the inauguration of a Communist People's Republic of China only five months earlier. Contributors to the first debate endorsed an initiative taken by Spender at a recent British Commonwealth Foreign Ministers' meeting, from which developed the Colombo Plan whereby prosperous members of the Commonwealth were to provide financial, technical and professional help to less developed Asian members. The new Government based its foreign policy on Australian participation in co-ordinated British Commonwealth schemes of defence, and on close co--operation with the United States. Dr Evatt reaffirmed his habitual faith in the United Nations, and on the question of China said that although the new regime would have to be recognised sooner or later, recognition need not carry with it the recognition of Formosa.

The most memorable speech in this debate was delivered by the intelligent and ambitious 'Victorian', Stan Keon. It was memorable because young

Keon had the temerity to rebuke his own leader. Chifley had said earlier in the debate that the Christian churches had not done sufficient to combat social injustice in pre-war Central Europe. 'That statement does not represent my view', said Keon,

> and I hope that it does not represent the view of any substantial section of the community ... We owe it to the memory of men like Cardinal Mindszenty and Archbishop Stepinac, when such an allegation is made, to point out that today, when other defences have failed, the Christian Church is the only force that is standing firm in the defence of humanity, spiritual rights and freedom.

The significance of this brash departure from party solidarity was not lost upon those who heard it. Least of all was it lost upon Chifley. 'Those new Melbourne fellows have a bug', he said. 'They have a bug—that's what's wrong with them.'

Australian awareness of Asia was further sharpened by the outbreak of war in Korea and, barely one month later, by a decision to provide Australian ground troops for service in that conflict. This came as a complete surprise to Menzies, who was crossing the Atlantic for defence talks in Washington when the decision was made and announced. Cabinet had considered the matter before his departure, and had decided against commitment in spite of some urging to the contrary by the Minister for External Affairs, Spender. On 26 July, however, Spender's department advised him that the British Government was about to announce its own unexpected decision to send troops to help United States forces in Korea. Spender telephoned the acting Prime Minister, Fadden, in Queensland and persuaded him that there was not time to call Cabinet together, or to get in touch with Menzies; an Australian announcement should be made immediately. Fadden overcame his concern about what 'the Big Fellow' might think, and issued a two-sentence statement that very night to the effect that Australia would provide ground troops for use in Korea under United Nations auspices. Only after the statement had been made did Spender telephone Menzies in mid-ocean. 'He said little', wrote the Baron of Bardia later, with just a hint of satisfaction, 'and in the circumstances I could not say much, but even over the distance of some 12,000 miles I was aware of the sourness in his voice'.

The Korean war, and more specifically the international wool boom generated by it, put paid to any chance the Government might have had of redeeming its election promise to 'put value back into the pound'. That embarrassment of riches brought inflationary pressures to bear on the Australian economy, caused an alarming increase in the volume of imports, and placed severe political strain on the coalition. By late 1950 Menzies and most of his Liberal colleagues were convinced that upward revaluation of the Australian pound offered the best means of restoring the balance of trade. But the Country Party, arguing that the export boom would soon subside and that a corrective devaluation might prove too difficult, was bitterly opposed to this course. Cabinet discussed the fate of the pound on at least seven occasions, and, according to Fadden's later account, in spite of appearances to the contrary, 'the survival of the composite government was seriously threatened'.

Although the Liberals outnumbered Labor by fifty-five to forty-seven in the lower house, they could not continue to govern without adequate support from the other nineteen full-voting representatives, all of whom belonged to the Country Party. Now two Country Party ministers, Page and Anthony, were carrying letters of resignation in their pockets in case of sudden need, and three Liberals were thought to be ready to side with the Country Party on financial policy. A solution was found by Fadden. He suggested to Menzies that, instead of revaluation, wool growers should pay to the Treasury 20 per cent of the total value of their domestic and export sales, to be held as credit against future tax assessments. The idea was embodied in a Wool Sales Deduction Scheme, to be repealed when the price of wool fell as expected; the Australian pound remained steady; and so did the Liberal–Country Party coalition.

Early in the life of this parliament the House of Representatives adopted the first permanent Standing Orders, or rules of procedure, in its half-century of existence. The Standing Orders which had come into operation in 1901 were designated as temporary, and various proposals to amend them had come to nothing. Only the imminent enlargement of parliament, and particularly the resulting need to shorten speeches, brought this matter to a head. The Chifley Government appointed an all-party Standing Orders Committee to prepare a permanent set, and its proposals, slightly amended, were adopted by the House on 22 March 1950. The changes affecting members most noticeably were concerned with speaking time. Henceforth ministers introducing bills would be allowed 45 minutes instead of an hour; speeches on the second reading would last only 30 minutes instead of 45; speeches on the adjournment, ten minutes instead of 15; no-confidence motion and Address-in-Reply speeches, 25 minutes instead of 35.

The interpreter of Standing Orders, Speaker Cameron, soon gave members cause to recall the warnings of his acceptance speech. A few Opposition members, led by the former Speaker, challenged his rulings at every opportunity. Fire came out of the bramble, and wild indiscretion too. On 30 March, in one of the angriest debates anyone could remember, Cameron deeply embarrassed the Government by making a statement from the Chair that was nothing less than a personal attack on the Governor-General. Archie Cameron did not do things by halves.

The prepared statement arose from a question asked at an earlier sitting by one of Cameron's most persistent critics, A. D. Fraser (Lab, Eden-Monaro, N), concerning a press report that after having presented the Address-in-Reply to the Governor-General Cameron had refused His Excellency's offer of refreshment and departed abruptly. In his statement the Speaker recalled an attack which McKell had made upon him at an A.L.P. conference ten years before, when McKell had been Leader of the Opposition in New South Wales and Cameron Leader of the federal parliamentary Country Party.

[This was] the most personal attack that I have ever been subjected to in my life [he said] . . . Among the terms which were used in regard to myself were "mistrusted", "detested", "narrow prejudice", "blindness", "personal jealousy", "intemperate", "blackmailing", "bushranging" . . . On assuming the Speakership of this House I took a calculated risk. I met the Governor-General for the second time in my life, and I trust that my conduct on that day was no disgrace to this House . . . On the 27th February last, in reply to an invitation, I called the attention of the Governor-General to his past attitudes to me. I informed His Excellency that I had no desire to accept the hospitality of those who spoke of me in the terms employed by him.

Chifley moved a motion of censure against the Speaker for what he described as a 'deplorable incident', but Menzies, although his heart could hardly have been in it, brought all his skills to the Speaker's defence. He called the censure motion 'arrant humbug', and applied the gag so that the motion could be defeated on party lines without further delay. Cameron made no apology, and continued to take on all comers for the rest of the year.

When parliament reassembled on 7 March 1951 its expectation of life was short indeed, for the Senate had overplayed its game of offering every provocation short of providing grounds for double dissolution, and the Government had nearly run out of patience. Menzies complained that the Labor Party was using a Senate majority which it had won in 1946 to frustrate a lower house elected in 1949. Soon after his return from the Commonwealth Prime Ministers' conference in London, the Prime Minister sought to arouse a truly horrendous fear—that World War III was just around the corner. With all the authority of supposed inside knowledge he told a special meeting of State Premiers on 2 March: 'If the Western Democracies, including ourselves, fail to prepare themselves completely within three years they may regard a war of aggression against them as in the highest degree probable'. With Communist Chinese troops by that time fighting an undeclared war against Americans in Korea, this was by no means inconceivable; and yet a National Service Bill, introduced in November to provide for compulsory military training, still lay before a Senate Select Committee. Early in March the Federal A.L.P. conference did instruct the parliamentary Labor Party to let that Bill pass; but it also congratulated Caucus on the Opposition's continuing stand against the Commonwealth Bank Bill.

The last straw for the Government came on 9 March, when the High Court ruled by six to one (Latham C.J. dissenting) that for various technical reasons the Communist Party Dissolution Act was invalid. In essence the majority held that in present circumstances the Act could not be supported, either as an exercise of the Commonwealth's defence power, or as an exercise of its Constitution maintenance power. At the next sitting of parliament, on Tuesday 13 March, Menzies rose after the dinner adjournment to make a statement on the Court's judgment. 'Let the machinery of the Constitution work', he concluded.

Let us go to our masters, the Australian people, and ask them to say where they stand on these crucial issues of the Communist conspiracy, of law and order in industry, of the public safety, of the preparedness of this country to meet as heavy a cloud of danger as free men have looked at for many long months . . . The government will welcome the verdict of the people.

Clearly the Prime Minister was intent upon seeking a double dissolution in accordance with Section 57 of the Constitution, as had been done only once before, by Joseph Cook in 1914. But the present circumstances were not quite as straightforward as in that precedent. Section 57 authorises the Governor-General to dissolve both houses simultaneously

> if the House of Representatives passes any proposed law, and the Senate rejects or fails to pass it, or passes it with amendments to which the House of Representatives will not agree, and if after an interval of three months the House of Representatives . . . again passes the proposed law . . . and the Senate [persists in its attitude].

In Cook's case the Labor-controlled Senate had decisively rejected one of his Government's bills on two adequately separate occasions. Menzies would have to rely on the Commonwealth Bank Bill, which had initially been passed by the Senate with amendments unacceptable to the lower house. A second identical bill had reached the Senate in October, and was still there.

On 14 March, the day after Menzies's statement, the Senate referred the bill to a select committee. Was that 'failure to pass'? Dr Evatt advised Caucus that reference to a select committee after second reading was a legitimate stage in the consideration of a bill as provided by Standing Orders; but his great rival Barwick, closely as ever in touch with the Liberal Party on legal matters, agreed with Menzies and Spicer that the Senate's procrastination would satisfy the Governor-General that its real intention was failure to pass. Another element of uncertainty was the Governor-General himself. Whereas Cook had dealt with a fellow conservative at Government House, Menzies would have to deal with a former Labor Premier. But Chifley took no comfort from that. 'Billy McKell will please his bloody self', he warned his colleagues.

On Thursday 15 March, while the National Service Act was passing through its final stages in the Senate without amendment, Menzies went to Yarralumla to tell the Governor-General that he intended advising him to dissolve both houses. On Friday he submitted that advice in writing, accompanied by opinions from the Attorney-General and Solicitor-General supporting his contention that the Senate's delay in passing the Commonwealth Bank Bill amounted to an expression of unwillingness to pass it, which was tantamount to failure. Unlike Munro-Ferguson in 1914, McKell sought no other advice. The Prime Minister had to wait 24 hours for his answer; but on Saturday morning he returned to Government House, received the answer he wanted, and took tea and cigars with His Excellency.

The main issue of the election on 28 April was Communism. Labor made some attempt to court what Calwell called the kitchen vote by accusing the Government of negligence in the face of inflation, and advocating wider use of price control. Menzies responded by attributing high prices to low productivity caused by Communist influence in the trade unions. He reaffirmed his Government's determination to ban the Communist Party ('the fifth column for a potential enemy'), if necessary by seeking new constitutional power for the Commonwealth; and to introduce secret ballots for trade unions. An amending Conciliation and Arbitration Bill had been introduced for the latter purpose (and, more truthfully, to provide a useful talking point for the coming election campaign) in the last week of parliament, but it bogged down in the Senate and lapsed at prorogation.

Chifley was not himself for this election. Only five months earlier he had suffered a coronary occlusion at home in Bathurst, and now, as he dragged himself around the country, weary and hoarser than ever, he seemed the perfect embodiment of a party whose heart had been broken. At every turn in the campaign he was out-talked and outmanoeuvred by his robust opponent. As at Government House, so too in the polling booths Menzies got what he wanted. The Government was returned to office with control of both houses. Party numbers in the new House of Representatives would be fifty-two Liberals (formerly fifty-five), fifty-two Labor (forty-seven) and seventeen Country Party (nineteen). In the Senate the coalition would have a majority of four.

Fission

It was now possible for any passer-by, if so disposed, to tell at a glance whether parliament was sitting into the night. Speaker Cameron had noticed on a visit to Westminster that this sort of information was conveyed by a red light above the Lords and a green one above the Commons; and when Australia's twentieth parliament opened, red and green lights could be made to glow above the roof of Parliament House. The obvious connotation of 'Stop' and 'Go' no longer applied as aptly as it would have done with a hostile Senate; but the air of festivity engendered by coloured lights was not inappropriate, for 1951 was the jubilee of federation and the Commonwealth parliament. The jubilee began with a commemorative ceremony in Sydney's Centennial Park attended by some three thousand people. There were jubilee church services, and for reasons not altogether clear a party of soldiers and civilians re-enacted Charles Sturt's 1000-mile row by whaleboat down the Murrumbidgee and Murray rivers.

On the night of 9 May eight thousand people went to Melbourne's Exhibition Building for a more pertinent re-enactment of the opening of the first federal parliament by the Duke of Cornwall and York. One month later, on the morning of Tuesday 12 June, the twentieth parliament was opened in Canberra with stateliness surpassing that of the previous year, though members of the royal family who might otherwise have added lustre to the occasion were prevented from doing so by illness of the King. That afternoon senators and members attended in the Senate chamber to hear the Governor-General's opening speech. The Chair of the Senate was now occupied by a new President—Senator E. W. Mattner, a Liberal farmer from South Australia, like Speaker Cameron—who had been elected unopposed earlier in the day. Agreement to the Address-in-Reply was moved next day by a new Victorian senator, also a farmer, Magnus Cormack. Like others on the Government side who followed him in this debate, Senator Cormack expressed the hope that the jubilee might prove to be, like 1901, a significant year in the constitutional development of the Commonwealth. 'Honorable senators who have been elected to represent the States', he said, 'should examine whether another Commonwealth convention should be held in

1951 in order to determine whether the Commonwealth is to continue its growth . . . and whether we should allow the States to wither away and atrophy and the nation of the next 50 years to become a monolithic State'. This sort of hope received wide and earnest expression during the jubilee, both in and out of parliament, but nothing was to come of it.

Billy Hughes was the only member of the original parliament present at a jubilee banquet in Parliament House on Tuesday night. W. G. Higgs had died only the day before, and the other survivors—Sir George Pearce and the seemingly immortal King O'Malley—had not been able to come. The climax of the jubilee was to be a ball in King's Hall on Wednesday night. One of the few parliamentarians not to attend was the Leader of the Opposition. 'Are you going to the ball tonight?' Fred Daley asked him as he was leaving Parliament House. 'No', Chifley replied. 'I'm going back to the Kurrajong to read a couple of Westerns, you can go and trip the light fantastic.' After dinner at the hotel Chifley retired to his room and went to bed. One or two colleagues looked in on their way to the ball, and at about 7 p.m. he was joined by the Bathurst woman who had been his personal secretary since 1928, Phyllis Donnelly. They listened to the ABC news and a 'Forum of the Air' programme in which Allan Fraser and Les Haylen were taking part. Then Chifley telephoned his wife in Bathurst, and Miss Donnelly made some supper. At 9.20 p.m. Chifley sat up in bed with a sudden pain in the chest. He tried to make light of it, but soon lapsed into unconsciousness. Miss Donnelly called a doctor and an ambulance, and he was taken to Canberra Hospital. When word reached Dr Evatt at the ball he left immediately for the hospital with a few others, including the Leader of the Oppositon in the Senate, Nick McKenna, Fred Daly, and the Member for West Sydney, Billy O'Connor. They were too late. A priest had been summoned, and he was coming out of Chifley's room as they arrived. 'Did you get here in time?' asked Daly. 'I think I did', said the priest.

Daly telephoned Mrs Chifley. He and the others then returned to Parliament House, entering inconspicuously through the Senate door, and Evatt told Menzies that Chifley was dead. Just before midnight the Prime Minister announced to the hushed crowd in King's Hall:

> It is my sorrowful duty to tell you that tonight, during the celebration, Mr Chifley, former Prime Minister and Leader of the Opposition, has died. I do not want to try even to talk about him, because, although we were political opponents, he was a great friend of mine and yours, and a fine Australian . . .

There was no more music, and the guests, some of them in tears, made their way home. Dr Evatt was said to have sobbed in his office for almost half an hour.

Chifley's coffin lay in King's Hall on Friday morning, and then, after being flown home with an escort of Spitfires, in Bathurst's Roman Catholic cathedral until the state funeral on Sunday. The cortège was accompanied by the Governor-General, the Prime Minister, the presiding officers of parliament and, among many others, a large contingent of railwaymen. It passed through the streets of Chifley's beloved Bathurst, and out along the Orange road to where a grave had been prepared on a small hill inside the cemetery. By chance Chifley was buried on the same day of the year as that on which the first Labor candidates had been elected to an Australian parliament, the New South Wales Legislative Assembly, sixty years before. He was mourned as one of Labor's best loved parliamentary leaders, but no one could say that he left the party any better than he had found it. On the contrary, Chifley had dared to take the socialist objective seriously, and the party had suffered in consequence. His death during the diamond jubilee of the parliamentary labour movement and the golden jubilee of federal parliament marked symbolically an end to the bowyang days of working-class heroism and socialist optimism. The holy ikon had been packed away out of sight, but that was not to say that dissension had also left the party room.

Dr Evatt was elected to the leadership unopposed, and his deputy was Arthur Calwell. They were an ill-sorted pair, this former High Court judge with no real power base in the labour movement, and former Victorian Treasury officer. Neither of them was remotely like Chifley, and neither was destined to follow in his path to the Prime Ministership. In spite of Evatt's reported tears when Chifley died, it was also said that he had the same capacity as E. G. Theodore for being genuinely compassionate towards humanity in the mass, yet often coldly lacking in feeling for individuals. When he was Minister for External Affairs, and his arrival in New York would be heralded by a message to the Australian Consulate-General saying 'MNSTR ARVG', the cablese was said to mean 'Monster Arriving'. For all his intellectual powers, or perhaps partly because of them, Evatt was in many ways temperamentally unsuited to politics. Impatient and suspicious, he could be downright churlish when the occasion called for at least some attempt at courtesy or charm. Once, on arrival in a country town for an election meeting, he was met by the local member and a Caledonian pipe band. 'What's this bloody menagerie for?' asked Dr Evatt.

While it was true that friendship of a kind had existed between Menzies and Chifley, there was only cold antagonism between Menzies and Evatt. They were natural enemies, and their antipathy was a blight on the general atmosphere of parliament. Sitting across the table from Menzies, Evatt used to surround himself with books, newspaper cuttings, notes, and at his feet a litter of screwed up paper. All that Menzies normally had with him before a speech was a neat handful of headline reminders. Evatt's speeches were strong on content, but they were delivered in a flat nasal voice without the slightest oratorical adornment.

Calwell's voice was even more unlovely, and was matched by the rather gawky features—beaky nose and skewed mouth—which during his stormy administration of wartime censorship led one cartoonist to portray Calwell as a cockatoo squawking 'Curse the press!' But he made more rhetorical effort than Evatt, and was indeed one of the House's more accomplished speakers. He was surprisingly erudite in the field of United States history, an interest inspired by his paternal grandfather having been American. His father, a Victorian policeman, was Anglican; his mother, born of Irish parents, was Roman Catholic, and she reared him in that faith. But in spite of his religious conviction Calwell was not one of the 'Victorians'. Like Evatt, he belonged nominally to the centre of the party. He had a sense of humour, but rather a mordant one. There was a bitterness about him that some attributed to the death of a much loved 11-year-old son from leukaemia in 1948. During that ordeal Calwell became a daily attendant at mass, and after the boy's death he wore a black tie for the rest of his life.

The Ministry had been enlarged from sixteen to twenty, and among its new members were Hasluck (Territories), Kent Hughes (Interior and Works) and McMahon (Navy and Air). Spender retired from parliament in order to succeed Norman Makin as Ambassador to the United States. There had been rumours of intrigue against Menzies by a cabal of New South Wales Liberals, including Spender, and although he always subsequently scouted the suggestion, it was assumed by many that he was leaving politics as a beaten pretender. The portfolio of External Affairs went to Casey, another Liberal with ambivalent feelings about his leader. Privately Casey wrote that the Prime Minister was ignoring his advice on the best means of dealing with inflation, and keeping the larger matters of policy in his own hands, without consulting Cabinet.

'The time has come when I must get out of this government', he wrote, probably late in 1951. 'I cannot serve any longer under M's leadership. I have struggled on for 2 years in an effort to adjust myself to his way of doing things but I cannot do so any longer.' Casey's gloom may well have been accentuated by periodic attacks of dysentery at this time, and by his reliance on sleeping pills at night and benzedrine by day. He did not leave the Government, of course, but served capably for nine years in the portfolio of External Affairs and also as Minister in charge of the Commonwealth Scientific and Industrial Research Organisation. One of his first major steps in the former capacity was to move in October 1951 for the establishment of an all-party Joint Committee on Foreign Affairs. The main purpose of this committee, serviced by the Department of External Affairs and entitled to call persons and documents in camera without ministerial concurrence, was to improve the quality of debate on foreign affairs by keeping a body of parliamentarians well informed in that field.

The twentieth parliament also saw the establishment of a new post in the House of Representatives—Leader of the House, initially in the person of Eric Harrison. Derived from the House of Commons, where the post had come into being when the Prime Minister was a member of the House of Lords, the Leader of the House is a minister responsible—in consultation with the Prime Minister, other ministers and the Government Whips—for the management of Government business in the House. He determines the order of business, allocates time for debates, and negotiates with the Opposition. Although created only by decision of the executive of the day, rather than decision of parliament, the post became entrenched by convention and was eventually endowed with special remuneration in addition to the normal ministerial allowance.

The first legislative programme arranged by the new Leader of the House included some unfinished business from the previous parliament, for which the way was now clear. In June the Government introduced another Conciliation and Arbitration Bill for the use of secret ballots in trade union affairs, and another Commonwealth Bank Bill identical with that which had triggered the double dissolution. Both received assent in August. Later in the same parliament, in 1953, yet another Commonwealth Bank Act was passed, to establish a separately incorporated Commonwealth Trading Bank in place of the existing General Banking Division of the Commonwealth Bank, and also, as Menzies said, 'to protect the trading banks, insofar as that protection can be given by statute, against unfair competition by the Commonwealth Bank'. Dr Evatt said that the government's real purpose was to weaken the people's bank on its trading side compared with the trading banks. But the Opposition was just as powerless to stop this banking Bill as it had been in 1951.

On 5 July 1951 the Government introduced a Constitution Alteration (Powers to Deal with Communists and Communism) Bill, and a Defence Preparations Bill. The former was intended, as Menzies said, to remedy 'grave defects in the power of . . . parliament . . . in time of peace to protect the safety of the nation against treacherous agents acting for a foreign power'—defects which had been disclosed by the High Court's recent ruling against the validity of the Communist Party Dissolution Act, and which could be remedied only by a referendum to amend the Constitution. Labor members shouted themselves hoarse against this Bill, to no avail, and the former President of the Senate, Senator Gordon Brown, suffered a stroke while speaking in the second reading debate. Sir Earle Page was called into the chamber to attend the unconscious 66-year-old. Brown recovered, and continued in the Senate for another fourteen years.

Labor was more successful at the referendum on 22 September, for not even fear of Communism could overcome the deeper Australian fear of constitutional amendment. Dr Evatt had opposed the Bill strenuously in parliament, and had been smeared for his pains. When he finished attacking the Government for wanting 'to adopt totalitarian methods in order to defeat the totalitarian doctrine of communism', Harold Holt rose to say, 'The House has just been listening to the most notable defender of communism in Australia'—a reference to Evatt's High Court appearance on behalf of the watersiders.

Evatt relished the referendum campaign, and the 'No' majority, narrow though it was (2 370 009 to 2 317 927, and three States to three), which rewarded the Opposition's efforts. But his active role also strengthened the kind of impression that Holt and others were conveying about him. It had been noticed, and reported by the press, that Keon and Mullens failed to attend his opening referendum meeting in Melbourne.

The measure introduced on the same day as the referendum Bill, the Defence Preparations Bill, was a minor version of Australia's wartime National Security Act, inspired at this time of 'ostensible peace' (as the High Court had termed it) by a recent Act of the United States Congress. Here was a self-proclaimed free enterprise government taking to itself the power to govern by regulation. In justification, Menzies spoke of the need to prepare the Australian economy against the danger of war; Evatt described the measure as a 'powers grab bill' representing 'an abdication by parliament of its authority', and 'a complete surrender by the Government, which was returned to power in 1949 on a pledge to abolish oppressive government controls of all kinds'. The Bill provided authority for the Government to make such regulations as were necessary for defence preparations, but explicitly excluded taxation, Commonwealth Government borrowing, compulsory direction of labour and compulsory military service. All regulations made under this measure would be subject to parliamentary disallowance, and the Act itself would be of limited duration, expiring on the last day of 1953. As it turned out, of course, World War III was not around the corner, and no regulations were ever proclaimed.

Another American example followed in the twentieth parliament by some Government members was the McCarthyist pursuit of alleged Communists and fellow travellers. The purpose may sometime have been well intended, but often the charge was ill-founded and damage was left unrepaired. H. B. S. Gullett attacked Dr J. J. Burton, who had been secretary of the Department of External Affairs when Evatt was the Minister, for proposing to visit Peking. W. C. Wentworth criticised the Commonwealth Literary Fund for awarding a grant to the novelist Kylie Tennant, whom he labelled an active Communist, to write a novel about intinerant bee-keepers. Miss Tennant, explaining that her membership of the Communist Party lasted only one month and had expired more than twenty years before, angrily refunded her grant. Admitting his mistake, the Honourable Member for Mackellar offered to waive privilege so that Miss Tennant might have the right to sue him. Speaker Cameron ruled, however, that once a member made a statement in the House he could not divest it of parliamentary privilege.

Keon and Mullens launched similar attacks against the authors Judah Waten, Vance Palmer and Frank Hardy. Menzies defended the Commonwealth Literary Fund and refrained from joining the witch-hunt. Casey, on the other hand, spurred the campaign along with undocumented allusions to the presence of 'traitors in our midst'. Using phrases that would have fitted perfectly into one of Senator McCarthy's diatribes, he told the House: 'The Government is endeavouring to unearth this small but extremely dangerous nest of traitors that exists in the Public Service'. For some months afterwards Eddie Ward, in his inimitable fashion, kept inviting Casey at Question Time to inform the House about progress of the inquiry into his nest of traitors; but the Minister had said all he was going to say on that subject.

In September 1951 Fadden introduced a Budget designed to curb inflation. The 'Horror Budget', as newspapers called it, adjusted taxation rates upward to achieve a substantial surplus for the year 1951–52. In 1952 parliament's Public Accounts Committee was also revived under the chairmanship of F. A. Bland (Lib, Warringah, N), to expose administrative waste. Austerity was the order of the day, but that did not deter parliament from approving, early in 1952, a recommendation by the Nicholas Committee of Enquiry that parliamentary salaries be raised from £1500 to £1750.

Two significant measures before parliament when it reassembled on 6 February 1952 were the Treaty of Peace (Japan) Bill and the Security Treaty (Australia, New Zealand and the United States of America) Bill, the latter to provide parliamentary approval of the ANZUS Pact. This pact, which had been signed four months previously, was partly intended to reconcile public opinion in Australia and New Zealand to the generous terms of the peace treaty which America wanted for Japan. The Bill was treated as a bipartisan measure, but some Labor speakers questioned the worth of the ANZUS treaty's vaguely worded clauses. Everything or nothing could be read into the main clause, depending upon the reader's faith or scepticism. 'Each party', said Article IV(i), 'recognises that an armed attack in the Pacific area on any of the parties would be dangerous to its own peace and safety and declares that it would act to meet the common danger in accordance with its constitutional processes'. Did that mean any more than each party acting as its own national interest might dictate? Dr Evatt asked in vain for some assurance that the treaty would not be 'merely a paper agreement', and Ward declared it to be 'a meaningless document'. But it was the best protection available, and parliament dutifully passed the Bill.

On the morning of 6 February Casey began his second reading speech on the peace treaty Bill, only to be interrupted by the arrival of news that King George VI had died. How aptly the events of this day symbolised Australia's changing international alignment: the King dead, a mortal enemy forgiven, and a new protector pledged. The sitting was suspended for twenty minutes, and then resumed for two minutes, during which the Prime Minister announced the news from London in words of deeply felt grief:

> It is my very melancholy task to inform the House that the news that ran in rumour a few minutes ago has now been officially confirmed. His Majesty the King died this morning. I, and I am sure every other honorable member, feel quite incapable at this moment of saying what should be said. Therefore, I consider that the House should adjourn until tomorrow, when we can express our feelings as they should be expressed.

In spite of Australia's developing ties with the United States, it would have been hard to exaggerate the strength of pro-British feeling that survived in parliament—particularly, of course, on the Government side. Even the outlook from parliament's front steps was now dominated by another statue of King George V, erected in 1953—as if the one already standing in King's Hall was not enough—on the lawn directly in front of Parliament House. And when Sir William McKell's term ended in 1953, he was naturally replaced by a British Governor-General, Field-Marshal Sir William Slim. The enthusiasm shown at this distinguished soldier's welcome to Canberra was exceeded only by that accorded to Queen Elizabeth II when she opened the third session of the twentieth parliament in February 1954, the first such opening by a monarch in Australian parliamentary history.

At the everyday level of parliamentary practice, both sides of both houses were dyed indelibly with Westminster red and green. When a new Labor member, elected for Werriwa (N) at a by-election, made his maiden speech early in 1953, McEwen had the effrontery to interject. The Speaker quickly reminded McEwen of the convention, borrowed from Westminster, that maiden speeches should be heard in complete silence. The new member was E. G. Whitlam, a Sydney lawyer whom Haylen had dubbed 'The Young Brolga' because of his height and dignity. Whitlam was probably as well versed in Westminster lore as anyone in the House. 'I thought that the Minis-

ter for Commerce and Agriculture had returned to the more congenial climate of Disraeli's day', he told the Speaker. 'I recollect that Disraeli said, on
the occasion of his maiden speech, "The time will come when you shall hear
me". Perhaps I should say, "The time will come when you may interrupt
me"'.

Westminster tradition was reinforced during this parliament by the presentation to the House of Representatives of a new Mace, a jubilee gift from
the House of Commons, and by the purchase of one of the few known copies
of Magna Carta. The new Mace was a close copy of the Westminster one, and
replaced that which had been borrowed in 1901 from the Victorian Legislative Assembly. It was delivered in November 1951 by a three-man delegation
from the House of Commons led by Richard Law, M.P., a son of Bonar Law.
Speaking from the floor of the House (a privilege extended to strangers on no
other occasion, before or since), Law and his colleagues described the Mace
as 'essentially the symbol of the Crown which unites our two parliaments
and our two peoples', and noted that whenever 'tragedy, war and disaster
have threatened the Old Country . . . our children overseas were with us for
good or ill'. The Magna Carta, purchased in 1952 by the National Library for
£15 600, was placed on permanent exhibition in King's Hall.

A greater tribute to Britain, paid promptly and with little consideration of
consequences, was the Defence (Special Undertakings) Bill, introduced in
June 1952 to facilitate the test explosion of Britain's first nuclear bomb near
the north-west coast of Australia. Menzies had agreed the previous year to a
British request that the explosion be allowed to take place in the Monte Bello
Islands, a barren group of small islands on a coral reef about 100 miles north-
east of Exmouth Gulf in Western Australia. Neither parliament nor Cabinet
was consulted about that basic decision; but to judge from the brevity of
debate on the subsequent Bill, it seemed that parliament was at one with the
Prime Minister about Operation Hurricane, as the test was known.

Dr Evatt told the House that the Opposition believed the measure was
urgent, because of the imminence of the test, and that there should be no
opposition to it. The only concern expressed about danger came from F. M.
Osborne (Lib, Evans, N), who suggested that birds on the islands should be
dispersed before the explosion; and from Dr Donald Cameron (Lib, Oxley,
Q), who worried that radioactive material released by nuclear fission might
damage photographic film unless precautions were taken by the owners.

The Hurricane device, slightly more powerful than that which destroyed
Hiroshima, was exploded on 3 October 1952 three metres below the water-
line in an old Royal Navy frigate, which was instantly vaporised. The test
authorities had no means of predicting the spread of fission material ('One of
the objects of the experiment', said a classified document made public thirty
years later, 'is to fill to some extent this gap in our knowledge'), and in fact
the radioactive cloud was carried by unexpected winds across mainland
Australia. During the next five years Hurricane was followed by two more
nuclear explosions in the Monte Bellos and nine more on the continent itself,
at the Emu and Maralinga sites in South Australia. For good or ill, the children overseas were compliant.

Because of the double dissolution, a half-Senate election became necessary sooner than usual. The Constitution provides that the term of senators elected after a double dissolution should date back to the preceding 1 July, and consequently the terms of half the senators elected in 1951 (those who had been allocated three-year terms in order to maintain the rotation of senators) expired on 30 June 1953. At the consequent election Labor made appreciable gains (50.61 per cent of the total valid vote compared with 45.88 per cent in 1951), but nonetheless gained only one extra seat. Henceforth the coalition would hold a Senate majority of only one vote. This was better than no majority, but the half-Senate result boded ill for the Government at the next House of Representatives election, which could not be delayed beyond the middle of the following year.

Both parliamentary leaders had reason to feel uneasy. Menzies, after less than four years in office, saw the electoral pendulum swinging back against his Government. He also had a restless back bench (three Tasmanian Liberals and one Queensland Country Party member had recently crossed the floor of the lower house to vote against the Government, though unavailingly, on a Land Tax Assessment Bill); and, not so worrying but certainly a distraction, the Speaker was getting on the Government's nerves. During a debate on civil aviation Menzies accused Calwell of conducting 'an organised smear campaign' against Australian National Airways, the free enterprise alternative to the Government-owned Trans-Australia Airlines. Calwell objected, and when the Speaker ordered withdrawal Menzies withdrew only the word 'organised'.

'The Prime Minister must either withdraw [all three words]', said the Speaker, 'or he must move dissent from my ruling'. Menzies moved dissent, and Ward then asked: 'If the motion is carried, Mr Speaker, will you leave the Chair?' To which the Speaker replied: 'It will not have the slightest effect on me'. And neither it did. The motion was carried, and Cameron stayed in the Chair.

Dr Evatt, although encouraged by the electoral swing, became increasingly conscious of friction inside his own party. He was suspicious of Calwell, who was performing well against the Government with accusations of 'pernicious inertia', and, in the hope of steadying his own rather unstable power base, he sought to regain some of the support he had lost on the right of the party through his opposition to the Communist Party Dissolution Act and the referendum proposal. He even contrived a meeting with Santamaria in Melbourne, but that was a vain hope. Something was about to happen that would identify Evatt inescapably with the left, destroying any possibility of reconciliation with the Catholic right and the Industrial Groups.

On 10 February 1954 Menzies was informed by the Director-General of the Australian Security and Intelligence Organisation, Colonel Charles Spry, that A.S.I.O. was negotiating the probable defection of a Russian diplomat in Canberra. The diplomat—Vladimir Petrov, third secretary in the Soviet Embassy, and resident officer of the Ministry of State Security, the M.V.D.—was secretly granted political asylum on 3 April. Ten days later, at peak radio time after the dinner adjournment, Menzies told parliament and the nation of this sensational coup. Petrov had brought with him 'a great number of documents and what may turn out to be much oral information', and enough of this material had already been examined 'to show that there are matters affecting Australia's security which call for judicial investigation'. The Government therefore proposed, said Menzies, 'to set up a royal commission of investigation into what I may call espionage activities in Australia'. The matter was too urgent to wait for the next parliament, he said, and a bill would be introduced immediately for the appointment of three royal commissioners.

Dr Evatt was in Sydney, receiving debutantes at the Fort Street Old Girls' Ball, when Menzies activated this time bomb. Evatt's press secretary, Fergan O'Sullivan, telephoned him there, and a short press statement was issued at about 9 p.m. As soon as parliament sat next morning Evatt was on his feet. The Opposition, he said, would support the fullest inquiry into all the circumstances connected with the Prime Minister's statement, and if anyone had been guilty of espionage or seditious activities a Labor Government would see that he was prosecuted.

GOVERNMENT SUPPORTERS.—Ha ha!

Mr SPEAKER.—Order!

Dr EVATT.—How extraordinary it is, Mr Speaker, that in a matter of supreme national importance we should hear a loud 'Ha ha!' from a few honorable members on the Government side of the House who are notorious for their activities in smear campaigns.

It was not clear whether the laughter was directed at the suggestion that Labor would regain office, or that, if so, it would be willing to prosecute suspected spies; probably both. Until Petrov's sudden materialisation, a Labor victory at the next election had been by no means out of the question. Five of the six States now in fact had Labor Governments. But the outcome of this election would almost certainly be affected by the existence of a Royal Commission into espionage, which opened its proceedings in Canberra twelve days before Australia went to the polls on 29 May. The Government campaigned on its improved economic performance, and promised a reduction in taxes. Menzies studiously avoided the Petrov case; but his faithful Achates, Sir Eric Harrison, asked voters whether they were willing to let a man who had appeared in court for Communists 'take charge of the Royal Commission into Communist espionage'. Evatt avoided both espionage and socialism, promising lower taxes, higher pensions and abolition of the means test. The latter was more than the 'Victorian' Bourke could tolerate. He differed publicly from his leader over the means test, and had to be warned off by the Victorian executive officers.

Labor won 50.03 per cent of the total vote, compared with 47.07 per cent by the coalition parties; but, due in large measure to the 1949 redistribution, this was not enough to gain office. The Government lost five seats (all held by Liberals), but still had a majority of seven in the lower house. This was a bitter blow to Dr Evatt, whose state of mind was already giving some of his colleagues cause for concern. It will not be possible here to trace in detail the path that lay ahead of Dr Evatt and his party. The path was tortuous, strewn with obstacles and ever more downward. To quote the historian of this melancholy period, Robert Murray, Labor now entered 'three terrible years, when it was to provide weekly, if not daily, sensations, and when men were to become parodies of themselves'.

On the day before the twenty-first Parliament opened on 4 August 1954 Evatt survived a leadership challenge from the Western Australian right-winger, Tom Burke, by 64 votes to 20. But Caucus remained highly volatile. Calwell appeared to be dissociating himself as much as possible from Dr Evatt, against the day when he might decide to issue a challenge of his own, and the left-winger, Ward, was also displaying symptoms of leadership ambition. At the next Caucus meeting Haylen told Ward to 'stop beating his chest as if he was running the Party', and Ward took a punch at him. On 16 August Evatt did something that rumour had been saying he might do, and that some of his colleagues feared would cost him the leadership: he appeared before the Petrov Royal Commission as counsel for two members of his own staff—Allan Dalziel, his personal private secretary; and Albert Grundeman, assistant private secretary—who had been mentioned in the proceedings. (A third member of his staff, O'Sullivan, had also been mentioned as author of a document tendered before the Commission.)

This seemed the height of folly, but greater heights were to come. For one thing, Evatt made a public statement which provoked the Commissioners into withdrawing his leave to appear before them, on grounds that there was too much conflict between his roles as politician and counsel. Realising that he had also alienated himself from the right wing, and that the left might now be tempted to support Calwell against him, he moved desperately to the left. On 5 October he issued a press statement which one newspaper referred to as a Hydrogen Bomb. In brief, he attacked the 'Victorians', calling them 'a small minority group of members, located particularly in the State of Victoria', which had, since 1949, become increasingly disloyal to Labor and the Labor leadership. 'Adopting methods which strikingly resemble both Communist and Fascist infiltration of larger groups', he said, 'some of these groups have created an almost intolerable situation—calculated to deflect the Labor Movement from the pursuit of established Labor objectives and ideals . . .'.

Project Hurricane had nothing on the disruptive power of this statement. It split the parliamentary Labor Party for the first time since 1931, and its fission products continued to poison the Labor Party for many years to come. The Split, to give that intricate event its deceptively simple name, might be said to have started in Caucus on 20 October. A motion by right-wing Senator George Cole (T) for a spill of leadership positions was before the meeting, with Calwell and Allan Fraser prepared to stand for Leader and Deputy. Keon, Mullens and Bourke fulminated against Evatt, but the motion for a spill was lost. Although it was clearly defeated on the voices, Ward called for a division. He and Evatt wanted all their enemies clearly identified. 'To everyone's amazement', wrote Daly, who had given his voice to the 'Noes', but was provoked by this tactic into changing his vote, 'Evatt leaped on to the table, pencil and paper in hand, red-faced and excited, and triumphantly called out, "Get their names, get their names!"' The motion was defeated by 52 to 28, and rightly or wrongly the twenty-eight affirmative voters were

Party Politics
Frith's Cartoon in the West Australian, *21 November 1958*

regarded henceforth by the rest of the party as 'Groupers', 'Catholic Action' or 'Movement'.

In the next five months the dimensions of the Split became more apparent. In November the A.L.P. federal executive withdrew official party recognition from the Industrial Groups, and authorised a special conference of the Victorian branch to elect a new Victorian executive in place of the current one, which included six members of the Movement. A new Victorian executive was elected in February 1955, but the party's Federal Conference held in Hobart the following month attracted both Victorian delegations, 'old' and 'new'. Federal Executive ruled that only the new one could attend, and the Conference endorsed Federal Executive's action against the Groups. Calwell expressed guarded criticism of his leader. A distorted report of this appeared in the press, and Dr Evatt was quoted as saying he would give Calwell 'a hiding' if the report was true. To which Calwell replied: 'Dr Evatt couldn't flatten an egg with a shovel'.

Later in March the new Victorian executive suspended four State ministers and thirteen backbench supporters of Victoria's Labor Government. At federal parliamentary level the Split was not so severe as that of 1916. Whereas Hughes had taken fourteen M.H.R.s and eleven senators out of the party with him, when the twenty-first parliament met again for the autumn sitting on 19 April Caucus was short of only seven Victorian M.H.R.s. Those missing were Keon, Bourke, Mullens, Robert Joshua (Ballarat), T. W. Andrews (Darebin), J. L. Cremean (Hoddle) and W. G. Bryson (Bourke). They had been expelled from A.L.P. membership by the new Victorian executive two weeks before, and now called themselves the Australian Labor Party (Anti-Communist). Presumably for tactical reasons, they chose as their leader the only non-Catholic among them—Joshua, a former bank clerk and wartime Lieutenant-Colonel, and a practising Anglican layman whose wife and children were Catholics. Much to the Opposition's resentment, and in spite of strong protest by Evatt, the Speaker gave them as a party room the Deputy Opposition Leader's suite, adjacent to Evatt's own suite. In August they were joined, though on the other side of Parliament House, by Senator Cole, to whom the Government accorded full status as a party leader. His fellow Tasmanian, Labor Senator O'Byrne, suggested that he should be known as Senator Maria.

Only two events from the remainder of this parliament need distract attention briefly from the fission process which continued inexorably during that time. In May a Government backbencher, Percy Joske (Lib, Balaclava, V) brought in the first private member's Bill since Curtin's amendment to the Defence Act in 1939. This was the Matrimonial Causes Bill, providing legal remedy for women whose husbands had deserted them and were domiciled at such a distance—perhaps overseas, as in the case of broken wartime marriages—as to render the task of divorcing them impossibly difficult or costly under existing law. The Bill was supported by both sides, and had an easy passage.

The second event was an unprecedented case of privilege in which parliament defended itself with a zeal that many outsiders regarded as excessive. It was rather as if the House had been annoyed by two blow-flies, and used its new Mace to swat them. On 3 May the Labor Member for Reid (N), Charles Morgan, drew the House's attention to an article in the *Bankstown Observer*, a free advertising weekly in his electorate owned by one Raymond Fitzpatrick and edited by Frank Browne. The article alleged that Morgan 'is, or was, mixed up in what can only be described as an Immigration Racket'. Fitzpatrick was a wealthy haulage contractor whose influence in local politics had earned him the nickname 'Mr Big'. He had supported Jack Lang when the 'Big Fella' temporarily wrested the electorate from Morgan in 1946, and was still feuding with Morgan.

Browne was a journalist notorious for a scandalous and widely read newsletter called *Things I Hear*. The newsletter was heavily political and gratuitously offensive. For example, it always referred to Calwell as 'Awful Arthur', and a recent issue had contained the following item about the Prime Minister.

> This week, trying to get a little reflected glory out of the Test-match, [Menzies] said that if he got to Valhalla he wanted to find a cricketer on either side of him. Tut, tut, Bob. Your knowledge of Norse mythology can't be as bad as all that. Valhalla is a Warriors' paradise. You tore up your admission ticket way back in 1914.

Browne had few if any friends in parliament, and plenty of enemies.

Morgan's complaint that the *Observer* article directly attacked his integrity and conduct as a parliamentarian was referred by the House to its Committee of Privileges. As was usual in such cases the Clerk of the House reported to the Committee as to whether in his opinion privilege was involved. In this case Clerk Green advised the Committee in writing that it would be absurd if parliamentary privilege protected a member against allegations about his conduct outside the House; Morgan's complaint was not a matter of privilege, and the proper place to resolve it was a civil court. Nevertheless, the Committee reported that there was no evidence of improper conduct by Morgan, and that Fitzpatrick and Browne were guilty of a serious breach of privilege by publishing articles intended to influence and intimidate a member in his conduct in the House.

On 9 June the House agreed without division to two motions by the Prime Minister: one endorsing the Committee's report, and the other resolving that Fitzpatrick and Browne be notified that the House would hear them at the Bar at 10 a.m. the following day before proceeding to decide what action it would take against them for their breach of privilege. No one had ever before been called to the Bar of the lower house, though Sir Robert Gibson had appeared in much different circumstances at the Bar of the Senate in 1931.

The Bar is a cylindrical brass rail which can be lowered across the main entrance to the chamber directly opposite the Speaker's Chair. Fitzpatrick was escorted to it first by the Serjeant-at-Arms (J. A. Pettifer), and he apologised briefly and humbly. When Browne's turn came, he went down like a true larrikin, giving cheek to the end. He spoke eloquently and at length about freedom of speech. The Speaker ordered him to take his hands off the Bar, and Browne went on to ask how it was that he had been convicted though never charged, had no legal representation, and no right to cross-examine his accuser. In these proceedings, he said, the Prime Minister had but one purpose—'Bring Browne in here to grovel for mercy, and if he does not grovel for mercy, put him in for life'. It was a spirited performance, but in the ensuing debate Menzies termed it 'an exhibition of unparalleled arrogance and impertinence'. He went on to say that parliament was 'the flower of Australian democracy, and the degree to which this House protects the freedom of its members to speak and to think will be the measure of its service to democracy'. Calwell called Browne 'an arrogant rat', and Fitzpatrick 'an illiterate lout'.

In separate motions Menzies moved that the offenders be committed to gaol for three months. Dr Evatt moved amendments to impose substantial fines in place of gaol sentences, and when those were defeated the motions were put and passed, by 55 to 12 in the case of Fitzpatrick and 55 to 11 in the case of Browne. A.L.P. members voted according to conscience; but many of them were absent or, like Calwell, abstained from the division. The 'No' voters were all A.L.P., and only three A.L.P. members voted for gaol. They were Norman Makin, the former Speaker who had re-entered parliament for the South Australian seat of Bonython after his return from Washington; Nelson Lemmon (Forrest, W); and E. G. Whitlam.

The offenders were transferred from custody of the Serjeant-at-Arms to that of the Australian Capital Territory's Chief Commissioner of Police, and finally taken to Goulburn gaol, where they completed their full sentences. Few Australians would have realised before this unique case that parliament had the power to imprison citizens. Such power was inherited from Westminster, through Section 49 of the Constitution, which provides that parliament's powers, privileges and immunities shall be such as are declared by parliament, 'and until declared shall be those of the Commons House of Parliament of the United Kingdom'. Fitzpatrick and Browne applied to the

High Court for writs of habeas corpus to release them, but their applications were dismissed. Allan Fraser tried in parliament to have their sentences reduced, but his efforts came to nothing.

The press and other channels of public opinion sided strongly against parliament. The *Sydney Morning Herald*, for example, said that 'by invoking the ancient and outmoded sanctions of privilege and applying them so harshly' parliament had 'risked making martyrs of two inconspicuous and rather contemptible persons' and had 'raised up a strong public feeling that no citizens of this free country, whatever their misdemeanours, should be gaoled except by due process of the law and the Courts'. According to a Gallup poll, 67 per cent of all Australians held that view, or something like it.

By coincidence, the day parliament sent two men to gaol was Frank Green's last day at the Table before his retirement, after thirty-four years on the staff of the House of Representatives and eighteen years as its Clerk. He was deeply depressed by the proceedings of that day. 'I had been dedicated to upholding parliamentary democracy against the interests controlling the Executive', he wrote after his retirement. 'Now I saw myself as a failure and Parliament as something meaningless, just a "front" for the dead democracy. As for Parliament House, I saw it as Frank Anstey had finally seen it—"The House of Dead Hopes; the habitation of Dead Souls"'.

Anstey's valediction could also have been applied to the parliamentary Labor Party at this time. On 20 April Evatt resigned the leadership in order to test his support, and was re-elected by 52 votes to 27. That afternoon Bill Bourke addressed the House on 'a definite matter of urgent public importance'—namely, 'the subservience of the Right Honourable Leader of the Opposition and his followers to the Communist Party, as evidenced by his acceptance of large sums of money from Communist sources to the funds of the party led by him'. Speaking for the Anti-Communist Labor Party, he referred to Evatt as 'the man who wrecked the Labor Party' and 'the best friend the Communists ever had'.

Two weeks later Keon returned to the attack in a debate on foreign affairs and defence. The debate dealt mainly with Australia's commitment of troops and aircraft, under its ANZAM agreement with Britain and New Zealand, to help combat Communist rebellion in Malaya, and with the Southeast Asia Treaty Organisation (SEATO), which had been established by agreement with the United States in the previous year. Keon took an extremely hard line on defence (he had earlier advocated the pre-emptive use of nuclear weapons against China), and contrasted his own party's fear of a Chinese Communist invasion of Southeast Asia with the A.L.P.'s misgivings about the Malayan commitment. When Keon's time expired, the Speaker gave the next call to the Government rather than Labor. Such was the resulting uproar from the Labor benches that at 9.08 p.m. Cameron suspended the sitting until the following afternoon, and for good measure ordered the Serjeant-at-Arms to remove the Mace from the chamber. The only other time a Speaker had suspended a sitting was in 1919, for fifteen minutes, during Mick Considine's celebrated fracas.

The report of the Royal Commission on Espionage, tabled on 14 September, was a distinct anticlimax. 'What is the upshot of this Petrov affair?' asked

Dr Evatt in the ensuing debate, which took place in October. 'There has been the attempted smearing of many innocent Australians, grave inroads have been made into Australian freedoms by attacks on political non-conformity . . . But after eighteen months of inquiry, at this great cost to the nation, no spies have been discovered. Not a single prosecution is recommended.' Dr Evatt should have left it at that. Instead, carried away by the not unreasonable belief that Menzies had stage-managed the affair for electoral gain, he told an incredulous House that he had written to the Foreign Minister of the U.S.S.R., Mr Molotov, asking whether the Petrov documents were genuine. To a gale of cat-calls and laughter he went on to read Molotov's reply—that the documents were 'falsifications fabricated on the instructions of persons interested in the deterioration of the Soviet–Australian relations and in discrediting their political opponents'.

This remarkable failure of political judgement on Evatt's part must have been partly the result of exceptional stress. But some were also reminded of an earlier assertion by Santamaria that Evatt's talk of Catholic conspiracy was the 'figment of a disordered mind'. Menzies elaborated on that theme:

> In brief, the right honorable gentleman would have us believe that months of investigation on oath, scores of thousands of questions and answers, and the meticulous examination of documents, should all be brushed aside because the nation found guilty of espionage says, "We are not guilty".
> What I have already said will, without any verbal decorations, satisfy all sane and sensible people that the right honorable gentleman, suffering from persecution delusions, is introducing us into a world of sheer fantasy.

On 26 October 1955 Menzies took advantage of the Split and the Molotov letter by calling an early general election. The new Governor-General proved no less obliging than the old, and writs were issued for an election on 10 December. The only real issue was the Leader of the Opposition, and his fitness to lead. In his crumpled suit, wide-brimmed old hat and red socks, Dr Evatt was an unappealing figure by comparison with his impregnable rival in well cut double-breaster. He held his own seat by only 226 votes, and his party, severely disadvantaged by Anti-Communist Labor preferences, lost ten seats. Labor's only consolation was that all seven M.H.R.s of the Joshua group were defeated. But one Anti-Communist Labor candidate, F. P. V. McManus, was elected to the Senate from Victoria. After July he and Senator Cole would hold the balance of power there.

The Ming Dynasty

Midway through the twenty-second parliament, on 3 April 1957, Menzies became Australia's longest-serving Prime Minister by any reckoning. If his pre-war Ministry was taken into account, he had broken the cumulative record two years earlier. Now he had been Prime Minister continuously for seven years three months and six days (one day longer than the total of W. M. Hughes's three consecutive ministries from 1915 to 1923), and he showed no sign of faltering. A few of his backbenchers went their own way from time to time, and the Senate was no longer under the coalition's absolute control. Compared to his hag-ridden rival, however, Menzies could look forward to relatively plain sailing. The 'magnificent voyage' which he had once predicted for the Liberal Party might run into a nasty squall, or run out of wind; but there were no shoals or reefs on the course ahead. The Menzies ascendancy, which some already called the Ming Dynasty, had the look of permanence. His public persona was as familiar and probably as highly approved as that of any previous prime minister. According to the Gallup poll his approval for leadership by non-Labor voters was 90 per cent, whereas only 51 per cent of Labor voters extended the same kind of approval to Dr Evatt. After the election Evatt had survived a leadership challenge by Allan Fraser, but his manner became more muddled and eccentric, intensifying the disadvantage at which he found himself in most encounters with Menzies.

With his colleagues, Menzies was friendly yet aloof; he could unbend more graciously than earlier in his life, but only a fool would have overstepped the mark with him. On one occasion he had been regaling some backbenchers with an anecdote. He was a superb raconteur, and the punchline brought peals of unaffected laughter. One of the group, Bruce Wight (Lib, Lilley, Q), forgot himself so far as to slap the Prime Minister on the back and say: 'You old bastard!' The laughter ceased. Menzies said, 'Good evening gentlemen', and left the room. As Leslie Haylen wrote about a similiar incident between the leader and some of his followers, 'the Godhead had withdrawn beyond the veil'.

In the party room he was courteous but masterful. If a member dug his heels in, wrote Jo Gullett, the Prime Minister would resort to his 'Old boy' technique.

> Don't think I do not appreciate your difficulties.' 'There is much substance in what you say.' 'We must consider it.' 'I am grateful to Geoff for reminding us of this' . . . If all this fails there are more drastic measures. A troublesome member like Wentworth can soon find himself isolated: 'He is disloyal . . . He gives information to the press. He has been heard to say this or that.' One way or another the party does pretty much as it is told.

Menzies also tightened his control of Cabinet by reducing it to more manageable size. With the swearing in of the new Ministry in January 1956, Cabinet was restricted to twelve of the twenty-two ministers, a practice borrowed in principle from Westminster.

The only member of the old ministry whose absence from the new occasioned much comment was the former Minister for the Interior, W. A. (later Sir Wilfrid) Kent Hughes. His omission, much as it shocked the man himself, was hardly surprising, for Billy Kent Hughes had blotted his ministerial escutcheon a year before while inspecting war graves in Asia. Colonel Kent Hughes had been a prisoner of war in Taiwan, and had since become a passionate supporter of the Chiang-Kai-shek regime on that island, and an opponent of the Chinese mainland government. To the embarrassment of Menzies, who was visiting London at the time, Kent Hughes took the opportunity while in Taiwan of publicly taking the British Government to task for its China policy. Menzies sent a cable asking him to refrain from making any more statements on foreign policy, and from then on his ministerial days were numbered. After being dropped from the ministry he became chairman of the Joint Committee on Foreign Affairs, and one of the main critics of low expenditure on defence.

In his opening speech on 15 February 1956 the Governor-General foreshadowed legislation for the introduction of television into Australia along lines recommended by a Royal Commission in 1954. He also referred to his advisers' concern, natural enough with the balance of power about to change in the Senate, that relations between the two houses should be reviewed. 'They are of opinion', said Sir William Slim,

> that a government requires a reasonable term of office and a reasonable period of stability in which it may give effect to its long-range plans for the nation. They will, therefore, propose the setting up of an all-party committee of both Houses to investigate the constitutional problems which may be referred to it. One of these problems is that of the Senate and its powers and the procedure to be followed in the event of a dispute between the two Houses.

The Governor-General's speech made no mention of banking legislation, which as it turned out was to be one of the twenty-second parliament's most controversial issues. This was no oversight on the part of His Excellency's advisers, for the issue was raised against the Government's wishes by some of its own backbenchers who wanted legislation to complete the administrative separation of the Commonwealth Bank and the Commonwealth Trading Bank. Menzies managed to curb most of these backbenchers ('There is much substance in what you say . . . '), but H. J. Bate (Lib, Macarthur, N) persisted in attempting to introduce a private member's bill in May. The Whips made sure he did not obtain a seconder, but that was not the last that was to be heard of the subject in this parliament.

Two Government senators abstained from voting on a Stevedoring Industry Bill, designed to replace the Australian Stevedoring Board with a new Stevedoring Industry Authority that would have no control over wages. This revolt was potentially more serious for the Government than Jeff Bate's insubordination, but the Bill passed all stages successfully in June. Another measure agreed to without amendment by the Senate that month was the Parliamentary Allowances Bill, approving a recommendation by the Richardson Committee that parliamentary salaries be increased by £600 per year. Although this was the second such increment in four years, it did little more than bring members' salaries into line with those of some State parliaments.

The Prime Minister was overseas for four months of this parliament's first session, and during that time he played an unexpectedly prominent role on the stage of international politics. He left Australia in May to attend the Commonwealth Conference, and was on his way home via the United States in July when Egypt, in repudiation of contractual concession, nationalised the Suez Canal. Back he went to London for a round of crisis meetings reminiscent of his wartime exploits there. On 23 August the 22-nation Suez

Canal conference appointed Menzies leader of a small delegation to negotiate with President Nasser in Cairo. The British Prime Minister, Sir Anthony
Eden, sent a message to Fadden, asking him to 'spare' Menzies for this task,
even though it would mean that the Prime Minister would not return to Australia in time for the opening of parliament's Budget sitting. Fadden sent
Menzies a cable saying: 'Good luck. We are heartened by the skill, honesty
and care with which we know you will approach this matter'. But no amount
of luck or skill could have saved this ill-fated mission from failure. It was
doomed on 28 August, six days before the delegation's first meeting with
Nasser, by a statement from the American Secretary of State, John Foster
Dulles, that 'the Suez Canal is not a primary concern to the United States'.
Menzies argued the case for international management of the canal, and
obliquely threatened Egypt; Nasser dismissed international control as a new
form of imperialism, accused Menzies of threatening him, and broke off
negotiations.

'My Cairo jaunt was a very stimulating and interesting one', wrote
Menzies to an old friend and long-time correspondent, the artist Lionel
Lindsay, 'and served to make me completely au fait with all sides of the Suez
problem. If it were not for official matters at home urgently requiring my
attention, I would have loved dearly to stay in London for further
conferences'. Parliament debated the Suez crisis on 25 September, and again
on 1 November, only a few hours after the Anglo-French bombing of Egyp-
tian airfields. Menzies maintained that Egypt's nationalisation decree was a
breach of international law, which justified the use of force. Evatt, speaking
after the bombing, returned in spirit to his presidency of the United Nations:

> I say that certain events are happening, and innocent people are being
> killed because of the action of the British and French governments. It is
> disgraceful to think that this should occur without the authority of the
> United Nations . . . The [Prime Minister] has postulated the theory that
> you can use force without the authority of the United Nations if you think
> it is right that it should be used . . . That is an absolutely intolerable and
> illegal doctrine, and no one who has any experience of the United Nations
> Charter or its working would put forward such a proposition.

On this point the Minister for External Affairs, Casey, was more in agreement with Evatt than with Menzies. His opposition to the invasion of Egypt
contrasted strongly with the Prime Minister's championship of Britain right
or wrong, and it may well have cost him the deputy leadership of the parliamentary Liberal Party when Sir Eric Harrison resigned to become High
Commissioner in London. In a preferential ballot on 26 September Casey
was the first candidate to be eliminated, followed by Sir Philip McBride
(Grey, S), and Senator W. H. Spooner (N). The new Deputy Leader, Leader
of the House and heir-apparent was the Melbourne lawyer, Harold Holt, a
protégé of Menzies who, although only forty-eight years old, had now been
in parliament for more than two decades. Holt was not only an able minister,
but sociable and debonair as well. When the Queen Mother attended a State
Ball in her honour during this parliament, it was the new Leader of the
House who danced a quick-step with her.

The House also had a new Speaker. Archie Cameron fought his last battle during the winter recess of 1956, and when parliament resumed another South Australian, Jack (later Sir John) McLeay, was elected in his place. Speaker McLeay was more fig than bramble. It was said, by Clyde Cameron, that Sir John knew less about Standing Orders than any other post-war Speaker; but he brought a welcome evenness of temperament to the Chair. At the same time, the House seemed to lose some of its verve as well as uproar. Indeed the twenty-second parliament was one of the least talented of its kind for many years. Some of the best debaters, notably the defeated 'Victorians', were no longer to be heard; and ministers were often notable for their absence when by rights they should have been in the chamber. In a ministerial statement on 19 March 1957, Holt drew attention to the scantiness of attendance. He said that Cabinet meetings and party committee meetings would be arranged to enable ministers and private members to spend more time in the House, but this did not eventuate. More than a year later the Liberal backbencher, Gullett, remarked upon the decline of parliament. 'The Prime Minister must accept a good deal of responsibility for this state of affairs', he wrote.

> To begin with, he and his Cabinet hardly ever attend debates. The general thing is for one bored minister to sit dejectedly at the table while debates are going on or to bring in a file of papers and attend to them without the least sign of paying attention to the speakers. Little by little the impression grows on the members that parliament does not matter and they bother about it less and less.

The issue of reorganising the Commonwealth-owned banks, raised initially by Bate and other Liberal backbenchers, was urged upon the Government with more success by some of the private banks most concerned about competition from that quarter. Fadden and his party were opposed to any weakening of the Commonwealth Bank, and the Government's eventual decision to proceed with changes in the banking structure was evidence of the extent to which Country Party influence had declined within the coalition. But the package of fourteen bills introduced on 25 October 1957 was not exactly what some free enterprise champions had expected.

The main measures were the Reserve Bank Bill, separating central banking from other functions, and renaming the central bank; the Commonwealth Banks Bill, setting up three banks (the Trading Bank, Savings Bank and Development Bank), all controlled by a Commonwealth Banking Corporation; and the Banking Bill, replacing special accounts by statutory reserve deposits, of which 25 per cent could be withdrawn by the central bank at short notice. Although these proposals would bring about the desired separation of functions, it became obvious that in some respects they would in fact strengthen the Commonwealth Bank rather than weaken it. This did not prevent Labor from attacking the bills as a 'sinister sellout', and when the package reached the Senate in November it encountered united opposition from twenty-seven A.L.P. senators and three Labor breakaways—Cole and McManus, and a Queensland senator, C. P. Byrne. When the Split spread to Queensland in 1957 the Premier of that State, V. C. Gair, and most of his ministers were expelled from the A.L.P. They formed the Queensland Labor Party, and it was to this counterpart of Victoria's Anti-Communist Labor Party that Senator Byrne now belonged.

Thirty negative votes would deadlock the Senate, and in that event under Standing Orders the banking legislation would be rejected. Obviously every vote would be needed, and one Labor senator, J. J. Arnold (N), was recovering from major surgery in a Newcastle hospital. He was flown to Canberra. At the last minute Holt offered Labor a pair, but the offer was declined and Senator Arnold, pale and hollow-eyed, voted from a wheelchair in the crucial division on 27 November. His convalescence did not appear to be affected, and he served another eight years in the Senate. More banking bills were guillotined through the lower house four months later, and again they were negatived by a tied vote in the Senate, this time without need of a wheelchair. Menzies could then have requested a double dissolution. He did not do so, presumably because dissolution of the whole Senate would have enhanced the breakaway Labor group's chances of retaining the balance of power.

Could anything be done to ameliorate this problem of disagreement between the houses? The Joint Committee on Constitutional Review, which had been established to examine that question among others, presented its report in October 1958. There had been only one previous constitutional review, by a Royal Commission appointed in 1927, and its recommendations had been completely ignored. The Joint Committee fared little better. On the question of disagreement it recommended that in certain circumstances the Governor-General in Council should be empowered to convene a joint sitting of the two houses to vote upon a proposed law in dispute, without the preliminary double dissolution as presently provided for by the Constitution. The number of members of the House of Representatives should no longer be tied to being as nearly as practicable twice the number of senators, and senators' terms should end at the expiry or prior dissolution of the lower house. The Joint Committee also reported widespread dissatisfaction with the present state of financial arrangements between the Commonwealth and the States, and recommended that a conference of political leaders should be held to discover whether any substantial adjustment of the relative financial positions could be achieved.

Although the Joint Committee's recommendations were not acted upon by the Government, the financial position of the States was improved in 1959 by the introduction of Financial Assistance Grants. These replaced the tax reimbursement grants which had been made by the Commonwealth since 1942, when the States relinquished income tax. They were determined by a formula taking into account population growth, wage rises and a 'betterment factor' allowing the States to improve their services. Financial Assistance Grants could be spent in any way the States wished, but since the early 1950s the Commonwealth had also been making greater use of specific purpose grants, which could be spent only as Canberra stipulated. From the federalist point of view, this represented a growth of central power and a further loss of State autonomy.

Several other events during the life of this parliament affected State finances. Two of them were judgments by the High Court. The former Chief Justice, Sir John Latham, once said that when he died, Section 92 of the Constitution would be found written on his heart. And that prescription of free trade within the Commonwealth continued to be a fertile source of transport cases after Latham was succeeded by Sir Owen Dixon in 1952. In *Hughes and Vale* v. *New South Wales* (1955), the Court had raised obstacles to the taxation of interstate trade; but in *Armstrong* v. *Victoria* (1957), Victoria's revised system of taxing interstate road hauliers was held to be valid. The second event, also in 1957, was a case brought by Victoria and New South Wales challenging the validity of the Commonwealth's monopoly of income tax. This was the second uniform tax case, and in its judgment the Court upheld the essential elements of uniform tax legislation. It gave a wide interpretation to the Commonwealth's grants power, and confirmed the view expressed by Latham in the 1942 case that the Commonwealth had power to determine the course of State administration by means of specific purpose grants.

Another event affecting Commonwealth–State financial relations was the appointment in 1957 of an expert committee, chaired by a British academic, Sir Keith Murray, to report on the future of Australian universities. Menzies wholeheartedly supported the Murray Committee's recommendations for radically increased federal expenditure on new and existing universities. In 1959 the Australian Universities Commission was established to advise the Government on triennial budgeting for Commonwealth contributions and matching grants for this long-overdue programme of university expansion.

Finally, in this recital of events affecting Commonwealth–State relations, parliament passed a Railway Standardisation (New South Wales and Victoria) Agreement Bill in September 1958, approving an agreement between the Commonwealth, New South Wales and Victoria for the standardisation of railway between Sydney and Melbourne. This followed the report of a Government Members' Rail Standardisation Committee, appointed in 1956 and chaired by W. C. Wentworth, which had recommended a practicable plan for overcoming Australia's costly break-of-gauge problem. The problem was that railway lines in New South Wales were built to standard-gauge or width; those in Victoria and part of South Australia to broad gauge; and those of Queensland, Tasmania and Western Australia to narrow gauge. Under the Standardisation Agreement Act, the Commonwealth initially provided all funds and bore seven-tenths of the cost of standardising the gauge between Albury in New South Wales and Melbourne. This part of the national undertaking was completed in 1961, and by 1969 a standard-gauge line via Broken Hill linked the east and west coasts of the continent.

At the next general election, on 22 November 1958, the Country Party had a new leader. After twenty-two years in parliament, and more Budgets than any other federal treasurer, Sir Arthur Fadden had announced in March that he would retire at the end of the parliament. His deputy, John McEwen, was elected to the leadership unopposed, but Menzies made it clear that, past custom notwithstanding, the Country Party had no exclusive claim to the Treasurership. This was a further indication of the Country Party's weaker standing in the coalition, but there was nothing weak about the new leader himself. 'Black Jack' McEwen was probably the only minister able to confront Menzies on anything like equal terms, and the Prime Minister privately considered him to be the ablest man, after himself, in the Government. Holt was appointed Treasurer after the election, and McEwen remained at Trade, where he had been notably successful. In July 1957 he had signed the Japan–Australia Trade Agreement, strongly opposed by manufacturing groups and trade unions. Later that year a visit to Australia by the Japanese Prime Minister, Mr Kishi, provided further evidence of a new relationship between the two countries.

The establishment of an office of Secondary Industry within McEwen's department led some to suspect him of seeking to extend his party's influence into the manufacturing sector—which was to say, into outer metropolitan electorates. He denied this, but the impression remained that he was much less in the Country Party's traditional low-tariff, anti-city mould than his predecessors.

Among candidates at the 1958 election were members of a new political party, the Democratic Labor Party, which had been established in New South Wales two years previously by Industrial Group sympathisers. In 1957 it joined forces with the Anti-Communist Labor Party, under its own name and the leadership of Senator Cole, and for the election it fielded a total of 113 candidates (counting those of its northern counterpart, the Queensland Labor Party) in all States. Its supporters were advised to give their second preferences to Liberal or Country Party candidates. That alone would probably have been enough to cruel any remaining hope for the A.L.P. on polling day. During the campaign Dr Evatt made an extraordinary offer to vacate the leadership after the election, win or lose, if the D.L.P. would give its second preferences to his party. Senator Cole rejected the offer by demanding that the A.L.P. should first abandon socialism, unity tickets with Communists, opposition to the Industrial Groups, and recognition of Communist China.

This was the first televised federal election campaign. Policy speeches were not televised, but Evatt and Calwell debated unemployment and migration against Holt and McMahon, and the Prime Minister made a solo appearance before a panel of four polite journalists. Two days before the election Labor published newspaper advertisements appealing again for D.L.P. second preferences and quoting Cardinal Gilroy to the effect that Christians were free to vote for any party except the Communist Party. Archbishop Mannix promptly put a stop to that by saying: 'Every Communist and every Communist sympathiser in Australia wants a victory for the Evatt party. This is alarming'.

As it happened, the Evatt party polled rather better than expected, but still poorly enough to satisfy the Government. In the lower house the Liberal and Country parties each made a net gain of one seat, increasing the government's majority to thirty-two. The Senate was now under coalition control as well, by a majority of four. Senator Cole was re-elected, and Senator McManus still had half of his six-year term to run. No other D.L.P. candidates were elected to either house, but in a negative sense the new party had achieved one of its most important objectives by depriving Labor of D.L.P. second preferences—88 per cent of them in Victoria, and 60 per cent in New

South Wales. At the next meeting of Caucus, Evatt was challenged by Ward. Calwell bided his time, no doubt drawing comfort from Ward's public reference to 'grave and continuing errors of leadership', and the reduced margin by which Evatt survived (46 votes to 32).

The twenty-third parliament opened on 17 February 1959, and for the first time this ceremony was televised to viewers in Sydney. Another innovation was the gentle but insistent ringing of division bells, accompanied by blinking red and green lights, which now replaced the buzzers used previously to summon members into their chambers. The legislative programme for the first session included the banking Bills from the previous parliament (these passed quickly though both chambers, with only minor amendments designed to provide some consolation for their backbench Liberal critics); another Parliamentary Allowances Bill, providing the third salary increment in seven years (£400 per annum), and accorded much hostile press comment on that account; and a Matrimonial Causes Bill, designed to establish uniform divorce law in place of the ten codes then existing in different parts of the Commonwealth.

Three Liberal and two D.L.P. senators opposed the salary proposals in the Senate, but the absence of ten A.L.P. senators allowed the Bill to pass without amendment. In spite of a Caucus decision that the basic salary increases should be allowed to pass, eight members spoke against them, or abstained from voting. This was probably no more than insurance against electoral hostility. The result was not in doubt.

The Matrimonial Causes Bill was the sequel to an earlier botched attempt at divorce reform. In 1957 the Government had agreed to let Joske introduce a private member's bill, but the price he had to pay for that permission was a bill so conservative that the legal profession campaigned against it. Menzies finally withdrew the bill, and gave an undertaking that the Government would put through one of its own. He now had the very man for that job: the greatest constitutional lawyer of his day, Garfield Barwick. Barwick had come into parliament at a by-election for Parramatta (N) in 1958, and was appointed Attorney-General in Menzies's new Ministry, as he had known he would be.

In handling this Bill, Barwick earned his spurs with distinction. Of fourteen proposed grounds for divorce, the most controversial was that which allowed divorce after separation for five years when there was no prospect of cohabitation being resumed. This concept of divorce without matrimonial fault was already embodied in the Western Australian code, but was new to the rest of Australia. Both sides treated the Bill as a non-party measure. Evatt strongly supported it; Calwell opposed it; and generally sides were taken according to religious conviction or lack of it. During the second reading debate Dr Evatt paid his old legal opponent a generous tribute. 'I have heard very many famous speeches, both in this chamber and elsewhere', he said. '[The Attorney-General's] speech appealed to me as one of the most impressive, important and decisive speeches of its kind that I have ever heard.' The Bill passed its second reading in the lower house by 84 votes to 16, and passed the Senate in December with only minor amendment.

Dr Evatt's time in the House of Dead Hopes was now almost over. In spite of doubts about his stability, the Heffron Labor Government of New South Wales loyally and irresponsibly offered him the Chief Justiceship of that State. At the end of his last day in Parliament House he walked down the steps alone, and never returned. He was installed as Chief Justice in February 1960 and remained there, a growing cause of concern and even alarm to his fellow judges, until he suffered a complete mental collapse in 1962. He then withdrew from public life and lived as an invalid in Canberra for only three more years. Sometimes he would wake up believing that he was still a justice of the High Court. Perhaps he wished, in so far as he could wish anything by then, that he had never left the High Court for politics. No parliamentarian's life ended more bleakly than Evatt's, except perhaps Alfred Deakin's.

Calwell was elected to succeed Evatt by 42 votes to 30, his only opponent being Reg Pollard, who was supported by those who feared that Calwell's Catholicism might lead him to seek a rapprochement with the D.L.P. In the ballot for Deputy Leader, Gough Whitlam had a narrower win against three rivals. The final vote, against Eddie Ward, was 38–34.

Labor's new leaders were generally regarded as a well balanced choice: a 63-year-old Victorian Catholic with trade union connections, and a 43-year-old non-Catholic (indeed agnostic) from the upper middle class. Under their tutelage the Parliamentary Labor Party could surely look forward to at least some improvement in its fortunes. It was doubtful, however, that this change of leadership perturbed the Lord Protector in his Lodge. Menzies seemed more secure than ever. He knew how to discern Australia's worries and assuage them, and he knew how to handle opponents on both sides of the House. Only a few weeks earlier his one-time rival for leadership of the U.A.P., Casey, had followed Spender and Harrison out of parliament. Menzies got him a life peerage, and he went to join his old patron, Bruce, in the House of Lords. There were no more pretenders to the Liberal throne, only an authorised and patient heir. The Ming dynasty seemed likely to flourish, if not for generations more, at least for parliaments more.

15

Changing of the Guard

Lion Passant

A newly appointed Governor-General, Viscount Dunrossil, ushered parliament into the 1960s with a speech that began—first things first!—with proper attention to the Royal Family. Before outlining his advisers' proposals for the second session of the twenty-third parliament, which opened on 8 March 1960, His Excellency rejoiced at the birth of a second son to Her Majesty the Queen, noted with pleasure the betrothal of Princess Margaret, and recalled the honour and delight felt by all Australians during the recent visit from Princess Alexandra of Kent. Such remarks were traditionally intended to inspire a sense of continuity and well being: the Queen's on her throne, God's in his heaven, and all's right with the world. Yet the 1960s held more surprises than Lord Dunrossil or his audience could have suspected. For one thing there would be a marked weakening of the British connection with Australia, a connection never more aptly symbolised than by the presence of a British Governor-General at Yarralumla. As if presaging the changes soon to come, Lord Dunrossil died in office before he could open another Australian parliament.

William Shepherd Morrison, as he was before elevation to the peerage, was a Governor-General in the mould of Munro-Ferguson: a Scot who distinguished himself as a soldier during World War I, and later entered the House of Commons. He was a Conservative member for thirty years, and Speaker of the House for eight of those years. During his short term of viceregal office in Canberra, Dunrossil travelled more widely than was perhaps wise for a man of sixty-seven. He visited all States of the Commonwealth, and the territory of Papua-New Guinea. Although his health had been good when he left England, he contracted a stomach infection in Port Moresby, and later developed symptoms of heart trouble.

His first anniversary as Governor-General, on 2 February 1961, was marred by illness; next morning, when his valet took a cup of tea to his bed-room, he was dead. Dunrossil was the first Governor-General to die in office, and he was buried in the churchyard of St John the Baptist, not far from the graves of Clerk Gale and Clerk McGregor. His successor was another viscount—Lord De L'Isle, a winner of the Victoria Cross, managing director of Schweppes (Home) Ltd, and descendant of the Elizabethan soldier and poet Sir Philip Sidney. A Gallup poll at the time showed that 63 per cent of respondents would have preferred an Australian appointment. They were soon to have their wish, for Lord De L'Isle was the last British Governor-General. His successor in 1965, the first Australian to be recommended for this office by a conservative government, was the eminently suitable Lord Casey.

During the first half of the 1960s, with which this chapter will be con-cerned, the British lion guardant seemed to become a lion passant, walking away towards Europe. Britain's application to join the European Economic Community may have been thwarted temporarily by France in 1963, but for many Australians the British intention alone was enough to dramatise the end of imperial protection, and to encourage greater reliance upon Austra-lia's wartime saviour. There was soon to be a changing of the guard, from lion to eagle; even the currency would be changed, from pound to dollar. Enemies would be revised according to America's estimate of danger. No longer would Indonesia be considered as dangerous as it was during the con-frontations in West New Guinea and Malaysia; the new foe would be Com-munist aggression, and the battlefield would be Vietnam. Finally, there would be a change of Prime Ministers in 1966. Menzies, still British to his bootheels, would be succeeded by someone more at ease in new company. Holt got on well with most people, but was temperamentally more in tune with Americans than Britons.

Before considering these events, we must return to the parliamentary session opened by Lord Dunrossil in 1960. Its two most controversial measures dealt with internal security: the Telephonic Communications (Interception) Bill, defining procedures by which ASIO could tap telephones in order to protect the Commonwealth from acts of espionage or subversion; and a bill to amend the Crimes Act. Barwick had a fair measure of success with these, but not without cost to his own parliamentary reputation. As Menzies was to say later about his Attorney-General, he was a good lawyer but a disappointing politician. '[Barwick] didn't understand parliament. He didn't understand the art of getting along with that fellow over in the corner, and making him think.' Furthermore, he could not withstand the Opposition's fire as coolly as those with longer parliamentary experience. Someone like Ward could get straight under his skin. During the Telephonic Communications debate, for example, Ward taunted him with the political applications of phone-tapping:

> much as I abhor this eavesdropping on telephones, I have no doubt that if I could listen to a few telephone conversations, including some to which the Attorney-General is a party, I would obtain some very

interesting information which would be of great interest to this Parliament. The Attorney-General who, obviously, is very uncomfortable at the moment, will have to be careful because, when you listen in to the telephone conversations you get all kinds of information. You can even hear conversations about bankruptcies, and probably the Attorney-General appreciates the matter to which I am referring.

Sir GARFIELD BARWICK.—I know how dirty that remark is.

Mr SPEAKER.—Order!

Mr WARD.—The Attorney-General—

Sir GARFIELD BARWICK.—I know how dirty that remark is.

Barwick, as Ward knew, had been made bankrupt for a few months at the age of twenty-seven because of unsuccessful efforts to help one of his brothers out of financial trouble. There was no shame in it, and a better parliamentary performer could easily have turned the attack back upon Ward. Instead, said Haylen in the House next day, Barwick 'went like a wet meringue'.

The phone-tapping Bill passed without amendment; but the Crimes Bill, introduced in September 1960, was modified to some extent. It was intended to make good what the Government had come to regard, during proceedings before the Petrov Royal Commission, as shortcomings in the Crimes Act. Not since the Latham amendments of 1926 had the Act been tightened to such an extent as this: Barwick's Bill redefined the offences of treason, treachery, sabotage and espionage, strengthening the State's defences but also weakening civil liberties. As with the Communist Party Dissolution Bill, there was heated argument in Caucus between left-wingers demanding outright opposition to the measure, and those who believed with Calwell and Whitlam that the party should accept the principle while arguing for extensive changes in detail. In one argument Eddie Ward chased Gough Whitlam, flung his glasses on to a lobby couch and aimed a punch at the deputy leader, missing him and bruising his own knuckles on the wall. (Ward later used to say that he first realised he was getting old when that punch missed Whitlam.) Caucus endorsed the Calwell–Whitlam approach, but the extra-parliamentary 'No' forces were nevertheless mobilised again. On 26 October a crowd of three hundred unionists from Sydney and Port Kembla demonstrated rowdily against the Bill in King's Hall.

Sir Garfield's chief parliamentary opponent, the towering shadow Attorney-General, drew attention to the incongruity of Barwick's legal and political careers. 'He is the person', said Whitlam, 'who inculcated in the courts of this country, more than anybody else has ever done, a distrust of government. He is now finding the same attitude being attributed to him as he has always protested about on the part of other State and Commonwealth governments'. On one occasion Whitlam and other Labor members reduced the one-time hero of High Court and Privy Council to tears of frustration.

During the committee stage of the Bill, on 17 November, Barwick asked: 'Would anybody contend that if an assassin was intercepted after he had made a pass at the Sovereign or the heir apparent, he could not be interfered with?'

Mr ALLAN FRASER.—Stop sheltering behind the Sovereign all the time.

Sir GARFIELD BARWICK.—That is a remarkable remark. I have heard it from the honorable member for Eden-Monaro. Let the public know it. He said, "Stop talking about the Sovereign so much".

Mr WHITLAM.—He did not say that. You are cashing in on the monarchy . . .

Sir GARFIELD BARWICK.—I heard it and so did my colleagues . . .

Mr WHITLAM.—He is a liar.

The TEMPORARY CHAIRMAN..—I call the Deputy Leader of the Opposition to order . . .

Mr WHITLAM.—I will not withdraw. This truculent runt thinks he can get away with anything.

The TEMPORARY CHAIRMAN.—Order! I ask the Deputy Leader of the Opposition to withdraw that remark.

Mr WHITLAM.—I will not withdraw when the Attorney-General will not withdraw his untruth.

The TEMPORARY CHAIRMAN.—Order!

Mr WHITLAM.—I withdraw.

Barwick had simply misheard Fraser's interjection, with most damaging consequences. The man was barely in control of himself at the ministerial table, and when he left the chamber a few minutes later, accompanied by McEwen, he was weeping. The Crimes Act received assent in December. Although containing less than Barwick had originally intended, it nonetheless greatly strengthened the State's power to defend itself. The real reduction was to Barwick's reputation. His discomposure at the table was only part of what the *Sydney Morning Herald* called 'a sad lack of political sense'. For three more years he continued to serve devotedly, taking on External Affairs as well as the Attorney-Generalship; but no longer was his name mentioned as freely as it had been formerly in speculation about the eventual succession to Menzies.

In the second half of this parliament the Government was vulnerable on two fronts: the economy and foreign affairs. Boom conditions since the mid-1950s had caused an alarming increase in the cost of living, and a drain on foreign reserves. The Budget which Holt brought down on 16 August 1960 was intended to have a mildly deflationary effect; but when that failed to check domestic inflation or ameliorate the balance of payments, he introduced, in November, a series of more determined fiscal measures to achieve those ends. There were cries of 'Stop-Go' from the press, and the Opposition moved a motion of no confidence immediately after the Treasurer's announcement. The Government fended that off, but in the Senate its position was weaker than appeared from the nominal party strengths—Government, thirty-two; A.L.P., twenty-six; D.L.P., two.

One of the more unpopular fiscal measures was a bill to increase sales tax on cars, and when this reached the upper house in December two self-willed Liberals, Senators R. C. Wright (T) and I. A. C. Wood (Q), crossed the floor to tie the crucial vote at 29–29, thus bringing about a negative result. Here was the Senate rejecting a money bill, no less. Two days later the Government reintroduced the bill, and when it reached the Senate in the last sitting week of the year Senator Wright had second thoughts. 'I record my opinion', he said in the debate, 'that it was proper, on the first occasion, to vote against the measure as an expression of Senate opinion on a national policy of importance; but now, in view of the insistence of the Government, with the support of the House of Representatives, it is no longer proper to continue that opposition'. He abstained from the division, and although Senator Wood stuck to his guns the absence of one Labor senator permitted the bill to pass its second reading 29–27.

Perhaps emboldened by its earlier 29–29 venture into territory usually regarded as out of bounds, the Senate now modified the customary financial distinction between the two houses of parliament. The custom had always been that the upper house would not consider a financial proposal until it had been passed by the House of Representatives. In September 1961, however, the Senate decided to consider the Estimates before the main Appropriation Bills (of which the Estimates are part) were received from the lower house. The purpose was to give the Senate more time to examine the Estimates in detail rather than having to do so amid the end-of-session rush. This step was well within the Senate's competence, but not surprisingly it incurred some criticism from the lower house on grounds of evading the spirit of the Constitution.

On the foreign policy front the Minister for External Affairs, still Menzies himself, made a statement to parliament in April 1961 about his recent discussions abroad. These had included meetings in Washington with President Kennedy and the Secretary of State, Dean Rusk; the Commonwealth Prime Ministers' Conference in London, where Menzies had taken a prominent and, some thought, clumsy part in discussion of South Africa's decision to leave the Commonwealth; and a SEATO meeting in Bangkok. In London he had opposed the principle of Commonwealth nations sitting in judgment on one of their number, and at a press conference after South Africa's withdrawal he said: 'To have a member of the Commonwealth virtually excluded on a matter of domestic policy [Apartheid] presents a rather disagreeable vista for the future . . . I have my own immigration policy'.

Calwell moved an amendment to the motion for printing Menzies's ministerial statement, which would have turned that motion into one of censure. The Prime Minister's support for South Africa, and his apparent equating of Australia's immigration policy with Apartheid, had done great damage to relations with Commonwealth and South-East Asian states, said Calwell, and had aggravated the position created by him while attending a recent session of the United Nations General Assembly. At the United Nations Menzies had antagonised certain neutralist Asian nations, and incurred the public wrath of India's President Nehru, by attempting unsuccessfully to widen a proposed United States–Soviet summit to include Britain and France. Sir Wilfrid Kent Hughes joined the attack on Menzies's conduct of the External Affairs portfolio, but Calwell's motion was inevitably defeated and a counter-motion in praise of the Prime Minister was passed by 60 votes to 37.

None of this was sufficiently controversial to be an issue in the campaign leading up to the next general election, held on 9 December 1961; and, for the first time since 1945, Communism was not an election issue either. The only real issue, at least on Labor's hustings, was the economy, and the recession into which it had been tipped by the Government's fiscal measures. Unemployment, which had been above 100 000 for some months, was still rising; and the output of manufacturing industry had declined alarmingly. Calwell's policy speech promised to restore full employment within twelve months, if necessary by means of a supplementary Budget for a £100 million deficit; and to finance social service benefits costing £150 million a year, without increasing taxation. He also covered himself against any coalition attempt to exploit the A.L.P. platform's commitment to nationalisation (banking, credit, insurance, monopolies, shipping, public health) by undertaking to ignore that plank if elected.

The Government, on the other hand, stood pat.

'Trust me,' said Mr Menzies in effect. 'I know best what's best for you, and what that is you will find out in due course.' There was something shocking, and even, to those concerned with the proper functioning of a parliamentary democracy, frightening, in the Prime Minister's lofty paternalism, his unshaken complacency, his bland dismissal of a major social and economic problem as 'some temporary unemployment'.

This reaction by the *Sydney Morning Herald* to Menzies's 'policy speech without a policy' was hardly surprising, for the *Herald* was an old foe of his. What did cause surprise was that traditionally conservative newspaper's enthusiastic support for Calwell. 'Labor presents the better case', said its climactic editorial. 'If the Government should survive this challenge it will be one of the luckiest in Australian history.'

There was a swing of 4.6 per cent to Labor, and the result was closer than at any previous federal election. 'Of course I am surprised', Menzies told the press. 'So is Mr Calwell. So are you. We are all surprised.' As vote counting and distribution of preferences continued for another week, a deadlocked House of Representatives or even a Labor victory seemed possible. But the Government was indeed the luckiest in Australian history. The outcome was finally decided in the Queensland seat of Moreton, where the sitting Liberal member, Jim Killen, was returned by 110 votes, thanks to a handful of Communist Party preferences. 'Killen, you are magnificent', the Prime Minister was reported to have said in a congratulatory phone call. Killen later confessed that, disappointed at not having received such a call, he had invented it for the *Courier-Mail*. His victory gave the Government a 62–60 majority in the lower house. One of the coalition's fifteen casualties there, and a casualty in more senses than one, was Sir Earle Page. He died on the very eve of the declaration of the poll in which an A.L.P. candidate, F. W. McGuren, ended the Doctor's 42-year sway over Cowper. In the Senate the state of the parties after July would be: Liberal-C.P., thirty; A.L.P., twenty-eight; D.L.P., one (Cole), Independent, one (Turnbull).

Ten days after the election President Sukarno issued his long-heralded 'Command for the Liberation of West Irian', an escalation of Indonesian confrontation with Dutch sovereignty in West New Guinea. Calwell, no doubt emboldened by the tantalising closeness of office, made a rather bellicose press statement. 'If Indonesia seeks to deny the principles of the United Nations Charter', he said, 'and to use force to create a potential threat to Australia's security, then I say, with all due regard to the gravity of the situation, that the threat must be faced'. Menzies called his bluff ('If Mr Calwell's statement means that, without any regard to what might be the attitude or action of the great Powers . . . Australia should . . . declare war against Indonesia, it is clearly crazy and irresponsible'), and nothing further was heard about war from the Opposition. The Prime Minister found greater merit in the economic policies which had served Labor so well, though not quite well enough, on polling day. After having derided them during the campaign, he now put them to work for the Government. Income tax was reduced by 5 per cent in order to stimulate spending, unemployment benefits were increased, and more credit was extended though the Development Bank for industrial expansion.

The Government made the best of its precarious position in the lower house, where, after providing the Speaker, it had a majority of only one. It lost several procedural motions, but imposed its will on more significant issues by resorting frequently to the gag—no fewer than fourteen times in the first fifteen sitting days of 1962. The Opposition hoped for an early dissolution, but did nothing definite to bring one about. Among the legislative measures passed by this twenty-fourth parliament were the Commonwealth Electoral Act of 1962, which finally, and not before time, removed the franchise prohibition against 'aboriginal natives of Australia', thus granting them the same voting rights as all other Australian citizens; the Papua and New Guinea Act of 1963, in effect a response to the United Nations Trusteeship Council's criticism of Australia's 'stubborn adherence to a policy of gradualism' in that benighted territory; and various defence measures, mainly concerned with the American alliance, which will be noted in the second part of this chapter. The Papua and New Guinea Act provided for election of an enlarged legislature, to be known as the House of Assembly, with a majority of indigenous members and a common roll of electors.

This was a relatively uneventful parliament, memorable only for events of no great political significance. On 29 August 1962 the Liberal Member for North Sydney, W. M. Jack, rose to make his first speech in seven years, and only his fourth since entering parliament in 1949. 'Silent Billy Jack' was popular with his electors and fellow parliamentarians, and ministers and even one or two senators hurried to hear him deliver a totally soporific defence of the Budget, beginning: 'I can remain silent no longer'.

On 6 December the acting Attorney-General, Gordon Freeth, tabled on behalf of Barwick, who was touring South-East Asia in his additional new capacity as Minister for External Affairs, a ministerial statement on restrictive trade practices. Barwick felt strongly that the free enterprise system ought to be protected from anti-competitive business practices, but Cabinet as a whole was not convinced of that. The most he had been able to obtain from his colleagues was permission to table this white paper for discussion. His proposals, involving compulsory disclosure by companies of prescribed anti-competitive practices, were vigorously opposed by business interests, and when a Trade Practices Act was eventually passed, in 1965, it was much narrower in application than Barwick had envisaged. But at least the Commonwealth had again taken up the task of 'trust-busting' which it had abandoned in 1909 after the High Court ruled that it lacked power in such matters. Barwick thought this narrow interpretation was wrong, and might now be reversed.

On the first day of the autumn session, 26 March 1963, Eddie Ward set a parliamentary record by submitting 118 questions without notice. They covered a wide range of subjects and were addressed to almost every minister in Cabinet. It was as if the Honourable Member for East Sydney knew his time was short, and was letting fly with as many parting shots as he could. Four months later he died of a heart attack. Once, while the House was passing a series of resolutions mourning deaths of members, Ward had muttered ironically to Calwell that when his time came he wanted only five words spoken—'He was loved by all'. Instead Menzies, who had suffered as much as anyone at Ward's hands, moved a conventional motion of condolence; and Calwell extolled him as a tribune, democrat and friend. With more candour, the *Sydney Morning Herald* said that Ward had reflected a characteristic element in the Australian scene—'the tough, boss-hating, one-eyed element of the militant trade unions, the Labor branches and the poor back streets, an element which is now, perhaps, slowly disappearing'.

Ward's friend, Leslie Haylen, whose own parliamentary career had only a few more months to run, was responsible during this session for probably the best practical joke ever played in parliament. On 2 May, while the House was in Committee of Supply considering an Appropriation Bill, W. C. Wentworth went off on his favourite tangent to allege that the Labor Party was 'infected with communism'. Gordon Bryant (Lab, Wills, V) retaliated by reading the following comment on Wentworth's great-grandfather by Sir Henry Parkes: 'Mr Wentworth exhausted his great powers of invective in denouncing the new party of reformers as Socialists, Communists, uprooters of law and order, and everything else for which a vile name could be found'. While W. C. Wentworth IV was on his feet repeating the charge of Communist infection Haylen entered the chamber and stood beside him. He wore a long white coat borrowed from the parliamentary dining room, and around his neck hung a stethoscope. 'I murmured softly that he should come with me', Haylen wrote later; 'we had the green cart waiting for him outside and a quiet rest and loving attention would be just the thing for his obviously overwrought condition. As I continued to talk softly Wentworth appeared amazed. For a second he really thought "They had come for him"'. Haylen was suspended for 24 hours, and withdrew from the chamber.

Unity within the Liberal–Country Party coalition, never more important to the Government than in a closely divided House, was set at some risk by two differences of opinion during the twenty-fourth parliament. One concerned a proposed electoral redistribution which came before the House in December 1963. McEwen had described it publicly as 'crazy' and 'cockeyed'. His party joined forces with Labor, and Menzies, acknowledging the futility of proceeding further, moved adjournment of the debate. The second difference of opinion was over the effect which Britain's proposed entry into the European Economic Community would have upon Australian primary producers, who were accustomed to selling about one-fifth of their output to the British market. Cabinet's view, conveyed to parliament by Menzies and McEwen, was that Australia stood to suffer very serious trading losses if Britain joined the European Economic Community without making special provision to safeguard its former suppliers. On 25 July 1962 the Minister for Air and Minister assisting the Treasurer, Leslie Bury (Lib, Wentworth, N), delivered a speech in Sydney containing this dissent from coalition orthodoxy: 'If Britain does enter [the E.E.C.], I do not believe the overwhelming majority of Australians will notice any change or be materially affected. Certain rural industries will have to adjust any plans for future expansion, but in the aggregate their output is only a minor element in the total economic scene'.

Bury, a tall English-born economist whose languid air belied his political ambition, was eventually to be proved right. But McEwen could hardly have been expected to ignore the dismissal of his constituency as 'a minor element'. He declared himself 'shocked that a ministerial colleague should completely undercut the strength of Australia's negotiating position by declaring that Australia had little to fear from Britain's entry, apparently irrespective of terms'. Menzies then called for Bury's resignation from the ministry, on the traditional ground that his attitude was incompatible with ministerial responsibility and cabinet solidarity. This seemed more rigorous than necessary. There were precedents for breaching the principle of Cabinet solidarity with impunity, and in any case Bury, although a minister, was not a member of Cabinet. His temporary banishment was attributed to the insistence of McEwen, who saw Bury as a willing agent of the Treasury, with which McEwen and his Trade Department were frequently at odds over economic policy. McEwen won this bout, but his chances of ever leading the coalition probably suffered for it.

While the impending realignment of British trade encouraged closer Australian alliance with the United States, there was no discernible lessening of traditional loyalties; on the contrary, it sometimes appeared that the weaker the British connection became in reality, the stronger it grew in sentiment and nostalgia. A prime example of this inverse proportion was provided by the Prime Minister himself during a visit to Canberra by Queen Elizabeth and the Duke of Edinburgh early in 1963. The visit coincided with Canberra's jubilee, and at a state reception in King's Hall on 18 February Her Majesty said that as she had flown over the city she had found it difficult to believe that 'all this [had] grown up in 50 short years'. In his speech of welcome, Menzies surprised many of those present, including the Queen, by quoting from the Elizabethan poet, Barnabe Googe:

> There is a lady sweet and kind,
> Was never face so pleased my mind;
> I did but see her passing by,
> And yet I love her till I die.

As the Queen blushed and lowered her eyes, the audience applauded spontaneously and, at the Prime Minister's call, gave three cheers for Her Majesty. A few days later, by private investiture at Government House, the

Queen conferred upon her Australian Prime Minister the Most Noble Order of the Thistle. This exclusive order of knighthood, second only to the Order of the Garter, is within the Sovereign's personal gift and not bestowed on ministerial advice.

Thus Sir Robert Menzies became the only knighted Prime Minister of Australia apart from Page and Barton. His wife, Dame Pattie Menzies, had been awarded the Dame Grand Cross of the Order of the British Empire nine years earlier. On his next visit to Britain, Sir Robert was installed in the Order's chapel at St Giles Cathedral, Edinburgh. His arms consisted of a shield with Southern Cross supported by lion guardant and kangaroo proper, and surmounted by the motto 'Vil God I Haif', a variation of the Clan Menzies motto, 'Vil God I Zal'.

The new knight's enthusiasm for royalty showed itself again when a Currency Bill was being prepared in 1963 for the introduction of decimal currency three years later. At his urging, Cabinet decided to name the major unit the 'royal'. That might have fetched three cheers after dinner in King's Hall, but it was too much for general public opinion. There was an outcry from the press, and in September Holt conceded that 'the name selected was not a popular choice'. As no indigenous name had suggested itself, the choice became 'dollar'.

Canberra in its jubilee year was well advanced in a phase of development for which the Prime Minister himself could fairly claim more credit than any other parliamentarian. Although when he first arrived in 1934 Canberra had been for him 'a place of exile', longer acquaintance bred affection for the capital and dedication to its improvement. In 1955 a Senate select committee on the development of Canberra urged the establishment of a single development authority for the city, construction of a lake in the Molonglo basin similar to the one planned by Burley Griffin, and preparation of a master plan for a 'government triangle' extending from an apex on Capital Hill to a base along the lake shore, and embracing the provisional Parliament House. On the Prime Minister's initiative a National Capital Development Commission was established in 1957. The British town planner, Sir William Holford, was also asked for advice on the city's future development. His recommendations included lakes along the Molonglo between northern and southern portions of the city, a new bridge at Commonwealth Avenue, a new and permanent Parliament House near the lakeside base of the government triangle, and a Royal pavilion, to be used by the Queen in her capacity as Queen of Australia, on Capital Hill. Fortunately Sir William's advice was taken with a grain of salt.

Menzies made it his business, however, to see that a lake came into being. In 1959 he ensured that an item of £1 million was included in the Budget estimates for a start to the project, but on returning from his annual visit to London he found that the item had been struck out during his absence. At the next meeting of Cabinet he asked:

> 'Am I rightly informed that when I was away the Treasury struck out this item of one million for the initial work on the lake?' The reply was yes, and that Cabinet had agreed. I said, 'Well, can I take it that by unanimous

consent of ministers the item is now struck in?' A lot of laughter ran around the Cabinet room; there were some matters on which they reasonably thought that the old man should be humoured.

A dam was built across the Molonglo River near Government House, and the basin began to fill, drowning a few farms and the Royal Canberra Golf Club, the latter of which built new links at Yarralumla. New bridges were opened at King's Avenue in 1962, and Commonwealth Avenue in 1963; the lake, nine kilometres long and covering a surface area of 678 hectares, was officially opened by the Prime Minister in 1964. The dam was named after Scrivener, Canberra's first surveyor. Some ministers wanted the lake named after Menzies, but he had the good grace (not to mention political sense) to insist that it be called Lake Burley Griffin. No decision was made about a permanent Parliament House, but near the site suggested by Holford a National Library building was erected. That institution had been separated from the Parliamentary Library by the National Library Act of 1960, and in 1968 the national librarian, H. L. (later Sir Harold) White, and his staff moved the library into its new home.

Between 1950 and 1960 the population of the Canberra city district rose from 22 000 to 50 000 and in the following decade it would more than double again, to 129 000. In response to this growth, all disabilities were removed from the Member for the Australian Capital Territory in 1966, placing Canberra on the same representational footing as the rest of the Commonwealth except the Northern Territory, which was brought into conformity two years later.

The next federal election was not due until late 1964, but as soon as the Government's borrowed economic policies had taken beneficial effect Menzies secured an early dissolution of the precariously balanced lower house, on the ground that he needed a more secure majority for the conduct of international affairs at a time of crisis between Indonesia and Malaysia. Labor not unreasonably felt that it had an excellent chance of winning what had escaped it by a hair's breadth only two years before, and when Menzies informed parliament of the election date, 30 November 1963, Calwell addressed him with appropriate belligerence. 'If I, as an ordinary Australian bloke, may address my noble Scottish friend, I would say to him, in the words of Macbeth—

> Lay on, Macduff;
> and damn'd be him that first cries, 'Hold, enough!'

Menzies had timed the election well. His government was no longer vulnerable on economic policy, whereas the Opposition had by now espoused electorally disadvantageous policies on certain international issues. These were the Malaysian crisis and—more importantly, as will be explained later in this chapter—a proposed United States naval communications station in Australia, and the concept of a nuclear-free southern hemisphere. Both major policy speeches were televised (Menzies's from a studio, Calwell's from a public meeting), and both contained a wide range of financial inducements. Calwell again eschewed nationalisation. That plank was still in the

A.L.P. platform, but the objective of 'democratic socialisation' had recently been shortened by the dropping of 'control of banking and credit by the Parliament of the Commonwealth'.

Menzies promised the first measure of state aid for independent schools ever offered at a federal election (scholarships and a science grant scheme), and Calwell had no option but to join in this auction for the independent school vote—which was to say, the Roman Catholic vote. The religious bigotry that would have prevented any party from making such an offer a few years earlier had now subsided to some extent, but there were still plenty of Protestants sufficiently unreconstructed to call a spade a spade. 'This is an undisguised attempt to capture the support of a particular section of the community', said the Anglican Coadjutor Bishop of Sydney, Marcus Loane. 'It is a straight-out bid for the preferences of the D.L.P. which may determine the final result of the election.'

Eight days before the election, President Kennedy was assassinated. Calwell later accused Menzies of attempting to 'link the fortunes of his degenerate party with [this] tragedy'. There was not much evidence of that in the Prime Minister's speeches, but commentators agreed that whatever influence the assassination might have on the Australian election would be more likely to favour the Government than the Opposition. As results were soon to show, however, the Government had no need of such marginal help as that. It romped home with a majority of twenty-one after the Speaker was elected. The new ministry was enlarged to twenty-five, with Hasluck replacing Townley as Minister for Defence, and the pardoned Bury taking a new portfolio of Housing. Athol Townley had resigned from parliament in order to become Australian Ambassador to the United States, but died before taking up that post. He had been one of the few parliamentary colleagues with whom Menzies could relax completely. Another was the Minister for Civil Aviation, Senator Shane Paltridge (Lib, W), who was also soon to die.

It was widely assumed that the twenty-fifth parliament would probably see Sir Robert's departure from political life. He was now in his seventieth year and, although still vigorous, was known to suffer from bouts of diverticulitis. Many believed that one of his reasons for calling an early election had been to give his successor an easier introduction to the leadership, and the most likely successor was still Harold Holt. Holt's main rival, Barwick, did not remain in parliament long enough to try his fortune whenever the time might come. In April 1964, at a farewell for the retiring Chief Justice, Sir Owen Dixon, Menzies was injudicious enough to remark: 'It is possible for a good lawyer to become a good politician. But reconversion is impossible'. Nine days later Cabinet agreed to appoint parliament's most eminent lawyer-turned-politician in Dixon's place.

The Prime Minister denied a suggestion made in some quarters that pressure had been applied to translate Barwick to the High Court because of differences between the two of them concerning American obligations under the ANZUS treaty if Australian troops in Malaysia should find themselves in action against Indonesian forces. Barwick had rashly asserted that the treaty would cover any Indonesian attack on Australian troops in Borneo; but the

United States Government, which had no intention of becoming embroiled in war with Indonesia, left Menzies in no doubt about its displeasure at Barwick's legalistic interpretation of the treaty.

Barwick was undoubtedly interested in the Chief Justiceship, and well qualified for it; but even so, there did seem to be some reluctance about his departure from parliament, 'The old man kicked me out', he told some of his friends. 'I don't know what else I could have done about it.' His successor as Attorney-General was a young Melbourne Q.C., B. M. Snedden (Lib, Bruce), and the new Minister for External Affairs was Paul Hasluck.

On the Opposition side, Calwell and Whitlam became increasingly edgy with one another after the party's electoral disappointment. The press drew attention to a party memorandum by Whitlam on the election, in which he said that Calwell had performed less impressively than Menzies during the previous parliament. According to press reports, Whitlam had also criticised Calwell while on a visit to New Zealand. He denied the accuracy of these reports, but soon hinted that he would be a candidate for the leadership at the first opportunity. Later in his life Calwell wrote: 'There has never been any real friendship between us . . . We have been acquaintances rather than comrades'.

Some of the 'ordinary Australian blokes' in Calwell's party disapproved of one of his actions at this time—the acceptance of a Papal decoration, Knight Commander of the Order of St Gregory the Great and the Grand Silver Star. Some thought that he was compensating for electoral failure with an alternative symbol of success; others, that he was using the Vatican to improve his standing in the eyes of Catholic voters. Santamaria's *News Weekly* assured its readers that the Order of St Gregory was handed out to all kinds of official recipients; even the Cuban Ambassador to the Vatican had received one.

The twenty-fifth parliament consisted of one continuous session, and it was the longest of all sessions in federal history, lasting two years and eight months. In the first year parliament enacted a record number of 130 bills, but sat for only sixty-five days. The average time spent on each of these bills by the House of Representatives was five hours and three minutes, and the following year's average was even less. Among the measures passed at this rate in 1964 and 1965 were bills giving effect to the Government's election promises of state aid for independent schools, amendments to the Income Tax Act, various defence measures which will be mentioned later, and two referendum bills.

The latter two were to remove Sections 24 and 127 from the Constitution. Section 24 required membership of the House of Representatives to be 'as nearly as practicable' twice the number of senators. Given the general reluctance to have more senators, this nexus provision had the effect of discouraging enlargement of the lower house, even though population growth would eventually make such enlargement necessary for the purpose of keeping electorates to a reasonable size. Only the D.L.P. was opposed to the Section 24 referendum bill; and all parties supported removal of Section 127, the anachronistic purpose of which was to avoid the necessity of counting 'Aboriginal natives' in reckoning the population of the Commonwealth. This section had made some sort of sense in the 1890s because of the practical difficulty of enumerating remote Aborigines at that time. But now there was no excuse for denying Aborigines the same demographic role as other Australians played in the determination of proportionate State representation in the lower house.

W. C. Wentworth attempted to have a guarantee against racial discrimination inserted in the Constitution. His private member's bill for this purpose was debated in 1966, but lapsed at prorogation. In 1967 the Government reintroduced its Constitution alteration bills for removal of Sections 24 and 127. It declined to incorporate Wentworth's guarantee in the latter measure, claiming that such a section would become almost as fertile a source of attack on the constitutional validity of legislation as Section 92; but it included a further proposal to remove the last ground for any belief that the Constitution discriminated against people of the Aboriginal race, while at the same time ensuring that parliament could enact special laws for such people. The latter proposal was to exclude the italicised words from Section 51 (xxvi): 'The people of any race, *other than the aboriginal race in any State,* for whom it is deemed necessary to make special laws'.

Both bills were submitted to referendum in May 1967. The one affecting Aborigines was approved; the other was not. Although it was doubtful whether the amendment of Section 51 (xxvi) really added much to Commonwealth power concerning Aborigines, the electorate's remarkable nine to one affirmation showed that voters wanted the federal government to assume responsibility for the welfare of Aboriginal Australians. Certainly the Commonwealth took it as a mandate to do so. For many years to come, the federal government would indeed give a national lead in this hitherto shamefully neglected field. Regrettably, however, the results were not to match the apparent intention of that rare 'yes' at referendum.

Because early dissolution of the House of Representatives had thrown elections for the two chambers out of gear, an election for half the Senate was held by itself when it came due, on 5 December 1964. The result changed the balance of power only slightly, to the advantage of the D.L.P.: Government thirty; Labor, twenty-seven; D.L.P., two; Independent, one. Senator Cole was defeated, but two other D.L.P. candidates were successful—V. C. Gair, the former Queensland Premier; and F. P. McManus, who was returning to the Senate after an absence of three years.

In both chambers the Government's backbenchers were the most restive of their kind that anyone could remember. This may have been because of their growing belief that Menzies would soon retire, or simply because of the cavalier way their leaders had treated them for so long. Twelve coalition senators, including Wright and Wood, forced the Government to re-examine a proposed amendment to the Repatriation (Special Overseas Service) Bill. In December 1965 Wright also joined Labor and the two D.L.P. senators to reject another money bill, by 25 votes to 24. This was an Income Tax Bill raising the rate of tax on the income of trust estates and superannuation funds, a proposal to which only Wright and the D.L.P. were opposed, and also raising personal income tax by 2½ per cent, to which Labor was opposed, but not the D.L.P. or Wright. The bill was resubmitted, and rejected again; but there was no prospect of a double dissolution, because the only party likely to benefit from a full Senate election was the D.L.P. The Government simply divided the bill in two: one for the rise in personal taxation, which passed 23–22, with Senator Wright and the D.L.P. supporting the Government; and one for the other tax, which passed 39–3, with Wright and the D.L.P. forming the minority.

In the lower house, Liberal backbenchers were responsible for several departures from Government orthodoxy in 1965. Killen moved that in the opinion of the House a referendum should be held on the fluoridation of Canberra's water supply, a project upon which the Government had already decided to embark. Government members were free to vote as they wished. The resolution was passed 56–52, but fluoridation went ahead anyway, without a referendum. During debate on proposals by the Joint Committee of Constitutional Review, H. B. Turner (Bradfield, N) supported the principle of 'one vote one value' in terms that caused some resentment in the Country Party; and when a report of the Standing Orders Committee came before the House, Wentworth moved that an additional rule be adopted to ensure that on days set aside for General Business and Grievance debates, these items should take precedence over 'matters of public importance'. He pressed his amendment to a division, but was supported by only eleven other Liberals. One recommendation of the Standing Orders Committee that was adopted by the House permitted members to read their speeches. Previously they had been allowed only 'reference to copious notes', which was all that the Senate continued to allow.

On the last sitting day of 1965, 10 December, Sir Robert Menzies rose without notes of any kind to move the adjournment. For a reason not yet announced but generally understood, his tone was more valedictory than usual. 'A good parliament cannot exist without good members', he said.

> A good parliament cannot exist without good debate—strong debate, strenuous debate and, every now and then, if you like, heated debate. But we all know from our experience that when the debates are over we look round the House and we on each side of the House know that we have a lot of close personal friends among our political opponents. This is as it should be . . . I am very proud to have served in this Parliament, because I think it has made its own invaluable contribution to the political history of Australia.

Calwell replied in kind. 'I think that this occasion could be an historic one', he said.

> I do not want to peer too far into the future, but I have what Carlyle would have called a preternatural suspicion that things might happen next year. Well, it is a rather sad occasion, but it is an important occasion. And in a sad and glorious sense I am proud to be here today before what I think might happen does happen.

On 26 January 1966 Mezies tendered his resignation to the Governor-General, Lord Casey, and the parliamentary Liberal Party elected a new leader, Harold Holt. Holt was unopposed, but the Deputy Leadership was contested by McMahon and Hasluck, with McMahon prevailing. Sir Robert did not resign his seat immediately, but simply moved to the back benches. Never had there been a prime ministerial departure like this one. Sir Robert had been Prime Minister continuously for sixteen years and two months, and cumulatively for eighteen years and six months—by either reckoning, more than twice as long as any of his predecessors. He was the first Australian Prime Minister to relinquish office voluntarily, and he did so while still firmly in control of his party and the Government. Whatever judgement might be made of his long protectorate, its ending was a memorable event, like the turn of a century. Press comment was uniformly respectful of the man himself, but more critical about the era over which he had presided. 'It was in many ways a splendid era', said the *Sydney Morning Herald*,

> '—dignified, prosperous, sedate. But it was not an era of political or intellectual excitement. Ideas were not welcomed. Debate was not encouraged. If the status of Federal Government steadily increased, the status of Parliament steadily declined. There was no ferment of ideas in the country to stimulate Ministers. Intellectuals were frowned on or snubbed. It is time for a change . . .

Menzies would be remembered for his political longevity, his Austral-Britishness, his faculty for creating contentment at home and peril abroad, the deftness with which he purloined Opposition policies, his timely assistance to the universities and, his fostering of the national capital—but not much else, for in the main he and his party had not been innovators. Fortunately for him the 'magnificent voyage' had been undertaken in fair economic weather, and its sailing instructions were 'Steady as she goes'.

Menzies presided over certain important policies inherited from his predecessors—notably Commonwealth predominance over the States, Commonwealth management of the economy, and perpetuation of Australia's wartime reliance on the United States. Yet somehow he managed to maintain the comforting illusion that nothing much had changed. Australians were still loyal members of the British Commonwealth, and free enterprise was not really being influenced by the central bank. One of his last acts as Prime Minister had been to table a long-awaited report by the Vernon Committee of Economic Enquiry and promptly repudiate it. The Vernon Committee—established two and a half years earlier under the chairmanship of Dr James Vernon, managing director of Colonial Sugar Refining Ltd—proposed a detailed strategy for economic growth, including the establishment of two new bodies, a National Economic Council to advise the Government on long-term economic planning, and a Special Projects Commission to advise on major developmental projects. That kind of advice was not welcome. Sir Robert told the house that the Vernon Committee had exceeded its terms of reference, and that its report proposed a degree of planning and direction in the economy which would be neither acceptable nor appropriate in Australia.

During the English summer of 1966, while the Australian parliament was in recess, Sir Robert Menzies arrived in London to accept another honour. It would have been hard to guess what more the United Kingdom could offer him. He was already a Master of the Bench of Gray's

Inn, a liveryman of the Worshipful Company of Goldsmiths, a life member of the East Molesey Cricket Club, President of the Lords Taverners, a Doctor of Laws of Oxford and Cambridge, a Burgess of Edinburgh and Freeman of Swansea, a Privy Councillor, Companion of Honour and Knight of the Thistle. But now, as if in recognition of his long protectorate, Sir Robert was to be installed as Lord Warden of the Cinque Ports, a ceremonial office traditionally associated with protection of the channel ports of Hastings, Romney, Hythe, Dover and Sandwich. Among past wardens were Wellington, Palmerston, Salisbury, Curzon and Churchill. On 20 July Sir Robert, wearing an admiral's gold-braided hat, green sash, red-piped frock coat uniform and sword, was led through the streets of Dover by the Serjeant of Admiralty, who carried a silver oar, to a hallowing service conducted in the church of St Mary-in-the-Castle by the Archbishop of Canterbury. What more fitting end could there have been to his voyage? He had resigned from parliament on 17 February and was succeeded in Kooyong by the 26-year-old President of the Victorian Liberal Party, Andrew Peacock.

Eagle Guardant

Back in March 1962, during a debate on the Netherlands-Indonesian dispute over West New Guinea, Menzies had remarked: 'No country in the world more than ours needs great and powerful friends'. By that well-worn phrase, he meant Britain and the United States; but before long Australia for all practical purposes would have only one great and powerful friend. Britain was unmistakably in retreat from Australia's part of the world, and the United States by contrast was taking more notice of the region. Only a few weeks after the debate on West New Guinea, the American Secretary of State, Dean Rusk, flew to Canberra for the annual ANZUS conference.

It was unusual for someone of Rusk's status to attend this conference. He had not come because of the trouble in West New Guinea, for the United States was no more perturbed about that than it had been about Egypt's seizure of the Suez Canal. Apparently Australia had been over-reacting to Indonesian nationalism; a greater danger to the region, declared Rusk at a State banquet held for him in Parliament House, was Communist aggression in South Vietnam. 'The stakes are greater than South Vietnam itself', he said.

The independence of all the peoples of South-East Asia is involved . . . You are helping there in significant and growing ways, but there is more for all of us to do in that situation. We should like to see many other free nations also lend a helping hand. Aggression against South-East Asia must not be allowed to succeed.'

Vietnam was almost a new name to the pages of Hansard. There had been mention of Indo-China during the 1950s, notably at the time of the Geneva Conference which ended French colonial rule there; but the first mention of Vietnam did not come until October 1961, when Sir Wilfrid Kent Hughes asked the Prime Minister whether the Government was aware that President Kennedy had sent his top military adviser to South Vietnam to assess the real strength of the present Communist attack on that country. In April 1962 Ward, speaking on the adjournment, asserted that the real danger of Australia being involved in a war was not, as many people believed, in West New Guinea against Indonesians, but in South Vietnam. And that was the sum total of parliament's interest in Vietnam before Dean Rusk's visit.

Before the end of May, however, the Minister for Defence announced the commitment of thirty Australian army instructors to work with South Vietnamese forces; the Minister for External Affairs gave details of aid to fortify South Vietnamese villages; and the Prime Minister announced that the Government had approved a United States request for permission to establish and operate a naval communications station in Western Australia. The station—to be built at North West Cape, not far from the Monte Bello Islands and their nuclear debris—had nothing specifically to do with Vietnam, but everything to do with relations between Australia and the United States. Its purported function, according to the Prime Minister's announcement in parliament, would be 'to provide radio communications for United States and allied ships over a wide area of the Indian Ocean and the Western Pacific'; more precisely, although this was not publicly known at the time, its primary function would be to communicate with nuclear missile-carrying submarines of the United States Navy.

The Opposition was not sure what to say about North West Cape at first, though some of its left-wingers were instinctively opposed to it. On 17 May one such Labor member, Tom Uren (Reid, N), said during a Grievance Day debate: 'The radio station to be established will be for war purposes and not for the purposes of peace. I condemn this action of the Government. I believe that we should not make our soil available to any foreign power whatsoever'. This was music to the Leader of the House's ears. Holt met Whitlam each sitting day to arrange the business of the House, and ever since the close-run 1961 election he had seemed depressed about the Government's prospects. 'His spirits, however, rose spectacularly on the last day of the autumn session', wrote Whitlam, 'when Uren attacked Menzies's announcement . . . Holt felt that he now had an issue which the Liberals could exploit'.

Seeking a new foreign policy which would be more clearly distinguishable from that of the coalition, Calwell proposed that Australia should take the initiative in bringing about a 'nuclear free southern hemisphere'. The A.L.P. federal executive later supported him in this, adding that Australia should neither 'make, acquire nor receive' nuclear weapons. When North West Cape became the focal point of controversy about American bases, with the Government claiming that opposition to the base would prejudice Australian security, Calwell adopted the position that establishment of the base was not against his party's policy providing that Australia retained sovereignty over the area and was admitted to full partnership in its use. The greatest damage to the A.L.P. in this controversy occurred when a special Federal Conference of the party was held at Canberra in February 1963 to decide whether Calwell was really on the right track. Calwell and Whitlam were not among the thirty-six delegates from State branches, for the A.L.P.'s constitution at that time did not extend ex-officio voting rights to either the leader or deputy leader of the parliamentary party. The press photographed them waiting outside the meeting to hear the outcome, and Menzies lost no time in claiming that A.L.P. policy on this important matter was being formulated by '36 faceless men'. Calwell, he said, was 'a minnow among the 36 Tritons'. Later in the year Federal Executive resolved that the leader and deputy leader of the parliamentary party could attend its meetings as observers, and in 1967 a special conference on party organisation decided that the leader and deputy leader in both houses could attend with full voting rights. But for the time being, in 1963, the damage had been done.

On 9 May 1963 Barwick introduced the United States Naval Communication Station Bill, to approve an agreement which he and the American Ambassador had signed earlier that day. The station, he said, was 'a wireless station, nothing more and nothing less'. Calwell subsequently moved an amendment along lines endorsed by the extra-parliamentary faceless men, which would have added the words

> with the understanding that the station will be operated in a way which will not bring Australia into war . . . without the knowledge and consent of the Government of the Commonwealth and in the spirit of the undertakings to consult and act which the governments have assumed in Articles III and IV of the ANZUS Treaty.

His motion was negatived by 57 votes to 53, and the Bill passed without amendment. Next time the United States concluded a similar agreement with Australia, concerning a highly classified satellite ground station at Pine Gap, near Alice Springs, there was not even formal reference to parliament. A secret agreement was signed by representatives of the two governments in September 1966, without legislation.

During the 1963 election campaign Menzies had criticised Labor's lack of enthusiasm for either North West Cape or Australia's part in the defence of Malaysia against Indonesian aggression; and presumably that had been

'I did but see her passing by, and yet I love her till I die': R. G. Menzies, soon to become Sir Robert, pays courtly tribute to the Queen at a state reception in King's Hall on 18 February 1963.

Sir Arthur Fadden

Sir John McEwen, painting by Sir William Dargie

Sir Alister McMullin, President of the Senate (1953–1971)

Archie Cameron, Speaker of the House of Representatives (1950–1956)

partly responsible for his comfortable win. In the following year Australian troops stationed in Malaysia engaged Indonesian forces in combat for the first time, and the war in Vietnam assumed more alarming dimensions. On 10 November 1964 Menzies delivered a ministerial statement based on reports by the defence and service departments and the Chiefs of Staff Committee. Placing greatest emphasis on the Malaysian crisis, but alluding also to a recent engagement between North Vietnamese and United States naval vessels in the Gulf of Tonkin, he concluded by announcing that the Government had decided there was no alternative to the introduction of selective compulsory service for the first time since World War II. The call-up would start about the middle of 1965, and 4200 young men would be required by the end of that year.

Labor's reaction was predictable. Clyde Cameron immediately reminded the House of the Prime Minister's failure to enlist in 1915; Fred Daly challenged McMahon and J. D. Anthony (C, Richmond, N) to enlist; and during the second reading debate on the National Service Bill Calwell described the call-up as a 'lottery of death'. But if Calwell hoped to revive the anti-conscription fervour of 1916 and 1917, he was no more successful than he had been in 1943. In spite of Labor opposition the Bill passed its final stage on 17 November, without major amendment.

By early 1965 the war in Vietnam had completely overshadowed Malaysia's troubles. On the night of 29 April Menzies informed parliament of a Cabinet decision to provide an Australian infantry battalion for service in South Vietnam—not conscripts, but the 1st Battalion of the Regular Army. 'The Australian Government', he said, 'is now in receipt of a request from the government of South Vietnam for further military assistance'. This was technically true, but not far removed from deception. The offer of troops was an Australian initiative, taken in order to comply with perceived American wishes, and the South Vietnamese request, organised with last-minute haste by the Australian embassy in Saigon, had reached Canberra by cable at 6 p.m.—three weeks after Cabinet had taken the decision, and only two hours before the Prime Minister rose in parliament to announce it.

On the next sitting day, 4 May, Calwell delivered one of his finest speeches, denouncing the commitment in terms which were to form the basis of Labor's sustained opposition to the Vietnam war over the next few years. He said:

> We do not think it is a wise decision. We do not think it is a timely decision. We do not think it is a right decision. We do not think it will help the fight against Communism. On the contrary, we believe it will harm that fight in the long term. We do not believe it will promote the welfare of the people of Vietnam. On the contrary, we believe it will help prolong and deepen the suffering of that unhappy people so that Australia's very name may become a term of reproach among them. We do not believe that it represents a wise or even an intelligent response to the challenge of Chinese power. On the contrary, we believe it mistakes entirely the nature of that power, and that it materially assists China in her subversive aims . . . We of the Labour Party do not believe that this decision serves, or is consistent with, the immediate strategic interests of Australia. On the

contrary, we believe that, by sending one quarter of our pitifully small effective military strength to distant Vietnam, this Government danger-ously denudes Australia and its immediate strategic environs of effective defence power . . .

The Government will try . . . to project a picture in which once the aggressive invaders from the North are halted, our men will be engaged in the exercise of picking off the Vietcong, themselves invaders from the North and stranded from their bases and isolated from their supplies. But it will not be like that at all. Our men will be fighting the largely indigen-ous Vietcong in their own home territory . . . They will be fighting at the request of, and in support, and presumably under the direction of an unstable, inefficient, partially corrupt military regime which lacks even the semblance of being, or becoming, democratically based . . . Our pre-sent course is playing right into China's hands, and our present policy will, if not changed, surely and inexorably lead to American humiliation in Asia.

The autumn sitting ended with an even more unseemly scramble than usual. In the last four days parliament was presented with no fewer than nineteen bills—including amendments to defence statutes, allowing con-scripts to be sent overseas—and was dragooned into pushing them through stages which, according to one newspaper, 'lacked even the dignity nor-mally accorded to ritual, however empty of meaning it may be'. The climax was a sitting of twenty-two hours, ending with adjournment for the winter recess at 8 a.m. on 26 May. Speaking on the adjournment, Holt attributed blame for the inconvenience of an all-nighter to the failure of Opposition members to observe an arrangement for the timing of business entered into on their behalf by Calwell, who by then was absent from the chamber.

> Mr HOLT.—When I asked the Leader of the Opposition why [the arrangement] had not been observed . . . he said, quite frankly, but, I thought, a little abjectly: "I just cannot control my party".
>
> Mr WHITLAM.—When does the right honorable gentleman allege that the Leader of the Opposition said that?
>
> Mr HOLT.—He said it during the suspension of the sitting for dinner, or just prior to the dinner interval, last evening. The honorable member for Moreton (Mr Killen) was with me at the time. This was in no sense a confidential statement. It was merely a statement of the facts.

Such an admission by Calwell would not have surprised or displeased Whitlam, for the two men were increasingly at loggerheads. Whitlam was now challenging the left wing, demanding that Labor modify or abandon its opposition to state aid for independent schools, and enforce its rules against unity tickets with Communist candidates. The more vigorously he pressed this attack, the more closely Calwell became identified with the left. At a meeting of the Federal Executive in June—held at the A.L.P.'s newly estab-lished Canberra office, in the Australian Workers' Union building—Whitlam threatened to resign his position as deputy leader if decisions about to be taken on unity tickets did not satisfy him. This would have precipitated a general spill of offices in the parliamentary party, including that of leader, in which event it was assumed that Whitlam would probably contest Calwell's position. His threat had the desired effect of deterring Victorian delegates to the ensuing Federal Conference from seeking rescission of the rules on unity tickets.

Labor's electoral hopes were revived somewhat in February 1966 by the unexpected success of Dr Rex Patterson at a by-election for the Queensland seat of Dawson, rendered vacant by the death of a sitting Country Party member, G. W. Shaw. This was the Government's first by-election defeat since 1952. It seemed to spur Whitlam's ambition, and conflict continued over the parliamentary party leadership. In February he publicly criticised the Federal Executive's recent reaffirmation of the party's opposition to state aid. With his customary disregard for caution, Whitlam referred to the Executive as 'twelve witless men', and said that next time there was a ballot for parliamentary leader he would submit his name.

In spite of his erudite, pedantic manner, Whitlam was given to forceful, impetuous action. During the recent Budget sittings, for example, he had an explosive exchange across the ministerial table with Paul Hasluck. The debate was about repatriation benefits, and Whitlam accused Hasluck of denying his own parents by voting against benefits for Salvation Army personnel who had served with the forces. Hasluck, whose father had been a Salvation Army officer, leant forward and said to Whitlam, who was in the act of raising a glass of water to his lips: 'You are one of the filthiest objects ever to come into this chamber'. As quick as a flash, Whitlam flung the water at Hasluck's face. 'I was provoked', he said, and left the chamber.

Whitlam was lucky not to be expelled from the Labor Party for his gratuitous remarks about the Federal Executive. He was called before the Executive to account for his 'gross disloyalty', but for internal party reasons was let off with a caution. The party's policy on state aid was changed at the next Federal Conference, to Whitlam's satisfaction. At a Caucus meeting on 27 April Calwell and Whitlam accused each other of disloyalty, and a spill motion by one of Whitlam's New South Wales supporters, Senator J. A. Mulvihill, was defeated by 49 votes to 24. Calwell told the meeting, however, that if Labor lost the next election he would not stand for leadership in the twenty-sixth parliament.

One indirect result of Whitlam's manoeuvring against Calwell was the expulsion from the Victorian A.L.P. of Captain Sam Benson (Batman), a master mariner who was active in the right-wing Defend Australia Committee. Benson's failure to abide by the Federal Executive's proscription of that organisation was one reason for his expulsion, and another was his support for the abortive spill motion. On 13 September he took his seat as an Independent, the first in the House since Dr Nott (A.C.T.) in 1951. There was little room for true independence in the partisan ranks of federal parliament, but the quasi-independence of backbench dissent made itself heard more loudly with every passing year of coalition rule. The Liberal Member for Franklin (T), C. W. J. Falkinder, decided after twenty years on the back bench to retire before the next election, and in his last Budget speech, on 31 August 1966, he explained why.

the fact is that we have a Cabinet, a Ministry, the members of which now believe and have believed for some time that in some kind of sense there is a divine right not of kings but of Cabinets. True it is that we frequently have discussions in our party meetings on both sides on bills dealing with matters of concern to us, but the fact is . . . that there are few of us who really take any part in deliberations concerning the country's business . . . In my experience of this place, it is a very rare occasion when any alteration to a bill is made . . . It has appeared to me that we have gradually, slowly but surely, given away our rights as individuals to have an expression in what becomes law through this Parliament . . .

This swan song expressed what was by now a familiar plaint. In the previous Budget debate, Harry Turner had spoken forcefully against executive regimentation, and in favour of close scrutiny of bills by committees, as practised in the American Congress. 'On account of the monolithic regimentation of parties', he said, 'any attempt by any honourable member on either side of the chamber to seek a reasonable amendment is regarded as an affront to the Government and as an undermining of the confidence of the Parliament in the Government'.

This final year of the twenty-fifth parliament was marked by increasing awareness of the war in Vietnam. In February 1966 the Vice-President of the United States, Hubert Humphrey, visited Canberra for much the same kind of purpose as Dean Rusk, and a few days later Holt announced that Australia would treble its Vietnam force to 4500, including conscripted national servicemen. On 21 June someone tried to kill Arthur Calwell after he had spoken on Vietnam at a public meeting in the Sydney suburb of Mosman. As his car was about to leave Mosman Town Hall a disturbed young man named Peter Kocan, who had been in the audience, fired a .22 bullet through the rear window, spattering Calwell's jaw with fragments of bullet and glass, but not seriously wounding him.

It was not clear whether Vietnam played any part in Kocan's motivation (all he said later was that he did not like Calwell's politics), but his half-hearted imitation of Lee Harvey Oswald certainly lent an air of heightened tension to the Vietnam protest movement in Australia. The Labor members most active in this movement were Tom Uren, a one-time prize-fighter who had been a prisoner of war on the Burma–Thailand railway and in Japan; and Dr J. F. Cairns (Yarra, V), a former Victorian decathlon champion and undercover policeman. After rising to become officer in charge of the C.I.B.'s Shadowing Squad, an intelligence group also known as 'The Dogs', Jim Cairns served briefly with the A.I.F., in 1945. Instead of returning to The Dogs after the war, he resumed an academic course which he had commenced while in the police force. Supporting himself as a tutor and eventually a lecturer in Economic History at the University of Melbourne, he gained a Master's degree in Commerce and a Ph.D., and distinguished himself on the left wing of the Labor Party by dint of intellect and radical passion. In 1955 he had defeated the incumbent D.L.P. member for Yarra, Stan Keon.

Calwell became fully opposed to the war in Vietnam only when conscription was introduced. Whitlam acknowledged the importance of the American alliance, but became more critical of the war as it escalated. On 13 October, for example, he clashed with one of the chamber's Vietnam hawks, Dr Malcolm Mackay (Lib, Evans, N). Mackay, a Presbyterian minister who was also an astute businessman with mining interests, accused Whitlam of having advocated the immediate withdrawal of Australian troops from Vietnam. Whitlam replied that it was no wonder the honourable gentleman had been unfrocked. When the Speaker ordered him to withdraw that untruth, he did so, but went on to explain in mock apology that he had been 'misled by the honourable gentleman's long ago having given up the divine for the divining rod'. Later in the day one of Mackay's colleagues, Dudley Erwin (Lib, Ballarat, V), referred to Whitlam as 'a petulant pansy'.

Anti-war and pro-American feelings combined incongruously when President Johnson himself arrived for a three-day visit. It was as if the American eagle had swooped on Canberra. The huge white and blue Air Force One landed at Fairbairn R.A.A.F. Base on 20 October, only a few days before the issue of writs for the next House of Representatives election. After a ceremonial welcome by the Governor-General, the President and the Prime Minister set out for the Canberra Rex Hotel in a bullet-proof Lincoln which had been flown in from Washington earlier that day. At King's Avenue the motorcade was halted by a cheering crowd. 'Long live American–Australian friendship', called the President though a loudspeaker in his car. 'Here's your Prime Minister—get up there, Harold, and say something.' Holt responded by saying how glad he was that L.B.J. was not standing for Prime Minister of Australia.

At a parliamentary luncheon next day, with yellow roses everywhere in honour of the President's home state, Johnson expatiated on the theme of American–Australian friendship. Responding to a toast from the Prime Minister, he recalled Holt's use of the slogan 'All the way with L.B.J.' during his recent visit to Washington—a use, incidentally, which many Australians, particularly those opposed to the war, had found acutely embarrassing:

> When your Prime Minister said in Washington, speaking on the course of the battle, that he will go all the way with LBJ there was not a single American who felt he was saying anything new. There is not a boy wearing uniform yonder today who does not know that when freedom is at stake, when brave men stand shoulder to shoulder in battle, Australia will go all the way—and America will go all the way—not part of the way, not a third of the way, not three parts of the way but all the way, when liberty and freedom are won.

After the dinner John McEwen and Jim Killen walked out through King's Hall together. 'You don't seem to like him', remarked McEwen, and Killen replied: 'Jack, ever since I saw that photograph of Johnson holding up one of his dogs by its ears I've put a big line through him'. McEwen nodded. 'He reckons it's good for them', he said, 'and he reckons some other things are good for us also'. A more favourable impression was recorded by the Minister for Air, Peter Howson (Lib, Fawkner, V). Howson was one of parliament's few consistent diarists, and that night he wrote: 'The President made an effective and telling speech . . . There can now be no doubt that Australia has an umbrella—or a shield (Three years ago, this was not nearly such a certainty) . . . This should in addition be good value for the election'.

The election of 26 November was fought mainly on the related issues of

conscription and Australian intervention in Vietnam, and opinion polls
suggested strongly that Labor's policies on those issues would ensure its
defeat. Calwell promised to abolish conscription immediately upon taking
office, and to bring Australian troops back from Vietnam as soon as practicable after consultation with Australia's allies. Holt restated the Government's foreign policy but did not emphasise the American alliance. After the
President's flying visit, that scarcely needed emphasis. A new splinter party,
the Liberal Reform Group, fielded twenty-one candidates on a platform of
opposition to the war and to the use of Australian conscripts in Vietnam.
Correctly assuming that they had little chance of being elected, the Liberal
Reformers sought to direct their preferences to Labor, but Labor was beyond
help of that kind. The coalition was returned with a majority of forty-one.
Even the hawkish Independent, Captain Benson, was returned by the Labor
voters of Batman. Electorally it was a season for hawks, and eagles.

16

Another Place

King Tide

For once in this narrative it is appropriate that parliament should be opened in the red chamber where, by seemingly illogical tradition, parliaments have always been opened. There is nothing in the Constitution or Standing Orders to say on which side of Parliament House the Governor-General or his deputy should declare parliament open. Although common sense would suggest the green chamber in which governments are made and unmade, custom borrowed from Westminster decrees otherwise. For symbolic reasons, the House of Commons and House of Representatives prefer to keep the Sovereign and the viceregal representative at arm's length. Consequently the Sovereign opens the United Kingdom parliament in the House of Lords, and the Governor-General does the same for Australia's parliament in the Senate. After seating himself in the viceregal chair and requesting the assembled senators to be seated, His Excellency commands the Usher of the Black Rod to let members of the House of Representatives know that he desires their attendance in the Senate chamber. On this occasion— the opening of the twenty-sixth parliament by Lord Casey, on 21 February 1967—it could still have been said that such a tableau made the Senate seem more important in the parliamentary scheme of things than in fact it was. But the scheme of things was changing. After decades of relative quiescence, broken in the main only by Opposition majorities voting on party lines to frustrate the lower house, the Senate would, in the period covered by this chapter, assert itself as never before. It would reject some financial measures sent from the lower house, and would establish a wide-ranging system of standing committees. And for the first time in federal history the red chamber would provide Australia with a Prime Minister.

It will be remembered that the Senate, unlike the lower house, is pre-

469

vented under the Constitution from initiating or amending money bills, or amending any bill so as to increase a proposed charge or tax. But those are the only restraints upon it. The Senate may address requests to the lower house for amendment of money bills, and may press or repeat such requests. It may also reject any bill, whether financial or non-financial, no matter how seriously that might embarrass a Government. Thus, despite frequent appearances to the contrary, it is one of the most powerful upper houses in the world.

This was sometimes difficult to believe. With the establishment of the Tariff Board in 1921, the Senate had been relieved of much routine work on behalf of its nominal constituencies, the States. Preferential voting resulted in overwhelming majorities for one major party or the other, party discipline tightened, and many senators came to regard themselves as little more than party hacks. On the other hand, proportional representation produced senates from 1949 onwards that were more evenly, indeed often too evenly, balanced between Labor and non-Labor. This encouraged a show of independence by some senators, which tended to attract candidates convinced that the Senate provided more scope for individual initiative than the lower house.

In 1952 the Government Leader and the Leader of the Opposition tried to confine the Senate's power to amend; but other senators narrowly thwarted their efforts. Although Section 53 of the Constitution states that the upper house may not amend 'proposed laws imposing taxation, or proposed laws appropriating revenue or moneys *for the ordinary annual services of the Government*', the Senate had always regarded appropriation (works and services) bills as appropriating not for 'the ordinary annual services of the Government', and consequently as being within its power to amend. But the Solicitor-General had recently expressed an opinion that most appropriations of this kind, dealing with new works and services involving capital expenditure, might be properly regarded as expenditure on the ordinary annual services of the Government. That would mean they were not amendable by the Senate.

A motion by Senator McKenna (Lab, T) with amendment proposed by Senator Spicer (Lib, V), which came before the Senate on 4 November 1952, would have had the effect of confirming the Solicitor-General's opinion and foregoing the right to amend appropriation (works and services) bills. In one memorable speech, Senator Wright (Lib, T) spoke for an hour without notes, drawing from memory upon the federal convention debates to contest the Solicitor-General's opinion. All senators were permitted to vote free from party duress, and the vote was tied 24–24, resolving the question in the negative and preserving the Senate's power.

Only rarely did senators vote along State rather than party lines, as the federal conventions had intended they should. In 1952, for example, all ten senators from Tasmania (five Liberals and five Labor) voted with the Opposition to pass an amendment concerning land tax assessment. In 1958 all South Australian senators voted together for an amendment to the Snowy Mountains Hydro-Electric Power Bill, safeguarding their State's share of the River Murray's water.

In 1967 two Liberal senators, Ian Wood (Q) and Magnus Cormack (V), led a campaign against the Government's ill-fated attempt to alter the Constitution so that the number of M.H.R.s could be increased without necessarily increasing the number of senators. Cormack and Wood were regarded as 'institutional senators' or 'good Senate men', prepared sometimes to put the Senate's welfare, as they saw it, above party considerations. Also in 1967 the Senate established two select committees, one to report on the container method of handling cargoes and the other on the metric system of weights and measures. In 1968 further select or *ad hoc* committees were appointed on water pollution, air pollution, and medical and hospital costs. This brought to only thirty-three the number of Senate select committees since 1901, but the Senate was soon to take much greater interest in committees of a more lasting kind. In 1969 the Standing Orders Committee instructed the Clerk of the Senate, J. R. Odgers, to report on the feasibility of establishing standing committees (not joint committees of both houses, but standing committees of the Senate) of a kind which had proved successful in the British, Canadian and New Zealand parliaments.

Odgers had been an officer of the Senate for twenty-seven years, and was the author of *Australian Senate Practice*, first published in 1953 and then in its third edition. He was a devoted 'Senate man', and so too, in his own way, was the current Opposition Leader, Senator L. K. Murphy. The A.L.P. platform still called for abolition of the Senate; but Lionel Murphy, a left-wing industrial lawyer from Sydney, had hitched his wagon to that star and did not mind how brightly it shone. At first Odgers was uncertain about the kind of system he ought to recommend. 'It's not good enough Jim', said Murphy, when Odgers showed him a draft report. 'Go for the big one. Go for the lot. I'll get it through my party.' Odgers rewrote the report and Murphy kept his part of the bargain, as will be recounted later in this chapter.

Lionel Murphy had the sort of Irish-Australian face—shrewd and beefy, with a big nose and protruding ears—that would not have looked amiss in Sydney Trades Hall, Tammany Hall or the Dail. But he had not come from a working-class background like some of the Balmain boys with whom he rubbed shoulders in the A.L.P. and at the New South Wales Bar. His father, a builder, was born in Tipperary, and his maternal grandfather, whose name was also Murphy, had emigrated from Ireland in the 1880s. The family was not Catholic. Lionel was educated at Kensington Public School, Sydney Boys' High School and, during World War II, at Sydney University, where he first took a Bachelor of Science degree with honours in Organic Chemistry and then a law degree. He was a man of infectious enthusiasm and great personal charm, a vigorous conversationalist who put forward constructive views in a deep, nasally resonant voice which many found instantly persuasive. He was elected to the Senate in 1962, and five years later replaced Senator D. R. Willesee (W) as Opposition Leader in that chamber. By then the Senate's balance of parties had been made even more precarious than usual by Senator D. C. Hannaford's resignation from the Liberal Party over the Vietnam issue. With Hannaford (S) sitting as an Independent, the numbers were: Coalition, 28; Labor, twenty-eight; D.L.P., two; Independent, two. Neither the Government nor the Opposition in the lower house wanted a double dissolution, which would be likely to help only the D.L.P. in the Senate; but in the Senate Murphy seemed eager to challenge the Government.

On 12 May 1967 Labor senators combined with the D.L.P. and one Independent (Turnbull) to defeat a Post and Telegraph Rates Bill, 24–25. 'There are no limitations on the Senate in the use of its constitutional powers', said Senator Murphy,

> except the limits self-imposed by discretion and reason. There is no tradition in the Australian Labor Party that we will not oppose in the Senate any tax or money Bill . . . Our tradition is to fight, whenever and wherever we can, to carry out the principles and policies for which we stand.

The Government warned that $17 million would be lost if rate increases provided for in the Bill were delayed until the Budget; but when a similar measure was sent to the Senate a week later it too was defeated, 24–26. The Government then tried to introduce the new rates by regulation, only to have the regulations disallowed by the Senate, 27–25. A third bill achieved the result sought by the Government, but not until the Budget session.

The Senate was only one of many difficulties confronting the Holt Government. Harold Holt had won a great electoral victory, amply securing his mandate and at last escaping from the vast shadow of his predecessor. But such is the volatility of political life that within a few months his triumph had turned to trouble.

Into the parliament came the largest contingent of new members since 1949, among whom were seventeen new Liberals, three new Country Party members, the first woman M.H.R. since Dame Enid Lyons's retirement (a South Australian public relations consultant, Miss Kay Brownbill, Liberal Member for Kingston), and the youngest member ever elected to the Australian parliament (another South Australian Liberal, the 22-year-old Member for Adelaide, Andrew Jones). Holt made some changes to his ministry, now enlarged by the addition of one portfolio, but not as many changes as his electoral success had led some to expect. H. F. Opperman (Immigration) and F. C. Chaney (Navy) were dropped from the Ministry. Snedden took over Immigration and Leadership of the House, and his Attorney-Generalship went to the Sydney Q.C., Nigel Bowen (Lib, Parramatta, N). A new portfolio of Education and Science went to Senator John Gorton (V), who later in the year became Leader of the Government in the Senate. One Country Party minister, C. E. Barnes (McPherson, Q), left Cabinet for the outer Ministry and the newly elected Deputy Leader of that party, J. D. Anthony (Minister for the Interior), was promoted to Cabinet. McMahon stayed at Treasury, Hasluck at External Affairs, and Bury at Labour and National Service. In parliament the former Government Whip, W. J. Aston (Lib, Phillip, N), a company director from the eastern suburbs of Sydney, was elected Speaker in place of Sir John McLeay, who had retired before the election.

Across the table from Holt there now sat a more dangerous opponent than Calwell. True to his word, Calwell stood down from leadership after the election, and Caucus took only fifteen minutes to elect Whitlam in his place, by 39 votes compared to the combined 29 of his two closest rivals, Jim Cairns and Frank Crean (Melbourne Ports). In the ballot for deputy leader, a relatively unknown Tasmanian, Lance Barnard, defeated Dr Cairns on the seventh count, by 35 votes to 33.

One of Holt's troubles in the new parliament concerned the terrible collision three years earlier between the flagship of the Australian fleet, the aircraft carrier H.M.A.S. *Melbourne*, and the destroyer H.M.A.S. *Voyager*, resulting in the deaths of eighty-one men on board the smaller vessel. Although a Royal Commission was not able to determine the cause of this disaster off the coast of New South Wales, its report found some personal fault in *Melbourne*'s commander, Captain R. J. Robertson. The Opposition moved in 1964 to censure the Government for its conduct of naval affairs, with particular reference to the collision, but inevitably lost the motion on party lines. Several Liberal backbenchers believed that an injustice had been done to Captain Robertson, who after being posted to a lesser command ashore had resigned from the navy. John Jess (Latrobe, V), whose wife was Robertson's cousin, sought to have the inquiry reopened. The case for this became stronger in 1967 when a former officer on the *Voyager*, Peter Cabban, alleged that the captain of the destroyer—Captain D. H. Stevens, who was killed in the collision—had frequently drunk to excess.

It happened that both Cabban and Robertson were constituents of the new Liberal Member for Warringah, E. H. St John, Q.C., and when St John rose to make his maiden speech on 16 May his subject was the *Voyager*. Seldom had any parliamentarian made such a bold debut as this. With all the forensic skill of a silk, and idealism exceeding prudence, St John accused the Goverment and the Navy of covering up, and demanded justice for Captain Robertson. The Prime Minister hurried into the chamber, red of face, while St John was still in full flight.

> When they came back from the Far Eastern cruise . . . when [H.M.A.S. *Voyager*] went in for its refit, [Captain Stevens] was perpetually drunk—if not asleep or sick, attempting to recuperate. Is this irrelevant? Is not this one of the facts and circumstances leading up to the 'Voyager' disaster? Or have I lost the meaning of the word 'irrelevant'? Are we playing a battle of semantics? What is the meaning of the word 'irrelevant'?
>
> Mr HAROLD HOLT.—What is the meaning of the word 'evidence'?
>
> Mr ST JOHN.—I did not expect to be interrupted by the Prime Minister. We all have been invited to debate what comes to us second hand. The Prime Minister's interruption demonstrates better than anything else that this kind of matter can be sifted only by a proper judicial inquiry, by a select committee or otherwise.

This was the first time anyone had broken the convention of maiden speeches being heard in silence since McEwen interrupted the young Whitlam in 1952. Three days later Holt announced the appointment of a second Royal Commission. It exonerated Captain Robertson and his fellow officers of the *Melbourne*, and, although scouting any suggestion that Captain Stevens had been under the influence of alcohol at the time of the collision, it laid responsibility for the collision clearly on the *Voyager*.

The baby of the House, Andrew Jones, devoted most of his maiden speech to his own generation, comparing the 'gutless wonders in society, the people who will buck anything, who will buck the establishment or the Government' with those young Australians serving in Vietnam, 'who do not buck, who settle down, apply themselves and do their job'. He was heard in silence, but a few weeks later the Opposition heckled him unmercifully as he apologised to the House for remarks which he had made about some of its members in a speech to the Liberal Party Dining Club in Adelaide. It seemed, according to the text of his Adelaide speech, that Jones had 'little in common with other politicians, many of whom are drunk half the time'.

> I was amazed to be in the House one day to see there nine members out of 124. Three were asleep, two were doing the crossword, and one was reading an outdated Donald Duck comic. A Minister was asleep in his chair. This is the way the Government was being run on that day. I have been disillusioned by the filth, smut, jealousy and friction I have seen in Canberra politics.

However poorly attended the House might have been on that day—and no one could deny that the House sometimes conducted business with less than a quorum present—young Mr Jones had undoubtedly spoken out of turn. He had omitted to mention the various demands which are placed upon members, often requiring them to spend more time outside the chamber than within, and worse still he had offended the House's dignity. In a speech punctuated with such interjections as 'Shame', 'Next time stay sober' and 'That'll teach you to keep off the grog', he apologised to the House for his 'inaccurate and ill-advised' remarks. 'I have learned a painful lesson which I shall not forget lightly', he said.

> It was never my intention to belittle any member or to cast any aspersions on this Parliament, and I admit that I was foolish and indiscreet. I apologise to the House for my behaviour, and promise all members faithfully that I will do my best to redeem myself in the eyes of my colleagues on both sides of the House.

Mr Jones then retired to his room, and the House settled down to another day's work—'happy in the thought', as one sardonic commentator remarked, 'that the dignity of the institution had been maintained'.

Two by-elections this year were the cause of greater dissatisfaction for the Government than might have been expected from the 1966 result, even allowing for the tendency of voters to chastise governments between general elections. In July a Labor candidate, Gordon Scholes, won the Victorian seat of Corio, which had fallen vacant when its Liberal occupant, the former bicycling champion Hubert Opperman, resigned to become High Commissioner in Malta. The swing to Labor was 11 per cent. The Liberal Party might have compensated for that loss when the Queensland seat of Capricornia became vacant through the sitting Labor member's death, for Capricornia had been held by a Liberal until 1961, and the new Labor candidate was a left-winger with widely publicised unconventional views, Dr Douglas Everingham. At the September by-election, however, Everingham improved slightly on his predecessor's vote.

In parliament the Government was embarrassed by the enormous cost of

F-111 strike bombers which had been ordered from the United States to impress Indonesia, the escalating war in Vietnam, and a controversy about No. 34 Squadron of the R.A.A.F., the so-called V.I.P. flight used by senior politicians. The cost of twenty-four F-111s had grown from an original $125 million to $237 million, and the Opposition lost no opportunity of protesting at this apparent exorbitance. In August the Attorney-General introduced a Defence Forces Protection Bill, making it an offence to send aid to North Vietnam or the National Liberation Front. The Opposition responded with an urgency motion in the Senate, charging the Government with inconsistency in permitting the sale of $4 million worth of steel to China while still declaring that nation to be a strategic threat. The motion failed on a vote of 25–25, with D.L.P. senators naturally enough supporting the Government's unswerving commitment to the American cause. The Treasurer was reported to have said in Washington, 'Where you go, we will go', a variation on 'All the way' which reminded Whitlam irresistibly of 'Ruth standing among the alien corn'. In October Holt announced the despatch of another seventeen hundred men to Vietnam, bringing the Australian military commitment to eight thousand.

The matter of the V.I.P. flight had attracted attention periodically in the Senate, particularly from the Independent Senator Turnbull, after the Government decided in 1965 to re-equip No. 34 Squadron with jet aircraft at a cost which grew from an initial estimate of $11 million to $21 million. On 27 September 1967 Senator Murphy sought to move a motion for the tabling of all accounts and papers relating to the use of V.I.P. aircraft by ministers and other parliamentarians. The Government forestalled this with an undertaking that the Prime Minister would make a ministerial statement, which he did on 4 October. He denied that catering was extravagant (on a recent flight from North West Cape he and his wife Zara had lunched on pies and sausage rolls), but claimed that it was actuarially impossible to separate the V.I.P. operation from other functions of the flight, such as training.

When the statement was read in the Senate next day, Labor proceeded with Senator Murphy's motion, which was carried by 25 votes to 15, with Liberal senators Lillico (T), Wright (T) and Wood (Q) supporting the Opposition, D.L.P. and Independents. This was the Government's worst numerical defeat in the Senate since 1949. On 24 and 25 October Senator G. C. McKellar (C, N), representing the Minister for Air, provided some of the particulars sought by the Senate resolution, but not passenger lists. On that subject, which the Opposition was especially keen to elucidate, Senator Mckellar said unequivocally: 'No detailed records have been kept of who travelled with an applicant on a particular flight'. This was consistent with a statement which Holt had made to parliament more than a year previously, on the basis of advice from the Minister for Air, Peter Howson. 'After a flight is completed', the Prime Minister said on that occasion, 'the list of names is of no value and is not retained for long. For similar reasons, no records are kept of the places to which craft in the V.I.P. flight have taken V.I.P. passengers. The answers to these questions are thus not available'.

Or so it had seemed. Five hours after McKellar's afternoon statement the Government Leader, Senator Gorton, tabled passenger manifests of the

V.I.P. flight for the last fourteen months. John Gorton had been left in an unenviable position, suspecting that the Government was withholding information which did exist, and apprehensive that at any moment a majority of senators might call the secretary of the Department of Air to the Bar of the chamber to be questioned about records. Howson was attending a meeting of the Commonwealth Parliamentary Association in Uganda, and during his absence the portfolio was being handled by the Minister for Civil Aviation, R. W. Swartz (Lib, Darling Downs, Q). Gorton, who had been an R.A.A.F. fighter pilot during World War II, found it hard to believe that 34 Squadron had not retained its manifests. He was also a man given to prompt action. Without bothering to consult the acting Minister, he telephoned the secretary of the Department and asked whether any passenger manifests existed. They did, and he tabled them that night.

This bold exercise in damage control enhanced Gorton's reputation with some of his party colleagues, but left Holt and Howson open to suspicion of having misled parliament. Howson had been a wartime pilot, too, with the Fleet Air Arm on Malta; but apart from that, and his being a Victorian, he had little in common with the extrovert, informal Gorton. He had a clipped English accent, for he had not come to Australia until after the war, and his manner was equally abrupt. Returning hurriedly from Uganda, he offered his resignation; but Cabinet, after hearing a statement from him, decided not to accept it. 'It was not an easy statement to unravel', he wrote in his diary, 'but there could be no doubt that the part I had played in it I had played honestly. I think the Cabinet were left realising that Gorton had behaved abominably in the matter, and his antagonism to me shone through the discussions we had this morning'.

The V.I.P. affair continued on its course, replete with inconclusive explanations and accusations, until the next half-Senate election, on 25 November. That was to be another disappointment for the Government. The A.L.P. made much of the Senate's new-found vigour in curbing executive power, and the D.L.P. pointed proudly to the impartiality of its two senators, who had voted sixty-four times with the A.L.P., sixty-six times with the Government, and nineteen times alone or with Independents against the rest of the Senate. Holt spoke mainly about foreign policy, and as little as possible about the V.I.P. flight.

Deeply resenting the way in which his own credibility had been called into question on that issue, he asserted, though not convincingly, that Whitlam had 'the unenviable reputation of being the least reliable in the statements he makes of any political leader I have known in the federation's history'. During one televised press conference he turned to a veteran political correspondent and asked whether he had ever known him to lie. The correspondent replied that Holt was a completely truthful man. Obviously the Prime Minister was also an anxious man, for no one who knew him would have felt that such a testimonial was necessary.

The election result was a mild rebuke to the Government rather than a vote of confidence in the Opposition. When new senators took their seats in July, the A.L.P. and D.L.P. would have the numbers, given the will, to outvote the Government even with Senator Turnbull supporting it.

In the lower house, the time-consuming V.I.P. controversy and recurrent debate on Vietnam had produced legislative congestion of extraordinary proportions. When the House met for the second last day of the session in November, its notice paper carried no fewer than forty-one separate items of business, including seven bills concerning offshore oil exploration and production, seventeen tariff proposals, three bills aimed at reorganising the waterfront industry, and a ministerial statement on Vietnam.

Soon after parliament rose, Cabinet was summoned urgently to consider a decision by the British Government to devalue the pound sterling. It decided not to follow suit, although many primary producers, and consequently the Country Party, would have preferred to see the Australian dollar devalued as well. Cabinet's decision meant that farmers would be disadvantaged under existing contracts, and exports of meat, dairy products and fruit to the United Kingdom would be affected in the longer term. McEwen was overseas when the decision was taken, and on his return he protested publicly about the damage it was likely to inflict upon his party's constituency. This imposed considerable strain on the coalition, but Holt dealt promptly and firmly with the situation. He met McEwen for seventy-five minutes, and later issued a statement, in effect a rebuke of the Deputy Prime Minister, which the latter accepted without public demur.

McEwen's main antagonist in the parliamentary Liberal Party was its deputy leader, McMahon. Great antipathy existed between these two men— the one aloof and austere, with 'a Corsican-like devotion to the pursuit of vendettas'; the other equally ambitious, younger and more than a little devious. McEwen regarded McMahon as a threat to the coalition, suspecting him of wishing to see the end of the Country Party, and of leaking Treasury information to discredit some of that party's initiatives. In this imbroglio he found an unexpected ally in the Governor-General, Lord Casey. On 8 December 1967 His Excellency, with the knowledge and approval of Holt and McEwen, invited the Treasurer to see him and warned that any more friction with the Country Party leader could affect the stability of the coalition, and consequently of the Government. When this later became known publicly, some observers held that stability of the Government was a legitimate concern of the Governor-General. Others wondered whether His Excellency would have taken quite the same trouble to prevent a split in a Labor Government. At any rate, Casey's warning was effective. McMahon undertook to do all he could to preserve the Liberal–Country Party coalition.

With that settled, the way seemed clear for the Prime Minister to enjoy a reasonably carefree Christmas holiday. On Friday 15 December he drove from his Melbourne home in Toorak to the beach house at Portsea where he and his wife spent as much of their leisure as political life allowed. 'This is the refreshment', he once said of the beach. 'If I didn't get this I'd go bonkers.' Portsea is at the entrance to Port Phillip Bay, just across the Rip from Point Lonsdale, where Alfred Deakin used to go for his kind of refreshment, a meditative re-charging of that 'inner life' so often curtailed by public responsibility. Holt's refreshment was more convivial and physical. Surrounded by what Zara called a 'witty, with-it crowd, very healthy and athletic', the Holts led an archetypal weekend existence at Portsea, composed largely of barbecues, impromptu drinks, tennis and swimming. Although in his sixtieth year, the Prime Minister was still fit enough for surfing on the ocean side of the peninsula, and spear-fishing for lobsters. On Sunday morning, which was overcast and windy, he went with some neighbours and their friends to watch the English yachtsman, Alec Rose, beating into Port Phillip Bay on his voyage around the world. A king tide was running out of Bass Strait, with huge waves dumping driftwood and kelp ashore. Even so, the Prime Minister wanted a swim. They drove to a strip of sand called Cheviot Beach; he changed into his swimming trunks behind a rock, and at 11.15 a.m. entered the surf alone. The others watched him bobbing between the waves for about ten minutes, then suddenly became aware that he had vanished. Despite an intensive search for almost three weeks, his body was never found.

There was something singularly Australian about this accidental, almost casual, death in the surf. It had nothing in common with President Kennedy's death, but the shock felt around Australia was probably no less than would have been occasioned by an assassin's bullet. What, if anything, did it mean? Press reaction ranged from anger that the nation had not provided better protection for its leader, to a certain pride in the fact that Australia's Prime Minister had been able to lead the relatively unfettered kind of life in which such a death was possible. Some thought Holt 'too nice a man to have been a great prime minister', while others more charitably said that he was 'an able man and an honest man who might well have led the country sensibly and wisely for many years'. Others again thought they discerned in that wild king tide the symbolic end of the Menzies era. 'Holt', according to one commentator,

> if not an extension of Menzies, was as Anthony Eden to Winston Churchill, a crown prince long kept waiting for the throne . . . [He] was finally given office, as was Eden, when political waters seemed calm, the weather set fair. All too soon skies began to darken, and the sea-storm that literally destroyed Harold Holt ushered in a decade of unprecedented disturbance.

Independence

On the two previous occasions when a conservative coalition government had suddenly been deprived of its leader—in 1939 by the death of Lyons, and 1941 by the resignation of Menzies—the Governor-General had commissioned the Deputy Prime Minister, who was a member of the Country Party, to serve as Prime Minister until the larger coalition partner chose its new leader. Lord Casey now followed this example. He could have commissioned a Liberal minister temporarily, but concurred in the view put to him by the Deputy Prime Minister, McEwen, that such an appointee would have an unfair advantage in the leadership election that was soon to be held by the parliamentary Liberal Party. Without doubt McEwen was well qualified, and more than willing, to lead the coalition indefinitely. But recognising the political difficulties this would pose (not least because of his antagonism towards McMahon), he agreed to accept an interim appointment provided there was no formal statement of time limit. He did, however, state publicly on the day he was sworn in, 19 December 1967, that he would step aside as soon as the Liberals had chosen their leader, and in the meantime would not alter policy or the ministry.

One thing he could do, and did, was to ensure that his successor would not be McMahon. He called the Treasurer to his office and told him that the Country Party would not continue to serve in government if McMahon became Prime Minister. This was pretty much what Sir Earle Page had done to Menzies in 1939, but more effective. Black Jack did not mince his words. 'Bill', he said, 'I will not serve under you because I don't trust you'. McMahon made no reply. He sat looking at McEwen for a moment, then left the room without a word. McEwen stated his decision publicly, though neither he nor McMahon revealed the simple reason he had given for it. Other reasons, real and imagined, also gained currency. McMahon stoically refrained from comment, and withdrew from the leadership race.

There were four contenders, but the race was really between two of them. Billy Mackie Snedden, although Leader of the House, was not even in Cabinet and he seemed to have little support in the party room. Leslie Bury had more support, particularly from New South Wales, but looked and sounded more like an Anglican parson than a prime minister. The other two made a better showing in the gauntlet of press and television interviews through which they approached the party election.

Paul Meernaa Caedwalla Hasluck, 62-year-old Western Australian journalist, diplomat and historian, had been a member of parliament since 1949, Minister for Territories for twelve years, and Minister for External Affairs for four years. Hasluck was a hard-working, intelligent minister who had the blessing of Sir Robert Menzies. On the debit side, his manner was rather stiff and he showed an unusual reluctance to promote his own cause. When McEwen asked who was working for him, Hasluck replied that he thought he had good support, but no one was actively campaigning on his behalf. 'In my experience you don't win party elections that way', said the realistic McEwen. 'If you want to win, you ought to get someone working for you straight away.' Perhaps Hasluck did not care one way or the other. Several years later he was to write that his long tenure of the thankless Territories portfolio had 'killed in me all personal political ambition and deadened my political interest'.

The fourth candidate was John Grey Gorton, the 56-year-old Government Leader in the Senate. Gorton was another 'fortyniner, but one who had not lost any of his ambition, and fully understood the process of winning. Two of his fellow Victorians—the Liberal Whip, Dudley Erwin, and the Minister for the Army, Malcolm Fraser, were mustering votes for him, but Gorton was also his own best supporter. He was a lanky, gregarious man with wry, rather battered features which were the legacy of a wartime injury. On television he projected an image of plain, no-nonsense egalitarianism; in person he was refreshingly informal, admittedly sometimes blunt to the point of rudeness, but nevertheless a 'good bloke'. His only obvious disadvantage in the leadership contest was membership of the Senate. There is nothing in the

Constitution to prevent senators from serving as ministers, and of course many of them, including Gorton, had done so. But by custom arising from the Senate's inability to initiate financial legislation, the majority of ministers, including the Prime Minister and Treasurer, had always been drawn from the House of Representatives. Thus if the Liberals were to choose Gorton as leader, and therefore Prime Minister, he would have to resign from the Senate and find a seat in the lower house.

They did choose him. According to unofficial estimates of the election held on 10 January 1968, Bury and Snedden were eliminated in a first ballot and Gorton then beat Hasluck by 43 votes to 38. He was sworn in as Prime Minister the same day, and resigned his place in the Senate on 1 February in order to contest the by-election for Higgins, left vacant by Holt's death. For the next three weeks, Prime Minister Gorton did not belong to either house of parliament. This state of limbo was permitted under Section 64 of the Constitution, but the only precedent for it was Barton's first three months in office before the first federal election. The by-election was held on 24 February, and on 1 March the new Member for Higgins, grinning from ear to ear, was escorted into the House by McEwen and McMahon, the former once again Deputy Prime Minister and the latter still Deputy Leader of the Liberal Party.

The new Prime Minister was eager for office, but not so eager for parliament. On his advice the Governor-General had prorogued parliament on 9 February 1968, terminating the first session of the twenty-sixth parliament and thus causing all bills to lapse. It seemed reasonable that the new Prime Minister should want to start with a clean notice paper, and make his own statement of policy. But no such statement was forthcoming, and in the months ahead Gorton treated parliament with a lack of interest amounting almost to disdain.

Nor did he show much respect for the public service. He dispensed with most of his predecessor's personal and senior departmental staff, replacing the permanent head of the Prime Minister's Department, Sir John Bunting, with C. L. S. (later Sir Lennox) Hewitt. He appointed as his private secretary a very capable woman of only twenty-two years, Ainsley Gotto, who had previously worked for Dudley Erwin, but he wisely retained the services of Holt's press secretary, Tony Eggleton.

On the other hand he made surprisingly few ministerial changes. Only D. L. Chipp (Navy) and Howson (Air) were dropped, presumably because of the *Voyager* and V.I.P. flight affairs. Among four newcomers were Senator M. F. Scott (Customs and Excise) and W. C. Wentworth (Social Services), both of whom had promoted his candidature. A young member of only two years' standing, P. R. Lynch (Lib, Flinders, V), was given the Army portfolio, probably for no other reason than Gorton's awareness that he needed a Catholic in his Ministry.

In making Gorton its leader, the Liberal Party had taken an unaccustomed risk. Hasluck would have been a more orthodox choice, but Gorton seemed likely to give a better account of himself against Whitlam. Gorton belonged to the species of Australian political leader that had come to be characterised as larrikin. According to one sociologist, such 'larrikin leaders' as Reid, Hughes, Fadden and Calwell were flash, irreverent, tough and earthy, in the tradition of mean streets and hungry kitchens. Yet not all of them came from deprived circumstances. Gorton did not, but his background was unusual.

His father, John Rose Gorton, was an English entrepreneur who prospered in South Africa, and after the Boer War emigrated to Australia with his wife, from whom he later obtained a judicial separation. She would not agree to a divorce and lived in Sydney, supported by her husband, while he maintained a home in Melbourne with Alice Sinn, the daughter of an Irish railway worker. Alice gave birth to a daughter and son out of wedlock, and died of tuberculosis when the son, John Grey Gorton, was seven. The boy then went to live with his father's wife in one of Sydney's more prestigious suburbs, Killara. He later boarded at Sydney Church of England Grammar School; went to live briefly with his father, who had become an orchardist at Kangaroo Lake, in the Victorian Mallee; and finished his secondary schooling at Geelong Grammar. He excelled at sport, and became a house captain. His school nicknames were 'Droop', because of his casual bearing, and 'Flick', because of a slight facial tic.

After matriculating, Gorton went to Brasenose College, Oxford. He graduated with second class honours in History, and married the sister of one of his college friends, an American. In 1936, the year his father died, Gorton and his wife Bettina took over the orchard at Kangaroo Lake. When war broke out he enlisted in the R.A.A.F., was posted to an R.A.F. Spitfire squadron in Britain, and later served in Singapore, northern Australia and New Guinea. Flight Lieutenant Gorton was lucky to survive the war. On one occasion he crashed on an island near Singapore, injuring his face and arms. The ship on which he left Singapore was torpedoed by a Japanese submarine, but he was lucky enough to be picked up from a raft by an Australian destroyer. After plastic surgery to his face he joined a Kittyhawk squadron in Darwin. On one flight he was forced down on Melville Island, and led a Crusoe-like existence for six days before being rescued. In New Guinea his Kittyhawk flipped over during take-off, but miraculously he escaped unharmed. After the war he returned to the orchard, became president of the local shire council, and was elected to the Senate.

The new Prime Minister's first extended performance in parliament took place on 14 March, during a debate on the use of torture by Australian soldiers in Vietnam. Some who heard this debate, or read it in Hansard, could scarcely believe that parliament was discussing such a subject; but the war had indeed brought army and parliament alike to such a shameful pass. Gorton had the unenviable task of defending Australia's military honour while answering the question of whether, so to speak, the army had stopped beating its wife. It was a no-win situation. Lynch, in a ministerial statement, confirmed that Australian troops had captured a woman dressed in civilian clothes who had been reporting their movements by radio to the Vietcong. 'The interrogator did no more than shout at the woman', he said, 'bang the table, use threats and proceed to pour some water down the woman's throat.

I say that this was done in an endeavour to secure answers to questions which could affect—'.

MR SPEAKER.—Order! The House will come to order . . .

MR LYNCH.—I say again that the interrogator did these things in an endeavour to secure answers to questions which could have been vital to the safety and security of Australian soldiers.

Mr CLYDE CAMERON.—We ought to pour water into you.

MR SPEAKER.—Order! The honourable member for Hindmarsh will cease interjecting.

Gorton spoke next. He conceded that the spirit of the Geneva Convention had been broken, but not 'to the point that any real torture had been applied'. There were members of the House who knew what real water torture was, he said, and those subjected to it could not walk away from an interrogation tent, as this woman had done. He added that such a thing should not have happened; that it had been done in the stress and strain of fighting by someone acting contrary to army instructions, who had consequently been removed from the position which he previously held; and that if it happened again, as it might, the reason and the consequence would be the same. This was not the stuff from which parliamentary reputations were made. But at least the Prime Minister had measured up to a difficult and odious task.

In May the Minister for Labour and National Service, Bury, introduced a bill to strengthen the National Service Act against those the Minister called 'draft dodgers' and 'self-styled conscientious objectors'. Whitlam said that few bills had ever been brought to parliament with so many objectionable provisions and with so little explanation or justification. Calwell, free from the constraints of leadership, gave full vent to his detestation of the conflict which had now involved Australia in torture as well as conscription—'a filthy, bloody war; a cruel, dirty war; an immoral, unjust, unwinnable civil war far removed from our shores'. The Government gagged debate to speed the Bill through all stages, but outside parliament sit-down demonstrations were staged at The Lodge and in Bury's Sydney office.

It had been widely assumed that Gorton would seek a mandate for his leadership by calling a general election before the end of 1968. But this was not his intention. On 19 November Whitlam moved want of confidence in the Government for its failure to make decisions about the defence, development and welfare of Australia, and its refusal to debate such matters in parliament. No Australian Government, he said, had been in such disarray since the fall of Fadden in 1941. That was drawing a rather long bow, for the motion was defeated by 67 votes to 35, and after five more sitting days parliament adjourned for the summer recess.

Whitlam's position had been stronger since April, when he confirmed his own mandate within the Labor Party by means of a 'back me or sack me' ultimatum to Caucus. He resigned as party leader over a dispute at federal executive level—about whether or not a right-wing Tasmanian delegate, Brian Harradine, should be permitted to attend executive meetings, as Whitlam and a minority of delegates believed he should—and stood for re-election. His margin over Dr Cairns was narrower than expected (38 votes to 32), but Whitlam interpreted this as a mandate to pursue his objectives, including reform of the left-wing Victorian branch. Others urged caution. Gil Duthie, a Methodist clergyman who had voted for Whitlam with some reservation, told him not to 'mount a white charger like Joan of Arc and set out on a one-man holy crusade against the A.L.P. machine'. 'He is too impulsive', wrote Duthie in his diary, 'too dictatorial, too scholastic, too messianic and must learn self-control'. It seemed that Whitlam did manage to control himself. There were no more fireworks on the federal executive, despite Harradine's presence, and the next federal conference, in July 1969, provided Whitlam with most of the decisions he wanted. He was now said to be more like one of the boys, and was even seen drinking with unionists in the bar.

That kind of socialising came more naturally to Gorton. He liked a drink and a good time, and saw no reason to change his ways simply because he had become Prime Minister. On the eve of his departure for the United States in May 1969 he was farewelled by the Leader of the D.L.P., Senator Gair, with the traditional Australian warning 'Behave yourself'. In reply the Prime Minister snarled: 'John Grey Gorton will behave precisely as John Grey Gorton bloody well decides he wants to behave'. He was understandably sensitive on this score because of recent events in parliament. On 19 March Bert James (Lab, Hunter, N) had spoken on the adjournment about certain scurrilous rumours concerning the Prime Minister's conduct, which had been mentioned in Frank Browne's *Things I Hear*. James had learnt the art of stirring the possum from an expert, his late father, Rowley James. Calwell moved that the matter be referred to the Committee of Privileges, which had dealt with Browne before. When debate on that motion was resumed next morning, the Prime Minister denied any misconduct on his part and McEwen accused the Opposition of wishing the Prime Minister to go to the United States for important discussions while under the cloud of his conduct being examined by a parliamentary committee. The motion was defeated.

Within a few minutes of Gorton's denial he received unexpected support from the Leader of the Opposition in another place, Senator Murphy. Without consulting his party colleagues in the lower house, Murphy asked the Government Leader in the Senate to inform the Prime Minister that he regarded the allegations as utterly untrue and accepted without reservation Gorton's assurance that his conduct had been entirely proper. 'The lesson we ought to learn from this incident', said Murphy,

is that the Parliament should be jealous to ensure that while public men are made to account for their public actions their right to privacy must be preserved equally with the rights of all other citizens. Every citizen should resent a slander against the Prime Minister as if it were a slander against himself.

Little more was heard about most of Frank Browne's scandal-mongering, for it was apparently groundless. But one rumour, concerning a visit by the Prime Minister to the American Embassy, had a certain amount of substance. On the adjournment that same night the Liberal Member for Warringah, St

John, gave the House a censorious account of it, based on information which he had obtained from members of the Press Gallery and confirmed in conversation with the Prime Minister himself. On the night of the day President Johnson announced the cessation of the bombing of North Vietnam, 1 November 1968, Gorton attended a Press Gallery dinner. The American Ambassador had also invited him to call in at the embassy after the dinner, as he had some more information to impart about the bombing pause. The dinner was a great success, and according to St John the Prime Minister did not reach the embassy until about 2.30 a.m. He was accompanied by his press secretary and a 19-year-old journalist, Geraldine Willessee, a daughter of the former Opposition Leader in the Senate, who had asked him for a lift home. They stayed until about 5.30 a.m.

Could such behaviour be excused by the right to privacy, or was it the public action of a public man and therefore open to censure? St John had no hesitation in asserting the latter.

> What would the American Ambassador and his wife think of a Prime Minister who being invited to a social or other occasion arrives at 2.30 in the morning or somewhere about that time with a young lady not his wife aged 19 and stays for some hours? Let honourable members laugh if they please. I do not worry; the Australian public will judge this. I leave it for them to say whether this would in fact prejudice relations between Australia and the United States, because I am quite sure it would have been the Ambassador's duty to report this incident to the President and I can imagine what the President thinks of a Prime Minister who would treat his Ambassador in this fashion . . . It is simply not good enough in a Prime Minister of Australia.

Gorton replied that he too would be happy to 'let the public of Australia judge how terrible that occurrence was'. That was the end of the matter in parliament. The public's judgement was not apparent immediately, but it was already obvious that, whatever damage Gorton may have sustained, the prosecutor had gravely damaged his own parliamentary career. Next day St John the Baptist, as Fred Daly called him, decided that he might as well be hanged for a sheep as a lamb. He issued a press statement saying that other Liberals shared his concern not only about the Prime Minister's personal life but about his conduct generally—his centralist tendency, shown in the Government's dealings with the States; the cronyism apparent in such appointments as those of Gordon Freeth (Lib, Forrest, W), to replace Hasluck as Minister for External Affairs when the latter succeeded Lord Casey as Governor-General, and Dudley Erwin to replace Freeth as Minister for Air; and the cavalier independence which he displayed towards the public service and the Liberal Party organisation. All this was probably true, but none of the Liberals sharing Ted St John's concern displayed any of his suicidal idealism. He went into the wilderness alone. Eight days after his speech on the adjournment he declined endorsement by the Warringah conference of the Liberal Party, and took up the uncertain life of an Independent.

During his visit to Washington the Prime Minister assured his hosts that Australia would 'go Waltzing Matilda' with the United States in resisting aggression. In spite of this rather gauche version of Holt's 'All the way' theme, Gorton was not in fact an orthodox Liberal on defence matters. He had stated publicly that, with Britain proposing to withdraw militarily from South-East Asia, Australia might have to abandon its traditional policy of forward defence and rely instead upon well-armed mobile forces at home which could be deployed in the region as required. He called this 'an Israeli-type capacity for defence'. Others dubbed it 'Fortress Australia', and although Gorton disavowed that term, he found that his views unnerved defence traditionalists, including D.L.P. voters.

As the next general election approached, D.L.P. uneasiness about the Government's defence and foreign policy thinking was compounded by the new Minister for External Affairs. On 14 August Gordon Freeth tabled a ministerial statement, which had not been seen by the Cabinet or the Minister for Defence, about Russia's growing interest in southern Asia and the Indian Ocean. It amply justified the misgivings many had expressed at Freeth's promotion to replace such a senior minister as Hasluck. 'Australia has to be watchful', it said in part,

> but need not panic whenever a Russian appears. It has to avoid both facile gullibility and automatic rejection of opportunities for co-operation . . . The Australian Government at all times welcomes the opportunity of practical and constructive dealings with the Soviet Union, as with any other country, and this has been the basis of our approach to each issue.

To judge from the ensuing outcry in Santamaria's *News Weekly*, Matilda might almost have been giving the next waltz to the U.S.S.R.. The D.L.P. went so far as to say that it would be thinking hard about assignment of its preferences at the next election.

After the shortest Budget session on record, parliament was dissolved on 26 September 1969 and its members took to the hustings for a month-long election campaign. The outlook for the Government was not auspicious. Most ominously, there was a sharp decline in popular support for Gorton. According to the Gallup poll, approval of him as Prime Minister over such possible alternatives as McMahon and the Minister for National Development, David Fairbairn (Lib, Farrer, N), had fallen from 64 per cent in April to 44 per cent in early October. On the other hand, approval of Whitlam as Leader of the Opposition had remained more or less steady at 53 per cent during the same period. The decline in Gorton's rating was almost certainly attributable to public disapproval of his behaving and acting as he bloody well wanted to behave and act. Such independence could sometimes be excused, even admired; but there was growing concern in the press, public service and business community about the way Gorton was inclined to make off-the-cuff policy decisions without due regard for expert advice or Cabinet approval. The latest example of this had been his one-man decision in September, against Treasury advice, to prevent an overseas takeover of the life insurance company, MLC Ltd. As the MLC was registered in Canberra, the Government was able to protect it against a share raid by amending the A.C.T. companies' ordinance. Treasury warned that such direct action might frighten foreign capital, but Gorton went ahead anyway. The decision enhanced his reputation for aggressive nationalism, but not for safe, reliable leadership.

In his policy speech Gorton tried to soothe the fears which Freeth's statement had aroused in the D.L.P. 'We believe that any military alliance or arrangement between Russia and a country in our region would pose a threat to ourselves', he said. 'For we cannot forget Czechoslovakia and Hungary and other occupied nations, and we believe that Russian Communism still has as its objective the spreading of its system throughout the world.' On the domestic front, he promised tax reductions for lower and middle income groups, but said nothing about the vexed question of Commonwealth–State financial relations, which had prompted some Liberals to question his commitment to federalism. Labor offered an attractive election policy including a plan to end poverty, a comprehensive health insurance scheme, pension rises, emergency grants to schools, and withdrawal of all Australian forces from Vietnam by mid-1970.

Although the D.L.P. did not withhold its usual preferential support, the coalition came within a few seats of losing office. As one observer wrote, Australian politics were no longer frozen; the thaw had arrived. The swing against the Government was the largest pro-Labor swing since federation, 7.1 per cent; but Gorton was saved by the size of his majority, which was reduced from forty to seven. St John and Freeth were both defeated, and among the seventeen new Labor members was Richard Klugman (Prospect, N), the first European-born member of the House since the German-Australians Stumm and Dankel during World War I. Dr Klugman, a medical practitioner in western Sydney, had emigrated to Australia with his Viennese parents in 1938. Elections for two casual Senate vacancies slightly altered the party numbers in that chamber to A.L.P., twenty-eight; Government, twenty-seven; D.L.P., four; Australia Party, one. The latter group was the latest manifestation of the Liberal Reform Group, which had become known as the Australian Reform Movement in 1967 and the Australia Party in 1969.

Soon after the Government's narrow escape, Gorton faced a challenge to his leadership in the Liberal party room. This crisis was precipitated by David Fairbairn, an English-born grazier, educated at Geelong Grammar and Jesus College, Cambridge, who was the grandson of two members of the first federal parliament, Sir George Fairbairn and Edmund Jowett, and a nephew of the Fairbairn who died in Canberra's 1940 air disaster. In a telegram to the Prime Minister, David Fairbairn said that, 'as a matter of personal integrity and with the best interests of the Government and the nation at heart', he could no longer serve under Gorton, and would consider contesting the leadership himself. The only other contender was McMahon. McEwen lifted his veto on McMahon and announced the Country Party's willingness to form a coalition with any of the three candidates. At an election on 7 November Gorton retained the leadership by a majority estimated at 33 or 34 out of 65 votes cast. McMahon polled better than Fairbairn, and in the ballot for deputy leader he defeated Snedden by 35 votes to 28.

In the new ministry McMahon replaced Freeth as Minister for External Affairs, Bury became Treasurer, and Malcolm Fraser took the Defence portfolio, left vacant by the retirement of Fairhall. Gorton dropped two of his staunchest supporters, Erwin and Senator Scott; but four of the five new Liberal ministers—D. L. Chipp, T. E. F. Hughes (Parkes, N), Killen and Peacock—were members of a Gortonite coterie known as the Mushroom Club. Fred Daly referred to this select company on the opening day of the new parliament. 'There are things like the Mushroom Club that we would have liked to explore today', said Daly.

> The former Minister for Air, the honourable member for Ballaarat (Mr Erwin), said that the Mushroom Club had a motto which was: 'Keep them in the dark and feed them bull' . . . He made a number of statements on his dismissal from the Ministry . . . When he was asked why he was dismissed from his position as Leader of the House and also as Minister for Air, he said: 'How was I dismissed? I describe it in these words.' He said: 'It is shapely; it wiggles; and it is cold-blooded.'

This was a reference to the Prime Minister's private secretary, Ainsley Gotto, whom Erwin blamed for his unceremonious dumping. The vulgarity of his statement probably cost Erwin whatever sympathy he might otherwise have received.

The twenty-seventh parliament was summoned on 25 November to comply with the constitutional requirement that parliament shall meet not later than thirty days after the return of writs; it was then prorogued, after a sitting of only thirteen hours, for the equally compelling reason that the Government needed time to collect itself before facing the Opposition in earnest. As Whitlam told the House, the Governor-General's speech was the shortest of its kind since Sir Ronald Munro-Ferguson had opened a one-day session in 1917. With his usual attention to detail, Whitlam remarked that the 21-gun salute had taken longer than Sir Paul Hasluck's 75-second speech. Indeed some members thought they detected a sardonic smile on Sir Paul's face as he ended that speech with the words: 'I now leave you to the discharge of your high and important duties, in the faith that Divine Providence will guide your deliberations and further the welfare of the people of the Commonwealth'.

With the help of Divine Providence and ten applications of the gag the Government survived censure motions in both houses, and soon after midnight fled into a summer recess that was to last for three and a half months. When the second session opened on 3 March 1970 His Excellency spoke for forty-five minutes. That was more like it. He foreshadowed many measures that were ready to be introduced in the lower house, but said nothing about some very significant steps that were soon to be taken in the Senate. Never before had the red chamber seemed so purposeful, so independent of the other place, as it did at the start of this historic session. On 17 March the Standing Orders Committee referred Clerk Odgers's report on standing committees to the Senate for consideration. Two days later, on a separate subject, Senator Murphy successfully moved that a select committee be appointed to inquire into and report upon the desirability and feasibility of the Commonwealth establishing a securities and exchange commission, either alone or in co-operation with the States. 'The background of this motion', he said,

> is the greatest speculative boom in Australia's history—one of the

greatest in world history. In the background also are a series of company crashes during the 'sixties and recent evidence of improper practices, notorious and harmful to the interests of this nation . . .

The turnover in shares through the stock exchanges is now running at thousands of millions, that is, billions of dollars, per year. The old-world calm of the stock exchange has changed to the air of a casino. The boom recalls the South Sea Bubble and the events preceding the great Wall Street crash. Where so many enter unknown waters, there are many who do not know how to swim, and there are many sharks—not only single sharks, but schools of sharks.

The eight-member Senate Select Committee on Securities and Exchange was chaired first by Senator Magnus Cormack, and for most of its four-year existence by Senator Peter Rae (Lib, T). Its private and public hearings, at which evidence was given by the protagonists in some of Australia's most spectacular company crashes, attracted great public attention. By the end of its work in 1975 the Committee had done much to create the environment in which a National Companies and Securities Commission was established.

Odgers's report was considered by the Senate in June. Senator Murphy, who had obtained from Caucus the approval for a full system of legislation and general purpose standing committees which he had assured Odgers would be forthcoming, moved for the immediate establishment of seven standing committees. 'People around the world are becoming more educated', he told the Senate,

and they will not tolerate the kind of nonsense that goes on where legislative bodies deal with important matters and at the end of a sitting or a sessional period have not got through a fraction of the business. They just will not tolerate it and if we do not see that this democratic system works then it will be replaced . . . Here is a great representative body, as there is across the corridor, and I think both of them can work. They can work if they start to adopt efficient procedures, and the standing committee system is the efficient procedure.

The Government Leader, Senator Sir Kenneth Anderson (N), while agreeing that a permanent system should be established, urged a more gradual approach. He moved as a first step the establishment of five committees to consider the Estimates. The D.L.P. Leader, Senator Gair, also advocated gradualism. As a compromise, the Senate established five estimates committees and two standing committees, all before the end of 1970, and resolved to establish the other five standing committees over a period of not less than twelve months. The standing committees would each consist of eight senators, with the chairman being a Government senator and the balance of party allegiance reflecting that of the Senate as a whole. Members would be appointed by resolution at the commencement of each parliament, and matters would be referred to them on motion by the Senate. The first two Standing Committees were on Health and Welfare, and Primary and Secondary Industry and Trade. The other five, all of which became fully operative by October 1971, were on Education, Science and the Arts; Social Environment; Foreign Affairs and Defence; Constitutional and Legal Affairs; and Finance and Government Operations.

According to the *Sydney Morning Herald*, these were 'the most fundamental and dramatic changes witnessed in the Commonwealth Parliament since the States decided to federate 70 years ago', making the Senate 'potentially the most powerful parliamentary chamber in Australia'. Even without its new committee system, the Senate had shown a degree of independence which excited its partisans and alarmed others. In the wake of the former Senator Gorton's accession to the Prime Ministership, Sir Robert Menzies warned that the Senate might be getting ideas above its station. 'In Australia we practise a system of responsible government', he wrote.

> In that system Ministers sit in and are responsible to Parliament; but Cabinet may be displaced by a vote of the House of Representatives (not the Senate) and therefore holds office at the will of the House of Representatives . . . It would be a falsification of democracy if, on any matter of Government policy approved by the House of Representatives, possibly by a large majority, the Senate, representing the States and not the people, could reverse the decision.

Such reversal was by no means unknown, of course, and another example of it occurred in June 1970. The States Receipts Duty Bills were intended to have the effect of enabling States to receive revenue from a tax on receipts, which otherwise they would have to forgo because of a High Court ruling that such taxes were basically excise duties and therefore a Commonwealth monopoly. The federal Government, already in more than enough trouble with the States on other matters, agreed to their request that it should impose the receipts taxes as part of its own budget and pass the amount collected to the States. Labor, however, decided to oppose the legislation and if necessary defeat it in the Senate. Whitlam had already declared the Opposition's willingness to defeat money bills in that chamber. 'We intend to press our opposition by all available means on all related measures in both Houses', he said during the Budget debate on 25 August. 'If the motion is defeated we will vote against the [Appropriation Bills] here and in the Senate. Our purpose is to destroy the Government which has sponsored it.' Later, speaking on the States Receipts Duty legislation on 1 October, he said: 'We all know that in British parliaments the tradition is that if a money Bill is defeated the government goes to the people to seek their endorsement of its policies'.

In the Senate, Labor attacked the Receipts Duty Bills on grounds that they were retrospective, would fall unfairly on consumers, and would be an administrative nightmare. In case any of his colleagues doubted the propriety of opposing a financial measure, Senator Murphy read into Hansard a list of 168 financial measures which Labor had opposed in the Senate since 1950. With D.L.P. support the bill was rejected, by 19 votes to 26, and the Government had to make other arrangements to help the States. It happened that in this same month the Standing Orders Committee of the House of Representatives recommended a lifting of the rule against referring directly to the Senate in proceedings of the lower house. Oblique terms such as 'another place' and 'members of another place' had probably come into use as a means of surmounting another standing order of the lower house, to the effect that allusions to debates of the current session in the other house were out of order. The latter rule, designed to prevent fruitless argument between members of two distinct bodies who were unable to reply to each other, had been relaxed in 1963. Now the House decided to go the whole hog and call the Senate by its name. This seemed eminently sensible, for the chamber that was blazing a new committee trail and rejecting financial bills was not simply another place but another place altogether.

On both sides of the lower house a substantial number of backbenchers envied the Senate its new versatility, and wanted to follow that example. The Prime Minister was not enthusiastic. When the Speaker, Sir William Aston, raised the matter of standing committees with him, the most Gorton would agree to support was another select committee or two. One of the most active proponents of a standing committee system was the Labor member for Perth, J. M. Berinson, a 38-year-old pharmacist who had come into parliament at the last election. Speaking in a Grievance Day debate on the morning of 21 May 1970, he said:

> on all sides I hear the Parliament denigrated as a charade, a farce, a hollow shell, a puppet show, and it is remarkably difficult in all honesty to construct a defence to this criticism. We are at a stage where most of a member's constructive work is done outside the Parliament, while a great deal of his time is still spent within it. Surely the question that has to be faced is that we spend so much time here, how can we make the best use of it? . . .
>
> Today listed on the Senate notice paper is a motion calling for the setting up of a comprehensive standing committee system in that House. Why should we not be doing that here? This House, by contrast, has twice the membership and hence at least twice the capacity to constitute committees and yet only one current committee is now functioning on a policy matter, namely, aircraft noise.
>
> Last week we agreed to set up a second select committee which will consider the preservation of the red kangaroo. What about the preservation of the Parliament? What about the preservation of the parliamentary member in some meaningful sense? If the Government will not agree to go straight to a comprehensive system of standing committees why not at least a short-term select committee to make recommendations on the subject?

Later that day, at the instigation of Berinson and the Liberal Member for Wakefield (S), C. R. Kelly, seven backbenchers from each side of the House met in a committee room to discuss the matter further. Two of the Liberals, A. A. Street (Corangamite, V) and D. J. Hamer (Isaacs, V), and one of the Labor members, Dr M. H. Cass (Maribyrnong, V), subsequently made representations to the Prime Minister, but nothing came of it. On 21 August the Labor Member for Wills (V), Gordon Bryant, moved in the House for the appointment of eight standing committees similar to those envisaged for the Senate. On the Government side Bryant's proposal was predictably supported by Harry Turner, but more significantly was opposed with great vehemence by John McEwen, whose parliamentary career was nearly over. Speaking at a meeting of the joint Government parties, McEwen said that he would 'vomit' if the Government took any lead on the management of parliamentary affairs from Bryant, a member who earlier in the year had 'compelled the Speaker to suspend a sitting by his refusal to leave the chamber when suspended'. In such a confrontation between the champions of government and parliament, one McEwen was worth ten Turners. Bryant's motion was left dormant on the notice paper.

The incident referred to by McEwen, Bryant's defiance of the Speaker, had occurred shortly after midnight of 8 April during debate on the River Murray Waters Bill. This measure, ratifying an amendment to the River Murray Waters Agreement, provided for the next major water storage in the Murray system to be built not at Chowilla in South Australia, as had earlier been contemplated, but at Dartmouth in Victoria. South Australia felt that it had been let down, and the Opposition intended helping its supporters in that State by moving several amendments during the committee stage of the debate.

The Opposition had received an assurance from the Leader of the House, Snedden, that time would be allowed for full debate. There was no obvious reason why Labor should not have been allowed to have its say, for the Government was winning the River Murray debate and had the numbers to defeat any unwanted amendments. But in the eleven sitting days so far that year Snedden had moved the gag no fewer than twenty-one times, and at one minute to midnight on 8 April he moved it again. The House turned into bedlam.

The Labor Member for Dawson, Dr Patterson, called Snedden a dingo. When called upon to withdraw, he substituted the words 'tame dog', and only after much prevarication did he withdraw and apologise for that. One of his colleagues, W. G. Hayden (Oxley, Q), was named for suggesting that the House was not being run democratically. When the question of his suspension was put, the tellers for the 'Noes' refused to act and the Speaker declared the question resolved in the affirmative. Hayden withdrew. Bryant then called the Speaker a disgrace to the Chair. He was named. The tellers for the 'Noes' again refused to act, and Speaker Aston directed the Serjeant-at-Arms to request the Honourable Member for Wills to leave the precincts of the chamber. Bryant refused to go, and Labor members crowded around him to keep the Serjeant at bay. The Speaker then suspended the sitting.

Next morning Bryant apologised and withdrew. Whitlam moved a motion of censure against Snedden for his 'mishandling of the business of the House and his repeated failure to honour agreements made between the Government and the Opposition'. This was amended on the Prime Minister's motion to censure Whitlam for not having used his influence to restrain 'an attack on the institution of parliament', and the motion as amended was passed by 61 votes to 49. Was it any wonder that Joe Berinson heard the Australian parliament described at this time as a charade, a farce and a hollow shell? In the aftermath of the River Murray fracas, parliament was sensitive to such remarks, and also to criticism that it sat only one-third as frequently as the British and Canadian parliaments. The Government proposed that sitting hours be extended to provide the equivalent of a fourth sitting day each week, and the Opposition for its part established a committee to determine in what way parliament could become 'an effective organ of democracy exercising a real supervision over the administration'. The latter objective had recently been incorporated in the A.L.P. platform, on a motion by Senator Murphy.

The most important measures dealt with by parliament in 1970 were the Australian Industry Development Corporation Bill, establishing 'McEwen's bank', the purpose of which was to raise overseas capital for loan funds which could be used by Australian companies to expand their operations; the National Health Bill, bringing into effect recommendations of the Nimmo Committee on medical benefits and the administration of voluntary health insurance organisations; and the Territorial Sea and Continental Shelf Bill, asserting the exclusive right of the Commonwealth to exercise sovereign control over resources of the sea-bed off the Australian coast, from low-water mark to the outer limits of the continental shelf. The latter measure was intended to redefine sovereignty over submerged lands, a matter on which parliament had previously acted only to the extent of providing a legislative framework—the Petroleum (Submerged Lands) Act and other associated measures of 1967—to govern the exploitation of offshore petroleum resources.

For the first time since 1909 Australia had not a single Labor government, though Labor was to win office in South Australia and Tasmania before the end of the year. In the meantime, six conservative State Governments were unwilling to make any further sacrifices on the altar of Moloch, and denounced the centralism which they discerned in the conservative Commonwealth Government's offshore policy, described by one State attorney-general as 'a sin against the spirit of Federalism'.

The Territorial Sea and Continental Shelf Bill was introduced in April 1970 by the Minister for National Development, Swartz. On 8 May his predecessor, David Fairbairn, declared that the Government had dishonoured an undertaking given by him to State ministers in March 1969. With the authorisation of Cabinet, said Fairbairn, he had made an offer to the States that they should retain control of the mineral resources of the territorial sea-bed (that is, from low-water mark to the three-mile limit offshore) while the Commonwealth would exercise total rights from the three-mile limit to the edge of the continental shelf. The States replied with a counter-offer. Fairbairn agreed to convey that to Cabinet, and gave an undertaking that the Commonwealth would consult the States again before taking any action.

That was the undertaking which, according to Fairbairn and other Liberals, the Government had broken. In a ministerial statement Gorton disputed Fairbairn's interpretation of events, and the Opposition moved quickly to take advantage of the situation. On 15 May Dr Patterson moved an amendment to a motion by Snedden that the Prime Minister's statement about Fairbairn's accusation be noted. The amendment amounted to a censure motion, and with the support of only four Liberal rebels it could have brought the Government down. McEwen saved the day by putting together a further amendment, acceptable to the rebels, which included the words 'that this House does not believe that there has been any failure on the part of the Government to honour any commitments'. All Liberals supported the Government except Fairbairn, who abstained, and the much amended motion was passed by 63 votes to 57. Debate on the Bill remained adjourned.

The atmosphere of crisis was heightened in the second half of 1970 by a half-Senate election which disappointed both Government and Opposition, and by intermittent Vietnam demonstrations. After July 1971 the Government and Opposition would each have 26 votes in the Senate; the D.L.P would have five; and, consonant with the new mood of the Senate, there would be three Independents. In addition to Senator R. J. D. Turnbull there would be another Tasmanian Independent, Michael Townley, and a Western Australian Independent, campaigning for abolition of death duties, S.A. Negus.

Protest against Australia's involvement in Vietnam, and particularly against conscription, was expressed as angrily and rowdily in Parliament House as in the streets of Sydney and Melbourne. On 10 June the Speaker was obliged to suspend sitting for half an hour while police cut free five women who had chained themselves to railings of the public gallery in protest against conscription. One woman shouted, 'Stop gaoling my son'. Moratorium rallies were held outside Parliament House, and at one of these Whitlam was photographed by the Commonwealth News and Information Bureau with a Vietcong flag clearly visible near him. A Government member later tabled the photograph, which the Opposition claimed had been falsified in order to embarrass Whitlam. On 29 September Lance Barnard moved the Opposition's second censure motion of the year against Gorton, alleging want of confidence on the ground that he had 'allowed a faked photograph to be tabled in the House'. It was defeated by 51 votes to 56.

Vietnam was an all-pervading issue, spreading like an indelible stain on Australia's political fabric. It bolstered the Opposition's confidence, weakened the Government, and contributed to the downfall of the Prime Minister. The latter event had become increasingly likely in recent months, and with McEwen's retirement from parliament in February 1971 it became inevitable. Sir John McEwen's departure, and the election of J. D. Anthony to lead the Country Party, freed McMahon from McEwen's residual disfavour, making him completely acceptable as a successor to Gorton. The crisis was precipitated by the Minister for Defence, Fraser, but if he had not done it someone else would. Gorton had offended too many friends ever to be short of enemies. The pass to which he had now come was as fraught with danger as his wartime flying career. If he did not crash, drown or run out of fuel, he was bound to flip over on take-off.

John Malcolm Fraser was an Oxford-educated grazier from the Western District of Victoria: a bigger and tougher version of David Fairbairn. He had helped to make Gorton Prime Minister, but relations between the two men had deteriorated in the past year. Gorton felt that the ambitious young Minister for Defence had not supported him sufficiently in the offshore minerals crisis, and for his part Fraser resented the Prime Minister's lack of enthusiasm for a tri-service training college. The sudden escalation of hostility between them was more evident to the press than to the public because it was expressed mainly in 'off the record' briefings to certain members of the Press Gallery.

Since the Menzies era a new generation of political journalists had arisen in Canberra. Veterans like Ian Fitchett (*Sydney Morning Herald*), Alan Reid

(Sydney *Daily Telegraph*) and Harold Cox (Melbourne *Herald*) were still widely respected. But their supremacy was being challenged by several formidable newcomers, notably Allan Barnes (*Age*), Laurie Oakes (Melbourne *Sun*), Alan Ramsey (the Murdoch group's *Australian*, which had been launched as a Canberra-based daily in 1964), Max Walsh (*Australian Financial Review*, a Fairfax publication which became a daily in 1963), David Solomon (*Canberra Times*, which had come under Fairfax control in 1964), and Peter Samuel (*Bulletin*). The Press Gallery now delved more deeply than in the past, with more expertise and greater independence from proprietorial direction. But the relationship between news makers and news breakers was just as symbiotic as ever, and politicians were still adept at using journalists for their own advantage. Sometimes, as in the fall of Gorton, the Press Gallery not only reported and analysed the news, but also helped to make it.

In February 1971 the ABC reported from Saigon that the Australian Army intended winding down its civil action programme in Vietnam. Fraser immediately contradicted this, and gave briefings which led to press reports of serious tension between himself and the army. One report said that Fraser had instructed the Defence Department's Joint Intelligence Organisation to investigate army activities in Vietnam because he did not trust the army's own information. The Prime Minister, who had been shown the latter report before its publication, hastened to assure the Chief of the General Staff, Lieutenant-General Sir Thomas Daly, that he did not share the Minister's reservations about the army. He then directed Fraser to deny the report, and rubbed salt into the wound by giving a briefing to Ramsey of the *Australian* from which the journalist prepared a report stating that Sir Thomas Daly had accused Fraser of disloyalty. Daly denied the report, and Gorton declined to comment on it. Ramsey claimed that the Prime Minister had been shown the report in typescript, and had made no attempt to stop publication.

Fraser resigned from Cabinet on 8 March, and next day made a statement of explanation in parliament accusing Gorton of disloyalty and criticising the general quality of his leadership. 'This man', he said, 'because of his unreasoned drive to get his own way, his obstinacy, his impetuous and emotional reactions, has imposed strains on the Liberal Party, the Government and the Public Service. He is not fit to hold the great office of Prime Minister'. Gorton's reply was interrupted by an unexpected and quite unprecedented interjection when he came to deal with Ramsey's story.

> . . . I therefore replied to that question: 'Had General Daly said what it was claimed he did say?' by saying that I thought it wrong to discuss or comment with Mr Ramsey on what a third party had said and Mr Ramsey replied: 'Fair enough'.
> A VOICE.—You liar.
> MR SPEAKER.—Order.
> MR CALWELL.—Why don't you deal with the animal?

The voice belonged to Alan Ramsey in the press gallery. He left in some confusion, and composed an apology to Gorton worded in such a way as to prevent the Opposition from moving that he be called to the Bar of the House to explain the meaning of his interjection.

'All the way with LBJ': Prime Minister Holt and the Governor-General, Lord Casey, welcome President Johnson at Fairbairn RAAF Base on 20 October 1966.

On the way to an election: the Clerk of the Senate, J. R. Odgers (left), the Clerk of the House of Representatives, A. G. Turner, the Deputy Clerk of the House of Representatives, N. J. Parkes, and the Serjeant-at-Arms, A. R. Browning, on the steps of Parliament House as a 19-gun salute is fired after the reading of the Governor-General's proclamation dissolving the twenty-fifth Parliament on 31 October 1966, seven days after President Johnson's departure.

John Grey Gorton, Prime Minister (1968–1971)

William McMahon, Prime Minister (1971–1972)

Sir Owen Dixon, sixth Chief Justice of the High Court (1952–1964)

Sir Paul Hasluck, Governor-General (1969–1974)

At a meeting of the parliamentary Liberal Party on 10 March a motion of confidence in Gorton's leadership, moved by his own faction, was opposed by several speakers including Fairbairn, Jess, Mackay, Turner, Howson and Bate. The vote was tied at 33–33. Gorton then used his casting vote against himself, presumably out of awareness that to survive by his own vote alone would fatally weaken the Government's ability to withstand a want of confidence motion by the Opposition. In the subsequent leadership ballot McMahon not surprisingly defeated his only opponent, Snedden. What did cause surprise was that Gorton nominated for the deputy leadership against Fairbairn and Fraser. There was much sympathy for him in the party room, and he won by a comfortable margin. 'I don't think any of us expected this', wrote Howson in his diary. 'It's a pity, as it will make it so much more difficult for us in the weeks ahead.'

Austerlitz

The Government's situation rapidly became even more difficult than pessimists had expected. Not since the U.A.P.'s declining years had the major coalition party been in such disarray as when William McMahon became Australia's twentieth Prime Minister. And he was hardly the man to work wonders of reconciliation and reconstruction, even if such a miracle had been feasible. Instead, he was destined to preside over the disintegration of a Government that had been far too long in office. He tried to rally the party by invoking the spirit of 1949, but it was too late for that. The magnificent voyage had lasted twenty-one years, and the good ship *Free Enterprise* was now being swept ever closer to the rocks, sails in shreds and more than a few men overboard.

At the age of sixty-three, McMahon was the oldest man apart from McEwen ever to become an Australian Prime Minister; but he was unusually fit for his years, and could acquit himself creditably on the squash court against men twenty years his junior. Billy McMahon was a dapper, balding figure of the same height (5ft 6ins) as another diminutive Prime Minister, Billy Hughes; and like Hughes, he had suffered from deafness. Although his hearing had been rectified by surgery in early adulthood, his manner of speaking was still affected by that early handicap. His voice quavered with an almost liturgical rhythm that would not have sounded out of place in St Mark's Church of England, Darling Point. He was a tireless talker who gathered and disseminated political intelligence with great facility. Whitlam once called him 'Tiberius with a telephone'. His friends spoke admiringly of his energy, shrewdness and patience; those who wished to denigrate him said that he was contrary, nervous and vain.

McMahon belonged to the upper crust of Sydney's eastern suburbs. Orphaned in early childhood, he was brought up by his uncle, Sir Samuel Walden, a prominent businessman and one-time Lord Mayor of Sydney. Although his father, a Sydney solicitor, had been Roman Catholic, young McMahon was educated at the non-denominational Sydney Grammar School and the Anglican St Paul's College, Sydney University, where he took a law degree. From 1928 to 1940 he worked at Sydney's oldest law firm—Allen, Allen and Hemsley—eventually becoming a junior partner acting as solicitor for the Commonwealth Bank of New South Wales. He then joined the A.I.F, did mainly staff work in Australia and attained the rank of major. After the war he visited the United States and Britain, and on his return to Australia in 1947 he took an economics degree.

Although reputed to be something of a playboy, for he was sometimes photographed at night clubs and had not yet married, McMahon was in fact a demon for work and intensely ambitious. After winning the new seat of Lowe in 1949, he had to wait only eighteen months before being admitted to Cabinet with two portfolios, Navy and Air. After those came Social Services, Primary Industry, Labour and National Service, Treasury, and External Affairs (the latter being renamed Foreign Affairs in 1970). McMahon's experience was immense. For most of his career it had seemed that he lived only for politics; but at the age of fifty-seven, he had married a prominent member of Sydney's *haut monde*, Sonia Hopkins, who was twenty-four years his junior. By the time he became Prime Minister he had two children, and a third was born during his term of office.

McMahon's Ministry was not a harmonious one. He himself kept Foreign Affairs for only twelve days, then moved Leslie Bury to that portfolio from Treasury, only to drop him from the ministry four months later. Bury had not distinguished himself in either post, but such an abrupt dismissal created the distinct impression that McMahon had not forgiven Bury for replacing him as Treasurer in Gorton's Ministry. Bury's only comment was that 'political life is full of hazards, even for prime ministers'. Snedden followed Bury as Treasurer, and Nigel Bowen followed him at Foreign Affairs. Howson was rewarded for his past support with an ill-sorted Ministry consisting of Aboriginal Affairs (regrettably transferred from the Minister for Social Services, Wentworth, who had done well in that field), Environment, Arts and Tourist Activities. Conversely, Hughes and Killen were repaid for their loyalty to Gorton by being sent to the back benches. Killen passed the time there by making orotund neo-Menzian speeches and exchanging erudite jests with the Leader of the Opposition, with whom he enjoyed good rapport.

Gorton had asked for and received Defence, which must have given him some satisfaction, while Fraser had to make do with Education and Science. The presence of a deposed Prime Minister in Cabinet was a continuing source of discomfort to McMahon. He ignored Gorton as much as possible; but when contact could not be avoided, they quarrelled about the defence budget. Before long, however, Gorton provided the Prime Minister with a reason to ask for his resignation. In August 1971 he wrote a newspaper article replying to a book by Alan Reid—an employee of McMahon's principal Sydney supporter, Sir Frank Packer—which had been severely critical of Gorton's Government. McMahon seized upon part of this article, dealing with the problem of leaks from Cabinet, as evidence that Gorton himself had breached Cabinet solidarity. Gorton thereupon tendered his resignation from the Ministry and the Deputy Leadership. Fairbairn became Minister for Defence, and Snedden Deputy Leader. For his part, Gorton assumed *de facto* leadership of the other ex-ministers sitting mutinously on the back benches.

The new Government lost a good deal of credit through its mismanagement of legislative business, particularly in the final week of the 1971 autumn sittings. Between 10 a.m. on Tuesday 4 May and 3.44 a.m. on Friday 6 May the House of Representatives sat for fifty hours. There were many more bills than would normally have been dealt with in that sitting time, even if spread over more days, and to facilitate this 'legislation by exhaustion', as the press called it, the new Leader of the House, Sir Reginald Swartz, lumped seventeen of them together for guillotining in a period of little more than fifteen hours. When Sir Reginald moved the suspension of Standing Orders for this purpose, Killen was among those who spoke in protest:

> I should take this opportunity, if for no other reason, to indicate to the House that recent events have not swept me into a state of docility, neither of servility. This is a disgraceful proceeding. It is a proceeding unworthy of the national Parliament and a proceeding which does great affront to this country. [Quorum formed]. This is the 16th year in which I have sat in this Parliament and in my recollection there is no precedent for this measure. True it is a precedent can be found dealing with the guillotine relating to Bills in the same genera but there is not, to my recollection, a precedent which offers an example where 17 Bills, many of them plainly different from one another, should be taken together . . .

Once during these truncated proceedings the House moved into and out of the committee stages without anyone saying anything, and the committee was taken to have accepted amendments which had been circulated by the Government, but never formally moved, let alone debated. Three income tax bills were disposed of in less than an hour, and a bill to change the Constitution of Papua New Guinea in less than half an hour. At one stage in the early hours of Thursday morning Speaker Aston threw a pencil at the Minister for Social Services, who had begun to snore on the front bench. It was, as Whitlam said, 'an utter travesty of what the parliament should endure'. Newspaper editorials condemned the Government for its abuse of parliament, and compared the sorry state of the lower house with the recent improvement of the Senate's reputation. Senators made the same comparison. Diligently they continued to sit for eight days after the House had tumbled into recess, and several speakers referred in passing to the recent disgraceful events in another place. During debate on the Ministers of State Bill, which increased the number of ministers by one, Senator Sir Magnus Cormack paid particular attention to the growing power of executive government in the lower house, as evidenced by the latest accretion of ministerial strength and the Prime Minister's announced intention of appointing six Assistant Ministers; the adverse effect of this upon parliamentary rule; and the importance of the Senate as a countervailing force. Sir Magnus, who was soon to be elected President of the Senate, drew attention to the Government's excuse for the recent legislative turmoil:

> [The excuse was] that the Bills had not emerged from the bureaucracy. In terms of parliamentary constitutionality, I have always believed that instructions for Bills to be prepared were given by Ministers of State. But there emerges in this significant statement that there is no policy direction from the Minister of State level; instead there is a policy direction emerging from the other end of the tunnel . . .
> There has been interposed between the Crown, as we have historically

understood it, and the Parliament as we have historically understood it, a
new power altogether. That power is the power of the bureaucracy or the
power emerging from the needs of individuals composing the Ministry. A
temporary marriage of convenience between the infallibility of the
bureaucracy and the temporary needs of the people who can be drawn
from Parliament is a new and damaging power in the concept of whether
Parliament should rule. That is the power of the Executive . . .

I like to think, much in the terms of Sir Robert Menzies, that I am a parliamentarian to my boot heels. But pre-eminently I am a senator to my
boot heels. Now I can see with great sorrow and an enormous amount of
apprehension that we are moving into an area where there is a new
component of power, namely, the convenient marriage of Ministers and
the bureaucracy, by which Parliament will be overruled. This can be prevented only by the existence of a Senate that is willing to accept the norms
of parliamentary rule as they have grown up in English speaking
countries over the past 300 or 400 years . . .

Never had the Opposition been more sure of itself, and with every passing
month its confidence increased. The Victorian branch of the A.L.P. had been
reconstructed, the federal conference had approved new election policies,
and during parliament's winter recess Whitlam led a delegation of Labor
members and officials on a visit to China. His timing could not have been
better. Although Australian and Chinese diplomats had been in cautious
communication in other parts of the world, there was no expectation in
Canberra that the United States (and inevitably also Australia) would soon
establish normal relations with the People's Republic of China, as Britain
had done two decades before. Taken unawares by Whitlam's visit, the Prime
Minister resorted to the hackneyed rhetoric of the 1950s and 1960s. On 12
July, while the delegation was in Beijing, McMahon said at a meeting of
Young Liberals in Melbourne:

It is time to expose the shams and absurdities of [Whitlam's] excursion
into instant coffee diplomacy. We must not become pawns of the giant
Communist power in our region. I find it incredible that at a time when
Australian soldiers are still engaged in Vietnam, the Leader of the Labor
Party is becoming a spokesman for those against whom we are fighting
. . .

Three days later President Nixon announced that he had accepted an invitation to visit China, because 'all nations [would] gain from a reduction of
tensions and a better relationship between the United States and the
People's Republic of China'. The Australian Government had no option but
to welcome this initiative, and Whitlam was able to claim that at least his
visit had made Australia appear 'less slow-footed, less imitative' than would
otherwise have been the case.

On the first day of the Budget sittings, 17 August, the Opposition attacked
McMahon with full force. At Question Time every Opposition call was taken
alternately by Whitlam and Barnard, who asked a total of nine questions,
each one beginning: 'I ask the Prime Minister a question'. All of them dealt
with either Gorton's recent resignation or the leaking of Cabinet infor-

mation. Bury had observed earlier in the year that Cabinet 'leaked like a ruddy sieve', and Gorton had referred publicly to someone called 'Billy the Leak'. In spite of such blatant disaffection, however, Gorton and the other ex-ministers had made it known that they would not vote in favour of a no-confidence motion. For this reason Whitlam argued that a motion which he moved after Question Time on 17 August was not strictly a no-confidence motion, and had not been accepted as such by the Prime Minister. But it did incorporate sentiments expressed by honourable and disaffected gentlemen opposite, said Whitlam hopefully, and accordingly they should feel free to vote for it. 'I put it to them', he said, 'that if they vote for this motion they will not destroy the Liberal Party, but rather they will give it a lease of life'. The motion was that, in the opinion of the House, 'the Prime Minister's methods and motives in removing his Ministers and his subservience to outside influence have destroyed trust in his Government at home and abroad'.

> This is a Prime Minister [said Whitlam] who has not the trust of his own Party and who has not and cannot have the trust of this House. It was an exquisite experience to watch the former Ministers—Ministers whom he has dismissed—looking at him when he gave his answers this afternoon and to see the intensity, to use as neutral a term as one can properly use on this occasion, that they showed as they listened to his replies.
> Mr GORTON.—It is so hard to hear from this far away.
> Mr WHITLAM.—I will concede that the right honourable gentleman's expression indicated incomprehension . . .

In spite of Whitlam's cajolery no one crossed the floor, and the motion was defeated by 56 votes to 62. Snedden then introduced the Budget, allowing for a considerable increase in Commonwealth spending offset by higher domestic receipts from taxation. On 26 August the House was counted out for want of a quorum. The last time this had happened during a Budget debate was in 1912. Sir Frank Packer's *Daily Telegraph* suggested that a group of Labor members had caused the interruption to proceedings by walking out of the chamber when the quorum was called. Denying this, the Opposition raised the *Telegraph*'s report as a matter of privilege. The Committee of Privileges found the author guilty of contempt, but the House decided that it would best consult its own dignity by taking no further action in the matter.

Earlier in the year the House had come to a similar conclusion about another breach of privilege—the imprisonment of the Labor member for Reid (N). Tom Uren, a former heavyweight boxer and prisoner-of-war of the Japanese, had been gaoled briefly in New South Wales for failing to pay $80 court costs in connection with his unsuccessful prosecution of a police officer for allegedly assaulting him during a Vietnam moratorium demonstration. Although Uren did not raise privilege in his own defence, the Committee of Privileges found that in such circumstances a member of the House of Representatives enjoyed the same immunity as had applied to members of the House of Commons in 1901—that is to say, immunity from imprisonment on a civil matter (but not a criminal one) during a session of parliament or in the 40-day period preceding or following a session. No further action was taken by the House.

On 7 September Whitlam raised as a matter of public importance 'the need to pass laws relating to trade practices, consumer protection, consumer credit, securities markets and overseas control under the Commonwealth's corporations power'. This debate arose from a decision of the High Court in *Strickland* v. *Rocla Concrete Pipes Pty Ltd*, which on the one hand held that the Trade Practices Act did not validly require registration of an agreement containing restrictive practices that had purely intrastate application, but on the other hand, and more importantly, overruled one of its own early decisions about the Commonwealth corporations power. In *Parker* v. *Moorehead* (1909), a case concerning the Australian Industries Preservation Act, the High Court had ruled in effect that parliament could not pass laws dealing with the intrastate operations of such corporations. This was an interpretation which Barwick, when he was Attorney-General, had thought too narrow. Now, as Chief Justice with a majority of the bench concurring, he was able to revive the corporation power. 'As a consequence', said Whitlam in the matter of public importance debate,

> the Australian Parliament now can pass laws such as the parliament of every other industrial or developed country has long been able to pass . . . The High Court judgment, it seems to me, does not permit the Australian Parliament to pass laws for the incorporation or nationalisation of companies. It does, it seems to me, permit the Australian Parliament to enact national codes on the operation of companies.

This judgment would not have been obtained but for the persistence of the former Attorney-General, Tom Hughes—'the honourable, learned and gallant member for Berowra', as Whitlam referred to him in the debate. Hughes was naturally more cautious than Whitlam about the use which parliament ought to make of the corporations power, but he expounded the Gortonian view of federalism:

> I heard on the radio this morning that one newspaper . . . described [the judgment] as a blow to federalism. Federalism is one of those Alice in Wonderland-Humpty Dumpty kind of words. One remembers that Humpty Dumpty said to Alice that words mean exactly what one wants them to mean. To me, federalism involves as a basic fact living under a federal constitution and if one is to live under a federal constitution it is one of the primary duties of the federal government, the national government, to explore the limits of constitutional power given to it under that constitution and then, having explored them with a view to ascertaining them by judicial decision, act within them in what one conceives to be the national interest . . .

The Prime Minister, who took no part in this debate, was less inclined than his predecessor to explore the limits of Commonwealth power; in fact, with Gorton's troubles *vis-à-vis* the States so fresh in mind, McMahon was positively disinclined on that score. The gap in restrictive practices legislation was closed easily enough by a new Trade Practices Act, but the Government did nothing to make further use of the corporations power. On 7 December 1971 Whitlam moved to bring on the long adjourned debate on the Territorial Sea and Continental Shelf Bill, for which Gorton said he was prepared to vote no matter what the Government's attitude might be. But McMahon was determined to keep out of the troubled waters between low tide and the edge of the continental shelf. The motion was defeated on party lines, and in spite of further prodding by the Opposition the Bill eventually lapsed at dissolution.

Although the latest possible time for the next election was still twelve months away, public opinion poll findings released early in the new year made dismal reading for the Government. During the last twelve months approval of McMahon as Prime Minister had dropped from 55 per cent to 25 per cent. A Gallup poll published in February 1972 showed support for Labor at 49 per cent; the Coalition, 40 per cent; and the D.L.P., 7 per cent. This was the first time Labor had exceeded the rest of the political spectrum combined.

Disapproval of Whitlam dropped from 41 per cent to 38 per cent, but some of his own followers still had reservations about his style of leadership. Although Whitlam had the ability to inspire devoted loyalty, he could also be—as the Opposition Whip, Gil Duthie, wrote in his diary—

tactless, arrogant, domineering. [He] accuses me of blathering about him & his willingness [to] approach McMahon on salaries', wrote Duthie. 'You are a weak man', sez he in my office after accusing me in my place in the House. Rather than make a scene, I explained all I'd done was to counter criticism that he was doing nothing to put the Opposition case [for higher parliamentary salaries] to the PM as previous A.L.P. leaders had done. What a blasted nerve, to belittle, condemn and insult me when actually I'd been defending him.

Parliamentary salaries and allowances, which had last been adjusted in 1968, generated strong feeling in this parliament. Mr Justice Kerr, a judge of the Commonwealth Industrial Court who had been appointed to report on the subject, recommended increases ranging from $3950 (combined salaries and allowances) for members and senators to more than $7000 for senior ministers. Although describing this as 'eminently fair' and 'in no way excessive', the Prime Minister, anxious to set an example of wage and salary restraint, at first proposed to reduce the recommended levels by 28 per cent and finally, on the last day of the 1971 Budget sittings, postponed the Parliamentary Allowances Bill because the Opposition intended to vote against the more substantial ministerial rises. These bills also lapsed at dissolution late in 1972.

Parliament reassembled on 22 February 1972, and on 29 February Whitlam moved a want of confidence motion alleging that the Prime Minister, in answering questions without notice, had 'deliberately misled the House' and 'harmed Australia's relations with other countries'. As the House divided, McMahon approached Gorton, with whom he had held no conversation since the latter's dismissal, and said: 'John, I'd like you to sit and talk to me during the division'. 'Go to buggery!' replied Gorton. He voted with the Government nevertheless, and the motion was defeated by 52 votes to 57.

Gorton was behaving more like a pretender than a former Prime Minister.

He toured the country, expounding his own brand of Liberalism, and when McMahon was unable to provide *Time* magazine with a list of national goals, Gorton obligingly compiled one. A 'Get Gorton Back Committee' came into being, but there was no real prospect of such a return. Killen had requested a meeting of the parliamentary party in April to consider 'the extreme political crisis'. The request was denied, and McMahon seemed certain to lead the party at the coming election.

The foremost domestic issues in the remaining few months of this parliament were industrial relations and Aboriginal land rights. On 26 April the Minister for Labour and National Service, Lynch, introduced the umpteenth Conciliation and Arbitration Bill, which was intended, among other things, to impede large-scale union mergers of the kind then being planned by the left-wing metal trades unions. The amalgamation provisions, inspired by the D.L.P., required a postal ballot of all members of all unions concerned, the return of valid ballot papers by at least half the members of each union, and at least half the returned ballot papers to support the proposed amalgamation before it could take place. Labor voted against many features of the Bill, and particularly the amalgamation provisions; but with D.L.P. and Independent support, the Bill passed the Senate late in May and received assent in August.

Metal trades unions pressed ahead with their merger regardless, and industrial relations continued to hold parliament's attention. On 23 August there was an angry debate about industrial violence, arising out of a statement to the House by the shadow Minister for Labour, Clyde Cameron. The wider but related issue of law and order was given prominence during the same month by a televised debate between the Attorney-General, Senator Ivor Greenwood (Lib, V), and the nation's best known trade union official, R. J. L. Hawke, who had been President of the A.C.T.U. since 1970. Senator Greenwood also clashed in parliament with Senator Murphy on the subject of terrorism, disputing Murphy's allegation that right-wing Croatian extremists had been responsible for recent bombings in Sydney. Murphy sought to refer the matter to the Senate's standing committee on foreign affairs and defence, but the D.L.P. and Senator Townley voted with the Government to defeat his motion.

The issue of Aboriginal land rights reached the twenty-seventh parliament in two ways: the tabling on 25 May of a report of the Gibb Committee of Review on the situation of Aborigines on pastoral properties in the Northern Territory, and the continuing presence of an Aboriginal tent 'embassy' on the lawn in front of Parliament House. On 2 June the Minister for the Interior, Ralph Hunt (C, Gwydir, N), announced that the Government would accept the Gibb Committee's main recommendations, and would lease land to the Gurindji people who had been squatting at Wattie Creek, on the Vestey Company's Wave Hill property, for the last six years. Hunt also announced the Government's intention to bring in an ordinance dealing with trespass on unleased land in Canberra.

The ordinance was proclaimed on 20 July, and police immediately dismantled the tents and arrested eight people, including five Aborigines. 'The Aboriginal embassy was removed from the lawns of Parliament House this morning with a small amount of violence', wrote the Minister for Aborigines, Howson, in his diary. 'Ralph Hunt is elated with the success of the project, but I have a feeling that this is only the first round of the battle.' The tents were re-erected three days later, dismantled again with more arrests, erected a third time on 30 July, and dismantled again. On 15 August, while the House debated a motion of no confidence in the Minister for the Interior for his handling of the affair, four Aboriginal women chained themselves to railings on the front steps of Parliament House. The motion was defeated on party lines.

Aborigines had made substantial political progress since the opening of Parliament House in 1927, when people in the crowd, on the very site of the dismantled 'embassy', threw coins to old Marvellous from Gundagai. They still had much to achieve, but at last their protests were effectively organised and articulate. Now there was even an Aboriginal in federal parliament, and not before time. Neville Bonner (Lib, Q), a former bridge carpenter, had been chosen in 1971 to fill a casual Senate vacancy caused by the resignation of Dame Annabelle Rankin. His mother was an Aborigine born on a mission station near Ipswich, and married to an English seaman and labourer who deserted her shortly before Neville, their second child, was born. The boy grew up in deprived circumstances at Lismore and later Beaudesert, in southern Queensland. 'I feel overawed by the obvious education of honourable senators within this august chamber', he said in his maiden speech.

I assure honourable members that I have not attended a university or a high school and, for that matter, I do not know that I can say that I have spent very much time at a primary school. But this does not mean that as a Senator from Queensland I am not able to cope. I have graduated through the university of hard knocks. My teacher was experience. However, I shall play the role which my State of Queensland, my race, my background, my political beliefs, my knowledge of men and circumstances dictates. This I shall do, through the grace of God, to the benefit of all Australians.

The Budget session was a prelude to the election. The Budget itself injected $740 million into the economy to stimulate growth and reduce unemployment. It raised pensions, and lowered income tax by an average of 10 per cent. There was to be a poverty inquiry, and the means test for age pensions would be abolished over a three-year period. A Companies (Foreign Take-overs) Bill was introduced in October, and received assent little more than a week later.

The Opposition had electoral bait of its own, and plans for prompt bureaucratic action in the expected event of a Labor victory. It also tried unsuccessfully to secure the enfranchisement of Australia's 650 000 18-year-olds, who on balance might reasonably have been expected to prefer Labor's policies to those of the conservative parties. The High Court had recently rejected an argument that 18-year-olds who were already enfranchised for some State elections were therefore eligible to vote federally in those States. A few days later Whitlam moved suspension of Standing Orders for resumption of debate on the Commonwealth Electoral Bill, which he had introduced in May for the enfranchisement of all 18-year-olds. When this motion was defeated, Senator Murphy introduced the Bill in the Senate. The Government put paid to that by having the debate adjourned, on a vote of 26–22.

On 10 October McMahon announced the date for a House of Representatives election, 2 December. Whitlam must have been expecting that date, for it was the latest one possible and he had something apposite to say about it. 'The second day of December is a memorable day', he told the House. 'It is the anniversary of Austerlitz. Far be it from me to wish, or to appear to wish, to assume the mantle of Napoleon, but I cannot forget that 2nd December was a date on which a crushing defeat was administered to a coalition—a ramshackle, reactionary coalition.'

During the adjournment debate, Whitlam made the customary adieux to colleagues who would not be nominating for election to the next parliament. One of these was his former leader and bugbear, Arthur Calwell, now concluding thirty-two years of distinguished if often abrasive parliamentary service. Whitlam's only reference to Calwell was a neat but half-mocking allusion to his Papal knighthood and his time as Minister for Immigration.

> There are among [our departing colleagues] three Knights Commander, one Commander and one Officer of the Most Excellent Order of the British Empire. There is one Knight Commander of the Order of St Gregory the Great who, it is appropriate in the circumstances to remark, was the first to extol the angelic qualities of English migrants.

The Prime Minister spoke about his own great respect for the institution of parliament, and Clyde Cameron replied that he had never heard such balderdash in all his life. Cameron was one of Labor's hardest-working shadow ministers—'my Carnot, the organiser of victory', said Whitlam, forgetting on that occasion that he had no wish to assume the mantle of Napoleon.

> Hundreds of questions have not been answered [said Cameron]—so much for respect for the institution. Information has been suppressed so that the Parliament could not learn the facts . . . The executive has constantly used the Parliament as a mere rubber stamp for decisions it had already made—so much for the Prime Minister's alleged respect for the institution of Parliament . . . Having said that, I want to dissociate myself completely from any good wishes that might have been extended to the Prime Minister and to the other people who have spent so much of their time during the last 23 years preventing the people of Australia from getting the kind of legislation they have long been hungering for.

And so to the hustings. Labor's campaign, well orchestrated on the theme of 'It's time', began with a wildly enthusiastic meeting in Sydney's western suburb of Blacktown, part of the underprivileged urban region at which many of the party's policies were aimed. Whitlam addressed his audience with the same words as Curtin had used when announcing the outbreak of war with Japan: 'Men and women of Australia . . . '. In the course of his speech he made 140 specific promises, including immediate abolition of conscription, recognition of China, a comprehensive free medical service, and greatly expanded Government spending on schools both public and private.

McMahon's policy speech, delivered on television without an audience, pointed to the Government's record, matched some of Labor's traditional welfare policies, and questioned Labor's ability to govern after so long a period in the wilderness.

The vote for Labor was by no means as strong as early returns on election night suggested, but it produced a historic victory nonetheless. Before the night was out McMahon conceded defeat in a dignified speech to a national television audience. He was the first conservative Prime Minister to lose an election since Bruce, and conversely this was the first time since 1929 that Labor had moved from Opposition into office by means of electoral victory. After more than a generation, the tide that Chifley used to talk about had come in again. Labor had a majority of nine in the House of Representatives, but it would not be able to rely on the Senate. The arithmetic of that regenerate chamber was unchanged: Labor, twenty-six; Liberal, twenty-one; Country Party, five; D.L.P., five; Independent, three.

17

Cyclones

Tracy

Out of the vast low-pressure system of the last nine parliaments there now came into being a disturbance of great intensity. The swing to Labor on 2 December 1972 was only 2.5 per cent, but that was enough to send warm moist air billowing upwards out of the doldrum trough. After twenty-three years in Opposition, the Labor Party was raring to go. It was replete with policy objectives, and imbued with an exhilarating sense of destiny and urgency. Given the extent of the new Government's aspirations, and the hostile aspect of the Senate, there was not a moment to be lost. Rather than wait for Caucus to elect a full ministry, Gough Whitlam and his deputy, Lance Barnard, were sworn in almost immediately as a two-man ministry, capable also of forming a three-man Executive Council with the Governor-General. McMahon tendered his resignation at 11 a.m. on 5 December, and at 3.30 p.m. Sir Paul Hasluck administered oaths of office to Whitlam as Prime Minister with twelve other portfolios and Barnard as Minister for Defence with the remaining thirteen portfolios. The 'duumvirate', as this interim ministry became known, was unique in Australian parliamentary experience; but there was a Westminster precedent. With his usual didactic precision, Whitlam declared the duumvirate to be the smallest ministry with jurisdiction over Australia since the Duke of Wellington held all imperial portfolios for a month in 1834.

The new Prime Minister justified his prompt assumption of power on grounds that certain executive decisions needed to be made without delay, that the Government had a mandate to implement its policies, and that a full ministry could not be chosen for at least several days. Under A.L.P. rules, ministers must be elected by the full parliamentary party. Nine members of that party were still waiting to learn whether they would be returned to parliament or not. Their fate was unlikely to be decided until preferences were distributed, and Whitlam was not prepared to wait as long as Scullin had done in similar circumstances after the 1929 election. In the aftermath of that election the Bruce–Page Ministry, although defeated overwhelmingly, had remained in office for ten days before the new ministry was sworn in.

But there was more to the duumvirate than that. By seizing the reins in so unorthodox a way, and blowing up a storm of executive action at a time when normally the pace of Australian life slowed down for the Christmas season, Whitlam was demonstrating to the world that Australia had indeed voted for a change of government. His scope of action was confined to what could be done without parliament, but that was scope enough. Many Australians were surprised to learn what could be done by regulation alone. In less than two weeks Whitlam and Barnard announced forty decisions, including an immediate end to conscription and the release of all gaoled draft resisters. Other decisions led quickly to the return of Australian troops from Vietnam, the transfer of Australia's China embassy from the charade of Taipei to the reality of Beijing, and a reversal of the Australian vote on resolutions concerning southern Africa in the United Nations General Assembly. The duumvirate stopped wheat exports to Rhodesia, took preliminary steps towards the granting of Aboriginal land rights, requested talks with the Premiers of New South Wales and Victoria to discuss plans for a regional growth centre at Albury-Wodonga, gave an R certificate to the previously banned film 'Portnoy's Complaint', removed the excise on wine, set about asking the Arbitration Commission to reopen its hearing on the A.C.T.U.'s application for equal pay to women, cancelled a New Year's Day honours list prepared by the previous Government, and initiated moves to replace the Imperial honours list with an Australian one. By the time Caucus assembled on 18 December it was clear to everyone that a new wind was not merely blowing but positively howling in Canberra.

This bold assertion of the Government's authority was also an assertion of Whitlam's personal ascendancy, and as such its effectiveness was little diminished by his having to share the limelight with Barnard. Whitlam once said that he did not mind how many prima donnas the Labor Party had so long as he was prima donna assoluta. The party possessed several prima donnas, but the Deputy Prime Minister was not one of them. Lance Barnard, a former Tasmanian high school teacher whose father had been one of Chifley's ministers, had become Deputy Leader because of his undoubted loyalty to Whitlam and his notable lack of enemies. He was conscientious, diffident and never likely to steal any of his leader's thunder. Others more ambitious than Barnard would soon be joining the second ministry, but even in that less harmonious company Whitlam's primacy would remain absolute.

Edward Gough Whitlam was a new kind of Labor Prime Minister, a product of the middle class, and as different from Chifley or Curtin as anyone could be. The Prime Minister whom he most resembled in terms of personal manner and parliamentary performance was Menzies. In some respects he even outdid that paragon. He was taller (6ft 5ins), more erudite, and perhaps even wittier. Where Menzies purveyed imperial *gravitas*, Whitlam dealt out radical bourgeois passion spiced with levity and malice. He spoke with a breathy kind of emphasis which some of his colleagues, including Barnard, found highly infectious. He addressed people as 'Comrade', but it was doubtful whether he ever broke the old rule that there are no friends in politics. Some worshipped him. Others could be disconcerted by his lack of small talk, or offended by his indifference and rudeness. Sometimes he acted impetuously, but he claimed there was method in his impetuosity. 'When you are faced with an impasse', he once told a television interviewer, 'you have got to crash through or you've got to crash'.

Whitlam made it known early that he would not accept appointment to the Privy Council, thus denying himself the 'Right Honourable' prefix which had been assumed by every previous Prime Minister except Deakin and Watson. He dispensed with a butler previously employed at The Lodge, and decided not to use the black Bentley with C1 numberplate which had served all prime ministers since Menzies. For the time being he made do with the white Ford Galaxie which he had used as Leader of the Opposition, and dropped the prime ministerial practice of flying an Australian flag on the bonnet. These egalitarian gestures put one commentator in mind of 'a grandly bedizened puce-coloured orchid trying to pass itself off as a shrinking violet'. And there was some truth in that. Before long the Ford Galaxie was replaced by a new white Mercedes-Benz.

Gough Whitlam was born in 1916 at Kew, in the Victorian electorate which later became the blue ribbon preserve of R. G. Menzies. The family was descended on his father's side from a great-grandfather who had come to Australia after service with the British Army in India, and on his mother's side from a long line of Shropshire farmers. His father, H. F. E. Whitlam, was a public servant in the Commonwealth Crown Solicitor's office. Fred Whitlam was later transferred to Sydney, where the family lived in Mosman, Chatswood and Turramurra, and the boy went to Knox Grammar School. In 1928 the Whitlams moved to Canberra, exchanging the comfort of Sydney's North Shore for a mock Tudor home in the raw but prestigious suburb of Forrest. Gough went first to Telopea Park High School, and then to Canberra Grammar School. He co-edited the *Canberran* school magazine with Brian Green, whose father was Clerk of the House of Representatives; after school hours he took Greek and piano lessons, the latter being given by Charles Scrivener, the surveyor who had pegged out the site of Canberra two decades earlier; and from his own father, a scholarly and puritanical man who eventually became Crown Solicitor, he acquired a genuine respect for the public service. In short, Gough Whitlam grew up breathing the air of Canberra.

His education was completed at the University of Sydney, in St Paul's College. After taking his B.A. (including Greek) and LL.B., he spent the last four years of the war as an R.A.A.F. navigator on Ventura bombers operating from northern Australia. This was uncomfortable work for an exceptionally tall man, and one who never managed to conquer air sickness. It was also dangerous. On one sortie against a Japanese base on the East Indies island of Sumbawa, a fuel line on Whitlam's Ventura was cut by anti-aircraft fire, forcing the pilot to make the return flight to Western Australia on one engine, sometimes barely fifty feet above the Timor Sea.

In 1944, while his squadron was based at Gove on Cape York Peninsula, Whitlam's political appetite was whetted by the '14 powers' referendum, through which Curtin tried to enlarge the authority of federal parliament. 'I was appalled by the spurious arguments put against the referendum by the conservative elements in Australia', said Whitlam many years later. 'I propagandised in my squadron in favour of the referendum [and] was really very upset and discouraged when it was beaten. From then on I decided to do something about it.'

After the war he was admitted to the Bar and worked for a time as junior to the prominent Bill Dovey, Q.C., whose daughter Margaret had become Whitlam's wife in 1942. The Whitlams went to live in Cronulla, which was far removed geographically and socially from the North Shore; he joined a local branch of the A.L.P., stood unsuccessfully for the State seat of Sutherland in 1950, and two years later, at the age of thirty-six, secured preselection for Werriwa, an outer Sydney electorate which then extended south to Helensburgh, near Wollongong. At a by-election in 1952 he more than trebled the majority of his predecessor, the late Bert Lazzarini.

Twenty years later Whitlam was to have the satisfaction of acknowledging a letter from Sir Robert Menzies congratulating him on Labor's election to office. 'You would, I think, be surprised to know', wrote Whitlam in reply, 'how much I feel indebted to your example, despite the great differences in our philosophies. In particular, your remarkable achievement in rebuilding your own party and bringing it so triumphantly to power within six years has been an abiding inspiration to me'. Whitlam had taken about the same time to cleanse the Augean stables in Victoria, wean his older colleagues away from the socialist objective, and attract the support not only of workers but of employees generally.

'The overthrow of the Victorian State Executive breaks the last link of Labor with socialism', wrote Les Haylen bitterly in 1970. 'We are now in the process of becoming a Kennedy-type party of millionaires, academics and careerists.' To Whitlam the holy ikon was anathema—not a relic of the true faith, but a sentence to perpetual Opposition. In place of it he advocated competition between public and private enterprise, Commonwealth aggrandisement at the expense of States, and the nourishing of local authorities directly from the centre. He spoke often about State neglect of public transport, hospitals, schools and sewerage. Another lesson he had learnt from Menzies was the use which the Commonwealth could make of Section 96 ('Parliament may grant financial assistance to any State on such terms and conditions as the Parliament thinks fit') to impose its will outside strict limits of the Constitution's heads of power. Conservative governments had used tied grants to circumvent Section 92 (free trade between the States) when they deemed it advisable, which admittedly had not been often. For the new Government, however, Section 96 was an open invitation accepted wholeheartedly. 'I went from the despair of Section 92 to the confidence of Section 96', wrote Whitlam. 'Ninety two was the barrier, 96 the avenue.'

The second Whitlam Ministry, elected by Caucus on 18 December 1972 and sworn in the next day, involved the most extensive departmental reorganisation for a quarter of a century. Whitlam kept Foreign Affairs for himself; Barnard kept Defence, which now included all three service departments; Dr J. F. Cairns was given the new portfolios of Overseas Trade and Secondary Industry; Frank Crean, Treasurer; Senator Murphy, who was one of six senators in the ministry, Attorney-General and Minister for Customs and Excise; Senator D. McClelland (N), the new portfolio of Media; Senator K. S. Wriedt (T), Primary Industry; Fred Daly, who was one of only four members surviving from the Caucus of 1949, Minister for Services and Property and Leader of the House of Representatives; Clyde Cameron, Labour; R. F. X. Connor (Cunningham, N), the new portfolio of Minerals and Energy; and Lionel Bowen (Kingsford-Smith, N), Postmaster-General. There were seventeen other ministers, and, in a departure from the coalition's practice of having an inner and outer ministry, all ministers were members of Cabinet.

The pace of government, far from slackening during Christmas and New Year, actually accelerated. There was a revaluation of the Australian dollar in response to an inflationary trend produced by the previous Government's failure to take similar action. The Minister for Immigration, A. J. Grassby (Riverina, N), announced a cut-back in migration because of a disturbing rise in unemployment; the Minister for Social Security, W. G. Hayden (Oxley, Q), announced a retraining scheme for the same reason; and the Treasurer took action to block certain tax loopholes. Ministerial staffs expanded, consultants were appointed, and task forces were set up with jurisdiction over various areas of 'the Program'. The impression was one of frantic activity, and there was nothing illusory about it. Indeed the interplay of government, parliament, judiciary and crown now takes on an intensity and velocity not previously encountered in this narrative. Our focus must therefore become more selective, ignoring some aspects of the Whitlam Government in order to treat adequately the extraordinary events soon to take place in parliament.

The twenty-eighth parliament was opened on 27 February 1973. Al Grassby wore a purple suit with lace cuffs, Bill Hayden wore a powder blue suit and white shoes, and the chastened Opposition, under the leadership of Billie Snedden, looked appropriately sombre in various shades of grey. Members of a religious sect stood on the front steps handing out pink carnations with prayers attached, and much to the agnostic Prime Minister's annoyance a combined Church service, organised by Duthie, Crean and other members of the Parliamentary Christian Fellowship, was held in the National Methodist Church before the opening ceremony. Whitlam and the Minister for Health, Dr Everingham, had tried unsuccessfully to secure Caucus support for abolition of the traditional reading of prayers by the new Speaker, J. F. Cope (Lab, Sydney, N), when he took the chair; but at least Whitlam managed to keep God out of the Governor-General's speech. Instead of 'relying on the blessings of Almighty God', as in the past, His Excellency concluded by saying: 'With the utmost confidence that you will fulfil to the utmost of your abilities the deep responsibility the Australian people have placed in you, I leave you to carry out your high and important duties'.

The legislative programme outlined by the Governor-General was to be 'the most comprehensive [of its kind] in the history of the Australian parliament . . . designed to achieve basic changes in the administration and structure of Australian society in the lifetime of this Parliament'. Measures would be introduced in the first session to repeal penal sanctions in the Conciliation and Arbitration Act and facilitate the amalgamation of trade unions, expand the activities of the Australian Industry Development Corporation, establish a National Pipeline Authority, settle the touchy matter of offshore sovereignty which the two previous governments had either bungled or ignored, eliminate all forms of racial discrimination, abolish capital punishment in the Australian Capital Territory and Northern Territory, and make the process of government less secret. But while parliament undoubtedly had a duty to consider the Government's measures, there was no guarantee that it would pass all of them. On the contrary, in fact, the Opposition in the Senate expressed clear reservations from the start.

The Leader of the Opposition, Senator Withers, questioned the Government's claim to have received a mandate, and threatened to use the chamber's full powers of rejection. Reg Withers, a former Government Whip, was genial, humorous but rigorous in matters of party discipline. He was known as 'The Toe-cutter', in macabre allusion to a gang of criminals notorious at that time for enforcing its writ by means of digital amputation with a bolt-cutter. 'Figures belie the claim that the whole nation has grasped the Labor Party to its breast', said Senator Withers during the Address-in-Reply debate on 8 March.

> The overall swing to the ALP was only 2.5 per cent, and for the information of honourable senators opposite, that was the smallest swing that has occurred to either this Government or the present Opposition in the past five elections. It is also terribly important to realise, particularly in the Senate, that this swing took place in only three States, namely New South Wales, Victoria and Tasmania. Western Australia, South Australia and Queensland indicated an enormous lack of enthusiasm for the call 'It's time' by swinging to the Liberal and Country Parties . . . So let us not talk overmuch of mandates. Let us also remember that the Senate was deliberately set up by the founding fathers with its enormous powers to act as a check and a balance to protect the interests of the smaller States from the excesses of the larger. Because of the temporary electoral insanity of the two most populous Australian States, the Senate may well be called upon to protect the national interest by exercising its undoubted constitutional rights and powers.

One week later Senator Withers's opposite number—the Leader of the Government and Attorney-General, Senator Murphy—did something which brought the Government's post-electoral honeymoon to an abrupt end. On the night of 15 March, after a parliamentary sitting, Murphy went without warning to the Canberra office of the Australian Security Intelligence Organisation and took possession of an interdepartmental committee's memorandum dealing with an impending visit to Australia by the Prime Minister of Yugoslavia, Djemal Bijedic. The Government was concerned for Mr Bijedic's security, bearing in mind the existence of right-wing Croatian terrorism in Australia. Murphy had frequently criticised the previous Attorney-General, Senator Greenwood, for his lack of concern about right-wing terrorism, and for A.S.I.O.'s apparent complacency. The issue was now revived by Murphy's melodramatic discovery of the interdepartmental memorandum, which suggested that any statement made by the new government on terrorism 'should not be at variance' with those made by the McMahon Government. Early next morning he flew to Melbourne and descended with Commonwealth police on A.S.I.O.'s headquarters, in search of more files.

The A.S.I.O. raid, as it became known, haunted the Government for weeks to come. Senator Greenwood declared that Murphy had acted illegally, as he had no authority over the Director-General of A.S.I.O., and Snedden said that Australian security had been damaged by the raid. On 5 April the Senate carried a motion by 29 votes to 25 censuring Murphy for his handling of the matter, and the House passed a motion of confidence in him. Four days later Murphy embarrassed the Government again when it became known that he had failed to inform Cabinet of news, communicated to him by the Yugoslav ambassador, that Yugoslavia intended to execute three naturalised Australians who had taken part in an armed incursion into Bosnia. On 9 May the D.L.P. leader in the upper house, Senator Gair, moved to set up a Senate select committee, with an Opposition majority, to inquire into the civil rights of migrant Australians. To Murphy this was further evidence of a political vendetta against himself. Earlier the Senate had also rebuffed its erstwhile champion by disallowing new divorce rules, on grounds that Murphy should have introduced them by legislation rather than executive regulation. Now it was sooling a hostile committee on to him.

'I think that all these things will come to be understood by the people of Australia', said Murphy in the debate on Senator Gair's motion,

> and that retribution will fall upon the heads of members of the Opposition. The sooner there is a double dissolution and the sooner the Senate is brought to the people, the better . . . the Senate has become unworkable due to the refusal of the Opposition to pay even ordinary respect to the traditions of the Senate.

He then called off pairs in order to defeat the motion by 28 votes to 27, which was arguably a worse breach of tradition than anything done recently by the Opposition. The Opposition was incensed. After Withers had spoken his mind on the adjournment, the Attorney-General said: 'The Leader of the Opposition speaks of honour in this place. I refer to the succession of events over the last few weeks . . .'

> Senator RAE.—We will never trust you again.
> Senator MURPHY.—You shut up, you little cur.
> Senator O'BYRNE.—A cur and a skunk . . . What is worse is that Senator Greenwood, who has had a classical education, is being led by a little toad from Queensland—
> The PRESIDENT.—Order! Senator O'Byrne will moderate his language.
> Senator O'BYRNE.— I will alter the description to bull frog—90 per cent frog—and ten per cent bull.

The bull frog was of course Senator Gair. The Senate later reversed its vote on his motion and did establish a select committee with a non-Government majority. It met several times, but never submitted a report. Other matters came to seem more important than the arcane politics of Croatia and A.S.I.O. On 17 May the Senate negatived the Commonwealth Electoral Bill (No. 2). An earlier Electoral Bill, lowering the federal franchise age to eighteen, had passed all stages in March. But the second one, designed to equalise urban and rural electorates by providing that the number of voters in any electorate should not be any more than 10 per cent higher or lower than the average number throughout Australia, met determined opposition in the Senate, particularly from the Country Party. The Senate rejected the Bill by 27 votes to 31. As future events would show, this was the first step towards a double dissolution.

On 30 May Senator Withers moved successfully to have debate on the Seas and Submerged Lands Bill adjourned until 1 August, arguing that the States should have adequate time to consider the significance of legislation affecting offshore sovereignty. There was much discussion of whether such deferral amounted for constitutional purposes to a first rejection of the Bill, as prescribed in Section 57. The Government had legal advice that it did; others, while agreeing that it did, were less dogmatic about 'fails to pass', which Section 57 mentioned somewhat imprecisely. Such quibbling was unnecessary, however, for the Senate in its present mood would provide unequivocal grounds for a double dissolution soon enough.

By the time the Senate adjourned on 8 June for the winter recess, it had rejected three more Bills regarded by the Government as potential double dissolution triggers: the Conciliation and Arbitration Bill, repealing penal sanctions; the Senate (Representation of Territories) Bill, proposing two senators each for the A.C.T. and Northern Territory, in line with representation of those territories in the lower house; and the Representation Bill, designed to prevent territorial senators from being counted when calculating the number of M.H.R.s for maintenance of the two-to-one ratio between House and Senate. The Electoral, Territories and Representation Bills were reintroduced after the required lapse of three months, and were rejected by the Senate a second time.

In spite of the Senate's mood, parliament passed a record volume of legislation during the autumn sittings. This was made possible by last-minute use of the guillotine in the Senate on forty-three bills which the Government, with D.L.P. support, managed to have declared Urgent Bills. They were dealt with at an average rate of one every eighteen minutes. The Death Penalty Abolition Bill, abolishing that penalty in all laws under the jurisdiction of the Australian parliament, except within Papua New Guinea, was passed earlier in the year on a free vote. In another free vote the Medical Practice Clarification Bill, intended to legalise abortion on request in the A.C.T., was defeated in the lower house by 23 to 98.

On the last sitting day before the winter recess Whitlam, in a statement of achievements entitled *Apologia pro Vita Sua*, reminded the House that so far the Government had put before parliament 118 bills, of which 103 had been passed. This compared with an average of only fifty-three bills introduced in all the autumn sittings between 1950 and 1972. The Leader of the Opposition replied by making a pun on the word 'sua', and translating Cardinal Newman's Latin as 'an apology for the life of a Prime Minister'. 'From the title', said Snedden about Whitlam's meticulous listing of his government's achievements both in and outside parliament,

> the whole tone is set—as sarcasm, a swollen head and confusion. The basic assumption is that multiplying members of boards, task forces, Bills and treaty ratifications is a measure of actual achievement. It rests on the Fabian view that a pamphlet changes and achieves, and pamphlets do not do that. It has the ring of rusting carriage wheels, it is so old.

What really rang false was Snedden's riposte, for he was in no position to be making mock of the Government. For the first time in its existence, his party no longer enjoyed its accustomed close relationship with the Country Party. The trouble began after the election when the Victorian Liberal Party, against Snedden's wishes, revoked the Coalition's electoral pact, and it was exacerbated by disagreement as to whether Anthony or Lynch should occupy the Deputy Leadership of the Opposition. That position went to Lynch. Snedden's shadow ministry was exclusively Liberal, and for the time being there were no joint party meetings.

At the Premiers' Conference in June, Whitlam avoided the kind of platitudes with which his predecessors had sought to disguise domination by the Commonwealth Government—or rather 'Australian Government', as Labor ministers now called it. Bluntly he stated the principles to be applied in specific purpose programmes of financial assistance under Section 96 of the Constitution. 'From now on', he said,

> we will expect to be involved in the planning of the function in which we are financially involved. We believe that it would be irresponsible for the national government to content itself with simply providing funds without being involved in the process by which priorities are set, and by which expenditures are planned and by which standards are met.

Such directness reminded one commentator, Dr Colin Hughes, of the distinction drawn by Governor Huey Long of Louisiana between the different centralist approaches of United States presidents. According to Long, President Hoover was a hoot owl who banged into the roost, knocked the hen off her perch and seized her as she fell. Roosevelt, on the other hand, 'slips into the roost and scrootches up to the hen and talks softly to her. And the hen just falls in love with him, and the first thing you know there ain't no hen'. Whitlam, wrote Hughes, was a hoot owl coming after a succession of Liberal scrootch owls which had left the state chickens bereft of feathers, if not yet consumed.

Australia's closest approximation to Huey Long—the Premier of Queensland, Johannes Bjelke-Petersen—led a chorus of State protests. 'The Commonwealth', he said,

> must cease regarding all revenue as 'our' money, in which it will dictate how the money will be spent by attaching strings and conditions . . . The Commonwealth should remember that it is a child of the States and

attained its pre-eminent position by controlling the purse strings. We've seen too much in the last three months of the use of the bludgeon and the carrot by Federal Ministers.

By that time, however, the hoot owl had left the roost.

The first Labor Budget for twenty-four years, brought down by Crean on 21 August, contained few major surprises. It was concerned more with honouring campaign promises than with addressing the problem of inflation—a problem soon to be compounded without warning by an international energy crisis. Economically more significant than anything in the Budget was an earlier Government decision, taken in July against Treasury advice, reducing tariffs on all imports by 25 per cent. This was effectively another revaluation of the Australian dollar against the United States dollar, and it was not a good idea. It alienated workers whose employment depended on tariff protection, alarmed the business community, and bedevilled the Government's future relations with the Treasury.

Although there was speculation that the Budget appropriation bills might be blocked in the Senate, the Opposition made no attempt to do so. On 30 August, however, Senator Withers successfully moved an amendment to the formal Address-in-Reply, adoption of which had been postponed earlier in the year though pressure of legislative business. The amendment criticised the Government's economic, defence and foreign policies. Only twice before, in 1905 and 1914, had such a discordant note been incorporated in the Address's formal anthem of loyalty to the Sovereign. Did this portend the forcing of an election? Snedden said definitely in September that the Opposition would not use the Senate for that purpose, and in October the President of the Senate, Sir Magnus Cormack, expressed the view that his chamber would be committing suicide if ever it blocked supply. On the other hand, it later emerged that in October Senator Withers sent a memorandum to Snedden outlining a strategy by which a change of government might be engineered.

The Withers memorandum was about supply, without which no executive can carry on the business of government. Only the two houses of parliament can provide supply by passing an Act to appropriate revenue or moneys from the Consolidated Revenue Fund for a stated purpose. Parliament does this by means of appropriation and supply bills, the main appropriation bills usually being introduced in August to provide for expenditure outlined in the Budget for the current financial year, and supply bills being introduced during the autumn sittings in order to provide temporary funds until new appropriation bills are passed at the next Budget sittings. The Senate undoubtedly has power to reject such bills, as it has the power to reject any bills. It may not originate or amend proposed money bills, or amend any bill so as to increase a proposed charge or tax; but in all other respects its legislative powers are equal under the Constitution with those of the lower house. The lower house may defer or reject Supply. Therefore so may the Senate.

What Withers suggested in his memorandum to Snedden was not that the Senate should reject appropriation or supply bills, but that it should *defer* them. This would have the same financially embarrassing effect on the Government as rejection. It would bring pressure to bear on the Governor-

General to resolve the deadlock and, equally important, would keep the money bills under Opposition control. If the Prime Minister could not obtain supply, then surely he would have to resign, and the Governor-General would either send for someone who could obtain it, or send the lower house to an election.

Because the Senate could not also be sent to an early election (unless, of course, grounds existed for a double dissolution), a convention had grown up that it should not exercise its power to reject or defer supply; and indeed, it had never yet done so. Conventions may be broken, however, and in any case, the *raison d'être* for this one was soon to be compromised. By November 1973 three bills had completed the requirements of Section 57. The Government had sent these bills back for the second rejection in the upper house as a warning to Opposition senators that they too could all be made to face election if they dared to block supply. And that kind of warning was itself a licence to break convention. If the Senate was no longer a coward's castle, and senators could be made to share the fate which they had the power to force upon the lower house, then the blocking of supply might not be such a dishonourable action after all.

In the normal course of events half the Senate would be due for election by mid-1974, but this was not a very normal parliament. The sword of deferral was suspended over the House of Representatives, and the double dissolution mechanism was ticking away like a time bomb.

The situation was nerve-racking. Tempers frayed, and the standard of parliamentary behaviour deteriorated. In November the House of Representatives invited Australia's most distinguished author, Patrick White, who had recently received the Nobel Prize, to be seated on the floor of the House in recognition of his personal achievement. The last time such an invitation had been extended was to the aviator Captain Hinkler, in 1928. Mr White declined, explaining that his nature could not easily adapt itself to such a situation. 'It is gratifying and moving that so many people from such varied walks of life should have wanted to express their enthusiasm', he wrote to the Speaker. 'So may we, please, leave it at that?' Perhaps this was just as well, for the House at that time was no place for a gentleman.

The Speaker, Jim Cope, was a former treasurer of the New South Wales branch of the Australian Glassworkers' Union who had graduated from the rough political school of inner Sydney, and had come to be regarded as one of the House's best and most amusing interjectors. He had a good grasp of Standing Orders, but it was often more than he could do to control the House. 'I am president of the Redfern Lonely Hearts Club', he said after one upheaval in October, 'and I get more decorum there than I get here'. Epithets like 'gutless wonder' and 'boofhead' were hurled from both sides. In one exchange across the table, Whitlam's effortless superiority provoked an uncharacteristic lapse of taste on Snedden's part. Chagrined at an agreement reached between the Government and the D.L.P. to secure passage though the Senate of referendum bills for the control of wages and prices, Snedden shouted at the Prime Minister: 'Who's churching the old whore now?' Whitlam had asked the same question some days earlier in connection with a proposed Country Party–D.L.P. amalgamation, which never eventuated.

'The old whore' had then been the Country Party, but in Snedden's clumsier hands the question carried unfortunate sectarian overtones which did nothing to improve relations between his own party and the predominantly Roman Catholic D.L.P. At about this time, incidentally, Senator Gair was replaced as Leader of the parliamentary D.L.P. by Senator McManus.

In spite of Whitlam's clear superiority over his main opponent, he too was capable of reckless departure from the accepted standards of parliamentary debate. Early in November he introduced four more referendum Bills: the Constitution Alteration (Simultaneous Elections) Bill, providing for federal elections to be held simultaneously for the House of Representatives and one half of the Senate; the Constitution Alteration (Democratic Elections) Bill, to establish electorates holding as nearly as practicable the same number of people, which was also the intention of the Commonwealth Electoral Bill (No. 2), now twice rejected by the Senate; the Constitution Alteration (Local Government Bodies) Bill, enabling the Commonwealth to make funds available directly to local government bodies rather than through State Governments; and the Constitution Alteration (Mode of Altering the Constitution) Bill, intended in part to make the Labours of Hercules somewhat easier by requiring referendum bills to be approved in only three of the six States, rather than four as at present, in addition to being approved as usual by a majority of voters nationally.

The Opposition opposed all four bills, but particularly the first, which Snedden said was intended to reduce the power of the Senate. It would make the Senate an appendage of the House of Representatives, he argued, because one half of the Senate could then be taken automatically to an election at the will of a Prime Minister by his obtaining dissolution of the lower house, to which half the Senate would be electorally synchronised. The Government had all four measures declared as urgent bills so that debate on them could be limited. This use of the guillotine aroused the usual strong feeling, which reached a disorderly climax when the House resumed after an official dinner for the Prime Minister of New Zealand on the evening of 14 November. Some members had dined too well. Next morning the Prime Minister expressed regret that his hospitality had been abused. One former Liberal minister, Dr A. J. Forbes, immediately took umbrage:

> On a point of order: on behalf of everybody on this side of the House, I find the Prime Minister's remark extremely insulting, and demand a withdrawal.
> Mr SPEAKER.—Order! There is no point of order involved.
> Mr WHITLAM.—I invite honourable gentlemen to look at the honourable gentleman's eyes, even this morning.
> Mr WENTWORTH.—On a point of order—
> Mr SPEAKER.—Order! The House will come to order.
> Mr SNEDDEN.—You must be ashamed of yourself.
> Mr WHITLAM.—You ought to be ashamed of yourself, too. Look at him: Look at his bleary face.
> Mr SNEDDEN.—You are being gutless.
> Mr WHITLAM.—It is what he put in his guts that rooted him.
> Mr SNEDDEN.—On a point of order. I ask the Prime Minister to repeat

the exact words he just used. I hope that Hansard wrote them down.
Did Hansard get those words? . . .
Mr SPEAKER.—Order! There was a personal reflection, and I ask the
Prime Minister to withdraw.
Mr WHITLAM.—Well, if it was heard, I will withdraw it, but do people
want to hear what it was? It is of no use withdrawing something that
was not recorded. Was it recorded? I understand that it was recorded.
Well, honourable members will be able to see what it was. I withdraw
it; it was out of order.

During December the Constitution Alteration Bills for price and income
control were rejected at referendum; the Simultaneous Elections, Democratic Elections and Local Government Bodies referendum Bills were
negatived in the Senate; and the Mode of Altering the Constitution Bill was
amended by the Senate, and consequently laid aside by the House. The Senate also adjourned debate on the second reading of a Petroleum and Minerals Authority Bill, authorising Commonwealth entry into petroleum and
minerals search and production through the agency of a Petroleum and Minerals Authority. It negatived a Health Insurance Bill, involving a scheme of
universal health insurance financed by a taxation levy; passed, with amendments accepted by the lower house, a Seas and Submerged Lands Bill; and
also, with acceptable amendments, passed several education bills. The latter,
based upon recommendations of the Karmel Committee, proposed aid to
schools on a needs basis instead of the existing per capita basis, and established a Schools Commission to implement the Karmel Committee's
recommendations.

In spite of the Senate's rejection of thirteen bills, deferral of seven and
amendment of nineteen, Whitlam had many achievements to record in his
second *Apologia pro Vita Sua*, which he delivered to a restless House on 13
December, the last sitting day of the year. Although the Government had
had to contend with 'dinosaurs in one place and schoolboys in the other', he
said, it had nonetheless introduced 253 bills, of which 203 had been passed.
The nearest previous approach to this had been in 1968, when 169 bills were
introduced and 157 passed.

The House had sat for more than nine hundred hours, the greatest number
of sitting hours in one year for more than half a century; the Government had
allowed seventy debates on the adjournment, the greatest number on
record; Cabinet had made 1675 decisions since January; the number of Commonwealth departments had been increased from twenty-seven to thirty-
seven; the texts of thirty-nine treaties and agreements with other countries
had been presented to parliament; and such organisations as the Industries
Assistance Commission (replacing the Tariff Board), Prices Justification Tribunal and Pipeline Authority had been given permanent statutory form.
When Whitlam sought leave to have the full list of such achievements incorporated in Hansard, the Opposition refused. He then read it out, taking the
better part of two hours to do so, while Snedden, the only Opposition member present, busied himself signing Christmas cards.

The record was undeniably impressive. Yet Whitlam's critics spoke of
legislation by exhaustion and saturation, and in one public opinion poll 74

per cent of respondents agreed with the proposition that the Government was 'trying to do too many things at once'. One commentator remarked that it was 'only in fairy stories that sleeping princesses fall in love with those who awaken them; it may be, too, that they should be awakened gently with a kiss even if the sleep has lasted only a quarter of a century'.

Another analogy was to be found in Aesop's fable of the frogs. Might the generation that had tired of King Log now be having second thoughts about King Stork? The only federal by-election of the year—in September, for the seat of Parramatta, rendered vacant by the resignation of the former Liberal Attorney-General, Nigel Bowen—showed a 7 per cent swing away from Labor. But this was at least partly attributable to the Government's insistence during the campaign that a new airport for Sydney would be located in the electorate—a decision which the President of the A.C.T.U. and newly elected President of the A.L.P., Bob Hawke, termed 'political imbecility'. The coming half-Senate election would presumably provide a less ambiguous verdict, but defeat of the prices and incomes referendums also revived press speculation during the Christmas recess that Whitlam might seek an earlier double dissolution.

The constitutional status of the three bills that had been twice rejected by the Senate was thrown into some doubt by the prorogation of parliament on 14 February 1974. This action, taken so that the Queen could open a new session during her forthcoming visit to Australia, had the effect of causing all bills still before parliament to lapse. Some maintained that this destroyed the potential efficacy of the twice rejected bills for the granting of a double dissolution, but the High Court was later to rule unanimously that prorogation does not interrupt the sequence of events required by Section 57.

Her Majesty opened the new session on 28 February. Among other announcements in her speech, she confirmed that on the advice of her Australian and British ministers she had decided not to refer to the Privy Council petitions from the Queensland and Tasmanian governments concerning rights to the sea-bed as defined in the recently passed Seas and Submerged Lands Act. The High Court, she said, was the appropriate tribunal for such a dispute between the States and the Commonwealth. All States later challenged the validity of this Act, whereby sovereignty over the territorial sea-bed was vested in the Commonwealth; but in *New South Wales* v. *the Commonwealth* (1975) the High Court ruled against them. Submerged lands between the low-water mark and the edge of the continental shelf were the domain of Moloch.

In the new session the Government guillotined its four remaining referendum bills through the House again, and introduced a fifth one—the Constitution Alteration (Interchange of Powers) Bill, to allow reference of powers from the Commonwealth to the States. When these bills reached the Senate in March, three of the original four were again negatived, and the other was amended unacceptably and laid aside. The Interchange of Powers Bill was deferred by the Senate until consideration could be given to its proposals by the States and by an Australian Constitutional Convention, the latter of which had begun deliberations during the previous year but was not destined to achieve much. Among thirty-four other bills which the House passed during this session (only nineteen of which the Senate also passed) was another Petroleum and Minerals Authority Bill. The first such bill had been adjourned by the Senate in December, reinstated on the Senate's notice paper at the request of the House in March, and negatived on 2 April. The second bill reached the Senate on 8 April, and two days later was deferred for six months.

On 21 March the Prime Minister told the House that a normal half-Senate election would be held in May, and that the Governor-General had agreed that the four Constitution Alteration Bills which the Senate had either defeated or amended unacceptably could be submitted to referendum on the same day. The latter was in accordance with Section 128 of the Constitution, which provides that a Constitution Alteration Bill passed by one house but not the other may be submitted to the electors if it has been again passed and rejected in the same manner after an interval of three months. As it turned out, all four would be defeated.

By the time Whitlam announced the half-Senate election, he had some reason to hope that it might result in Government control of the upper house. The reason lay in what became known as the Gair Affair, a bizarre political manoeuvre sponsored principally by Senator Lionel Murphy. Sponsorship by the invader of A.S.I.O. should have been warning enough for the Prime Minister, but the prospect of Senate control was so alluring that caution, scruple and common sense all went overboard.

Early in March 73-year-old Senator Vince Gair complained to the Government Whip in the Senate, Justin O'Byrne, that the D.L.P. had treated him shabbily; he was thinking of getting out, he said, and would not be averse to a diplomatic post if the Government would let bygones be bygones and offer him one. Senator O'Byrne reported this conversation to Murphy, who immediately discerned its relevance to the coming half-Senate election, and suggested a plan to Whitlam. At present Labor could hope to win only two of the five vacancies in Queensland. But if there were six vacancies in that State, as there would be if Gair resigned and caused a casual vacancy before the election, the party would almost certainly win three of them. If Labor also polled as expected in the other States, it would then have thirty-one senators in the new chamber, a bare majority.

Senator Gair, once an implacable enemy of the A.L.P., was promptly offered the post of Ambassador Extraordinary and Plenipotentiary to Ireland, and he accepted it. The Executive Council approved his appointment on 14 March, and the Irish Government accepted him as ambassador-designate on 20 March, the day before the half-Senate election date was announced. All this was a closely kept secret until a Melbourne newspaper broke the story on the morning of 2 April. At Question Time that morning Whitlam confirmed the appointment, and Snedden labelled it 'the most shameful act ever perpetrated by an Australian government'. This was hardly true, for Hughes had tried to manipulate the Senate numbers even more blatantly in 1917; and in any case, as soon became apparent, the Gair manoeuvre was unlikely to achieve its intended effect. Shrewder minds than Snedden's quickly found a flaw in Murphy's plan: Gair had not yet formally resigned from the Senate.

Senator Withers, Senator Greenwood and the Leader of the National Country Party (as the Country Party had become known in March), Doug Anthony, telephoned the Country Party Premier of Queensland, Bjelke-Petersen, and persuaded him to have writs for the half-Senate election issued that very evening. While a Country Party senator plied the Ambassador-designate with beer and prawns to ensure that he did not resign too soon, the writs were issued in Brisbane. As Senator Withers put it, the Premier had trumped the ace. Senator Gair's resignation, when it came, would now cause a vacancy that could not be filled at the election in May. It would have to be filled by a vote of the Queensland parliament, which would be certain to return a non-Labor senator. Next day, in the Senate, Withers taunted Murphy with the fact that the Executive Council had approved Gair's appointment almost a year to the day after Murphy's ill-fated A.S.I.O. raid. In the House, Anthony asked Whitlam whether the Premier of Queensland, who was a qualified pilot, had ever taken him for a ride.

On that day, 3 April, the parliamentary D.L.P. expelled its former leader—but not before he had delivered one of the most sincere valedictions in Australia's parliamentary history. 'I've carried you bastards for years', he told his four erstwhile colleagues, 'and now you can go to buggery!' Later in the day Sir Magnus Cormack read to the Senate a letter from Gair asserting that because an ambassadorship was an office of profit under the Crown the effect of his appointment had been to render vacant his place as a senator by virtue of Section 45 of the Constitution. That section provides for the disqualification of any senator who 'agrees to take any fee or honorarium for services rendered to the Commonwealth'. Next day Senator Murphy moved that the High Court be asked to determine whether, and if so, when, Senator Gair's seat had become vacant; but instead the Senate decided the matter for itself. An Opposition amendment to Murphy's motion, resolving that Gair had not resigned or vacated his place before 3 April, was carried by 30 votes to 26.

All this became irrelevant when, on 4 April, Snedden announced that the Opposition would endeavour to force an election for the lower house by opposing, and if necessary defeating in the Senate, an Appropriation Bill which was then before the House of Representatives. For some weeks past Snedden had been under pressure to do this from the National Country Party, which was worried about the effect of Labor's intended electoral reforms on its own disproportionate representation; and now the Gair Affair ('This shameful episode, this deceitful episode') had provided a convenient issue. 'If [an Appropriation Bill] is opposed in the Senate it will be defeated', said Snedden. 'Then we would make appropriate arrangements for the money to be made available after the Prime Minister has announced a dissolution of this House and the calling of an election so that the people can decide.'

As soon as Snedden resumed his seat, Whitlam rose to trump that particular ace with the threat of a double dissolution. 'If the Senate rejects any money Bill', he said,

—the first time that the Senate would have rejected a money Bill in the history of our nation—I shall certainly wait upon the Governor-General and I shall advise the Governor-General not merely to dissolve the House of Representatives but to dissolve the Senate as well . . . At this stage, as honourable members know, there are all the ingredients for a double dissolution.

The Government now increased the number of ingredients by reintroducing and guillotining the Health Insurance Bill, the Health Insurance Commission Bill and the Petroleum and Minerals Authority Bill. It did this not so much for the sake of a double dissolution, but rather to increase the number of bills that could be voted upon at a joint sitting of both houses which would be held in accordance with Section 57 in the event of continued disagreement between the houses after the election. While tension continued to mount, the Deputy Leader of the Opposition, Phillip Lynch, asked the Prime Minister an embarrassing question about Supply. Was he aware, asked Lynch on 8 April, of a statement made by Senator Murphy in 1970 declaring that it was the Labor Party's tradition to oppose in the Senate any 'money bill or other financial measure whenever necessary to carry out our principles and policies', and furthermore that Murphy had listed no fewer than 168 financial measures which the Labor Opposition had opposed between 1950 and 1970. 'I do remember that Senator Murphy tabled such a list in the Senate', replied Whitlam. 'I did not approve of his tabling it . . . I have not always agreed with Senator Murphy in the past and I did not at that time.' He must have counted himself lucky that Lynch had overlooked the fact that Whitlam himself had spoken in much the same vein that year.

On the afternoon of 10 April the first of three Appropriation Bills came before the Senate. To a Government motion at about 4.15 p.m. that debate on the Bill should be resumed at a later hour, Senator Withers moved an amendment adding the words 'but not before the Government agrees to submit itself to the judgment of the people at the same time as the forthcoming [half] Senate election', and criticising the Government on several counts including the Gair Affair. After a brief debate Senator Murphy moved that the Government's motion be put without amendment, declaring that if it was not put and passed the Government would treat that as a denial of Supply. At 5.25 p.m. Murphy's motion that the question be now put was defeated by 26 votes to 31, and at 8.30 p.m. the Prime Minister told the House that the Governor-General had granted him a double dissolution. The grounds consisted of six bills which had twice been rejected by or had failed to pass the Senate.

The result of the election held on 18 May was close enough for Snedden to make the rather fatuous claim: 'We were not beaten. We didn't win enough seats to form a government, but I do not believe that what has occurred was in any sense a defeat'. Yet the fact was that Whitlam had become the first Labor prime minister ever to win two successive elections. His Government had scraped back into office with its lower house majority reduced from nine to five and its Senate position, although slightly improved, still short of control. The Labor Party, and the combined Liberal and Country Parties (which now resumed coalition), would each have twenty-nine Senate votes. As the Independent Senator Townley was expected to support the Opposition, the best that Labor could hope for in the new Senate was a tie whenever Senator Steele Hall (Liberal Movement, S) chose to support it. Vince Gair was on his leisurely way to Dublin, and the D.L.P. had reached the destination which he had wished upon it. All D.L.P. senators were defeated, and the party was wound up four years later.

Three more women joined Margaret Guilfoyle in the Senate. They were Senators Ruth Coleman (Lab, W), Kathryn Martin (Lib, Q) and Jean Melzer (Lab, V). In the lower house Mrs Joan Child (Henty, V), a former union liaison officer, became Labor's first woman M.H.R. Another Labor member, John Dawkins, was elected from a new Western Australian electorate named after the first woman senator, Dorothy Tangney. This was the scant measure of women's parliamentary participation in the mid-1970s. Only five of the 187 federal seats were held by women, and only two of the 127 electorates were even distinguished by female names. The other seat was Chisholm (V), named after the colonial philanthropist, Caroline Chisholm.

At the first Caucus meeting after the election the Victorian left-winger, Jim Cairns, challenged Barnard for the Deputy Leadership, and defeated him by 54 votes to 42. As a response by the right wing, Ken Wriedt challenged Murphy for the party's leadership in the Senate, but lost by 41 votes to 55. Senator J. M. Wheeldon (W) was elected to the ministry in place of Al Grassby, who had lost his seat at the election. Senator Justin O'Byrne was also chosen to challenge Sir Magnus Cormack as President. Thanks to Steele Hall and one defector, O'Byrne later received thirty-one of the sixty senators' votes and became the first Labor President for twenty-three years.

The twenty-ninth parliament was opened by Sir Paul Hasluck on 9 July 1974, but two days later his successor, Sir John Kerr, was sworn in as Australia's eighteenth Governor-General. Sir John, until recently Chief Justice of New South Wales, was the fifth Australian to be appointed Governor-General, and the first lawyer in that office since Sir Isaac Isaacs. He was also the first Australian-born Governor-General not to have served in parliament. Aged fifty-nine, silver-haired and rubicund of face, Sir John cut a suitably viceregal figure, though his father had been a Balmain boilermaker. Like Evatt, Spender and Barwick, Kerr was a product of Fort Street High School and Sydney University. Although he was built like a basso profundo, his voice was surprisingly thin and high; and by the same token, although he had belonged to the A.L.P. until the mid-1950s, his political tone was not so predictable as Whitlam seemed to imply when he sometimes referred to Kerr possessively as 'My Viceroy'. In his days at the bar, Kerr, Q.C., had represented right-wing unions in the anti-Communist struggles of the early post-war period. He became a judge of the Commonwealth Industrial Court in 1966, and Chief Justice of the Supreme Court in 1972.

The first business of the Government was now to reintroduce the six bills which had occasioned the double dissolution so that, after their rejection by the Senate, the Governor-General could convene a joint sitting to vote upon them. At this sitting, the like of which had never been held before, the Government could expect to receive ninety-five of the 187 votes—just one more than the absolute majority required by the Constitution in such circumstances. The six bills—three dealing with electoral matters, two with health insurance, and the Petroleum and Minerals Authority Bill—were duly guillotined though the lower house, and negatived by the Senate between 16 and 24 July. Six days later the Governor-General convened a joint sitting to commence on the morning of 6 August, in the House of Representatives.

Certain preliminaries had to be gone through first. Two legal challenges were launched in the High Court—one, by Senators Cormack and James Webster (C, V), denying that more than one bill could be presented to a joint sitting, and seeking an injunction to prevent the sitting being held; the other, by the Queensland Government, questioning whether the Petroleum and Minerals Authority Bill had complied with all constitutional provisions for a bill to be presented to a joint sitting. On 5 August the Court rejected the senators' application, and ruled that the Queensland Government lacked standing to test the eligibility of the Petroleum and Minerals Authority Bill at that stage. The way was left open, however, for a challenge after the Bill had been passed.

As Standing Orders provided little guidance on how a joint sitting should be conducted (Fred Daly had likened the situation to 'a Surry Hills preselection: there are no rules'), special rules were drawn up after discussion between leaders and officers of the two houses, and were adopted by both houses. Furthermore, parts of the joint sitting were to be televised in colour. This would be the first time that any proceedings of the Australian parliament had been shown live on television, and the Parliamentary Proceedings Broadcasting Act had to be amended accordingly.

The joint sitting lasted for eighteen and a half hours, on 6 and 7 August, and filled 175 pages of Hansard. All members attended on both days, and a total of sixty-six members took part in the debates. The Governor-General's proclamation convening the sitting was read at the outset by the Clerk of the Senate. Clerk Odgers also conducted proceedings for the appointment of a chairman. There was only one nomination, Speaker Cope, and he presided from his chair as usual. All bills were affirmed by votes ranging between 95 and 97. Members comported themselves with great decorum, and the television debut was generally accounted a success.

After this interlude of enforced co-operation, the two houses resumed their state of intermittent mutual hostility. As quickly as possible the Government sent to the Senate several bills which, if rejected, would begin the process of obtaining grounds for another double dissolution in case the Senate should try to force an early dissolution of the lower house alone by withholding or rejecting supply. The Senate obliged by rejecting no fewer than fifteen bills in the next few weeks. Three of these, supplementary bills pertaining to the health insurance scheme, were rejected a second time early in December. That provided the Government with grounds for another double dissolution at any time it chose.

The Senate blocked a Remuneration and Allowances Bill, which proposed increasing the basic parliamentary salary from $14 500 to $20 000 in accordance with recommendations by a Remuneration Tribunal which had been established in the previous year. It also negatived two more Conciliation and Arbitration Bills, including the one facilitating union amalgamations. On the other hand, by perseverance and adroit management, Senator Murphy managed to get some of his own most cherished bills through the red chamber. These included the Trade Practices Bill, a compromise between Murphy and Greenwood which was nevertheless the most important legislation affecting the business community and consumers yet passed by parliament; and the Family Law Bill, abolishing the fault concept in divorce proceedings and replacing it with a single ground for the dissolution of marriage—having separated and lived apart for twelve months or more. How Sir Garfield Barwick must have envied Murphy those particular legislative trophies! The Family Law Bill passed the Senate on a free vote in November; the House of Representatives deferred it until the autumn session, but passed it then.

Another of Murphy's laws—the Racial Discrimination Bill, enabling Australia to ratify the International Convention on the Elimination of All Forms of Racial Discrimination—had a more tortuous but ultimately successful passage. It was introduced in the Senate in 1973, but lapsed at prorogation in February 1974; was reintroduced in the Senate, discharged from the Senate notice paper, introduced in the lower house early in 1975, and eventually passed by both houses, though not without some amendment.

The 1974–75 Budget was brought down later than usual, on 17 September. If Treasury's advice had been heeded, such a Budget would not have been brought down at all. Frank Crean's budgetary measures were aimed at easing unemployment rather than lowering the inflationary pressures which had been produced by the oil shock which followed the Israeli–Arab conflict of October 1973. The price of oil quadrupled by the end of that year, and did not decrease. The resulting inflationary pressures were an economic incubus which Australia shared with the rest of the oil-buying world. In vain the Treasury argued that the Budget would escalate inflation, making it even harder to achieve full employment; would worsen a prospectively difficult balance of payments problem; and would push the economy further into recession. Once again there was speculation about the Senate's attitude on Supply, but this time the Opposition made no obstruction.

Crean's days in charge of the Budget were numbered. Although shrewd and conscientious, he was regarded by some of his most influential colleagues as a weak Treasurer. In the Cabinet reshuffle following the May election, Whitlam had offered the Treasury to his new deputy, the eloquent and emotional left-wing economist, Dr Jim Cairns. Cairns declined; but few of his peers, and certainly not Crean, doubted that he aspired to the post. On 21 November Whitlam called Crean and Cairns to his office and said, 'Well, we have got to decide'.

'I am afraid I just bowed to the inevitable', Crean later recalled.

> I said, 'Well Gough, you and Jimmy both want it to happen', and Jimmy didn't say 'No', so when he had gone I said: 'Well Gough, you will be sorry about this . . . You will be sorry that you ever made Jimmy Treasurer; and secondly, for goodness sake don't have anything to do with this loan business'.

And so we come to 'The Loans Affair', a series of events which did more than anything else to determine the eventual fate of the Whitlam Government. On the night of Friday 13 December, eight days after the House had risen for the summer recess, the Prime Minister and two of his most senior ministers held what purported to be a meeting of the Executive Council. The Executive Council consists of the Governor-General and his ministers. Its function is to give formal approval, and thus legal form, to executive decisions made by those same ministers in Cabinet. 'Exco' meetings are usually attended by the Governor-General and only two or three ministers. A quorum is three.

On this occasion, when the Prime Minister requested a meeting at about 7 p.m., he found that the Governor-General was in Sydney, attending a performance of the ballet 'Romeo and Juliet'. The matter was urgent, for Whitlam was due to begin an extended journey overseas the following day, and so he convened a meeting at The Lodge with the Attorney-General, and the Minister for Minerals and Energy, Rex Connor, to prepare a minute for the Governor-General's signature. The meeting was also attended by the departmental heads of Treasury and Minerals and Energy, Sir Frederick Wheeler and Sir Lenox Hewitt, but not by the new Treasurer, although at the time Dr Cairns was no further away than another room of The Lodge, where a meeting of the A.L.P. national executive was in progress. His absence was surprising, for one of the Treasurer's main functions is to raise loans for the Commonwealth, and the Executive Council minute of 13 December authorised the borrowing of $4000 million in non-equity capital from abroad. This was the largest loan ever contemplated in Australian history, and authority to raise it was being vested in the Minister for Minerals and Energy.

Reginald Francis Xavier Connor was a huge man remarkable for his intimidating physical presence and his passionate nationalism. He took pride in having been born on Australia Day—in the coal and steel centre of Wollongong, where his great-great-grandfather had been an Irish cobbler— and in having been named after Australia's patron saint. At the age of sixty-eight he was a tribal elder of the Labor Party, one of the few remaining bowyang boys, not ashamed to wear braces, and able to talk knowledgeably about Jack Lang. Yet he was anything but a has-been. Rex Connor knew more about petroleum, uranium and coal than any of his colleagues. He dazzled the Cabinet with science, statistics and brutal argument. His nickname was 'The Strangler'.

It was an obsession with Connor, and one which he propagated in Caucus and Cabinet, that Australia's mineral resources should be recovered, processed and distributed without recourse to foreign equity ownership. This was what the Pipeline Authority, the Petroleum and Minerals Authority and the $4000 million dollars of non-equity capital were all about. Australia's capital market could not possibly provide the enormous sums required; but there did seem a good chance that overseas lenders, particularly the new rich of the Arab oil revolution, would fill the bill.

Under the Financial Agreement the Commonwealth is obliged to consult the States on all overseas borrowing with the exception of funds sought for 'defence purposes' or 'temporary purposes'. With two Labor State Governments represented on the Loan Council and the Commonwealth's two votes and a casting vote, the Government could have obtained a 5–4 vote of approval. But it would be much simpler to avoid that formality, and so the Executive Council minute described Connor's purposes as 'temporary'. This was a rather specious way of describing national gas pipelines, coal loading facilities and the electrification of railways. But the Attorney-General assured the meeting that 'temporary purposes' could be substantiated, or at least argued in court if necessary, by reference to Australia's temporary economic situation. In addition to the purpose of providing 'protection for Australia's supplies of minerals and energy, the Exco minute cited such purposes as '[strengthening] Australia's external financial position' and '[dealing] with current and immediately foreseeable unemployment'.

The minute was sent next morning to Admiralty House in Sydney, with advice from the Prime Minister that the Governor-General could validate the previous night's meeting by approving the holding of it. His Excellency doubted this, and his doubt was later shared by others. Professor Geoffrey Sawer, for example, wrote that only the Governor-General or the Vice-President of the Executive Council could validly call a Council meeting, and he doubted whether the Governor-General could validate one retrospectively. (The Vice-President at the time was the Minister for Tourism and Recreation, Frank Stewart. He was in Canberra on 13 December, but took no part in the Exco meeting.) In spite of his doubt, which in any case he rightly regarded as a justiciable matter that should be left to the courts, the Governor-General approved the meeting and signed the minute.

Little suspecting the troubles that had thus been set in train, the Prime Minister and his entourage departed by Qantas jet on Saturday afternoon for a five-week tour of the European Economic Community. Two years had now passed since the Whitlam Government swept into office, and, as if to commemorate that political cyclone, something ominous began building up over Australia's northern approaches. This was a tropical depression like the one which Clement Wragge had named Amok in 1901. It was first detected on 20 December over the Arafura Sea between Timor and West Irian. Next day the satellite photographs showed a cyclone moving slowly in a south-westerly direction, towards Darwin. The Bureau of Meteorology's Tropical Cyclone Warning Centre at Darwin issued an alert, and named the cyclone Tracy.

The eye of the cyclone, measuring twelve kilometres across, was tracked by radar as it passed over Melville and Bathurst Islands, still moving south west. The wind reached Darwin soon after midnight on Christmas Day, attaining a maximum velocity of 217 kilometres per hour at 3 a.m., and did not abate until 6.30 a.m. Cyclone Tracy was the most devastating natural disaster ever to occur in Australia. Ninety per cent of Darwin's homes were destroyed, sixty-six lives were lost, and twenty-five thousand people had to be evacuated by air almost immediately. The Director-General of the Natural Disasters Organisation, Major-General Alan Stretton, was placed in supreme control of the stricken city. The acting Prime Minister, Dr Cairns, flew there on Boxing Day. No fewer than six Commonwealth ministers showed the flag in Darwin and on 27 December, amid the rubble, they held a Cabinet meeting to authorise the offer of return fares as an added inducement to the homeless to accept evacuation at Government cost. The Prime Minister himself flew back from London on the eve of a sightseeing visit to the Mediterranean. He inspected the areas of worst damage, then headed for the older ruins of Sicily and Crete.

Trixie

There was more of the same still to come. Within a few weeks another disturbance developed over the Indian Ocean, sending Cyclone Trixie, potentially even more destructive than Tracy, swirling towards the Western Australian coast. The eye was four times wider than Tracy's, and its maximum velocity (246 kilometres per hour) was the highest ever recorded in Australia. On 18 February 1975 Trixie passed dangerously close to the town of Onslow, unroofing a few houses, then veered out to sea without further damage. Overshadowed though it was by the Darwin disaster, Cyclone Trixie provided a suitably strident overture for the autumn sitting of parliament which began at roughly the same time on the other side of the continent. Indeed the year 1975 was to produce one political gust after another, banging at the doors and windows of a government increasingly under attack.

The first blow was a reduction of the Government's Senate strength from twenty-nine to twenty-eight. This was brought about by Senator Murphy, who resigned on 10 February to accept appointment to a vacancy on the High Court created by the death of Mr Justice Sir Douglas Menzies. Murphy's appointment was first suggested to the Prime Minister early in December by the Attorney-General's friend, Dr Cairns. The Prime Minister had no reason to show such preferment, except to rid himself of a source of trouble and of course to install a politically sympathetic mind on the bench which in all likelihood would soon have to pass judgment on some of the Government's legislation. He and Murphy had been antagonists since the 1960s. Whitlam acknowledged Murphy's success in getting bills through the Senate, but had been sorely embarrassed by such matters as the A.S.I.O. raid and the Gair appointment.

The final decision on Murphy's future was delayed for some weeks, probably because of his involvement during December in what the press dubbed 'Cyclone Junie'. Ms Junie Morosi was a Eurasian of considerable beauty and mental toughness. She had worked on Murphy's personal staff, but had now been appointed office co-ordinator (in effect, private secretary) to the new Treasurer, a position formerly filled by a senior officer of the Treasury. The appointment was unconventional, for as the Treasurer himself admitted, 'one of the things she isn't interested in is economics'. Opposition senators became increasingly inquisitive about Ms Morosi at Question Time, and on 11 December, the last sitting day of the Senate and the day on which Cairns became Treasurer, Senator Greenwood took advantage of the adjournment debate to read into Hansard no fewer than thirty-three questions about her, addressed to the Attorney-General. They were never answered. By the time parliament resumed on 11 February Lionel Murphy had been translated to the High Court, presumably beyond the reach of controversy.

The full effect of Murphy's resignation started to become apparent when the Liberal Premier of New South Wales, Tom Lewis, intimated that the replacement to be chosen by State parliament might be a 'political neuter'. And that was exactly what happened. In spite of a unanimous vote by the Senate urging New South Wales to observe the convention that a casual Senate vacancy should be filled by someone from the same party as the former incumbent, the seat went to the 72-year-old Mayor of Albury, Cleaver Bunton, a man well known for his lack of party attachment. Senator Bunton was not averse to supporting the Government on some issues, but his appointment did more harm to the Government than merely reducing the number of votes upon which it could rely in all circumstances. Bunton's appointment established a precedent for the filling of a casual vacancy by someone not simply neutral but hostile to the former incumbent's party.

Then Cyclone Junie blew up again. On the morning of 20 February W. C. Wentworth raised as a matter of public importance the propriety of Ms Morosi's appointment to the Treasurer's staff. He drew upon a statement which had been made by some of her former employees and business associates, accusing her and her husband of having fraudulently misappropriated public money. The Treasurer, who had recently spoken in a press interview about the 'kind of love' he felt for Ms Morosi, vouched for her in this debate as a person of 'integrity, honour and competence'. Before the Opposition could take the matter further, the Leader of the House called on the business of the day.

The Government suffered further damage when, at the height of one of the shouting matches that had become commonplace in the House, the Prime Minister virtually forced the Speaker to resign. Jim Cope commanded a good deal of affection, but not much obedience. His voice did not carry well, and for the last two years he had been subjected by the Opposition to a campaign of regular disruption. One day he had to name no fewer than three members: Gorton, Forbes and Peter Nixon (C, Gippsland, V). Another time he was reduced to telling the House: 'I have had you blokes!'

On the morning of 27 February Speaker Cope was again having trouble with Dr Forbes, who accused Clyde Cameron of telling 'a monstrous lie' and then tried to evade making an unconditional withdrawal.

Dr FORBES.—I withdraw it and substitute 'an untruth'.
Mr CAMERON.—Mr Speaker, I—.
Mr SPEAKER.—Order!
Mr CAMERON.—Look, I don't give a damn what you say, I—.
OPPOSITION MEMBERS.—Name him! Name him!
Mr SPEAKER.—Order! I ask the Minister for Labour and Immigration to apologise to the Chair. I ask the Minister for Labour and Immigration to apologise to the Chair. I ask the Minister for Labour and Immigration to apologise to the Chair. Order! Is the Minister going to apologise?
Mr WHITLAM.—No.
Mr SPEAKER.—I name the Minister for Labour and Immigration.
Mr SINCLAIR.—I move: That the honourable gentleman be suspended from the services of this House.

As the House divided, Whitlam paused at the Chair and said three words to Cope: 'You should resign'. Recalling that moment years later, Cope said:

I had the running out of the sand in the glass for two minutes, and I knew I'd have five or six minutes approximately for the taking of the division, which gave me ample time to think it over. What should I do? It did pass my mind that I could wait for this division, knowing I'd lose it, and then name the Prime Minister for intimidating the Chair. I thought if I do that it might precipitate a crisis in the party and . . . we were in enough trouble at that particular time as it was without exacerbating the position any further . . . So I thought rather than injure the party I'd take it on the chin and just resign my place as Speaker of the House.

This was not the first time a Government had challenged a Speaker's authority. In 1953, when the House dissented from a ruling by Speaker Cameron that a statement by Menzies was unparliamentary, Cameron carried on as if nothing had happened. Cope could have done the same without harm to the Labor Party, but he was no Archie Cameron. After announcing that the motion for suspension had been resolved in the negative by 55 votes to 59, he told the House that he would submit his resignation to the Governor-General and asked the Deputy Speaker, Gordon Scholes (Lab, Corio, V), to take the Chair. Snedden moved suspension of Standing Orders so that he could move to censure the Prime Minister for 'his disgraceful conduct in abusing the Speaker and attempting, by intimidation, to have the Speaker favour the Government and Ministers'. When that failed he moved, also unsuccessfully, that the Committee of Privileges should be asked to decide 'the manner in which the [Prime Minister] should be dealt with for his intimidation of the Speaker'. Debate on each of these motions was gagged by the Government.

After dinner adjournment the Clerk read a message from Yarralumla inviting the House to choose a new Speaker. It thereupon elected Scholes, a former locomotive engine driver and amateur heavyweight boxing champion of Victoria. Scholes already had five years' experience as Deputy Chairman of Committees and Deputy Speaker, and was clearly able to control the House.

Snedden came out of the Cope affair with less advantage than might have been expected, given the Government's vulnerability. The fact was that in most confrontations with the Government he came off second best. Whitlam had his measure, and pounded him unmercifully. In this unequal contest Snedden's worst performance was his disastrous attempt, during an exchange with Whitlam about the filling of casual Senate vacancies, to ridicule the Prime Minister's fluffily emphatic delivery:

> Mr WHITLAM.—The first casual vacancy to arise after proportional representation was introduced in the Senate arose in December 1951. It occurred in Western Australia. A Labor senator died. The Liberal Premier—.
>
> Mr SNEDDEN.—Come on. Woof, woof!
>
> Mr SPEAKER.—Order! Interjections will cease or I will take the appropriate action. That applies to every member of the House.
>
> Mr WHITLAM.—The right honourable gentleman seems to be more than usually hysterical. I have never known even him to giggle so much. He is going ga-ga.

On 4 March Snedden managed to get his censure motion before the House, but again his performance was not impressive. Whitlam moved an amendment turning the motion into censure of the Opposition for its disruptive and unruly parliamentary conduct, and the motion as amended was passed by 64 votes to 59. During this debate the Leader of the House made a prediction. 'Honourable members opposite have put the Leader of the Opposition on show today', said Daly,

and all the time I could see by the smirk on the face of the honourable member for Wannon [Malcolm Fraser] that he is saying to himself 'Would not I be a lot better? I look better, I stand taller, I talk more intelligently. You have seen what he can do. Give me a go.' In a week or so there may well be a motion brought forward in the party room to remove the Leader of the Opposition.

And so there was. Snedden had already survived one such attempt four months earlier. On that occasion the motion for a spill had been defeated, and Fraser had neither confirmed nor denied that he was to have been the alternative put forward by the dissidents, chief of whom was Tony Staley (Chisholm, V). This time the plotters were more resolute, and came mainly from the Senate. They included Senators Cormack, Withers and Greenwood, Senator Robert Cotton (N), Senator Peter Durack (W) and R. V. Garland, (Curtin, W). The Deputy Leader, Phillip Lynch, continued to support Snedden but took the precaution of also attending a crucial gathering in Senator Cormack's flat at Toorak. Peacock and Chipp were unreservedly on Snedden's side. At a party meeting on 21 March Fraser defeated Snedden by 37 votes to 27, and Lynch retained the Deputy Leadership.

Fraser was fourteen years younger than Whitlam, and could look him squarely in the face from a height of almost six feet five inches. Try though he did to soften his austere image, aptly likened to one of the great stone images on Easter Island, he still deserved a nickname that had been bestowed upon him by Labor members, 'The Prefect'. Fraser said that he wanted to 'catch Mr Whitlam with his pants down', but spoke respectfully about responsible government. 'I generally believe', he said at his first press conference, 'if a government is elected to power in the lower house and has the numbers and can maintain the numbers in the lower house, it is entitled to expect that it will govern for the three-year term unless quite extraordinary events intervene'.

Fraser rallied the parliamentary Liberal Party around him, except for the recalcitrant Gorton, who resigned from the party and sat as an Independent until the next election, when he intended to stand for one of the two A.C.T. seats in the Senate. In June an adventitious but nonetheless plausible seal was set upon Fraser's leadership at a by-election for the Tasmanian seat of Bass. The last thing the Government needed was an electoral verdict from a textile-manufacturing region where many Labor voters had lost employment as a result of the 1973 tariff cut. The sitting member, Barnard, had pleaded medical reasons for leaving parliament, and the Ambassadorship to Sweden was made available for him. The President of the A.L.P., Hawke, termed this by-election 'an act of political lunacy', and so it was. The swing against Labor was 17 per cent.

Two other windfalls for Fraser were the Deputy Prime Minister's removal from the Treasurership (which made Cairns the only Treasurer never to present a Budget), and soon afterwards his removal from the Ministry altogether. Crean had been proved right: the Prime Minister was indeed sorry that he had appointed Jimmy Cairns as Treasurer. There were several reasons for this, including Cairns's increasing isolation from his ministerial colleagues; the Morosi controversy; a certain lack of discretion in business dealings shown by his private secretary, who was also his stepson; and a loans affair of his own making, which understandably became confused in the public mind with the wider petro-dollar loans affair that had been dogging the Government ever since parliament resumed.

The Opposition's shadow Treasurer, Lynch, began asking parliamentary questions about the petro-dollar loans affair in February. On 23 April he extracted the information that Connor had been given authority to borrow up to $4000 million, but that the limit had been reduced in January to $2000 million so as not to interfere with efforts being made by the Treasury to finance a loan in Germany.

Connor's negotiations were indeed likely to give orthodox lenders the wrong impression. Some of the people he was dealing with might have stepped off the Orient Express, or out of the pages of Ian Fleming's *Goldfinger*. His first contact had been Gerasimos Karidis, an Adelaide builder who dabbled in the commodities market and had been recommended to him by Cameron and Cairns. From Karidis the path led to such denizens of the international money market as Theo Cronendonk, Yu Shat Fuk, Dr Ako, Sheik Sikkar Gassan and, most notably, a Pakistani money broker based in London, Tirath Hassaram Khemlani, who seemed to spend much of his time on board intercontinental jets in quest of 'funny money'. During May, while the Treasury was trying to raise $100 million in New York, Sir Frederick Wheeler persuaded Cairns that Connor's authority ought to be revoked in case his emissaries should alarm Wall Street. Cairns went into the House and mentioned this to Whitlam at the Table.

'I think everyone would be happier if the Khemlani affair was ended soon', said the Treasurer. 'All right', replied the Prime Minister, 'but you'll have to be the bastard and tell him'.

Cairns moved back to the front bench and put the proposition to 'The Strangler', who was surprisingly ready to oblige.

'Rex says OK', Cairns reported back to the Prime Minister, 'we can bring the Khemlani discussions to an end'.

'Jesus Christ', said Whitlam, 'Did he?'

Connor's authority was revoked on 20 May. Nine days later the Prime Minister wrote to all ministers involved in loan raising, instructing them not to initiate further borrowings without first referring the proposals to him. But the damage had already been done. As one commentator said, 'a whole host of middlemen across the world had become involved in the Australian government's loan-raising activities'. One of these was a Melbourne financier named George Harris. On 4 June—the day before a Cabinet reshuffle, occasioned by Barnard's departure, in which Cairns already knew that he would be demoted to the portfolio of Environment and Conservation—Lynch asked the latest in a series of questions without notice directed to the Treasurer, concerning overseas loans. Had he, in a letter dated on or about 5 March, offered a commission or brokerage fee of 2½ per cent on any loan money arranged by the recipient of the letter or his company? Dr Cairns denied this categorically. Next day he was succeeded as Treasurer by W. G. Hayden, a 42-year-old Queenslander who had completed his education the hard way. Hayden matriculated while a member of the Queensland police force, and completed his economics degree as an external student while serving in parliament.

On 2 July Whitlam confronted Cairns about two matters: a letter dated 7 March from Cairns to the financier Harris, offering a brokerage fee of 2½ per cent; and a newspaper report about his stepson's connection with a company that was trying to raise money overseas for a housing project in Cairns's electorate. Concerning the letter, which was the more important of the two issues, for it involved the charge of misleading parliament, all Cairns could say was that he had no recollection of ever having signed it, and that it was completely contrary to his previously expressed intention to Mr Harris. Considering this explanation inadequate, and finding Cairns unwilling to resign, Whitlam advised the Governor-General to terminate his commission as a Minister of the Crown. Cairns tried to reach Sir John Kerr by telephone, intending to ask for a hearing, only to be informed that His Excellency was at dinner. Clyde Cameron had made a similar request in writing at the time of the Cabinet reshuffle, when he was reluctant to move from Labour and Immigration to Science and Consumer Affairs. On both occasions Sir John Kerr accepted the Prime Minister's advice that he should not hear the ministers concerned.

This was the first time a Prime Minister had ever sacked a Deputy Prime Minister (Crean was elected in Cairns's place at the next Caucus meeting), but in spite of such drastic action the loans affair continued to rage out of control. The press, particularly the Melbourne *Age*, scoured the world for telexes dealing with the activities of Khemlani and others of that stripe. On 9 July Whitlam recalled parliament from its winter recess for a one-day 'put up or shut up' sitting on the loans allegations. He tabled documents filling thirty-seven pages of Hansard, challenged the Opposition to do its worst, and spoke warmly of the late minister whose political career he had been obliged to destroy:

> This is the tribunal in which the Opposition as much as the Government will be judged—in the highest court, by the jury of the people. We are all on trial now. There is a special and overriding reason why this Parliament is the proper place. For it is upon the very question of proper parliamentary conduct that the one authentic event in a week of squalid intrigue turned—not the pseudo events of the media but the one definite event, tremendous in the life of a party, of a nation; supremely tragic in the life of a man . . . The fault was grievous but it lies not in his integrity or reputation as a man of honour. He has rendered remarkable service to his Party and the nation. But the lapse from the standards which the Prime

Minister at least, and this Government at least, insist upon left me with no choice.

Fraser's reply contained no revelations, but plenty of damaging rhetoric. In place of 'Woof, woof' the Government now faced snapping jaws. 'We have had enough of this nonsense from the Prime Minister', said Fraser.

We have had enough words without substance . . . The people of Australia no longer trust this Government. The affair arises from an appalling attempt to keep secret one of the worst scandals of Australia's history—a scandal compounded with stupefying incompetence and brazen deceit. The whole country is concerned with the ineptitude, intrigue and deception. The whole country is demanding answers.

He incorporated forty-four questions in Hansard, and to a motion by Whitlam that the matter of overseas loan negotiations be considered by the House he moved an amendment calling for a Royal Commission.

An even more incisive attack came from a member of the shadow ministry, R. J. Ellicott (Lib, Wentworth, N), who was a former Commonwealth Solicitor-General and a cousin of Sir Garfield Barwick. Concentrating on the Executive Council meeting of 13 December 1974, Ellicott said: 'I believe there is a prima facie case against the Government that it has deceived the Governor-General . . . The action was unconstitutional, unlawful and based on deception. That is the charge. There is a prima facie case'.

In a speech tinged with self-pity, Dr Cairns presented himself as being

perhaps too willing to encourage those who want to break through the rigours of the establishment. Perhaps I do wear my heart too easily on my sleeve. Perhaps if I do that I am not suitable to be a Minister of this nation. If that is the decision of the Government of the nation I accept it because I will not cease to wear my heart on my sleeve.

Connor wore his heart more like a boxing glove. He incorporated in Hansard ten pages of telex messages, mainly between himself and Tirath Khemlani, and concluded with a defiant protestation of good faith. 'I am an honest man', he said.

I deal with honest people. Throughout my 2½ years as a Minister of the Crown I have stood in the path of those who would have grabbed the mineral resources of Australia. I have no apologies whatever to make for what I have done . . . I fling in the face of little men of the Opposition the words of an old Australian poem:

> 'Give me men to match my mountains,
> Give me men to match my plains,
> Men with freedom in their vision,
> And creation in their brains'.

Ironically, these lines were misquoted from a patriotic ballad written not in Australia but in one of the very countries which Connor accused of trying to grab Australia's mineral resources. They were from 'The Coming American', by one Sam Walter Foss of Boston.

At 10 p.m. the Leader of the House withdrew Whitlam's original motion, with the result that Fraser's amendment lapsed. Although the House then resumed its broken recess, the Senate, which had also been recalled on 9 July, held four more sittings during the following two weeks. In a motion amended by Senator Withers, and carried by the Opposition and two Independents, the Senate resolved on 9 July that in view of the Government's refusal to appoint a Royal Commission into overseas loan activities the Senate should call to the Bar and examine twelve senior public servants, including the permanent heads of the Treasury, Minerals and Energy, and Attorney-General's departments. The Usher of the Black Rod was despatched to Adelaide to serve a similar summons on Gerasimos Karidis.

Such a challenge to the principle of responsible government had never been issued so bluntly in Australia before, although the calling of the chairman of the Commonwealth Bank board to the Bar of the Senate in 1931 provided precedent of a sort. By convention, public servants appearing before parliamentary committees could answer some questions of fact, but not of policy. Various politicians, including Whitlam, had asserted while in Opposition that parliament should be able to examine public servants more thoroughly. From the vantage point of office, however, Whitlam saw things differently. 'In taking this course', he said,

> [the Senate is challenging] the fundamental character of Ministerial responsibility. It is the Government—not the Public Service—that will answer in the Parliament any request, any challenge put to it. It is the Government—not the Public Service—that is responsible to the people. This is in accord with the principles on which our democracy is based. If these principles are successfully challenged, Government would become unworkable.

Accordingly the Prime Minister instructed all public servants called as witnesses by the Senate that they were to claim Crown privilege in respect of all questions about matters mentioned in the Senate's resolution of 9 July. On the afternoon of 16 July the eleven witnesses were called consecutively to the Bar by Black Rod, were asked to state their names and occupations, and were then questioned by Opposition senators. They all claimed privilege on matters covered by their instructions, and were eventually discharged from further attendance. From start to finish, these fruitless formalities took three hours and twenty minutes.

At another sitting on 22 July Mr Karidis, accompanied by Counsel, answered questions freely, but did not add much to the Opposition's store of knowledge. Asked by Senator Steele Hall how Khemlani's commission was to have been divided, the witness replied: 'Mr President, we did not know how much we was getting, what we was getting and when we got it and when the deal we will finish, but it has never been finalising yet. It is too early for all these things to discuss'. And there the matter rested for the moment. Not a dollar of the original $4000 million had been raised, and not a cent paid in commission; but the potential of the loans affair to damage the Government was not exhausted yet.

In this recital of misadventures, the sword and the time bomb should not be forgotten. Despite Fraser's repeated affirmation that only in 'extraordinary' or 'reprehensible' circumstances should a Government elected to power in the lower house be prevented by a hostile Senate from governing for a full three-year term, the Senate's power to refuse or defer Supply remained a fact of parliamentary life. As if to remind the Government of that, the Senate delayed consideration of Supply Bills in May, purportedly to give the Treasurer time to explain his needs more fully. 'I want it to be understood quite clearly', said Senator Cotton, the Opposition spokesman on Manufacturing Industry,

> that there is no intention on the part of the Opposition to refuse to pass the Supply Bills . . . [But] the Opposition feels that the time has come when this matter should not be passed over lightly, should not be treated casually, but should be looked at far more critically, and that a little more time should be taken on it.

The time bomb was of course the stockpile of bills which had failed to pass the Senate on two occasions and could therefore be used to obtain a double dissolution. By the end of the autumn sittings there were fifteen such bills, including a National Health Bill; two Conciliation and Arbitration Bills; a Superior Court of Australia Bill, to establish a court exercising federal jurisdiction in place of the Australian Industrial Court and the Federal Court of Bankruptcy, and to assume some of the functions of the High Court and State Supreme Courts; and another Constitution Alteration (Simultaneous Elections) Bill.

The latter, designed to ensure that Senate elections were always held at the same time as elections for the House of Representatives, had failed to obtain the necessary approval at referendum in 1974. But it had failed only narrowly to obtain an overall majority of the votes, and Whitlam argued that it should be put to the people again. The Opposition in the Senate still believed that the real purpose of this amendment would be to let a Government drag half the Senate with it every time it faced a lower house election.

The balance of power in the Senate was tipped further in favour of the Opposition by the death of Senator B. R. Milliner (Lab, Q) during the winter adjournment. In choosing a replacement, the Premier of Queensland, Bjelke-Petersen, went one better than Premier Lewis's recent breach of convention in filling Senator Murphy's casual vacancy. His choice, duly ratified by a vote of the Queensland parliament, fell upon Albert Patrick Field, a member of the A.L.P. who had no sympathy with the Whitlam Government and professed his willingness to vote against it at every opportunity. Pat Field, a French-polisher by trade but also an employee of the Queensland public service, was expelled by the Labor Party for accepting nomination against the official Labor candidate, and took his place in the Senate as an anti-Labor Independent. Once again the Prime Minister had been taken for a ride by the Queensland Premier. No wonder he forgot propriety and denounced that crafty, bucolic Lutheran as 'a bible-bashing bastard', a 'humbug' and a 'hypocrite'.

Senator Field cut a sorry figure in Canberra. The Government tried to prevent him being sworn in on 9 September by moving that the question of his eligibility be referred to the Senate's Standing Committee of Disputed Returns and Qualifications. But the 'Ayes' and 'Noes' being equal, this passed in the negative. Government senators then left the chamber while Field was sworn in, and thereafter they ostracised him. He asked one question about the superphosphate bounty ('superphosphorus', as he called it); but before he was able to deliver his maiden speech, proceedings were started in the High Court to challenge the validity of his appointment. The ground for this was that Field might not have resigned in the correct manner from his position in the public service, and would therefore have held an office of profit under the Crown when the State parliament elected him. On 1 October Field was granted leave of absence until the High Court could hear the case. In fact it never came on for hearing, and for reasons to be explained later Senator Field never returned to the Senate. Merely by his absence, however, he was destined to earn a modest niche in parliamentary history.

The High Court did not impinge upon the Whitlam Government nearly as much as it had upon Labor's two earlier reforming Governments—those of Chifley, whose judicial casualties included bank nationalisation and free medicine; and Fisher, many of whose legislative achievements were struck down by the Court. As one commentator wrote, 'the Whitlam Government survived its own explorations and adventures with Commonwealth legislative and financial powers—nearly all aimed at expanding the role of the Commonwealth at the expense of the States—almost completely unscathed'.

The only major casualty was the Petroleum and Minerals Authority Bill, which the Court overturned in June 1975—not on substantive grounds, but for the procedural reason that the Bill had not been passed in accordance with the deadlock provisions of the Constitution. The Government then announced that the Petroleum and Minerals Authority's existing commitments would be honoured by the Petroleum and Minerals Company of Australia Pty Ltd, wholly owned by the Government and incorporated in the Australian Capital Territory, and that the Petroleum and Minerals Authority Bill would be submitted to parliament again. The Strangler was not a man to give in easily.

In October 1975 the High Court delivered two judgments favourable to the Government. First, it dismissed a challenge by the State of Victoria to the validity of the Australian Assistance Plan. The A.A.P. was intended to regionalise social welfare by co-ordinating it at the local level, a service hitherto usually performed by State authorities. It was financed by direct money grants which bypassed the States, a stratagem depending for its constitutional validity on Section 81, which gives the federal Government power to appropriate money from the Consolidated Revenue Fund 'for the purposes of the Commonwealth'. However, the Justices were much divided in their reasoning, and their opinions provided no guarantee that the plan could be properly underpinned by a regulatory Act.

In its second October judgment the Court upheld the validity of the Senate (Representation of Territories) Act, which provided for the election of four more senators—two from the Australian Capital Territory, and two from the Northern Territory. The question at issue was whether Section 122 of the

Constitution permitted territorial senators to have full voting rights, as provided by the Act, or whether they should be non-voting delegates. A majority of four justices—including Murphy J., but not Barwick C.J.—interpreted the word 'representation' in that section to mean the same as it meant elsewhere in the Constitution, which was to say full voting rights. The Chief Justice and two of his brethren thought such an interpretation would 'subvert the Constitution and seriously . . . impair its federal character'.

As it was possible that Labor might win the lion's share of territorial representation, the High Court's Senate judgment was of particular concern to the National Country Party, which was still very apprehensive about the Government's electoral redistribution proposals. The case for a whole-hearted attempt to put the Government out of office was consequently being urged again by Anthony, and there was speculation about the likely fate of the Budget bills. A counter-speculation was that if the Senate Opposition blocked or deferred Supply, the Government might call an election for half the Senate (which was due before 30 June 1976) and the four territorial senators, and just possibly that might give the Government temporary control of the Senate.

On 19 August the new Treasurer, Bill Hayden, presented a Budget that was generally well received, and led the Prime Minister to regret not having made Hayden Treasurer from the outset. The domestic deficit at the end of 1974–75 had been $1949 million, nine times more than the previous record. It was hardly surprising, then, that Hayden's Budget speech proposed consolidation and restraint instead of further expansion in the public sector. The estimated domestic deficit for 1975–76 was $2068 million. 'Inflation is this nation's most menacing enemy', said Hayden. 'We aim to curb it. Unless this aim is achieved, the nation's productive capacity will run down and job opportunities will diminish.'

Fraser was guarded in his early comment on the Budget. 'We'll be following normal procedure in the Senate', he said, 'and with the knowledge we have at the moment, at this stage it would be our intention to allow it a passage through the Senate'. The implication was clear, however, that normal procedure could quickly be rendered inappropriate by the advent of 'extraordinary' or 'reprehensible' circumstances. While Appropriation Bills 1 and 2 were going through committee stages in the lower house during September and October the loans affair continued to evolve in ways that were beyond the Government's control. Khemlani, apparently believing that he had authority to do so, was still trying to raise capital for the Australian Government, and the press knew about it. Legend would later depict a vivid image of poor deluded Connor sitting in his office late at night waiting for the telex to bring him petro-dollars. Whether or not that was true, it now became known that at least to some extent he had ignored the withdrawal of his loan-raising authority on 20 May.

On 8 October Lynch asked the Prime Minister without notice whether any senior ministers were at present involved in major overseas loan raisings. Whitlam replied: 'No'. Fraser then asked whether he would reaffirm his confidence in Connor's administration of the Minerals and Energy portfolio. Whitlam replied: 'Certainly I will. I do not quite understand what the honourable gentleman is driving at . . . '. Next day the Prime Minister told parliament that Connor had assured him in June that all loan discussions had been terminated, and that all communications of substance between himself (Connor) and Khemlani had been tabled on 9 July.

Then Khemlani came to Australia, bringing with him a number of telexes which the Melbourne *Herald* published on 13 October. One of these, which had not been tabled on 9 July, showed that Connor had been in communication with Khemlani about loans at least until 23 May, three days after the withdrawal of his authority. On the afternoon of 14 October Whitlam informed the House that the Governor-General had accepted Connor's resignation and appointed Senator Wriedt in his place. (Connor left the ministry altogether, and to fill that vacancy Caucus chose one of his strongest supporters, 31-year-old Paul Keating, who represented the Sydney electorate of Blaxland.)

Immediately after Whitlam's announcement, Fraser asked him whether, in view of the events which had led first to Cairns's dismissal and then to Connor's resignation, he now considered that his own participation in the same events obliged him to resign also.

> Mr WHITLAM.—Mr Speaker, no . . .
> Mr LYNCH.—Why did the Prime Minister mislead the House on 9 October with an assurance that all communications of substance between the Minister for Minerals and Energy and the original Government intermediary were tabled on 9 July?
> Mr WHITLAM.—I regret to say that I myself was misled.

'At last', as one headline put it, 'the footprints of a giant reprehensible circumstance!' On 15 October Malcolm Fraser announced outside the chamber that the Opposition would refuse to pass the Budget bills in the Senate until the Government called an election. At 4.35 p.m. Senator Withers rose to speak on the Loan Bill, a measure which had been in the Senate for several weeks and was closely linked with Appropriation Bills No. 1 and No. 2, which the Senate had received on the previous day. The Opposition, he said, would attempt to delay these three Bills because it had decided that the people must be given a chance to express their will.

> The only way to force the Government to submit to the people is by this device . . . This is a Government that lurches not just from crisis to crisis but from scandal to scandal. Nothing is worse than this incredible loans affair. It is an affair which involved an attempt to go behind the Constitution and the Loan Council. It was an attempt to defy the Parliament and an attempt to impose massive debt repayments on future Australians without either their knowledge or their approval. It is not enough for the Prime Minister to claim that the affair has ended because the people involved have been removed. The Prime Minister has hidden behind his Ministers and has refused to take the responsibility himself . . . His Ministers have been made sacrifices on the altar of his ego. Yet still he survives. Not only does he survive, but also he now threatens to defy the Parliament by refusing to go to the electorate. Never has a Prime Minister evinced such cowardly disgraceful behaviour . . .

The Opposition believes that both Houses should go to the people. We challenge the Prime Minister to arrange for that to happen. He has the opportunity because the Parliament is now in a state of total deadlock. It has been deadlocked on 21 Bills so far and it now faces a deadlock on the most important legislation of all—the Appropriation Bills.

Senator Withers then moved an amendment to the Government's motion that the Loan Bill be read a second time, so that the motion stated instead that the Bill 'be not further proceeded with until the Government agrees to submit itself to the judgment of the people'. The amended motion was passed by 29 votes to 28, Senators Steele Hall and Bunton voting with the Government, Senator T. C. Drake-Brockman (NCP, W) being absent overseas and paired with Senator W. W. Brown (Lab, V), and Senator Field still on leave of absence. Field was crucial to the Opposition's stategy of deferral, even though he was not there. If Senator Milliner had not died, or had been replaced by a genuine Labor senator, the deferral motion would have been defeated on a tied vote of 29–29. The only way in which the Opposition could then have brought pressure to bear upon the Government would have been the far less preferable one of rejecting the Budget bills outright by using a tied vote to defeat the motion for a second reading. That course of action would have run the risk of defection by a few Opposition senators who were believed to be uneasy about or definitely opposed to rejection. It would also have removed the bills from the Senate's control, whereas deferral, as Senator Withers had pointed out to his colleagues in 1973, kept the bills conveniently at hand in case a new Government should suddenly want them passed.

Next day, while the Senate dealt with Appropriation Bills No. 1 and No. 2, Whitlam moved a motion of confidence in the Government, asserting 'the basic principle that a Government that continues to have a majority in the House of Representatives has a right to expect that it will be able to govern'. These were Fraser's own words. 'He has professed that principle again and again', said Whitlam.

There is the really 'reprehensible circumstance' today—a man who knows what is honourable, yet who does the thoroughly dishonourable—the exact definition of a man without honour, a man without principle. As another self-indulgent wool grower said in putting personal interests ahead of the nation's interest, *video meliora proboque; deteriora sequor.*

Not many in the House would have known the tag from Ovid ('I see and approve better things, but follow worse'), but some would surely have remembered that five years earlier Whitlam himself had spoken against the very principle he was now denouncing Fraser for having abandoned. The motion of confidence was passed on party lines, by 62 votes to 57, and on the lawn outside Parliament House a crowd of several thousand people demonstrated against the denial of Supply. Both gestures were unavailing. The Senate voted 29–28 to defer the two Appropriation Bills.

That evening, 16 October, Whitlam attended a State banquet at Government House in honour of the Prime Minister of Malaysia, Tun Abdul Razak. During a preliminary conversation with Sir John Kerr and the guest of honour in the Governor- General's study, Whitlam spoke of the day's events with unexpected candour. As Sir John was later to reveal in a book about the 1975 crisis, '[the Prime Minister] said to me with a brilliant smile, "It could be a question of whether I get to the Queen first or you get in first with my dismissal." We all laughed'.

What followed in the next few weeks was a war of nerves between an Opposition determined to force dissolution by withholding Supply in the Senate and a Government equally determined to 'tough it out'—and on the sidelines a third force, the Governor-General, who possessed constitutional power to resolve the deadlock if and when he judged that to be expedient. Each contender made out a good case in support of his position; they must have been good cases, for on earlier occasions each contender had used the other's argument when it suited his purpose.

The issues were confused, however, by the oblique way in which the Constitution gives the Senate power to withhold or reject money bills, and gives the Governor-General power to dismiss his ministers. They were also confused by the fact that neither of these powers had ever yet been used in the Commonwealth, although there were some rare precedents for refusal and dismissal in the States. The Governor-General's power to dismiss ministers is implied, without saying so in as many words, by Section 64, which gives His Excellency power to 'appoint officers to administer departments of State of the Commonwealth'. These officers, who are ministers, 'shall hold office during the pleasure of the Governor-General': no pleasure, no office. Apart from Sir Philip Game's dismissal of Lang in 1932, and an earlier but less exact parallel in Canada, the power to dismiss was widely regarded as a reserve power, like an indulgent father's strap, to be used only in circumstances so extreme as to be almost inconceivable.

Because of these ambiguities there was a wide range of opinion about the developing crisis. Eight professors of law, including Geoffrey Sawer, urged the Senate to observe not the strict letter of the law but rather the convention that denial of Supply should not be reduced to the level of a routine political tactic. Sir Robert Menzies, who several years earlier had spoken against the rising power of the Senate, now sided with Fraser. In doing this he was returning to a view which he had expressed in 1947, when he too had been Leader of the Opposition: 'Surely it is a curious argument to say that a power deliberately and specifically conferred on the Upper House is in no circumstances to be exercised'. On the other hand, Killen deplored the Senate's breach of convention. The former Liberal–Country League Premier of South Australia, Sir Thomas Playford, also warned Liberal senators against blocking the Budget. Those who were known to have misgivings about it included Senators Alan Missen (V), Don Jessop (S), Neville Bonner (Q), Eric Bessell (T) and Condor Laucke (S).

Probably the most influential opinion expressed at this stage came from the Opposition frontbencher, Ellicott. In a press statement issued on 17 October, this former Solicitor- General strongly affirmed the existence of the Senate's and the Governor-General's powers. He then went on to assert that in the present circumstances the Governor-General's only possible course was to require Whitlam either to satisfy him that he could obtain Supply, or to advise a double dissolution. If Whitlam did not comply, the Governor-General should dismiss him and commission someone who would advise dissolution. Ellicott sent a copy of this statement to the Governor-General's official secretary.

At His Excellency's request, the incumbent Solicitor-General, Maurice Byers, Q.C., later prepared a statement commenting on the Ellicott opinion. While not disputing the deferral and dismissal powers, Byers said there was a strong case for believing that the Senate was acting contrary to convention, and expressed the view that viceregal intervention would compromise the neutrality of the Crown.

On the next sitting day, 21 October, the battle was joined in earnest on the parliamentary and viceregal fronts. The House considered a message from the Senate concerning the deferral, and returned a message of its own, asserting that such action was contrary to constitutional convention, and requesting the Senate to reconsider and pass the Bills without delay. Whitlam referred to great constitutional struggles of the past—'1640, 1688, 1832 and 1910'—and quoted Abraham Lincoln's solemn oath to preserve and defend the Constitution. Fraser needed no such grand allusions. He simply quoted Whitlam's own words of 1970: 'We will vote against the Bills here and in the Senate. Our purpose is to destroy this Budget and to destroy the Government which has sponsored it'.

Also on this day the Governor-General held separate discussions with the Prime Minister and, with Whitlam's ready approval, Fraser. He told Whitlam that in his view the situation had not yet crossed the threshold into a true constitutional crisis because the Senate had only deferred the Budget, not rejected it, and money had not started to run out. Whitlam replied that even if money were to run out he believed he could manage with the help of the banks, backed by Commonwealth guarantee. At his meeting with Fraser, Sir John inquired about the possibility of defection in the Senate. Fraser replied that the coalition would remain firm on deferral. When Sir John asked why deferral had been preferred to rejection, Fraser said Supply had been deferred so that, should there be a change of government, he would be able to guarantee Supply by immediately securing passage of the Appropriation Bills through the Senate.

Two more Appropriation Bills, identical with the first two, were sent to the Senate on 23 October, and deferred on a vote of 29–28. A similar test of nerve took place on 5 November, and again the Bills were deferred by an undivided coalition, this time on a vote of 30–29. Drake-Brockman and Brown voted with their respective parties, and Field was still absent. The Senate rang with epithets like 'dingo', 'swine', 'mongrel', and 'cur'; and in the House, Whitlam and Fraser locked horns like two bull mooses. The Governor-General held further discussions with each of them separately on 30 October and 3 November. On 3 November, at Government House in Melbourne, Fraser told His Excellency that the Opposition was willing to grant Supply if the Prime Minister would agree to hold an election for the House of Representatives at the same time as the normal half-Senate election. When

Sir John Kerr leaves Parliament House after being sworn in as Governor-General, 11 July 1974.

Government House, Yarralumla

The third Whitlam Ministry: (clockwise from left front) R. F. X. Connor, C. R. Cameron, J. F. Cairns, E. G. Whitlam, Senator L. K. Murphy, Senator D. R. Willesee, F. Crean, F. R. Stewart, F. M. Daly, W. G. Hayden, W. L. Morrison, R. A. Patterson, L. Barnard, L. F. Bowen, Senator D. McClelland, D. N. Everingham, Senator R. Bishop, Senator J. L. Cavanagh, L. R. Johnson, M. H. Cass, J. M. Bryant, Senator J. M. Wheeldon, T. Uren, K. E. Enderby, C. K. Jones, K. E. Beazley, Senator K. S. Wriedt

Whitlam in extremis: in the foreground, the Governor-General's official secretary, David Smith, is reading the viceregal proclamation dissolving both houses of parliament on 11 November 1975, and in the background, to the left of Mr Whitlam, are J. D. Anthony and Ian Sinclair.

Fraser in excelsis: *the New Prime Minister leaves Parliament House on 11 November 1975.*

The Lodge

Queen Elizabeth opening the second session of the twenty-eighth Parliament, 28 February 1974

The President of the Senate, Senator Justin O'Byrne, welcomes Senator Cleaver Bunton to the chamber, 27 February 1975

J. F. Cope, Speaker of the House of Representatives (1973–1975)

Sir John put that to the Prime Minister half an hour later, Whitlam said he would never advise an election for the lower house unless he himself was ready to do so. The only way such an election could occur, he said, would be if the Governor-General were willing 'to do a Philip Game'.

That very course was urged by Fraser during another meeting with the Governor-General, at Yarralumla on Thursday 6 November. The Government still had 24 days' Supply left, and on the day of this meeting, when the Senate refused to pass the Appropriation Bills for the third time, the Treasurer was negotiating with the banks to obtain what the Government hoped would be a legal and satisfactory alternative to Supply. According to Sir John Kerr's subsequent account, Fraser told him that

> if I failed to act in the situation which existed I would be imperilling the reserve powers of the Crown for ever; he accepted that the decision was mine but inaction on my part, with Supply running out, the Senate firm on deferral, and the Government asserting the right to govern without Supply, would destroy the reserve powers.

'I [now] had no doubt', wrote Kerr, ' . . . that the leaders were on the point of collision. I knew on 6 November that I would have a weekend of very serious private deliberations which I intended to undertake alone.' This he did at Admiralty House, the sandstone mansion looking across Sydney Harbour towards Circular Quay, where an earlier Governor-General, Munro Ferguson, had once met a worried Prime Minister, Hughes. And just as Munro Ferguson on another occasion had sought advice from the Chief Justice of the High Court, Sir Samuel Griffith, so now, on Sunday evening, did Sir John Kerr telephone Sir Garfield Barwick, Menzies's one-time Attorney-General, asking him to call at Admiralty House on his way to court next morning.

But the circumstances were different. Munro Ferguson had been new to the country when Joseph Cook asked him for a double dissolution on relatively trivial grounds, and Griffith advised him to make up his own mind, adding: 'Although [a Governor-General] cannot act except upon the advice of Ministers, he is not bound to follow their advice, but is in the position of an independent arbiter'. Kerr was no stranger to Australian law and politics, and he was about to take the kind of action which had been urged upon him, not by his ministers but by the Leader of the Opposition. Sir John had probably come to this conclusion through his own deliberations, regardless of the pressure which Fraser had sought to apply. All he asked the Chief Justice on Monday morning was whether he could lawfully withdraw a Prime Minister's commission.

Sir Garfield prefaced his response with the dubious statement that, as the question was not one which a court could decide, he would be prepared to answer it. After requesting that his visit be recorded publicly in the daily announcement of viceregal engagements, he took himself off to sit in court at Darlinghurst. While hearing a matter concerning the liability of company directors, with Justices Mason and Jacobs, he drafted a written answer to Sir John's question, and took it to Admiralty House at lunch time. In brief, the answer was that 'if Your Excellency is satisfied in the current situation that the present Government is unable to secure supply, the course upon which Your Excellency has determined is consistent with your constitutional authority and duty'. That afternoon the Governor-General returned to Canberra.

The morning of Tuesday 11 November was resplendent with sunlight shining along the east–west axis of Lake Burley Griffin, rose gardens in full bloom, and magpies singing on Capital Hill. At 9 a.m., by arrangement made the previous day, Whitlam, Crean and Daly met Fraser, Lynch and Anthony in the Prime Minister's suite to propose a compromise. If the Senate Opposition would pass the Budget and the electoral redistribution, he would defer the half-Senate election as long as possible, which meant until mid-1976; if not, he would call it immediately. Anthony seemed to think there was merit in a late election, but Fraser and Lynch rejected the proposal out of hand.

'They seem very cocky', remarked Crean after Fraser and his companions had left. Whitlam immediately telephoned the Governor-General to ask for an appointment, saying that he now wanted a half-Senate election before Christmas. Sir John had to attend the Remembrance Day service at the War Memorial at 11 a.m., and Whitlam would have to be in the House soon after that as there was a notice of motion to censure the Government. He arranged to ring the Governor-General again as soon as he could leave the chamber.

The House sat at 11.45 a.m. Fraser moved the censure motion, Whitlam moved an amendment turning the motion into one of censure against Fraser for procuring the action of coalition senators to defer Supply, and the House suspended for lunch at 12.55 p.m. By that time both men were at Yarralumla. His Excellency had arranged to see Whitlam at 12.45 p.m., and Fraser at 1 p.m. Fraser actually arrived first because his staff, keeping an eye on Whitlam's car at the side of Parliament House, drew the wrong conclusion from its early departure and sent Fraser on his way too soon. The Prime Minister's car was not carrying Whitlam and by the time it returned for him Fraser had been ushered into a side room at Government House to wait for his appointment. This later gave rise to suspicion that Fraser had been summoned first, to be concealed in waiting. Although that particular suspicion was unfounded, there was undeniably an air of ambush at Yarralumla. As the Prime Minister entered the Governor-General's study, intending to ask formally for an immediate half-Senate election accompanied by a referendum on the Constitution Alteration (Simultaneous Elections) Bill, Sir John Kerr said to him:

> Before you say anything Prime Minister, I want to say something to you. You have told me this morning on the phone that your talks with the leaders on the other side have failed to produce any change and that things therefore remain the same. You intend to govern without parliamentary supply.

'He said, "Yes", wrote Kerr later. I replied that

> in my view he had to have parliamentary supply to govern and as he had failed to obtain it and was not prepared to go to the people [at a general election], I had decided to withdraw his commission'.

According to Sir John's account, Whitlam then jumped up, looked at the telephones and said, 'I must get in touch with the Palace at once'.

'It is too late', replied His Excellency.

'Why?'

'Because you are no longer Prime Minister. These documents tell you so and why.'

Sir John handed Whitlam his statement of reasons, which had been typed earlier in the day; but the Prime Minister did not read them. 'I see', was all he said.

'The Chief Justice agrees with this course of action', said Kerr.

'So that is why you had him to lunch yesterday. I advised you that you should not consult him on this matter.'

'We shall all have to live with this.'

'You certainly will.'

In his own subsequent account of this conversation, Whitlam dismissed as 'a concoction and an absurd one' Sir John's recollection of the words 'I must get in touch with the Palace'. 'I was trapped in an ambush', wrote Whitlam.

> My sole instinct was to escape, to depart at once from the place where the deed had been done and the presence of the man who had done the deed. When he offered his hand and said, 'Anyway, good luck,' it was from ordinary habit and simple courtesy that I shook hands.

Events now moved with cyclonic speed and turbulence. Whitlam departed for The Lodge, and Fraser was brought into the study. The Governor-General asked Fraser whether he could obtain Supply if he were commissioned to form a caretaker government, and Fraser said that he could. He agreed not to initiate any new policies or hold any inquiries into activities of the previous Government before an election, and undertook to advise a double dissolution if he was unable, as he surely would be, to get the confidence of the lower house. Fraser then signed a prepared letter setting out the terms agreed upon, and the Governor-General swore him in as the Commonwealth's twenty-second Prime Minister. 'I think we ought to dispense with the traditional glass of champagne', said His Excellency. 'I feel sure you would rather get back to your desk—there's a lot to be done.' Fraser permitted himself a tight smile, and as he walked towards the door he told the Governor-General that he believed he could obtain Supply during the afternoon.

At The Lodge, Whitlam urgently summoned several of his senior colleagues and assistants who would be involved in action which he was planning to take 'in the only place which had any meaningful role, the House of Representatives'. He telephoned his wife in Sydney, and then tucked into a steak. To most of those who now began arriving, Whitlam said simply: 'The bastard's sacked us'. Those called to The Lodge included Crean, who was due to speak in the censure debate immediately after lunch; Speaker Scholes; the Leader of the House, Fred Daly; the Attorney-General, K. E. Enderby (A.C.T.); the A.L.P.'s national secretary, David Combe; Whitlam's speech writer, Graham Freudenberg . . . but not one senator. Incredible though it would seem in retrospect, no one thought it necessary to inform

Senator Wriedt, his deputy leader, Senator Douglas McClelland, or the President of the Senate, Senator O'Byrne. So little time had passed that the news was still known only to a select few members of the Government which had suddenly become an Opposition. During the luncheon adjournment Mr Justice Murphy telephoned his friend Senator James McClelland, who had replaced Cameron as Minister for Labour and Immigration, and in that capacity was successfully damping down the inflationary wage combustion which had flared up under his predecessor's administration. Murphy asked whether it was true, as he had just heard, that the Government had been dismissed. 'Of course not', replied McClelland. 'That's not going to happen. All sorts of rumours are flying around, but we're still in control.'

Both Houses resumed sitting at 2 p.m., and contrary to Whitlam's expectation the place that had the more meaningful role to play was the Senate. Unlike Senator Wreidt, Senator Withers knew exactly what had happened; he had heard the news in the pandemonium of Fraser's office at lunch time, and had warned the Opposition Whip, Senator Fred Chaney (W), to make certain that every coalition senator was present in the chamber. Senator Doug McClelland, who was manager of Labor's business in the Senate, had earlier warned Withers that the Appropriation Bills would be presented again after lunch. Soon after 2 p.m., inside the chamber, he asked Withers: 'What are you going to do?'

There are differing versions of what followed in the next few minutes, but according to one account Withers replied: 'We'll let them through'.

When word of this reached Senator Wriedt he came across to sit beside Withers, and said with a smile: 'You've buckled at last have you?'

'Yes, we have buckled.'

'Well I'll be damned. Why?'

'Gough's been sacked and Malcolm's Prime Minister.'

Wriedt took this as a joke, but between 2.10 p.m. and 2.15 p.m. either he or Doug McClelland received a message that removed all misunderstanding. The Clerk read the order of the day for consideration of the latest message from the House, which called upon the Senate to pass the Appropriation Bills without delay. Senator Wriedt was ready to move suspension of Standing Orders so that a motion for the passage of the two bills could be put forthwith, without debate or amendment. In view of the news which had just reached him, it may be said with hindsight that Wriedt could and should have delayed the calling on of the Appropriation Bills. He could, for instance, have moved motions to bring on other business. And the President, although hitherto punctilious in his conduct of that office, might conceivably have responded to the Opposition's departure from convention by ignoring convention himself and calling only Labor senators to speak. This would have delayed matters, perhaps enabling the Government to take counter action in the House of Representatives; but failing some Government initiative in the lower house, the Senate Opposition, possessing a majority, would eventually have taken charge of business there and procured the passage of the Appropriation Bills on its own motion. In any case, nothing of the sort happened. Senator Wriedt, disoriented by the sudden reversal of fortune, moved his motion and then moved the closure. The main question—that the

Bills be now passed—was agreed to on the voices and the sitting was suspended at 2.45 p.m.

In the House at that time Frank Crean was still delivering his speech on the censure motion which Fraser had moved before lunch, and delivering it as if nothing untoward had happened. The division bells rang, and the amended motion (in effect a censure of Fraser) was passed by 63 votes to 56. At 2.34 p.m. the Speaker called the Honourable Member for Wannon, and Fraser, knowing that he now had Supply, rose to announce that the Governor-General had commissioned him to form a Government until elections could be held, and that the House would be dissolved as soon as double dissolution papers could be prepared. Amid uproar he moved that the House adjourn. The bells rang again, and the motion was defeated by 55 votes to 64.

The new Prime Minister did not bother to vote in a division which he could not possibly win; he had more important things to do outside the House. Coalition members then began moving to the Government side of the chamber. As Labor members had moved to the Opposition side of the chamber to vote against the motion for adjournment Speaker Scholes suggested that they stay there. They returned to the Government side, however, and the Speaker made no objection.

With hindsight once again, Labor might have been able to use its majority in the lower house to put through a motion rescinding all previous votes on the Appropriation Bills and sending a message to the Senate acquainting it of that decision and asking it to return the Bills before voting on them. If the Senate ignored such a message and passed the Bills, the House could then have instructed the Speaker not to present them to the Governor-General for assent. In that event Fraser would not have had Supply and the Governor-General might have felt obliged to reinstate Whitlam. A double dissolution would certainly have followed, but Labor would at least have been saved from the political disadvantage of being sent to the polls as a dismissed government, which to many voters meant a disgraced Government.

But that opportunity had passed. At 2.48 p.m. Daly moved suspension of Standing Orders so that Whitlam could move a want of confidence motion in the new Government without notice. The motion read simply: 'That this House expresses its want of confidence in the Prime Minister and requests Mr Speaker forthwith to advise His Excellency the Governor-General to call the honourable member for Werriwa to form a government'. The question was put soon after 3 p.m., and passed by 64 votes to 54. Speaker Scholes announced that he would convey the resolution of the House to the Governor-General as soon as possible, the Appropriation Bills were returned from the Senate without amendment, and at 3.15 p.m. the sitting was suspended until 5.30 p.m. In the event, however, it was not to be resumed.

During the next hour and a half several white Commonwealth cars sped down Dunrossil Drive, the wide avenue lined with English elms leading to Government House. Sir John Kerr believed, in his own words, that 'speedy action was advisable, even necessary'. His first priority was to see Fraser and the secretary of the Attorney-General's Department, Clarence Harders, who presented him with the formal material for a double dissolution. Fraser's car was already parked outside Government House when a member of the House staff arrived at 3.50 p.m. with the Appropriation Bills, for signature by the Governor-General. The Speaker at first had difficulty in arranging an appointment for himself, to present the House's resolution. But after he sent a telephone message to the official secretary, saying that unless an audience was granted he would recall the House and seek further guidance from members about subsequent action, an appointment was made for 4.45 p.m. When he handed the Governor-General a copy of the resolution, Sir John informed him that he had already dissolved both houses of parliament and that there would be a general election on 13 December.

At that moment, or very close to it, the Governor-General's secretary, David Smith, was standing in front of microphones on the crowded front steps of Parliament House, reading His Excellency's proclamation dissolving the two Houses. The steps were surrounded by several hundred people, almost all Whitlam supporters, who had been cheering and chanting 'We want Gough!' Whitlam had soon appeared at the top of the steps; but Mr Smith, a slim figure in dark formal jacket and grey tie, had not been able to make his way up through the crowd. A Senate officer, and later Clerk of the Senate, Alan Cumming Thom, had seen Smith's difficulty and ushered him through a door on the veranda next to the front steps and taken him to the office of the Clerk, where he waited until he could take his place on the steps.

The proclamation, which could barely be heard above the din, began with a recital of the dissolution requirements of Section 57 and of their fulfilment by twenty-one twice-rejected bills. It concluded with the words 'God save the Queen'. Only a speaker as practised and angry as Whitlam could have turned that venerable phrase back upon the man whom he had once called 'My Viceroy'.

'Well may we say "God Save the Queen"', he burst out, 'because nothing will save the Governor-General'. He called his successor 'Kerr's cur', and urged his listeners: 'Maintain your rage and your enthusiasm through the campaign for the election now to be held and until polling day'.

Next day the Speaker wrote to the Queen, asking that she should act to restore Whitlam to office. This had no more chance of altering the course of events than oratory outside Parliament House. Five days later Her Majesty's private secretary returned a letter to Scholes stating that the Australian Constitution places the prerogative powers of the Crown in the hands of the Governor-General as the representative of the Queen of Australia, and that 'it would not be proper for her to intervene in person in matters which are so clearly placed within the jurisdiction of the Governor-General by the Constitution Act'.

The election, held on the anniversary of the executive council meeting which had authorised Rex Connor to raise $4000 million, was a triumph for the coalition. It produced the greatest landslide in federal history, leaving the coalition with 72 per cent of seats in the lower house. This compared with 61 per cent won by the Menzies–Fadden coalition in 1949, 66 per cent by Labor in the smaller House of 1943, 68 per cent by the Bruce–Page Government in 1925, and 71 per cent by the Nationalists in 1917. In the next parliament

Fraser's Government would have a lower house majority of fifty-five, compared with Labor's recent majority of three. The party strengths would be Liberal, sixty-eight; National Country Party, twenty-three; Labor, thirty-six. In the Senate the coalition would have a clear majority of eight over Labor. It would not have to rely upon two non-aligned senators, Steele Hall (Liberal Movement) and a new Tasmanian Independent, the former Labor right-winger Brian Harradine; nor would it have to put up with an Independent John Gorton, for he failed in his attempted return to the Senate. Six former Labor ministers lost their seats, but Connor and Cairns were not among them.

As the full dimensions of the landslide became apparent on election night one television commentator in the central tally room at Canberra, Bob Hawke, said with tears running down his cheeks: 'We've had the guts ripped out of us'. Next morning one of the twenty-four Labor parliamentarians who lost their seats, Gil Duthie, delivered the sermon at Laurence Vale Methodist Church in Tasmania. The subject he had chosen was 'The Secret of Serenity', and before going to church he prayed for 'strength and purpose to face the appointment after the shock of last night'.

If there was any serenity to be salvaged from outrage and defeat, perhaps it could be attained through recollection of what the Whitlam Government had achieved. Despite the Senate's hostility, that Government had brought into being more fruitful legislation than even Deakin's 'finest harvest'. Throughout its first seventy-one years of existence the Senate had rejected only sixty-eight government bills; in the next three years, it rejected no fewer than ninety-three Whitlam bills. Yet in spite of this obstruction, and the political cyclones of 1974 and 1975, Labor was able to secure the enactment of 508 measures—compared with 404 in the previous three-year period, and 383 in the period before that. It did more for education, health, social welfare, women and Aboriginal Australians than any previous government. It abolished the means test for pensioners aged seventy years or more. It renovated Australia's anachronistic foreign policy, invigorated national consciousness, and fostered the arts as never before.

The Whitlam Government took too many initiatives; achieved a great deal nevertheless; and went down fighting, against the Senate, against inflation, and against the ineptitude of some of its own members. Towards the end it seemed to be getting the upper hand economically, and to have cut its ministerial losses. By then, however, too much had gone wrong. Circumstances were ripe for intervention by the Governor-General and intervene he did, sending Labor to its second election in nineteen months, and the third in as many years. This time it was an election that Labor could not possibly hope to win.

While Duthie preached on serenity that Sunday after the election, Whitlam was at The Lodge conferring with staff and contemplating his resignation from leadership of the parliamentary party. During the morning he telephoned Bill Hayden in Ipswich, to sound him out about taking over. Hayden, who was the only Labor M.H.R. in Queensland to have retained his seat, said he was not interested at that stage. The only other possible successor in Whitlam's opinion was the A.L.P. federal president, Bob Hawke;

but although Hawke was an extremely popular national figure, he was not yet a member of parliament. When Hawke came to The Lodge on Sunday afternoon, Whitlam offered to stand down before the next election if in the meantime Hawke entered parliament and gained the confidence of Caucus. Hawke's response was favourable.

The Governor-General spent Sunday at Yarralumla, without visitors. Earlier he too had broached the subject of resignation, with Fraser, who had urged him to do nothing before the election. Now, fortified by the electorate's apparent vindication of his actions, he was more inclined to remain in office. According to his subsequent autobiography, *Matters For Judgment*, Sir John had no regrets. On the contrary he took pride in having, as he saw it, saved Australia from catastrophe. The constitutional crisis had been produced by the coalition's denial of Supply, and by Labor's determination to keep governing regardless; he had dealt with this crisis 'by getting the issue to the people, who resolved it'. 'In the result', he wrote,

> it is now difficult to remember how truly threatening that crisis was. We can remember terrible tragedies, depressions and wars which actually happened but it is harder to remember crises which would have been disastrous had they happened. The blade may pass within a millimetre, but we will not remember it, because it did not strike.

To Whitlam and his supporters the true catastrophe was not one that may have been avoided, but one that had actually happened. The blade had struck, and it was wielded by the Governor-General. In his reply to Kerr, a book entitled *The Truth of the Matter*, Whitlam denied that the Governor-General's intervention had been either inevitable or necessary. The crisis, he wrote, had been caused by the coalition's refusal to accept the electorate's verdict of December 1972, reaffirmed in May 1974; but the crisis could not have ended the way it did 'save for the conduct of one man, the Governor-General of Australia, Sir John Kerr, conduct which I have publicly described as dishonourable and deceitful'.

There was no hope of reconciling such divergent opinions. On this issue the nation was divided as bitterly as it had been over Vietnam, or conscription for the Great War, and it was too early yet for objectivity. Had the Governor-General acted wisely, and just in the nick of time; or should he rather have let the politicians fight out their war of nerves? Might a less interventionist Governor-General have guided the belligerents towards a parliamentary solution? Had Sir John Kerr merely done his duty? Or was he influenced by other considerations, not least his own position, in carrying out what some called a constitutional *coup d'état*? A lot of time would have to pass before the answers could be determined by anything other than the answerer's own politics.

18

Atlas

Cabinet

Coming after the Whitlam years, Fraser's term of office was bound to seem rather an anti-climax. In some respects it was a period of recovery, of regaining breath after the unaccustomed exertion of widespread reform and constitutional jeopardy. Gone were all the high hopes of Whitlam's term, the daredevilment of crashing through, and finally crashing. Fraser set out to revive the economy and to restore public confidence in governmental integrity. Like Lyons after Scullin, he was the elected alternative to catastrophe; and like Lyons, he held office for seven years. But there the resemblance ended. In character and political style, no two men could have been less alike. As Stanley Bruce had once remarked, Lyons lacked three qualities which every prime minister should have: 'a hide like a rhinoceros, an overpowering ambition, and a mighty good conceit of himself'. This hardly mattered in the wake of the great Depression, when no Australian Government could do much more than mark time, follow the Premiers' Plan, and wait for the world to recover from its economic wounds. Fraser, on the other hand, was amply endowed with hide, ambition and a conceit of himself amounting to arrogance. Far from marking time, he was in some ways even busier than Whitlam.

During Fraser's term of office the average number of House of Representatives sittings per year was eighty-one, compared with seventy for each of the preceding three years. The average number of sitting hours per year was 654, compared with 778, and the average number of Acts passed per year was 180, compared with 169. If it had been in Fraser's nature to compose a Whitlam-style *Apologia pro Vita Sua*, he could also have cited a comparison of Cabinet business. The Fraser Cabinet held an average of 345 meetings per year, compared with 159 by Whitlam's Cabinet. It received an average of

1431 submissions, memoranda and other papers per year, compared with 851; and it made an average of 2693 decisions per year, compared with 1391.

These were indicators of activity rather than achievement, but they nevertheless demonstrated one of the main differences between Whitlam and Fraser. The former was essentially a parliamentarian, despite his rough handling of parliament on occasion; the latter, although he could perform effectively in the House when necessary, was far more at home with the executive, and especially with Cabinet. Both leaders paid due attention to their party rooms, and to their extra-parliamentary parties. But for Fraser, to a greater extent than Whitlam, the main instrument of political power was Cabinet.

Never before had the Cabinet room, conveniently close to the Prime Minister's suite on the eastern side of Parliament House, been used with such resolute purpose as it was during these years. Fraser would badger his ministers when they were not meeting there, and dragoon them when they were. According to the somewhat partial account of his Minister for Defence, Jim Killen, any conversation around the Cabinet table would invite prime ministerial displeasure ('Can we have one meeting please?'), though Fraser himself never hesitated to converse in an undertone while some other minister was speaking. Sometimes he would leave the Cabinet room abruptly, without apology, then burst back in, asking, 'Where were we?' Votes were not taken often; and when they were, the result was not always a matter of simple arithmetic. On one occasion Cabinet voted eight to six against a proposal, endorsed by the Prime Minister, to ban cigarette advertising from television.

'Well, there *is* to be a ban', said Fraser after the vote had been taken.

'Cut it out, Prime Minister', said the Minister for Transport, Peter Nixon (NC, Gippsland, V). 'It was the other way around.'

'You have lost it, Peter, and that's all there is to it.'

Fraser followed the earlier coalition practice of having a relatively small Cabinet, from which more than half his ministers were omitted, though they might be invited to attend its meetings whenever appropriate. His second ministry, sworn in on 22 December 1975, numbered twenty-five, of whom twelve were Cabinet ministers. His closest colleagues were the Minister for Employment and Industrial Relations and Minister assisting the Prime Minister in public service matters, A. A. Street (Lib, Corangamite, V); the Minister for Primary Industry and Deputy Leader of the National Country Party, Ian Sinclair (New England, N); and, cigarette vote notwithstanding, Peter Nixon. Tony Street was a former captain of Fraser's old school in Melbourne. Like Fraser he was nominally a grazier, and Corangamite adjoined the Prime Minister's own electorate in south-western Victoria. Sinclair and Nixon were graziers, too, and tough exponents of *realpolitik*. Fraser had much affinity with them. He was not quite so close to Doug Anthony, but on the whole his relations with the lesser coalition party were excellent. Indeed some Liberals thought that he took too much notice of their country cousins.

Anthony was Deputy Prime Minister, Minister for National Resources and Minister for Overseas Trade. Other members of Cabinet included Phillip

Lynch, Treasurer and Deputy Leader of the parliamentary Liberal Party; Senator Withers, Minister for Administrative Services, Vice-President of the Executive Council, and Government Leader in the Senate; Senator Cotton, Industry and Commerce; Senator J. L. Carrick (Lib, N), Education; Andrew Peacock, Foreign Affairs; Robert Ellicott, Attorney-General; John Howard (Lib, Bennelong, N), Business and Consumer Affairs; and Senator Margaret Guilfoyle (Lib, V), the first woman in Cabinet since Dame Enid Lyons, Social Security. Two Liberals who might reasonably have expected portfolios, but were passed over because of Fraser's personal dislike, were Don Chipp and Senator Peter Rae. Only five ministers came from the Senate, one fewer than in Whitlam's last Ministry.

As the volume of Cabinet business increased, the Cabinet system and the supporting role played by the Cabinet Office underwent various changes. The Cabinet Office staff was increased from twenty-five to thirty-three, and the position of Secretary to Cabinet, previously held by a much overworked secretary of the Department of the Prime Minister and Cabinet, A. T. (Sir Alan) Carmody, was taken over by the Deputy Secretary of that department, G. J. (later Sir Geoffrey) Yeend, and was accorded the status of permanent head. Standing committees were reorganised to distribute the Cabinet's workload more evenly, and the Department of the Prime Minister and Cabinet improved its liaison with other departments so that decisions of the Cabinet could be followed through more effectively. As its power increased, 'PM and C' took on some of the attributes of a White House in a presidential system of government. Fraser made heavy demands upon it, and used its information to bring pressure to bear on his ministers.

John Malcolm Fraser was naturally enough influenced by that great exemplar of his time, Sir Robert Menzies. But the Prime Minister whom he resembled more closely in dourness of spirit and toughness of hide was John McEwen. He also had some of Bruce's 'born to rule' superiority, and haughty diction to go with it. Although coming to office at the same relatively early age as Menzies, forty-five, Fraser had already served twenty years in parliament—almost twice as long as Menzies had before he became Prime Minister, and four times longer than Bruce. A grazier he may have been, but most of his adult life had been spent in politics. Born in Melbourne, he was the son of a non-practising lawyer, J. Neville Fraser, who owned and worked a property in the New South Wales Riverina, and a grandson of Sir Simon Fraser, the pastoralist and land speculator who had represented Victoria in the Senate for twelve years. The Frasers came from Nova Scotia, and earlier still from Scotland, where their forebears were said to have had some connection with the traditional chiefs of Clan Fraser, the Lords Lovat.

Malcolm's mother, née Una Woolf, was the daughter of a Perth accountant, who had been born in New Zealand. Malcolm, after early years with his parents on the Riverina property, Balpool, was educated at a preparatory school in Toorak, a boarding school in the New South Wales town of Moss Vale, and finally Melbourne Church of England Grammar. He was a better than average student at school, but did less well at Magdalen, his father's old college at Oxford, taking third class honours in Philosophy, Economics and

Politics. Returning to Australia in 1952, he lived at Nareen, a property with 20 000 sheep in Victoria's Western District, near the town of Hamilton, to which his parents had moved after a bad drought in the Riverina.

After joining the Liberal Party in 1954, he gained preselection for the local seat of Wannon, which Labor had recently won from the Liberals. He failed to win it back by only seventeen votes, and won comfortably at the next election, in 1955, with the help of preferences from the Anti-Communist Labor Party. A year later he married Tamara Beggs, daughter of a prominent Western District family, and bought a home in Canberra.

Little was heard about the Honourable Member for Wannon until he became Minister for the Army in 1966; but in the pages of Hansard he could be found at conscientious intervals speaking thoughtfully on economic matters and foreign affairs. He inveighed against the Soviet Union with as much conviction as any of his Liberal colleagues, but verged on heresy when it came to South Africa. During the debate about South Africa's decision to leave the British Commonwealth in 1961, Fraser was the only member of his party to condemn apartheid and pronounce good riddance on the new republic. He also displeased Menzies by espousing some of Casey's pro-American views, disagreed with Holt on immigration, and argued with Gorton about State rights. In due course he engineered the latter's downfall, and ultimately brought down two others who stood between himself and the Prime Ministership, Snedden and Whitlam.

As the journalist Peter Bowers remarked, Fraser was the most predatory figure in federal history—'a tiger in a bamboo forest, often hard to see but always hugely, hungrily present'. Tigers are not as a rule noted for ideology, but Fraser expounded a stern kind of philosophy that matched his ruthless political style and formidable physical presence. In his 1971 Alfred Deakin Lecture he echoed Arnold Toynbee's theory of challenge and response with the memorable assertion that life was not meant to be easy. '[Toynbee's] thesis', he said,

> can be . . . simply stated: That through history nations are confronted by a series of challenges and whether they survive or whether they fall to the wayside depends on the manner and character of their response . . . It involves a conclusion about the past that life has not been easy for people or for nations, and an assumption for the future that that condition will not alter. There is within me some part of the metaphysic, and thus I would add that life is not meant to be easy.

On another occasion, in 1972, he spoke respectfully of *Atlas Shrugged*, an American novel by Ayn Rand which had become something of a conservative cult. Ms Rand's book was an indictment of 'big government', and a celebration of rational selfishness. 'The basis of the argument', said Fraser, 'was that people with energy, the people who want to get on and want to work . . . are the people to be encouraged. In the book they ultimately go on strike because they are fed up with being milched by people who won't work'. Ayn Rand likened those reluctant strikers to an Atlas who disowns responsibility for the burden he has been bearing so thanklessly. One of her characters asks another:

If you saw Atlas, the giant who holds the world on his shoulders, if you saw that he stood, blood running down his chest, his knees buckling, his arms trembling but still trying to hold the world aloft with the last of his strength, and the greater his effort the heavier the world bore down upon his shoulders—what would you tell him to do?

'I don't know. What could he do? What would *you* tell him?'
'To shrug.'

There is a parallel to be drawn between Atlas, a Titan rich in flocks and herds at the western limit of the classical world, and Fraser, proud owner of merinos and herefords in the Western District. Fraser was built for a heavy load, but like the Rand version of Atlas he was not averse to stepping out of character. The next three parliaments would in fact show him to be a pragmatist who ignored his own rhetoric whenever he deemed it necessary, and shrugged off all complaints.

Sir John Kerr opened the thirtieth parliament on 17 February in an atmosphere of unprecedented bitterness. His Excellency was booed by several hundred Labor sympathisers as he entered Parliament House, his speech was boycotted by the Opposition, and at afternoon tea in the Senate garden neither Sir John nor the Leader of the Opposition acknowledged the other's presence. For the first time since federation there was no evening reception to mark the opening. In the Senate, where a South Australian flour miller, Senator Condor Laucke, was elected to the President's Chair, Sir Magnus Cormack likened the Opposition to a lot of chimpanzees. Senator J. L. Cavanagh (Lab, S) then defended the boycott as a legitimate response to the disruption of parliamentary democracy 'by the unconstitutional action of a person who calls himself a Kerr'.

Senator WITHERS.—I raise a point of order, Mr President. I ask under Standing Order 417 that the honourable member withdraw that remark.

The PRESIDENT.—Standing Order 417 precludes any disrespectful reference to His Excellency the Governor-General or to Her Majesty.

Senator CAVANAGH.—Apparently Government senators take exception to the word 'a'. I will address him as Mr Kerr . . . Contrary to the whole Constitution a government that was given a mandate to operate for 3 years was dismissed by an individual who came into this House today expecting us to pay homage to him. We find no credit in that, but Government senators cannot accept the fact that we should not have been there to pay homage and to condone the action that was taken on that occasion.

In the lower house Whitlam congratulated the new Speaker, his old opponent Snedden, but doubted Snedden's willingness and capacity to assert the rights of the House. 'After all', he said, 'you yourself abetted the first attempt by the Senate to usurp the rights of this House in April 1974. The attempt failed because you, unlike your successor, did not corral the complete conservative coalition of newspaper proprietors, Chief Justice and Governor-General'. The rage was maintained faithfully for months and years to come. Sir John was awarded the Grand Cross of St Michael and St

George by a Government which quickly restored the practice of recommending Australian citizens for imperial honours; but the public derision
and execration regularly visited upon His Excellency became a growing
embarrassment to himself, his family and the Government.

The Governor-General's opening speech foreshadowed the implementation of some Government policies, but said nothing of others: 'my Government', he said,

> believes that the Australian people have given it a strong directive to bring
> under control the highest unemployment for forty years and the worst
> prolonged inflation in the nation's history. The Government believes that
> excessive government intervention in the life of the nation is a major fac-
> tor in economic instability . . . The Government's long term objective is to
> prevent the growth of centralised bureaucratic domination in Australia,
> the increasing dependence of individuals on the state. It is to encourage
> the development of an Australia in which people have maximum freedom
> and independence to achieve their own goals in life, in ways which they
> decide.

There was to be a major direction of resources away from Government
towards individuals and private enterprise. An Administrative Review Committee would recommend ways to make the federal bureaucracy more econ-
omical and effective; reforms would be introduced to reverse the
concentration of power in the federal Government, and increase the autonomy of local and State Governments; the Budget deficit would be lowered;
and individuals would be protected, by means of tax indexation, against
massive unlegislated tax increases resulting from inflation.

There was no mention of wage indexation, the system introduced by
Whitlam's Government whereby the Arbitration Commission conducted a
national wage case hearing after each quarterly publication of the consumer
price index. Fraser had promised to retain wage indexation; but the latest
consumer price figures had shown an increase of 5.6 per cent, and on the
advice of John Stone, deputy secretary and later secretary of the Treasury,
Fraser decided in January that the Government should intervene in the wage
case and oppose a full flow-on of the increase. In extenuation of this reversal,
the Treasurer said that Fraser had promised only to 'support the wage
indexation agreement', which permitted any party to argue for less than full
indexation. As it turned out, the Arbitration Commission disregarded the
Government's submission and granted full indexation. Nevertheless a
promise seemed to have been broken.

There were other examples of the new Government's 'flexibility' or pragmatism. After having promised to abolish the Prices Justification Tribunal,
Fraser now sought to mollify the unions by leaving it intact; and after having
promised to maintain Medibank, he proceeded slowly but surely to dis-
mantle it. In a mini-Budget brought down by Lynch on 20 May, full tax
indexation was introduced immediately, instead of being phased in over a
period of three years as the Government had originally intended. Then, as
circumstances changed during the next few years, and to the disillusionment
of many taxpayers, it was phased out.

On 20 May the Government also introduced the Social Services Amendment Bill (No. 2), greatly increasing the rate of child endowment, which henceforth was to be called family allowance. In accordance with recommendations by Professor Ronald Henderson's Commission of Inquiry into Poverty, whose reports had been tabled in 1975 and early 1976, the weekly family allowance for a first child was to be increased from 50 cents to $3.50; second child, from $1 to $5; third and fourth children, $2 to $6; fifth and later children, $2.50 to $7. This measure, which had a quick passage through parliament, was one of the Fraser Government's most important social reforms. The new rates increased the annual cost of child endowment/family allowance from $235 million to $1020 million, and the increase was offset by abolition of taxation rebates for children and students.

Most of the inquiries left in action by Labor fared worse than Professor Henderson's commission. The Fraser Government disbanded fourteen of them, and imposed deadlines on twenty-six others. It resurrected the term 'Commonwealth Government' in place of Whitlam's 'Australian Government', dispensed with the diplomatic services of Vincent Gair in Dublin, disavowed Rex Connor's vision splendid, abolished the Social Welfare Commission and the Australian Housing Corporation, and transferred the Australian Assistance Plan to the States. Some members of the Government's Social Welfare Committee wanted the Assistance Plan retained, but most of them soon succumbed to Fraser's unremitting pressure. He invited them to dinner at The Lodge. 'At the cigar and cognac stage', wrote one member who did not change his mind, Don Chipp, 'the Prime Minister would nonchalantly suggest that the AAP was a socialist initiative, centralist in nature, and should be administered by the States. Only the brave or the stupid could resist such persuasion'.

The Government reduced expenditure on everything except defence—even going so far as to propose the abolition of a $40 funeral benefit for pensioners. This was more than some of its own backbenchers could take. In the lower house two Tasmanian Liberals—Bruce Goodluck (Franklin) and Michael Hodgman (Denison)—threatened to cross the floor. The gesture would have been futile, given the Government's overwhelming majority, and in any case they did not make it. But in the Senate, where crossing the floor was not a waste of time, six Liberals—Senators Missen (V), Wood (Q) Bonner (Q), Jessop (S), Rae (T) and Townley (T)—threatened to help the Opposition delete the relevant section of the Social Services Amendment.

Faced with such a revolt, Atlas shrugged. While the Minister for Social Services, Margaret Guilfoyle, was earnestly assuring her fellow senators that the bill would have to be passed intact or not at all, she was embarrassed to learn that the Government had backed down. How piquant it was to see the biter bit! 'The irony has to be savoured,' said the Melbourne *Age*.

It is unkind to scratch fresh wounds, but it is perhaps fitting that Malcolm Fraser's Government should have suffered its first major defeat at the hands of some of its supporters in the Senate. The man who became Prime Minister through a misuse of Senate power has now been forced into an embarrassing retreat as a result of a proper use of Senate power.

The *Canberra Times* predicted that 'the successful assertion by the Senate of its independence as a house of review will give heart to Government backbenchers who were beginning to resent the overwhelming ascendancy of the Cabinet'.

After parliament's autumn sitting the Prime Minister visited China, and then the United States, where he exchanged felicities with President Ford and Ayn Rand. Although Fraser had said during the election campaign that he would not be a tourist Prime Minister, his travels were in fact more than a match for those of his wide-roving predecessor. Sometimes it seemed as though Atlas was indeed shouldering the cares of the world, and not merely those of the antipodes.

It was Fraser rather than his Foreign Minister who delivered the Government's first ministerial statement of foreign policy, the main theme of which was the threat posed to world peace by the Soviet Union. In the ensuing debate on 1 June Whitlam wondered why the statement had not been delivered by Andrew Peacock, and asked: 'Was its mixture of cold war rhetoric and apocalyptic doom-saying, all this rattling of antique sabres and blowing of rusty bugles . . . too much for the trendy pretensions and superficial urbanities of the Foreign Minister?' The Government reversed Labor's recognition of Soviet rule in Latvia, Lithuania and Estonia; abandoned Labor's support for a zone of peace and neutrality in the Indian Ocean; and encouraged the American presence on Diego Garcia in order to maintain a naval balance with the Soviet Union in the Indian Ocean. On certain international issues, however, Fraser's attitude was not antique or rusty. He assisted at the birth of Zimbabwe, under Marxist auspices; he supported the black African struggle against apartheid; and in the continuing North–South dialogue about international economic issues he sided with the southern underdogs. No one quite understood why the grim apostle of challenge and response should hold these sympathies, but hold them he did.

The Budget brought down by Lynch on 17 August concerned itself mainly with the fight against inflation. Much of its effect in that regard was undone, however, by Cabinet's decision three months later to devalue the Australian dollar by 17.5 per cent, in spite of contrary advice from Treasury. Fraser was not one to be over-awed by Treasury even when its advice proved to be sound. Before the end of the year he had divided it into two departments—Treasury and Finance—thus diversifying the sources of economic advice, and strengthening the position of his own department. That strength was further augmented in the following year by the establishment of the Office of National Assessment, an agency responsible to the Department of Prime Minister and Cabinet, and providing it with intelligence analysis and advice on foreign affairs.

Although the Fraser Government dismantled some of Labor's proudest achievements, it left much intact, and parliament carried to completion certain measures which had been set in train by the previous government. Examples of this during the 1976 Budget session were the Aboriginal Land Rights (Northern Territory) Bill and the Ombudsman Bill. Labor had appointed an Aboriginal Land Rights Commissioner, Mr Justice A. E.

Woodward, to report on appropriate means of satisfying the 'reasonable aspirations' of Aborigines in relation to land rights, but it was left to the Fraser Government to implement some of his recommendations.

The Ombudsman Bill closely resembled a Labor measure which had foundered in the Senate. Like the Administrative Appeals Tribunal Act, which had been passed in 1975, this Bill had its origin in the 1971 report of the Commonwealth Administrative Review Committee, chaired by Mr Justice Kerr before his viceregal accession. Its purpose was to establish an office of Commonwealth Ombudsman, empowered to investigate grievances by members of the public about administrative actions by officials of Commonwealth departments, statutory authorities and other government agencies. The office of Ombudsman, established in 1977, complemented an Administrative Appeals Tribunal which, since July 1976, had been dealing with appeals against administrative decisions and actions under Acts and ordinances providing for such appeals.

Thus the executive was not having everything its own way. In 1976 the Government also implemented a proposal for a House of Representatives Standing Committee on Expenditure. This proposal, emanating from the Prime Minister himself, seemed at odds with the executive's usual attitude to parliamentary scrutiny. In fact, however, it was a pre-emptive concession designed to forestall a comprehensive committee system which a Joint Committee on the Parliamentary Committee System was about to recommend. The House of Representatives had lagged behind the Senate in this regard, partly because of the inherent distaste of governments for parliamentary scrutiny, and also because of the Senate's changing character. As the Senate had become more independent, so governments had tightened their control of the lower house.

In 1973 the House had been allowed to establish a Standing Committee on Aboriginal Affairs and another on Environment and Conservation. But Fraser did not want to go far along that path. By taking the initiative he was able to pigeonhole the joint committee's report for the time being, and to restrict the expenditure committee's terms of reference. Its main term of reference was to examine the cost-effective implementation of government policies, not the policies themselves. 'This coincided', wrote one observer of the parliamentary committee system, 'with the understandably minimalist view of the role of parliament adopted by the Fraser government—to legitimise the policies of the executive, not to determine them'.

On the night of 30 November parliament debated the first report of the Fox Commission, which Labor had appointed in 1975 to inquire into the environmental aspects of uranium mining in the Northern Territory. Rarely had there been a more futile debate, for the Government had already announced its intention to honour existing contracts for the export of uranium from Mary Kathleen mine. Labor Caucus had also given its blessing to that, although the party's National Executive had recommended a moratorium on all uranium mining. During the brief and poorly attended parliamentary debate the Liberal Member for Hotham (V), Don Chipp, moved an amendment to the motion under discussion, expressing the House's opinion that there should be a two-year moratorium on the mining and exporting of uranium, to allow sufficient time for public debate and further research into the risks involved.

> If this means voting against the Government and against my Party, so be it [said Chipp]. I say this after having read the Fox report thoroughly on at least 4 occasions. The question posed to me is: Should Australia mine and mill its uranium deposits? I believe that this is the most important subject discussed in this Parliament since the Vietnam war.
>
> Mr Justice Fox says that it is one of the most important things discussed by this Parliament. As I speak, Mr Deputy Speaker, Mr Speaker is not in the Chair, the Prime Minister is not in the House, the Leader of the Opposition is not in the House, Cabinet is meeting, only two ministers are in the House and since this debate began . . . the attendance of members of Parliament in the chamber has ranged from eleven to nineteen. Indeed there are only 5 representatives of the Press in the Press Gallery. Not for the first time, my judgment of what is an important issue facing Australia is wrong.

Chipp did not have to vote against his party, because the debate was adjourned after only two hours and the motion he sought to amend lapsed with all other business when parliament was prorogued three months later, so that the Queen might open a second session. But Chipp did more than vote against the Liberal Party; he resigned from it. Donald Leslie Chipp was a former management consultant who had taken a major part in organising the Melbourne Olympic Games. He had been in parliament for sixteen years and had served capably as Minister for the Navy, Minister for Customs and Excise, Deputy Leader of the House, and briefly in 1972 as Leader of the House. Fraser gave him three portfolios in the six-week-long interim ministry, then left him out of the second ministry altogether. The Prime Minister had not forgiven Peacock and Chipp for their loyalty to Snedden. He could not vent this feeling on a colleague as influential as Peacock, but he could and did penalise Chipp. This was a mistake, for Don Chipp—whose deeply-carved features and emotional temperament were probably inherited from an Italian great-grandmother—was not a suitable subject for chastisement. He stored up grievances, and the uranium debate was his last straw.

On 24 March 1977 Chipp announced his resignation in the House, criticising the Government on several counts: its policy of industrial confrontation, particularly the Prime Minister's determination to replace the Arbitration Inspectorate with a stronger Industrial Relations Bureau, which was already being condemned as needlessly provocative by employees and employers alike; its breach of promises to continue the Australian Assistance Plan and wage indexation; failure to allow a full debate on uranium mining; and passive acceptance of the subjugation of Portuguese Timor, which Indonesia had invaded in December 1975, when Australia was preoccupied with other matters. He then embarked on a nationwide speaking tour which led to the formation of a new centre party—the Australian Democrats, incorporating the Australia Party and the Liberal Movement, both of which had fared badly in the elections of 1974 and 1975. The party's national president was a Victorian industrialist, John Siddons, formerly national convenor of the Australia Party; but the real driving force was Chipp. He declared himself deeply concerned about the failure of parliament to be anything more than a rubber stamp, and said that the new party would direct its ambitions toward the Senate.

Even without a third party, the Senate had been causing the Government trouble enough. Early in the autumn sitting of 1977 four Tasmanian Liberals had joined forces with Labor and the Independent Senator Harradine, who was also a Tasmanian, to defeat a measure dealing with stabilisation payments for apples and pears, a measure which the Tasmanians regarded as insufficiently helpful to the Apple Isle. Next the Senate balked at part of the Government's 'New Federalism' policy, which was being held out to the States as the best way to increase their autonomy and responsibility. The first proposed stage was to guarantee the States a fixed percentage of Commonwealth tax receipts, and in this connection the federal Government introduced legislation empowering the Grants Commission to recommend a new formula for distribution of funds to the States. To the smaller States it seemed that using the Grants Commission for such a purpose as this would compromise their chances of making a case later for further grants, as they would in effect by appealing from Caesar to Caesar. When several Liberal senators threatened to cross the floor on this issue, Fraser shrugged his shoulders and held the matter over until the next Premiers' Conference. The second proposed stage of 'New Federalism', in accordance with the Liberal principle that governments ought to raise the money they spend, was to give back some of the income-taxing power which the States had lost through the advent of uniform taxation in 1942. The States did not like the sound of that at all. New South Wales and South Australia threatened to challenge any legislation which might force them to tax income, and this matter too was held over for discussion with the Premiers.

'New federalism' did not have much effect on the balance of power between Commonwealth and States. As one commentator wrote, the Whitlam Government had produced a comparatively minor anti-federal shift away from the regions towards the centre; Fraser, on the other hand, 'produced a movement back along the spectrum towards the regions, but again not very far'. The Fraser Government reduced the quantum of conditional grants to the States by way of Section 96, but did not increase unconditional grants by the same proportion. It gave the States the right to impose their own income tax surcharge; but the State governments, fearing their opponents would condemn any such move as double taxation, shied well away from it.

An Advisory Council for Inter-Governmental Relations was established in 1977, with a secretariat in Hobart. This body, consisting of five federal parliamentarians, one member from each of the State parliaments, one from the Northern Territory and one local government representative from each State, met three times a year until 1986, when it was deemed not to be earning its keep and was disbanded. Perhaps the Fraser Government's most significant federal action was its transfer of the Commonwealth's hard-won powers over the territorial sea and offshore resources. Although the High Court had upheld these powers, the Commonwealth voluntarily returned them to the States in October 1977. This was either magnanimity or surrender, depending on one's point of view; but, either way, it did not greatly alter the concentration of power at the centre.

A third conflict between Senate and Government during the autumn sitting concerned a package of four Constitution Alteration Bills emanating from deliberations by the Constitutional Convention in Hobart, Sydney and Melbourne. The first Bill provided for simultaneous elections of the Senate and House of Representatives, a proposal which had been rejected at referendum by all States except New South Wales in 1974. The second Bill sought to ensure that a casual vacancy in the Senate was filled by a person of the same political party as the former incumbent—in other words, that there should be no more Senator Buntons. The third sought to allow electors in Territories to vote at referendums on proposed laws to alter the Constitution, and the fourth sought to provide a maximum retiring age of seventy for justices of the High Court and any other court created by parliament.

There was no opposition to any of these Bills in the lower house. In the Senate, however, three of them were opposed by a few non-Labor senators—the first by a minority of ten, the second by eight, and the fourth by two. Some of the dissenters also campaigned against the Bills in their home States. At a referendum held on 21 May 1977 three of the proposals were carried, but the Simultaneous Elections Bill, although it received a clear majority of the national vote, failed to pass because it was rejected in Queensland, Western Australia and Tasmania.

The Budget sitting of 1977 was notable for debates on uranium and Timor, neither of which had any discernible effect upon the course of Government action, or rather, in the latter case, inaction; a rushed passage through parliament for the Commonwealth Employees (Employment Provisions) Act, giving ministers discretion to stand down public servants who, although not themselves on strike, were prevented from working by the industrial action of others; and another amendment of the Conciliation and Arbitration Act to further strengthen the Industrial Relations Bureau, which the Opposition now described as 'an enormous police force, which will be there to impose a whole array of pains and penalties upon the unions'. The C.E.E.P. Act was not proclaimed until 1979, during a strike by employees of the Australian Telecommunications Commission. As its critics had predicted, it merely worsened the Government's relations with public service unions. The Act was repealed after the next change of government, the Industrial Relations Bureau was abolished, and the Arbitration Inspectorate was re-established.

During the 1977 Budget sitting two of Fraser's most senior ministers left Cabinet in dramatic circumstances. On 6 September Robert Ellicott informed the House that he had resigned as Attorney-General in protest at Cabinet's decision to put an end to certain protracted legal proceedings known as the Sankey case. In 1976 a Sydney solicitor named Danny Sankey had brought a private action against Gough Whitlam and three of his former ministers—Mr Justice Murphy, Cairns and Connor—charging them with having conspired in the 1974–75 Loans Affair to effect an unlawful purpose. Sankey's lawyers had now asked the Government to take over his proceedings. Cabinet, presumably of the view that there was no political advantage to be gained in pursuing the matter further, and perhaps also feeling that use of the criminal law against political opponents was a dangerous precedent for any government to establish, decided that Ellicott should take over the proceedings and terminate them.

Ellicott maintained, however, that as first law officer of the Crown he alone should decide what action to take. 'I regarded Cabinet as preventing me from exercising my duty', he said.

> I had an application to take over the proceedings. I needed to know all the evidence. I regarded Cabinet as trying to control me in the exercise of my discretion by suggesting that there was only one option—termination of the proceedings. I have to say with great regret that I regard Cabinet as having acted wrongly on that occasion. I do not believe that Cabinet should prevent the Law Officer from investigating any criminal matter. This is a criminal matter. There are politicans involved; in that sense one can say that it is political. But the fact is that these are committal proceedings before a court. It is a criminal matter and I believe that a basic principle is involved.

Another factor in Ellicott's resignation was probably his certainty, first proclaimed in the sound and fury of 1975, that there was a prima-facie case. As Whitlam said in the House, the matter had become an obsession with Ellicott. 'I believe that the whole core of this matter', said Whitlam, 'is that the former Attorney-General has had an obsession about it extending over more than two years. He has taken an excessively vain attitude about his legal opinions'. In spite of Cabinet's efforts to end the case as soon as possible, it dragged on for another three years in the Queanbeyan magistrate's court, the Supreme Court of New South Wales and the High Court, the last of which ruled against the notion that absolute Crown privilege protects federal Cabinet papers from being produced in judicial proceedings. The case eventually concluded in August 1980 when the magistrate held that on the evidence, and having regard to the High Court decision on preliminary legal points, there was no prima-facie case to answer.

The second resignation from Cabinet was that of the Treasurer. It had become known that Lynch, and incidentally the Prime Minister and Deputy Prime Minister too, were using family trusts to minimise their tax obligations. Neither Fraser nor Anthony regarded this as anything more than a minor political embarrassment, though an inconvenient one, given the imminence of another election. But the Treasurer's position was complicated by other factors. He was known to have made windfall profits from land speculation, and among his business associates were some who had been involved in a Victorian land scandal.

With the Lynch affair threatening to affect the election, Fraser demanded his resignation. Lynch, who was in hospital for a kidney stone operation, reluctantly complied on 19 November. 'I have at no time withheld from you the nature of my pecuniary interests', he told Fraser in his letter of resignation, 'and it has at all times been open to you to seek further information from me, or to let me know that my statement of affairs was not consistent, in your view, with my ministerial responsibilities'. The Prime Minister was unmoved, and too busy even to visit his deputy party leader in hospital. The

Minister of State for Special Trade Negotiations, John Howard, was appointed Treasurer.

On the Opposition side, Whitlam had barely managed to retain his party leadership. Early in the first session his position was jeopardised by bizarre allegations that he had been involved, together with the party's national secretary, David Combe, and a left-wing Victorian member of the National Executive, Bill Hartley, in an attempt to obtain $500 000 from the Government of Iraq to help cover Labor's recent election campaign costs. After careful inquiry, the National Executive strongly censured Whitlam for his part in this affair. At the Caucus meeting which considered the National Executive's report, Whitlam was retained as leader; but one shadow minister, Kim Beazley, resigned from his position on the Opposition front bench in protest at the leader's conduct. Beazley's place was taken by Hayden, who became spokesman on defence. In May 1977 Hayden challenged Whitlam for the leadership which he had declined to accept immediately after the 1975 election. Whitlam survived, but only by 32 votes to 30—that is, effectively by his own vote and the vote of his son, A. P. (Tony) Whitlam, who had been elected for Fred Daly's former seat, Grayndler.

The other main protagonist of 1975, Sir John Kerr, was soon to leave office prematurely and be succeeded by a constitutional lawyer, the former Vice-Chancellor of Queensland University, Sir Zelman Cowen. Before departing, however, Sir John acceded to the Prime Minister's request for an early dissolution. This showed a distinct change of mind on Sir John's part, for in a speech delivered to the Indian Law Institute in 1975 he had said:

> It is, of course, not sufficient for [a prime minister] to seek a dissolution of parliament simply because he would like to have an election long before it is due. The essential question is whether the Governor-General can be satisfied that parliament has, in fact, become unworkable. The country should not be forced to an early election merely to help leaders solve internal party questions but only when it is necessary to deal with a situation which parliament itself cannot solve.

The thirtieth parliament was perfectly workable, and still had a year to run. Fraser's only justification for going early, and for guillotining nineteen bills through the Senate in four hours to clear the decks in time, was that an election for the lower house could thus be held at the same time as one for half the Senate. Other less presentable but more relevant considerations were the perceived advantages for the Government in going to the polls before Hayden replaced Whitlam, before the next quarterly consumer price index, and before the employment figures deteriorated further. At the general election on 10 December the coalition was returned with a reduced but still massive majority of forty-eight in the lower house, and a majority of nine in the Senate, provided no one crossed the floor. From 1 July the Senate would consist of twenty-nine Liberals, six Nationals, twenty-six Labor, two Democrats, and one Independent. The successful Democrats were Don Chipp (V) and an author and journalist named Colin Mason (N). Another member of the new party, Janine Haines, had been chosen by the South Australian parliament in December to fill a casual vacancy created by the resignation of Steele Hall. Her term expired before Chipp and Mason took their seats, but she was to be returned to the Senate by popular vote three years later.

Soon after the election a report on Phillip Lynch's financial affairs revealed nothing illegal or improper. He returned to Cabinet as Minister for Industry and Commerce, and easily survived a challenge by Killen for the Deputy Leadership of the parliamentary Liberal Party. Ellicott became Minister for Home Affairs and Capital Territory, but was no longer a member of Cabinet. In Caucus, Bill Hayden defeated Lionel Bowen (Kingsford Smith, N) for the leadership, by 36 votes to 28, and Bowen defeated Tom Uren, Mick Young (Port Adelaide, S) and Ralph Willis (Gellibrand, V) for the Deputy Leadership.

Whitlam became a backbencher for the few months remaining before he resigned from the House in which he had served for more than a quarter of a century. Like Eddie Ward he seemed to go out in a storm of interrogation, placing 581 questions on the notice paper of the new parliament, about everything from whaling and uranium to trachoma and the Kurile Islands. He also spread his adieux widely, making official parliamentary visits to Andorra, Argentina, Belgium, Brazil, Chile, China, France, Hong Kong, Indonesia, Japan, New Caledonia, the New Hebrides, Poland, Spain, Switzerland, Thailand, Turkey, the United Kingdom, the U.S.S.R. and Vietnam. As it happened, Whitlam's last few weeks as a member of parliament coincided with the death and funeral of his only parliamentary peer, Sir Robert Menzies. Whitlam was absent from Australia when the traditional condolence debate was held on 23 May, but fifteen other members paid tribute to the Lord Warden of Australia. Fraser mentioned every aspect of his career except the parliamentary one, but the Leader of the Opposition placed proper emphasis on Menzies's 'clear, consistent and impressive devotion to the parliamentary institution'. The Honourable Member for Mallee, Peter Fisher (NC), also recorded the fact that councillors and staff of Dimboola Shire had observed one minute's silence at the Menzies Memorial in Jeparit, a steel spire surmounted by a purple thistle.

There were no farewell speeches for Whitlam before parliament went into the winter recess during which he resigned his seat. But on the first adjournment of the next sitting Barry Jones (Lab, Lalor, V) delivered a formal valediction with proper affection and respect. 'Gough Whitlam', he said, 'was, by universal consent, the greatest member of the present Parliament—the largest in spirit, the loftiest in aspiration, the greatest orator and the member with the widest and deepest range of interests . . . His judgment was not infallible. Nevertheless, in a political Lilliput he was our Gulliver'.

High Court

The thirty-first parliament, which ran its full course for a change, from 1978 to 1980, was notable particularly for legislation concerning the third arm of government, the judiciary. In 1979 parliament enacted the most important changes made to the High Court since its establishment in the third year of federation; and in 1980 the Court moved into a building of its own in Canberra. Under the Judiciary Act of 1903, the principal seat of the High

Court was required to be at the seat of government—and so it had been, in Melbourne, until the legislature and executive moved to Canberra in 1927. For the next four decades the Court held hearings in all State capitals, though most frequently in Melbourne and Sydney. In 1968 the Gorton Government decided that the Court should have a permanent home in the national capital, and in 1970 it chose the site for such a home in the north-eastern corner of the parliamentary triangle, between the Administrative Building and Lake Burley Griffin.

Although the National Capital Development Commission originally envisaged 'a very small building', perhaps not much larger than the Court's modest *pieds-à-terre* in Melbourne and Sydney, that idea was quickly dispelled by the Chief Justice. Sir Garfield Barwick wanted a building that would symbolically express the judiciary's independence and unique relationship to the legislature. An architectural competition was held in 1972–73, and construction of the winning design—by the Australian firm Edwards, Madigan, Torzillo and Briggs—began two years later.

The building was to be a massive pile of concrete and glass, no less conspicuous than the provisional Parliament House, and separated from it by a few hundred yards of lawn and trees. Sir Garfield tried to have the concrete covered with a paste of crushed white marble, so that it would match or even outshine the walls of Parliament House; but Whitlam would not hear of that. The building was to be approached by way of a long ceremonial ramp, flanked by a parallel waterfall. Inside its southern façade there would be a lofty public hall with concrete pillars 24 metres high and another ramp ascending to two of the buildings' three elegant courtrooms. For reasons best known to Sir Garfield, an enormous British coat of arms was etched on to the northern façade, so that seemingly Mt Ainslie was guarded by a ghostly lion and unicorn. Whitlam had laughed this out of court, but the determined Chief Justice later talked Fraser into it.

Although Sir Garfield achieved more or less the kind of home he wanted for the Court, he was thwarted in other ways. He failed in a rather high-handed attempt to take over the National Trust homestead, Lanyon, as a Yarralumla-style residence for the Chief Justice; and the High Court legislation passed by parliament in 1979 was not entirely to his liking. The High Court of Australia Act made provision for the Court, rather than government departments, to be responsible for its building, staff and finances, the latter being provided by parliament in accordance with a budget proposed by the Court. Although Court administration was not formally incorporated, the justices now for the first time took collective responsibility for their own affairs. This had the effect of reducing the Chief Justice's administrative power, for his voice was only one of seven. The Act also made provision for the Court to hold sittings anywhere in Australia and the external Territories, as it saw fit. Barwick wanted the Court's registries closed in the States, and hearings to be held only in Canberra. His learned brethren argued strongly to the contrary, and the upshot was that the Court continued to hold hearings in all capital cities except Sydney and Melbourne.

Another measure, the Evidence Amendment Act, affirmed parliament's right to disallow Rules of Court made by the High Court. This amendment resulted from a view expressed by the Senate Standing Committee on Constitutional and Legal Affairs, that the relevant wording of the Evidence Act left parliament's power open to doubt.

The High Court building was formally opened by the Queen on 26 May 1980, in the presence of a large judicial and parliamentary assembly. In the course of his speech, Sir Garfield drew Her Majesty's attention to the huge painting by Tom Roberts, transferred from Parliament House and now hanging in the new public hall, depicting the opening of the first Australian parliament by her grandfather, when he had been Duke of York. Sir Garfield then referred to some of the changes which had taken place recently in the relationship between parliament and the High Court on the one hand, and lion and unicorn on the other. 'From the inception', he said,

> the Court had, and has been grateful for, the assistance of the learning, wisdom and experience of their Lordships of the Privy Council except in cases involving the distribution of power between the elements of the federation. In those cases, to use the language of the Constitution, cases involving questions *inter se* of the constitutional power of those elements, the Court's decision is by the Constitution made final unless the Court certifies the case to be one proper for decision by the [Privy Council]. In practice, with but one exception, such cases have been finally decided by the Court itself.

Access to all that learning, wisdom and experience in London had been curtailed considerably by two Acts of the Australian parliament—the Privy Council (Limitation of Appeals) Act, and the Privy Council (Appeals from the High Court) Act. Since the passing of these measures in 1968 and 1975 respectively, no appeal could be brought from the High Court to the Privy Council in any case except one involving an *inter se* question which the High Court certified as being proper for decision in Downing Street. Although appeals of purely State concern could still be taken direct from certain State courts to the Privy Council, a decision by the High Court bound all other Australian courts in point of precedent. 'The [High] Court has thus become the final court of appeal in Australia in all matters', said Sir Garfield. 'Apart from the possibility of appeals to the [Privy Council] from State courts in matters of exclusively State concern, the Court is at the apex of the judicial systems of Australia, that of the Commonwealth and those of the several States as well.' (The very few remaining formal constitutional and legal links between Australia and the United Kingdom were all to be removed five years later by the Australia Act. These included appeals to the Privy Council from State supreme courts, the Queen's power to disallow State acts, and the power of the United Kingdom parliament to legislate for Australia.)

Only a month before the opening of the new building, Sir Garfield had been embroiled in one of the very few controversies ever occasioned by the conduct of a High Court judge. Some felt that he was unfairly impugned, and indeed he emerged unscathed from what became known as the Mundroola affair. Others rightly discerned in this affair a new and healthier public attitude towards the High Court. To an earlier generation the idea of impropriety, partiality or even political bias by knights of the realm in full-bottomed wigs had been almost inconceivable. By 1980, thanks not least to Sir Garfield's participation in the constitutional crisis of 1975, judges were no longer above suspicion and could be called to account.

On 26 April 1980 the Melbourne *Age* published an article alleging that the Chief Justice, without declaring an interest, had heard cases involving corporations—Ampol, Brambles and Colonial Sugar, to be precise—in which shares were held by a Barwick family company, Mundroola Pty Ltd. The Opposition had been aware of this matter for several weeks, and at the next sitting of parliament, on 28 April, Senator Gareth Evans (Lab, V) gave notice that on the following day he would move a lengthy motion about it. His motion began by taking note of one of the findings of a recent Committee of Inquiry on Public Duty and Private Interest: 'It is now accepted that Judges should not engage in business or in any way be associated with business institutions, for example as director, trustee or adviser'. This committee, chaired by the Chief Judge of the Federal Court of Australia, Sir Nigel Bowen, had been appointed in the wake of Phillip Lynch's resignation over matters of private interest, and its report had been tabled late in 1979.

Starting from that assumption, Senator Evans's motion invited the Senate to resolve that a joint select committee of parliament be appointed to inquire into and report on 'the hearing and adjudication by the Chief Justice of matters involving companies . . . in which Mundroola Pty Ltd held shares'; 'the extent to which the Chief Justice heard and adjudicated matters involving questions of law in taxation, real property, company law and other areas of relevance . . . to the conduct of business activities by Mundroola Pty Ltd'; 'whether in all the circumstances public confidence in the administration of justice has been imperilled by the Chief Justice'; and if so, what action parliament should take by way of censure, or by proceedings under Section 72 of the Constitution, the section providing for an address by both houses to the Governor-General asking for the removal of a High Court judge on the ground of 'proved misbehaviour or incapacity'.

Next day the Prime Minister beat the Opposition to the draw by incorporating in Hansard a letter of explanation from the Chief Justice. Mundroola, Sir Garfield said, had been established many years before to benefit his two children, who had always been the sole proprietors of its shares and assets. He himself had never derived any income, or personal advantage in taxation, from the company; he had ceased to be one of its directors in 1974; and was 'certainly quite sure that no decision of [his had] been in the least influenced by the fact that Mundroola Pty Ltd had any shares in companies in litigation before the Court'. The Prime Minister went further by saying that four of the six cases in question had gone against the companies concerned on votes by the Chief Justice and other Justices, and that none of the six decisions had turned on the views of the Chief Justice alone. 'There is no case in anything that has been presented, said Fraser in conclusion, 'for the establishment of a joint parliamentary committee, a parliamentary inquiry or any other inquiry'.

Senator Evans moved his motion half an hour later. Without definitely imputing conflict of interest, he canvassed several grounds for thinking that there might be 'a possiblility of something less than impartiality' on Sir

Garfield's part. 'It might be thought', he said, 'that the standards I am suggesting are unreasonably high and not such that lesser mortals could reasonably be expected to attain. But the fact remains that the standards we require of our judiciary are higher than might be reasonable to require of anyone else'. He then quoted from a speech by Sir Winston Churchill in the House of Commons:

> A form of life and conduct far more severe and restricted than that of ordinary people is required from judges and, though unwritten, has been most strictly observed . . . The judges have to maintain, though free from criticism [in Parliament], a far more rigorous standard than is required from any other class that I know of in this Realm.

Not even by calling such testimony as that did Senator Evans persuade a single Government senator to cross the floor on this matter. The motion was defeated by 32 votes to 22, with the two Democrats supporting the coalition and the Chief Justice. Little more was heard about Mundroola, and in any case Sir Garfield Barwick's judicial career was almost over. He retired on 31 January 1981, after having served as Chief Justice for sixteen years and nine months—slightly longer than either of the two other contenders for that distinction, Latham and Griffith. During that time he had cemented into permanent place the 'keystone of the federal arch', as Deakin called the High Court; encouraged the tax avoidance industry by judicial decision; and, more constructively, presided over a continuing tendency of High Court judgments to enlarge Commonwealth power at the expense of the States.

On Sir Garfield's last day in office, the Court handed down judgment in the so-called DOGS (Defence of Government Schools) case, a challenge launched eight years previously against Commonwealth aid to church schools. This was the first time the High Court had dealt with Section 116 of the Constitution, which forbids the Commonwealth to make any law for 'establishing any religion'. Barwick and five other justices, with Murphy dissenting, held that a law providing for financial aid to the educational activities of church schools was not a law for establishing a religion, even though its operation might indirectly assist the practice of religion; and all seven justices agreed that a statute granting money to a State was a valid exercise of Commonwealth power under Section 96, notwithstanding that the statute required the State to apply the money for a particular purpose or pay it to a particular recipient. Both the Fraser Government and the Opposition had promised a referendum if the Court had ruled against state aid, but now that controversy was virtually over.

Two other examples of judicial enlargement of Commonwealth power during Fraser's term of office were *Murphyores Inc Pty Ltd* v. *Commonwealth of Australia* (1976) and *Koowarta* v. *Bjelke-Petersen* (1982). In the first of these the Court upheld the Commonwealth's power to prohibit the export of minerals obtained from sands on Fraser Island, a surpassingly beautiful part of the national heritage which was in danger of being despoiled by sand mining. In Koowarta's case, an Aborigine named John Koowarta had brought an action in the Supreme Court of Queensland for damages against the Queensland Government because of its refusal to transfer the lease of a pastoral property to members of his tribal community. He submitted that this refusal, based as it was on a State government policy of preventing Aborigines from acquiring large isolated areas of land, was a breach of the Racial Discrimination Act, which had been introduced in parliament by Senator Murphy before his appointment to the bench. The Queensland government demurred, and brought an action against the Commonwealth in the High Court seeking a declaration that the Racial Discrimination Act was invalid. The new Chief Justice and five other justices, with Murphy dissenting, held that the relevant sections of the Act were not valid laws under Section 51 (xxvi), which gives parliament power to make laws with respect to 'the people of any race for whom it is deemed necessary to make special laws'. But it also held by four votes to three, and thus found for Koowarta, that because the Act gave effect to the International Convention on the Elimination of all Forms of Racial Discrimination, to which Australia is a party, it was a valid exercise of parliament's constitutional power to make laws with respect to external affairs. On that point Murphy was in the majority, and the new Chief Justice voted with the minority.

The new Chief Justice was Sir Harry Gibbs, a former Justice of the Supreme Court of Queensland who had been appointed to the High Court in 1970. Fraser had favoured Barwick's cousin, the former Attorney-General Ellicott, but Ellicott's candidature was tarnished by the prominent part he had played in the crisis of 1975. Most of the States preferred the equally conservative but relatively non-political Queenslander, and under Sir Harry's tactful leadership the Court became a more harmonious institution than it had been under Barwick.

If the High Court had stolen a march on parliament architecturally, it was not to enjoy that superiority for long. Only a few days after the official opening, the Government announced details of the design for a new and permanent Parliament House which would not only dwarf every other building in the country but outdo most of them architecturally as well. In 1974 parliament had at last chosen the site for its permanent home—not beside the lake, a site fancied by some members for its evocation of Westminister beside the Thames; nor on Camp Hill, the rise immediately behind the provisional building; but on the still higher ground behind that rise, Capital Hill. This choice was given legislative form by means of a private member's bill, the Parliament Bill (No 2), initiated by the Labor member for Burke (V), Keith Johnson.

A Joint Standing Committee on the New and Permanent Parliament House was established in 1975 to act as client in all matters of planning, design and construction. In May 1977, coinciding with the fiftieth anniversary of the opening of the provisional building, the Joint Committee presented parliament with a report recommending unanimously that a permanent building be constructed and occupied by 26 January 1988, the two hundredth anniversary of European settlement in Australia. The Prime Minister and Treasurer considered the proposal too costly in existing economic and political circumstances. Cabinet was evenly divided for and against a new building, but the Government's backbenchers voted overwhelmingly in favour of it. So did the Opposition. Fraser acquiesced in the face of such bipartisan enthusiasm, and in November 1978 the Government announced that funds would be made available to implement the Joint Committee's proposal. In 1979 the Parliament House Construction Authority, established to control design and construction in association with the National Capital Development Commission, held an international design competition for a building to cost approximately $151 million at current prices. The winning design, which the assessors regarded as being far superior to all others, was submitted by the New York firm of Mitchell/ Giurgola in partnership with an Australian-born architect, Richard Thorp.

The permanent Parliament House, designed principally by the distinguished Italian-American architect Romaldo Giurgola, was to be a concrete massif partly covered by the excavated and restored crest of Capital Hill. The effect was intended to be both natural and monumental. 'Our concept of the building', said the architects' submission,

> is not as a monumental structure imposed on the landscape, but rather one which is closer in spirit to the Greek monumentalisation of the acropolis, in which there is a continuity from the most minute elements of the architectural order to the massive forms of the building itself, yet all of which is congruent with the landscape.

Standing on Burley Griffin's north–south land axis, the building would face directly across the provisional Parliament House and the lake to the War Memorial and Mt Ainslie. A central zone containing forecourt, veranda, foyer halls, Cabinet room, Cabinet committee rooms, the Prime Minister's office and ministerial suites would be circumscribed by two boomerang-shaped walls facing outwards, and within these concavities would stand the legislative chambers, Senate on the western side and House of Representatives on the east. Resolutions authorising the preparation of detailed designs and specifications were passed by parliament during the Budget sitting of 1980, and site preparation began in January 1981.

The thirty-first parliament was notable also for a permanent tightening of security precautions in the provisional Parliament House, and for some tentative essays at procedural reform in the House of Representatives. Only eight days before the new Governor-General opened the parliament on 21 February 1978, most of the innocence still left to Australia had gone up in smoke outside Sydney's Hilton Hotel, where the first Commonwealth Heads of Government Regional Meeting was being held. A very powerful bomb had exploded in George Street, killing three men and confirming previous Croatian evidence that Australia was as vulnerable to terrorism as any other part of the world. As a result of this, security for the opening of parliament was tightened to an unprecedented extent by the deployment of troops in and around Parliament House. On 2 March the Speaker announced plans to control entry into the building and its non-public areas by means of a pass system, and to check all incoming baggage. People entering the public galleries of the chambers would also have to pass through detection equipment, and internal and external surveillance of the building would be increased.

As for procedural reform, it will be remembered that Fraser pre-empted the 1976 report of the Joint Committee on the Parliamentary Committee System by establishing a Standing Committee on Expenditure. In June 1978, however, the Government initiated a change in Standing Orders, as recommended by the Joint Committee, so that bills could be referred to legislation committees for scrutiny after the second reading stage in the House of Representatives. These committees, consisting of between thirteen and nineteen members nominated by the parties in proportion to their numerical strength, were to be formed on an *ad hoc* basis to deal with particular bills. By the end of 1978 seven bills, including the Great Barrier Reef Marine Park Bill, had been referred for this kind of scrutiny. But deciding whether or not to refer bills to legislation committees was the prerogative of the Government, not of the House. In 1979 only two bills were referred, and in 1981 the practice ceased altogether.

Other attempts were made to reform House procedure. In 1979 the House of Representatives made its first use of Estimates Committees to examine, more closely than was possible in the committee of the whole, the proposed expenditures contained in the main Appropriation Bill for each year. These two committees were distinct from the Standing Committee on Expenditure, whose main functions were to consider any papers on public expenditure presented to the House; to consider how, if at all, policies implied in figures of expenditure might be carried out more economically; and to examine the costs and benefits of implementing Government programmes. As with the legislation committees, the Government made sure that it would have little to fear from Estimates committees. Not only would their activities be restricted to the main Appropriation Bill, but the committees could do no more than express an opinion about the estimates, and debate in the House on their reports would be limited to three hours.

Also in 1979 the Speaker commissioned a discussion paper by the Clerk of the House, J. A. Pettifer, canvassing the possible establishment of eight standing committees which would subsume the legislation and Estimates committees. At about the same time, Speaker Snedden distributed to all members a paper in which he advocated adoption of the convention of an independent Speaker, as observed at Westminster. The main elements of this convention were that the Speaker would not engage in partisan controversy inside or outside the chamber, even at general elections; that he would always be re-elected unopposed as Speaker if he so wished; that he would not be opposed by the major parties at general elections; and that he would always cast his vote in accordance with established conventions, without regard to the merits of the question. Neither of these initiatives by the Speaker bore any fruit.

Throughout the thirty-first parliament the Opposition concentrated its fire on one of the Prime Minister's few personal weaknesses, his credibility. From broken election promises in the previous parliament, the attack now moved to Fraser's alleged perfidy, his propensity to mislead, and many inventive variations of the same theme, up to and including the ultimate accusation of lying, which time and again caused the Speaker to demand withdrawal.

Mr KEATING.— . . . in the 1975 election campaign, I was in Mossman in Queensland. At the end of a hard day's campaigning, I was leaning on a bar of a hotel with an old farmer beside me. The Prime Minister appeared on television and I asked: 'What do you think of this fellow?' He looked hard at him and said: 'Son, if I had a dog with eyes as close together as that I would shoot it.'

Mr SPEAKER.—Order! The honourable member will withdraw that imputation.

Mr KEATING.—I will withdraw it, Mr Speaker. The Government ought to realise that the hardest job it has is marketing Malcolm Fraser as a believable commodity because he is now regarded as the most untrustworthy Prime Minister in the history of this Federation.

On 29 May 1978 Hayden moved the Opposition's seventh motion of censure, with emphasis on the Government's alleged dishonesty and the Prime Minister's 'extravagent self-indulgence in the matter of his personal overseas travel'. Fraser was about to embark on his eleventh trip abroad in twenty-seven months. 'It is a government of lies', said Hayden, who was himself about to embark on a tour of seven Asian countries, 'of little lies and big lies and, most often, stupid lies. If truth were hard cash this Government would live in rags and the Prime Minister die a pauper'. He was not called upon to withdraw, for the charge of lying had been made against the Government, not against an individual member.

Moving another censure motion on 4 June 1979, Hayden returned to the same theme in an attempt to bring about the resignation of the Minister for National Development, Kevin Newman (Lib, Bass, T), who had been caught out in what appeared to be an attempt to mislead the House. Newman and the Minister for Science and the Environment, Senator Jim Webster (NC, V), had given contradictory answers to identical questions in their respective chambers as to whether or not proclamation of the Great Barrier Reef Marine Park was being delayed because oil drilling permits had been issued inside the area. Fraser defused the issue by announcing that there would be no further exploration for petroleum in the Barrier Reef region, but not before Hayden had accused him of telling 'half-truths, untruths, big lies, little lies and stupid lies'.

Again, when asking a question without notice on 26 February 1980 concerning the Prime Minister's alleged misrepresentation of Labor's attitude towards the recent Soviet invasion of Afghanistan, Hayden described Fraser as 'a compulsive liar'. In a subsequent debate on Afghanistan, the Opposition accused Fraser of selling Nareen wool to the Soviet Union while at the same time expecting Australian athletes to boycott the impending Olympic Games in Moscow. After a discourse from Mick Young on the different wool brands used by graziers in the Nareen district, purporting to show that some of the Prime Minister's wool had gone to Leningrad, Paul Keating demonstrated the savage virtuosity for which he was becoming notorious.

Let the Judas tell us how many pieces of silver he will get. Let him say . . .
My colleague mentioned the markings. The following are the markings

on wool out of Nareen: A. Neeson, whose brand is N/Nareen; E. Neeson, whose brand is JFN/Nareen; P. Cox, whose brand is PC/Nareen; and J.M. Fraser whose brand is simply Nareen . . . It was his filthy wool that was sold. He is a phoney; he is a humbug.

Fraser did not answer this unfair but effective attack immediately. He ignored it during the Afghanistan debate; but at a later sitting, goaded by a question without notice, he pointed out that the wool in question had been sold before the Soviet invasion. It had been sold by open auction, with upwards of two hundred buyers bidding, and in such circumstances no grazier could tell where his wool was likely to go.

By the end of 1979 Fraser's approval rating in the Morgan Gallup poll had fallen below 30 per cent. Nearly 60 per cent of respondents 'disapproved' of him, while only 13 per cent were 'undecided'. His public image was that of a strong, ruthless leader who nonetheless disconcerted his followers by frequent lapses from the stern religion that he preached. The credibility problem arose mainly from his willingness to make promises which he would patently, and for the best of reasons, not be able to keep; and the impression of ruthlessness was reinforced periodically by yet another departure from Fraser's ministry. During the thirty-first parliament—partly because of the Prime Minister's determination to avoid at all cost the kind of ministerial imbroglios which had proved so damaging to the previous Government, and also for other reasons—three more ministers left the Cabinet.

On 7 April 1978 the Liberal member for Fadden (Q), Donald Cameron, alleged in the House that a fellow Queenslander and member of his own party—the Minister for Finance, and Member for McPherson, Eric Robinson—had interfered with the redistribution process and had also caused the Electoral Commissioners to change back the name of his (Robinson's) electorate from Gold Coast to McPherson during the previous year's distribution of seats. Perennial friction between Nationals and Liberals in Queensland had spread into the federal sphere, and wherever possible under the existing coalition agreement the National Country Party was engaging in three-cornered campaigns against Liberal candidates. Robinson, a millionaire owner of sports stores in Queensland, was a former President of the Liberal Party in that State. Although it was traditional for Liberal ministers not to be opposed by N.C.P. candidates, Robinson feared that any change in the name of his electorate might be used as an excuse to break that tradition. Cameron for his part was incensed at having had to move from the electorate of Griffith, a former Labor seat which he had won against all odds on five occasions, to the new seat of Fadden, which he barely managed to win against Labor and N.C.P. candidates at the 1977 election. As a result of Cameron's allegations in the House, Robinson was suspended from his portfolio, and a royal commission was appointed.

One of the witnesses called before the royal commission was the Government Leader in the Senate, Senator Reg Withers, who in his capacity as Minister for Administrative Services was responsible for electoral matters. Senator Withers revealed to the royal commissioner that in conversation with the Chief Electoral Officer he had expressed an opinion that 'Gold

'Keystone of the federal arch': the High Court building in Canberra

Sir Garfield Barwick, seventh Chief Justice of the High Court (1964–1981)

Mr Justice Murphy

The first woman Speaker. Mrs Joan Child, follows the first woman Serjeant-at-Arms, Mrs Lynette Simons, into the House for the swearing-in ceremony on 11 February 1986, passing Sir Robert Menzies on the way.

The Usher of the Black Rod (1970–1980), Guy Smith

Sir Billy Snedden, Speaker of the House of Representatives (1976—1983)

D. L. Chipp, Member of the House of Representatives and Senator

H. B. Turner, Member of the House of Representatives

Sir Magnus Cormack, President of the Senate (1971–1974)

Senator R. G. Withers

J. R. Odgers, Clerk of the Senate (1965–1979)

The Prime Minister, R. J. L. Hawke, and the Attorney-General, L. F. Bowen, at a Cabinet meeting

Parliament Houses, provisional and permanent, seen from above Lake Burley Griffin

Coast' was not as good a name as 'McPherson'. This conflicted to some extent with an assurance which Senator Withers had given some months previously in the Senate that he had not contacted the Electoral Commissioner about the change of name. Technically he had not, but the Chief Electoral Officer, according to his evidence at the royal commission, had passed the Senator's opinion on to the Electoral Commissioner. That was enough for the Prime Minister, no matter how much gratitude he may have owed Withers for the latter's crucial help in 1975. On 7 August Fraser asked him to resign in the interests of ministerial propriety, and when he refused Fraser called a meeting of senior ministers to secure his dismissal. It was all done with the abruptness of a bolt-cutter. Withers was summoned to the Prime Minister's office. Fraser offered him a cigar and said: 'The meeting has decided you must go. I am therefore withdrawing your commission tonight'. 'As you like', replied Senator Withers, 'thanks for the cigar'.

Withers later showed more emotion in talking to the journalist, Paul Kelly. He said: 'When the man who's carried the biggest knife in this country for the last ten years starts giving you a lecture about propriety, integrity and the need to resign, then he's either making a sick joke or playing you for a mug'. Anthony and Lynch thought the punishment too harsh, and argued for Withers's reinstatement, but the Prime Minister would not relent. Robinson was exonerated by the Royal Commissioner. He resumed his portfolio in August 1978, only to resign six months later, explaining to one of his colleagues, Jim Killen: 'I just can't work with the big bastard any more'. His main grievances appeared to be Fraser's closeness to the National Country Party, in Queensland as well as in Canberra; his autocratic administrative style; and his lack of respect for ministers. Thanks to intercession by Lynch, however, the breach was quickly repaired. Robinson, having received some sort of assurance from the Prime Minister, rejoined the Cabinet within three days of leaving it.

The third departure from Cabinet was that of the Deputy Leader of the National Country Party and Minister for Primary Industry, Ian Sinclair. 'Sinkers' was a formidable grazier-cum-businessman, treated with wary respect by most of his fellow members. He resigned his portfolio on 27 September 1979 after a commissioner appointed by the Labor Government of New South Wales concluded that he had committed forgery and other offences in connection with four family companies of which he was a director. Criminal proceedings were brought against him, but in August 1980 he was acquitted of all charges and immediately restored to Cabinet, as Minister for Special Trade Representations.

As the thirty-first parliament approached its full term, a rare event occurred. Senator Peter Rae saw through all stages a private member's bill, the Wireless Telegraphy Amendment Bill, designed to ameliorate certain anachronistic and draconian provisions of the original 1905 Act. This was the first private member's bill since 1974, and only the ninth since federation to be passed by both houses. It was not much of a triumph for the back benches, but was savoured nonetheless.

With a general election due on 18 October, the Morgan Gallup poll showed 46 per cent support for the coalition and 45 per cent for Labor. During the six-week-long campaign, Labor concentrated on the decline in family living standards, and projected in its publicity not merely one leader but three: Hayden, of course; Bob Hawke, the retiring A.C.T.U. president, who had won preselection for the blue ribbon seat of Wills, in Melbourne; and the Premier of New South Wales, Neville Wran, who was now President of the A.L.P. Relations between Hayden and Hawke had been decidedly uneasy since the party's last national conference, in 1979, when Hayden had made a deal with left-wing delegates to amend proposals of a committee chaired by Hawke for a 'social contract' between the unions and a Labor Government, involving wage restraint. Hawke had been humiliated, and that was not an experience to which he was much accustomed.

The Government stood on its record, and tried to label Hayden as 'wishy washy' and a prisoner of the Victorian socialist left. The Democrats contested almost every seat in the lower house, and with more hope of success ran twenty-two candidates for the half-Senate election. Senator Chipp said that his party would not vote to block supply, but would, if it gained the balance of power, ensure that the elected Government kept its promises. 'In other words', he said, 'we will keep the bastards honest'.

The coalition was returned to office for a third term, but its lower house majority was further reduced, from forty-eight to twenty-three, and its Senate majority would disappear when Senators Chipp and Mason were joined in July 1981 by three more Democrats: Janine Haines (S), Michael Macklin (Q) and John Siddons (V). Party strengths in the Senate would then be Liberals, twenty-eight; N.C.P., three; A.L.P., twenty-seven; Australian Democrats, five; Independent, one. Thus Labor and the Democrats together would be able to block Government bills, and would also be able to initiate legislation whenever they could enlist the Independent support of Senator Harradine. The Labor Party now felt more at ease with the chamber that had mortally wounded the Whitlam Government, and to whose abolition the party had until recently been pledged. In 1975 the A.L.P. platform still called for amendment of the Constitution 'to abolish the Senate'. Two years later this was altered to read: 'The Senate and Legislative Councils to be abolished, this aim not to be interpreted in such a way as to prevent steps being taken to effect reform of those houses'. Since 1979, however, the platform had contained no reference to abolition—only to support for Constitutional amendments to ensure 'that the Senate has no power to reject, defer or otherwise block money bills', and that it 'may delay for up to six months, but not reject, any other proposed law'.

Senate

After being elected Speaker for a third term on the opening day of the thirty-second parliament, 25 November 1980, Sir Billy Snedden spoke on a familiar theme: the need to strengthen parliament's ability to withstand pressures from executive government. The Speaker, he said, should be permitted to withdraw from political party membership; he should be guaranteed continuity of office; and should have discretion over whether or not to let a Government apply the gag to parliamentary debate. Sir Billy himself had been a proficient and impartial Speaker for the last five years, and he seldom let an opportunity pass without speaking up strongly for the rights of parliament *vis-à-vis* those of the other two constitutional arms, particularly the executive. One of those rights, as he saw it, was control of parliament's own funds. 'The Executive', he had said in 1978,

> controls funds for the purposes of the Parliament and that control is excessive and contrary to the concept of an independent legislature. Parliament, through its Presiding Officers, must have greater independence in obtaining the funds necessary to do its job as a Parliament. We need a separate parliamentary budget. Parliamentary estimates should not be subject to change by the Executive. Accountability of the Parliament for the funds expended ought to be directly to the public, not to the Executive.

Sir Billy's heart was in the right place, but the perennially Government-controlled House of Representatives was not an advantageous chamber from which to advocate reforms of this kind. The better place for that was the Senate, and senators were of course well aware of their greater ability to challenge and even curb the executive. In a preface to the fifth edition of his *Australian Senate Practice* (1976), the Clerk of the Senate, J. R. Odgers, who retired during the thirty-first parliament, had written: 'As at 1976 the Senate is at the zenith of its powers'. This certainly had seemed true in the euphoria induced by the Senate's having brought about the dismissal of a government, but that victory had represented only the height of the Senate's power as a party house. As a house of review, exercising its power in order to monitor and restrain the government of the day, but not to expel it from office, the Senate was still going from strength to strength.

A number of senators, even some whose consciences were troubled by the events of 1975, now thought of their chamber as parliament's last and best hope against the executive. This thesis was elaborated in academic and parliamentary circles by the Professor of Politics at the University of Western Australia, Professor G. S. Reid, who later became Governor of Western Australia and earlier in his life had been a Serjeant-at-Arms in the House of Representatives. Professor Reid maintained that the elected parliament was 'a weak and weakening institution', that the chief beneficiary of its decline was the executive government, but that the judiciary was tending to compete with the executive in exploiting parliament's weakness. 'The House of Representatives . . . has become the captive of the Executive Government of the day', he wrote,

> and is now a sadly repressed and debilitated parliamentary chamber. The Senate, owing to a variety of circumstances, had developed the ability to check, to question, even obstruct the government of the day, but as a result it has become a widely criticised and frequently maligned and threatened parliamentary body.

One of the most earnest advocates of Senate activism was David Hamer, the former M.H.R. for Isaacs (V), who had been elected to the Senate from Victoria in 1978. Senator Hamer was the eighteenth Australian parliamentarian to have made the transition from lower to upper house (only nine had gone the other way), and he proclaimed his faith in the Senate with all the zeal of a convert. In his maiden speech he urged the Senate to find a new role in place of its outmoded one as 'States' House'—but not to set itself up again as a rival lower house, with all the disruptive consequences that such a role was now known to entail.

> As we are operating at the moment we are accepting responsibility without power [he said]. I think the answer lies in the gradual development of the Westminster system to a point somewhat closer to the American system, with a strong questioning Senate balancing the Executive. In this process the Senate, unlike any other chamber in the Westminster system, is uniquely placed to play a key role. Unlike any other second chamber, we cannot effectively be whipped into line by the threat of an election or of abolition.
>
> For this role an effective committee system is essential . . . This Senate has become a remarkable instrument of public inquiry into key political issues. I believe we must turn away from the role of trying to compete with the House of Representatives on its level, for the end product of that will be the destruction of responsible government. Let that House remain the electoral college for the government and a rubber stamp for the decisions of the Executive. Those prizes are not very rewarding; let it have them. We are desperately needed in roles which we alone can perform, as a watchdog on the proper decentralisation of Executive power and as a public chamber of review of the implementation of the policy decisions of the Executive. We have the chance over the next few years to make the most important and dramatic advances in the system of parliamentary government to occur this century. I hope we will seize our chance.

During the three-month-long autumn sitting of 1981, the Government rushed 118 bills through parliament while it still had nominal control of the Senate. The last vestiges of Medibank and tax indexation were laid to rest, in final breach of promises half-forgotten by almost everyone. An Airlines Agreement Bill passed though all stages, in spite of defection by eight Government backbenchers in the lower house, who voted for an amendment moved unsuccessfully by the Opposition. This measure was designed to maintain the two-airline policy introduced by the Menzies Government in 1952—a policy that was daily made manifest in the sky over Canberra by the parallel vapour trails of commercial Ansett Airlines and Commonwealth-owned Trans Australia Airlines (later to become Australian Airlines), flying in tandem between Sydney and Melbourne—and to increase competition between the duopolists. The Opposition defined the Bill's purpose more succinctly as 'to ensure the profitability of Ansett Airlines for at least the next eight years'.

A Freedom of Information Bill, which also passed in spite of defections, this time by five Government senators, was a new version of a measure that had been introduced in 1978. That Bill had been referred to the Senate's Standing Committee on Constitutional and Legal Affairs, which had found it wanting in many respects. Freedom of information had been one of Fraser's election campaign promises. The new measure was said by its sponsor, Senator Durack, to create a general though limited right of public access to official documents in the possession of ministers, departments and public authorities. But as ministers would retain the right to refuse certain broad categories of information, subject only to an appeal by the applicant to the Administrative Appeals Tribunal, which had in such cases no power to enforce its own recommendations, critics of the measure were soon calling it the Freedom from Information Bill.

One of the most contentious measures introduced during the autumn sitting, the Broadcasting and Television Amendment Bill, was opposed more successfully in the upper house by four Liberals—Senators Missen, Rae, Withers and Puplick. In fact the mere threat of opposition was enough to achieve the result desired by these four rebels. The original Act, passed in 1977, provided that regulatory functions in the broadcasting industry, such as the guarding of public interest in issuing broadcasting licences, should rest not with the Government but with an autonomous statutory authority, the Australian Broadcasting Tribunal. The amending Bill of 1981 proposed to modify that procedure. It contained legislative guidelines as to what constituted public interest, and proposed that the Minister for Communications should be able to lay down additional criteria on public interest simply by writing to the Chairman of the Broadcasting Tribunal. As it happened, the media magnate, Rupert Murdoch, was then at loggerheads with the Broadcasting Tribunal about his proposed takeover of a television station in Melbourne.

The 'Murdoch Bill', as the Opposition labelled this measure, had not yet been introduced by the Minister for Communications, Ian Sinclair, when Senator Chris Puplick (N) gave notice that he and other Liberal senators would oppose any amendment that seemed to have been inspired by Mr Murdoch. This was a warning that could not be ignored, for the Government knew that the Labor Party and the Democrats were of the same mind. When the Bill reached the Senate it had been shorn of ministerial right to give directions to the Broadcasting Tribunal about public interest.

On 5 May 1981 a joint sitting of both houses was held in the Senate chamber. Its purpose, quite different from that of the only previous joint sitting, in 1974, was to fill a casual vacancy caused by the death of one of the two Australian Capital Territory senators, J. W. Knight (Lib). Voting *en bloc*, as State parliaments do in similar circumstances, the joint sitting elected another Liberal—a Canberra barrister, Margaret Reid. There were now more women than ever in parliament, yet the total was still only twelve out of a combined membership of 189. In addition to Senator Reid, Senators Florence Bjelke-Petersen (N.C.P., wife of the Queensland Premier) and Jean Hearn (Lab, T) had been appointed to fill casual vacancies, and were elected in 1980 as well. The term of Senator Jean Melzer (Lab, V) was due to expire on 30 June, but Senator Janine Haines (D, S) would keep the number of women senators up to nine when she resumed her seat on 1 July. The others, who had been in the Senate since the 1970s, were Margaret Guilfoyle (V), Kathryn Martin (Q) and Shirley Walters (T), all Liberals; Ruth Coleman (W) and Susan Ryan (A.C.T.), Labor.

Three women had also been elected to the lower house in 1980: Joan Child (re-elected for Henty, V), Elaine Darling (Lilley, Q) and Roslyn Kelly (A.C.T.), all Labor. On the urging of Mrs Child, the Speaker promised to adopt the usage of 'honourable members' in place of 'honourable gentlemen'. 'The point is well made', he said. 'I apologise deeply and profusely.'

Loss of control in the Senate was first brought home to the Government by that chamber's opposition to measures associated with the Budget introduced by Howard on 18 August—the Sales Tax Amendment Bills (Nos 1A to 9A). This legislative package imposed a sales tax of 2½ per cent on such 'essential' items as clothing, footwear, books and newspapers. At the instigation of the Australian Democrats, now five strong, the Senate returned these Bills to the lower house on 24 September, requesting deletion of sales tax on the essential items. Declining, the House sent the Bills back to the Senate, which then pressed its request.

The Democrats announced that they would not vote against the package if it reached the Senate again, but during the Christmas recess they had a change of mind. An identical package of Sales Tax Amendment Bills arrived from the lower house early in the autumn sitting of 1982, and on 10 March the A.L.P., Democrats and Senator Harradine combined to defeat it by 29 votes to 27. This provided ground for a double dissolution, should the Government want one. A second ground was provided two weeks later when the same alignment of senators defeated a Social Services Amendment Bill for the second time. The purpose of this measure was to deny social service benefits to the wives and children of employees on strike, presumably as a means of discouraging industrial action. On 19 May a third ground was provided when non-Government senators rejected for a second time, by 29 votes to 28, the States Grants (Tertiary Education Assistance) Bill. This measure would have introduced fees for second and higher degrees, and was regarded in some quarters as a prelude to the reintroduction of fees for first degrees.

Clearly the Senate could also have tried to force a general election by blocking supply, if it had been so minded. The pragmatic member for Blaxland, Paul Keating, advocated just such a course of action after the favourable augury of a by-election in Lowe, on 13 March, when a Labor candidate, Michael Maher, won Sir William McMahon's old seat with a surprisingly large majority. The shadow Cabinet reconsidered its stance on this issue. While still opposed in principle to the blocking of supply, it decided that the tactic could be used as a means to obtain constitutional change, particularly removal of the Senate's power over supply. Fraser denounced this as hypocrisy, but the question was largely academic so long as the Democrats adhered to their professed determination never to take part in a repetition of 1974–75.

Although the Fraser Government was firmly against any major constitutional change at present, Labor used its Senate advantage to introduce in that chamber a Constitution Alteration (Fixed Term Parliaments) Bill. The Bill proposed not only a fixed parliamentary term of four years but also removal of the Senate's right to block supply, and the Governor-General's right to dismiss a Government. Vain hopes! 'It is perhaps easy', said Senator Evans in a well-timed second reading speech on 11 November 1981,

. . . to dismiss the Bill as essentially some kind of academic pipe-dream with no ultimate chance of attracting the broad cross-party support which we know to be a necessary—if not sufficient—condition of securing constitutional reform. But I remain reasonably confident that when its implications are fully absorbed and understood ... a new fixed term parliament system will be seen by most members and senators as the only presently realistic solution to the institutional problems inherent in our present Constitution.

His confidence was misplaced. The Leader of the Government, Senator Sir John Carrick (N), announced that the Government would oppose the Bill. Slowly it moved through all Senate stages, as in a dream, and by the time it reached the lower house in December 1982 its references to denial and dismissal had been deleted by amendment. Even so, the House left the Bill to lapse when parliament was dissolved.

One of the most eventful sittings of the Senate during this parliament was that of 19 November 1981. The order of general business for that day was rearranged so that the Senate could deal with two matters concerning its relationship with the executive. Senator Don Jessop, an independently-minded South Australian Liberal who was chairman of the Senate Select Committee on Parliament's Appropriations and Staffing, then presented the report of that committee calling on the Government to agree that appropriations for parliament be removed from the bill for the ordinary annual services of the Government and included in a separate Parliamentary Appropriation Bill. This was the sort of reform which Speaker Snedden had been advocating for some years. But coming from an independent-minded Senate, where the concept had been under discussion since the 1960s, it was now likely to carry more weight with the Government than anything a Speaker might say.

Later the same night the Senate debated and voted on a motion by Senator Alan Missen (Lib, V) to establish a Standing Committee for the Scrutiny of Bills, which the Government had been blocking for the last three years. The purpose of such a committee would be to ensure that legislation did not trespass unduly on personal rights and liberties, or make such rights and liberties 'unduly dependent upon insufficiently defined administrative powers or non-reviewable administrative decisions'. This was to be consistent with and parallel to the activities of the long-established and notably efficacious Senate Regulations and Ordinances Committee, concerning delegated legislation. Senator Missen's motion was opposed by the Government, but was none the less passed by 35 votes to 21, with Labor and the Democrats supported by five Liberals—Missen, Bonner, Hamer, Martin and Rae.

A motion to endorse the conclusions contained in the Jessop Committee's report was adopted by the Senate on 26 November, and the Government agreed to introduce a separate Parliamentary Appropriation Bill, although limiting its scope to functions administered by the five parliamentary departments: the Senate, House of Representatives, Parliamentary Library, Parliamentary Reporting Staff (Hansard) and Joint House Department. The Government also agreed that the Bill would not be treated as a Bill for the ordinary annual services of the Government, which in the past had been a sore point with defenders of parliamentary independence. Subsequent amendments to the Public Service Act vested in the Presiding Officers power to create, classify and abolish offices and to make appointments below the level of permanent head. The first Appropriation (Parliamentary Departments) Bill was introduced for the financial year 1982–83 and during that period a few functions were transferred from executive departments to administration by the Senate and House of Representatives.

One other exercise of Senate power remains to be mentioned in this parliament. On 17 August 1982 the chairman of the Senate Standing Committee on Regulations and Ordinances, Senator A. W. R. Lewis (Lib, V), gave notice of a motion to disallow one of the High Court's rules of court. This was the first time such action had ever been contemplated in parliament, though rules of court, like other forms of delegated legislation such as regulations and ordinances, were subject to disallowance by either house. The 'Regs and Ords' Committee had been surprised to find that one of the High Court's new rules, fixing a rate of interest on judgment debts, doubled the rate of interest which had previously applied, with retrospective effect to 1980. The Committee wrote to the Chief Justice expressing its concern about retrospectivity, and inquiring whether there had been any special circumstances causing delay in the making of this rule. After further communication with Sir Harry Gibbs, Senator Lewis withdrew his notice of disallowance on 23 September, explaining that the Court had agreed to amend the rule to overcome the problem identified by the Senate Committee.

Senate obstruction was by no means the only difficulty now encountered by Fraser's Government. The Government seemed also to have lost control in two spheres where formerly it had claimed superiority over its predecessor—the spheres of economic management, and governmental integrity. Australia had achieved moderate economic growth during Fraser's first six years; but the improvement was not structural, and in 1982, for reasons including severe drought and overseas recession, the economy deteriorated alarmingly. For six years Fraser had asserted the importance of 'fighting inflation first', yet often he had called a truce in order to pursue some politically expedient course such as tax relief or lower interest rates. As someone said, he talked like Ayn Rand but acted like Santa Claus. By the end of 1982 Australia's inflation rate had risen to 11 per cent, and the unemployment rate was higher than at any time since the 1930s.

Fraser had come to office as the champion of small government. Yet here again his rhetoric had not been matched by action. In 1976–77 his Government spent 29 per cent of Australia's gross domestic product, which was only slightly less than the 30 per cent budgeted for by Labor in 1975–76. The comparable figure for 1982–83 was 28.7 per cent. Admittedly Fraser had kept the deficit reined in for six years, but this was not to be the case in 1982–83. As a result of spending decisions made by Cabinet after the Budget had been brought down, and disastrous effects of the economic recession on revenue, the Treasurer was obliged in December 1982 to revise the Budget's deficit figure of $1674 million to almost $4000 million. And even that would turn out later to have been a gross underestimate.

In keeping with the Government's professed commitment to the cause of smaller government, a Committee of Review of Government Functions had been appointed soon after the last election to identify areas in which Government spending could be reduced. This so-called 'Razor Gang' was chaired by Sir Phillip Lynch, and its members included the Treasurer, John Howard, and the Minister for Finance, Dame Margaret Guilfoyle. Its report, presented in April 1981, proposed the abolition, scaling down and merging of various Government undertakings to achieve an estimated annual saving of $560 million, or 1.5 per cent of the Government's current annual expenditure. Most commentators felt that the razor was not sharp enough. 'The whole exercise is a waste of time', said the *Australian Financial Review*. 'The sum is so small in relation to government outlays and revenues that it is derisory.'

The issues of smaller Government and less Government intervention were dealt with during 1981 by two other reports, producing much discussion but no immediate action. The Campbell Committee of Inquiry into the Australian Financial System was the first of its kind since 1936. Its report, starting from the premise that 'the most efficient way to organise economic activity is through a competitive market system which is subject to a minimum of regulation and government intervention', recommended removal of many Government controls including those on interest rates, foreign banks, cheque accounts and the rate of exchange for the Australian dollar.

This report was acclaimed enthusiastically by a group of free market Government backbenchers—the 'dries', as they were known—who had been criticising the Government over tariffs, public spending and failure to deregulate the two airlines. Fraser sympathised ideologically; but when he had to deal with electoral expectations, Santa Claus kept getting in the way of Ayn Rand. The dries also gave their seal of approval to a report by the Industries Assistance Commission, recommending a more efficient structure for the automobile industry, with much reduced protection. This differed markedly from a plan for that industry sponsored by the Minister for Industry and Commerce, Sir Phillip Lynch. Lynch opposed the I.A.C. report, thereby forfeiting support which he had formerly received in the parliamentary Liberal Party from such 'dries' as Jim Carlton (Mackellar, N) and John Hyde (Moore, W). It was a loss which the Deputy Leader of the party could ill afford.

As the economy declined, so too did the Government's reputation for administrative competence and probity. In September 1981 the Senate Standing Committee on Finance and Government Operations, chaired by Senator Rae, presented a 377-page report on the Australian Dairy Corporation, a statutory body operating under the aegis of the Department of Primary Industry. The report contained accusations of tax evasion and other malpractices; the breach of an international trade treaty by a subsidiary of the Corporation, Asia Dairy Industries (HK) Ltd; and conflict between evidence given on oath to the Senate Committee by the Corporation's chairman, and public statements made by the former Minister for Primary Industry, Ian Sinclair, who had refused to appear before the Committee. Sinclair criticised the report, and was strongly supported by the Prime Minister and other ministers when the Opposition unsuccessfully moved want of confidence in the Government for 'its failure to ensure proper and adequate standards of administration by senior Government Ministers'.

In April 1982 two of the more able members of Fraser's Ministry—Michael MacKellar (Lib, Warringah, N), and John Moore (Lib, Ryan, Q)—resigned over a relatively trivial but politically damaging incident. Some months earlier, on his return from a trip to Japan, MacKellar, who was Minister for Health, had failed to declare a colour television set to Customs, thereby avoiding the payment of duty which applied to colour sets but not to black and white ones. His inadvertent mistake was noticed by a customs officer, but MacKellar was allowed to leave the airport without paying duty. The officer later reported the incident to the Minister for Business and Consumer Affairs, Moore, who was then responsible for the customs service. Moore reprimanded MacKellar, but decided not to take the matter any further. The press did that for him, and after a vain attempt by Fraser to defuse the crisis both ministers tendered their resignations.

Further evidence of administrative malpractice and incompetence emerged later in the year. The Woodward Royal Commission into the meat export industry, appointed after disclosure that horse and kangaroo meat was being exported to the United States as beef, reported in September the existence of bribery and corruption among meat inspectors in the Department of Primary Industry. Two witnesses stated in evidence that they had made a specific allegation about such matters to the Minister for Primary Industry—Sinclair's successor, Peter Nixon—without any appropriate action being taken. 'In my view', reported Commissioner Woodward, '[the Minister[did not deal with this allegation in a manner that was adequate or effective'. The exigencies of ministerial propriety, which had required the resignation of Senator Withers, did not extend as far as the National Party Member for Gippsland. (The National Country Party had recently dropped its middle name, though not of course its rural constituency.) Nixon offered to resign, but the Prime Minister would not hear of it. 'I cannot accept that one adverse finding against the minister has been substantiated', he said of the Woodward report. 'I unequivocally reject it.' Also in September the Joint Parliamentary Public Accounts Committee, inquiring into medical fraud and over-servicing by medical practitioners, heard evidence of 'a sorry saga of laggard responses, inaction, incompetence and possibly worse by the Government and the Department of Health'. According to some witnesses, the cost of 'medifraud' to taxpayers and health insurance funds may have been as high as $1000 million over the previous ten years.

Embarrassing though these revelations were for the Government, they paled beside another documentation of massive fraud—the fourth interim report of the Costigan Royal Commission on the Activities of the Federated Ship Painters' and Dockers' Union. This was presented to the Governor-General on 27 July 1982 and tabled by the Attorney-General, Senator Durack, on 25 August. The delay was understandable, for among other things the Costigan Report charged the Commonwealth Crown Solicitor's Office with 'gross negligence' in relation to the politically explosive matter of tax evasion.

The Royal Commissioner, Frank Costigan, Q.C., had been appointed largely at the Prime Minister's behest to enquire into allegations of violence and pay fraud against the notorious Painters and Dockers, a union said to be involved in such sidelines as drug smuggling and arms running. In an earlier report, Costigan had found illicit links between this union and the tax evasion industry which had flourished in the benign climate created by certain High Court judgments. He recommended amendment of the Income Tax Act to let the Royal Commission examine confidential tax records, and the Government agreed. The main revelation in Costigan's fourth report was the magnitude of the tax revenue which had been evaded through 'bottom-of-the- harbour' schemes. The term 'bottom-of-the-harbour' described the practice of stripping companies of all their assets, selling them off as tax losses in order to evade taxation, and then conveniently misplacing the company records—at the bottom of Sydney Harbour, as one operator put it, or alternatively in the Swan River or Port Phillip Bay.

'The amount of money likely to be lost to the revenue of the Commonwealth', reported Costigan, 'was of enormous amounts and even today I do not believe any sensible estimate can be made of its extent, save to say that it is measured in hundreds if not thousands of millions of dollars'. This extraordinary report helped to rule out the possibility of an early election, which Howard's benevolent Budget had led many to believe was in the offing. Its ramifications continued to concern Government and parliament for the rest of the year.

Even before Costigan's report, the Fraser Government had taken certain legislative steps against tax evasion. The Crimes (Taxation Offences) Act of 1980 had outlawed the stripping of untaxed profits by way of 'bottom-of-the harbour' schemes, and the Income Tax Laws Amendment Bill (No. 2) of 1981 added a new Part IV(A) to the Income Tax Assessment Act. Part IV(A) replaced Section 260 of the Income Tax Assessment Act, which a series of High Court decisions had shown to be inadequate. It established administrative procedures for distinguishing blatant, artificial or contrived anti-tax schemes from legitimate arrangements such as a husband and wife running a business as partners, thus setting the scene for more effective prevention of tax fraud than in the past.

Spurred on by the Costigan Report, Fraser was determined to act, as he said, 'with vehemence and strength in eradicating this unmitigated evil from the body politic in Australia'. In spite of special pleading by elements of the Liberal Party, the Government appointed a task force to pursue 'bottom-of-the- harbour' schemers, and prepared retrospective legislation for the collection of tax revenue from those who had benefited from the schemes between 1972 and 1980, when the Crimes (Taxation Offences) Act came into force. During 1982 parliament passed fifteen Acts concerned with income tax or company tax.

The Prime Minister was still firmly in control of Cabinet and the parliamentary party despite the emergence of a pretender to the leadership, in the spruce, sun-tanned person of Andrew Peacock. The Member for Kooyong, who at the age of thirty had been the youngest minister in federal history, sometimes practised a less conservative form of Liberalism than Fraser. As Minister for Foreign Affairs in 1980 he had argued in vain with the Prime

Minister, even threatened to resign, over Australia's adherence to the American policy of not withdrawing diplomatic recognition from the monstrous Pol Pot regime in Kampuchea. And as Minister for Industrial Relations, in the short time he held that portfolio after the 1980 election, he favoured a consensual approach to the trade unions rather than Fraser-style confrontation.

After the 1980 election John Howard prepared to challenge Lynch for the Deputy Leadership, apparently with Fraser's tacit approval. Peacock altered the probable course of events, however, by unexpectedly throwing his own hat into the ring, a move rightly interpreted by others as being also a challenge to Fraser's authority. Fraser then swung his support behind Lynch, who retained the Deputy Leadership by forty-seven votes to Peacock's not inconsiderable thirty-five.

On 16 April 1981 Peacock resigned from Cabinet. This was the fifteenth resignation, dismissal or suspension from Fraser's Ministry. Peacock's immediate grievances concerned some recent criticism of his private secretary by the Prime Minister, and his belief that Fraser had not adequately repudiated a press report to which Peacock had taken exception. But more substantial reasons were contained in his explanation to the House on 28 April. In a speech reminiscent of Fraser's attack on Gorton ten years before, Peacock accused the Prime Minister of disloyalty, riding roughshod over ministers, and weakening Cabinet government and the parliamentary system by centralising power around himself. Cabinet's Co-ordination Committee and its other committees were all part of this centralisation, he said.

> The [Co-ordination] Committee is in fact an extension of the Prime Minister's well known lobbying of Ministers before issues are brought to Cabinet. Therefore, when Cabinet meets a significant number of Ministers have already determined many matters concerning government strategy . . . The decision of Cabinet is a foregone conclusion and, so, collective wisdom of Cabinet is aborted. I remind the House that the Prime Minister himself, after he resigned from the Ministry in 1971, said, 'the most important part of cabinet government is collective wisdom'.
> Regrettably, by-passing the system of government does not stop there . . . Apart from individual caucusing by the Prime Minister and apart from the use of the Co-ordination Committee the Prime Minister also uses ad hoc committees. Provided an ad hoc Committee of Cabinet reports back to the full Cabinet there can be absolutely no objection to the use of it to examine a complex issue. The method should be used only to unravel complexities to save time for the full Cabinet. Since the Fraser Government came to power there has been a plethora of ad hoc committees. Even worse, these ad hoc committees make Cabinet decisions. I am informed that between June 1977 and July 1979 there were approximately 5,900 Cabinet decisions of which more than 1,200 were ad hoc decisions. I do not have later figures. But it is damning evidence and an indictment of the erosion of the Westminster system. What I in fact have shown reveals the Prime Minister's determination to centralise power and satisfy a mania for getting his own way.

In reply, Fraser insisted that Cabinet was operating precisely according to the principles of cabinet government, and said that he was puzzled and saddened at what Peacock had now done. The Opposition then moved a want of confidence motion in the Prime Minister, which after three hours of debate was negatived by 71 votes (including Peacock's) to 49. Peacock later announced that in the event of a leadership contest he would stand against Fraser, but otherwise he did nothing to bring matters to a head. Fraser did that about a year later, calling a special party meeting on 9 April 1982 to vote for the positions of Leader, which no one seriously believed he would lose, and Deputy Leader, which Lynch could no longer hope to retain. Fraser realised that if he again supported Lynch the 'dries' of the party, fearful for their preferred candidate in the Deputy Leadership ballot, Howard, might very well support Peacock, who was at that time displaying certain dry tendencies, in his bid for the Leadership. Fraser therefore withdrew his support from Lynch, who consequently did not stand for re-election. Fraser retained the Leadership by fifty-four votes to Peacock's twenty-seven, and Howard was elected Deputy Leader with a margin of twelve votes over MacKellar, whose colour television ordeal was soon to begin. Peacock accepted defeat gracefully and seven months later, in a closing of ranks for the next election, was readmitted to Cabinet as Minister for Industry and Commerce in place of Sir Phillip Lynch, who had resigned his seat for reasons of health.

On the other side of the House, Bill Hayden had a more formidable rival in his own nest—a Hawke in place of a Peacock, though Hayden's rival was in fact endowed with qualities of both those birds. The new Member for Wills, Robert James Lee Hawke, had gone straight into the shadow ministry as spokesman on Industrial Relations, Employment and Youth Affairs. He was more than well qualified for this preferment, having been a Western Australian Rhodes Scholar, the brightest and most abrasive advocate to have appeared in the wage cases of the 1960s, President of the A.C.T.U. from 1970 to 1980, and president of the A.L.P. from 1973 to 1978. Not only had Hawke achieved all this before the age of fifty but, by virtue of the uninhibited, irreverent persona which he projected, particularly on television, he was also something of a folk hero: the wild colonial boy with an Oxford education.

If some of Australia's past political leaders had been larrikins or prima donnas, Bob Hawke was a bit of both. He drank and swore like a trooper, but knew when to change his dissonant tune—acting more like a tycoon or merchant prince in the company of such friends as Sir Peter Abeles or Sir Roderick Carnegie, and like a statesman when the need for that arose. His forte was consensus, and when the Australian Broadcasting Commission invited him to deliver the 1979 Boyer Lectures he chose as his title 'The Resolution of Conflict'.

He also knew when to stop drinking. His favourite hotel in Melbourne was the John Curtin, named after the political leader whom Hawke most admired. The very name of Curtin had been a spur to his political ambition (one of his uncles, Albert Hawke, could have inherited Curtin's seat of Fremantle, but chose instead to become Premier of Western Australia) and was also a reminder of the incubus that alcohol could be to a politician. In May 1980 he switched to mineral water.

Hawke had stood unsuccessfully for the federal seat of Corio in 1963. If he had won then, he would have had almost as much parliamentary experience as Hayden. As it was, he came to parliament with no previous experience of the institution and certain reservations about it. In one of his Boyer lectures, for example, he had advocated the American-style appointment of some ministers from outside parliament. 'No one . . . would believe that the men and women with the best available administrative capacity for the government of the country repose exclusively in the two Houses of Parliament', he said. 'I would advocate that as an initial step one quarter of the positions in the Ministry should be open to be filled by persons not elected to the Parliament . . . [but] responsible to Parliament.'

Yet Hawke was by no means at a disadvantage in his new environment. Anyone who had risen to the top of the A.C.T.U. and the A.L.P. would soon have felt at home there in even the most disorderly circumstances. On 18 February 1982, for example, Hawke called the Prime Minister a liar and got away with it. During Question Time Fraser had sought to influence the outcome of a Victorian State election by asserting that the Labor Premier, John Cain, had described the Royal Commission into the Painters and Dockers and another Royal Commission into the Builders Labourers' Federation as 'political stunts', and that Labor therefore could not be relied upon to implement their recommendations if returned to office.

'That is a lie', interjected Hawke, and the familiar chant was taken up by other Opposition members—'Lies, lies, lies'. 'You are a liar', continued Hawke in his grating, incisive voice that could be heard clearly above the others. 'He did not say anything of the sort and you know he didn't. Why don't you tell the truth for once, you liar?' Speaker Snedden called upon Hawke to withdraw; he refused, the Speaker named him, and Sinclair moved his suspension. Hayden told the Speaker that Hawke would withdraw the words to which exception had been taken if the Prime Minister withdrew his allegation, but Fraser refused to do that. Bowen pointed out that if the Speaker were to name every member who had called 'liar' the House would become unworkable. As the uproar continued, Sir James Killen passed a note to the Speaker reading: 'Take the Mace and leave'. But Snedden waited until the noise abated and then wisely called the next question. 'I have reflected on the matter', he said,

> and I have come to the conclusion that I need to take a solution which is going to enable the Parliament to proceed and I am therefore not going to put the motion in relation to the honourable member for Wills. I will not call the [Prime Minister] to continue with the answer. I will call the next question. I call the honourable member for Kalgoorlie.

Snedden later came under considerable pressure from the Government to put the motion, but he practised what he had been preaching about independence, and did not back down as Speaker Cope had done seven years earlier.

It was obvious to Fraser that sooner or later Hawke would assume the leadership which Whitlam had offered him after Hayden had declined it in 1975, and that it was in the Government's interest to call the next election before that happened. Hayden commanded respect and affection in Caucus, but already some of his colleagues doubted that Labor could win under his leadership. Competent, intelligent, witty and compassionate though he was, Hayden was also a solitary man, distrusting those around him. And of course he had good reason to be distrustful. There was more speculation about his position in mid-1982 when he changed his stance on visits by American nuclear warships to Australian ports. After first asserting that visits of this kind were contrary to A.L.P. policy, which in any case some of his colleagues denied, he abruptly accepted them as being essential to preservation of the American alliance.

Reacting to adverse comment, Hayden called a special Caucus meeting to vote for the leadership on 16 July. Hawke—whose approval rating as a leader, according to the latest Morgan Gallup poll, was exactly twice as high as Hayden's—contested this ballot with support from Paul Keating and other members of the powerful New South Wales right wing. The left faction and some uncommitted members—particularly the diminutive Leader of the Opposition in the Senate, John Button (V), and Hayden's deputy, Lionel Bowen, remained loyal to their leader, who survived the ballot by 42 votes to 37. 'Is it enough?' he asked his friend Button anxiously. Button shook his head, but Hayden rose to his feet anyway and accepted the narrow victory.

It might have been enough for stable leadership, had there not been a by-election for Lynch's electorate on 4 December 1982. The Liberal candidate, Peter Reith, won by a bigger margin than had been expected, considering the calamitous state of the economy. This had the twin effects of encouraging Fraser to seek a double dissolution quickly, and removing much of Hayden's remaining support within the Labor Party. Fraser had held back from an election so far because of the economy, the Costigan Report, and illness in the Ministry. Lynch had undergone bowel surgery before his resignation, and Senator Durack had suffered a heart attack. Fraser himself was virtually immobilised by sciatica from November to January—a stricken Atlas, 'knees buckling . . . arms trembling, but still trying to hold the world aloft with the last of his strength'.

Parliament sat for six more days after the Flinders by-election. The Taxation (Unpaid Company Tax) Assessment Bill for the recoupment of tax evaded illegally since 1972 passed its final stage although six Liberal senators and a National had crossed the floor at the second reading to vote unavailingly against its retrospectivity. As a final gesture of independence, four Liberal senators (Missen, Rae, Bonner and Robert Hill, S) crossed the floor to vote for the World Heritage Properties Protection Bill, which had been introduced by the Democrat Senator Mason and supported by Labor.

The purpose of the Bill was to prevent construction of the Franklin dam, a matter of great concern to those who held the dam's economic justification to be outweighed by the damage it would do to the wilderness of south-west Tasmania. The Liberal Tasmanian Government was determined to build this hydro-electric dam, and the Fraser Government, caving in to States' rights pressure, had decided not to stop it doing so by exercise of the Commonwealth's external affairs power, which had been upheld by the High Court in Koowarta's case. As a sop to the conservationist vote, however, Fraser had taken steps to place the south-west wilderness area on the World Heritage List maintained under the Convention for the Protection of the World Cultural and National Heritage, which Australia had ratified in 1974. Senator Mason's bill put into legislative form the responsibilities which Australia had accepted by ratification. It was sent to the House of Representatives on 14 December, the last sitting day before the Christmas recess, and made an order of the day for the next sitting. But as it turned out, there were not to be any more sittings of that parliament.

A race now began between Fraser, who wanted the next election held while Hayden was still his main antagonist, and the parliamentary Labor Party, most of whose members felt they must have Hawke as their leader at that election. After recuperating from an operation to relieve pressure on the sciatic nerve in his lower back, Fraser resumed active work in January. On 24 January he warned the federal director of the Liberal Party, Tony Eggleton, to prepare for an election in March. In the Opposition camp, Hayden's two closest associates—the Deputy Leader, Lionel Bowen, and Senator Button— were urging him to step down voluntarily in favour of Hawke. Button visted Hayden twice in Brisbane and finally, on 28 January, reinforced his arguments in a letter which Hayden later described as 'brutal but fair'. The hard candour of this letter may be judged from one of its eight enumerated points:

> You said to me that you could not stand down for a 'bastard' like Bob Hawke. In my experience in the Labor Party the fact that someone is a bastard (of one kind or another) has never been disqualification for leadership of the party. It is a disability from which we all suffer in various degrees.

Acknowledging the situation, Hayden decided to announce his resignation at a meeting of the shadow ministry in Brisbane on 3 February. Fraser also chose that day to advise the Governor-General to dissolve both houses of parliament for an election on 5 March; but the Opposition stole his thunder. The Prime Minister reached Yarralumla unannounced at 12.20 p.m., only to find the new Governor-General—a former Justice of the High Court, Sir Ninian Stephen—unwilling to act quite as expeditiously as Fraser wished. His Excellency was about to sit down to lunch with the Polish Ambassador, and would need time to consider the request for a double dissolution, which was based upon thirteen bills twice rejected by the Senate in 1982. Fraser returned to Parliament House. Later in the afternoon Sir Ninian sought clarification of some points, and it was not until 5 p.m. that the Prime Minister was able to announce the fifth double dissolution in federal history.

Meanwhile, Hayden had announced his resignation at 1.25 p.m. 'At best I could win [in Caucus] by only a very narrow margin', he told the press. 'It would have been unconvincing to the community and it would have resolved nothing.' He went on to say, however, that he was not convinced the Labor Party could not have won the forthcoming election under his leadership. 'I believe', he said, 'that a drover's dog could lead the Labor Party to victory the way the country is and the way the opinion polls are showing up for the Labor Party'. Five days later Caucus formally elected Hawke, unopposed by any of the party's factions. Here was a good example of Hawke-style consensus.

A drover's dog probably *could* have led Labor to some sort of victory; but with Bob Hawke on the job instead—'Bringing Australia Together', as the A.L.P.'s consensual slogan put it—the victory was on a grand scale. Hawke's policy speech, delivered in the concert hall of the Sydney Opera House, contained policies appropriate to 'Australia's worst economic crisis for 50 years'. He promised a national economic summit conference, representing management, work-force and governments; a genuine prices and income policy, based upon an accord that had already been reached betwen the A.L.P. and the A.C.T.U.; a Medicare programme to be financed by tax levy; higher unemployment benefits and pensions, and tax cuts for lower income earners. The Liberal Party offered drought relief, tougher industrial policies, lower company tax, and the placement of unemployed people in the armed services.

The poll of 5 March 1983 was Labor's greatest election victory since 1943, and far greater than that of 1972. Labor had needed a swing of only 1.4 per cent to win. In fact, it had achieved 5 per cent. The twenty-third Prime Minister of the Commonwealth would have a working majority of twenty-four in the House of Representatives, and party strengths in the Senate would be: Labor, thirty; Liberal, twenty-three; National, four; Democrats, five; Independent (Harradine), one. Given the Democrats' past record, and the mutual regard existing between Hawke and Chipp, this seemed proximate to control of the Senate.

So ended the Fraser years, all seven of them. Malcolm Fraser had been Prime Minister longer than Deakin's three terms combined, longer than Lyons or Hughes, or indeed anyone except Menzies. He had worked grimly, and by his lights conscientiously; he had been an efficient administrator, and had dealt summarily, even harshly, with colleagues who transgressed his standards of governmental rectitude. But what battles had he won, apart from three general elections? Government was still as big as ever, inflation was unchecked, taxes were still so high that people evaded them, and the Budget deficit—as Hawke and his Treasurer, Paul Keating, were soon to learn—had blown out to an astounding $9000 million. At the Southern Cross Hotel in Melbourne on election night Fraser accepted defeat stoically, as if it were nothing more than another spasm of back pain. He said the right things in front of television cameras, answered questions with stony impatience—and then, suddenly, Atlas wept.

Adjournment

This narrative must now break the all too familiar rhythm of election, session and dissolution. The rhythm goes on, of course, but for us to explore the thirty-third, thirty-fourth and thirty-fifth parliaments would be a mistake. Both halves of the spectrum are changing rapidly. A Labor Government staking its fortune on the businesslike management of a deregulated capitalist economy has been re-elected for an unprecedented third successive term, while a conservative coalition, formerly the regular winner of multiple terms, is dislocated by the sort of factionalism once regarded as the special incubus of Labor. It is too early to interpret all this. Rather, it is time to move the adjournment, and in so doing to note only a few concluding acts by our three main protagonists—executive, judiciary and parliament.

Capital Hill

On 4 October 1983 the Prime Minister, R. J. L. Hawke, laid the foundation stone of the new Parliament House which was to be completed in Australia's bicentennial year, 1988. Such a ceremony would not have been complete without some reference to Parliament itself, and the Prime Minister's speech was appropriately respectful. 'The Parliament is, and I trust will always be, the highest forum in the land', he said. 'Ultimately, the government *must* face the Parliament because the Parliament alone has the right to approve or disapprove legislation and the funds which are the means by which a government governs at all. Through the Parliament, and most particularly the House of Representatives, the will of the people finds expression . . . The design of this new Parliament House and its siting in this prominent location in the national capital must enhance the traditional place of the Parliament in our society.'

Four years later, as parliament was preparing to enter its third and permanent home, visitors to the circular Capital Hill site could see for themselves the extent of that enhancement. The cost of the project started modestly enough with a target figure of $151 million set upon the notional building for which designs were invited. The winning design was costed at $220 million in 1978 prices, and over the next nine years, mainly as a result of inflation, strikes and the additional cost of non-building items (for example, furniture, security systems and art works), the figure rose million by million to more than $1000 million.

So immense was the undertaking, however, that such a cost was plausible. Admittedly some effort of imagination was still required to visualise the finished building with parliament in session: the Great Hall, two storeys high with one and a half times the floor area of King's Hall; the Members' Hall, three storeys high, with three times the floor area of King's Hall; the two legislative chambers, with slightly more floor space than their counterparts in the provisional building, but four times as much cubic space, and furnished respectively in reds and greens more characteristic of the Australian landscape than the traditional Westminster colours; and to the south of these chambers, executive accommodation for the Prime Minister and other ministers, the Cabinet Room, and a Cabinet committee room. Much of what would soon become marble, parquetry and carpet was still raw concrete; but already it was plain to see how much the building would enhance the traditional place of parliament, and, even more significantly, the place of the executive.

With Camp Hill bulldozed out of the way, the front of the new building could be seen looming above the provisional Parliament House. It presented a similar but more imposing line of solids and voids, surmounted by four stainless steel legs meeting high overhead to support a flagpole. Inside, there were to be 4500 rooms in connected buildings. A central zone built on three levels along Burley Griffin's north–south axis was defined by two great curved walls, each facing outwards. Seen from above in diagrammatic form, the outline of the structure bore some resemblance to a human figure spread-eagled, its head to the south, and the limbs defined by grassed and paved ramps which would provide continuous access to the top of the building. The lower part of this body, to the north, contained the Foyer, Hall and Members' Hall; the chest, head and shoulders belonged to the executive government; and the arms were spread, possessively it seemed, around a legislative complex in each of the concavities formed by the central zone's retaining walls, the Senate chamber and offices to the west, and the House of Representatives chamber and offices to the east.

Architecturally, there was no mistaking who was head of this house. The two-level executive area, which would provide accommodation for up to twenty-nine ministers and their staffs, covered more than fifteen times the area of the new House of Representatives chamber. The Prime Minister's suite alone occupied 750 square metres, a larger area than either the Senate chamber (450 square metres) or the House of Representatives chamber (537 square metres). Most ministerial office suites would accommodate up to eleven people in an area of about two hundred square metres. On a lower level there was parking space for more than a hundred ministerial cars, a

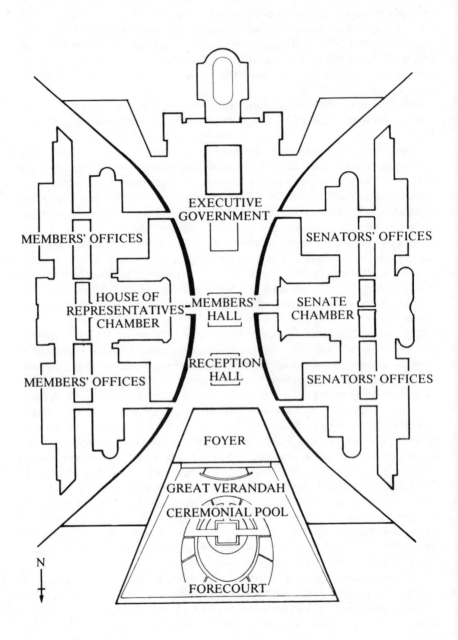

Floor plan of the new Parliament House

security area through which ministers could enter and leave the building without ever encountering the press or the general public. All this showed just how far the executive had come—to the point, in fact, where some likened its quarters on Capital Hill to a White House built inside the Capitol, or 10 Downing Street in the Palace of Westminster. 'The Executive will assume an entrenched position within its own enclave', wrote one commentator, 'and Ministers will be physically more remote from Backbenchers. The physical arrangements of the Executive entrance and the Prime Minister's suite will encourage a presidential-style status in the office'.

Of total working space in the new building, excluding public areas, 17 per cent was reserved for the Executive. How strange it was to reflect that sixty years earlier there had been only a few ministerial offices in the provisional Parliament House, and that the eleven-member Cabinet had been obliged to meet elsewhere, in West Block. Earlier still, in Melbourne, executive accommodation in Parliament House had consisted of one small room which was made available to the Prime Minister. Barton and his colleagues sometimes cooked chops there.

Parliament and Judiciary

During the years of the thirty-third and thirty-fourth parliaments, the High Court upheld Commonwealth power in the Tasmanian dam case; but it also defined the limits of such power in a judgment concerning federal and state industrial awards. In *Commonwealth of Australia* v. *State of Tasmania* (1983) a majority consisting of Mason, Murphy, Brennan and Deane JJ., with Dawson and Wilson JJ. and Gibbs C.J. dissenting, held that an act giving effect to obligations assumed by Australia under a bona fide international treaty or convention was a valid exercise of legislative power under the external affairs section of the Constitution. The question had arisen whether it was lawful for the Hydro-Electric Commission of Tasmania to construct a dam on the Gordon River downstream from its junction with the Franklin River. This wilderness area had been entered on the World Heritage List, thereby imposing certain treaty obligations upon the Commonwealth. As the World Heritage Committee had declared that flooding the Gordon and Franklin valleys would destroy significant cultural and natural features, and had recommended that the Australian Government take all possible measures to protect the area, the Government had made certain regulations under two conservation acts which would, if valid, render it unlawful to construct the dam except with consent of a Commonwealth minister. The principles were similar to those of *Koowarta* v. *Bjelke-Petersen*, and as in that earlier case the strongest argument for the assertion of Commonwealth power was expressed in Mr Justice Murphy's judgment.

For reasons soon to be explained, Justice Murphy was absent from the Bench for the case of *Queensland Electricity Commission* v. *the Commonwealth* (1985), in which the Court unanimously ruled against the central provision of the Conciliation and Arbitration (Electricity Industry) Act and, by a majority of four to two, declared the whole Act invalid. During the course of a bitter dispute in the Queensland power industry, the Hawke Government had attempted by means of this Act to facilitate the rapid transfer of Electrical

Trades Union members from their state award to a federal one, thus removing them from the Queensland Government's sphere of influence. The High Court ruled, however, that the Act disadvantaged Queensland by limiting its room to manoeuvre in industrial disputes. Commonwealth laws would be invalid, said the Court in effect, if they prevented a State from continuing to exist and function as such, and if they discriminated against a State by imposing some special burden or disability upon it. For all the sacrifices Moloch had exacted from the States, Australia was still a federation.

Mr Justice Murphy's absence from the Bench in 1985, and for most of his remaining judicial career, falls outside our main narrative. For that reason the allegations made against him in 1984, and the consequent parliamentary and judicial proceedings which took place one after another during the next two and a half years, will not be traversed fully here. Certain aspects of the matter should be mentioned, however, because of their parliamentary significance.

To summarise as briefly as possible, the allegations raised the question of what Parliament's responsibility might be in relation to Section 72 of the Constitution. This section provides for the removal of a High Court judge by the Governor-General on receipt of an address from the houses of Parliament praying for such removal on grounds of 'proved misbehaviour or incapacity'. The Government was not at first disposed to pursue the matter; but the Senate, controlled by non-Government parties, took it up tenaciously.

Thus did Mr Justice Murphy come under the kind of Senate scrutiny which he himself had once worked so tirelessly to invigorate. First, the Senate appointed a six-member Select Committee on the Conduct of a Judge; then, in the light of evidence given to that Committee, it appointed a four-member Select Committee on Allegations Concerning a Judge. The latter was virtually a royal commission operating within the framework of an investigating committee. Unlike any previous committee of the Senate this one had attached to it two independent commissioners, retired Supreme Court judges, with power conferred upon them by Senate resolution to examine witnesses and to advise on evidence to be called.

After examining evidence presented to the second committee, the Director of Public Prosecutions decided that Mr Justice Murphy should be prosecuted on two charges of attempting to pervert the course of justice in the Magistrates' Court of New South Wales. Apart from the judicial consequences of that decision, the question of parliamentary privilege also became involved. To senators and Senate officials, it seemed likely that the defence and prosecution would try to cross-examine witnesses and the accused on evidence given before the Senate committees. In the view of the President of the Senate, leading senators of all parties and the Speaker of the House of Representatives, this would be a breach of parliamentary privilege.

Under Section 49 of Australia's Constitution the powers, privileges and immunities of the two houses are such as Parliament may declare, and until so declared are the same as were those of the British House of Commons in 1901. In this way Parliament is protected by Article 9 of the 1689 Bill of

Rights: 'That the freedom of speech and debates or proceedings in Parliament ought not to be impeached in any court or place out of Parliament'.

Counsel instructed by the President of the Senate appeared at the committal hearing of the New South Wales Supreme Court, on each occasion submitting the parliamentary view that no use ought to be made in court of any Senate Committee evidence which would be contrary to the intention of Article 9. Counsel for Mr Justice Murphy submitted that the accused could not be cross-examined on his committee evidence. The magistrates supported these views, but the trial judge, Mr Justice Cantor, held that witnesses and the accused could be questioned as to what they had said before a Senate committee, for in his view that would not constitute a breach of Article 9.

The test by which he came to this conclusion was whether or not cross-examination would adversely affect freedom of speech in parliament, or parliamentary proceedings. In concluding that it would not, the judge dismissed as 'somewhat strained and artificial' one of two adverse effects which had been postulated by the Senate's counsel—that cross-examination of this kind would discourage other witnesses from giving evidence in future parliamentary proceedings. The second postulated effect, not referred to in the Cantor judgment, was that an attack upon the credibility of a witness by comparing his past parliamentary evidence with present judicial evidence may be damaging to him, thus in effect penalising him for having given evidence to Parliament in the first place.

At the trial, witnesses and the accused were cross-examined on evidence which they had given before the Senate committees, not only in public session but also in camera. In July 1985 a Supreme Court jury found Mr Justice Murphy guilty of one charge, and acquitted him of the other. He was sentenced to eighteen months' imprisonment, but was granted bail pending an appeal. The New South Wales Court of Appeal quashed his conviction on grounds unrelated to the question of privilege (misdirections of law by the trial judge) and ordered a new trial.

At the second trial in April 1986 Senate counsel again argued the parliamentary case for privilege, and again, though for reasons different from Mr Justice Cantor's, the judge, Mr Justice Hunt, was not persuaded. He too permitted witnesses to be cross-examined on parliamentary evidence. His judgment would have allowed the accused to be similarly cross-examined, but Justice Murphy chose not to give evidence. The jury acquitted Murphy, but that was not the end of either the controversy surrounding him or the parliamentary issue which had been raised by his trials.

Although the Senate had refrained from challenging the Cantor and Hunt judgments in the courts for fear of prejudicing Murphy's trial, it later took legislative action seeking to put into statutory form the long-established interpretation of Article 9 which those judgments had called into question. This was intended to have the effect of preventing such use of parliamentary proceedings as had been permitted in the Murphy trials. The Parliamentary Privileges Bill, introduced unprecedentedly by the President of the Senate in October 1986, also embodied certain changes in the law relating to parliamentary privilege which had been recommended by the Joint Select Com-

mittee on Parliamentary Privilege. After passing all stages in the Senate, the
Bill was received by the House of Representatives in March 1986. There too
the second reading speech was delivered in unprecedented fashion, by the
Speaker from the despatch box. The Bill was passed by the House on 6 May
1987.

The Murphy affair continued to unfold as inexorably as a classical tragedy,
evoking more partisan emotion than any other Australian event since the
Whitlam dismissal. The Government, in spite of its wish to end a former
colleague's unconscionably long ordeal, was prevented from doing so by a
combination of press criticism, the Judge's determination to resume his seat
on the Bench, and what appeared to be the reluctance of some of his fellow
judges to sit with him again. On 8 May the Attorney-General, Lionel Bowen,
introduced a bill to establish a Parliamentary Commission of Inquiry, consisting of three former superior court judges, to advise Parliament whether
any conduct of Mr Justice Murphy amounted to 'proved misbehaviour'
within the meaning of Section 72.

Before the Commission could make a full report, Mr Justice Murphy
rejoined his colleagues on the Bench, looking tired and pale, and later the
same day, 1 August 1986, confirmed reports that he was dying of inoperable
cancer. The Parliamentary Commission was disbanded, and on 21 October
Lionel Murphy's remarkable life came to its end.

The vacancies caused by his death and by the retirement of the Chief Justice, Sir Harry Gibbs, were filled by a former Judge of the Federal Court, Justice John Toohey, and the former New South Wales Solicitor-General, Miss
Mary Gaudron, Q.C. The new Chief Justice was Sir Anthony Mason. Justice
Gaudron, the first woman among the Court's thirty-seven judges since 1903,
was known to share some of Murphy's beliefs. In so far as such things could
be predicted, it seemed likely that the Commonwealth's prevailing majority
of four–three on the Court would be increased to five–two by the new
appointments.

Halley's Comet

By celestial providence our narrative may now conclude as it began, with a
comet: not the Great Southern Comet (for no one knew when that visitant of
1901 might reappear) but the predictable Halley's Comet, returning on its
majestic orbit for the first time since 1910. This most famous of all comets
arrived in Australia's eastern night sky early in 1986. Canberra doused its
lights for the occasion, and on one of the best viewing nights the Minister for
Science and Technology, Barry Jones, took most of his fellow parliamentarians by bus to Mount Stromlo Observatory for a closer look. Although the
Minister had wryly assured the House that Halley's Comet would be one of
the Hawke Government's most memorable achievements, it disappointed
the expectations inspired by its previous transit. Something of the same sort
could perhaps have been said about parliament. The institution presaged by
the Great Southern Comet had more than doubled its original membership;
it was soon to take up residence in a building of opulent proportions; and yet,
by all accounts, it now shone less brightly than in its infancy.

Soon after coming to office, the Hawke Government established a Joint Select Parliamentary Committee on Electoral Reform, under the chairmanship of Richard Klugman. Although neither its terms of reference nor the A.L.P. platform mentioned enlargement of the parliament, Dr Klugman's Committee regarded one of its terms ('the conduct of elections ... and matters related thereto') as justifying consideration of size. Among other electoral proposals, it recommended enlargement of both houses for the first time since 1949.

The case for enlargement rested mainly on the workload of members who by then were individually representing many more constituents than had been the case a quarter of a century earlier, and more than in other Westminster parliaments. Australian M.H.R.s represented an average of 74 989 electors each; British M.P.s, 65 692; members of the Canadian House of Commons, 56 349; and New Zealand parliamentarians, 22 117. Furthermore, the ratio between ministers and backbenchers in the Australian parliament had been altered to the latter's disadvantage by expansion of the ministry from nineteen in Chifley's time to the existing figure of twenty-seven. To some of those who regarded parliament as a weakening institution undermined by executive domination, its enlargement offered the chance of stronger pressure for parliamentary reform, and more parliamentarians to share the task of scrutinising legislation, possibly by means of a more effective committee system in the House of Representatives. At a partisan level, the Labor and National parties both expected to benefit electorally from the creation of more electorates.

The Committee recommended an increase in the number of lower house seats from 125 to 148, and, because of the nexus still ordained by the Constitution, a consequent increase in Senate numbers from sixty to seventy-six. If this proposal was to be implemented before completion of the permanent Parliament House, a new annexe would need to be constructed on the eastern side of the provisional building. Undeterred, the Government took that course at the next election. A Representation Bill providing for the recommended enlargement passed the House by 75 votes to 26 and the Senate by 30 to 24, the Nationals voting with Labor in both chambers. The Liberals and Democrats opposed it, on grounds that the cost of enlargement could not be justified in the prevailing economic climate. A second measure, the Commonwealth Electoral Legislation Amendment Bill, introduced several other changes recommended by the Klugman Committee, including simplification of Senate ballot papers and establishment of the Australian Electoral Commission, an independent statutory authority which would administer elections and referendums in place of the Australian Electoral Office.

Among the new electorates contested at a general election on 1 December 1984 were Menzies (V), McEwen (V), Lyons (T), Page (N), Calwell (V), Forde (Q), Makin (S) and Charlton (N). Four other new electorates were named after women (Gilmore, Goldstein, Moncrieff and Rankin), three after artists (Dobell, Lindsay and Streeton), one after the aviator Hinkler, and one after an Aborigine, Jagajaga. In spite of expectations, the relative positions of the parties were little changed by enlargement. Party strengths in the new Senate were Labor, thirty-four; Liberals, twenty-eight; Nationals, five; Democrats, seven; and Independents, two. In the House of Representatives Labor held eighty-two seats; Liberals, forty-five; and Nationals, twenty-one.

Two referendums were held at the 1984 election: one again seeking to require elections for both houses to be held simultaneously, and the other enabling the Commonwealth and States to refer powers to each other voluntarily. Both were rejected. This brought to thirty-eight the number of Constitution alteration bills submitted to the Australian electors, and to thirty the number that had been rejected. Constitutional change remained, as Menzies had observed, one of the labours of Hercules; but herculean efforts were still being made. After six biennial constitutional conventions had failed to achieve any significant reforms, a six-number Constitutional Commission, complete with secretariat and advisory committees, was established in 1986 with a brief to report by June 1988 on proposals for revising the Constitution.

Not surprisingly, the thirty-fourth Parliament differed in several respects from the institution when it had last been enlarged, in 1950. For one thing it now contained twenty-three women, which was more than two-thirds of the entire female membership since Federation.

Of the women in the new parliament, fifteen were in the Senate; fourteen were Labor, six Liberal, one Nationalist, one Democrat (Don Chipp's successor as the leader of that party, Senator Janine Haines), and one Nuclear Disarmament Party. At the opening of this parliament, on 21 February 1985, members of the lower house were led into the Senate chamber by the first woman Serjeant-at-Arms, Mrs Lyn Simons. One year later Mrs Joan Child (Lab, Henty, V) was elected to succeed Dr Harry Jenkins (Lab, Scullin, V) in the Chair of the lower house, thus becoming the federal Parliament's first Madam Speaker. In the upper house, Senator Douglas McClelland was succeeded a year later as President by Senator Kerry Sibraa (Lab, N).

Members of the new Parliament were somewhat younger than their predecessors in 1950, and, if the statistics of 1980 were any guide, they were better educated, less religious and more likely to have been born in Australia. Ninety-three per cent of members in 1980 were Australian-born, compared with 91 per cent in 1950, and their ethnic origins were still overwhelmingly Anglo-Saxon-Celtic. The only non-British European-born members in 1985 were Dr Klugman, who had been born in Austria; Dr Andrew Theophanous (Lab, Calwell, V), Cyprus; Lewis Kent (Lab, Hotham, V), Yugoslavia; and Senator David Vigor (D, S), France. Senators Arthur Gietzelt (Lab, N) and Norman Sanders (D, T) had been born in the United States.

The largest occupational category in 1980 was no longer 'business and commercial', but 'professionals' (45 per cent of all members, compared with 25 per cent in 1950 and 50 per cent in 1901), and the largest professional subgroup was still that of lawyers (16 per cent of all members, compared with 11 per cent and 27 per cent). The basic member's salary during the thirty-fourth parliament was $44 519; and the 1985–86 expenditure on parliament, excluding expenditure on the new building, amounted to about $170 million.

As the time approached for their ascent to Capital Hill, members of parliament had reason to be well satisfied with their material lot, but also, unless they were ministers, to be dissatisfied with their role in the scheme of things formed by cabinet, party rooms, parliament and the public service. Only one out of every four parliamentarians since 1901 had attained ministerial rank. Unless the lures of such possible preferment, better than average remuneration, and generous retirement privileges, were sufficient reward (and for some, of course, they were) parliament could be a tedious and frustrating place for backbenchers. In spite of its camaraderie, its unpredictable excitement, and the pertinacity or idealism of such private members as Hawker, Turner, Berinson and St John, parliament could also be what the disillusioned Frank Anstey had called 'that awful Dead House, that habitation of decayed souls'. Leslie Haylen said after twenty years as a backbencher that parliament lived 'only under the heavy sedation of forms and orders, ritual and out-moded procedures so that one must place one's ear to the parliamentary chest to hear the heart-beat at all'

During the 1970s and 1980s the lower house had come increasingly under the ministerial yoke, bullocking its way through more and more business in less sitting time than ever before. One hundred and thirty-eight acts of parliament were passed in 1971, and 202 in 1985; yet the annual average number of sitting hours for the House of Representatives fell from 543 during the 1970s to 480 between 1981 and 1985. A Standing Committee on Procedure, appointed by the House of Representatives in 1985, proposed a 40 per cent increase over the latter average, to a minimum of 670 hours. If adopted, that would still be far less than the latest average sitting times for the United Kingdom House of Commons (1550 hours) and the Canadian House of Commons (1125 hours).

Independents remained an endangered species (there were only three: Senator Brian Harradine; Senator Josephine Vallentine, who had resigned from the Nuclear Disarmament Party; and Senator George Georges, who had resigned from the Labor Party), and so did private member's bills, of which only three had been passed since 1980. Party discipline was as rigid as ever; the Speakership still lacked the kind of independence for which Sir Billy Snedden had campaigned; and the prospect of financial and administrative autonomy for parliament proved to have been largely an illusion. Reversing the trend of recent years, the Hawke Government circumscribed parliament's administrative responsibilities and set a total appropriation which the two houses could distribute among the various parliamentary departments, but could not alter. Also, at the time of this writing significant changes to the structure of parliamentary administration were also being proposed by the Presiding Officers.

Perhaps the most chastening experience for the thirty-fourth parliament came on 31 May 1985. After having treated the House of Representatives more brusquely than usual during the autumn sittings, and having guillotined eight bills on the last sitting day, 23 May, the Government recalled members of the House of Representatives from all over the continent eight days later to deal with a Repatriation Bill which had been returned by the Senate with an unexpected amendment after the House had risen. The Speaker summoned members to meet at 3 p.m., the amendment was passed, and at 4.18 p.m. the House adjourned until August.

During that recess, the House of Representatives chamber was occupied for four days by 160 people who, with the exception of federal ministers, were almost entirely 'strangers' to the House—in the main, State politicians, businessmen, trade union leaders, tax experts, Treasury officials, consumer representatives and academics. This National Tax Summit, chaired by the Prime Minister and the Treasurer, was intended to focus public attention on the need for tax reform. Like the National Economic Summit Conference of 1983, which had also been held in the House of Representatives, the Tax Summit led some parliamentarians to complain that the matter might well have been dealt with by the Government in the normal course of consultation, and in some other forum than Parliament House.

In circumstances such as these it was easy to belittle the significance of parliament. Most decisions of importance were made by Government party, Cabinet or public service. Admittedly parliament occasionally prevailed upon governments to alter their decisions in the course of debate, and the Senate had brought one government completely undone; but the day seemed to have gone when governments could be defeated on the floor of the lower house. There had been eight such defeats since 1901, but none since 1941.

For all its shortcomings, however, the much criticised institution of parliament still performs certain indispensable functions. In the words of Speaker Snedden, it is the all important link between the executive government and the people, a manifestation of the people's sovereignty to which any democratic government must be accountable. Parliament explains and justifies government decisions, and continually reminds the electors that alternative leadership and policies exist. As Professor Geoffrey Sawer has remarked, this is far from unimportant. 'So long as the actual function of parliament is understood', he wrote, 'one cannot dismiss it as a farce nor advocate its abolition'.

Furthermore there is nothing wrong with parliament that cannot be fixed, given the will to do so by Government and the electorate. If a more effective institution is wanted, the Constitution permits each House to make rules for the order and conduct of its business. In this connection it is worth remembering that comets vary in appearance from one visitation to another. There is always the chance that they will be brighter next time around.

Appendix 1

Parliaments

Parliament	Elected	Opened	Dissolved
First	29–30.3.01	9.5.01	23.11.03
Second	16.12.03	2.3.04	5.11.06
Third	12.12.06	20.2.07	19.2.10
Fourth	13.4.10	1.7.10	23.4.13
Fifth	31.5.13	9.7.13	30.7.14
Sixth	5.9.14	8.10.14	26.3.17
Seventh	5.5.17	14.6.17	3.11.19
Eighth	13.12.19	26.2.20	6.11.22
Ninth	16.12.22	28.2.23	3.10.25
Tenth	14.11.25	13.1.26	9.10.28
Eleventh	17.11.28	6.2.29	16.9.29
Twelfth	12.10.29	20.11.29	27.11.31
Thirteenth	19.12.31	17.2.32	7.8.34
Fourteenth	15.9.34	23.10.34	21.9.37
Fifteenth	23.10.37	30.11.37	27.8.40
Sixteenth	21.9.40	20.11.40	7.7.43
Seventeenth	21.8.43	23.9.43	16.8.46
Eighteenth	28.9.46	6.11.46	31.10.49
Nineteenth	10.12.49	22.2.50	19.3.51

Twentieth	28.4.51	12.6.51	21.4.54
Twenty-first	29.5.54	4.8.54	4.11.55
Twenty-second	10.12.55	15.2.56	14.10.58
Twenty-third	22.11.58	17.2.59	2.11.61
Twenty-fourth	9.12.61	20.2.62	1.11.63
Twenty-fifth	30.11.63	25.2.64	31.10.66
Twenty-sixth	26.11.66	21.2.67	29.9.69
Twenty-seventh	25.10.69	25.11.69	2.11.72
Twenty-eighth	2.12.72	27.2.73	11.4.74
Twenty-ninth	18.5.74	9.7.74	11.11.75
Thirtieth	13.12.75	17.2.76	10.11.77
Thirty-first	10.12.77	21.2.78	19.9.80
Thirty-second	18.10.80	25.11.80	4.2.83
Thirty-third	5.3.83	21.4.83	26.10.84
Thirty-fourth	1.12.84	21.2.85	5.6.87
Thirty-fifth	11.7.87	14.9.87	

Appendix 2

Ministries

Barton	1.1.01–24.9.03
Deakin	24.9.03–27.4.04
Watson	27.4.04–17.8.04
Reid–McLean	18.8.04–5.7.05
Deakin	5.7.05–13.11.08
Fisher	13.11.08–2.6.09
Deakin	2.6.09–29.4.10
Fisher	29.4.10–24.6.13
Cook	24.6.13–17.9.14
Fisher	17.9.14–27.10.15
Hughes	27.10.15–14.11.16
Hughes	14.11.16–17.2.17
Hughes	17.2.17–8.1.18
Hughes	10.1.18–9.2.23
Bruce–Page	9.2.23–22.10.29
Scullin	22.10.29–6.1.32
Lyons	6.1.32–7.11.38
Lyons	7.11.38–7.4.39
Page	7.4.39–26.4.39
Menzies	26.4.39–14.3.40
Menzies	14.3.40–28.10.40
Menzies	28.10.40–29.8.41

Fadden	29.8.41–7.10.41
Curtin	7.10.41–21.9.43
Curtin	21.9.43–6.7.45
Forde	6.7.45–13.7.45
Chifley	13.7.45–1.11.46
Chifley	1.11.46–19.12.49
Menzies	19.12.49–11.5.51
Menzies	11.5.51–11.1.56
Menzies	11.1.56–10.12.58
Menzies	10.12.58–18.12.63
Menzies	18.12.63–26.1.66
Holt	26.1.66–14.12.66
Holt	14.12.66–19.12.67
McEwen	19.12.67–10.1.68
Gorton	10.1.68–28.2.68
Gorton	28.2.68–12.11.69
Gorton	12.11.69–10.3.71
McMahon	10.3.71–5.12.72
Whitlam	5.12.72–19.12.72
Whitlam	19.12.72–11.11.75
Fraser	11.11.75–22.12.75
Fraser	22.12.75–20.12.77
Fraser	20.12.77–3.11.80
Fraser	3.11.80–7.5.82
Fraser	7.5.82–11.3.83
Hawke	11.3.83–13.12.84
Hawke	13.12.84–22.7.87
Hawke	22.7.87

Abbreviations

A.B.C.	Australian Broadcasting Commission
A.C.T.	Australian Capital Territory
A.C.T.U.	Australian Council of Trade Unions
A.I.F.	Australian Imperial Force
A.J.P.H.	*Australian Journal of Politics and History*
A.L.P.	Australian Labor Party
A.S.I.O.	Australian Security Intelligence Organization
A.W.U.	Australian Workers' Union
C	Country Party
CP	Country Party
CPD	*Commonwealth Parliamentary Debates*
C.S.I.R.O.	Commonwealth Scientific and Industrial Research Organisation
D.L.P.	Democratic Labor Party
F	Free Trade; Free Trader
HRD	*House of Representatives Debates*
Lab	Labor Party
Lib	Liberal Party
M.H.R.	Member of the House of Representatives
M.L.C.	Mutual Life & Citizens' Assurance Company Limited
M.P.	Member of Parliament
N	New South Wales
Nat	National Party
N.C.P.	National Country Party
N.T.	Northern Territory
P	Protection; Protectionist
Q	Queensland

R.A.A.F.	Royal Australian Air Force
S	South Australia
SD	*Senate Debates*
T	Tasmania
U	United Australia Party
U.A.P.	United Australia Party
V	Victoria
W	Western Australia

Notes

6 Transfer of posts, telegraphs and telephones to the Commonwealth: Section 69 of the Constitution provided for the transfer of State departments dealing with posts, telegraphs and telephones, naval and military defence, lighthouses and quarantine on dates to be proclaimed by the Governor-General. Section 51 (viii) gave parliament power to make laws with respect to astronomical and meteorological observations.

S.S. *Federal*: This steel-screw steamer, carrying 3486 tons of coal, was believed to have foundered near Rain Head. A submerged object fouled by minesweepers during World War II six kilometres off shore, at a depth of 73 metres, may have been its hulk.

7 Josiah Symon at the 1897 federal convention: Convention *Debates*, p. 515.

9 Government House: The Governor-General used Victoria's Government House as his Melbourne residence until 1930, during which time the Governor of Victoria resided at 'Stonnington', a mansion in the suburb of Malvern. In the same way, the Governor of New South Wales vacated Sydney's castle-like Government House in the Botanical Gardens from 1901 until 1912, making his own temporary residence at 'Cranbrook'.

10 'at least one cinematographer': This unidentified cameraman, whose cine-film is preserved at the National Library, was commissioned by the Federal Government from the well-established Limelight Department of the Salvation Army. The *Sydney Morning Herald*, 27 November 1900, also reported that 'in addition to local artists we are promised a visit from several cinematographists from London'.

11 B. R. Wise, *Industrial Freedom: A Study in Politics* (Cassell, London, 1982), p. 57.

12 Confederations and federations: R. R. Garran. *The Coming Commonwealth*, pp. 17-19.

Conversation between Parkes and Carrington: Extracts from Lord Carrington's Diary, Sydney, 1890 (Mitchell Library).

13 The Tenterfield oration: H. Parkes, *The Federal Government of Australasia: Speeches delivered on various occasions* (Sydney, 1890).

16 'a system which has never in the history of the world been tried . . . ': The combination of responsible government and a powerful upper house was not quite as unique as the delegates seemed to believe. Sir Samuel Griffith spoke of 'launching upon an unknown sea', yet the House of Lords at that time possessed the power to reject money bills, and did so. Deadlock between the two British houses had not been unknown. Such was also the case with the upper

611

houses of all Australian colonial legislatures except that of New South Wales. They could not initiate or amend money bills, but they could and occasionally did reject them. What *would* be unique about this combination of responsibility and a strong upper house would be that the Australian upper house, unlike the House of Lords or the colonial legislative councils, would be elected on manhood suffrage unrestricted by property qualification.

18 Labor's parliamentary debut: The first Labor member of an Australian parliament was Thomas Glassey, elected to the Queensland Legislative Assembly in 1888. He was followed in 1890 by J. P. Hoolan. Thirty-five Labor candidates were elected to the New South Wales Assembly in 1891, and 16 more to the Queensland Assembly in the general election of 1893.

21 Isaac Isaacs: Convention *Debates*, 13 April 1897, p. 545.
   Josiah Symon: Convention *Debates*, 13 April 1897, p. 518.

23 Procedure for altering the Constitution by referendum: Section 128 of the Constitution provides that a proposed law for alteration must be passed by an absolute majority of each house of parliament. It shall then, not less than two months and not more than six months after passing through both houses, be submitted in each State to the electors qualified to vote for the House of Representatives. But if either house passes any such proposed law, and the other house rejects or fails to pass it, or passes it with any amendment unacceptable to the first-mentioned house—and does so again after an interval of three months, with the same result—then the Governor-General may submit to the electors the proposed law as last proposed by the first-mentioned house. If the proposed law is approved by a majority of the six States and also by a majority of all the electors voting in all the States it shall be presented to the Governor-General for the Queen's assent.

24 Appeals from the High Court to the Privy Council: The Secretary of State for the Colonies, Joseph Chamberlain, objected to Clause 74 of the proposed Constitution which prevented (except for the Queen's right to grant special leave by Royal prerogative, which in any case the federal parliament would be empowered to limit at its legislative discretion) appeals proceeding from the High Court to the British Privy Council on matters involving interpretation of the constitutions of the Commonwealth and any State, unless those matters involved the public interest of some part of the British Empire other than the Commonwealth or State. In spite of its safeguards, this clause was regarded by the Colonial Office as a threat to imperial interests, or more specifically the private interests of British investors, inside the new Commonwealth. Their interests, it was felt, might be affected by constitutional cases, and should therefore be protected by leave to appeal.

   The compromise accepted by both sides was that only the High Court should have authority to grant or withhold leave to appeal from its own decisions in constitutional cases involving the relative powers of the Commonwealth and States. In other matters the Judicial Committee of the Privy Council could issue special leave to appeal to itself from the High Court, though the Commonwealth would also have power to bring down legislation restricting the kind of matters on which these non-constitutional appeals could be made by leave from the Privy Council.

25 'carrying . . . so heavy and restricting a burden of nineteenth century Colonial thinking': L. F. Crisp, *Australian National Government*, p. 82.
   J. Bryce, *Studies in History and Jurisprudence*, pp. 530-1.

27 Quick and Garran, p. 706.

29 P. M. Glynn, Diary, 4 January 1901 (National Library of Australia).

31 The right of Aborigines to vote in 1901: Western Australia and Queensland had a property qualification of £100, with which few if any Aborigines could have complied. In New South Wales, Victoria, Western Australia and Queensland Aborigines receiving charitable relief were excluded from the vote.

35 Two Independents in the House of Representatives: James Wilkinson (Moreton, Q), who described himself as Independent Labor, joined the Labor

Party in 1904. Alexander Paterson (Capricornia, Q) who was the only true Independent in the first parliament, retired after one term.

38 The *Talune* case: Jane Smith was tried twice more in June 1901, but at neither of her subsequent trials could the jury agree. The Crown then abandoned proceedings against her.

Clerk of the Parliaments: This title, used only by the first Clerk of the Senate and not by his successors, dates back to English parliamentary practice before the Lords and Commons were formed into separate houses. Parliament in the modern sense had its beginnings during the reigns of King John and his son Henry III. The sealing of Magna Carta by King John in 1215, embodying the principle that a monarch overrule the law, was an essential prerequisite to the rise of parliament as a law-making body. The word 'parliament', originally meaning a talk, from the French verb *'parler'*, was first applied to the meeting of the Great Council of prelates, earls and barons summoned to advise Henry III. The first recorded use of the word was in 1236.

Lords and Commons began sitting as distinct and separate houses in 1341, and the Commons established its precedence over the Lords in matters of taxation in 1395.

In some latter-day Westminster-style parliaments, including some of the colonial and State Australian parliaments, either the Clerk of the upper house or the senior Clerk of the legislature has carried the title of Clerk of the Parliaments in addition to his own title.

40 Paintings of the opening of Parliament: Tom Roberts's painting may be seen in the High Court at Canberra, and the original canvas by Charles Nuttall is in the possession of the trustees of the Exhibition Building, Melbourne.

44 'asserted their right to deliberate': The Senate, while free to adopt this practice of bringing up a 'privilege' bill for first reading if it wished, has never done so.

Address-in-Reply, May 1901: 'May It Please Your Excellency: We, the House of Representatives, in Parliament of the Commonwealth of Australia, in Parliament assembled, beg to express our loyalty to our Most Gracious Sovereign, and to thank Your Excellency for the gracious speech which you have been pleased to address to Parliament'. An almost identical Address-in-Reply was drafted by the Senate on 21 May, and the same basic form, with minor variations, has remained in use ever since.

45 Poem by George Essex Evans: *Argus*, 18 May 1901.

47 Ithuriel on Deakin: *Argus*, 1 June 1901.

Deakin's description of Reid: *The Federal Story*, ed. J. A. La Nauze (Melbourne, 1963), p. 60.

48 Speakers' mannerisms: J. H. Hume Cook papers, Ms 601, Series 9, Folder 46 (National Library).

50 Barton and Braddon: *CPD* (23.5.01) p. 295.

Hughes and O'Malley: *CPD* (23.5.01) p. 325, with Hansard's omissions restored from *Age*, 24 May 1901.

51 J. C. Watson's father: For further details about Johan Christian Tanck and the second husband of Watson's mother, George Watson, see J. C. Watson, a Genealogical Note', by Bede Nairn, *Labor History*, no. 34, May 1978, pp. 102–3. Tanck was a ship's officer, of unknown nationality.

53 'As someone wrote': Bede Nairn, *Civilising Capitalism* (Canberra, 1973), p. 204.

57 Peacock's laughter: R. A. Crouch Ms (La Trobe Library).

58 Hansard: Unlike the practice in the British, American and Canadian parliaments, where the separate chambers had their own reporting staffs, the Senate and the House of Representatives were served by the same staff, under direct control of the President and Speaker. The federal chambers proved to be more talkative than expected, and one additional parliamentary reporter was employed in 1907. From 1938 Hansard appeared daily, and from 1953 the cumulative debates were published in separate bound volumes.

61 Barton's trout: Hume Cook, Ms 601, Series 9, Folder 46, p. 141 (National Library).

64 Boer War debate: On 14 January 1902 Barton moved a two part motion—'That this House takes its first opportunity, in view of the despatch of a Federal Contingent to South Africa, to express its indignation at the baseless charges made abroad against the honour of the people and the humanity and the valour of the soldiers of the Empire', and 'That this House affirms the readiness of Australia to give all requisite aid to the Mother Country, in order to bring the present war to an end'.

The question on the first part was agreed to on the voices, and the second part was agreed to on a division 45 to 5. The 'Noes' were Higgins (P), Bamford (L), Ronald (L), Thomas (L) and McDonald (L).

65 Deakin's letter of resignation: Deakin diary, 9 April, 23 April 1902 (National Library).

68 Kingston on adultery in the heart. Hume Cooke papers, Ms 601, Series 9, Folder 46 (National Library).

70 Precedence: In the 1901 order of precedence, the President of the Senate came after the Governor-General, the State Governor and the Prime Minister, and immediately before the Speaker of the House of Representatives.

President of the Senate: Although entitled to a substantive vote, the President does not have a casting vote. In the case of an equal vote in the Senate, the motion is negatived.

73 Conciliation and Arbitration Bill: This Bill had been initiated earlier, in June 1901, and was later withdrawn.

74 Deakin's second reading speech on the Judiciary Bill: *CPD* (18.3.02) p. 10967.

High Court: Although the Judiciary Act stated that the principal judicial seat should be 'at the seat of Government', the early court sat in Sydney and Brisbane as well, incurring high travelling expenses in the process.

77 Ballaarat and Ballarat: Although Hansard used both spellings on occasion, the name of the electorate remained officially 'Ballaarat' until 1977, when it, like its principal city, dropped one of its middle vowels.

Deakin's 'Clues': These are contained in the Deakin papers held by the National Library of Australia.

78 Electoral Divisions: New divisions for the House of Representatives in New South Wales, Victoria, Queensland and Western Australia were accepted by parliament in 1906.

80 Women's franchise: Women received the right to vote at colonial or State elections in South Australia, 1894; Western Australia, 1899; New South Wales, 1902; Queensland, 1905; Victoria, 1908.

81 Court of Disputed Returns: The Electoral Act was amended in 1902 and 1907 to give the High Court jurisdiction over disputed election returns. Consequently the House of Representatives disbanded its Elections and Qualifications Committee, but the Senate continued to appoint such a committee for each parliament. The petitioners in 1904, both alleging ballot irregularities, were J. M. Chanter (P), the sitting Member for Riverina, and Dr W. Maloney, the unsuccessful Labor candidate against the sitting Member for Melbourne, Sir Malcolm McEacharn (P). The court declared both elections void, and the petitioners were successful in the resulting by-elections. Chanter's rival in Riverina, R. O. Blackwood (F), had one of the shortest parliamentary careers in federal history, three months and twenty-nine days. The briefest parliamentary career was that of C. R. Howroyd (Darwin, T), who died six days after his election, before he could be sworn in.

82 *Morning Post*: Deakin's article was written 22 December 1903 and published 28 January 1904.

83 Three elevens speech: *Age*, 2 February 1904.

90 'The voice was the voice of Esau': *CPD* (20.9.04) p. 4709.

91 'Here is the dagger': *CPD* (29.6.05) p. 73.

94 Closure of member: The motion that a member who is speaking 'be not further heard' cannot be moved while a member is giving a notice of motion or formally moving the terms of a motion. Nor may it always be accepted by the Speaker

when a member is speaking to a point of order, or making a formal explanation, as both those matters are within the control of the Chair.

99   The Senate's active role: In 1906 the Senate had also taken issue with the Governor-General. In the first exercise of his constitutional power to return a proposed law to parliament with a request for amendment, Lord Northcote had requested deletion from the Customs Tariff (British Protection) Bill of a racial provision likely to offend Indian opinion. The House of Representatives agreed, but the Senate disagreed. The Governor-General therefore reserved the Bill for the King's assent, which was never given.

'fair and reasonable' wages: Although New Protection was found to be unconstitutional by the High Court, Mr Justice Higgins's concept of a needs-based minimal wage remained virtually unchanged until 1931, when 'capacity to pay' was given currency by tribunals in response to the Depression.

Mr Justice Higgins: L. F. Fitzhardinge, *The Little Digger*.

101   'a rather highly coloured balloon': *CPD* (22.9.08) p. 203.

111   Liberal-Protectionist caucus meeting: Hume Cook's verbatim account may be found at the Australian National University, La Nauze collection, Ms 5248, Folder 70. Those who voted in favour of fusion were J. H. Hume Cook, Jabez Coon, R. A. Crouch, Alfred Deakin, Sir Thomas Ewing, L. E. Groom, Robert Harper, Samuel Mauger, C. C. Salmon, David Storrer, John Thomson, and Senators Sir Robert Best and J. H. Keating. The two absent Liberals, Austin Chapman and Senator C. St C. Cameron were both fusionists.

113   'Judas! Judas! Judas!': *Age*, 28 May 1909. The Hansard report, *CPD* (27.5.09) p. 114, limits itself to one 'Judas!'

114   Judas did not fail 'to hang himself afterwards': *CPD* (28.5.09) p. 175. Hughes's punchline was not original. It was used first by Henry Labouchère, Secretary of State for the Colonies in Palmerston's Ministry.

119   'one of the few parliamentarians to have held a seat in both houses': The first, moving from the lower house to the Senate in 1907, was James McColl (P, V). In 1910 W. G. Higgs and Sir Robert Best were elected to the House of Representatives, Higgs having previously been a senator from 1901 to 1907, and Best a senator from 1901 to 1910. Nine members in all changed houses during the first three decades of parliament—four in a downward direction, and five upwardly.

'A long effort tired his brain': Memoirs of M. L. Shepherd, A 1632 (Australian Archives, Canberra).

121   'suspended . . . from service of the House': J. H. Catts was suspended for 24 hours on 18 August 1910, and Senator Arthur Rae for the same period on 1 November 1912. For a second offence in the same year, a member may be suspended for seven consecutive days; and for a third, twenty-eight consecutive days. The maximum suspension has only been applied once, in 1919 to Michael Considine (Lab, Barrier, N).

124   Senator Sir Josiah Symon: Symon was defeated at the 1913 election.

125   'dispensed temporarily with wigs, buckles, ruffles and other traditional paraphernalia': The President of the Senate resumed wearing traditional garb in 1921, again at the request of a majority of senators. In the lower house, tradition (including use of the Mace) was restored by Speaker Johnson (Lib) in 1913, discontinued by Speaker McDonald from 1914 to 1917, but restored by Speaker Johnson in 1917.

126   Greece and Rome on the Nullarbor Plain: King O'Malley, *CPD* (20.9.11) p. 648.

127   King O'Malley's claim to have founded the Commonwealth Bank: Kim E. Beazley, *A.J.P.H.*, May 1963.

128   Deakin's reliance on notes: Although members could refer to notes, they were not at this time allowed to read their speeches, except for published matter which they read into Hansard. Speaker Holder required all such matter to be read rather than presented to the Hansard reporter. Speaker Salmon allowed statistical material to be incorporated in Hansard unread, but Speaker McDonald reverted to Holder's practice.

135   'Munro Ferguson sought advice from the Chief Justice': Sir Samuel Griffith

gave his advice orally at first, but on 5 October 1914 supplied the Governor-General with a written précis of it. For later opinions as to the propriety of Munro Ferguson's request for this advice, see L. F. Crisp, *The Parliamentary Government of the Commonwealth;* G. Sawer, *Australian Federal Politics and Law (1901–1929).*

136   B. S. B. Cook: 'Memoirs of a Pioneer Pressman', Mss 1453 (National Library).

141   Anstey v. Hughes: *CPD* (29.4.15) pp. 2765, 2769.

143   'They can all go to --, George': G. F. Pearce, *From Carpenter to Cabinet*, p. 128.

146   Inducements offered to Hughes to stay in England: J. H. Hume Cook, 'The Australian Party', 1930, Series III (7) 2C (National Library).

147   'now believed to have been arranged by Hughes': L.F. Fitzhardinge, *The Little Digger*, pp. 184-5.

150   The 24 Labor members who left the Caucus meeting with Hughes on 14 November 1916: House of Representatives: W. Archibald, F. Bamford, R. Burchell, E. Carr, J. Chanter, G. Dankel, J. Jensen, J. Lynch, A. Poynton, J. Sharpe, W. H. Smith, W. G. Spence, W. Webster. Senate: R. Buzacott, H. DeLargie, T. Givens, G. Henderson, P. Lynch, G. F. Pearce, E. Russell, W. Senior, W. Storey, J. Newlands, R. Guthrie.

157   The 1917 referendum decision: The national margin of 'No' votes over 'Yes' was 166 588, compared with 72 476 in 1916. The only States to vote 'Yes' in 1917 were Western Australia and Tasmania.

159   Lieutenant Burchell's Military Cross: This was awarded for 'conspicuous gallantry and devotion to duty in controlling railway operations, which involved the moving of troops and rolling stock and also the evacuation of wounded'. Burchell's citation said that he worked, with limited facilities, for three days and nights continuously.

163   Anstey and the Commonwealth police: This account was given by F. C. Green, a former Clerk of the House of Representatives, in *Overland*, August 1965. The wartime Commonwealth police force was disbanded in 1921, and another federal police body, the Peace Officers, came into being four years later. In 1960 the Peace Officers and the Commonwealth Investigation Service (a security service formed in 1911) became part of the present Commonwealth Police.

165   Corangamite (V) by-election: J. H. Scullin, the Labor member who had been defeated in 1913, regained this seat at the by-election in December 1918, under the preferential system. There were three eliminations and distributions of preferences.

    Parliamentary records: In addition to the longest speech, 1918 provided parliament's shortest and longest sitting. The shortest was 17 April 1918 in the Senate. It lasted one minute, long enough for prayers and tabling of the Commonwealth Bank's balance sheet. The Government Leader then moved adjournment because legislation expected from the other place was not likely to arrive that day. Sittings often lasted longer than temporal days. The longest, in the House of Representatives, lasted from 11 a.m. on Friday 18 January 1918 until 6.22 p.m. on Friday 25 January 1918—a period of 175 hours 22 minutes. But this period included a suspension of the sitting for arcane parliamentary reasons from 3.09 a.m. on 19 January until 3 p.m. on 25 January. The longest continuous sitting, 57 hours and 30 minutes, was on 16–18 November 1905.

166   Tudor's privilege motion: *CPD* (5.4.18) pp. 3646-79.

    Prosecution of J. H. Catts, M.H.R.: Catts was prosecuted seven times under the War Precautions Act for discussing the prosecution of others, and saying that Japan had designs on Australia. On each occasion he was bound over, but not fined. During one case he received the following telegram of encouragement from his friend King O'Malley: 'Brother Catts. Congratulations on courageous stand. If you need bail or boodle wire the King'.

    Five deletions from Hansard: *CPD* (3.12.18) p. 8626; (4.12.18) pp. 8753, 8764; (10.12.18) p. 8953; (13.12.18) p. 9299.

167   Hughes on Hansard: *CPD* (5.8.09) pp. 2101-2.

    Additions to Hansard proofs: R. F. Sholl, 'The Hand Behind the Mask:

Memoirs of Press and Parliament', in W. M. Hughes papers, Mss 1538, Series 5, Folder 80 (National Library).

172 Dismissal of J. A. Jensen from the Hughes Ministry: The Royal Commission referred to Jensen's use of his authority, while Minister for the Navy in 1916, to procure the purchases of a radio factory and ships. There was evidence of maladministration and the possibility (though this was not proven) of corruption. Jensen refused to resign, and then became the first Commonwealth minister to be dismissed from office, though not of course from parliament. He stood as an Independent at the 1919 general election and was defeated.

173 The 1919 referendums: The Constitution alteration (Legislative Powers) Bill sought, *inter alia*, to extend the trade and commerce power to intra-State as well as inter-State trade and commerce, and to give the Commonwealth a general power over industrial matters in place of its limited arbitration power. These powers, like those proposed in the Constitution Alteration (Nationalisation of Monopolies) Bill, were to last only three years or until a proposed constitutional convention made similar recommendations and they were approved at referendum, whichever came sooner.

177 Moses Gabb's maiden speech: *CPD* (4.3.20) p. 187.

179 The Engineers' case: Separate opinions were delivered by Higgins and Duffy JJ., Higgins J. concurring in substance with the majority and Duffy J. dissenting. The respondents later applied to the High Court for certificate of appeal to the Privy Council. The case was of the kind which could be appealed to the Privy Council only with the High Court's consent, and that consent was denied.

180 'Gum Arabic': Frank C. Green. *Servant of the House*, p. 60.

181 Speaker Holder's ruling on 'strangers': *CPD* (11.9.07) p. 3095.

'Lousy List': B. S. B. Cook, 'Memoirs of a Pioneer Pressman', Mss 1453 (National Library).

183 Anstey's speech on Mahon's expulsion: *CPD* (11.11.20) pp. 6468-72.

184 Later opinion of Hugh Mahon's expulsion: H. J. Gibbney, Hugh Mahon: A Political Biography, ANU thesis, MS 3131 (National Library); and report of Joint Select Committee on Parliamentary Privilege, June 1984. The Joint Select Committee's report stated, *inter alia*:

> The Mahon decision was made on party lines and it is a decision which we find troubling. We believe that if the power to expel is to remain . . . it should be exercised only in the most outrageous and compelling of cases. This follows both from the great severity of the sanction and the consideration that it is for the electors to determine who should be in parliament, rather than the houses themselves. This latter consideration may be answered by the argument that it would be quite competent for the expelled Member to re-contest his seat and to be re-elected. This argument overlooks the political reality that the mere fact of expulsion may so blight the expelled Member's political reputation that his prospects of successfully re-contesting an election are negligible.

185 'a definite matter of urgent public importance': Standing Order 38 of the House of Representatives, under which members could move adjournment of the House for the purpose of discussing a definite matter of urgent public importance, was amended in 1951 to enable a discussion to be initiated by submitting to the House 'a definite matter of urgent public importance' instead of a motion, thus removing the possibility that such discussion could end in a government's defeat.

187 Bells: The ringing of bells for a division or to establish a quorum is timed by a two-minute sandglass. In 1907 parliament temporarily abandoned bells in favour of a gong, but soon returned to bells.

190 Barcaldine . . . birthplace of Australia's labour movement: This notion, commemorated on a plaque beneath Barcaldine's 'Tree of Knowledge', is a tribute to the shearers' role in forming a radical political consciousness rather than a group or party. Concurrently with the shearers' strike of 1891, efforts were being made in various colonies to launch a political labour party. In Queensland

the Australian Labour Federation and the Australian Workers' Union came together in 1892 at a convention from which emerged the Queensland Labor Party, the first of its kind in Australia. The 'Tree of Knowledge' is an old cabbage gum under which 'the stalwart men and women of the west' are said to have held meetings during the strike.

191   'Drop the loot': *Age*, 22 September 1922.
195   Anstey on the first Australian-born ministry: *CPD* (1.3.23) p. 69.
199   Charlton on rural socialism: *CPD* (4.7.23) p. 655.
        Photograph of the House of Representatives at work: Melbourne *Herald*, 16 June 1923.
200   'one Speaker of a later generation': Speaker Snedden, unpublished speech to Law School, University of Western Australia, 1978.
202   Yates on film censorship: *CPD* (25.6.24) p. 1567.
203   Compulsory voting: The first Australian State to introduce compulsion was Queensland, in 1915, and the last was South Australia in 1944. The Victorian politician and diplomat, Sir Frederic Eggleston, once remarked that 'complusory voting assists a government which is moving with a live popularity: it punishes severely a government which is unpopular'.
205   'Serbonian bog': Mr Justice Higgins in the *Australian Boot Trade Employees' Federation* v. *Whybrow and Co and Others* (1910): 'At present, the approach to this Court is through a veritable Serbonian bog of technicalities, and the bog is extending'. Higgins was referring to the great morass mentioned in *Paradise Lost*, 'where armies whole have sunk'.
207   Senator Needham on States' rights: *CPD* (16.3.27) p. 465.
        Parliament's last sitting in Melbourne: *CPD* (23.3.27) p. 1085.
209   Aborigines on the Limestone Plains: Ngunawal and Ngarrugu were language groups, the former inhabiting the country between Queanbeyan, Yass and Goulburn, and the latter further south, from Queanbeyan to Delegate. Canberry and Pialligo were the scenes of smaller population groups and the land they inhabited. See F. W. Robinson, *Canberra's First Hundred Years and After*; W. P. Bluett, 'The Aborigines of the Canberra District at the arrival of the White Men', a paper read to the Canberra and District Historical Society, 29 May 1954.
210   Lhotsky's prophecy: J. Lhotsky, *A Journey from Sydney to the Australian Alps* (Blubber Head Press, Hobart, 1979) pp. 67-8.
213   A 'third-rate Luna Park': Patrick Abercrombie, quoted in Lionel Wigmore's *The Long View*, p. 56.
        'Then what name is to be given to the capital?' *CPD* (12.12.12) p. 6961.
217   American federal government buildings in the late Classical Revival style: One building particularly reminiscent of Canberra's Parliament House and the two secretariat buildings on either side of it is the Cannon House Office Building in Washington (1908).
219   'innocent pastimes of early federal Canberra': Diary of Clabon W. Allen, made available by the author. Dr Allen was later appointed Perren Professor of Astronomy at the University of London.
221   'including Walter Burley Griffin': Although it was sometimes stated that through an oversight Griffin was not invited, he and his wife were allocated a room at the Hotel Ainslie, and their names appeared on the published list.
222   Depictions of the opening of Parliament House, 9 May 1927: The painting by H. Septimus Power, which is reproduced on the jacket of this book, hangs in Parliament House, as also does a painting by W. B. McInnes of the Duke and Duchess of York in the Senate chamber. The DeForest Phono Film newsreel of the opening ceremony, silent and black and white, is held by the National Library Film and Sound Archive.
        Red ensign: Although the blue ensign was Australia's national flag, and the red ensign was the flag of the Australian merchant service, the latter was often flown on public occasions, presumably because of its more festive appearance.

231 Delegated legislation: Baron Hewart, *The New Despotism*; K. H. Bailey, *Australian Law Journal*, 15 May and 15 June 1930.
234 'Tragic Treasurer': *CPD* (16.11.27) pp. 1490, 1495.
238 Anstey on Theodore: Anstey memoirs, MS 4636 (National Library).
241 Bruce's biographer: Cecil Edwards, *Bruce of Melbourne*.
242 The 1928 referendum: The proposed insertion of Section 105A in the Constitution, empowering the Commonwealth to make agreements with the States concerning the Commonwealth's taking over and management of State debts, was approved by an uncharacteristic majority of voters in all States.
245 Hughes offers to lead the Country Party: *CPD* (15.3.29) p. 1307.
250 Hughes and Mann on the Maritime Industries Bill: *CPD* (30.8.29) p. 470; (5.9.29) p. 596.
251 Walter Marks on Armageddon: *CPD* (3.11.21) p. 12407.
252 Bruce and Latham visit the Governor-General: Latham to his wife, 10 September 1929, MS 6409, Folder 17 (National Library).
253 Labor's 'offer' to support Latham as Prime Minister: Memoir by Latham, *Meanjin Quarterly*, 21, 1962.
259 Rowley James moves the adjournment: *CPD* (3.12.29) p. 576
263 Duntroon: The Royal Military College returned from Sydney to Duntroon in 1937.
264 'I bloody well won't': *Smith's Weekly*, 4 October 1930.
266 'Scullin's absence . . . was . . . unavoidable': J. R. Robertson, 'Scullin as Prime Minister: Seven Critical Decisions', *Labor History*, no. 17, 1970.
   'like a couple of rabbits': Peter Love, 'Niemeyer's Australian Diary and other English records of his Mission', *Historical Studies*, no. 79, 1982.
   'he may not find it here when he returns': W. Denning, *Caucus Crisis*, p. 57.
268 Scullin's Buckingham Palace interviews: L. F. Crisp, 'The appointment of Sir Isaac Isaacs as Governor-General of Australia, 1930', *Historical Studies*, no. 42, 1964.
271 Scullin–Lyons cables: *Sydney Morning Herald*, 15 March 1931.
277 Adjournment as mark of respect: The practice of adjourning until the next sitting day for the death of a sitting member was later modified to suspension of the sitting for a few hours, but the death of a minister continued to warrant adjournment to the next sitting day.
278 W.A. Flying Corps Association: *Launceston Examiner*, 16 March 1931. Sir John Monash as dictator: G. Serle, *John Monash: A Biography* (Melbourne University Press, 1982). The Bishop of Willochra: *Sydney Morning Herald*, 3 July 1931.
281 Sir Robert Gibson at the Bar of the Senate: *CPD* (6.5.31) p. 1615. The last summoning to the Bar of an Australian parliament before this one was in 1906, when the Victorian Legislative Assembly summoned Rev. H. Worrall, to explain a sermon he had delivered at the Golden Square Methodist Church, Bendigo, on the subject, 'Who slaughtered the body and murdered the soul of Donald McLeod, bookmaker?' In the course of it he had said: 'There are men sitting in our Houses of Parliament, on whose heads will rest his blood . . . Sir Samuel Gillott stands in high authority, and I impeach that man tonight in God's name with the blood that has been flowing from the wounds of gamblers'.
284 Remaking ordinances previously disallowed: In 1933 the Acts Interpretation Act was amended to provide that a disallowed regulation could not be remade unless the resolution of disallowance was rescinded.
288 Scullin's biographer: J. R. Robertson, 'Scullin as Prime Minister: Seven Critical Decisions', *Labor History*, no. 17, 1970.
289 'a dreadful splash of milk and blood': Dame Enid Lyons, *So We Take Comfort*, p. 52.
292 The High Court upheld the first garnishee Act: The Lang Government argued that judgments of the High Court under the Financial Agreements Enforcement Act could not be executed against a State government without the passing of an

Appropriation Act by State parliament. A majority of the High Court held, however, that debts incurred by the States under the Financial Agreement were properly enforceable without a State Appropriation Act because Section 105A (5) of the Commonwealth Constitution made such obligations binding 'notwithstanding anything contained in this Constitution or the Constitution of the several States or in any law of the Parliament of the Commonwealth or of any State'.

Lang's efforts to evade the federal garnishee process: Expedients adopted by the Lang Government to keep New South Wales money away from the Commonwealth included a circular to State public servants requiring them in breach of the New South Wales Audit Act to forward all collected money to the Treasury rather than pay it into the banks. When Sir Philip Game consulted the New South Wales Chief Justice, Sir Philip Street, about the legality of this circular, the judge replied that he would have to make up his own mind. The Governor decided it was not legal.

295 'first child born to the wife of an Australian Prime Minister in office': The only other birth of this kind was to the McMahons in 1972.

298 'Membership of the House of Representatives had been reduced by redistribution': The Constitution provided that seventy-five members were to be elected to the House of Representatives, that parliament could make laws to vary that number, and that the number of members should be, as nearly as practicable, twice the number of senators. Under the Representation Act (1905), the process of redistribution begins with a quota obtained by dividing the population of the Commonwealth by twice the number of senators. The number of members to be chosen for each State is then determined by dividing each State population by the quota.

There were seventy-five full-voting seats for the elections between 1901 and 1922, seventy-six from 1925 to 1931, and seventy-five from 1934 to 1946.

Redistribution is conducted by three commissioners for each State, appointed by the Governor-General. In proposing new electoral boundaries, the commissioners take into account representations lodged in response to public advertisement and various economic, social and demographic considerations. Their proposals, submitted to the Minister, are proclaimed by the Governor-General if both houses of parliament pass resolutions approving them. If either house disallows the proposals, the Minister may call for a new redistribution.

301 Curtin and the army: During the 1917 anti-conscription campaign it was rumoured that Curtin had enlisted, but had been rejected. According to his biographer, Lloyd Ross, the foundation for this was that in 1915 Curtin and a friend walked into a recruiting office, but were turned away because of drunkenness.

302 Curtin on defence in the Pacific: *CPD* (5.11.36) pp. 1548-9.

306 Moffat diary, 1935–37: MS G 7251 (National Library).

308 A later generation of economic opinion: C. B. Schedvin, *Australia and the Great Depression*.

310 The Governor-General rebukes the Chief Justice: Lyons papers, MS 4851, Box 2, Folder 12 (National Library).

313 Conversations between Joseph Lyons, Enid Lyons and Menzies: Enid Lyons oral history transcript (National Library).

317 Lyons grave: The body of Joseph Lyons was later reburied, together with that of his wife, at Mersey Vale lawn cemetery, Spreyton, on the outskirts of Devonport.

320 Page's attack on Menzies: *CPD* (20.4.39) p. 16.

321 The Menzies brothers: Both elder brothers, Captain Frank Menzies and Sergeant-Major James Menzies, survived A.I.F. service in France. Robert Menzies had another brother, Sydney, who was ten years younger, and a sister, Isobel.

328 Menzies's private secretary: Sir Cecil Looker, oral history transcript (National Library).

332 'joint secret meetings': These took place on 12 March, 29 May and 20 August 1941, and on 20 February, 3–4 September and 8 October 1942.
334 Menzies was not blitzed by Churchill: P. G. Edwards, 'Menzies and the Imperial connection, 1939–41', *Australian Conservatism: Essays in Twentieth Century Political History*, ed. Cameron Hazlehurst (Canberra, 1979).
335 'the Baron of Bardia': *Sydney Morning Herald*, 27 January 1941.
338 Curtin's self-doubt: See Allan Fraser's remarks about diffidence and insecurity in *On Lips of Living Men*, ed. J. Thompson; diary of Henry Boote, Mss 2070, Series 2, Items 1 and 2 (National Library).
  'a chamber of ageing party hacks': D. Whitington, *Strive to be Fair*.
340 'and dash'd him on the craggy shore': Don Whitington, in his *Strive to be Fair*, said that Menzies quoted the lines in Greek and was nonplussed when Leo McClennan of the *Argus* continued the quotation in Greek: 'Torn was his skin, nor had the ribs been whole/But instant Pallas enter'd in his soul?' Menzies had done Greek at Junior school level, but not beyond.
344 The American and Japanese Ministers: The American legation was in Canberra, and the Japanese minister was based in Melbourne. When war broke out, Kawai and his staff were confined to their legation until August 1942, when they were repatriated via the neutral Portuguese colony of Mozambique.
351 Uniform tax scheme: The relevant acts were the Income Tax (War-time Arrangements) Act, Income Tax Assessment Act (1), and States Grants (Income Tax Reimbursement) Act, all passed between 15 May and 4 June 1942.
358 'I think you'll find he's had a miraculous recovery': Alan Reid, oral history recording 1:2/12 (National Library).
360 Members of parliament in the armed forces: Those who served overseas were Acting Sergeant A. M. Blain (Independent, Northern Territory); Captain Cyril Chambers (Lab, Adelaide), a dentist by profession, who served in New Guinea; and Senator Major K. C. Wilson (Lib, S), who served in the Middle East. Those who served only in Australia were Major Archie Cameron, Gunner Harold Holt, Major-General G. J. Rankin (C, Bendigo, V), Senator Captain A. S. Foll (Lib, Q), Captain E. J. Harrison, Wing Commander T. W. White, and Pilot Officer S. M. Falstein (Lab, Watson, N). All remained members of parliament during their periods of service except Senator Major Wilson, who was defeated in 1943.
  Max Falstein's air force career was marred by court martial while he was an aircraftman at air training school in 1942. It was alleged that he had said to the school's administrative officer: 'You are the most hated man on the station. I am going to Canberra next week and will have you shifted'. An R.A.A.F. court martial found him guilty of using insubordinate language, and sentenced him to 28 days' detention. His appeal to the Air Board was dismissed, but he was nonetheless re-elected in 1943, and qualified as a Pilot Officer.
367 Menzies as Hamlet: W. O. Fairfax, *Sydney Morning Herald*, 17 August 1943.
  Crayton Burns on the Liberal Party: *Argus*, 18 December 1944.
370 Curtin's choice of Governor-General: See P. G. Edwards, 'Labor's Vice-Regal Appointments: The Case of John Curtin and the Duke of Gloucester', *Labor History*, May 1978.
378 Parliamentary Standing Committee on Broadcasting: This was established in 1942, on the recommendation of a special wartime joint parliamentary committee on wireless broadcasting. Its main initial purpose was to retain some measure of parliamentary control over the semi-autonomous Australian Broadcasting Commission.
379 Rowley James's dentist: *Sydney Morning Herald*, 31 October 1947.
380 Dedman calls Morgan a 'bloody bastard': *CPD* (16.3.44) p. 1478.
384 'My dear Jack': R. G. Casey to Latham C.J., 29 October 1948, MS 1009/1/6726 (National Library).
391 'seven incompetent septuagenarians': *CPD* (9.10.47) p. 589.
392 Senator Amour in San Francisco: *CPD* (24.9.47) p. 167; (16.10.47) p. 847.
  'Congratulations, old man': A. A. Calwell, *Be Just and Fear Not*, p. 217.

394 Aboriginal franchise: *CPD* (3.3.49) p. 964.
399 Sir Earle Page and the Commonwealth Literary Fund: *CPD* (8.5.47) p. 2099.
402 'The Seven Dwarfs': These diminutive but powerful bureaucrats were H. C.
     Coombs, J. G. Crawford, Henry Bland, Frederick Wheeler, Allen Brown,
     Roland Wilson and Richard Randall.
409 Louis Quatorze: Edgar Holt, *Politics Is People*, p. 104. 'Roman senator': H.B.S.
     Gullett, *Observer*, 3 May 1958. 'Ming': Provenance uncertain, but believed to
     have first appeared in the Australian Communist Party's *Tribune, circa* 1951.
410 Parliament's most common surname: The list of parliamentarians since 1901
     includes twelve Camerons, eight Browns, seven Frasers, six McDonalds or
     MacDonalds, five Smiths and five Reids.
411 'Don't take any notice of all that bullshit': Russel Ward, *A Nation for a Continent*,
     p. 300. Personal communication from Fadden and Coombs.
413 Burke's telephone call to Chifley: L. F. Crisp, *Ben Chifley*, p. 394.
         'The Führer has spoken': *CPD* (4.5.50) p. 2219. 'Heil Menzies' was reported
     by the press, but not by Hansard.
415 'the survival of the composite government was seriously threatened': A. W.
     Fadden, *They Called Me Artie*, p. 116.
416 Speaker Cameron's statement about the Governor-General: *CPD* (30.3.50) p.
     1415.
422 Casey's difficulty with Menzies: W. J. Hudson, *Casey*, pp. 213-14.
427 Government backbenchers cross the floor, 4 June 1952: C. W. J. Falkinder (Lib,
     Franklin, T), B. H. Kekwick (Lib, Bass, T), A. W. G. Luck (Lib, Darwin, T), B. H.
     Corser (C, Wide Bay, Q).
         Motion of dissent from Speaker Cameron's ruling: *CPD* (6.3.53) p. 671.
429 'Evatt leaped on to the table': F. Daly, *From Curtin to Kerr*, p. 128.
433 The pre-emptive use of nuclear weapons: Unknown to most Australians until
     the release of Cabinet papers in 1986, Menzies was not averse to nuclear diplo-
     macy either. In 1955 he secretly suggested to Washington that the United States
     should use nuclear bombs on China if its forces threatened Malaya.
         Suspension of sitting: *HRD* (3.5.55) p. 362. It should be noted here that in
     1953 the consolidated Hansard was divided into two separate series, one for
     each chamber.
434 Evatt's letter to Molotov: *HRD* (19.10.55) p. 1695; Menzies, (25.10.55) p. 1860.
435 Gullett on Menzies: *Observer*, 3 May 1958.
         Sir Wilfrid Kent Hughes: Kent Hughes was a man of remarkable attainments.
     He had been a Victorian Rhodes Scholar, an Olympic athlete, the youngest
     major in the first A.I.F., and was the last original Anzac in the House of Rep-
     resentatives. While a prisoner of the Japanese with the 8th Division, he com-
     posed in microscopic handwriting on odd scraps of paper an epic poem, *Slaves
     of the Samurai*, which was published after the war by Oxford University Press.
437 Evatt on Suez crisis: *HRD* (31.10.56) p. 2062.
445 'British to his bootheels': Answering a question in the House on 29 October
     1963 about whether the R.A.A.F.'s new fighter replacement should be the
     American F-111 or the British TSR-2, Menzies said: 'As I have said before, I am
     British to the bootheels . . . But . . . I have always esteemed my prime duty to be
     to my own country and to the safety of my own country'. The provenance of the
     earlier reference is unknown.
         '[Barwick] didn't understand parliament': D. McNicoll, *Luck's a Fortune*
     (Wildcat Press, Sydney, 1979), p. 225.
447 'Stop sheltering behind the Sovereign all the time': *HRD* (17.11.60) p. 3032.
451 Haylen in white coat and stethoscope: L. C. Haylen, *Twenty Years' Hard Labor*,
     p. 136.
453 'Am I rightly informed?': Sir Robert Menzies, *The Measure of the Years*, p. 147.
455 American obligations under ANZUS: A statement by Menzies in parliament on
     21 April 1964, to the effect that Australia should not try to involve the United
     States in Malaysia 'in a cheap way', was regarded by some as contradicting
     earlier statements by Barwick.

456 'The old man kicked me out': David Marr, *Barwick*, p. 209.
462 'Holt felt that he now had an issue': Gough Whitlam, *The Whitlam Government 1972–1975*, p. 33.
464 'lacked even the dignity normally accorded to ritual': *Sydney Morning Herald*, 28 May 1965.
465 'You are one of the filthiest objects over to come into this chamber': HRD (30.9.65) p. 1462.
473 Censure motion concerning the collision between H.M.A.S. *Melbourne* and H.M.A.S. *Voyager*, *HRD* (12.9.64) p. 1473.
St John's maiden speech: *HRD* (16.5.67) p. 2169.
474 'one sardonic commentator': Don Aitkin, 'Political Review', *Australian Quarterly*, June 1967.
476 'unenviable reputation': 'Australian Political Chronicle', *A.J.P.H.*, Sept.–Dec., 1967.
477 'a Corsican-like devotion to the pursuit of vendettas': A. Reid, *The Power Struggle*, p. 19.
Lord Casey's warning to McMahon: A. Reid, *The Power Struggle*, p.109.
478 '"Holt", according to one commentator': W. F. Mandle, *Going It Alone* (Allen Lane, Melbourne, 1978) p. 204.
480 'The Prime Minister . . . had always been drawn from the House of Representatives': Two senators each had served as acting Prime Minister: Senator George Pearce in 1916, and Senator W. H. Spooner in 1962.
481 'larrikin leaders': S. Encel, *Nation*, 25 May 1968.
Debate on the use of torture: *CPD* (14.3.68) p. 155.
483 *Sydney Morning Herald*: 3 November 1970.
489 Menzies on the Senate's power: *Daily Telegraph*, 18 February 1968.
The committee was taken to have accepted amendments which had never been formally moved: D. Solomon, *Canberra Times*, 11 May 1971.
501 'tactless, arrogant, domineering': G. Duthie, *I Had 50,000 Bosses*, p. 266.
'Go to buggery!': *Australian*, 3 May 1972; *Sunday Independent* (WA), 11 June 1972; 'Australian Political Chronicle', *A.J.P.H.*, vol. 18, no. 2.
503 Senator Bonner's maiden speech: *SD* (8.9.71) p. 553.
507 Australian honours list: Letters patent establishing an Order of Australia were approved by the Queen on 14 February 1975. The Order originally consisted of Companion, Officer and Member; was amended by the Fraser Government in 1976 to include Knight and Dame, both of which were later removed by the Hawke Government; and now consists of Companion, Officer, Member and Medal.
508 'a grandly bedizened puce-coloured orchid': J. B. Paul, 'Political Review', *Australian Quarterly*, March 1973.
Whitlam's early life: Much of this detail comes from L. Oakes, *Whitlam PM*.
513 Death penalty: The death penalty had been carried out twice in the Northern Territory, but never in the Australian Capital Territory. By 1973 it had been abolished in Queensland (1922) and Tasmania (1968). Victoria and South Australia followed the Commonwealth's example in 1975, Western Australia in 1984, and New South Wales in 1985.
514 Scrootch owls and hoot owls: C. A. Hughes, 'Australian Political Chronicle', *A.J.P.H.*, Jan.–April 1973.
519 Sleeping princess: Hughes, C. A., 'Australian Political Chronicle', *A.J.P.H.*, Sept.–Dec. 1973.
526 The Executive Council meeting of 13 December 1974: G. Sawer, *Federation Under Strain* (Melbourne University Press, 1977), pp. 98, 102. The validity of the meeting was never tested in the High Court.
530 'the running out of the sand in the glass': Parliament's Bicentenary Publications Project, oral history interview with J. F. Cope, 1983.
'Woof, woof!': *HRD* (19.2.75), p. 427.
532 'you'll have to be the bastard and tell him': J. Cairns, *Oil in Troubled Waters* (Widescope International Publishers Pty Ltd, Melbourne, 1976), p. 100.

'a whole host of middlemen . . . ': P. Kelly, *The Unmaking of Gough*, p. 168.

533 A housing project in Cairns's electorate: *Age*, 1 July 1975.

537 'the Whitlam Government survived its own explorations and adventures with Commonwealth legislative and financial powers ... almost completely unscathed': Senator G. Evans in *The Whitlam Phenomenon* (McPhee Gribble/ Penguin, Melbourne, 1986), p. 160.

539 'the footprints of a giant reprehensible circumstance!': *Nation-Review*, 17–23 October 1975.

541 'It could be a question of whether I get to the Queen first or you get in first with my dismissal': John Kerr, *Matters for Judgment*, p. 258.

Precedents for the refusal of Supply by the upper houses of State Parliaments: Victoria in 1947 and Tasmania in 1948.

543 Barwick's visit to Admiralty House: G. Barwick, *Sir John Did His Duty*.

544 'Before you say anything Prime Minister, I want to say something to you': The following conversation derives mainly from Sir John Kerr's book, *Matters for Judgment*, and E. G. Whitlam's *The Truth of the Matter*.

546 'You've buckled at last have you?': This conversation comes from *Kerr's King Hit!* by Clem Lloyd and Andrew Clark. Other accounts of the events in the Senate between 2 p.m. and 2.24 p.m. are contained in Paul Kelly's *The Unmaking of Gough* and Alan Reid's *The Whitlam Venture*.

552 'Cut it out, Prime Minister': Sir James Killen, *Killen: Inside Australian Politics*, p. 257.

554 Fraser's speech on South Africa: *HRD* (12.4.61) p. 769.

Fraser on *Atlas Shrugged*: *Financial Review*, 28 June 1972.

559 'the understandably minimalist view of the role of parliament': 'Making Government Responsible: The Role of Parliamentary Committees', a chapter by Martin Indyk in *Responsible Government in Australia*, edited by Patrick Weller and Dean Jaensch (Melbourne, 1980).

561 'a movement back along the spectrum towards the regions': Jeffrey Scott, in *Australian Federation: Future Tense*, edited by Allan Patience and Jeffrey Scott (Oxford University Press, Melbourne, 1983).

565 Barry Jones's eulogy of Whitlam: *HRD* (15.8.78) pp. 286-7.

573 'if I had a dog with eyes as close together as that I would shoot it': *HRD* (22.11.78) p. 3177.

574 Ministerial dismissals and resignations: In addition to resignations by Withers, Robinson and Sinclair, Senator Glenister Sheil's (NCP, Q) appointment to the Executive Council without portfolio was terminated on 22 December 1977, only two days after it had been made. Fraser took this drastic action because of public statements made by the senator in support of South African apartheid.

An earlier casualty, not previously mentioned, was the Minister for Posts and Telecommunications, R. V. (later Sir Victor) Garland, who resigned in February 1976 after allegations of electoral impropriety had been made by an Independent candidate for the Australian Capital Territory. Garland and a former Liberal senator, George Branson, were charged with a breach of the Electoral Act, but the case proceeded no further than a magistrate's ruling that a jury properly directed would not convict them. Garland was readmitted to the ministry in 1977, and two years later resigned from Parliament to become Australian High Commissioner in London.

575 'When the man who's carried the biggest knife . . . ': Paul Kelly, *The Hawke Ascendancy*, p. 57.

Wireless Telegraphy Amendment Bill: Second reading, *SD* (16.5.80) p. 2463.

577 'We need a separate parliamentary budget': Sir Billy Snedden, addressing the National Press Club, 8 June 1978.

'a weak and weakening institution': G. S. Reid, 'The Changing Political Framework', *Quadrant*, Jan.–Feb. 1980.

578 Senator Hamer's maiden speech: *SD* (13.9.78) pp. 548-9.

582 'talked like Ayn Rand but acted like Santa Claus': Brian Buckley, secretary to Phillip Lynch.

589 'Is it enough?': Paul Kelly, *The Hawke Ascendancy*, p. 240.
590 Senator Button's 'brutal but fair' letter to Hayden: Paul Kelly, *The Hawke Ascendancy*, pp. 2-4.
595 'The Executive will assume an entrenched position': T. Fewtrell, 'A New Parliament House—A New Parliamentary Order', *Australian Journal of Public Administration*, December 1985, p. 323.
600 Birth-place and occupation of members of parliament: As with similar percentages quoted for earlier parliaments in Chapters 1, 8 and 14, most of these figures come from Professor Joan Rydon's *A Federal Legislature. The Australian Commonwealth Parliament 1901–1980.*

Non-British European-born members: The first non-British post-war migrant in Federal Parliament was Senator M. E. Lajovic (Lib, N), an accountant by profession, who was born and educated in Yugoslavia, and served in the Senate from 1976 to 1983.
602 In the words of Speaker Snedden: Patrick Weller and Dean Jaensch (eds), *Responsible Government in Australia* (Drummond, Melbourne, 1980), p. 71.

'one cannot dismiss it as a farce . . .': G. Sawer, *Australian Government Today*, 1977, p. 45.

Bibliography

Aitkin, D. *The Country Party in New South Wales: A Study of Organisation and Survival*. Australian National University Press, Canberra, 1972.

Australasian Federal Conference, *Official Record of the Proceedings and Debates*. Government Printer, Melbourne, 1890.

Australasian Federal Convention. *Official Record of Debates*. First Session, Government Printer, Adelaide, 1897; Second Session, Government Printer, Sydney, 1897; Third Session, Melbourne, 1898.

Australia. *Parliamentary Debates*. 1901–1987. Commonwealth Government Printer, Canberra.

Barwick, Garfield. *Sir John Did His Duty*. Serendip, Sydney, 1983.

Beale, Howard. *This Inch of Time: Memoirs of Politics and Diplomacy*. Melbourne University Press, 1977.

Beazley, K. E. 'The Labor Party and the Origin of the Commonwealth Bank', *Australian Journal of Political History*, IX, i, May 1963.

Bennett, J. M. *Keystone of the Federal Arch*. Australian Government Publishing Service, 1980.

Birrell, J. *Walter Burley Griffin*. University of Queensland Press, Brisbane, 1964.

Browning, H. O. *1975 Crisis: an Historical View*. Hale & Iremonger, Sydney, 1985.

Bryce, J. *Studies in History and Jurisprudence*. Clarendon Press, Oxford, 1901.

Burger, Angela. *Neville Bonner, a Biography*. Macmillan, Melbourne, 1979.

Calwell, A. A. *Be Just and Fear Not*. Lloyd O'Neil, Melbourne, 1972.

——. *Labor's Role in Modern Society*. Lansdowne, Melbourne, 1963.

Chipp, Don, and Larkin, John. *Don Chipp: The Third Man*. Rigby, Adelaide, 1978.

Cowen, Zelman. *Isaac Isaacs*. Oxford University Press, Melbourne, 1962.

Crisp, L. F. *The Australian Federal Labor Party 1901–1951*. Longmans, Green and Co., London, 1955.

——. *Australian National Government*. Longman Cheshire, Melbourne, 1978.

——. *Ben Chifley. A Political Biography*. Longmans, Green & Co. Ltd., Sydney, 1961.

——. *George Houston Reid: Federation Father, Federal Failure?* Australian National University, Research School of Social Sciences, Canberra, 1979.

Crowley, F. K. (ed.). *A New History of Australia*. Heinemann, Melbourne, 1974.

Cunneen, Christopher. *Kings' Men: Australia's Governors-General from Hopetoun to Isaacs*. George Allen & Unwin, Sydney, 1983.

d'Alpuget, Blanche. *Robert J. Hawke: a Biography*. Schwartz, Melbourne, 1982.

Dalziel, Alan. *Evatt the Enigma*. Lansdowne, Melbourne, 1967.

Daly, F. M. *From Curtin to Kerr*. Sun Books, Melbourne, 1977.

Deakin, Alfred. *The Federal Story; the Inner History of the Federal Cause*. Robertson and Mullens, Melbourne, 1944.

——. *Federated Australia: Selections from Letters to the Morning Post 1900–1901*. Melbourne University Press, 1968.

Denning, Warren. *Capital City*. Publicist Publishing, Sydney, 1938.

——. *Caucus Crisis: The Rise & Fall of the Scullin Government*. Hale & Iremonger, Sydney, 1982.

Dick, George. *Parliament House Canberra, Golden Jubilee*. Australian Government Publishing Service, Canberra, 1977.

Duthie, G. W. A. *I Had 50,000 Bosses*. Angus & Robertson, Sydney, 1984.

Edwards, Cecil. *Bruce of Melbourne: Man of Two Worlds*. Heinemann, London, 1965.

Edwards, John. *Life Wasn't Meant To Be Easy: a Political Profile of Malcolm Fraser*. Mayhem, Sydney, 1977.

Ellis, Ulrich. *A History of the Australian Country Party*. Melbourne, 1963.

Emy, Hugh V. *The Politics of Australian Democracy. Fundamentals in Pursuit*. Macmillan, Melbourne, 1974.

Evans, Gareth (ed.). *Labor and the Constitution 1972–1975*. Heinemann, Melbourne, 1977.

Evatt, H. V. *The King and his Dominion Governors*. Cassell, London, 1967.

——. *Liberalism in Australia: An Historical Sketch of Australian Politics Down to the year 1915*. Law Book Co., Sydney 1918.

Fabian Papers. *The Whitlam Phenomenon*. McPhee Gribble/Penguin, Melbourne, 1986.

Fadden, A. W. *They Called Me Artie*. Jacaranda, Brisbane, 1969.

Fitzhardinge, L. F. *St John's Church and Canberra*. St John's Parish Council, Canberra, 1959.

——. *William Morris Hughes, Vol. I: That Fiery Particle 1862–1914*. Angus & Robertson, Sydney, 1964.

——. *William Morris Hughes, Vol. II: The Little Digger 1914–1952*. Angus & Robertson, Sydney, 1979.

Freudenberg, Graham. *A Certain Grandeur*. Macmillan, Melbourne, 1977.

Garran, R. R. *Prosper the Commonwealth*. Angus & Robertson, Sydney, 1958.

——. *The Coming Commonwealth, an Australian Handbook of Federal Govern-*

ment. Angus & Robertson, Sydney, 1897.

Gibbney, H. J. Hugh Mahon: A Political Biography. M.A. thesis, Australian National University, 1970.

Gollan, Robin. *Radical and Working Class Politics: A Study of Eastern Australia, 1850–1910*. Melbourne University Press, 1960.

Graham, B. D. *The Formation of the Australian Country Parties*. Australian National University Press, Canberra, 1966.

Green, F. C. *Servant of the House*. Heinemann, Melbourne, 1969.

——. 'Changing Relations between Parliament and the Executive', *Public Administration* (Sydney), June 1954.

Groom, Jessie (comp.). *Nation Building in Australia; the Life and Work of Sir Littleton Groom*. Angus & Robertson, Sydney, 1941.

Hancock, W. K. *Australia*. Ernest Benn, London, 1930.

Hart, Philip. J. A. Lyons, a Political Biography. Ph.D. thesis, Australian National University, 1967.

Hasluck, Paul. *The Government and the People 1939–1941*. Australia in the War of 1939–45: Series IV, Vol. 1, 1952. *The Government and the People 1942–1945*. Australia in the War of 1939–45: Series IV, Vol. II, 1970. Australian War Memorial, Canberra.

——. *Mucking About: an Autobiography*. Melbourne University Press, Melbourne, 1977.

Hawke, R. J. L. *The Resolution of Conflict: 1979* Boyer Lectures. Australian Broadcasting Commission, Sydney, 1979.

Haylen, Leslie. *Twenty Years' Hard Labor*. Macmillan, Melbourne, 1969.

Hazlehurst, Cameron. *Menzies Observed*. Allen & Unwin, Sydney, 1979.

Hewart, Baron. *The New Despotism*. Ernest Benn, London, 1929.

Heydon, P. R. *Quiet Decision: a study of George Foster Pearce*: Melbourne University Press, 1965.

Holt, Edgar. *Politics Is People: the Men of the Menzies Era*. Angus & Robertson, Sydney, 1969.

Howard, Colin. *Australia's Constitution*. Penguin, Melbourne, 1978.

Howson, Peter. *The Howson Diaries: the Life of Politics* (Don Aitkin, editor). Viking Press, Ringwood, Victoria, 1984.

Hudson, W. J. *Casey*. Oxford University Press, Melbourne, 1986.

Hughes, Colin A. *Australian Federal and State Portfolio Lists: 1855–1982*. Department of Political Science, Research School of Social Sciences, Australian National University, 1983.

——. *A Handbook of Australian Government and Politics: 1965–1974*. Australian National University Press, Canberra, 1977.

——. *Mr Prime Minister: Australian Prime Ministers 1901–1972*. Oxford University Press, Melbourne, 1976.

——. *1977–83 Supplement to a Handbook of Australian Government and Politics: 1965–1974*. Department of Political Science, Research School of Social Sciences, Australian National University, 1984.

——. and Graham, B. D. *A Handbook of Australian Government and Politics: 1890–1964*. Australian National University Press, Canberra, 1968.

Hughes, W. M. *Crusts and Crusades: Tales of Bygone Days*. Angus & Robertson, Sydney, 1947.

——. *Policies and Potentates*. Angus & Robertson, Sydney, 1950.

Hutchison, J. M. The Australian Senate. Ph.D. thesis, Australian National

University, 1976.

Jaensch, Dean, and Teichmann, Max. *The Macmillan Dictionary of Australian Politics*. Second edition, Macmillan, Melbourne, 1984.

Journals of the Senate, 1901 to date. Commonwealth Government Printer, Canberra.

Kelly, Paul. *The Hawke Ascendancy*. Angus & Robertson, Sydney, 1984.

——. *The Unmaking of Gough*. Angus & Robertson, Sydney, 1976.

Kerr, John. *Matters for Judgment: An Autobiography*. Macmillan, Melbourne, 1978.

Kiernan, Colin. *Calwell: A Personal and Political Biography*. Nelson, Melbourne, 1978.

Killen, Sir James. *Killen: Inside Australian Politics*. Methuen Haynes, Melbourne, 1985.

La Nauze, J. A. *Alfred Deakin*. Melbourne University Press, 2 vols, 1965.

——. *The Making of the Australian Constitution*, Melbourne University Press, 1972.

Lang, J. T. *The Turbulent Years*. Alpha Books, Sydney, 1970.

Little, G. 'Fraser and Fraserism', *Meanjin*, 41, 3.

——. 'Hawke in Place: Evaluating Narcissism', *Meanjin*, 42,4.

Lloyd, C. J. The Formation and Development of the United Australia Party, 1929–37. Ph.D. thesis, Australian National University, Canberra, 1984.

——. and Reid, G. S. *Out of the Wilderness: the Return of Labor*. Cassell, Melbourne, 1974.

——. and Clark, Andrew. *Kerr's King Hit!* Cassell, Sydney, 1976.

Lyons, Dame Enid. *Among the Carrion Crows*. Rigby, Adelaide, 1972.

——. *So We Take Comfort*. Heinemann, London, 1965.

Marr, David. *Barwick*. Allen & Unwin, Sydney, 1980.

May, Erskine. *Treatise on the Law, Privileges, Proceedings and Usage of Parliament* (Sir Charles Green, editor). Butterworths, London, 1983.

Menzies, Robert. *Afternoon Light: Some Memories of Men and Events*. Cassell, Melbourne, 1967.

——. *The Measure of the Years*. Cassell, Melbourne, 1970.

Morgan, Carol. The First Minister of Australia, Studies of the Office in Crisis, 1920–41. Ph.D. thesis, Australian National University, Canberra, 1960.

Murphy, Denis. *Hayden: A Political Biography*. Angus & Robertson, Sydney, 1980.

Murray, R. *The Split: Australian Labor in the Fifties*. Cheshire, Melbourne, 1970.

Oakes, Laurie. *Crash Through or Crash: The Unmaking of a Prime Minister*. Drummond, Melbourne, 1976.

——. *Whitlam PM: a Biography*. Angus & Robertson, Sydney, 1973.

——. and Solomon, David. *The Making of an Australian Prime Minister*. Cheshire, Melbourne, 1973.

O'Collins, Gerald. *Patrick McMahon Glynn, a Founder of Australian Federation*. Melbourne University Press, 1965.

Odgers, J. R. *Australian Senate Practice* (Fifth Edition). Australian Government Publishing Service, 1976.

Ormonde, Paul. *A Foolish Passionate Man: A Biography of Jim Cairns*. Penguin, Melbourne, 1981.

Page, Sir Earle. *Truant Surgeon: the Inside Story of Forty Years of Australian*

Political Life (Ann Mozley, editor). Angus & Robertson, Sydney, 1963.
Palmer, N. *Henry Bournes Higgins: A Memoir*. London, 1931.
Parliament House, Victoria. Government Printer, Melbourne, n.d.
Parliamentary Handbook of the Commonwealth of Australia. 23 editions from 1915 to 1987. Australian Government Publishing Service, Canberra.
Patience, Allan, and Scott, Jeffrey. *Australian Federalism: Future Tense*. Oxford University Press, Melbourne, 1983.
——. and Head, Brian. *From Whitlam to Fraser: Reform and Reaction in Australian Politics*. Oxford University Press, Melbourne, 1979.
Pearce, Sir George. *From Carpenter to Cabinet*. Hutchinson, London, 1951.
Pettifer, J. A. (ed.). *House of Representatives Practice*. Australian Government Publishing Service, 1981.
Quick, John, and Garran, Robert. *The Annotated Constitution of the Australian Commonwealth*. Legal Books, 1976.
Reid, Alan. *The Gorton Experiment*. Shakespeare Head Press, Sydney, 1971.
——. *The Power Struggle*. Shakespeare Head Press, Sydney, 1969.
——. *The Whitlam Venture*. Hill of Content, Melbourne, 1976.
Reid, Sir George. *My Reminiscences*. Cassell, London, 1917.
Reid, G. S. 'The Changing Political Framework', *Quadrant*, January–February 1980.
Reynolds, J. *Edmund Barton*, Angus & Robertson, Sydney, 1948.
Robertson, John. *J. H. Scullin: A Political Biography*. University of Western Australia Press, 1974.
Robinson, F. W. *Canberra's First Hundred Years and After*. W. C. Penfold, Sydney, 1927.
Ross, Lloyd. *John Curtin: a Biography*. Macmillan, Melbourne, 1977.
Rydon, Joan. *A Biographical Register of the Commonwealth Parliament 1901–1972*. Australian National University Press, Canberra, 1975.
——. *A Federal Legislature: The Australian Commonwealth Parliament 1901–1980*. Oxford University Press, Melbourne, 1986.
St John, E. H. *A Time to Speak*. Sun Books, Melbourne, 1969.
Sawer, Geoffrey. *The Australian Constitution*. Australian Government Publishing Service, Canberra, 1975.
——. *Australian Federal Politics and Law 1901–1929*. Melbourne University Press, 1956.
——. *Australian Federal Politics and Law 1929–1949*. Melbourne University Press, 1963.
——. *Australian Government Today*. Melbourne University Press, 1977.
——. *Federation Under Strain*, Melbourne University Press, 1977.
Schedvin, C. B. *Australia and the Great Depression: a Study of Economic Development and Policy in the 1920s and 1930s*. Sydney University Press, 1970.
Schneider, Russell. *The Colt from Kooyong: Andrew Peacock, a Political Biography*. Angus & Robertson, Sydney, 1982.
——. *War Without Blood: Malcolm Fraser in Power*. Angus & Robertson, London, 1980.
Solomon, David. *Inside the Australian Parliament*. Allen & Unwin, Sydney, 1979.
——. *The People's Palace: Parliament in Modern Australia*. (Parliament's Bicentenary Publications Project) Melbourne University Press, 1986.
Spender, Percy. *Politics and a Man*. Collins, Sydney, 1972.

Spratt, E. *Eddie Ward; Firebrand of East Sydney*. Rigby, Adelaide, 1965.

Tennant, Kylie. *Evatt, Politics and Justice*. Angus & Robertson, Sydney, 1970.

Thompson, J. (ed.). *On Lips of Living Men*. Cheshire, Melbourne; 1962.

Trengove, Alan. *John Grey Gorton: an Informal Biography*. Cassell, Melbourne, 1969.

Turner, H. G. *The First Decade of the Australian Commonwealth: A Chronicle of Contemporary Politics 1901–1910*. Melbourne, 1911.

Votes and Proceedings of the House of Representatives, 1901 to date. Commonwealth Government Printer, Canberra.

Walsh, Maximilian. *Poor Little Rich Country: The Path to the Eighties*. Penguin, Melbourne, 1979.

Ward, Russel. *A Nation For a Continent: The History of Australia 1901–1975*. Heinemann, Melbourne, 1977.

Weller, Patrick (ed.). *Caucus Minutes 1901–1949*. 3 volumes. Melbourne University Press, 1975.

Whitington, Don. *The House Will Divide*. Melbourne, 1954.

——. *The Rulers: Fifteen Years of the Liberals*. Lansdowne, Melbourne, 1964.

——. *Strive to be Fair*. Canberra, 1977.

——. *The Witless Men*. Sun Books, Melbourne, 1975.

Whitlam, E. G. *The Truth of the Matter*. Penguin, Melbourne, 1979.

——. *The Whitlam Government 1972–1975*. Viking, Melbourne, 1985.

Wigmore, Lionel. *The Long View: A History of Canberra Australia's National Capital*. Cheshire, Melbourne, 1963.

Wise, B. R. *The Commonwealth of Australia: The Inner History of the Federal Cause*. Pitman, London, 1909.

Yarwood, A. T., *Asian Migration to Australia: The Background to Exclusion 1896–1923*. Melbourne University Press, 1964.

Young, I. E. *Theodore: His Life and Times*. Alpha Books, Sydney, 1971.

Manuscripts

National Library of Australia: Anstey, Frank; Barton, Sir Edmund; Beale, Sir Howard; Boote, H.; Broinowski, R. A.; Catts, J. H.; Cole, G. R.; Cook, B. S. B.; Daly, F. M.; Deakin, A.; Dedman, J. J.; Fairbairn, D. E.; Fisher, A.; Glynn, P. McM.; Groom, Sir Littleton; Gullett, H. B. S.; Hawker, C. A. S.; Haylen, L. C.; Hughes, W. M.; Hume Cook, J. H.; Isaacs, Sir Isaac; Kent Hughes, Sir Wilfrid, Latham, Sir John; Lyons, Dame Enid; Lyons, J. A.; Menzies, Sir Robert; McEwen, Sir John; Mahon, H.; Moffat, J. P.; Page, Sir Earle; Parkhill, Sir Archdale; Pearce, Sir George; Scullin, J. H.; Spender, Sir Percy; Ward, E. J.

Australian Archives: Cabinet papers; Shepherd, M. L., memoirs.

La Trobe Library, Melbourne: Crouch, R. A., memoirs.

Oral History Transcripts

National Library of Australia: Abbott, C. L. A.; Alexander, J. A.; Burmester, C.; Binns, K.; Cox, H.; Dedman, J. J.; Evatt, M.; Looker, Sir Cecil, Lyons, Dame Enid; Reid, A.; Rodgers, D.

Parliament's Bicentenary Publications Project: Cope, J. F.; Crean, F.

Index

by
Dorothy F. Prescott